Second Edition

POLITICAL THEORY

Classic and Contemporary Readings

VOLUME I

Thucydides to Machiavelli

Joseph Losco
Ball State University

Leonard Williams
Manchester College

OXFORD
UNIVERSITY PRESS

OXFORD
UNIVERSITY PRESS

Oxford University Press, Inc., publishes works that further Oxford University's
objective of excellence in research, scholarship, and education.

Oxford New York
Auckland Cape Town Dar es Salaam Hong Kong Karachi
Kuala Lumpur Madrid Melbourne Mexico City Nairobi
New Delhi Shanghai Taipei Toronto

With offices in
Argentina Austria Brazil Chile Czech Republic France Greece
Guatemala Hungary Italy Japan Poland Portugal Singapore
South Korea Switzerland Thailand Turkey Ukraine Vietnam

First published by Roxbury Publishing Company
Published by Oxford University Press, Inc.
198 Madison Avenue, New York, New York 10016
http://www.oup.com

Oxford is a registered trademark of Oxford University Press

Library of Congress Cataloging-in-Publication Data available

ISBN 978-0-19-533015-1

Dedication

For Marcia and Michael for their continued love and support, and for my Uncle Sam, who first introduced me to the wisdom of the ages (J.L.)

For my sons, Christopher and Jason, whom I cherish deeply, and for Robert Pettit, a dear friend through joys and trials alike (L.W.)

Acknowledgments

At Roxbury: Thanks to Claude Teweles for his confidence in our approach to these volumes, Sacha Howells for meticulous care of the manuscript, and Stephanie Villavicencio for help in securing reprint permissions.

At Ball State University: Thanks to Stephanie Painter for her long, hard hours in manuscript preparation and to Jim Huffman and Patrick Breen for help in tracking down research materials.

At Manchester College: Thanks to Alicia Brant for research and secretarial assistance, to the College for a research grant that aided the completion of this project, and to numerous colleagues for their support and friendship. ✦

Contents

---

*New to the Second Edition

Part II: The Age of Empire—Civil and Religious

---

*New to the Second Edition

*New to the Second Edition

Part III: Enter Modernity

*New to the Second Edition

---

*New to the Second Edition

Introduction

Consider the following questions: What do we mean by *freedom*, *human rights*, *equality*, and *justice*? Is there a *best* form of government? Why, and under what conditions, should citizens obey the state? How can a society's institutions and political life be changed for the better?[1] It does not take long to recognize that these questions raise some of our most enduring issues. Nor should it surprise anyone that courses in political theory address just such questions and concerns. Indeed, political theory courses have always met students' need for guidance as they face the extraordinary changes the world has witnessed in recent years. As a result, interest in political theory has increased greatly among college and university students in political science, philosophy, and many other disciplines.

This volume and its companion are intended to introduce undergraduate students to the history of Western political thought and the enterprise of political theory. For most students, this will be their only class in political theory; for all, it will likely be a new experience. Political science majors, for instance, will have studied the structures and processes of American politics, those of other nations, and the complexities of the international political arena. Their education will have focused on the debates surrounding a host of policy issues or on the empirical regularities of political behavior. Philosophy majors, on the other hand, will have had access to the history of Western thought about aesthetics, epistemology, logic, and metaphysics. For most undergraduate students, regardless of their disciplinary background, the study of political theory will no doubt be little more than a sideshow in a busy educational carnival. Nevertheless, it is our hope that by presenting the works of some of the West's most prominent political thinkers, as

well as commentaries engaging in the debates these thinkers continue to generate, another generation of students will come to see political theory as a rich storehouse of ideas for addressing our enduring social and political concerns.

The Nature of Political Theory

What is political theory? What is it that political philosophers do?[2] Significant answers to these questions have been given by two prominent scholars, Leo Strauss and Sheldon Wolin.[3] Strauss, the originator of a widely influential approach to studying theory, believed that the task of political philosophy is to gain wisdom about the nature of human beings and politics. "Doing" political theory thus involves learning to read the classics so that one may effectively distinguish between mere opinion and authentic knowledge. Wolin, on the other hand, argued that the study of political theory is best understood as a reflective discourse on the meaning of the political. As a dialogue among philosophers, political theory seeks to highlight the relation between continuity and change in political life.

Two more recent conceptions of political theory simultaneously echo and refine the ideas advanced by Strauss and Wolin. Robert Fowler and Jeffrey Orenstein, for instance, suggest that political theory involves reflection on basic political concepts, the analysis of alternative views about human beings and politics, and the pursuit of normative truth about the nature of the best regime.[4] Dante Germino points to the ongoing nature of the theoretical enterprise when he characterizes political philosophy as a "conversation of many voices"—that is, a dialogue "between different orientations toward political reality as a whole."[5] Viewed in this way, political philosophy is both a criti-

1

cal and creative activity in which each generation participates in a continuous tradition that unites present and past.

Regardless of what one believes theory to be, it is all too clear that there are many different approaches to studying the history of political thought.[6] For instance, one may choose to study the theorist as a person with unique concerns and motivations (a biographical approach); or, one could study the theories themselves—locating them in their cultural contexts, accounting for their conceptual development and change, and tracing complex patterns of their influence and impact (an historical approach). Still other approaches have focused on great problems or eternal questions presumed to face all political thinkers without regard to time, place, or circumstance (a perennial-issues approach).

In the face of these diverse approaches, we believe that the undergraduate student's best option is to adopt a problem-solving orientation to the study of political theory. We therefore tend to define political theory as the systematic effort to understand the meaning and significance of political life. Motivated by a given political or philosophical problem, one turns to the history of political theory (or even contemporary political thought and political science), and then shows its relevance to that problem. That done, the task becomes one of reflecting on the ideas offered by theorists in order to solve the problem, or at least, to clarify it in some important way. In sum, the student of political theory regards "interpretations as alternative solutions to some puzzle or problem, and then goes on to assess their adequacy *vis-à-vis* each other and in relation to one's own proposed solution."[7] Studying political theory, then, is not simply about reading a body of authoritative texts (though it includes such authority); it is also about reflecting on the meaning of political life itself.

In a similar vein, John Nelson presented a useful list of goals for the practice of political theory.[8] He argued that political theory's aims can be summarized in terms of three Cs: *comprehend, conserve,* and *criticize. Comprehend* here refers to the twin objectives of explanation and understanding. The-ories provide a conceptual vocabulary for describing and accounting for the most important features of political life and their interrelations, as well as for accounting for the forms and behaviors typically found in political practice. Simply put, political theory explores political phenomena by placing them in the context of human experience. The second aim, to *conserve,* connotes that the historical study of political thought helps preserve a cultural heritage. Lastly, to identify *criticize* as an aim for students of political theory underscores the fact that theory analyzes and evaluates both theoretical arguments and political phenomena.

To Nelson's list, we would add a fourth C: *create.* Theory shapes the way we view politics and gives insight into the problems and opportunities presented by political life. It can either restrict our vision or broaden our horizons. At all times, theorists must be aware that they are not engaging in pure philosophy, not living in a rarefied atmosphere of complete abstraction. As Benjamin Barber has observed,

> politics remains something human beings *do,* not something they possess or use or watch or talk or think about. Those who would do something about it must do more than philosophize, and philosophy that is politically intelligible must take full political measure of politics as conduct.[9]

Thus, theorists must be attuned to the political world, the world of praxis and action.[10] They should pay heed to the specific practices, behaviors, or orders recommended or implied by the political theories under investigation.

In the end, consensus on the essential definition of concepts such as politics, or of practices such as political theory, will likely elude our grasp. This does not mean, however, that conceptual definitions or political judgments are wholly subjective matters of whim or taste. Far from it. There are certain criteria good theories ought to meet, standards by which we can evaluate the political theories you will encounter in this book. We have in mind such criteria as logical consistency, breadth or comprehensiveness, clarity of thought and argument, and degree of insight, as well as acceptable implications for political practice. No matter which criterion you choose, though, take the time to argue with the theorists in this book, with your classmates and your instructor, or even with yourself.

About This Book

Like most books, the second edition of *Political Theory: Classic and Contemporary Readings* was inspired by a perceived need. Until recently, political theory instructors had a number of unsatisfactory options in selecting readings for their students. They could, for example, exclusively use primary works by the classic political theorists. Doing so usually meant, however, that students had to purchase as many as a dozen books in order to cover the major theorists in the traditional canon. Nor has the option of using a volume containing abridged selections from those works offered a solution to the problem. All too many students simply lack the background or context for making sense of the selections or for seeing their relevance to political life today.

Another option for the teacher of political theory has been to use a textbook of summary and commentary by a contemporary scholar. Such works certainly treat a large number of theorists in a short span of time, and they may provide students with insights into the classic writings. Yet, many instructors believe that students who read commentaries without encountering the texts themselves have not really learned political theory. Students should develop firsthand evaluations of the works of political philosophers, no matter how useful a scholar's commentary may be in placing those works in social and historical contexts.

We believe that *Political Theory: Classic and Contemporary Readings* brings together the best features of each of the above approaches, while minimizing their liabilities. For loyal users of the first edition, we believe you will be pleased with the enhancements in the present set of volumes. We have increased the number of entries of both canonical figures and nontraditional authors. We have updated a substantial number of commentaries to reflect more recent scholarship. There are new section introductions that provide an overview of the historic and intellectual currents giving rise to each generation of thinkers. Finally, we have improved the pedagogical section by adding web sites, class discussion and activity items, and annotated bibliographies. We believe all of these features make the second edition more comprehensive and easier to use.

For newcomers, let us review the basic features that distinguish this anthology from others. For one thing, this collection provides significant excerpts from classic writings for students to confront directly. The thinkers presented extend from Thucydides to Rawls, allowing instructors to pick and choose from a significant range of political theorists. Further, we have chosen commentaries that present multiple viewpoints from which to evaluate the tradition of Western political thought. These commentaries, representing a high degree of both scholarship and accessibility, raise important issues concerning the relevance of the classics to today's political problems.

By combining primary texts with scholarly commentaries, then, we allow students to study both the content and the practice of political theory. They should therefore be able to understand not only what classic theorists have had to say about politics, but they can also learn how contemporary theorists have approached the study of classic works.

Finally, because some classes in political theory are divided along traditional timelines of "ancient" and "modern," we have chosen to present this work in two volumes. We believe this will best accommodate the needs of students without sacrificing coverage. Students taking a class in only one time period can avoid the expense of a longer volume, while those involved in a two-semester sequence will find that most major political theorists have been covered by both volumes.

Where to split the volumes was initially a problem. Traditionalists and Straussians usually anoint Machiavelli or Hobbes as the initiator of the "modern era." On the other hand, theorists who are more historically inclined often speak of the modern period as properly beginning in the 18th century with the American and French Revolutions. While contemporary theorists are themselves divided over the proper interpretation of modernity, other works on the history of political thought have provided a solution to this problem. Many popular books divide the history of political thought around the work of Machiavelli, with some of them placing his work at the end of a volume on ancient political theory and others placing it at the beginning of a "modern" volume. Because his work is transitional in many respects, we have chosen to cover Machiavelli in both volumes. Purists may object, but again, we believe this provides flexibility for both professors and students.

Each unit in *Political Theory: Classic and Contemporary Readings* contains an introduction to a philosopher (his or her life and major theoretical contributions), selected readings from his or her work, and commentaries illuminating critical aspects of his or her thought. Though our selections are consistent with the type and extent of difficulty encountered in most undergraduate theory courses, some of the readings will undoubtedly require students to stretch themselves intellectually. We have sought to help students by summarizing the key arguments in our introductory essays and presenting brief annotated bibliographies. Further assistance for both the student and the instructor can be found in the discussion questions and World Wide Web addresses that we have included in each unit.

One important issue remaining to be addressed concerns how we selected the readings presented here. In selecting both philosophers and representative texts, our goal has been to provide a fairly comprehensive introduction to political theory, not a compendium of the world's political thought. We chose selections that represent the broad scope of the classics of Western political thought from Thucydides to the present day. These works are the subject of most of the teaching and commentary done by political theorists and philosophers today. They are works which have made singular contributions to our collective understanding of poli-tics, works to which we often return when seeking answers to questions about political life.

As such, this book of readings follows a well-established pattern for textbooks in the history of Western political thought. Though we reject the idea that each theorist plays a specific role in a grand drama, we do believe that each has made a distinctive and indispensable contribution to understanding politics. Certainly, we could not include the writings of everyone who has had anything of interest to say about politics. Many works of classic or near-classic status simply had to be left aside. For instance, we have not felt competent enough to include material expressing the unique insights of Asian, African, or Middle Eastern political thought. Our own philosophical tastes and relative levels of ignorance may result in some taking us to task.

However, a more difficult problem with selection emerges from the limitations of political theory as a scholarly community and an intellectual enterprise.[11] Like much other historical writing, and like a good bit of political practice, political theory has derived its language and outlook from a largely masculine experience. The writers that traditionally have been accorded classic status have all been male; they have all emerged from the conventionally masculine preserve of politics; and they have all employed non-inclusive language to talk about political life. Thus, many works of political theory either said nothing about women, or if they did, what they had to say was dismissive, derogatory, and sexist. We do not share such sentiments, and have been pleased that the writings taught in political theory courses have been expanded to include works by women. We have reflected that enlarged canon in this volume and its companion.

We selected the commentaries for each of the chosen philosophers by basing our decisions on the following considerations: (1) We wanted commentaries that reflected important ideas or controversies associated with the philosopher under study, especially where the concepts advanced are rather murky. (2) We sought commentaries that represented significant recent scholarship in political theory. In this way, students may get a sense of the current state of the field. However, when we felt that earlier commentaries were superior in illuminating key ideas or controversies, currency took a back seat. (3) Finally, we included commentaries that would be within the grasp of the average student approaching political theory for the first time.

Thus, the readings we have selected for this volume are a mix of classic writings and contemporary views. We believe this mix will acquaint students with the writings of a representative set of political theorists; provide them with contemporary analyses and interpretations of those works; and raise the major issues or questions associated with a particular theorist's contributions to understanding political life. We hope to stimulate students' interest so that they will read in and about the theorists we do present, as well as the many thinkers we have been forced (through limits imposed by convention, space, and time) to omit from this collection.

A Note to the Student on Reading *Political Theory*

As you begin your study of political theory, keep in mind that this book is not a road atlas providing detailed directions to every theoretical city of consequence. Instead, it is a guidebook offering some useful perspectives on places of potential interest to you. Of course, no guidebook can ever substitute for the experience of going to those places yourself. You must use the book merely as an aid in finding your own destinations in the world of political thought.

Still, as you read this book, you will find that some of the material will appear rather complex or dense; it may even seem to be phrased in an alien tongue. To help you cope with the welter of words that you will find in political philosophy readings, let us present a few hints on how to read actively and critically.[12] In general, critical reading involves both identifying and evaluating the argument an author makes in a text. An argument consists of a thesis or conclusion and the evidence or reasons given that warrant or support the thesis. Any argument will thus show a chain of reasoning:[13]

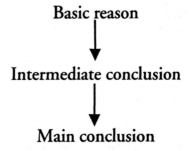

Basic reason
↓
Intermediate conclusion
↓
Main conclusion

Thus, the first step in reading complex texts is to locate the author's central argument or to read for his or her main point. Once you identify that primary conclusion, you should then think backward, as it were, to identify the evidence or reasons necessary to support that conclusion.

Specifically, for each text, ask yourself the following sets of questions:

1. What is the author's focus? What issue is being addressed? What problem is to be resolved?

2. What body of literature or belief does the author rely upon? What theoretical tradition has shaped the author's outlook or approach?

3. What is the author's primary conclusion? What evidence or reasons are given to support that conclusion?

4. Does the author's argument make sense? Is it logical and well-reasoned? Does it solve the problem the author initially raised?

5. What evidence or considerations has the author overlooked or neglected? What value assumptions has the author made that may or may not bear scrutiny?

6. What are the practical, theoretical, and ethical implications of the author's argument? Are those implications desirable? Why or why not?

In addition to these procedural guidelines, it might be helpful as you read to focus upon the answers to a set of key substantive questions. According to Dante Germino, political philosophers must grapple with at least three major concerns:[14] 1) What is the nature of human beings such that they engage in politics to coordinate their social dealings with others? While some political theorists are explicit regarding human nature, others (even those who discard the concept) often adopt implicit assumptions about human nature that inform their perspective. 2) What is the best regime for structuring human political relations? Here political theorists propose a wide range of options, as you will see; however, these options must conform to assumptions about human nature in order to be consistent and constructive. Some proposals are meant to broaden our perspective about the realm of human possibilities, but not all ideas about the "best" regime are meant to be realistic. Some ideas are meant only as goals more to be wished for than realized; others are intended to show inherent limits to what is humanly possible. 3) What role do historic forces play in the evolution and shaping of political solutions? Some have proposed that great individuals make history by force of their ideas, virtue, or skills; others assert that long-term social and economic developments play the major role in shaping not only political solutions but the ideas that inform them.

To this list of questions, we might add one more: How do the authors conceptualize the relationship between the individual good and the common good? Some theories assert that the innate sociality of the human animal mitigates potential conflicts along this dimension. By serving the common good, I am serving my own as well. An example might be contributing to a social insurance policy in which my contributions will combine with those of others to produce benefits for all those who need them, including myself. Other theorists focus on the difficulties involved in accommodating the individual and common good. During warfare, some individuals might be called upon to die so that others can live. Over the course of the history of political thought, there have been periods in which the place of one or the other type of good has assumed prominence. This question is no less important in the current era in which libertarian and communitarian ideals come into conflict.

This is the "stuff" of political theory. These are among the central ideas good political theorists explore. As you read each philosopher, try to discover the answers he or she provides to these questions. This will provide a basis for understanding the scope and breadth of ideas that have informed the Western tradition of political thought.

Notes

1. For similar queries, see Glenn Tinder, *Political Thinking: The Perennial Questions*, 6th ed. (New York: Longman, 1996); and Larry Arnhart, *Political Questions: Political Philosophy from Plato to Rawls*, 2nd ed. (Prospect Heights, IL: Waveland Press 1993).

2. Though the term *theory* frequently has been applied to both normative and empirical studies, some political scientists reserve the term *philosophy* for studies of the former sort (e.g., what is the best regime?) and apply *theory* to the latter sort (e.g., what models best explain voter turnout?). Nonetheless, empirical theorists must make normative assumptions in generating explanatory models, and normative philosophers clearly must take empirical data into account in formulating defensible views. Therefore, for our purposes, we treat the terms *political theory* and *political philosophy* as more or less interchangeable.

3. Leo Strauss, *What is Political Philosophy?* (Glencoe, IL: Free Press, 1959), 10–12; and Sheldon Wolin, *Politics and Vision* (Boston: Little Brown, 1960), 2–5.

4. Robert B. Fowler and Jeffrey R. Orenstein, *Contemporary Issues in Political Theory*, rev. ed. (New York: Praeger, 1985), 2.

5. Dante Germino, "The Contemporary Relevance of the Classics of Political Philosophy." In Fred Greenstein and Nelson Polsby, eds., *Handbook of Political Science*, vol. 1 (Reading, MA: Addison-Wesley, 1975), 229–281.

6. Daniel Sabia, "Political Education and the History of Political Thought," *American Political Science Review* 78 (December 1984): 985–999.

7. Terence Ball, *Reappraising Political Theory* (Oxford: Oxford University Press, 1995), 29.

8. John Nelson, "Natures and Futures for Political Theory," in Nelson, ed., *What Should Polit-*

ical Theory Be Now? (Albany: State University of New York Press, 1983), 3–24.

9. Benjamin Barber, *The Conquest of Politics: Liberal Philosophy in Democratic Times* (Princeton, NJ: Princeton University Press, 1988), 11, emphasis in the original.

10. Of course, political theorists have not always lived up to this charge. For a recent critique of the alienation of political theory from political practice, see Jeffrey C. Isaac, "The Strange Silence of Political Theory," *Political Theory* 23 (November 1995): 636–652.

11. For a discussion of the limits of political theory, see Judith Evans, Jill Hills, Karen Hunt, Elizabeth Meehan, Tessa ten Tusscher, Ursula Vogel, and Georgina Waylen, *Feminism and Political Theory* (London: Sage, 1986).

12. These hints are drawn from our teaching experiences and Anthony Daley, "On Reading," *PS: Politics and Political Science* 28 (March 1995): 89–100; Alec Fisher, *The Logic of Real Arguments* (Cambridge: Cambridge University Press, 1988); and Diane Schmidt, *Expository Writing in Political Science* (New York: HarperCollins, 1993).

13. Fisher, op. cit., 10.

14. Adapted from Dante Germino, "The Contemporary Relevance of the Classics of Political Philosophy," in Fred Greenstein and Nelson Polsby, eds., *Handbook of Political Science,* vol. 1 (Reading, Mass.: Addison-Wesley, 1975), 229–281.

Further Reading

Fowler, Robert Booth, and Jeffrey R. Orenstein. 1993. *An Introduction to Political Theory.* New York: HarperCollins.

Frank, Jason A., and John Tambornino, eds. 2000. *Vocations of Political Theory.* Minneapolis: University of Minnesota Press.

Galston, William. 1993. "Political Theory in the 1980s: Perplexity Amidst Diversity." In *Political Science: The State of the Discipline II,* ed. Ada Finifter, pp. 27–53. Washington, D.C.: American Political Science Association.

Gunnell, John. 1983. "Political Theory." In *Political Science: The State of the Discipline,* ed. Ada Finifter, pp. 3–45. Washington, D.C.: American Political Science Association.

Klosko, George. 1994. *History of Political Theory: An Introduction,* 2 vols. Fort Worth, TX: Harcourt Brace.

Morrow, John. 1998. *A History of Political Thought: A Thematic Introduction.* New York: New York University Press.

Nelson, John, ed. 1983. *What Should Political Theory Be Now?* Albany: State University of New York Press.

Okin, Susan Moller. 1979. *Women in Western Political Thought.* Princeton, NJ: Princeton University Press.

Portis, Edward. 1998. *Reconstructing the Classics: Political Theory from Plato to Marx,* 2nd ed. Chatham, NJ: Chatham House.

Shanley, Mary Lyndon, and Carole Pateman, eds. 1991. *Feminist Interpretations and Political Theory.* University Park, PA: Penn State University Press.

Skinner, Quentin, ed. 1985. *The Return of Grand Theory in the Human Sciences.* Cambridge: Cambridge University Press.

Spragens, Thomas. 1976. *Understanding Political Theory.* New York: St. Martin's Press.

Thiele, Leslie Paul. 1997. *Thinking Politics: Perspectives in Ancient, Modern and Postmodern Political Theory.* Chatham, NJ: Chatham House. ✦

Part I

Greek Roots

Tell Me, O Muse, of that ingenious hero who traveled far and wide after he had sacked the famous town of Troy. Many cities did he visit, and many were the nations with whose manners and customs he was acquainted; moreover he suffered much by sea while trying to save his own life and bring his men safely home; but do what he might he could not save his men, for they perished through their own sheer folly in eating the cattle of the Sun-god Hyperion; so the god prevented them from ever reaching home. Tell me, too, about all these things, O daughter of Jove, from whatsoever source you may know them.

—Homer's *Odyssey*

Why begin with the ancient Greeks? This is a fair enough question but incredibly difficult to answer. Scholars point to a confluence of forces making ancient Hellas a likely spot for cultural development and exchange. For example, her location at the crossroads of East and West made possible a fortuitous blending of ideas and artifacts, especially in light of her maritime prowess. Faith in her gods provided a basis for the imperialism that resulted in the wide expansion of her influence throughout the Mediterranean world. That same imperial impulse necessitated the development of military and political institutions sufficient to maintain her aspirations. But surely, similar constellations of forces predated the Greek city-states and serious political discourse certainly took place elsewhere in both East and West, as Ar-

istotle's collection of world constitutions attests.

If we want to understand why ancient Greece is traditionally the starting point for the study of political philosophy we might more profitably turn to the present. Our continued interest in self-rule, our fascination with institutions of democracy, the paradox between self-interest and the necessity of collective action, the interplay between ethics and politics, our primal concern for fairness, and our preoccupation with justice—all direct our attention back to ancient Greece as the source of the very vocabulary of politics we use today. We look to ancient Greece for an understanding of the perennial problems facing a free people and for insight into the foundations of social life itself. It is because the philosophy of the ancient

Greeks continues to speak to the concerns of Western society that we turn back to those who left one of the first records of their struggle to forge a good society. This is not to say that earlier history does not matter, nor that it is unimportant to set the historic context in which Western traditions emerged.

The roots of Greek civilization can be traced to the island of Crete during the Bronze Age in about the third millennium B.C.E. King Minos conquered most of the Cyclades and ruled the seas from his labyrinthine fortress at Knossos. By the mid-15th century B.C.E., Minoan civilization had spread to the mainland and was reflected in the developing Mycenaean culture. But the Classic Age of Greece did not commence until much later at the beginning of the first millennium B.C.E., when the Dorian tribes from the Northwest and North Central regions of the mainland invaded Mycenaean strongholds. This invasion affected the language, art, and social customs that were to develop as the Classic Age began. Much of the myth and religion that were to dominate the Homeric and Hellenistic ages emerged at this time. Homer's works reflect the struggles of this period and the imperial desires of leaders to reach outward for both commerce and control.

By the 7th century B.C.E., tribal systems gave way to the city-state, distinctive units of government and culture that dotted the Greek peninsula and surrounding areas. The following description by C. M. Bowra (1957: 21–2) gives a sense of what life in the city-state was like:

> It is customary to speak of the units of Greek polity as city-states, and the phrase is apt enough if we recognize that such a state consisted of a good deal more than a city. If the city, usually walled, was the center of government and justice and of many handicrafts and trades, other activities went on outside. If there were fertile plains, people would live in villages near their work. Beyond the plains was rising land, usually covered by scrub, hard to cultivate, except in patches and pockets, and useful chiefly for pasturing goats. Beyond this, and still higher up, were the rough slopes of the mountains, perhaps here and there enclosing some isolated hamlet, but for the most part desolate, the haunt of hunters in summer and snow-covered in winter. Since many Greek cities lay close to the sea, there would be ports where ships could be built and harboured and a maritime population could have its home. In general, the inhabitants of a city-state would be formed of farmers, craftsmen, and sailors, and many would combine two or even three of the roles. Because all members of a city-state lived in close proximity within a more or less enclosed space, they had a strong sense of unity and kinship. This did not save them from internecine struggles or from class war, but it meant that respect for local tradition made them look on the men of other cities as somehow different from themselves. . . .

City-states developed their own distinct identities. It is hard to overestimate the sense of identity that one felt for one's city-state or the distaste some citizens experienced for members of neighboring communities. By the 5th century B.C.E., two of the most significant and distinct city-states were Sparta and Athens.

Sparta prided herself on her military prowess. Her soldiers were well-trained and dedicated. Yet, her economic position was weak, her intellectual life neglected, and her political leadership uninspired. Social life demanded an austere uniformity and abhorrence of luxury. Control and balance were cardinal virtues. In politics, the demands of royalty and commoners were kept in check by a council of elders (Vernant, 1982: 66). Athens, by contrast, established herself as an impressive naval power after her role in beating back the Persian invasion late in the 5th century B.C.E. In trade, she became a commercial giant. Her government underwent a series of dramatic reforms and, under the leadership of the statesman Cleisthenes, and later, Pericles, her culture flourished. The scope of her democratic operations was breathtaking. Perhaps as many as 50,000 male citizens were expected to participate in politics and to fill numerous offices by lot. As many as 500 citizens were required to fill positions on the Boule, a body that reviewed state business for discussion by the popular

Assembly. More dramatic, however, was the fact that important policies could be discussed at large open-air meetings of the Assembly, at some of which a quorum of 6,000 was required. For all its democratic reforms, however, slaves and women were without political voice and Athens ruled its possessions autocratically. Still, Athenians prided themselves on their sophistication, love of art, and dedication to the discovery of truth. These differences between Sparta and Athens contributed to a mutual suspicion that ended in a war that was to last for 27 years.

Athenian expansion after her success in ousting the Persians gave the Spartans cause for concern. The two powers stood at the center of great alliances, each with designs on regional hegemony. According to the historian Thucydides, it was Athenian imperialism in attempting to secure alliances with former allies of the Spartan League that led to the long siege known as the Peloponnesian War. For 27 years, the fortunes of two great alliances, the Peloponnesian League and the Athenian Alliance, seesawed back and forth. Ultimately, according to Thucydides, the steadiness of Spartan rule in the face of Athenian debate and indecision led to the defeat of Athens. Not long afterward, however, both leagues were eclipsed by the power of the Macedonians under Alexander the Great, who invaded from the North and subdued the entire peninsula. Throughout the entire period of conquest, however, Athens managed to sustain her cultural prominence.

The Pre-Socratics

No one is quite sure exactly how the search for truth wrested itself free from the religious tradition which had long guided understanding of the sensual world. By the 6th century B.C.E., however, Milesian thinkers like Thales, Anaximander and Anaximenes surely played a prominent role in the transformation of knowledge.

With the Milesians, the origin and ordering of the world for the first time took the form of an explicitly posed problem to which an answer must be supplied without mystery, an answer gauged to human intelligence, capable of being aired and publicly debated before the mass of citizens like any question of everyday life. They thus posited a function of understanding free of any concern with ritual. The "natural philosophers" deliberately ignored the domain of religion. Their quest no longer had anything to do with those religious practices to which myth, despite its relative autonomy, always remained bound to some degree (Vernant, 1982: 107).

Secular knowledge required not revelation but dialogue in order to permit refutation. Public debate became the forum for testing one's ideas. The world of the soothsayer gave way to the intellectual and the teacher.

Various theories were offered regarding the components that make up the universe and how they are constructed. Air, water and fire contended for prominence in one or another materialist theory. Pythagoras (570–490 B.C.E.) shifted interest from material to form and developed mathematical tools to uncover the harmonious relations alleged to underlie the perceptible world. Heraclitus (c. 500 B.C.E.) emphasized not unity but strife and opposition as components giving rise to certain change in the universe. The philosophers of the Eleatic school following the ideas of Parmenides (c. 515–448 B.C.E.) distrusted sensory perception and favored the use of deductive reasoning and logic as more certain pathways to knowledge.

Sophistic philosophers moved away from the abstract study of nature to the more practical considerations of living. Sophists were traveling instructors who contracted with young men willing to pay for instruction in reasoning and discourse. These teachers no doubt shared much with later philosophers who tried to displace them since both appealed to reason and both focused on the problems of living rather than on the study of natural phenomena that preoccupied their immediate predecessors. However, the portrait of the sophists left by philosophers is not flattering, and theirs is perhaps the most indelible portrait to survive.

Sophists were depicted as crass merchants of intellectual sleight-of-hand, more concerned with appearances than with truth. They were exemplified by opponents, like Plato, as extolling self-interest over community good. Power and ambition were their motivation, not truth and genuine virtue. They denied intrinsic good and proclaimed a conventionalist view in which rhetoric and debate were the surest means to individual happiness and success (Nelson, 1982: 7). Justice had no independent standard outside of the will of the stronger. Men like Gorgias, Protagoras, and Thrasymachus came to symbolize this school and the cynical perspective attributed to them became the dominant view until their later incarnation in the 2nd century C.E. and subsequent rehabilitation much later by Hegel (Kerferd, 1981). Despite this contemptuous vision, the preeminent philosophers of the Classic Age clearly thought of the sophists as able foes and lost no opportunity to defeat them in argument. This "pre-Socratic" point of view is present not only in the antagonists in Plato's dialogues but in the words and deeds attributed to leaders and warriors by the historian Thucydides.

As the term implies, "pre-Socratics" paved the way for the more substantial work to follow by the great names in political philosophy: Socrates, Plato and Aristotle. Putting their contributions in perspective, one scholar notes (Guthrie, 1967: 445–6):

. . . a dispassionate assessment of their contribution to the history of philosophy would probably show that, to use a metaphor, although they manufactured many of the pieces and set them on the board, Plato and Aristotle were the first players who learned the rules and started the game. The pieces are those opposed concepts by means of which philosophical discussion is maintained: being and becoming, sensible and intelligible, analytic and synthetic, appearance and reality, time and eternity, materialism and idealism, mechanism and teleology, and so forth. Once these stand out, a philosopher may champion one or another, but the pre-Socratics could not yet do this.

References

Bowra, C. M. 1957. *The Greek Experience.* New York: Mentor.

Guthrie, W. K. C. 1967. *The Encyclopedia of Philosophy.* New York: Collier-MacMillan and the Free Press.

Nelson, Brian. 1982. *Western Political Thought: From Socrates to the Age of Ideology,* 2nd ed. Englewood Cliffs, NJ: Prentice Hall.

Kerferd, G. B. 1981. *The Sophistic Movement.* New York: Cambridge University Press.

Vernant, Jean-Pierre. 1982. *The Origins of Greek Thought.* Ithaca, NY: Cornell University Press. ✦

Thucydides

Thucydides was probably born in Thrace, in the northern part of the Greek mainland, in about 460 B.C.E. Information about his early life is sketchy, but it is probable that he was born of noble stature with ties to Athens and personal ties with her leaders. He was elected to the post of general and served the Athenian Alliance in the opening phases of the Peloponnesian War. Saddled with losing the city of Amphipolis—until then an Athenian stronghold—in battle, he was banished into exile for 20 years. During this period, he traveled behind battle lines among Spartans and Athenians using his contacts and privileged position to write a history of the war that reflected decisions made by both sides. The work ends abruptly in the 20th year of the war. It is probable he did not live beyond 399 B.C.E.

His history of the war is important not simply as a chronicle but for the approach it took toward understanding complex events. Poetry and myth were shunted aside in favor of a type of empiricism in which the author employed first-hand reports, recollections, and trusted observations to reconstruct events. This is not to say that his methods insured accuracy. For instance, he says that when he was not present at speeches, he made the speakers "say what in [his] opinion was called for by each situation." Nevertheless, his crude empiricism added an important dimension to the development of Western thought. He believed, as do many modern historians, that an accurate understanding of the past can help us anticipate the future.

Thucydides also brought to his treatment a sophistic perspective that suffused his reporting of events. His actors reflect the sophistic view that human action is motivated by three great drives: fear, honor, and self-interest. People who steadfastly hold these forces in balance are likely to be politically successful. In their dealing with others, they must calculate risk and advantage carefully before entering into alliances or risking their security in war. They must remember that the victor ultimately determines the terms of justice. In advancing this perspective through examples in his history, Thucydides anticipates the perspective of "realpolitik" in international relations. As for domestic politics, the trouble with democracy, he believes, is that it awakens individualism and extended discourse in ways that destabilize the *polis* even as these forces contribute to cultural advance. "By giving less freedom to the individual, a closed society like Sparta, based on the principle of status and governed by unquestioned tradition, develops less creative initiative, less intelligence, and less energy than a democracy and, hence, only a modest empire. But its traditional norms are a more stable vehicle of rationality than Athenian enlightened self-interest" (Bluhm, 1967: 123).

History of the Peloponnesian War

Thucydides begins his account of the great world war of his time with an explanation of his method, portions of which are reproduced here. He carefully states his reasons for rejecting other approaches common to his day and describing the method he plans to employ. Banished are poetry and the tradition of the epic chronicle. Instead, he proposes an empirically based account made possible by his travels and ties to disputants on both sides of the conflict. He then turns his attention to conditions that led to the outbreak of war.

A web of alliances characterized the Greek city-states well before the outbreak of the great Peloponnesian War (431–404 B.C.E.). About the time Athens expelled the

Persians from the Greek peninsula (449 B.C.E.), the two great superpowers, Athens and Sparta, along with their allies, signed a "30 Years' Peace" in which each power abandoned its designs on colonies of strategic importance to the other and unaligned colonies were allowed to enter whichever alliance they chose. Three years later, a skirmish over several rebellious colonies in the central portion of the mainland led to a brief confrontation between the superpowers followed by yet another "30 Years' Peace" accord.

A series of events involving colonies of Corinth, aligned with Sparta, led to a final breakdown of peace. The first of these was over Corcyra. Fearful of forceful occupation by Corinth, the Corcyrans approached the Athenians for help. Unwilling to allow Corcyran strength to be absorbed by its enemies, Athens sent a fleet to help Corcyra turn back a Corinthian attack in 433 B.C.E. In response, Corinth immediately set about fomenting rebellion in Potidaea, a member of the Athenian league, in hopes of bringing Sparta into a larger conflict. With the help of a poorly executed Athenian response, revolt broke out and Athens used force to bring Potidaea back in line. Corinthian intrigue had been successful, however. No longer trusting Athenian intentions, Sparta was now induced to declare war and the great Peloponnesian War was on.

Over the period of this long war, the fortunes of each alliance continually rose and fell. Athenian strength lay in her naval superiority and the wealth she collected from tribute abroad. Sparta's strength was in her army, but forces could not fight year-round and Spartan troops were needed back home for harvest. While the course of the war cannot be detailed here, a few additional events relevant to the accompanying readings will be highlighted. Early Spartan attacks on the mainland were met by token resistance as the Athenians fortified population centers and settled in for a war of attrition. Simultaneously, she attempted to cut off Spartan supply lines by sea. The strategy, employed by Pericles, the Athenian leader, was successful in repelling Spartan troops. However, the price was a great plague visited upon the residents of the city crowded behind Athens's defensive walls. It is estimated that one-third of the population died as a result of disease. Pericles's famous oration to the city, in which he honors not so much the war dead as the idea of Athens for which the dead devoted their lives, is reproduced here.

In 416 B.C.E., as fortunes continued to seesaw between the superpowers, Athens sent several generals to Melos, a neutral island suspected of harboring Spartan sympathies, to negotiate terms of surrender. In open debate between representatives of the invading force and the Melian people, the subject turned quickly to justice. The Athenians warned the Melians to consider only their self-interest and their capacity for withstanding an Athenian attack and not to argue abstract principles of fair play. The Melians refused to take this advice and were laid waste by the invading Athenian troops.

Ultimately, a war-weary Athens, her citizens openly divided, set out on an ill-conceived course of appeasement. One of her own generals, Alcibades, deserted and took up arms against his old city for the cause of Sparta. Spartan determination held steady, and the course of the war turned decidedly in her favor.

Commentaries

In his commentary, C. D. C. Reeve explores passages from *History of the Peloponnesian War* to reveal a more complex understanding of Thucydides's view of human nature than the reader may first consider. Reed asserts that Thucydides's view is not simply static and pessimistic. Instead, he argues, the elements of human nature, reason and passion, re-assort themselves in response to social situations. Thus, in periods of civil disruption, balance is lost and extreme behavior takes over. With proper leadership and guided by proper laws, harmony between the elements of human motivation can be achieved even if this does not imply innate goodness. This nuanced view suggests potentially greater relevance of Thucydides's work for the study of politics today.

Laurie Johnson takes a detailed look at the Melian Dialogue with an eye toward uncovering Thucydides's own understanding of justice. Unlike modern realists in the field of international relations who assume uniformity of egoistic motivation and disparage all considerations save for self-interest in the conduct of foreign relations, Thucydides, Johnson asserts, adds regard for *enlightened self-interest* along with a sense of justice promulgated by good character and wise leadership as additional components of rational policy. In fact, blind adherence to narrow self-interest can sometimes obscure the function of justice as a means of preserving mutual interests and maintaining the kind of moral leadership necessary to earn a modicum of respect at home and abroad. While the most obvious lesson from this section of Thucydides's work would seem to be that "might makes right," Johnson argues that Thucydides wanted to demonstrate the limits of this view when it is taken to extremes. Despite the arrogance and brutality shown by the Athenians to the Melians, continued immoderation led to missteps and the final defeat of Athens. By comparing the Melian argument with that of Diodotus, an able Athenian orator, she also demonstrates the power and limits of rhetoric.

References

Bluhm, William T. 1967. "Thucydides." *Encyclopedia of Philosophy, Vol. 8.* New York: Collier MacMillan, 123–4.

Kuhlmann, Kurt. "Historical Commentary on the Peloponnesian War." http://www.warhorsesim.com/epw_hist.html. May 18, 2001.

Thucydides. [1980.] *History of the Peloponnesian War.* Translated by Charles Forster Smith. Cambridge, MA: Harvard University Press.

Web Sources

http://www.classictexts.net
ClassicTexts.net. This site provides full texts of major literary and philosophic texts, including Thucydides's *History of the Peloponnesian War.* The site requires registration, but it is free.

http://www.warhorsesim.com/epw_hist.html
Epic of the Peloponnesian War: Historical Commentary. Warhorse Simulations provides Kurt Kuhlmann's commentary and useful historical overview of the causes and events of the Peloponnesian War.

http://members.home.net/georgefrank/War/Index.html
The Peloponnesian War. Simon Frank presents a list of battles and related links on this famous war between Athens and Sparta.

http://www.fordham.edu/halsall/ancient/eb11-thucydides.html
Ancient History Sourcebook: Thucydides. This is an excellent review of the life and times of Thucydides taken from the 11th Edition of the Encyclopedia Britannica.

http://www.mygale.org/sdelille/gdpa.html
The Peloponnesian War. Sven Delille's home page presents ancient sources about Thucydides and the war in general, reviews, bibliographies, and discussions.

Class Activities and Discussion Items

1. Research and discuss current trends in historiography. To what extent would Thucydides's account be considered "good history" today? Which of his methods stands up over time? Which would be considered unacceptable by modern historians? Is Thucydides's account more like scholarly history or "pop" history?

2. History is written by the winners. To what extent does Thucydides's account reflect this point of view? Discuss.

3. Attrition and war weariness led to internal debate and uncertainty regarding the course of the war among Athenians. According to Thucydides, these elements, in the face of Spartan steadfastness, led to the defeat of Athens. To what extent have similar events played a part in the results of recent wars and skirmishes throughout the world? Does historical example always support Thucydides's view that nations must not undertake war unless they are prepared to pay any price to see it to the end?

4. One implicit lesson from Thucydides's account of the Peloponnesian War is that acts of nations reflect interests and not morals. This may be particularly clear in his account of the Melian Dialogue. Research the views of modern realists in the study of international rela-

tions like Hans Morgenthau, Robert Gilpin, and John Herz, and neo-realists like Richard K. Ashley, Robert O. Keohane, and Stanley Hoffman. How do their views on the nature of international relations compare with those of Thucydides?

5. Should morality play a part in foreign policy? Discuss this question with support drawn from contemporary conflicts around the world.

Further Reading

Ahrensdorf, Peter J. 1997. "Thucydides's Realistic Critique of Realism." Polity 30 (2): 231–265. For the last half-century foreign policy thinking in the United States has been dominated by the realist school. Part of its prestige has rested on its adherents' ability to trace their intellectual pedigree back to Thucydides. Read carefully, however, Thucydides is a theoretical realist who provides a sharp critique of political realism. He does support 20th-century realists' claims about the weakness of justice in international affairs and the dangers of moralism in foreign policy.

Boucher, David. 1998. *Political Theories of International Relations: From Thucydides to the Present.* New York: Oxford University Press. Examines currents in international relations theory and Thucydides's place within its evolution.

Forde, Steven. 1995. "International Realism and the Science of Politics: Thucydides, Machiavelli and Neorealism." *International Studies Quarterly* 39 (2): 141–160. Contemporary structural realism, or "neo-realism," has become influential in the study of international relations, due in part to claims of being more scientific than its predecessors. The arguments of Thucydides and Machiavelli are used to assess the claims of contemporary realism.

Johnson, Laurie M. 1993. *Thucydides, Hobbes and the Interpretation of Realism.* DeKalb, IL: Northern Illinois University Press. Compares, contrasts, and assesses the realistic theories advanced by Thucydides and Hobbes.

Monoson, Sara, and Michael Loriaux. 1998 "The Illusion of Power and the Disruption of Moral Norms: Thucydides's Critique of Periclean Policy." *American Political Science Review* 92 (2): 285–297. Thucydides's view of the Athenian leader Pericles is examined. Antithetical reasoning is present in the treatment of Pericles and is manifested in the opposition between the statesman's brilliance and the infelicitous consequences of his statecraft.

Orwin, Clifford. 1994. *The Humanity of Thucydides.* Princeton, NJ: Princeton University Press. Orwin explores Thucydides's understanding of the interplay between justice and compulsion and argues that the human motivations of fear, honor, and self-interest do not exonerate human action from blame.

Palmer, Michael. 1992. *Love of Glory and the Common Good: Aspects of the Political Thought of Thucydides.* Lanham, MD: Rowman & Littlefield Publishers. Part of the Perspectives series on classical political and social thought.

Pangle, Thomas L. and Peter J. Ahrensdorf. 1999. *Justice Among Nations: On the Moral Basis of Power and Peace.* Lawrence, KS: University Press of Kansas. A review and discussion of theories on international relations from classical to modern neo-realism.

Schofield, Malcolm. 1999. "Realism and Realpolitik." *Times Literary Supplement* (May 7):34. Useful reviews of *Thucydides: Narrative and Explanation* by Tim Rood, *The Humanity of Thucydides* by Clifford Orwin, and *Thucydides and the Ancient Simplicity: The Limits of Political Realism* by Gregory Crane.

Singer, Peter. 1999. "The Thucydides Tapes." *PS* 32(3):596–601. Thucydides and other scholars discuss the origins of the Peloponnesian War in a fictitious conference. ✦

1
Excerpts from *History of the Peloponnesian War*

Thucydides

Book One

20 In investigating past history, and in forming the conclusions which I have formed, it must be admitted that one cannot rely on every detail which has come down to us by way of tradition. People are inclined to accept all stories of ancient times in an uncritical way—even when these stories concern their own native countries. Most people in Athens, for instance, are under the impression that Hipparchus, who was killed by Harmodius and Aristogeiton, was tyrant at the time, not realizing that it was Hippias who was the eldest and the chief of the sons of Pisistratus, and that Hipparchus and Thessalus were his younger brothers. What happened was this: on the very day that had been fixed for their attempt, indeed at the very last moment, Harmodius and Aristogeiton had reason to believe that Hippias had been informed of the plot by some of the conspirators. Believing him to have been forewarned, they kept away from him, but, as they wanted to perform some daring exploit before they were arrested themselves, they killed Hipparchus when they found him by the Leocorium organizing the Panathenaic procession.[1]

The rest of the Hellenes, too, make many incorrect assumptions not only about the dimly remembered past, but also about contemporary history. For instance, there is a general belief that the kings of Sparta are each entitled to two votes, whereas in fact they have only one; and it is believed, too, that the Spartans have a company of troops called 'Pitanate'. Such a company has never existed. Most people, in fact, will not take trouble in finding out the truth, but are much more inclined to accept the first story they hear.

However, I do not think that one will be far 21 wrong in accepting the conclusions I have reached from the evidence which I have put forward. It is better evidence than that of the poets, who exaggerate the importance of their themes, or of the prose chroniclers, who are less interested in telling the truth than in catching the attention of their public, whose authorities cannot be checked, and whose subject-matter, owing, to the passage of time, is mostly lost in the unreliable streams of mythology. We may claim instead to have used only the plainest evidence and to have reached conclusions which are reasonably accurate, considering that we have been dealing with ancient history. As for this present war, even though people are apt to think that the war in which they are fighting is the greatest of all wars and, when it is over, to relapse again into their admiration of the past, nevertheless, if one looks at the facts themselves, one will see that this was the greatest war of all.

In this history I have made use of set 22 speeches some of which were delivered just before and others during the war. I have found it difficult to remember the precise words used in the speeches which I listened to myself and my various informants have experienced the same difficulty; so my method has been, while keeping as closely as possible to the general sense of the words that were actually used, to make the speakers say what, in my opinion, was called for by each situation.

And with regard to my factual reporting of the events of the war I have made it a principle not to write down the first story that came my way, and not even to be guided by my own general impressions; either I was present myself at the events which I have described or else I heard of them from eyewitnesses whose reports I have checked with as much thoroughness as possible. Not that even so the truth was easy to discover: different eyewitnesses give different accounts of the same events, speaking out of partiality for one side or the other or else from imperfect memories. And it may well be that my history will seem less easy to read because of the absence in it of a romantic element. It will be enough for me, however, if these words of mine are judged useful by those who want to understand clearly the events which happened in the past and which (human nature being what it is) will, at some time or other and in much the same ways, be repeated in the future. My work is not a piece of writing designed to meet the taste of an immediate public, but was done to last for ever.

23   The greatest war in the past was the Persian War; yet in this war the decision was reached quickly as a result of two naval battles and two battles on land. The Peloponnesian War, on the other hand, not only lasted for a long time, but throughout its course brought with it unprecedented suffering for Hellas. Never before had so many cities been captured and then devastated, whether by foreign armies or by the Hellenic powers themselves (some of these cities, after capture, were resettled with new inhabitants); never had there been so many exiles; never such loss of life—both in the actual warfare and in internal revolutions. Old stories of past prodigies, which had not found much confirmation in recent experience, now became credible. Wide areas, for instance, were affected by violent earthquakes; there were more frequent eclipses of the sun than had ever been recorded before; in various parts of the country there were extensive droughts followed by famines; and there was the plague which did more harm and destroyed more life than almost any other single factor. All these calamities fell together upon the Hellenes after the outbreak of war.

War began when the Athenians and the Peloponnesians broke the Thirty Years Truce which had been made after the capture of Euboea.[2] As to the reasons why they broke the truce, I propose first to give all account of the causes of complaint which they had against each other and of the specific instances where their interests clashed: this is in order that there should be no doubt in

anyone's mind about what led to this great war falling upon the Hellenes. But the real reason for the war is, in my opinion, most likely to be disguised by such an argument. What made war inevitable was the growth of Athenian power and the fear which this caused in Sparta. As for the reasons for breaking the truce and declaring war which were openly expressed by each side, they are as follows. . . .

The Dispute over Corcyra

In Corinth tempers were running high 31 over the war with Corcyra. All through the year following the sea battle and in the year after that the Corinthians were building ships and doing everything possible to increase the efficiency of their navy. Rowers were collected from the Peloponnese itself, and good terms were offered to bring them also from the rest of the Hellas.

In Corcyra the news of the preparations provoked alarm. They had no allies in Hellas, since they had not enrolled themselves either in the Spartan or in the Athenian league. They decided therefore to go to Athens, to join the Athenian alliance, and see whether they could get any support from that quarter.

When the news of this move reached Corinth, the Corinthians also sent representatives to Athens, fearing that the combined strength of the navies of Athens and Corcyra would prevent them from having their own way in the war with Corcyra. An assembly was held and the arguments on both sides were put forward. The representatives of Corcyra spoke as follows:

'Athenians, in a situation like this, it is 32 right and proper that first of all certain points should be made clear. We have come to ask you for help, but cannot claim that this help is due to us because of any great services we have done to you in the past or on the basis of any existing alliance. We must therefore convince you first that by giving us this help you will be acting in your own interests, or certainly not against your own interests; and then we must show that our gratitude can be depended upon. If on all these points you find our arguments unconvincing, we must not be surprised if our mission ends in failure.

'Now Corcyra has sent us to you in the conviction that in asking for your alliance we can also satisfy you on these points. What has happened is that our policy in the past appears to have been against our own present interests, and at the same time makes it look inconsistent of us to be asking help from you. It certainly looks inconsistent to be coming here to ask for help when in the past we have deliberately avoided all alliances; and it is because of this very policy that we are now left entirely alone to face a war with Corinth. We used to think that our neutrality was a wise thing since it prevented us being dragged into danger by other people's policies; now we see it clearly as a lack of foresight and as a source of weakness.

'It is certainly true that in the recent naval battle we defeated the Corinthians single-handed. But now they are coming against us with a much greater force drawn from the Peloponnese and from the rest of Hellas. We recognize that, if we have nothing but our own national resources, it is impossible for us to survive, and we can imagine what lies in store for us if they overpower us. We are therefore forced to ask for assistance, both from you and from everyone else; and it should not be held against us that now we have faced the facts and are reversing our old policy of keeping ourselves to ourselves. There is nothing sinister in our action; we merely recognize that we made a mistake.

33 'If you grant our request, you will find that in many ways it was a good thing that we made it at this particular time. First of all, you will not be helping aggressors, but people who are the victims of aggression. Secondly, we are now in extreme peril, and if you welcome our alliance at this moment you will win our undying gratitude. And then, we are, after you, the greatest naval power in Hellas. You would have paid a lot of money and still have been very grateful to have us on your side. Is it not, then, an extraordinary stroke of good luck for you (and one which will cause heartburning among your enemies) to have us coming over voluntarily into your camp, giving ourselves up to you without involving you in any dangers or any expense? It is a situation where we, whom you are helping, will be grateful to you, the world

in general will admire you for your generosity, and you yourselves will be stronger than you were before. There is scarcely a case in history where all these advantages have been available at the same time, nor has it often happened before that a power looking for an alliance can say to those whose help it asks that it can give as much honour and as much security as it will receive.

'In case of war we should obviously be useful to you, but some of you may think that there is no immediate danger of war. Those who think along those lines are deceiving themselves; they do not see that facts that Sparta is frightened of you and wants war, that Corinth is your enemy and is also influential at Sparta. Corinth has attacked us first in order to attack you afterwards. She has no wish to make enemies of us both at once and find us standing together against her. What she wants is to get an initial advantage over you in one of two ways—either by destroying our power or by forcing us to use it in her interests. But it is our policy to be one move ahead, which is why we want you to accept the alliance which we offer. It is better to have the initiative in these matters—to take our own measures first, rather than be forced to counter the intrigues that are made against us by others.

'If the Corinthians say that you have no 34 right to receive one of their colonies into your alliance, they should be told that every colony, if it is treated properly, honours its mother city, and only becomes estranged when it had been treated badly. Colonists are not sent abroad to be the slaves of those who remain behind, but to be their equals. And it is quite clear that Corinth was in the wrong so far as we are concerned. We asked them to settle the affair of Epidamnus by arbitration; but they chose to prosecute their claims by war instead of by a reasonable settlement. Indeed, the way in which they are treating us, their kinsmen, ought to be a warning to you and ought to prevent you from falling into their deceitful traps or listening to what may appear to be their straightforward demands. When one makes concessions to one's enemies, one regrets it afterwards, and the fewer concessions one makes the safer one is likely to be.

35 'It is not a breach of your treaty with Sparta if you receive us into your alliance. We are neutrals, and it is expressly written down in your treaty that any Hellenic state which is in this condition is free to ally itself with whichever side it chooses. What is really monstrous is a situation where Corinth can find sailors for her ships both from her own allies and from the rest of Hellas, including in particular your own subjects, while we are shut off from a perfectly legitimate alliance, and indeed from getting help from anywhere: and then, on top of that, they will actually accuse you of behaving illegally if you grant our request. In fact it is we who shall have far greater reason to complain of you if you are not willing to help us; you will be rejecting us, who are no enemies of yours, in the hour of our peril, and as for the others, who are enemies of yours and are also the aggressors, you will not only be doing nothing to stop them, but will actually be allowing them to build up their strength from the resources of your own empire. Is this right? Surely you ought either to stop them from engaging troops from your own subjects, or else to give us, too, whatever assistance you think proper. Best of all would be for you to receive us in open alliance and help us in that way.

'We have already suggested that such a course would be very much in your own interests. Perhaps the greatest advantage to you is that you can entirely depend on us because your enemies are the same as ours, and strong ones, too, quite capable of doing damage to those who revolt from them. And then it is quite a different matter for you if you reject alliance with a naval power than if you do the same thing with a land power. Your aim, no doubt, should be, if it were possible, to prevent anyone else having a navy at all: the next best thing is to have on your side the strongest navy there is.

36 'Some of you may admit that we have shown that the alliance would be in your interests, and yet may still feel apprehensive about a breach of your treaty with Sparta. Those who think in this way should remember that, whether you feel apprehensive or not, you will certainly have become stronger, and that this fact will make your enemies

think twice before attacking you; whereas if you reject us, however confident you may feel, you will in fact be the weaker for it, and consequently less likely to be treated with respect by a strong enemy. Remember, too, that your decision is going to affect Athens just as much as Corcyra. At the moment your thoughts are on the coming war—a war, in fact, which has almost broken out already. Certainly you will not be showing very much foresight for your own city if, at this time, you are in two minds whether to have on your side a power like Corcyra, whose friendship can be so valuable and whose hostility so dangerous to you. Apart from all other advantages, Corcyra lies in an excellent position on the coastal route to Italy and Sicily, and is thus able to prevent naval reinforcements coming to the Peloponnese from there, or going from the Peloponnese to those countries.

'The whole thing can be put very shortly, and these few words will give you the gist of the whole argument why you should not abandon us. There are three considerable naval powers in Hellas—Athens, Corcyra, and Corinth. If Corinth gets control of us first and you allow our navy to be united with hers, you will have to fight against the combined fleets of Corcyra and the Peloponnese. But if you receive us into your alliance, you will enter upon the war with our ships as well as your own.'

After this speech from the Corcyraean 37 side, the representative of Corinth spoke as follows: 'These Corcyraeans have not confined their arguments to the question of whether or not you should accept their alliance. They have named us as aggressors and have stated that they are the victims of an unjust war. Before, therefore, we go on to the rest of our argument, we must deal first with these two points. Our aim will be to give you a clear idea of what exactly we are claiming from you, and to show that there are good reasons why you should reject the appeal of Corcyra.

'"Wisdom" and "Moderation" are the words used by Corcyra in describing her old policy of avoiding alliances. In fact the motives were entirely evil, and there was nothing good about them at all. She wanted no allies because her actions were wrong, and she was ashamed of calling in others to witness her own misdoings. The geographical situation of Corcyra gives its inhabitants a certain independence. The ships of other states are forced to put in to their harbours much more often than the Corcyraean ships visit the harbours of other states. So in cases where a Corcyraean has been guilty of injuring some other national, the Corcyraeans are themselves their own judges, and there is no question of having the case tried by independent judges appointed by treaty. So this neutrality of theirs, which sounds so innocent, was in fact a disguise adopted not to preserve them from having to share in the wrong-doings of others, but in order to give them a perfectly free hand to do wrong themselves, making away with other people's property by force, when they are strong enough, cheating them, whenever they can manage to do so, and enjoying their gains without any vestige of shame. Yet if they really were the honourable people they pretend to be, this very independence of theirs would have given them the best possible opportunity of showing their good qualities in the relations of common justice.

38 'In fact they have not acted honourably either towards us or towards anyone else. Though they are colonists of ours, they have never been loyal to us and are now at war with us. They were not sent out in the first place, they say, to be ill treated. And we say that we did not found colonies in order to be insulted by them, but rather to retain our leadership and to be treated with proper respect. At all events our other colonies do respect us, and indeed they treat us with great affection. It is obvious, then, that, if the majority are pleased with us, Corcyra can have no good reason for being the only one that is dissatisfied; and that we are not making war unreasonably, but only as the result of exceptional provocation. Even if we were making a mistake, the right thing would be for them to give in to us, and then it would be a disgrace to us if we failed to respect so reasonable an attitude. As it is, their arrogance and the confidence they feel in their wealth have made them act improperly towards us on numerous occasions, and in particular with regard to Epidamnus, which belongs to us. When this place was in distress, they took no steps towards bringing it under control; but as soon as we came to relieve it, they forcibly took possession of it, and still hold it.

39 'They actually say that they were prepared in the first place to submit the matter to arbitration. The phrase is meaningless when used by someone who has already stolen an advantage and makes the offer from a safe position; it should only be used when, before opening hostilities, one puts oneself on a real and not an artificial level with one's enemies. And in their case there was no mention of this excellent idea of arbitration before they started to besiege Epidamnus; they only brought the word forward when they began to think that we were not going to let them have their own way.

'And now, being in the wrong themselves over Epidamnus, they have come to you and are asking you not so much for alliance as for complicity in their crime. They are asking you to welcome them at a time when they are at war with us. What they should have done was to have approached you in the days when they were really secure, not at this present moment, when they have wronged us and when danger threatens them. Under present circumstances you will be giving aid to people who never gave you a share in their power, and you will force us to hold you equally responsible with them, although you took no part in their misdeeds. Surely, if they expect you to join fortunes with them now, they should have shared this power with you in the past.

40 'We have shown, I think, that we have good reasons for complaint, and that the conduct of Corcyra has been both violent and grasping. Next we should like you to understand that it would not be right or just for you to receive them as allies. Though there may be a clause in the treaty stating that any city not included in the original agreement is free to join whichever side it likes, this cannot refer to cases where the object of joining an alliance is to injure other powers; it cannot refer to a case where a city is only looking for security because it is in revolt, and where the result of accepting its alliance, if one looks at the matter dispassionately, will be,

not peace, but war. And this is what may well happen to you, if you will not take our advice. You would not only be helping them, but making war on us, who are bound to you by treaty. If you join them in attacking us, we shall be forced to defend ourselves against you as well as them.

41 'The right course, surely, is either for you to preserve a strict neutrality or else to join us against them. At least you have treaty obligations towards Corinth, whereas you have never even had a peace treaty with Corcyra. What you ought to do is to establish a precedent by which a power may receive into its alliance that revolted from you and when the Peloponnesian states were divided on the question whether to help them or not, we were not one of those who voted against you; on the contrary, we openly opposed the others and said that every power should have the right to control its own allies. Now, if you are going to welcome and assist people who have done wrong to us, you will find just as many of your own people coming over to our side, and you will be establishing a precedent that is likely to harm you even more than us. All this we have a perfect right to claim from you by Hellenic law and custom. We should like also to give you some advice and to mention that we have some title to your gratitude. We are not enemies who are going to attack you, and we are not on such friendly terms that such services are quite normal. We say, therefore, that the time has come for you to repay us for what we did for you in the past.

'You were short of warships when you were fighting Aegina, just before the Persian invasion. Corinth then gave you twenty ships. As a result of this act of kindness you were able to conquer Aegina, and as a result of our other good turn to you, when we prevented the Peloponnesian states from helping Samos, you were able to punish that island. And these acts of ours were done at critical periods, periods when people are very apt to turn upon their enemies and disregard every other consideration except victory. At such times people regard even former enemies as their friends, so long as they are on their side, and even genuine friends as their enemies, if they stand in their way; in fact their overmastering desire for victory makes them neglect their own best interests.

'We should like you to think carefully over 42 these points; we should like your young men to ask their elders about them, and for you to decide that you ought to behave towards us as we have behaved towards you. Do not think: "the Corinthians are quite right in what they say, but in the event of war all this is not in our interest." It is generally the best policy to make the fewest errors of judgement, and you must remember that, though Corcyra is trying to frighten you into doing wrong by this idea of a coming war, there is no certainty that a war will come. You may think that Corinth will be your enemy in the future, but it is not worth your while to be carried away by this idea and to make open enemies of us now. A much wiser course would be to remove the suspicions which we already feel towards you in connection with Megara. And you will find that an act of kindness done at the right moment has a power to dispel old grievances quite out of proportion to the act itself.

'Do not be influenced by the fact that they 43 are offering you a great naval alliance. The power that deals fairly with its equals finds a truer security than the one which is hurried into snatching some apparent but dangerous advantage. We ourselves are now in that position that you were in at the time when, during the discussions at Sparta, we laid down the principle that every power should uphold this principle, and, since our vote helped you then, you should not injure us now by voting against us. No, you should deal with us as we have dealt with you, and you should be conscious that we are in one of those critical situations where real friendship is to be gained from helping us and real hostility from opposing us. Do not go against us by receiving these Corcyraeans into your alliance. Do not aid and abet them in their crimes. Thus you will be acting as you ought to act and at the same time you will be making the wisest decision in your own interests.'

This was the speech of the Corinthian del- 44 egation. The Athenians, after listening to both sides, discussed the matter at two assemblies. At the first of these, opinion seemed to incline in favour of the Corinthian arguments, but at the second there was a change, and they decided on entering into some kind of alliance with Corcyra. This was not to be a total alliance involving the two parties in any war which either of them might have on hand; for the Athenians realized that if Corcyra required them to join in an attack on Corinth, that would constitute a breach of their treaty with the Peloponnese. Instead the alliance was to be of a defensive character and would only operate if Athens or Corcyra or any of their allies were attacked from outside.

The general belief was that, whatever happened, war with the Peloponnese was bound to come. Athens had no wish to see the strong navy of Corcyra pass into the hands of Corinth. At the same time she was not averse from letting the two Powers weaken each other by fighting together; since in this way, if war did come, Athens herself would be stronger in relation to Corinth and to the other naval Powers. Then, too, it was a fact that Corcyra lay very conveniently on the coastal route to Italy and Sicily.

45   So, with these considerations in mind, Athens made her alliance with Corcyra. The Corinthian representatives returned to Corinth, and soon afterwards Athens sent ten ships as reinforcement to Corcyra. These ships were under the command of Lacedaimonius, the son of Cimon, Diotimus, the son of Strombichus, and Proteas, the son of Epicles. Their instructions were to avoid battle with the Corinthians except under the following circumstances. If the Corinthians sailed against Corcyra with the intention of landing on the island itself or at any point in Corcyraean territory, then they were to do whatever they could to prevent it. These instructions were given in order to avoid breaking the existing treaty.

46   The ten ships reached Corcyra, and now the Corinthians had completed their preparations and sailed for the island with a fleet of 150 ships. Ten of these came from Elis, twelve from Megara, ten from Leucas, twenty-seven from Ambracia, one from Anactorium, and ninety from Corinth herself. Each contingent had its own officers; the Corinthian admiral, who had four subor-

dinate commanders, was Xenoclides, the son of Euthycles.

This fleet sailed out from Leucas to the mainland opposite Corcyra and came to anchor at Chimerium in the territory of Thesprotis. There is a harbour here, and above it, at some distance from the sea, the city of Ephyre in the Elean district. Near Ephyre the waters of the Acherusian Lake flow into the sea. It gets its name from the river Acheron, which flows through Thesprotis and falls into the lake. The other river in the district is the Thyamis, which forms the boundary between Thesprotis and Cestrine. Between the mouths of these two rivers is the high promontory of Chimerium. It was at this point of the mainland that the Corinthians came to anchor and made an encampment.

47   The Corcyraeans, as soon as they heard of their enemies' approach, manned 110 ships, commanded by Miciades, Aisimides, and Eurybatus, and made a camp on one of the group of islands which are called 'Sybota.' The ten Athenian ships were with them. Their land forces were posted on the headland of Leukimme and had been reinforced by a contingent of 1,000 hoplites from Zacynthus. The Corinthians, too, on the mainland received considerable reinforcements from the natives of those parts, who had always been on friendly terms with them.

48   When the Corinthians had finished their preparations, they took with them rations for three days and put out to sea by night from Chimerium with the intentions of engaging the enemy. At dawn they came in sight of the Corcyraean ships already in the open sea and bearing down upon them. As soon as they saw each other, both sides took up their positions for battle. The Athenian ships were on the right side of the Corcyraean line, which otherwise consisted of their own ships in three squadrons, each under the command of one of their admirals. This was the Corcyraean order of battle. On the other side the ships of Megara and of Ambracia were on the right, the other allies were variously distributed in the centre, and the Corinthians themselves, with the best ships at their disposal, held the left of the

line, facing the Athenians and the right wing to the Corcyraeans.

49   Then, after the signals had been hoisted on both sides, they joined battle. The fighting was of somewhat old-fashioned kind, since they were still behindhand in naval matters, both sides having numbers of hoplites[3] aboard their ships, together with archers and javelin throwers. But the fighting was hard enough, in spite of the lack of skill shown: indeed, it was more like a battle on land than a naval engagement. When the ships came into collision it was difficult for them to break away clear, because of the number engaged and of their close formation. In fact both sides relied more for a victory on their hoplites, who were on the docks and who fought a regular pitched battle there while the ships remained motionless. No one attempted the manoeuvre of encirclement; in fact it was a battle where courage and sheer strength played a greater part than scientific methods. Everywhere in the battle confusion reigned, and there was shouting on all sides.

The Athenian ships would come up in support of the Corcyraeans whenever they were hard pressed and would so help to alarm their enemies, but they did not openly join the battle, since the commanders were afraid of acting contrary to the instructions they had received at Athens.

The right of the Corinthian line was in the greatest difficulties. Here a Corcyraean squadron of twenty ships routed their enemies and drove them back in confusion to the mainland. Sailing right up to their camp, they landed, set fire to the empty tents, and plundered the property they found there. Here, then, the Corcyraeans won a victory and the Corinthians and their allies suffered a defeat. But on the left, where the Corinthians themselves were, things went very differently. The Corcyraeans were in any case in inferior numbers, and they also lacked the support of the twenty ships engaged in the pursuit. And now the Athenians, seeing that the Corcyraeans were in difficulties, began to support them more openly. At first they refrained from actually ramming any Corinthian ship; but finally, when there was no doubt about the defeat and the Corinthians

were still pressing on, there came a point where everyone joined in and nothing was barred. Thus a situation inevitably came about where Corinthians and Athenians were openly fighting with each other.

After their victory, the Corinthians, instead of taking into tow and dragging away the ships that they had put out of action, turned their attention to the men. They sailed in and out of the wreckage, killing rather than taking prisoners. Thus they unknowingly killed some of their own friends, since they did not realize that those on the right side of their line had been defeated. Many ships had been engaged on both sides and the action had been an extensive one, so that, once battle was joined, it was not easy to make out who were winning and who were being defeated. Indeed, so far as numbers of ships were concerned, this was the biggest battle that had ever taken place between two Hellenic states.   50

After they had driven the Corcyraeans to the land, the Corinthians gave their attention to the wrecks and to their own dead, most of whom they were able to recover and bring back to Sybota, not an inhabited place, but a harbour in Thesprotis, where the land army of their native allies was stationed in their support. They then formed up again and sailed out against the Corcyraeans.

The Corcyraeans, fearing that they might attempt to make a landing on their island, came out to meet them with every available ship, including the ten Athenian ships as well as the remainder of their own fleet.

It was already late in the day, and both sides had sung the paean before attacking, when suddenly the Corinthian ships began to back water. They had seen in the distance twenty more Athenian ships approaching. These had been sent out later from Athens to reinforce the original ten, since the Athenians feared (quite rightly, as it turned out) that the Corcyraeans might be defeated and that their own ten ships would not be enough   51
to support them. It was this new force that the Corinthians saw. They suspected that they came from Athens, and thought that there might be still more behind the ships that were visible. Therefore they began to retire.

The Corcyraeans were making their attack from a direction where visibility was not so good, and had not sighted the ships. They were amazed when they saw the Corinthians backing water. Finally someone sighted them and shouted out that there were ships ahead. Then they also retired, since it was already getting dark and the Corinthians had turned and broken off contact with them. The Corcyraeans went back to their camp on Leukimme, and the twenty Athenian ships, which were under the command of Glaucon, the son of Leagrus, and Andocides, the son of Leogoras, sailed up to their camp, making their way through the wrecks and the dead bodies. They arrived not very long after they had originally been sighted, but it was now night and the Corcyraeans feared that they might be enemy ships. However, they were recognized and came safely to anchor.

52 Next day the thirty Athenian ships with all the Corcyraean ships that could put to sea sailed out to the harbour of Sybota, where the Corinthians lay at anchor, to see whether they were prepared to fight. The Corinthians put out from shore and formed a line in the open sea. There they remained, having no intentions of starting an engagement. They saw that a fresh fleet had arrived from Athens, and they were conscious of their own difficulties: the prisoners whom they had aboard their ships had to be guarded, and in the desolate place where they were there were no facilities for repairing their vessels. What particularly worried them was the thought of how they were to make their voyage home. They feared that the Athenians might consider that the treaty had been broken by the recent fighting and might intercept them on their way back. They therefore 53 decided to put some of their men, not carrying a herald's wand, on board a boat and to send them to the Athenians to find out how matters stood.

This was done, and the Corinthian messengers made the following speech: 'Athenians, you are putting yourselves in the wrong. You are starting a war and you are not abiding by the treaty. We are here in order to deal with our own enemies, and now you are standing in our path and have taken up arms against us. Now if your intention is to prevent us from sailing against Corcyra or anywhere else that we wish, if, in other words, you intend to break the treaty, then make us who are here your first prisoners, and treat us as enemies.'

After this speech of the Corinthians, all those in the Corcyraean forces who had been within hearing shouted out in favour of making prisoners of them at once and then putting them to death. The Athenians, however, replied as follows: 'Peloponnesians, we are not starting a war and we are not breaking the treaty. These Corcyraeans are our allies, and we came here to help them. We shall do nothing to stop you if you wish to sail in any other direction; but if you sail against Corcyra or against any part of her territory, then we shall do our best to prevent you.'

When they received this reply from the 54 Athenians, the Corinthians began to prepare for their voyage home. They also put up a trophy to commemorate their victory on the part of Sybota that is on the mainland. Meanwhile the Corcyraeans salvaged the wreckage of their ships and took up the bodies of their own dead. These had been washed towards them by the current and by a wind which got up during the night and scattered them in all directions. They then put up a trophy on the island of Sybota, claiming that the victory had been theirs.

The reasons that each side had for claiming the victory and setting up a trophy were as follows. The Corinthians had had the upper hand in the fighting until nightfall: thus they had brought in most of the disabled ships and their own dead: they held at least 1,000 prisoners and they had sunk about seventy enemy ships. The Corcyraeans had destroyed about thirty ships and, after the arrival of the Athenians, they had recovered off their coast their own dead and their disabled vessels. Then on the day after the battle the Corinthians, on seeing the Athenian fleet, had backed water and retired before them, and after the Athenians had arrived, had not come out from Sybota to fight. So both sides claimed the victory.

On their voyage home the Corinthians 55 took Anactorium, at the mouth of the Ambracian Gulf. It was a place in which both

Corinth and Corcyra had rights and it was given up to the Corinthians by treachery. Before sailing home the Corinthians put settlers of their own into Anactorium. They sold 800 of the Corcyraean prisoners who were slaves, and they kept in captivity 250 whom they treated with great consideration, hoping that a time would come when they would return and win over the island to Corinth. Most of them were in fact people of great power and influence in Corcyra.

So Corcyra remained undefeated in her war with Corinth and the Athenian fleet left the island. But this gave Corinth her first cause for war against Athens, the reason being that Athens had fought against her with Corcyra although the peace treaty was still in force. . . .

The Debate at Sparta and Declaration of War

66 Both the Athenians and the Peloponnesians had already grounds of complaint against each other. The grievance of Corinth was that the Athenians were besieging her own colony of Potidaea, with Corinthians and other Peloponnesians in the place; Athens, on the other hand, had her own grievances against the Peloponnesians; they had supported the revolt of a city which was in alliance with her and which paid her tribute, and they had openly joined the Potidaeans in fighting against her. In spite of this, the truce was still in force and war had not yet broken out. What had been done so far had been done on the private initiative of Corinth.

67 Now, however, Corinth brought matters into the open. Potidaea was under blockade, some of her own citizens were inside, and she feared that the place might be lost. She therefore immediately urged the allies to send delegates to Sparta. There her own delegates violently attacked the Athenians for having broken the truce and committed acts of aggression against the Peloponnese. The people of Aegina were on her side. Out of fear of Athens they had not sent a formal delegation, but behind the scenes they played a considerable part in fomenting war, saying that they had not been given the independence promised to them by the treaty. The Spartans also issued an invitation to their own allies and to anyone else who claimed to have suffered from Athenian aggression. They then held their usual assembly, and gave an opportunity there for delegates to express their views. Many came forward with various complaints. In particular the delegates from Megara, after mentioning a number of other grievances, pointed out that, contrary to the terms of the treaty, they were excluded from all the ports in the Athenian empire and from the market in Athens itself. The Corinthians were the last to come forward and speak, having allowed the previous speakers to do their part in hardening Spartan opinion against Athens. The Corinthian speech was as follows:

'Spartans, what makes you somewhat re- 68 luctant to listen to us others, if we have ideas to put forward, is the great trust and confidence which you have in your own constitution and in your own way of life. This is a quality which certainly makes you moderate in your judgements; it is also, perhaps, responsible for a kind of ignorance which you show when you are dealing with foreign affairs. Many times before now we have told you what we were likely to suffer from Athens, and on each occasion, instead of taking to heart what we were telling you, you chose instead to suspect our motives and to consider that we were speaking only about our own grievances. The result has been that you did not call together this meeting of our allies before the damage was done; you waited until now, when we are actually suffering from it. And of all these allies, we have perhaps the best right to speak now, since we have the most serious complaints to make. We have to complain of Athens for her insolent aggression and of Sparta for her neglect of our advice.

'If there were anything doubtful or obscure about this aggression on the whole of Hellas, our task would have been to try to put the facts before you and show you something that you did not know. As it is, long speeches are unnecessary. You can see yourselves how Athens has deprived some states of their freedom and is scheming to do the same thing for others, especially among our own allies, and that she herself has for a long time been preparing for the eventuality of war.

Why otherwise should she have forcibly taken over from us the control of Corcyra? Why is she besieging Potidaea? Potidaea is the best possible base for any campaign in Thrace, and Corcyra might have contributed a very large fleet to the Peloponnesian League.

69 'And it is you who are responsible for all this. It was you who in the first place allowed the Athenians to fortify their city and build the Long Walls after the Persian War. Since then and up to the present day you have withheld freedom not only from those who have been enslaved by Athens but even from your own allies. When one is deprived of one's liberty one is right in blaming not so much the man who puts the fetters on as the one who had the power to prevent him, but did not use it—especially when such a one rejoices in the glorious reputation of having been the liberator of Hellas.

'Even at this stage it has not been easy to arrange this meeting, and even at this meeting there are no definite proposals. Why are we still considering whether aggression has taken place instead of how we can resist it? Men who are capable of real action first make their plans and then go forward without hesitation while their enemies have still not made up their minds. As for the Athenians, we know their methods and how they gradually encroach upon their neighbours. Now they are proceeding slowly because they think that your insensitiveness to the situation enables them to go on their way unnoticed; you will find that they will develop their full strength once they realize that you do see what is happening and are still doing nothing to prevent it.

'You Spartans are the only people in Hellas who wait calmly on events, relying for your defence not on action but on making people think that you will act. You alone do nothing in the early stages to prevent an enemy's expansion; you wait until your enemy has doubled his strength. Certainly you used to have the reputation of being safe and sure enough: now one wonders whether this reputation was deserved. The Persians, as we know ourselves, came from the ends of the earth and got as far as the Peloponnese before you were able to put a proper force into the field to meet them. The Athenians, unlike the Persians, live close to you, yet still you do not appear to notice them; instead of going out to meet them, you prefer to stand still and wait till you are attacked, thus hazarding everything by fighting with opponents who have grown far stronger than they were originally.

'In fact you know that the chief reason for the failure of the Persian invasion was the mistaken policy of the Persians themselves; and you know, too, that there have been many occasions when, if we managed to stand up to Athenian aggression, it was more because of Athenian mistakes than because of any help we got from you. Indeed, we can think of instances already where those who have relied on you and remained unprepared have been ruined by the confidence they placed in you.

'We should not like any of you to think that we are speaking in an unfriendly spirit. We are only remonstrating with you, as is natural when one's friends are making mistakes. Real accusations must be kept for one's enemies who have actually done one harm.

'Then also we think we have as much right 70 as anyone else to point out faults in our neighbours, especially when we consider the enormous difference between you and the Athenians. To our minds, you are quite unaware of this difference; you have never yet tried to imagine what sort of people these Athenians are against whom you will have to fight—how much, indeed how completely different from you. An Athenian is always an innovator, quick to form a resolution and quick at carrying it out. You, on the other hand, are good keeping things as they are; you never originate an idea, and your action tends to stop short of its aim. Then again Athenian daring will outrun its own resources; they will take risks against their better judgement, and still, in the midst of danger, remain confident. But your nature is always to do less than you could have done, to mistrust your own judgement, however sound it may be, and to assume that dangers will last for ever. Think of this, too: while you are hanging back, they never hesitate; while you stay at home, they are always abroad; for they think that the farther they go the more they will get, while you think that any movement may endanger what you have already. If they win a victory, they follow it up at once, and if they suffer a defeat, they scarcely fall back at all. As for their bodies, they regard them as expendable for their city's sake, as though they were not their own; but each man cultivates his own intelligence, again with a view to doing something notable for his city. If they aim at something and do not get it, they think that they have been deprived of what belonged to them already; whereas, if their enterprise is successful, they regard that success as nothing compared to what they will do next. Suppose they fail in some undertaking; they make good the loss immediately by setting their hopes in some other direction. Of them alone it may be said that they possess a thing almost as soon as they have begun to desire it, so quickly with them does action follow upon decision. And so they go on working away in hardship and danger all the days of their lives, seldom enjoying their possessions because they are always adding to them. Their view of a holiday is to do what needs doing; they prefer hardship and activity to peace and quiet. In a word, they are by nature incapable of either living a quiet life themselves or of allowing anyone else to do so.

71 'That is the character of the city which is opposed to you. Yet you still hang back; you will not see that the likeliest way of securing peace is this: only to use one's power in the cause of justice, but to make it perfectly plain that one is resolved not to tolerate aggression. On the contrary, your idea of proper behaviour is, firstly to avoid harming others, and then to avoid being harmed yourselves, even if it is a matter of defending your own interests. Even if you had on your frontiers a power holding the same principles as you do, it is hard to see how such a policy could have been a success. But at the present time, as we have just pointed out to you, your whole way of life is out of date when compared with theirs. And it is just as true in politics as it is in any art or craft: new methods must drive out old ones. When a city can live in peace and quiet, no doubt the old-established ways are best: but when one is constantly being faced by new problems,

one has also to be capable of approaching them in an original way. Thus Athens, because of the very variety of her experience, is a far more modern state than you are.

'Your inactivity has done harm enough. Now let there be an end of it. Give your allies, and especially Potidaea, the help you promised, and invade Attica at once. Do not let your friends and kinsmen fall into the hands of the bitter enemies. Do not force the rest of us in despair to join a different alliance. If we did so, no one could rightly blame us—neither the gods who witnessed our oaths nor any man capable of appreciating our situation. The people who break a treaty or alliance are the ones who fail to give the help they swore to give, not those who have to look elsewhere because they have been left in the lurch. But if you will only make up your minds to act, we will stand by you. It would be an unnatural thing for us to make a change, nor could we find other allies with whom we have such close bonds. You have heard what we have to say. Think carefully over your decision. From your fathers was handed down to you the leadership of the Peloponnese. Maintain its greatness.'

This was the speech of the Corinthians. 72 There happened to be already in Sparta some Athenian representatives who had come there on other business. When they heard the speeches that had been made, they decided that they, too, ought to claim a hearing. Not that they had any intention of defending themselves against any of the charges that had been made against Athens by the various cities, but they wished to make a general statement and to point out that this was an affair which needed further consideration and ought not to be decided upon at once. They wanted also to make clear how powerful their city was, to remind the elder members of the assembly of facts that were known to them, and to inform the younger ones of matters in which they were ignorant. In this way they hoped to divert their audience from the idea of war and make them incline towards letting matters rest. They therefore approached the Spartans and said that, if there was no objection, they, too, would like to make a speech before the assembly. The Spartans invited them to do so, and they came forward and spoke as follows:

73 'This delegation of ours did not come here to enter into a controversy with your allies, but to deal with the business on which our city sent us. We observe, however, that extraordinary attacks have been made on us, and so we have come forward to speak. We shall make no reply to the charges which these cities have made against us. Your assembly is not a court of law, competent to listen to pleas either from them or from us. Our aim is to prevent you from coming to the wrong decision on a matter of great importance through paying too much attention to the views of your allies. At the same time we should like to examine the general principles of the argument used against us and to make you see that our gains have been reasonable enough and that our city is one that deserves a certain consideration.

'There is no need to talk about what happened long ago: there our evidence would be that of hearsay rather than that of eyewitnesses amongst our audience. But we must refer to the Persian War, to events well known to you all, even though you may be tired of constantly hearing the story. In our actions at that time we ventured everything for the common good; you have your share in what was gained, do not deprive us of all our share of glory and of the good that it may do us. We shall not be speaking in the spirit of one who is asking a favour, but of one who is producing evidence. Our aim is to show you what sort of a city you will have to fight against, if you make the wrong decision.

'This is our record. At Marathon we stood out against the Persians and faced them single-handed. In the later invasion, when we were unable to meet the enemy on land, we and all our people took to our ships, and joined in the battle at Salamis. It was this battle that prevented the Persians from sailing against the Peloponnese and destroying the cities one by one; for no system of mutual defence could have been organized in face of the Persians themselves. Once they had lost the battle at sea they realized that their force was crippled and they immediately with-
74 drew most of their army. That, then was the result, and it proved that the fate of Hellas depended on her navy. Now, we contributed to this result in three important ways: we produced most of the ships, we provided the most intelligent of the generals, and we displayed the most unflinching courage. Out of the 400 ships, nearly two-thirds were ours: the commander was Themistocles, who was mainly responsible for the battle being fought in the straits, and this, obviously, was what saved us. You yourselves in fact, because of this, treated him with more distinction than you have ever treated any visitor from abroad. And the courage, the daring that we showed were without parallel. With no help coming to us by land, with all the states up to our frontier already enslaved, we chose to abandon our city and to sacrifice our property; then, so far from deserting the rest of our allies in the common cause or making ourselves useless to them by dispersing our forces, we took to our ships and chose the path of danger, with no grudges against you for not having come to our help earlier. So it is that we can claim to have given more than we received. There were still people living in the cities which you left behind you, and you were fighting to preserve them; when you sent out your forces you feared for yourselves much more than for us (at all events, you never put in an appearance until we had lost everything). Behind us, on the other hand, was a city that had ceased to exist; yet we still went forward and ventured our lives for this city that seemed so impossible to recover. Thus we joined you and helped to save not only ourselves but you also. But if we, like others, had been frightened about our land and had made terms with the Persians before you arrived, or if, later, we had regarded ourselves as irretrievably ruined and had lacked the courage to take to our ships, then there would no longer have been any point in your fighting the enemy at sea, since you would not have had enough ships. Instead things would have gone easily and quietly just as the Persians wished.

'Surely, Spartans, the courage, the resolu- 75 tion, and the ability which we showed then ought not to be repaid by such immoderate hostility from the Hellenes—especially so far as our empire is concerned. We did not gain this empire by force. It came to us at a time when you were unwilling to fight on to the end against the Persians. At this time our allies came to us of their own accord and begged us to lead them. It was the actual course of events which first compelled us to increase our power to its present extent: fear of Persia was our chief motive, though afterwards we thought, too, of our own honour and our own interest. Finally there came a time when we were surrounded by enemies, when we had already crushed some revolts, when you had lost the friendly feelings that you used to have for us and had turned against us and begun to arouse our suspicion: at this point it was clearly no longer safe for us to risk letting our empire go, especially as any allies that left us would go over to you. And when tremendous dangers are involved no one can be blamed for looking to his own interest.

76 'Certainly you Spartans, in your leadership of the Peloponnese, have arranged the affairs of the various states so as to suit yourselves. And if, in the years of which we were speaking, you had gone on taking an active part in the war and had become unpopular, as we did, in the course of exercising your leadership, we have little doubt that you would have been just as hard upon your allies as we were, and that you would have been forced either to govern strongly or to endanger your own security.

77 'So it is with us. We have done nothing extraordinary, nothing contrary to human nature in accepting an empire when it was offered to us and then in refusing to give it up. Three very powerful motives prevent us from doing so—security, honor, and self-interest. And we were not the first to act in this way. Far from it. It has always been a rule that the weak should be subject to the strong; and besides, we consider that we are worthy of our power. Up till the present moment you, too, used to think that we were; but now, after calculating your own interest, you are beginning to talk in terms of right and wrong. Considerations of this kind have never yet turned people aside from the opportunities of aggrandizement offered by superior strength. Those who really deserve praise are the people who, while human enough to enjoy power, nevertheless pay more attention to justice than they are compelled to do by their situation. Certainly we think that if anyone else was in our position it would soon be evident whether we act with moderation or not. Yet, unreasonably enough, our very consideration for others has brought us more blame than praise. For example, in law-suits with our allies arising out of contracts we have put ourselves at a disadvantage, and when we arrange to have such cases tried by impartial courts in Athens, people merely say that we are overfond of going to law. No one bothers to inquire why this reproach is not made against other imperial Powers, who treat their subjects much more harshly than we do: the fact being, of course, that where force can be used there is no need to bring in the law. Our subjects, on the other hand, are used to being treated as equals; consequently, when they are disappointed in what they think right and suffer even the smallest disadvantage because of a judgement in our courts or because of the power that our empire gives us, they cease to feel grateful to us for all the advantages which we have left to them: indeed, they feel more bitterly over this slight disparity than they would feel if we, from the first, had set the law aside and had openly enriched ourselves at their expense. Under those conditions they would certainly not have disputed the fact that the weak must give in to the strong. People, in fact, seem to feel more strongly about their legal wrongs than about the wrongs inflicted on them by violence. In the first case they think they are being outdone by an equal, in the second case that they are being compelled by a superior. Certainly they put up with much worse sufferings than these when they were under the Persians, but now they think that our government is oppressive. That is natural enough, perhaps, since subject peoples always find the present time most hard to bear. But on one point we are quite certain: if you were to destroy us and to take over our empire, you would soon lose all the goodwill which you have gained because of others being afraid of us—that is, if you are going to stick to those principles of behaviour which you showed before, in the short time when you led Hellas against the

Persians. Your own regulated ways of life do not mix well with the ways of others. Also it is a fact that when one of you goes abroad he follows neither his own rules nor those of the rest of Hellas.

78 'Take time, then, over your decision, which is an important one. Do not allow considerations of other people's opinions and other people's complaints to involve you in difficulties which you will feel yourselves. Think, too of the great part that is played by the unpredictable in war: think of it now, before you are actually committed to war. The longer a war lasts, the more things tend to depend on accidents. Neither you nor we can see into them: we have to abide their outcome in the dark. And when people are entering upon a war they do things the wrong way round. Action comes first, and it is only when they have already suffered that they begin to think. We, however, are still far removed from such a mistaken attitude; so, to the best of our belief, are you. And so we urge you, now, while we are both still free to make sensible decisions, do not break the peace, do not go back upon your oaths; instead let us settle our differences by arbitration, as is laid down in the treaty. If you will not do so, we shall have as our witnesses the gods who heard our oaths. You will have begun the war, and we shall attempt to meet you in any and every field of action that you may choose.'

79 The Athenians spoke as I have described. Now the Spartans had heard the complaints made by their allies against Athens and also the Athenian reply. They therefore requested all outsiders to leave and discussed the situation among themselves. Most people's views ended to the same conclusion—namely, that Athens was already acting aggressively and that war should be declared without delay. However, the Spartan King Archidamus, a man who had a reputation for both intelligence and moderation, came forward and made the following speech:

80 'Spartans, in the course of my life I have taken part in many wars, and I see among you people of the same age as I am. They and I have had experience, and so are not likely to share in what may be a general enthusiasm for war, nor to think that war is a good thing or a safe thing. And you will find, if you look carefully into the matter, that this present war which you are now discussing is not likely to be anything on a small scale. When we are engaged with Peloponnesians and neighbours, the forces on both sides are of the same type, and we can strike rapidly where we wish to strike. With Athens it is different. Here we shall be engaged with people who live far off, people also who have the widest experience of the sea and who are extremely well equipped in all other directions, very wealthy both as individuals and as a state, with ships and cavalry and hoplites, with a population bigger than that of any other place in Hellas, and then, too, with numbers of allies who pay tribute to them. How, then, can we irresponsibly start a war with such a people? What have we to rely upon if we rush into it unprepared? Our navy? It is inferior to theirs, and if we are to give proper attention to it and build it up to their strength, that will take time. Or are we relying on our wealth? Here we are at an even greater disadvantage: we have no public funds, and it is no easy matter to secure contributions from private sources. Perhaps 81 there is ground for confidence in the superiority which we have in heavy infantry and in actual numbers, assets which will enable us to invade and devastate their land. Athens, however, controls plenty of land outside Attica and can import what she wants by sea. And if we try to make her allies revolt from her, we shall have to support them with a fleet, since most of them are on the islands. What sort of war, then, are we going to fight? If we can neither defeat them at sea nor take away from them the resources on which their navy depends, we shall do ourselves more harm than good. We shall then find that we can no longer even make an honourable peace, especially if it is thought that it was we who began the quarrel. For we must not bolster ourselves up with the false hope that if we devastate their land, the war will soon be over. I fear that it is more likely that we shall be leaving it to our children after us. So convinced am I that the Athenians have too much pride to become the slaves of their own land, or to shrink back from warfare as though they were inexperienced in it.

82 'Not that I am suggesting that we should calmly allow them to injure our allies and should turn a blind eye to their machinations. What I do suggest is that we should not take up arms at the present moment; instead we should send to them and put our grievances before them; we should not threaten war too openly, though at the same time we should make it clear that we are not going to let them have their own way. In the meantime we should be making our own preparations by winning over new allies both among Hellenes and among foreigners—from any quarter, in fact, where we can increase our naval and financial resources. No one can blame us for securing our own safety by taking foreigners as well as Greeks into our alliance when we are, as is the fact, having our position undermined by the Athenians. At the same time we must put our own affairs in order. If they pay attention to our diplomatic protests, so much the better. If they do not, then, after two or three years have passed, we shall be in a much sounder position and can attack them if we decide to do so. And perhaps when they see that our actual strength is keeping pace with the language that we use, they will be more inclined to give way, since their land will still be untouched and, in making up their minds, they will be thinking of advantages which they still possess and which have not yet been destroyed. For you must think of their land as though it was a hostage in your possession, and all the more valuable the better it is looked after. You should spare it up to the last possible moment, and avoid driving them to a state of desperation in which you will find them much harder to deal with. If now in our present state of unpreparedness we lay their land waste, hurried into this course by the complaints of our allies, I warn you to take care that our action does not bring to the Peloponnese still more shame and still greater difficulties. As for complaints, whether they come from cities or from private individuals, they are capable of arrangement; but when war is declared by our whole confederacy for the sake of the interests of some of us, and when it is impossible to foresee the course that the war will take, then an honourable settlement is not an easy thing at all.

'Let no one call it cowardice if we, in all 83 our numbers, hesitate before attacking a single city. They have just as many allies as we have, and their allies pay tribute. And war is not so much a matter of armaments as of the money which makes armaments effective: particularly is this true in a war fought between a land power and a sea power. So let us first of all see to our finances and, until we have done so, avoid being swept away by speeches from our allies. It is we who shall bear most of the responsibility for what happens later, whether it is good or bad; we should therefore be allowed the time to look into some of these possibilities at our leisure.

'As for being slow and cautious—which is 84 the usual criticism made against us—there is nothing to be ashamed of in that. If you take something on before you are ready for it, hurry at the beginning will mean delay at the end. Besides, the city in which we live has always been free and always famous. "Slow" and "cautious" can equally well be "wise" and "sensible". Certainly it is because we possess these qualities that we are the only people who do not become arrogant when we are successful, and who in times of stress are less likely to give in than others. We are not carried away by the pleasure of hearing ourselves praised when people are urging us towards dangers that seem to us unnecessary; and we are no more likely to give in shamefacedly to other people's views when they try to spur us on by their accusations. Because of our well-ordered life we are both brave in war and wise in council. Brave, because self-control is based upon a sense of honour, and honour is based on courage. And we are wise because we are not so highly educated as to look down upon our laws and customs, and are too rigorously trained in self-control to be able to disobey them. We are trained to avoid being too clever in matters that are of no use—such as being able to produce an excellent theoretical criticism of one's enemies' dispositions, and then failing in practice to do quite so well against them. Instead we are taught that there is not a great deal of difference between the way we think and the way others think, and that it is impossible to calculate accurately events that are determined by chance. The practical measures that we take are always based on the assumption that our enemies are not unintelligent. And it is right and proper for us to put our hopes in the reliability of our own precautions rather than in the possibility of our opponent making mistakes. There is no need to suppose that human beings differ very much one from another: but it is true that the ones who come out on top are the ones who have been trained in the hardest school.

85 'Let us never give up this discipline which our fathers have handed down to us and which we still preserve and which has always done us good. Let us not be hurried, and in one short day's space come to a decision which will so profoundly affect the lives of men and their fortunes, the fates of cities and their national honour. We ought to take time over such a decision. And we, more than others, can afford to take time, because we are strong. As for the Athenians, I advise sending a mission to them about Potidaea and also about the other cases where our allies claim to have been ill treated. Especially is this the right thing to do since the Athenians themselves are prepared to submit to arbitration, and when one party offers this it is quite illegal to attack him first, as though he was definitely in the wrong. And at the same time carry on your preparations for war. This decision is the best one you can make for yourselves, and is also the one most likely to inspire fear in your enemies.'

After this speech of Archidamus, Sthenelaidas, one of the ephors of that year, came forward to make the final speech, which was as follows:

86 'I do not understand these long speeches which the Athenians make. Though they said a great deal in praise of themselves, they made no attempt to contradict the fact that they are acting aggressively against our allies and against the Peloponnese. And surely, if it is the fact that they had a good record in the past against the Persians and now have a bad record as regards us, then they deserve to pay double for it, since, though they were once good, they have now turned out bad. We are the same then and now, and if we are sensible, we shall not allow any aggression against our allies and shall not wait before we come to their help. They are no longer waiting before being ill treated. Others may have a lot of money and ships and horses, but we have good allies, and we ought not to betray them to the Athenians. And this is not a matter to be settled by law-suits and by words: it is not because of words that our own interests are suffering. Instead we should come to the help of our allies quickly and with all our might. And let no one try to tell us that when we are being attacked we should sit down and discuss matters; these long discussions are rather for those who are meditating aggression themselves. Therefore, Spartans, cast your votes for the honour of Sparta and for war! Do not allow the Athenians to grow still stronger! Do not entirely betray your allies! Instead let us, with the help of heaven, go forward to meet the aggressor!'

After this speech he, himself, in his capacity of ephor, put the question to the Spartan assembly. They make their decisions by acclamation, not by voting, and Sthenelaidas said at first that he could not decide on which side the acclamations were the louder. This was because he wanted to make them show their opinions openly and so make them all the more enthusiastic for war. He therefore said: 'Spartans, those of you who think that the treaty has been broken and that the Athenians are aggressors, get up and stand on one side. Those who do not think so, stand on the other side', and he pointed out to them where they were to stand. They then rose to their feet and separated into two divisions. The great majority were of the opinion that the treaty had been broken.

They then summoned their allies to the assembly and told them that they had decided that Athens was acting aggressively, but that they wanted to have all their allies with them when they put the vote, so that, if they decided to make war, it should be done on the basis of a unanimous resolution.

Afterwards the allied delegates, having got their own way, returned home. Later the Athenian representatives, when they had finished the business for which they had come, also returned. This decision of the assembly that the treaty had been broken took place in the fourteenth year of the thirty years' truce which was made after the affair of Euboea.

88 The Spartans voted that the treaty had been broken and that war should be declared not so much because they were influenced by the speeches of their allies as because they were afraid of the further growth of Athenian power, seeing, as they did, that already the greater part of Hellas was under the control of Athens. . . .

Book Two

Pericles' Funeral Oration

34   In the same winter the Athenians, following their annual custom, gave a public funeral for those who had been the first to die in the war. These funerals are held in the following way: two days before the ceremony the bones of the fallen are brought and put in a tent which has been erected, and people make whatever offerings they wish to their own dead. Then there is a funeral procession in which coffins of cypress wood are carried on wagons. There is one coffin for each tribe, which contains the bones of members of that tribe. One empty bier is decorated and carried in the procession: this is for the missing, whose bodies could not be recovered. Everyone who wishes to, both citizens and foreigners, can join in the procession, and the women who are related to the dead are there to make their laments at the tomb. The bones are laid in the public burial place, which is in the most beautiful quarter outside the city walls. Here the Athenians always bury those who have fallen in war. The only exception is those who died at Marathon, who, because their achievement was considered absolutely outstanding, were buried on the battlefield itself.

When the bones have been laid in the earth, a man chosen by the city for his intellectual gifts and for his general reputation makes an appropriate speech in praise of the dead, and after the speech all depart. This is the procedure at these burials, and all through the war, when the time came to do so the Athenians followed this ancient custom. Now, at the burial of those who were the first to fall in the war Pericles, the son of Xanthippus, was chosen to make the speech. When the moment arrived, he came forward from the tomb and, standing on a high platform, so that he might be heard by as many people as possible in the crowd, he spoke as follows:

'Many of those who have spoken here in 35 the past have praised the institution of this speech at the close of our ceremony. It seemed to them a mark of honour to our soldiers who have fallen in war that a speech should be made over them. I do not agree. These men have shown themselves valiant in action, and it would be enough, I think, for their glories to be proclaimed in action, as you have just seen it done at this funeral organized by the state. Our belief in the courage and manliness of so many should not be hazarded on the goodness or badness of one man's speech. Then it is not easy to speak with a proper sense of balance, when a man's listeners find it difficult to believe in the truth of what one is saying. The man who knows the facts and loves the dead may well think that an oration tells less than what he knows and what he would like to hear: others who do not know so much may feel envy for the dead, and think the orator over-praises them, when he speaks of exploits that are beyond their own capacities. Praise of other people is tolerable only up to a certain point, the point where one still believes that one could do oneself some of the things one is hearing about. Once you get beyond this point, you will find people becoming jealous and incredulous. However, the fact is that this institution was set up and approved by our forefathers, and it is my duty to follow the tradition and do my best to meet the wishes and the expectations of every one of you.

'I shall begin by speaking about our ances- 36 tors, since it is only right and proper on such an occasion to pay them the honour of recalling what they did. In this land of ours there have always been the same people living from generation to generation up till now, and they, by their courage and their virtues, have handed it on to us, a free country. They certainly deserve our praise. Even more so do our fathers deserve it. For to the inheritance they had received they added all the empire we have now, and it was not without blood and toil that they handed it down to us of the present generation. And then we ourselves, assembled here today, who are mostly in the prime of life, have, in most directions, added to the power of our empire and have organized our State in such a way that it is perfectly well able to look after itself both in peace and in war.

'I have no wish to make a long speech on subjects familiar to you all: so I shall say nothing about the warlike deeds by which we acquired our power or the battles in which we or our fathers gallantly resisted our enemies, Greek or foreign. What I want to do is, in the first place, to discuss the spirit in which we faced our trials and also our constitution and the way of life which has made us great. After that I shall speak in praise of the dead, believing that this kind of speech is not inappropriate to the present occasion, and that this whole assembly, of citizens and foreigners, may listen to it with advantage.

37 'Let me say that our system of government does not copy the institutions of our neighbours. It is more the case of our being a model to others, than of our imitating anyone else. Our constitution is called a democracy because power is in the hands not of a minority but of the whole people. When it is a question of settling private disputes, everyone is equal before the law; when it is a question of putting one person before another in positions of public responsibility, what counts is not membership of a particular class, but the actual ability which the man possesses. No one, so long as he has it in him to be of service to the state, is kept in political obscurity because of poverty. And, just as our political life is free and open, so is our day-to-day life in our relations with each other. We do not get into a state with our next-door neighbour if he enjoys himself in his own way, nor do we give him the kind of black looks which, though they do no real harm, still do hurt people's feelings. We are free and tolerant in our private lives; but in public affairs we keep to the law. This is because it commands our deep respect.

'We give our obedience to those whom we put in positions of authority, and we obey the laws themselves, especially those which are for the protection of the oppressed, and those unwritten laws which it is an acknowledged shame to break.

'And here is another point. When our 38 work is over, we are in a position to enjoy all kinds of recreation for our spirits. There are various kinds of contests and sacrifices regularly throughout the year; in our own homes we find a beauty and a good taste which delight us every day and which drive away our cares. Then the greatness of our city brings it about that all the good things from all over the world flow in to us, so that to us it seems just as natural to enjoy foreign goods as our own local products.

'Then there is a great difference between 39 us and our opponents, our attitude towards military security. Here are some examples: Our city is open to the world, and we have no periodical deportations in order to prevent people observing or finding out secrets which might be of military advantage to the enemy. This is because we rely, not on secret weapons, but on our own real courage and loyalty. There is a difference, too, in our educational systems. The Spartans, from their earliest boyhood, are submitted to the most laborious training in courage; we pass our lives without these restrictions, and yet are just as ready to face the same dangers as they are. Here is a proof of this: When the Spartans invade our land, they do not come by themselves, but bring all their allies with them; whereas we, when we launch an attack abroad, do the job by ourselves, and, though fighting on foreign soil, do not often fail to defeat opponents who are fighting for their own hearths and homes. As a matter of fact none of our enemies has ever yet been confronted with our total strength, because we have to divide our attention between our navy and the many missions on which our troops are sent on land. Yet, if our enemies engage a detachment of our forces and defeat it, they give themselves credit for having thrown back our entire army; or, if they lose, they claim that they were beaten by us in full strength. There are certain advantages, I think, in our way of meeting danger voluntarily, with an easy mind, instead of with a laborious training, with natural rather than with state-induced courage. We do not have to spend our time practising to meet sufferings which are still in the future; and when they are actually upon us we show ourselves just as brave as these others who are always in strict training. This is one point in which, I think, our city deserves to be admired. There are also others:

40 'Our love of what is beautiful does not lead to extravagance; our love of the things of the mind does not make us soft. We regard wealth as something to be properly used, rather than as something to boast about. As for poverty, no one need be ashamed to admit it: the real shame is in not taking practical measures to escape from it. Here each individual is interested not only in his own affairs but in the affairs of the state as well: even those who are mostly occupied with their own business are extremely well-informed on general politics—this is a peculiarity of ours: we do not say that a man who takes no interest in politics is a man who minds his own business; we say that he has no business here at all. We Athenians, in our own persons, take our decisions on policy or submit them to proper discussions: for we do not think that there is an incompatibility between words and deeds; the worst thing is to rush into action before the consequences have been properly debated. And this is another point where we differ from other people. We are capable at the same time of taking risks and of estimating them beforehand. Others are brave out of ignorance; and, when they stop to think, they begin to fear. But the man who can most truly be accounted brave is he who best knows the meaning of what is sweet in life and of what is terrible, and then goes out undeterred to meet what is to come.

41 'Again, in questions of general good feeling there is a great contrast between us and most other people. We make friends by doing good to others, not by receiving good from them. This makes our friendship all the more reliable, since we want to keep alive the gratitude of those who are in our debt by showing continued good-will to them: whereas the feelings of one who owes us something lack the same enthusiasm, since he knows that, when he repays our kindness, it will be more like paying back a debt than giving something spontaneously. We are unique in this. When we do kindnesses to others, we do not do them out of any calculations of profit or loss: we do them without afterthought, relying on our free liberality. Taking everything together then, I declare that our city is an education to Greece, and I declare that in my opinion each single one of our citizens, in all the manifold aspects of life, is able to show himself the rightful lord and owner of his own person, and do this, moreover, with exceptional grace and exceptional versatility. And to show that this is no empty boasting for the present occasion, but real tangible fact, you have only to consider the power which our city possesses and which has been won by those very qualities which I have mentioned. Athens, alone of the states we know, comes to her testing time in a greatness that surpasses what was imagined of her. In her case, and in her case alone, no invading enemy is ashamed at being defeated, and no subject can complain of being governed by people unfit for their responsibilities. Mighty indeed are the marks and monuments of our empire which we have left. Future ages will wonder at us as the present age wonders at us now. We do not need the praises of a Homer, or of anyone else whose words may delight us for the moment, but whose estimation of facts will fall short of what is really true. For our adventurous spirit has forced an entry into every sea and into every land; and everywhere we have left behind us everlasting memorials of good done to our friends or suffering inflicted on our enemies.

'This, then, is the kind of city for which these men, who could not bear the thought of losing her, nobly fought and nobly died. It is only natural that every one of us who survive them should be willing to undergo hardships in her service. And it was for this reason that I have spoken at such length about our city, because I wanted to make it clear that for us there is more at stake than there is for others who lack our advantages; also I wanted my words of praise for the dead to be set in the bright light of evidence. And now the most important of these words has been spoken. I have sung the praises of our city; but it was the courage and gallantry of these men, and of people like them, which made her splendid. Nor would you find it true in the case of many of the Greeks, as it is true of them, that no words can do more than justice to their deeds.

'To me it seems that the consummation which has overtaken these men shows us the meaning of manliness in its first revelation and in its final proof. Some of them, no doubt, had their faults; but what we ought to remember first is their gallant conduct against the enemy in defence of their native land. They have blotted out evil with good, and done more service to the commonwealth than they ever did harm in their private lives. No one of these men weakened because he wanted to go on enjoying his wealth: no one put off the awful day in the hope that he might live to escape his poverty and grow rich. More to be desired than such things, they chose to check the enemy's pride. This, to them was a risk most glorious, and they accepted it, willing to strike down the enemy and relinquish everything else. As for success or failures they left that in the doubtful hands of Hope, and when the reality of battle was before their faces, they put their trust in their own selves. In the fighting, they thought it more honourable to stand their ground and suffer death than to give in and save their lives. So they fled from the reproaches of men, abiding with life and limb the brunt of battle; and, in a small moment of time, the climax of their lives, a culmination of glory, not of fear, were swept away from us.

43   'So and such they were, these men—worthy of their city. We who remain behind may hope to be spared their fate, but must resolve to keep the same daring spirit against the foe. It is not simply a question of estimating the advantages in theory. I could tell you a long story (and you know it as well as I do) about what is to be gained by beating the enemy back. What I would prefer is that you should fix your eyes every day on the greatness of Athens as she really is, and should fall in love with her. When you realize her greatness, then reflect that what made her great was men with a spirit of adventure, men who knew their duty, men who were ashamed to fall below a certain standard. If they ever failed in an enterprise, they made up their

minds that at any rate the city should not find their courage lacking to her, and they gave to her the best contribution that they could. They gave her their lives, to her and to all of us, and for their own selves they won praises that never grow old, the most splendid of sepulchres—not the sepulchre in which their bodies are laid, but where their glory remains eternal in men's minds, always there on the right occasion to stir others to speech or to action. For famous men have the whole earth as their memorial: it is not only the inscriptions on their graves in their own country that mark them out; no, in foreign lands also, not in any visible form but in people's hearts, their memory abides and grows. It is for you to try to be like them. Make up your minds that happiness depends on being free, and freedom depends on being courageous. Let there be no relaxation in face of the perils of the war. The people who have most excuse for despising death are not the wretched and unfortunate, who have no hope of doing well for themselves, but those who run the risk of a complete reversal in their lives, and who would feel the difference most intensely, if things went wrong for them. Any intelligent man would find a humiliation caused by his own slackness more painful to bear than death, when death comes to him unperceived, in battle, and in the confidence of his patriotism.

'For these reasons I shall not commiserate 44 with those parents of the dead, who are present here. Instead I shall try to comfort them. They are well aware that they have grown up in a world where there are many changes and chances. But this is good fortune—for men to end their lives with honour, as these have done, and for you honourably to lament them: their life was set to a measure where death and happiness went hand in hand. I know that it is difficult to convince you of this. When you see other people happy you will often be reminded of what used to make you happy too. One does not feel sad at not having some good thing which is outside one's experience: real grief is felt at the loss of something which one is used to. All the same, those of you who are of the right age must bear up and take comfort in the thought of having more children. In your own homes these new children will prevent you from brooding over those who are no more, and they will be a help to the city, too, both in filling the empty places, and in assuring her security. For it is impossible for a man to put forward fair and honest views about our affairs if he has not, like everyone else, children whose lives may be at stake. As for those of you who are now too old to have children, I would ask you to count as gain the greater part of your life, in which you have been happy, and remember that what remains is not long, and let your hearts be lifted up at the thought of the fair fame of the dead. One's sense of honour is the only thing that does not grow old, and the last pleasure, when one is worn out with age, is not, as the poet said, making money, but having the respect of one's fellow men.

45   'As for those of you here who are sons or brothers of the dead, I can see a hard struggle in front of you. Everyone always speaks well of the dead, and, even if you rise to the greatest heights of heroism, it will be a hard thing for you to get the reputation of having come near, let alone equalled, their standard. When one is alive, one is always liable to the jealousy of one's competitors, but when one is out of the way, the honour one receives is sincere and unchallenged.

46   'Perhaps I should say a word or two on the duties of women to those among you who are now widowed. I can say all I have to say in a short word of advice. Your great glory is not to be inferior to what God has made you, and the greatest glory of a woman is to be least talked about by men, whether they are praising you or criticizing you. I have now, as the law demanded, said what I had to say. For the time being our offerings to the dead have been made, and for the future their children will be supported at the public expense by the city, until they come of age. This is the crowning prize which she offers, both to the dead and to their children, for the ordeals which they have faced. Where the rewards of valour are the greatest, there you will find also the best and bravest spirits among the people. And now, when you have mourned for your dear ones, you must depart.' . . .

Book Five

The Melian Dialogue

Next summer Alcibiades sailed to Argos 84 with twenty ships and seized 300 Argive citizens who were still suspected of being pro-Spartan. These were put by the Athenians into the nearby islands under Athenian control.

The Athenians also made an expedition against the island of Melos. They had thirty of their own ships, six from Chios, and two from Lesbos; 1,200 hoplites, 300 archers, and twenty mounted archers, all from Athens; and about 1,500 hoplites from the allies and the islanders.

The Melians are a colony from Sparta. They had refused to join the Athenian empire like the other islanders, and at first had remained neutral without helping either side; but afterwards, when the Athenians had brought force to bear on them by laying waste their land, they had become open enemies of Athens.

Now the generals Cleomedes, the son of Lycomedes, and Tisias, the son of Tisimachus encamped with the above force in Melian territory and, before doing any harm to the land, first of all sent representatives to negotiate. The Melians did not invite these representatives to speak before the people, but asked them to make the statement for which they had come in front of the governing body and the few. The Athenian representatives then spoke as follows:

'So we are not to speak before the people, 85 no doubt in case the mass of the people should hear once and for all and without interruption an argument from us which is both persuasive and incontrovertible, and should so be led astray. This, we realize, is your motive in bringing us here to speak before the few. Now suppose that you who sit here should make assurance doubly sure. Suppose that you, too, should refrain from dealing with every point in detail in a set speech, and should instead interrupt us whenever we say something controversial and deal with that before going on to the next point? Tell us first whether you approve of this suggestion of ours.'

86   The Council of the Melians replied as follows:

'No one can object to each of us putting forward our own views in a calm atmosphere. That is perfectly reasonable. What is scarcely consistent with such a proposal is the present threat, indeed the certainty, of your making war on us. We see that you have come prepared to judge the argument yourselves, and that the likely end of it all will be either war, if we prove that we are in the right, and so refuse to surrender, or else slavery.'

87   *Athenians:* If you are going to spend the time in enumerating your suspicions about the future, or if you have met here for any other reason except to look the facts in the face and on the basis of these facts to consider how you can save your city from destruction, there is no point in our going on with this discussion. If, however, you will do as we suggest, then we will speak on.

88   *Melians:* It is natural and understandable that people who are placed as we are should have recourse to all kinds of arguments and different points of view. However, you are right in saying that we are met together here to discuss the safety of our country and, if you will have it so, the discussion shall proceed on the lines that you have laid down.

89   *Athenians:* Then we on our side will use no fine phrases saying, for example, that we have a right to our empire because we defeated the Persians, or that we have come against you now because of the injuries you have done us—a great mass of words that nobody would believe. And we ask you on your side not to imagine that you will influence us by saying that you, though a colony of Sparta, have not joined Sparta in the war, or that you have never done us any harm. Instead we recommend that you should try to get what it is possible for you to get, taking into consideration what we both really do think; since you know as well as we do that, when these matters are discussed by practical people, the standard of justice depends on the equality of power to compel and that in fact the strong do what they have the power to do and the weak accept what they have to accept.

Melians: Then in our view (since you force   90
us to leave justice out of account and to confine ourselves to self-interest)—in our view it is at any rate useful that you should not destroy a principle that is to the general good of all men—namely, that in the case of all who fall into danger there should be such a thing as fair play and just dealing, and that such people should be allowed to use and to profit by arguments that fall short of a mathematical accuracy. And this is a principle which affects you as much as anybody, since your own fall would be visited by the most terrible vengeance and would be an example to the world.

Athenians: As for us, even assuming that   91
our empire does come to an end, we are not despondent about what would happen next. One is not so much frightened of being conquered by a power which rules over others, as Sparta does (not that we are concerned with Sparta now), as of what would happen if a ruling power is attacked and defeated by its own subjects. So far as this point is concerned, you can leave it to us to face the risks involved. What we shall do now is to show you that it is for the good of our own empire that we are here and that it is for the preservation of your city that we shall say what we are going to say. We do not want any trouble in bringing you into our empire, and we want you to be spared for the good both of yourselves and of ourselves.

Melians: And how could it be just as good   92
for us to be the slaves as for you to be the masters?

Athenians: You, by giving in, would save   93
yourselves from disaster; we, by not destroying you, would be able to profit from you.

Melians: So you would not agree to our   94
being neutral, friends instead of enemies, but allies of neither side?

Athenians: No, because it is not so much   95
your hostility that injures us; it is rather the case that, if we were on friendly terms with you, our subjects would regard that as a sign of weakness in us, whereas your hatred is evidence of our power.

Melians: Is that your subjects' idea of fair   96
play—that no distinction should be made between people who are quite unconnected with you and people who are mostly your

own colonists or else rebels whom you have conquered?

97 *Athenians:* So far as right and wrong are concerned they think that there is no difference between the two, that those who still preserve their independence do so because they are strong, and that if we fail to attack them it is because we are afraid. So that by conquering you we shall increase not only the size but the security of our empire. We rule the sea and you are islanders, and weaker islanders too than the others; it is therefore particularly important that you should not escape.

98 *Melians:* But do you think there is no security for you in what we suggest? For here again, since you will not let us mention justice, but tell us to give in to your interests, we, too, must tell you what our interests are and, if yours and ours happen to coincide, we must try to persuade you of the fact. Is it not certain that you will make enemies of all states who are at present neutral, when they see what is happening here and naturally conclude that in course of time you will attack them too? Does not this mean that you are strengthening the enemies you have already and are forcing others to become your enemies even against their intentions and their inclinations?

99 *Athenians:* As a matter of fact we are not so much frightened of states on the continent. They have their liberty, and this means that it will be a long time before they begin to take precautions against us. We are more concerned about islanders like yourselves, who are still unsubdued, or subjects who have already become embittered by the constraint which our empire imposes on them. These are the people who are most likely to act in a reckless manner and to bring themselves and us, too, into the most obvious danger.

100 *Melians:* Then surely, if such hazards are taken by you to keep your empire and by your subjects to escape from it, we who are still free would show ourselves great cowards and weaklings if we failed to face everything that comes rather than submit to slavery.

101 *Athenians:* No, not if you are sensible. This is no fair fight, with honour on one side and shame on the other. It is rather a question of saving your lives and not resisting those who are far too strong for you.

102 *Melians:* Yet we know that in war fortune sometimes makes the odds more level than could be expected from the difference in numbers of the two sides. And if we surrender, then all our hope is lost at once, whereas, so long as we remain in action, there is still a hope that we may yet stand upright.

103 *Athenians:* Hope, that comforter in danger! If one already has solid advantages to fall back upon, one can indulge in hope. It may do harm, but will not destroy one. But hope is by nature an expensive commodity, and those who are risking their all on one cast find out what it means only when they are already ruined; it never fails them in the period when such a knowledge would enable them to take precautions. Do not let this happen to you, you who are weak and whose fate depends on a single movement of the scale. And do not be like those people who, as so commonly happens, miss the chance of saving themselves in a human and practical way, and, when every clear and distinct hope has left them in their adversity, turn to what is blind and vague, to prophecies and oracles and such things which by encouraging hope lead men to ruin.

104 *Melians:* It is difficult, and you may be sure that we know it, for us to oppose your power and fortune, unless the terms be equal. Nevertheless we trust that the gods will give us fortune as good as yours, because we are standing for what is right against what is wrong; and as for what we lack in power, we trust that it will be made up for by our alliance with the Spartans, who are bound, if for no other reason, then for honour's sake, and because we are their kinsmen, to come to our help. Our confidence, therefore, is not so entirely irrational as you think.

105 *Athenians:* So far as the favour of the gods is concerned, we think we have as much right to that as you have. Our aims and our actions are perfectly consistent with the beliefs men hold about the gods and with the principles which govern their own conduct. Our opinion of the gods and our knowledge of men lead us to conclude that it is a general

and necessary law of nature to rule whatever one can. This is not a law that we made ourselves, nor were we the first to act upon it when it was made. We found it already in existence, and we shall leave it to exist for ever among those who come after us. We are merely acting in accordance with it, and we know that you or anybody else with the same power as ours would be acting in precisely the same way. And therefore, so far as the gods are concerned, we see no good reason why we should fear to be at a disadvantage. But with regard to your views about Sparta and your confidence that she, out of a sense of honour, will come to your aid, we must say that we congratulate you on your simplicity but do not envy you your folly. In matters that concern themselves or their own constitution the Spartans are quite remarkably good; as for their relations with others, that is a long story, but it can be expressed shortly and clearly by saying that of all people we know the Spartans are most conspicuous for believing that what they like doing is honourable and what suits their interests is just. And this kind of attitude is not going to be of much help to you in your absurd quest for safety at the moment.

)6 *Melians:* But this is the very point where we can feel most sure. Their own self-interest will make them refuse to betray their own colonists, the Melians, for that would mean losing the confidence of their friends among the Hellenes and doing good to their enemies.

)7 *Athenians:* You seem to forget that if one follows one's self-interest one wants to be safe, whereas the path of justice and honour involves one in danger. And, where danger is concerned, the Spartans are not, as a rule, very venturesome.

)8 *Melians:* But we think that they would even endanger themselves for our sake and count the risk more worth taking than in the case of others, because we are so close to the Peloponnese that they could operate more easily, and because they can depend on us more than on others, since we are of the same race and share the same feelings.

)9 *Athenians:* Goodwill shown by the party that is asking for help does not mean security for the prospective ally. What is looked for is a positive preponderance of power in action. And the Spartans pay attention to this point even more than others do. Certainly they distrust their own native resources so much that when they attack a neighbour they bring a great army of allies with them. It is hardly likely therefore that, while we are in control of the sea, they will cross over to an island.

Melians: But they still might send others. 110 The Cretan sea is a wide one, and it is harder for those who control it to intercept others than for those who want to slip through to do so safely. And even if they were to fail in this, they would turn against your own land and against those of your allies left unvisited by Brasidas. So, instead of troubling about a country which has nothing to do with you, you will find trouble nearer home, among your allies, and in your own country.

Athenians: It is a possibility, something 111 that has in fact happened before. It may happen in your case, but you are well aware that the Athenians have never yet relinquished a single siege operation through fear of others. But we are somewhat shocked to find that, though you announced your intention of discussing how you could preserve yourselves, in all this talk you have said absolutely nothing which could justify a man in thinking that he could be preserved. Your chief points are concerned with what you hope may happen in the future, while your actual resources are too scanty to give you a chance of survival against the forces that are opposed to you at this moment. You will therefore be showing an extraordinary lack of common sense if, after you have asked us to retire from this meeting, you still fail to reach a conclusion wiser than anything you have mentioned so far. Do not be led astray by a false sense of honour—a thing which often brings men to ruin when they are faced with an obvious danger that somehow affects their pride. For in many cases men have still been able to see the dangers ahead of them, but this thing called dishonour, this word, by its own force of seduction, has drawn them into a state where they have surrendered to an idea, while in fact they have fallen voluntarily into irrevocable disaster, in dishonour that is all the more dishonourable because it has come to them from their own folly rather than their misfortune. You, if you take the right view, will be careful to avoid this. You will see that there is nothing disgraceful in giving way to the greatest city in Hellas when she is offering you such reasonable terms— alliance on a tribute-paying basis and liberty to enjoy your own property. And, when you are allowed to choose between war and safety, you will not be so insensitively arrogant as to make the wrong choice. This is the safe rule—to stand up to one's equals, to behave with deference towards one's superiors, and to treat one's inferiors with moderation. Think it over again, then, when we have withdrawn from the meeting, and let this be a point that constantly recurs to your minds—that you are discussing the fate of your country, that you have only one country, and that its future for good or ill depends on this one single decision which you are going to make.

112   The Athenians then withdrew from the discussion. The Melians, left to themselves, reached a conclusion which was much the same as they had indicated in their previous replies. Their answer was as follows:

'Our decision, Athenians, is just the same as it was at first. We are not prepared to give up in a short moment the liberty which our city has enjoyed from its foundation for 700 years. We put our trust in the fortune that the gods will send and which has saved us up to now, and in the help of men—that is, of the Spartans; and so we shall try to save ourselves. But we invite you to allow us to be friends of yours and enemies to neither side, to make a treaty which shall be agreeable to both you and us, and so to leave our country.'

113   The Melians made this reply, and the Athenians, just as they were breaking off the discussion, said: 'Well, at any rate, judging from this decision of yours, you seem to us quite unique in your ability to consider the future as something more certain than what is before your eyes, and to see uncertainties as realities, simply because you would like them to be so. As you have staked most on and trusted most in Spartans, luck, and hopes, so in all these you will find yourselves most completely deluded.'

114   The Athenian representatives then went back to the army, and the Athenian generals,

finding that the Melians would not submit, immediately commenced hostilities and built a wall completely round the city of Melos, dividing the work out among the various states. Later they left behind a garrison of some of their own and some allied troops to blockade the place by land and sea, and with the greater part of their army returned home. The force left behind stayed on and continued with the siege.

About the same time the Argives invaded 115 Phliasia and were ambushed by the Phliasians and the exiles from Argos, losing about eighty men. Then, too, the Athenians at Pylos captured a great quantity of plunder from Spartan territory.

Not even after this did the Spartans renounce the treaty and make war, but they issued a proclamation saying that any of their people who wished to do so were free to make raids on the Athenians. The Corinthians also made some attacks on the Athenians because of private quarrels of their own, but the rest of the Peloponnesians stayed quiet.

Meanwhile the Melians made a night attack and captured the part of the Athenian lines opposite the marketplace. They killed some of the troops, and then, after bringing in corn and everything else useful that they could lay their hands on, retired again and made no further move, while the Athenians took measures to make their blockade more efficient in future. So the summer came to an end.

In the following winter the Spartans 116 planned to invade the territory of Argos, but when the sacrifices for crossing the frontier turned out of unfavourably, they gave up the expedition. The fact that they had intended to invade made the Argives suspect certain people in their city, some of whom they arrested, though others succeeded in escaping.

About this same time the Melians again captured another part of the Athenian lines where there were only a few of the garrison on guard. As a result of this, another force came out afterwards from Athens under the command of Philocrates, the son of Demeas. Siege operations were now carried on vigorously and, as there was also some treachery from inside, the Melians surrendered unconditionally to the Athenians, who put to death all the men of military age whom they took, and sold the women and children as slaves. Melos itself they took over for themselves, sending out later a colony of 500 men.[4]

Notes

1. In VI, 53–9 there is a lengthy digression on the assassination of Hipparchus in 514 B.C.

2. In 446–5 B.C.

3. The hoplites were the heavily accoutred infantry. Since they were responsible for providing their own arms and armour, they were drawn solely from the wealthier sections of the population.

4. That there were Melian survivors, who were restored by Lysander at the end of the war, is stated by Xenophon (*Hellenica,* ii, 2, 9).

Reprinted from: Thucydides, *History of the Peloponnesian War,* translated by Rex Warner, pp. 46–49, 53–67, 72–87, 143–151, 400–408. Copyright © 1954 by Rex Warner. Reprinted by permission of The Penguin Group: London. ✦

2
Thucydides on Human Nature

C. D. C. Reeve

"War," Thucydides says in a famous phrase, "is a violent teacher." Some of the lessons he learned at its bloody hands are contained in his great unfinished *History of the Peloponnesian War.* They are by no means easy to extract from it, however, for Thucydides is an unusually difficult writer, whose "search for truth," as he puts it himself, "strains the patience of most people, who would rather believe the first things that come to hand" (1.21). When the truth is about a war fought over two-and-a-half millennia ago in a faraway land, patience is no doubt strained even further.

Besides what he has to tell us about that war, however, Thucydides also aims to tell us something of more general interest and application.

> This history may not be the most delightful to hear, since there is no mythology in it. But those who want to look into the truth of what was done in the past—which, given the human condition, will recur in the future, either in the same fashion or nearly so—those readers will find this History valuable enough, as it was composed to be a lasting possession and not to be heard for a prize at the moment of a contest. (1.22)

What is it, then, that we should learn about ourselves from what happened to strangers long ago? What is the human condition—the human nature—we share with them that ensures the pertinence of their history to ours? If we can answer these questions, perhaps some of what Thucydides wanted to bequeath us will survive after we have forgotten or failed to learn the details of his account of what the Spartans and the Athe-

nians did to each other in the years between 431 and 404 B.C.

The natural and best place to begin is with the justly famous description of the civil war that took place in Corcyra in 427 B.C., which has been characterized, quite rightly in my view, as "the most substantial expression of direct personal opinion" in all Thucydides.[1] Here we find Thucydides himself doing some of the work for us, telling us directly what he thinks human nature is really like wherever it is found. A representative translation presents what he has to say as follows:

> Then, with the ordinary conventions of civilized life thrown into confusion, human nature, always ready to offend even where laws exist, showed itself proudly in its true colours, as something incapable of controlling passion, insubordinate to the idea of justice, the enemy to anything superior to itself. (3.84.2)[2]

The idea irresistibly conveyed is that human beings are naturally bad[3] and that only culture, in the form of the laws or conventions of civilized life—the very things that are destroyed in a civil war—prevents them from showing themselves in their very nasty true colors. When the veneer of culture and civilization [is] peeled away and our nature stands revealed, the passage seems to say, we see how really bad in the bone we actually are.

Patience, however, reveals Thucydides' message to be much more complex. Here is the passage—labeled (B)—more carefully translated and restored to its larger context:[4]

> [A] These atrocities, then, were mostly committed first in Corcyra, including all the acts of revenge people take, when they have the opportunity, against rulers who have shown more arrogance (*hubris*) than good sense (*sophrosunê*), and all the actions some people unjustly choose to escape long-standing poverty. Most of these acted from a passionate desire for their neighbor's possessions,[5] but there were also those who attacked the wealthy not out of a desire for more than their fair share (*pleonexia*), but primarily out of zeal for equality, and they were the most carried away by their undisciplined passion (*orgê*) to commit savage and pitiless attacks. [B] Now that life had been

thrown into confusion in the city, human nature—which is accustomed to violate justice and laws—came to vanquish law altogether, and gladly showed itself enslaved to passion (*orgê*), stronger than justice, and enemy of any superior. [C] Without the destructive force of envy (*phthonos*), you see, people would not value revenge over *to hosion*,[6] or profits over justice. When they want revenge on others, people are determined first to destroy without a trace the laws that commonly govern such matters, though it is only because of these laws that anyone in trouble can hope to be saved, and even though anyone might be in danger someday and stand in need of such laws. (3.84)

This entire text is obviously difficult, but there is another sort of problem with it: it is thought to be an interpolation by an imitator rather than by Thucydides himself. The evidence for inauthenticity is not entirely compelling, in my view, but I am not interested in rebutting it.[7] What I do want to rebut, however, is the oft-made claim, which bolsters the case for inauthenticity, that the thoughts expressed in the passage are not genuinely Thucydidean. A recent translator has put the issue well: "Could the Thucydides who in 3.82–83 saw the development of civil-war mentality as a macabre perversion of progress . . . [be the] Thucydides who in 3.84 viewed mankind as depraved from the outset?"[8] If 3.84 does view mankind in this way, I agree that it is not Thucydidean. When properly analyzed, however, it does not say that. And what it does say, as we shall see, is not only consistent with the rest of Thucydides' account of what took place in Corcyra, but allows us to see it, and much else in the *Histories*, in a new and compelling light.

Let us begin with (A) and what it has to say about *poverty*. Prior to civil war, some are rich and powerful (the pro-Spartan oligarchs we shall meet later) and some are poor and powerless (the pro-Athenian democrats). When conflict between the Spartans and Athenians changes the balance of power, civil war breaks out between the rich and the poor, and the poor take the opportunity unjustly to seize what belongs to the rich. They are motivated to do so either by *pleonexia*—a

passionate desire for more than their fair share of their neighbor's possessions—or by "zeal for equality" coupled with "undisciplined passion" aroused by those who had arrogantly used the greater wealth and power they enjoyed before the war.

Focus now on *injustice*. Why is it unjust for the poor to seize the possessions of the rich? The answer must surely be that the underlying motives, *pleonexia* in one case, undisciplined passion in the other, lead the poor to go beyond what equality itself demands. They do not rest content with a fair redistribution of wealth, but take more than their fair share or inflict unjust or unfair retribution on the rich. But unjust or unfair by what standard?

Turn next to *revenge*. It motivates people to attack any leader or any superior who showed arrogance rather than good sense when he was in power. It thus leads people to destroy the laws described in the final sentence of the passage, which are the only hope of those who have no other power to defend themselves. Now these laws are not the conventional, man-made laws of Corcyra or of any other city-state, since they are laws to which anyone in danger anywhere might need to appeal. What, then, are they?

In the Melian Dialogue, we find out:

Well, then, since you [Athenians] put your interest in place of justice, our [Melians'] view must be that it is your interest not to subvert this rule that is good for all: that a plea of justice and fairness should do some good for a man who has fallen into danger, if he can win over his judges, even if he is not perfectly persuasive. And this rule concerns you no less than us: if you ever stumble, you might receive a terrible punishment and be an example to others. (5.90)

The claim the Melians make is that it is the self-interest of a superior to be at least somewhat moved by the appeals to justice and fairness of weaker people he has the power to treat arrogantly, since he may find himself needing to make such appeals if he falls from power. What kind of rule exactly is this? What gives it its authority? The answer cannot be that it has been enacted by some duly constituted legislative body with jurisdiction over the Athenians and the Melians, since there is no such body. Instead, whatever authority the rule has is that of a rule of rational prudence or good sense (*sophrosunê*): Exercise power nonarrogantly lest you be the victim of revenge should you fall from power. Arrogance in the exercise of power leads to revenge, then, whereas good sense has at least the potential to lead to just and fair treatment. That appeals to fairness and justice should have at least some influence on those in power is, therefore, "good for all."

What is at issue in 3.84, then, are not the "ordinary conventions of civilized life" (a phrase that corresponds to nothing in the Greek text) or the conventional laws of some particular polis or city-state, but a notion of justice and fairness rooted in good sense and such known facts about human nature as that arrogance leads to revenge, and poverty to *pleonexia* and undisciplined passion.

The role (C) assigns to envy is that of explaining the actions of those motivated either by *pleonexia* or by zeal for equality coupled with undisciplined passion. Moreover, the envy itself has an explanation, namely, the pre-civil war distribution of wealth and power, which left some in lifelong poverty and others the impotent victims of arrogance. In other words, the distribution was unfair or unjust by the very standards of equality, fairness, and justice that recommend themselves to good sense and to piety. No doubt, power and wealth naturally attract some envy, but unfairly or unjustly held or arrogantly used power and wealth attract something else. They attract righteous indignation—and, indeed, that seems to me to be close to the proper sense of *phthonos* here, as in the familiar *phthonos tôn theôn*. What the gods feel is not so much envy at the legitimate success of mortals, but indignation at their arrogant, unfair, unjust success.

We are now ready to interpret (B) itself. When human nature is said to be "enslaved to passion," we naturally think of that nature as divided into the passion that is, so to speak, the slave master, on the one hand, and whatever it is that is the slave, on the other. Here, as one might think, human nature is something good (or at least not bad) that just

happens to be overcome or enslaved by something bad: the passion. On the other hand, when human nature is described as "accustomed to violate justice and laws," as "stronger than justice," and as "the enemy of any superior," human nature as a whole seems to be portrayed as intrinsically bad. When we look more closely into the passage, however, we see that only some elements in our nature are at issue here, not our nature as a whole. For what is an enemy to any superior is revenge sparked by the arrogant exercise of power; what is stronger than justice is *pleonexia* or zeal for equality coupled with passion sparked by unjust distributions of wealth and power; and what is accustomed to violate laws and justice are these very same things: passion, *pleonexia*, revenge. So our nature as a whole is not being characterized as bad, just certain things in it, and then only under certain circumstances.

Passage (C) identifies the element in our nature that passion overcomes as *to hosion*, which is standardly translated as "piety." This is not wrong, exactly, but it does obscure the real nature of Thucydides' thought. For the primary meaning of *hosios* is "sanctioned or approved by the law of nature, opp. to *dikaios* (established by human law)."[9] What passion does in reality, then, is this: it deafens people to appeals to the law, not of the state, but of nature. And that law, as we know, is the law based on good sense and a knowledge of that same nature. It is what Pericles, in his Funeral Oration, refers to as "the unwritten law that all people acknowledge it is shameful to break" (2.37).

A first stab at analyzing (B), then, might run as follows:

> Passion and *pleonexia*, kindled by inequalities of wealth and power, and set ablaze by the confusion of life caused by civil war, are stronger than the justice of good sense. Revenge, kindled by arrogance in the use of power, and set ablaze in the same manner, is the enemy of those who exercise power in that way.

Already this is a far cry from the pessimistic portrait of human nature with which we began. For good sense is as much a part of our nature as the revenge, *pleonexia*, and passion, which, especially in certain sorts of circumstances, overcome it.

Armed with this interpretation of 3.84, we are ready to look at some other famous passages from the Corcyra chapters, undoubtedly by Thucydides himself, which tell us more about the effects of civil war and the confusion that comes along with it. As before, I begin with a standard translation.

> In the various cities these revolutions were the cause of many calamities—as happens and always will happen while human nature is what it is, though there may be different degrees of savagery, and, as different circumstances arise, the general rules will admit of some variety. In times of peace and prosperity cities and individuals alike follow higher standards, because they are not forced into a situation where they have to do what they do not want to do. But war is a stern teacher; in depriving them of the power of easily satisfying their daily wants, it brings most people's minds down to the level of their actual circumstances. (3.82.2)[10]

The idea expressed in the passage, so translated, is this: people are morally better in times of peace and prosperity, but when their daily wants are not satisfied, their minds are brought down to the level of their actual circumstances—that is to say, they give over their minds entirely to thinking up ways of satisfying their daily wants by any means whatsoever. More succinctly: starve a human being and you will discover just what his true motivations are—motivations that peace and prosperity hide from view. The confusion of life that war brings, then, must be disorder in the means of satisfying our desires for our daily needs.

When the passage is translated more carefully, however, and our findings about 3.84 are used as a guide, it tells an altogether different story.

> Civil war brought many hardships to the city-states, such as happen and will always happen as long as the nature of human beings is the same, although they may be more or less violent or take different forms, depending on the circumstances in each case. In peace and prosperity, cities and private individuals alike have better judgment (*tas gnômas*) be-

cause they are not plunged into constraining necessities; but war, which takes away the everyday resources (*tên euporian tou kath' hêmeran*) is a violent teacher, i.e. it tends to assimilate most people's passions (*tas orgas*) to their conditions (*ta paronta*). (3.82.2)

Notice the difference. It is precisely *gnomê*, judgment (good sense or prudence) that, because of the absence of the sort of constraining necessities that come with civil war, tends to function better in peace and prosperity. The final clause tells us what these necessities are and how they operate to worsen judgment. Civil war assimilates most people's passions to their conditions, which are, since there is a war, violent conditions. By doing so, it takes away the everyday resources available to judgment, namely, calm passions and satisfied appetites. The result is that judgment or good sense is unbalanced by strong and undisciplined passion.

Further evidence that it is our judgment and its control by our passions that is at issue in the passage is provided by what Thucydides goes on to say. Again, I begin with a representative translation.

> So revolutions broke out in city after city, and in places where the revolutions occurred late the knowledge of what had happened previously in other places caused still new extravagances of revolutionary zeal, expressed by an elaboration in the methods of seizing power and by unheard-of atrocities in revenge. (3.82.3) To fit in with the change of events, words, too, had to change their usual meanings. What used to be described as a thoughtless act of aggression was now regarded as the courage one would expect to find in a party member; to think of the future and wait was merely another way of saying one was a coward. (3.82.4)[11]

Notice that, so translated, 3.82.4 does not connect in any obvious way with its predecessor, 3.82.3. In particular, no mechanism is specified to explain why or how words come to change their meanings as a result of the previously described effects of civil war on human nature.

Things change, however, when the passage is translated with greater care and consistency.

> Civil war ran through the city-states; those it struck later heard what the first cities had done and far exceeded them in inventing artful means for attack and bizarre forms of revenge. And they exchanged their usual verbal evaluations of actions for new ones, in the light of what they thought justified; thus irrational daring (*tolma . . . alogistos*) was considered courage (*andreia*) and loyalty to one's party. (3.82.3–4)

Words did not change their meanings at all, then; rather, human beings applied words with the old meanings to new things.[12] For example, they applied the word *courage*, with its old meaning, not to genuinely courageous acts, but to acts of *irrational daring*. And the reason they did so was that their judgment was impaired by their passions. Hence, the ready intelligibility of Thucydides' own diagnosis of what occurred:

> The cause of all this was a desire to rule arising out of *pleonexia* and ambition, and the love of victory that proceeds from these two. Those who led their parties in the cities promoted their policies under decent-sounding names: "political equality for the multitude" on one side, and "moderate aristocracy" on the other. And though they pretended to serve the public in their speeches, they actually treated it as the prize for their competition; and striving by whatever means to win, both sides ventured on the most horrible outrages and exacted even greater revenge, without any regard for justice or the advantage of the city-state. Each party was limited only by its own appetite at the time, and stood ready to satisfy its ambition of the moment either by voting for an unjust verdict or seizing control by force. (3.82.8)

As before, then, it is passion, *pleonexia*, ambition—powerful human feelings and emotions—that are to blame, not just for the distortion of judgment, but for the corruption of the very language of appraisal on which judgment relies. The judgment is as much a part of our nature, however, as are the strong passions that, under certain circumstances, cause it to pay insufficient heed to the voice of natural justice and fairness cautioning us not to be arrogant in the exercise of power.

With just this much to go on, we might think that *strong* emotions, at least, are bad in the bone, so that our natures include some intrinsically bad elements, although they also include some intrinsically good ones. But even this would be a mistake. Witness the general effect that civil wars are said to have:

> Thus was every kind of criminality afoot throughout all Greece because of civil wars, and the simplicity, which is so large an element in a noble character (*kai to euêthes, hou to gennaion pleiston metechei*),[13] was laughed at and disappeared. Citizens were sharply and mistrustfully divided from one another with respect to judgment (*tê(i) gnômê(i)*) because they were in separate ideological camps. No rational argument (*logos*) was so powerful, no oath so terrible, as to overcome this mutual hostility, but everybody, when they found themselves more powerful than their enemies, rationally calculating (*logismô(i)*) that security was not to be hoped for [from argument or oath], took precautions against injury, and were incapable of trusting anyone. For the most part, those of inferior judgment (*gnômên*) had the greatest success, since a sense of their own inferiority and of the sharp wits of their opponents put them into great fear that they would be overcome in rational argument (*logos*) or by the resourcefulness of their enemies' judgment (*gnômês*). They therefore went daringly (*tolmêrôs*) to work against them in action (*erga*), while the thinkers, i.e. those used to exercising foresight, thought that nothing should be got by action what could be got by judgment (*gnômê*). They were therefore unprotected and more easily killed. (3.83)

The poor pro-Athenian democrats and the rich pro-Spartan oligarchs have become divided by the civil war into separate ideological camps. And because of this, each of them is weakened, albeit in different ways. The poor have passion without judgment, which leads to bad action, while the rich have judgment without the passion necessary for action, which leads to equally fatal inaction. The clear implication is that both judgment and passion, in proper relation, are needed for success.

In Pericles' Funeral Oration, this implication is present yet again.

> We [Athenians] believe that what spoils action (*ergois*) is not rational argument (*logous*), but going into action without first being instructed by rational argument. In this too we excel over others: ours is the daring of people who rationally calculate (*tolman . . . eklogizesthai*) about what they will take in hand, whereas other people are made rash by ignorance and cowardly by rational calculation (*logismos*). But the people who most deserve to be judged tough-minded are those who know exactly what terrors or pleasures lie ahead, and are not turned away from danger by that knowledge. (2.40.2–3)

What civil war does, then, in separating the rich oligarchs from the poor democrats, is to separate those most capable of sound judgment, good sense, rational calculation, and foresight from those with the strong passions that make judgment effective in action. The result is people who are made "rash by ignorance," on the one side, and people who are made "cowardly by rational calculation," on the other. The ideal, which is the tough-minded "daring of people who rationally calculate," is found only when there is harmony between rich and poor, oligarchy and democracy, Sparta and Athens.

It is no surprise, therefore, to find that when Thucydides expresses his own political preference, it is for a blended constitution, which serves the interests of both rich oligarchs and poor democrats. Consider, for example, what he says about the government of the Five Thousand at Athens, which deposed that of the Four Hundred oligarchs in 411 B.C.:

> And now for the first time, at least in my lifetime, the Athenians clearly had their best government: for a moderate (*metria*) blending of the few [oligarchs] and the many [democrats] came about. And this was the first thing, after so many misfortunes had occurred, that made the city raise her head again. (8.97.2)

Such a constitution is fair or just, notice, by the standards of the unwritten law based in good sense and sound judgment, because, like that law, it is in everyone's interest.

What I want to claim, finally, is that the simplicity that 3.83 characterizes as "so large an element in a noble character" is the analogue in the individual soul of this sort of constitution in which judgment and passion are both present and properly related. Thucydides' assessment of Pericles, who he thinks to have a soul of this very type, provides strong evidence in favor of this view.

> Such were the rational arguments by which Pericles tried to cure the Athenians of their passionate anger (*orgês*) at him and draw away their judgment (*gnômên*) from [being influenced by] their terrible conditions (*tôn parontôn deinon*).[14] . . . As long as he was at the head of the city-state in time of peace, he governed it in a moderate way (*metriôs*) and guarded it securely; and it was greatest under him. . . . The reason for Pericles' success was this: he was powerful because he deserved to be, i.e. because of his judgment (*gnômô*), and also because he was known to be highly incorruptible. He therefore controlled the multitude like free men, and was not so much led by them, as he led them. He would not gratify the people in his speeches so as to get power by improper means, but because of their esteem for him he could risk their passion (*orgê*). Therefore, whenever he saw them unreasonably and arrogantly rash (*para kairon hubrei tharsountas*), he would make them afraid with his speeches; and, again, when they were unreasonably afraid, he would raise up their spirits and make them daring (*tharsein*). . . . But those who came later, by contrast since they were more on an equal level with one another, and each was striving to become first, were even ready to sacrifice the whole conduct of affairs to gratify the common people. (2.65.1–10)[15]

Pericles governed in a moderate way, satisfying the interests of the (many) poor and the (few) powerful alike. He was able to do so because he was not himself overcome by ambition or *pleonexia* and because he was "known to be highly incorruptible." Hence, he was able to guide the Athenian citizens, too, toward making good judgments, by arousing emotions in them that counteracted the ones that were leading their judgment astray. But those who replaced him lacked this harmony, because they were themselves riven by ambition and a pleonectic desire for gain that incapacitated their judgment. As a result, they sought to gratify the many in order to gain their support, harming the city-state as a whole by alienating the few, whose good judgment was thereby made unavailable to it.

The simplicity, which is so large an element in a noble character, is thus precisely what was missing from both sides during the civil war in Corcyra and in Athens after Pericles. Indeed, its absence is the personal or psychological equivalent of civil war: it is what is missing when one's emotions and appetites, rather than being in harmony with one's judgment or good sense, overpower it. Simplicity is thus a name for the proper relationship between reason and feeling or emotion that results in the harmony, unity, and simplicity that Pericles praised in the Athenians in his Funeral Oration and manifested in himself. Even strong emotions have a place in the best human life, then, and are bad only when they escape from that place.

Thucydides is not a pessimist, not someone who takes an unrealistically dark view of human nature. He does not think it inevitable that things go badly. But he is not an optimist either. He does not think that there are any cosmic guarantees that good judgment will be effectively exercised. What aids good judgment and strengthens it is knowledge of human nature and how it is likely to respond in different sorts of circumstances. For when we see what its tendencies are, our judgment, like Pericles', is provided with some of the resources it needs to weaken or strengthen our feelings as required, so that our capacity for effective action is reinforced. Even the best planning in the world, however, cannot take account of such things as plagues, which have comparable effects on human character to those of civil war.[16] Indeed, the idea that rational planning can take account of every contingency is one of the illusions that Thucydides tries to dispel.[17]

Is Thucydides right about us? Are human beings the way he says they are? This is an empirical matter; it cannot be settled just by thinking about it. To see whether Thucydides is right, we must look at history and how people behave in the kinds of circumstances he describes. There is no shortcut, therefore, to self-knowledge. If we want to know what we are, we must study what we have been. We must study the conclusions Thucydides drew from his own studies of the Peloponnesian War, to be sure, but we must also investigate the war for ourselves to see if the various events he and others describe bear out his general claims. But that is as complex a task, requiring just as much patient investigation as the proper interpretation of the general claims themselves. There is no easy path to good sense and good judgment. But there is a hard one, and Thucydides' *History* is permanently on it. If we read it with some of the immense care with which it was written, we will already have acquired something more valuable than rubies—a dissatisfaction with easy answers and a deep appreciation for the complexity of human affairs.

Notes

1. Simon Hornblower, *A Commentary on Thucydides*, vol. 1 (Oxford, UK: Clarendon, 1991), 478.

2. Rex Warner, *Thucydides: The Peloponnesian War* (Harmondsworth: Penguin, 1972), 245.

3. This implication is present in all the best-known English translations. Richard Crawley, *The Landmark Thucydides* (New York: Free Press, 1996): "human nature, always rebelling against the law, and now its master, showed itself ungoverned in passion, above respect for justice, and the enemy of all superiority." Steven Lattimore, *Thucydides, The Peloponnesian War* (Indianapolis, IN: Hackett, 1998): "human nature always ready to act unjustly even in violation of laws, overthrew the laws themselves and gladly showed itself powerless over passion but stronger than justice and hostile to any kind of superiority."

4. My translations are based, with modifications, on those given in Paul Woodruff's excellent *Thucydides on Justice, Power, and Human Nature* (Indianapolis, IN: Hackett, 1993).

5. That is, *pleonexia,* as the next clause makes clear.

6. I leave *to hosion* untranslated for a reason.

7. The evidence is reviewed in Hornblower, *A Commentary on Thucydides,* ad loc. W. R. Connor, *Thucydides* (Princeton, NJ: Princeton University Press, 1984), 102 n. 60, rightly asks who the author of 3.84 is if not Thucydides and how the chapter got into our text. The authenticity of the passage is defended in M. Christ, "The Authenticity of Thucydides 3.84," *Transactions of the American Philological Association* 119: 137–48.

8. Lattimore, *Thucydides: The Peloponnesian War,* 171 n. 3.84.

9. H.G. Liddell, R. Scott, and H. S. Jones, *Greek English Lexicon* (Oxford, UK: Clarendon, 1968), s.v. *hosios.*

10. Warner, *Thucydides: The Peloponnesian War,* 242. Crawley, *The Landmark Thucydides:*

    in peace and prosperity states and individuals have better sentiments, because they do not find themselves suddenly confronted with imperious necessities; but war takes away the easy supply of daily wants and so proves a rough master that brings most men's characters to a level with their fortunes.

    Lattimore, *Thucydides: The Peloponnesian War:*

    in peace and good circumstances, both states and individuals have better inclinations though not falling into involuntary necessities; but war, stripping away the easy access to daily needs, is a violent teacher and brings most people's passions into line with the present situations.

11. Warner, *Thucydides: The Peloponnesian War,* 242. Crawley, *The Landmark Thucydides:* "words had to change their ordinary meanings and to take that which was now given to them."

12. See J. Wilson, "The Customary Meanings of Words Were Changed—Or Were They? A Note on Thucydides 3.82.4," *Classical Quarterly* 32 (1982). Lattimore, *Thucydides: The Peloponnesian War,* gets it right: "men inverted the usual verbal evaluations of actions."

13. Literally, "the simple, in which the noble above all participates." That the simple is being said to participate in the noble, and not vice versa (as is grammatically possible), is convincingly argued in Martha Nussbaum, *The Fragility of Goodness* (Cambridge, UK: Cambridge University Press, 1986), 507–8 n. 24.

14. See 3.82.2 above.

15. The passage should be compared point by point with 3.82.8 above.

16. In 2.53 this is made particularly plain:

    The plague was the starting point for greater lawlessness (*anomia*) in the city. For everyone was ready to be more daring (*etolma*) about things they had previously enjoyed only in secret, since they saw the sudden change both for those who were prosperous and suddenly died and for those who previously owned nothing but immediately got their property. And so they thought it appropriate to use what they had quickly and with a view to pleasure, considering their persons and their possessions equally ephemeral. No one was enthusiastic over additional hardship for what seemed a noble objective, considering it uncertain whether he would die before achieving it. The pleasure of the moment, and whatever was conducive to that were deemed both noble and useful. Neither fear of the gods nor law of man was a deterrent, since it was judged all the same whether they were pious or not because of seeing everyone dying with no difference, and since no one anticipated that he would live till trial and pay the penalty for his crimes, but that the much greater penalty which had already been pronounced was hanging over them, and it was reasonable to get some satisfaction from life before that descended. (trans. by Lattimore, with minor changes)

17. A topic that merits an essay of its own, which might begin with Lowell Edwards, *Chance and Intelligence in Thucydides* (Cambridge, MA: Harvard University Press, 1975), and Colin Macleod, "Reason and Necessity: Thucydides III 9–14, 37–48," *Journal of Hellenic Studies* 98 (1978): 64–78.

3
The Melian Dialogue

Laurie Johnson

... Whereas the Plataean Debate took place in the fifth year of the war, the dialogue between representatives of Melos and Athens took place in the sixteenth year. Yet the central issue had altered little. The most noticeable difference between the Plataean Debate and the Melian Dialogue is form: the Melian Dialogue is the only *dialogue* in Thucydides' entire work. The dialogue form is chosen by the Athenians in order to avoid the "fair words" of most speech making. Hence, the dialogue itself is a denial of the worth of the explanations, justifications, and ornamentations of rhetoric. Another noticeable difference is not that self-interest informed the final decision but that it did so openly and was argued extensively on both sides. In the fifth year of the war, the Thebans and Plataeans had argued about justice: the justice of their past deeds as well as their present undertakings. In the sixteenth year, the style of argumentation in a similar situation had changed dramatically, reflecting changed beliefs. Past deeds, according to the Athenians, were irrelevant to present demands. Deeds and justice should not be an issue in the dialogue, but only force and safety. The Melians agreed to abide by these Athenian rules but resorted to a variety of arguments. As we will see, like the Plataeans, they had nothing to lose by doing so.

The Melians were an independent island people, and as such they were unique in their refusal to submit to Athenian rule. At first they took a neutral stance in the war, but after the Athenians plundered their territory, they became openly hostile to Athens. Accordingly Athens sent two generals, Cleomedes and Tisias, to subdue the Melians. Before doing any harm to their land, the generals decided to send envoys to negotiate with the Melians. The Melians did not want to bring these envoys before the people, preferring to restrict the dialogue to the Melian magistrates and the few.

The Athenians begin the dialogue by criticizing the Melians for thinking that Athenian arguments would seduce the common people and thus keep them out of the proceedings. Then they add a condition of their own: that the discussion should be a dialogue in which the Melians reply to any Athenian statement they find unsatisfactory: "Take up each point, and do not you either make a single speech, but conduct the inquiry by replying at once to any statement of ours that seems to be unsatisfactory" (5.85). The choice of the dialogue form might represent Athenian anger over the Melians' refusal to submit to their request to speak before the people. It is also an acknowledgment that a different venue requires a different mode of proceeding. The Athenians suspect that the Melians do not want their people hearing Athenian speeches because they think the commons are more readily moved by oratory, by "arguments that are seductive and untested." But they also suspect that the Melian oligarchs will be persuaded more easily by unadorned talk, and so they insist on the dialogue form just as they accept the Melians' request that the commons not be present.

The Melians accept this proposal, but they note that the fairness of it is really not open to discussion. They say that the Athenians contradict themselves by choosing the form of a dialogue, since the eminence of their force makes a true exchange of opinions impossible. This statement indicates that the Melians, from the very beginning, understand their situation: the presence of Athenian force makes the entire exchange something of a farce. They comment:

> For we see that you are come to be yourselves judges of what is to be said here, and that the outcome of the discussion will in all likelihood be, if we win the debate by the righteousness of our cause and for that very reason refuse to yield,

war for us, whereas if we are persuaded, servitude. (5.86)

The Melians say they might "win" the debate based on the facts presented if it were heard by an impartial judge. But even if they win in this way and thus resolve not to submit, war will be the result. Yet servitude will be the result of being "persuaded" by the Athenians' arguments. For the Melians, servitude must mean at least being tribute-paying allies of Athens (when the Athenians finally offer the fairly moderate terms of servitude, the Melians refuse). No terms have yet been offered by the Athenians, so it is possible that the Melians are thinking of something more dreadful. Why did the Athenians wait so late to deliver their terms? Perhaps it was because they had found the Melians more difficult to persuade than they had originally estimated. Or perhaps it was because the terms really did not matter to them in the context of the immediate question, which was whether or not Melos would be destroyed. If the terms had been put up front, it is possible that the Melians, more aware of what their "servitude" would have been like, might have given in. But it seems the Athenians' point really was that only safety should have been important to the Melians, not the particular terms of the settlement.

From the Athenians' point of view, there is nothing farcical about the dialogue. They are there to persuade the Melians to act in a rational manner to save themselves, now that they are faced with overwhelming superior force. But they do not take the dialogue form as seriously as the Melians. For the Melians, a dialogue means an exchange of views with the aim of reconciling differences. For the Athenians it is a one-way act of persuasion. The Melians object; the Athenians tell them why they are wrong. As it turns out, the dialogue evolves exclusively along these lines, even though the Melians constantly try to turn it into a meaningful two-way exchange.

The Athenians make it clear that they wish to persuade the Melians to give up without a fight. If the Melians want to talk about anything besides their present predicament and how to safely escape it, they might as well stop right now (5.87). The Melians respond

that it is natural for men in their position to use many kinds of arguments. However, they acknowledge that the question at hand is their safety, and they agree to abide with the Athenians' requirement. At this point, the only thing the Melians can do to keep the conversation going is to say they agree with the Athenians' conditions. The Athenians say they will not speak of their conduct in the Persian War, nor of how the Melians have wronged them, since the Melians would never accept their claims anyway. The Athenians' abandonment of justifications, including their heroism in the Persian War, indicates what little value they now place on the usual demands of rhetoric. That they say they will not speak of how the Melians have harmed them suggests that there may have been more grounds for their action than we are given here.[1] But since Thucydides gives us little background for the Athenian decision to confront Melos, we are encouraged to see it as without just cause.

The Athenians ask the Melians to omit claims that they did not aid the Spartans or that they have done Athens no real harm. Let us dispense with all customary formalities, they seem to be saying, "since you know as well as we know that what is just is arrived at in human arguments only when the necessity on both sides is equal, and that the powerful exact what they can, while the weak yield what they must" (5.89). The Athenians insist that the traditional trappings of Greek oratory be done away with, since they have nothing to do with the "real thoughts" of human beings and since the real thoughts of human beings dwell not on justice or honor but on safety and power. They do not claim here, or anywhere in the dialogue, that there is no such thing as justice or that both sides are incapable of agreeing on what it is. They argue only that justice is not applicable in the situation the Melians now encounter. To say that the strong do what they can and the weak do what they must is not to say that justice is applicable only when might makes right. But to say that both sides are equal subordinates justice to relationships of power and thus destroys its meaning.

If all talk of justice and honor are mere trappings, why are the Athenians so eager to see them eliminated? The Spartans listened to the Thebans and Plataeans speak of justice, all the while knowing that all parties were aware of the underlying issue of power interests. They allowed the debate to happen as if it were a mere embellishment to their predetermined actions. In a way this apathetic stance shows more disrespect for such debate than the Athenians' refusal to allow it. What harm would come from letting the Melians engage them in moral argument if the Athenians are likewise convinced that such arguments carry no weight? Instead, it seems that the Athenians understand that political rhetoric is fundamentally opposed and presents an alternative to their mode of conduct.

The Melians next try to turn the dialogue into a genuine argument by turning the Athenian requirements for relevancy around. They distinguish between Athens's apparent interest and true interest. If we must speak of interest and not of right, they say, then we must tell you that it is in *both* our interests not to eliminate arguments from justice or arguments that do not measure up to the criteria of strict rationality. In other words, it is expedient for the Athenians not to rule out the principle of morality as a common good:

> As we think, at any rate, it is expedient (for we are constrained to speak of expediency, since you have in this fashion, ignoring the principle of justice, suggested that we speak of what is advantageous) that you should not rule out the principle of the common good, but that for him who is at the time in peril what is equitable should also be just, and though one has not entirely proved his point he should still derive some benefit therefrom. And this is not less for your interest than for our own, inasmuch as you, if you shall ever meet with a reverse, would not only incur the greatest punishment, but would also become a warning example to others. (5.90)

Like Diodotus, the Melians have redefined "expediency" to mean enlightened self-interest. But they have taken this argument one step further; enlightened self-interest now means upholding common principles. It means not denying the coincidence of justice and expediency but embracing justice as the ultimate public good. If the Athenians' luck should ever run out, they would greatly benefit from such a rule and thus they should now uphold it. Likewise, if they are overly cruel now, they may be treated in a like manner in defeat. Thus the Melians bring up the possibility that the true Athenian interest lies in upholding the general rules of decency that forbid such behavior. A claim the Plataeans made only weakly is more fully put forward by the Melians, though with similarly ill results.

The Athenians deny that such a long-range view would benefit them in their particular situation. Athens is a great power. If she falls it will be to another great power, Sparta. But such a power has less reason to be vengeful than Athens's own subjects, if they ever were allowed to get the upper hand. Anyway, they say, they are prepared to take their chances, and they remind the Melians again that they want to talk about the preservation of Melos and nothing else. Reversing the Melian argument, they say that it is in both their interests for the Athenians to rule over Melos without trouble (5.91). The Melians would gain by not being destroyed, and Athens would profit by not having to destroy them (5.92–93).

The Athenians reject the suggestion that they should allow Melos to be neutral in the war and declare its friendship for Athens. They insist that Melian friendship would be worse than hostility, since it would tell the other islanders that Athens is not powerful enough to make Melos submit. Melian hostility would at least speak of Athenian power: "for in the eyes of our subjects that would be a proof of our weakness, whereas your hatred is a proof of our power" (5.95).

The Athenians seem now to be implementing the policy Diodotus rhetorically outlined earlier, in order to save the Mytilenaeans: only the threat of ever-present force would persuade the allies not to revolt. The purpose of destroying Melos would be to spread terror throughout the allied cities. But Melos is independent; therefore Athens's colonial possessions would not expect it to act the same way as themselves, say the

Melians. The Athenians maintain that the colonial states think that those states are independent that can ignore Athens's power. The fact that Melos is insular and rather weak makes it imperative that Athens show she is strong enough to control her (5.97). Melos is one of two neutral island cities. The Athenians' strategy, therefore, is to show her allies that they should not entertain rebellion by attacking a city that has not rebelled because she was independent to begin with—a city that has done nothing to warrant punishment. The Athenians are conforming in deed to the true, final implications of their own thesis. What could be more in accordance with Diodotus's prescription for how to avoid rebellion than the subjugation of Melos? How far is this policy from his suggestion that Athens, by everpresent vigilance, should prevent her allies from even thinking of revolt? The Athenian action at Melos is not an act of punishment—it is an act of repression, designed to expand the empire and add tribute if possible but chiefly to let the allies know that Athens is strong enough to keep subject all the island cities. If they remain impressed by the power of Athens, they will not revolt. But they will not believe that Athenian power is overwhelmingly superior or that it will necessarily be used against them if there are weak cities that are still independent, flouting that power. What could be a better example of ever-present vigilance than this? Isn't the rationale behind the attack on Melos the necessary outcome of Diodotus's logic that neither rule of law nor punishment will deter rebellion but only constant supervision and notice of force?

The Melians defiantly say that they would be great cowards if they did not resist as much as possible before submitting to servitude. In saying this, they sound familiar: the Plataeans made the question of honor the largest part of their argument. But the Athenians disagree, because their definitions of honor and justice are very different from the Melians' or the Plataeans': "No, not if you take a sensible view of the matter; for with you it is not a contest on equal terms to determine a point of manly honour, so as to avoid incurring disgrace; rather the question be-

fore you is one of self-preservation to avoid offering resistance to those who are far stronger than you" (5.101).

For the Athenians, pursuit of honor as well as justice is reasonable only among equals, a position that makes honor and justice depend on relationships of power. This is an unconventional view of both, a view the Athenians insist is inwardly held by all men, even if they do not admit it or hide it in flowery speeches. However, it is not a view they held in Pericles' time, in which they accorded justice to their inferiors by allowing allies equal treatment in their own courts. But toward the end of the dialogue, when we hear the Athenians repeat the old formula, a part of which is that the stronger should treat the weaker with moderation, it has a hollow ring. It is not true that the Athenians are absolved from having to be moderate because the Melians have violated the other part of the equation: that the weaker should step lightly around their superiors. The Athenians at the beginning of the war did not renounce the practice of letting the allies be judged by the same impartial standards of Athenian justice just because this made the allies impudent. They complained, but they treated this as the price that a great power paid for honor.

The Melians, like so many other characters in the *History*, next mention that fortune sometimes upsets the advantage of numbers. Besides, they say, to give up would be a sign of despair, while resistance at least offers some hope (5.102). The Athenians, doggedly, will let the Melians have no solace. Hope is for those who have abundant resources. But "those who stake their all on a single throw" are more likely to meet disaster than success. They warn against "divination, oracles, and the like" that might inspire undue hopes.

The Melians never mention divination or oracles, although next they do mention hope in the gods themselves. Because they are "god-fearing men standing [their] ground against men who are unjust," the Melians expect the gods to help even out their disadvantage. They also look to the Spartans to help them out of a sense of kinship and, if nothing else, "for very shame" (5.104). But the Athenians have an especially cutting answer for this objection. In the case of the Spartans, they say, if their interest or their own laws are in question, they will give their all. But they are most notable in considering "what is agreeable to be honourable, and what is expedient just."

The gods seem to have an even worse reputation than the Spartans. The Athenians do not expect to be favored any less than the Melians by the gods:

> For of the gods we hold the belief, and of men we know, that by a necessity of their nature wherever they have power they always rule. And so in our case since we neither enacted this law nor when it was enacted were the first to use it, but found it in existence and expect to leave it in existence for all time, so we make use of it, well aware that both you and others, if clothed with the same power as we are, would do the same. (5.105)

Thus the Athenians attribute to the gods the same drive for power they attribute to men. In making this claim, the Athenians seem to expound a natural law. They insist that this law is universally applicable in all times to all peoples and even to the gods. There is a fine line between admitting that neither gods nor men can help themselves and making out of justice an empty shell. If urges are compelling, how can anyone succumbing to them be called unjust? We come full circle to the question Diodotus raised in the Mytilenaean Debate.

The Melians choose not to object to these comments, perhaps because the Athenians' suggestions are too disconcerting to contemplate, but they do object to their doubts about the Spartans. They seem to have more trust in the Spartans than in the gods. Because Melos is a colony of Sparta, it would be in Sparta's interest not to betray the Melians, an act that would earn them the distrust of other friendly cities and would only strengthen the power of their enemies (5.106). The Athenians reply that to follow justice and honor is a dangerous course, while the Spartans are the least disposed to risk themselves (5.108–9). They are surprised that, after the Melians promised to talk about their country's safety they said

nothing that ordinary mortal men might hope to be saved by. Surely they will not succumb to that emotion "which most often brings men to ruin when they are confronted by dangers that are clearly foreseen and therefore disgraceful—the fear of such disgrace" (5.111.3–4). Besides, it is no disgrace to submit to the greatest city in Hellas.

For the first time in the dialogue the Athenians offer the Melians concrete terms: to become tribute-paying allies while keeping their own territory. They then offer their own code of conduct for the Melians to consider: not to submit to equals, to defer to superiors, and to treat inferiors with moderation. One wonders how the Athenians can claim both that one should not submit to one's equals and that honor and justice are applicable only among equals. Honor and justice both often require a form of submission: a discontinuation of unabated hostilities and not insisting on total victory. One also wonders at how the Athenians' definition of moderation has changed. It now means warning the enemy before destroying him. With these words, the Athenians end the dialogue, urging the Melians to consider how serious their predicament is and to choose wisely (5.111). Despite the Athenians' efforts the Melians decide to stand their ground. They offer their neutrality, something the Plataeans had refused the Spartans, but they will not quickly be robbed of one hundred years of liberty (5.112). To this the Athenians respond that the Melians are the only men who regard the future as more certain than the present and who "look upon that which is out of sight, merely because [they] wish it, as already realized" (5.113).

The Athenians followed through on their threat to Melos; they besieged it until it surrendered. Then they killed all the adult males and sold the women and children into slavery. Later they colonized the island themselves. The Melians were in a short time robbed of their liberty in a brutal fashion. An act like this would have been considered cruel and excessive by the standards eventually arrived at in the Mytilenaean Debate. That is, the Athenians, when they repented of their initial decision to execute all male Mytilenaeans and sell the women and children into slavery, did so because they felt that this sentence was cruel and excessive as well as unwise. And yet this is the very sentence that was actually passed on the Melians, and for much less reason. The Athenians could make a sound argument that the Mytilenaeans had done them an injustice. They could not and did not make any such argument about Melos.

But in the end, had the Melians not also shown their own kind of immoderation? They had refused to yield even after it was clear that they had no other choice between submission and death. They chose not to live to fight another day. Thucydides does not openly praise the Melians' bravery in accepting their fate, but to do so would be out of character for him. He simply reports their fates in brief and stern tones. The fact that he records the dialogue and the eventual destruction of the Melians, however, does make something valuable of the Melians' deaths; they did not die completely in vain. The Melian episode is an enduring black stain on the Athenians' history, a reminder of the ugliness of injustice as well as a warning of where such excess can lead. The Melian Dialogue is followed by the Sicilian Expedition, in which the Athenians in their hubris go too far. How could the Melians' lives have purchased any more meaning? Their attachment to honor, piety, and courage contribute to the Thucydidean lesson that moderation and justice are often profitable as well as right. The Melians, through Thucydides' eyes, appear more like martyrs than victims. Their deaths illustrate the failure of the Athenian thesis when that thesis is taken to its ultimate conclusions. . . .

Note

1. Arnold W. Gomme, *A Historical Commentary on Thucydides*, vol. 5 (Oxford: Clarendon Press, 1959), 157.

Plato

If, as Cicero claims, it was Socrates who "called down philosophy from the skies," then it was Plato who summoned humans to respect philosophy as their earthly guide. The name of Plato is with good reason equated with the onset of political philosophy, for it was Plato, in the West, who advocated the study of politics with the same devotion and rigor used by physicians to investigate the health of the body. While many of Plato's ideas seem anachronistic in modern society, we must remember that it was Plato who laid the groundwork for future discussions of politics by pointing to the importance of ideas like justice and prudence and by generating the very vocabulary of political discourse we use to this day.

Plato was born in Athens in approximately 420 B.C.E. of a wealthy and noble family. While few of the details of his life are certain, we know that he grew up during the final stages of the Peloponnesian War, the great war between the rival factions of Athens and Sparta; that he probably never married; that he traveled widely, especially in Egypt and Sicily; that he founded a school known as the Academy; and that he was greatly influenced by the teachings of his master, Socrates. Plato died in 347 B.C.E. at about the age of 81.

Of Socrates even less is known, since Socrates did not record his own philosophy. Much of what we know of Socrates comes from the works of his pupil, whose portrayal no doubt idealizes him, and by some of his critics, like Aristophanes, who ridiculed him. The latter, for example, portrays Socrates in his *Clouds* as an unwashed vagrant, constantly provoking argument through incessant and useless questioning. A group of itinerant teachers known as sophists came to regard Socrates' questioning as particularly bothersome. They argued that terms like morality and justice were hopelessly subjective and used by leaders merely to attain their own selfish ends. As a result, they specialized in training young well-to-do boys in how to use rhetoric in manipulating others. Socrates, on the other hand (at least the Socrates we know through Plato), insisted that objective standards could be set for morality and justice through philosophic reflection and that neither the good of the city nor the health of the soul could be attained without practicing these virtues. Socrates was eventually accused of impiety, not paying proper respect to the gods, and convicted by a democratic court. Much of Plato's work may be read as a vindication of the Socratic position that philosophy is the highest form of human activity that survives even the death of the philosopher. Plato's school, the Academy, stood as a testament to this truth.

Among the most significant political works of Plato are the *Republic*, the *Statesman*, and the *Laws*. These were written in the form of dialogues, partly in an attempt to capture the liveliness of philosophy as practiced by his tutor. This form exemplifies the Socratic dialectic, a manner of argumentation that begins by investigating a commonly held opinion and proceeds to illustrate its flaws and virtues by subjecting it to rigorous questioning. New truths about the original proposition realized in this way are then subjected to a new round of questioning, and so on.

While Plato was among the first thinkers to investigate politics in a philosophic manner, the true goal of philosophy, as he saw it, was to understand the good, to which particular political concepts like justice were related as parts to the whole. The Platonic cosmology (one not shared by Socrates) divided the world into two realms, the realm of ideas or forms and the realm of those things that come into being and pass away (what we might today call the material world). For Plato, the realm of ideas was the perfection and cause of those things that the ideas represented. For example, the idea of "chair" is in some ways prior to and "more real" than any *particular* chair—the material object is transitory and owes its origin to a thought that must have existed prior to the time any particular workman manufactured chairs. This theory of forms was attacked by later thinkers like Aristotle. Nevertheless, justice, like the good, was held by Plato to be an ideal or form, the content of which can be investigated philosophically and at least partially realized through the skill of the good ruler in the actual *polis* or city.

Crito

As discussed above, Socrates was tried for not paying proper respect to the gods of Athens. At his trial and sentencing, he refused to show contrition, foreswear allegiance to his own divinities (the "forms" or ideas), or to promise forbearance in "infecting" the youth of Athens with his incessant questioning. As a result, he was sentenced to death. In the *Crito*, reproduced here in full, Socrates rejects attempts to free him on the grounds that Athenian law demands it.

The *Republic*

The subject of the *Republic* is justice. The format is the dialogue. Socrates agrees to accompany a group of Athenians to the house of Polymarchus where a discussion commences with his host, his host's father Cephalus, the sophist Thrasymachus, the young Glaucon and Adeimantus, and several others regarding the proper definition of justice. In the process of discussion, Socrates agrees to "save" the reputation of justice attacked by Thrasymachus and others by showing its true nature. His approach is to make a comparison between the individual soul and a city, arguing that if justice could be identified in the larger unit, the city, it would be easier to find in the soul.

As discussion continues, Socrates engages Glaucon and Adeimantus in the creation of an imaginary utopian city wherein justice might be found. This is a city with three classes: the wise rulers (the best of the guardians), the courageous warriors, and the skillful artisans and merchants. The parts of the city are analogous to the parts of the soul. That part of the soul which desires material objects is the counterpart to the moneymaking class; the spirited part which experiences intense passion like anger is the counterpart of the guardian class; and reason corresponds to the city's ruling class. Much of the discussion centers around the education of the guardians who must be trained to love their own citizens but defend to the death against enemies. Socrates goes to great lengths to guarantee discipline, including a community of wives and children to insure that each guardian defends every citizen as his or her own without preference, the same lifestyle for men and women (including community training in the nude), and the pairing of the most fit men and women for mating to insure quality progeny. Socrates builds the city's creation so skillfully that he meets with little resistance from his interlocutors.

The principle of justice applicable to both city and soul is that justice requires each part to mind its own business; that is, each part must play its own role and not attempt to perform the function of other parts. Just as the wise rulers must lead the other classes in the city, so too must reason lead the other parts of the soul in order to insure harmony and happiness. The search for justice in the city is complete with the assertion that the good city can only come into being if the truly wise rule. The scope and gravity of this last proposal is crystallized in Plato's allegory of the cave, in which the philosopher comes to recognize that the world of material objects generally thought to be real is only the dim reflection of the sun's rays on the walls of the cave which houses the residents of the *polis*.

Four passages are presented from the *Republic*. In the first excerpt, taken from Book I, Socrates confronts Thrasymachus's assertion that justice is in the advantage of the stronger. In this selection, which demonstrates the Socratic dialectic, Socrates maneuvers the argument in a direction which elicits important concessions from Thrasymachus and ultimately undermines the sophist's entire position. The second passage is from Book IV. There, Socrates and his interlocutors search for the virtues in their newly created city, a search that ends with a new definition of justice. In the third selection, from Book V, Socrates makes his boldest proposal for the governance of the good city, rule by the philosopher king. The passage explores some of the reasons why this was considered such an unconventional proposal and sheds light on the nature of philosophy itself. Finally, Socrates summarizes his teaching about the good city in a selection from Book VII. In his "allegory of the cave," Socrates hopes to convince Glaucon and Adeimantus of the necessity of having philosophers rule.

Commentaries

In the following commentaries, Dale Hall attacks the influential interpretation that Plato's utopian city in the *Republic* is meant to illustrate the "limits of politics" generally and the impossibility of Plato's perfectly good *polis* in particular. Central to his attack is the contention that the analogy between the soul and the city entertained in the *Republic* is genuine and not meant to be ironic. The philosopher uses reason to harmonize the desirous and spirited part of his own nature and applies these same principles in ruling the populace. Allan Bloom responds to Hall's criticism by suggesting that there is irony in Socrates's utopian scheme and that the very suggestion that philosophers rule (i.e., mind the business of others) violates the strict standard of justice (minding one's own business) advanced by Plato. Bloom believes that Plato is really suggesting that the ideal political regime is hopelessly unattainable.

The debate over the proper interpretation of the *Republic* contained in these readings illustrates a broader debate regarding the proper reading of political philosophy in general. While Bloom calls for strict adherence to the text, Hall suggests that proper interpretation requires greater attention to historical and social factors at the time of the writing as well.

Web Sources

http://users.erols.com/jonwill/
Utopia on the Internet. This site links the user to a variety of on-line sources of utopian literature including the full text of the *Republic* and other classics like Sir Thomas More's *Utopia*. Includes links to discussion communities fostering utopian views.

http://plato.evansville.edu/
Exploring Plato's Dialogues. Developed by the University of Evansville, this site provides links to major works by Plato and incorporates the use of a powerful search engine that allows the user to request help in understanding terms, perform a word search, or discover bibliographic sources for further research.

http://classics.mit.edu/Plato/republic.html
The Internet Classics Archive: The Republic *by Plato.* This site provides the full text of the Benjamin Jowett translation of Plato's *Republic*.

http://www.perseus.tufts.edu
The Perseus Digital Library. This site provides background on classic themes, a timeline for source location, and links to classic texts in Greek and Latin as well as more modern sources.

Class Activities and Discussion Items

1. Compare and contrast social and political relations within Plato's utopian world with those advanced by any other utopian thinker (e.g., Sir Thomas More, Henry David Thoreau, Edward Bellamy, B. F. Skinner, Robert Heinlein, and others). In what ways is Plato's utopia more or less attractive than that advanced by a comparative author? Why?

2. Create a legal brief to defend Socrates in a court of law. Consider carefully how you would construct an argument that balances the state's right to regulate behavior it deems inappropriate with your client's right to question authority. Can such an argument easily be constructed without the use of modern concepts like the right to free speech, freedom of assembly, freedom of conscience, and the possibility of "unjust" laws?

3. Create your own utopia in speech. Be sure to include a discussion of the role of economic class structure, means of defense, role of citizens, and structures of decision-making and authority. What social and political conditions would need to be in place for your utopia to be realized?

4. Socrates builds commitment to community by divorcing the guardians from individual attachments to family. How adequate is this approach in insuring equal protection for citizens? How similar to or different from this approach is military training employed in the United States today? How similar to or different from this approach is military training employed today in parts of the world following fundamentalist religious traditions?

5. How do Plato's views on the political status of the intellectual compare with the role the intellectual plays in today's society?

6. Describe Plato's theory of human nature. In what ways does his conception succeed, and in what ways does it fail? Given your analysis, what is the relationship between Plato's theory of human nature and his theory of politics? Is this an adequate formulation? Is it a formulation you support? Why or why not?

Further Reading

Annas, Julia. 2000. *Platonic Ethics, Old and New.* Ithaca, N.Y.: Cornell University Press. Annas shows how the Middle Platonists viewed Plato's dialogues as multiple presentations of a single ethical philosophy, differing in form and purpose but ultimately coherent.

Barker, E. 1918. *Greek Political Theory: Plato and His Predecessors.* London: Methuen. Excellent background on pre-Socratic world view and Plato's impact on the ancient world.

Bloom, Allan. 1968. *The Republic of Plato* (Translated with Notes and an Interpretive Essay). New York: Basic Books. Bloom's essay is a scholarly chapter-by-chapter analysis of the work from the perspective of a follower of Leo Strauss.

Cai, Zong-qi. 1999. "In quest of harmony: Plato and Confucius on Poetry." *Philosophy: East and West* 49 (3): 317–345. Cai examines how Plato and Confucius formulate their views on poetry in light of their overriding concerns with harmony.

Hall, R.W. 1981. *Plato.* London: Allen & Unwin. Good review of the life and times of the great thinker.

Lewis, V. Bradley. 1998. "*Politeia kai Nomoi*: On the Coherence of Plato's Political Philosophy." *Polity* 31 (2): 331–349. Lewis disputes the often held view that Plato's *Republic* and *Laws* are conventionally understood to offer rival and incompatible views of the best political regime.

Nussbaum, Martha C. 2000. "Four Paradigms of Philosophical Politics." *Monist* 83 (4): 465–490. Nussbaum explores four distinct conceptions of the philosopher's public role in the ancient Greco-Roman world.

Smith, Nicholas D. 2000. "Plato on knowledge as a power." *Journal of the History of Philosophy* 38 (2): 145–168. Smith argues that the relationship between the cognitive powers and their various objects has been fundamentally misunderstood in Plato's *Republic*, leading scholars into one or more misinterpretations of important and explicit features of the text.

Stauffer, Devin. 2001. *Plato's Introduction to the Question of Justice.* Albany, N.Y.: State University of New York Press. Focusing on the crucial opening sections of the *Republic*, Stauffer argues that the dialectical confrontations with ordinary opinion presented in these sections provide the basis for Plato's view of justice, and that they also help to show how Plato's thought remains relevant today, especially as a rival to Kantianism.

Strauss, L. 1964. *The City and Man.* Chicago: Rand McNally. An analysis of the major differences between ancient and modern political thought in the West and Strauss's own reasons for preferring important elements of the ancient tradition. ✦

4
Crito

Plato

Characters

Socrates
Crito

Scene—The Prison of Socrates

St. I
p. 43
Socrates. Why have you come at this hour, Crito? Is it not still early?

Crito. Yes, very early.

Socr. About what time is it?

Crito. It is just daybreak.

Socr. I wonder that the jailer was willing to let you in.

Crito. He knows me now, Socrates; I come here so often, and besides, I have given him a tip.

Socr. Have you been here long?

Crito. Yes, some time.

Socr. Then why did you sit down without speaking? Why did you not wake me at once?

Crito. Indeed, Socrates, I wish that I myself were not so sleepless and sorrowful. But I have been wondering to see how soundly you sleep. And I purposely did not wake you, for I was anxious not to disturb your repose. Often before, all through your life, I have thought that your temperament was a happy one; and I think so more than ever now when I see how easily and calmly you bear the calamity that has come to you.

Socr. Nay, Crito, it would be absurd if at my age I were disturbed at having to die.

Crito. Other men as old are overtaken by similar calamities, Socrates; but their age does not save them from being disturbed by their fate.

Socr. That is so; but tell me why are you here so early?

Crito. I am the bearer of sad news, Socrates; not sad, it seems, for you, but for me and for all your friends, both sad and hard to bear; and for none of them, I think, is it as hard to bear as it is for me.

Socr. What is it? Has the ship come from Delos, at the arrival of which I am to die?

Crito. No, it has not actually arrived, but I think that it will be here today, from the news which certain persons have brought from Sunium, who left it there. It is clear from their report that it will be here today; and so, Socrates, tomorrow your life will have to end.

Socr. Well, Crito, may it end well. Be it so, II if so the gods will. But I do not think that the 44 ship will be here today.

Crito. Why do you suppose not?

Socr. I will tell you. I am to die on the day after the ship arrives, am I not?[1]

Crito. That is what the authorities say.

Socr. Then I do not think that it will come today, but tomorrow. I am counting on a dream I had a little while ago in the night, so it seems to be fortunate that you did not wake me.

Crito. And what was this dream?

Socr. A fair and beautiful woman, clad in white, seemed to come to me, and call me and say, "O Socrates—

On the third day shall you fertile Phthia reach."[2]

Crito. What a strange dream, Socrates!

Socr. But its meaning is clear, at least to me, Crito.

Crito. Yes, too clear, it seems. But, O my III good Socrates, I beg you for the last time to listen to me and save yourself. For to me your death will be more than a single disaster; not only shall I lose a friend the like of whom I shall never find again, but many persons who do not know you and me well will think that I might have saved you if I had been willing to spend money, but that I neglected to do so. And what reputation could be more disgraceful than the reputation of caring more for money than for one's friends? The public will never believe that we were anxious to save you, but that you yourself refused to escape.

Socr. But, my dear Crito, why should we care so much about public opinion? Reasonable men, of whose opinion it is worth our while to think, will believe that we acted as we really did.

Crito. But you see, Socrates, that it is necessary to care about public opinion, too. This very thing that has happened to you proves that the multitude can do a man not the least, but almost the greatest harm, if he is falsely accused to them.

Socr. I wish that the multitude were able to do a man the greatest harm, Crito, for then they would be able to do him the greatest good, too. That would have been fine. But, as it is, they can do neither. They cannot make a man either wise or foolish: they act wholly at random.

IV *Crito.* Well, as you wish. But tell me this, Socrates. You surely are not anxious about me and your other friends, and afraid lest, if you escape, the informers would say that we stole you away, and get us into trouble, and involve us in a great deal of expense, or perhaps in the loss of all our property, and, it may be, bring some other punishment upon us besides? If you have any fear of that kind, 45 dismiss it. For of course we are bound to run these risks, and still greater risks than these, if necessary, in saving you. So do not, I beg you, refuse to listen to me.

Socr. I am anxious about that, Crito, and about much besides.

Crito. Then have no fear on that score. There are men who, for no very large sum, are ready to bring you out of prison into safety. And then, you know, these informers are cheaply bought, and there would be no need to spend much upon them. My fortune is at your service, and I think that it is adequate; and if you have any feeling about making use of my money, there are strangers in Athens whom you know, ready to use theirs; and one of them, Simmias of Thebes, has actually brought enough for this very purpose. And Cebes and many others are ready, too. And therefore, I repeat, do not shrink from saving yourself on that ground. And do not let what you said in the court— that if you went into exile you would not know what to do with yourself—stand in your way; for there are many places for you to go to, where you will be welcomed. If you choose to go to Thessaly, I have friends there who will make much of you and protect you from any annoyance from the people of Thessaly.

And besides, Socrates, I think that you v will be doing what is unjust if you abandon your life when you might preserve it. You are simply playing into your enemies' hands; it is exactly what they wanted—to destroy you. And what is more, to me you seem to be abandoning your children, too. You will leave them to take their chance in life, as far as you are concerned, when you might bring them up and educate them. Most likely their fate will be the usual fate of children who are left orphans. But you ought not to bring children into the world unless you mean to take the trouble of bringing them up and educating them. It seems to me that you are choosing the easy way, and not the way of a good and brave man, as you ought, when you have been talking all your life long of the value that you set upon human excellence. For my part, I feel ashamed both for you and for us who are your friends. Men will think that the whole thing which has happened to you— your appearance in court to face trial, when you need not have appeared at all; the very way in which the trial was conducted; and then last of all this, the crowning absurdity of the whole affair—is due to our cowardice. It will look as if we had shirked the danger out of miserable cowardice; for we did not 46 save you, and you did not save yourself, when it was quite possible to do so if we had been good for anything at all. Take care, Socrates, lest these things be not evil only, but also dishonorable to you and to us. Reflect, then, or rather the time for reflection is past; we must make up our minds. And there is only one plan possible. Everything must be done tonight. If we delay any longer, we are lost. Socrates, I implore you not to refuse to listen to me.

Socr. My dear Crito, if your anxiety to save vi me be right, it is most valuable; but if not, the greater it is the harder it will be to cope with. We must reflect, then, whether we are to do as you say or not; for I am still what I always have been—a man who will accept no argument but that which on reflection I find to be truest. I cannot cast aside my former arguments because this misfortune has come to me. They seem to me to be as true as ever they were, and I respect and honor the same ones as I used to. And if we have no better argument to substitute for them, I certainly shall not agree to your proposal, not even though the power of the multitude should scare us with fresh terrors, as children are scared with hobgoblins, and inflict upon us new fines and imprisonments, and deaths. What is the most appropriate way of examining the question? Shall we go back first to what you say about opinions, and ask if we used to be right in thinking that we ought to pay attention to some opinions, and not to others? Were we right in saying so before I was condemned to die, and has it now become apparent that we were talking at random and arguing for the sake of argument, and that it was really nothing but playful nonsense? I am anxious, Crito, to examine our former argument with your help, and to see whether my present circumstance will appear to me to have affected its truth in any way or not; and whether we are to set it aside, or to yield assent to it. Those of us who thought at all seriously always used to say, I think, exactly what I said just now, namely, that we ought to respect some of the opinions which men form, and not others. Tell 47 me, Crito, I beg you, do you not think that they were right? For you in all probability will not have to die tomorrow, and your judgment will not be biased by that circumstance. Reflect, then, do you not think it reasonable to say that we should not respect all the opinions of men but only some, nor the opinions of all men but only of some men? What do you think? Is not this true?

Crito. It is.

Socr. And we should respect the good opinions, and not the worthless ones?

Crito. Yes.

Socr. But the good opinions are those of the wise, and the worthless ones those of the foolish?

Crito. Of course.

VII   *Socr.* And what did we say about this? Does a man who is in training, and who is serious about it, pay attention to the praise and blame and opinion of all men, or only of the one man who is a doctor or a trainer?

Crito. He pays attention only to the opinion of the one man.

Socr. Then he ought to fear the blame and welcome the praise of this one man, not of the multitude?

Crito. Clearly.

Socr. Then he must act and exercise, and eat and drink in whatever way the one man who is his director, and who understands the matter, tells him; not as others tell him?

Crito. That is so.

Socr. Good. But if he disobeys this one man, and disregards his opinion and his praise, and respects instead what the many say, who understand nothing of the matter, will he not suffer for it?

Crito. Of course he will.

Socr. And how will he suffer? In what way and in what part of himself?

Crito. Of course in his body. That is disabled.

Socr. You are right. And, Crito, to be brief, is it not the same in everything? And, therefore, in questions of justice and injustice, and of the base and the honorable, and of good and evil, which we are now examining, ought we to follow the opinion of the many and fear that, or the opinion of the one man who understands these matters (if we can find him), and feel more shame and fear before him than before all other men? For if we do not follow him, we shall corrupt and maim that part of us which, we used to say, is improved by justice and disabled by injustice. Or is this not so?

Crito. No, Socrates, I agree with you.   VIII

Socr. Now, if, by listening to the opinions of those who do not understand, we disable that part of us which is improved by health and corrupted by disease, is our life worth living when it is corrupt? It is the body, is it not?

Crito. Yes.

Socr. Is life worth living with the body corrupted and crippled ?

Crito. No, certainly not.

Socr. Then is life worth living when that part of us which is maimed by injustice and benefited by justice is corrupt? Or do we consider that part of us, whatever it is, which has to do with justice and injustice to be of less consequence than our body?   48

Crito. No, certainly not.

Socr. But more valuable?

Crito. Yes, much more so.

Socr. Then, my good friend, we must not think so much of what the many will say of us; we must think of what the one man who understands justice and injustice, and of what truth herself will say of us. And so you are mistaken, to begin with, when you invite us to regard the opinion of the multitude concerning the just and the honorable and the good, and their opposites. But, it may be said, the multitude can put us to death?

Crito. Yes, that is evident. That may be said, Socrates.

Socr. True. But, my good friend, to me it appears that the conclusion which we have just reached is the same as our conclusion of former times. Now consider whether we still hold to the belief that we should set the highest value, not on living, but on living well?

Crito. Yes, we do.

Socr. And living well and honorably and justly mean the same thing: do we hold to that or not?

Crito. We do.

IX   *Socr.* Then, starting from these premises, we have to consider whether it is just or not for me to try to escape from prison, without the consent of the Athenians. If we find that it is just, we will try; if not, we will give up the idea. I am afraid that considerations of expense, and of reputation, and of bringing up my children, of which you talk, Crito, are only the opinions of the many, who casually put men to death, and who would, if they could, as casually bring them to life again, without a thought. But reason, which is our guide, shows us that we can have nothing to consider but the question which I asked just now—namely, shall we be acting justly if we give money and thanks to the men who are to aid me in escaping, and if we ourselves take our respective parts in my escape? Or shall we in truth be acting unjustly if we do all this? And if we find that we should be acting unjustly, then we must not take any account either of death, or of any other evil that may be the consequence of remaining here, where we are, but only of acting unjustly.

Crito. I think that you are right, Socrates. But what are we to do?

Socr. Let us examine this question together, my friend, and if you can contradict anything that I say, do so, and I shall be persuaded. But if you cannot, do not go on repeating to me any longer, my dear friend, that I should escape without the consent of the Athenians. I am very anxious to act with your approval and consent. I do not want you to think me mistaken. But now tell me if you agree with the premise from which I start, and try to answer my questions as you think best.   49

Crito. I will try.

Socr. Ought we never to act unjustly vol- X untarily? Or may we act unjustly in some ways, and not in others? Is it the case, as we have often agreed in former times, that it is never either good or honorable to act unjustly? Or have all our former conclusions been overturned in these few days; and did we at our age fail to recognize all along, when we were seriously conversing with each other, that we were no better than children? Is not what we used to say most certainly the truth, whether the multitude agrees with us or not? Is not acting unjustly evil and shameful in every case, whether we incur a heavier or a lighter punishment as the consequence? Do we believe that?

Crito. We do.

Socr. Then we ought never to act unjustly?

Crito. Certainly not.

Socr. If we ought never to act unjustly at all, ought we to repay injustice with injustice, as the multitude thinks we may?

Crito. Clearly not.

Socr. Well, then, Crito, ought we to do evil to anyone?

Crito. Certainly I think not, Socrates.

Socr. And is it just to repay evil with evil, as the multitude thinks, or unjust?

Crito. Certainly it is unjust.

Socr. For there is no difference, is there, between doing evil to a man and acting unjustly?

Crito. True.

Socr. Then we ought not to repay injustice with injustice or to do harm to any man, no matter what we may have suffered from him. And in conceding this, Crito, be careful that you do not concede more than you mean. For I know that only a few men hold, or ever will hold, this opinion. And so those who hold it and those who do not have no common ground of argument; they can of necessity only look with contempt on each other's belief. Do you therefore consider very carefully whether or not you agree with me and share my opinion. Are we to start in our inquiry from the premise that it is never right either to act unjustly, or to repay injustice with injustice, or to avenge ourselves on any man who harms us, by harming him in return? Or do you disagree with me and dissent from my premise? I myself have believed in it for a long time, and I believe in it still. But if you differ in any way, explain to me how. If you still hold to our former opinion, listen to my next point.

Crito. Yes, I hold to it, and I agree with you. Go on.

Socr. Then, my next point, or rather my next question, is this: Ought a man to carry out his just agreements, or may he shuffle out of them?

Crito. He ought to carry them out.

XI *Socr.* Then consider. If I escape without 50 the state's consent, shall I be injuring those whom I ought least to injure, or not? Shall I be abiding by my just agreements or not?

Crito. I cannot answer your question, Socrates. I do not understand it.

Socr. Consider it in this way. Suppose the laws and the commonwealth were to come and appear to me as I was preparing to run away (if that is the right phrase to describe my escape) and were to ask, "Tell us, Socrates, what have you in your mind to do? What do you mean by trying to escape but to destroy us, the laws and the whole state, so far as you are able? Do you think that a state can exist and not be overthrown, in which the decisions of law are of no force, and are disregarded and undermined by private individuals?" How shall we answer questions like that, Crito? Much might be said, especially by an orator, in defense of the law which makes judicial decisions supreme. Shall I reply, "But the state has injured me by judging my case unjustly" Shall we say that?

Crito. Certainly we will, Socrates.

XII *Socr.* And suppose the laws were to reply, "Was that our agreement? Or was it that you would abide by whatever judgments the state should pronounce?" And if we were surprised by their words, perhaps they would say, "Socrates, don't be surprised by our words, but answer us; you yourself are accustomed to ask questions and to answer them. What complaint have you against us and the state, that you are trying to destroy us? Are we not, first of all, your parents? Through us your father took your mother and brought you into the world. Tell us, have you any fault to find with those of us that are the laws of marriage?" "I have none," I should reply. "Or have you any fault to find with those of us that regulate the raising of the child and the education which, you, like others, received? Did we not do well in telling your father to educate you in music and athletics?" "You did," I should say. "Well, then, since you were brought into the world and raised and educated by us, how, in the first place, can you deny that you are our child and our slave, as your fathers were before you? And if this be so, do you think that your rights are on a level with ours? Do you think that you have a right to retaliate if we should try to do anything to you? You had not the same rights that your father had, or that your master would have had if you had been a slave. You had no right to retaliate if they ill-treated you, or to answer them if they 51 scolded you, or to strike them back if they struck you, or to repay them evil with evil in any way. And do you think that you may retaliate in the case of your country and its laws? If we try to destroy you, because we think it just, will you in return do all that you can to destroy us, the laws, and your country, and say that in so doing you are acting justly—you, the man who really thinks so much of excellence? Or are you too wise to see that your country is worthier, more to be revered, more sacred, and held in higher honor both by the gods and by all men of understanding, than your father and your mother and all your other ancestors; and that you ought to reverence it, and to submit to it, and to approach it more humbly when it is angry with you than you would approach your father; and either to do whatever it tells you to do or to persuade it to excuse you; and to obey in silence if it orders you to endure flogging or imprisonment, or if it sends you to battle to be wounded or to die? That is just. You must not give way, nor retreat, nor desert your station. In war, and in the court of justice, and everywhere, you must do whatever your state and your country tell you to do, or you must persuade them that their commands are unjust. But it is impious to use violence against your father or your mother; and much more impious to use violence against your country." What answer shall we make, Crito? Shall we say that the laws speak the truth, or not?

Crito. I think that they do.

XIII   *Socr.* "Then consider, Socrates," perhaps they would say, "if we are right in saying that by attempting to escape you are attempting an injustice. We brought you into the world, we raised you, we educated you, we gave you and every other citizen a share of all the good things we could. Yet we proclaim that if any man of the Athenians is dissatisfied with us, he may take his goods and go away wherever he pleases; we give that privilege to every man who chooses to avail himself of it, so soon as he has reached manhood, and sees us, the laws, and the administration of our state. No one of us stands in his way or forbids him to take his goods and go wherever he likes, whether it be to an Athenian colony or to any foreign country, if he is dissatisfied with us and with the state. But we say that every man of you who remains here, seeing how we administer justice, and how we govern the state in other matters, has agreed, by the very fact of remaining here, to do whatsoever we tell him. And, we say, he who disobeys us acts unjustly on three counts: he disobeys us who are his parents, and he disobeys us who reared him, and he disobeys us after he has agreed to obey us, without persuading us that we are wrong. Yet we did not tell him sternly to do whatever we told him. We offered him an alternative; we gave him his choice either to obey us or to convince us that we were wrong; but he does neither.

XIV   "These are the charges, Socrates, to which we say that you will expose yourself if you do what you intend; and you are more exposed to these charges than other Athenians." And if I were to ask, "Why?" they might retort with justice that I have bound myself by the agreement with them more than other Athenians. They would say, "Socrates, we have very strong evidence that you were satisfied with us and with the state. You would not have been content to stay at home in it more than other Athenians unless you had been satisfied with it more than they. You never went away from Athens to the festivals, nor elsewhere except on military service; you never made other journeys like other men; you had no desire to see other states or other laws; you were contented with us and our state; so strongly did you prefer us, and agree to be governed by us. And what is more, you had children in this city, you found it so satisfactory. Besides, if you had wished, you might at your trial have offered to go into exile. At that time you could have done with the state's consent what you are trying now to do without it. But then you gloried in being willing to die. You said that you preferred death to exile. And now you do not honor those words: you do not respect us, the laws, for you are trying to destroy us; and you are acting just as a miserable slave would act, trying to run away, and breaking the contracts and agreement which you made to live as our citizen. First, therefore, answer this question. Are we right, or are we wrong, in saying that you have agreed not in mere words, but in your actions, to live under our government?" What are we to say, Crito? Must we not admit that it is true?

Crito. We must, Socrates.

Socr. Then they would say, "Are you not breaking your contracts and agreements with us? And you were not led to make them by force or by fraud. You did not have to make up your mind in a hurry. You had seventy years in which you might have gone away if you had been dissatisfied with us, or if the agreement had seemed to you unjust. But you preferred neither Sparta nor Crete, though you are fond of saying that they are well governed, nor any other state, either of the Greeks or the Barbarians. You went away from Athens less than the lame and the blind and the crippled. Clearly you, far more than other Athenians, were satisfied with the state, and also with us who are its laws; for who would be satisfied with a state which had no laws? And now will you not abide by your agreement? If you take our advice, you will, Socrates; then you will not make yourself ridiculous by going away from Athens.

XV   "Reflect now. What good will you do your-self or your friends by thus transgressing and breaking your agreement? It is tolerably certain that they, on their part, will at least run the risk of exile, and of losing their civil rights, or of forfeiting their property. You yourself might go to one of the neighboring states, to Thebes or to Megara, for instance—for both of them are well governed—but, Socrates, you will come as an enemy to these governments, and all who care for their city will look askance at you, and think that you are a subverter of law. You will confirm the judges in their opinion, and make it seem that their verdict was a just one. For a man who is a subverter of law may well be supposed to be a corrupter of the young and thoughtless. Then will you avoid well-governed states and civilized men? Will life be worth having, if you do? Will you associate with such men, and converse without shame—about what, Socrates? About the things which you talk of here? Will you tell them that excellence and justice and institutions and law are the most valuable things that men can have? And do you not think that that will be a disgraceful thing for Socrates? You ought to think so. But you will leave these places; you will go to the friends of Crito in Thessaly. For there is found the greatest disorder and license, and very likely they will be delighted to hear of the ludicrous way in which you escaped from prison, dressed up in peasant's clothes, or in some other disguise which people put on when they are running away, and with your appearance altered. But will no one say how you, an old man, with probably only a few more years to live, clung so greedily to life that you dared to break the highest laws? Perhaps not, if you do not annoy them. But if you do, Socrates, you will hear much that will make you blush. You will pass your life as the flatterer and the slave of all men; and what will you be doing but feasting in Thessaly?[3] It will be as if you had made a journey to Thessaly for a banquet. And where will be all our old arguments about

54 justice and excellence then? But you wish to live for the sake of your children? You want to bring them up and educate them? What? Will you take them with you to Thessaly, and

bring them up and educate them there? Will you make them strangers to their own country that you may bestow this benefit of exile on them too? Or supposing that you leave them in Athens, will they be brought up and educated better if you are alive, though you are not with them? Yes, your friends will take care of them. Will your friends take care of them if you make a journey to Thessaly, and not if you make a journey to Hades? You ought not to think that, at least if those who call themselves your friends are worth anything at all.

"No, Socrates, be persuaded by us who XVI have reared you. Think neither of children nor of life, nor of any other thing before justice, so that when you come to the other world you may be able to make your defense before the rulers who sit in judgment there. It is clear that neither you nor any of your friends will be happier, or juster, or more pious in this life, if you do this thing, nor will you be happier after you are dead. Now you will go away a victim of the injustice, not of the laws, but of men. But if you repay evil with evil, and injustice with injustice in this shameful way, and break your agreements and covenants with us, and injure those whom you should least injure, yourself and your friends and your country and us, and so escape, then we shall be angry with you while you live, and when you die our brothers, the laws in Hades, will not receive you kindly; for they will know that on earth you did all that you could to destroy us. Listen then to us, and let not Crito persuade you to do as he says."

Be sure, my dear friend Crito, that this is XVII what I seem to hear, as the worshippers of Cybele seem, in their passion, to hear the music of flutes; and the sound of these arguments rings so loudly in my ears, that I cannot hear any other arguments. And I feel sure that if you try to change my mind you will speak in vain. Nevertheless, if you think that you will succeed, speak.

Crito. I have nothing more to say, Socrates.

Socr. Then let it be, Crito, and let us do as I say, since the god is our guide.

Notes

1. Criminals could not be put to death while the sacred ship was away on its voyage. [Church]

2. Homer, *Iliad,* ix, 363.

3. The Athenians disdained the Thessalians as heavy eaters and drinkers. [Church]

Adapted from: Plato, *Euthyphro, Apology, Crito,* translated by F. J. Church, pp. 51–65. Copyright © 1956. Reprinted by permission of Pearson Education, Inc. ✦

5
Excerpts from the *Republic*

Plato

Book I

[Socrates:] . . . "As it is, Thrasymachus, you
345c see that—still considering what went before—after you had first defined the true
doctor, you later thought it no longer necessary to keep a precise guard over the true
shepherd. Rather you think that he, insofar
as he is a shepherd, fattens the sheep, not
looking to what is best for the sheep, but, like
d a guest who is going to be feasted, to good
cheer, or in turn, to the sale, like a money-maker and not a shepherd. The shepherd's
art surely cares for nothing but providing the
best for what it has been set over. For that the
art's own affairs be in the best possible way is
surely adequately provided for so long as it
lacks nothing of being the shepherd's art.
And, similarly, I for my part thought just now
that it is necessary for us to agree that every
kind of rule, insofar as it is rule, considers
what is best for nothing other than for what
is ruled and cared for, both in political and
e private rule. Do you think that the rulers in
the cities, those who truly rule, rule willingly?"

[Thrasymachus:] "By Zeus, I don't think
it," he said. "I know it well."

"But, Thrasymachus," I said, "what about
the other kinds of rule? Don't you notice that
no one wishes to rule voluntarily, but they
demand wages as though the benefit from
ruling were not for them but for those who
346a are ruled? Now tell me this much: don't we,
at all events, always say that each of the arts
is different on the basis of having a different
capacity? And don't answer contrary to your
opinion, you blessed man, so that we can
reach a conclusion."

"Yes," he said, "this is the way they differ."

"And does each of them provide us with
some peculiar benefit and not a common

one, as the medical art furnishes us with
health, the pilot's art with safety in sailing,
and so forth with the others?"

"Certainly."

"And does the wage-earner's art furnish b
wages? For this is its power. Or do you call
the medical art the same as the pilot's art? Or,
if you wish to make precise distinctions according to the principle you set down, even if
a man who is a pilot becomes healthy because sailing on the sea is advantageous to
him, nonetheless you don't for that reason
call what he does the medical art?"

"Surely not, " he said.

"Nor do you, I suppose, call the wage-earner's art the medical art, even if a man
who is earning wages should be healthy?"

"Surely not," he said.

"And, what about this? Do you call the
medical art the wage-earner's art, even if a
man practicing medicine should earn
wages?"

He said that he did not.

"And we did agree that the benefit of each c
art is peculiar?"

"Let it be," he said.

"Then whatever benefit all the craftsmen d
derive in common is plainly derived from
their additional use of some one common
thing that is the same for all."

"It seems so," he said.

"And we say that the benefit the craftsmen
derive from receiving wages comes to them
from their use of the wage-earner's art in addition."

He assented with resistance.

"Then this benefit, getting wages, is for
each not a result of his own art; but, if it must
be considered precisely, the medical art produces health, and the wage-earner's art
wages; the housebuilder's art produces a
house and the wage-earner's art, following
upon it, wages; and so it is with all the others:
each accomplishes its own work and benefits that which it has been set over. And if pay
were not attached to it, would the craftsman
derive benefit from the art?"

"It doesn't look like it," he said. e

"Does he then produce no benefit when he
works for nothing?"

"I suppose he does."

"Therefore, Thrasymachus, it is plain by now that no art or kind of rule provides for its own benefit, but, as we have been saying all along, it provides for and commands the one who is ruled, considering his advantage—that of the weaker—and not that of the stronger. It is for just this reason, my dear Thrasymachus, that I said a moment ago that no one willingly chooses to rule and get mixed up in straightening out other people's troubles; but he asks for wages, because the 347a man who is to do anything fine by art never does what is best for himself nor does he command it, insofar as he is commanding by art, but rather what is best for the man who is ruled. It is for just this reason, as it seems, that there must be wages for those who are going to be willing to rule—either money, or honor, or a penalty if he should not rule."

"What do you mean by that, Socrates?" said Glaucon. "The first two kinds of wages I know, but I don't understand what penalty you mean and how you can say it is a kind of wage."

"Then you don't understand the wages of b the best men," I said, "on account of which the most decent men rule, when they are willing to rule. Or don't you know that love of honor and love of money are said to be, and are, reproaches?"

"I do indeed," he said.

"For this reason, therefore," I said, "the good aren't willing to rule for the sake of money or honor. For they don't wish openly to exact wages for ruling and get called hirelings, nor on their own secretly to take a profit from their ruling and get called thieves. Nor, again, will they rule for the sake of honor. For they are not lovers of honor. c Hence, necessity and a penalty must be there in addition for them, if they are going to be willing to rule—it is likely that this is the source of its being held to be shameful to seek to rule and not to await necessity—and the greatest of penalties is being ruled by a worse man if one is not willing to rule oneself. It is because they fear this, in my view, that decent men rule, when they do rule; and at that time they proceed to enter on rule, not as though they were going to something good, or as though they were going to be well d off in it; but they enter on it as a necessity and

because they have no one better than or like themselves to whom to turn it over. For it is likely that if a city of good men came to be, there would be a fight over not ruling, just as there is now over ruling; and there it would become manifest that a true ruler really does not naturally consider his own advantage but rather that of the one who is ruled. Thus everyone who knows would choose to be benefited by another rather than to take the trouble of benefiting another. So I can in no way agree with Thrasymachus that the just is the advantage of the stronger. But this we shall consider again at another time. What Thrasymachus now says is in my own opin- e ion a far bigger thing—he asserts that the life of the unjust man is stronger than that of the just man. Which do you choose, Glaucon," I said, "and which speech is truer in your opinion?"

"I for my part choose the life of the just man as more profitable."

"Did you hear," I said, "how many good things Thrasymachus listed a moment ago 348a as belonging to the life of the unjust man?"

"I heard," he said, "but I'm not persuaded."

"Then do you want us to persuade him, if we're able to find a way, that what he says isn't true?"

"How could I not want it?" he said.

"Now," I said, "if we should speak at length against him, setting speech against speech, telling how many good things belong to being just, and then he should speak in return, and we again, there'll be need of count- b ing the good things and measuring how many each of us has in each speech, and then we'll be in need of some sort of judges who will decide. But if we consider just as we did a moment ago, coming to agreement with one another, we'll ourselves be both judges and pleaders at once."

"Most certainly," he said.

"Which way do you like?" I said. "The latter," he said.

"Come now, Thrasymachus," I said, "answer us from the beginning. Do you assert that perfect injustice is more profitable than justice when it is perfect?"

"I most certainly do assert it," he said, c "and I've said why."

"Well, then, how do you speak about them in this respect? Surely you call one of them virtue and the other vice?"

"Of course."

"Then do you call justice virtue and injustice vice?"

"That's likely, you agreeable man," he said, "when I also say that injustice is profitable and justice isn't."

"What then?"

"The opposite." he said.

"Is justice then vice?"

"No, but very high-minded innocence."

d   "Do you call injustice corruption?"

"No, rather good counsel."

"Are the unjust in your opinion good as well as prudent, Thrasymachus?" "Yes, those who can do injustice perfectly," he said "and are able to subjugate cities and tribes of men to themselves. You, perhaps, suppose I am speaking of cutpurses. Now, such things, too, are profitable," he said, "when one gets away with them; but they aren't worth mentioning compared to those I was just talking about."

e   "As to that," I said, "I'm not unaware of what you want to say. But I wondered about what went before, that you put injustice in the camp of virtue and wisdom, and justice among their opposites?"

"But I do indeed set them down as such."

"That's already something more solid, my comrade," I said, "and it's no longer easy to know what one should say. For if you had set injustice down as profitable but had nevertheless agreed that it is viciousness or shameful, as do some others, we would have something to say, speaking according to customary usage. But as it is, plainly you'll say that injustice is fair and mighty, and, since you also dared to set it down in the camp of virtue and wisdom, you'll set down to its account all the other things which we used to
349a set down as belonging to the just."

"Your divination is very true," he said.

"But nonetheless," I said, "one oughtn't to hesitate to pursue the consideration of the argument as long as I understand you to say what you think. For, Thrasymachus, you seem really not to be joking now, but to be speaking the truth as it seems to you."

"And what difference does it make to you," he said, "whether it seems so to me or not, and why don't you refute the argument?"

"No difference," I said. "But try to answer b this in addition to the other things: in your opinion would the just man want to get the better of the just man in anything?"

"Not at all," he said. "Otherwise he wouldn't be the urbane innocent he actually is."

"And what about this: would he want to get the better of the just action?"

"Not even of the just action," he said.

And does he claim he deserves to get the better of the unjust man, and believe it to be just, or would he not believe it to be so?"

"He'd believe it to be just," he said, "and he'd claim he deserves to get the better, but he wouldn't be able to."

"That," I said, "is not what I am asking, but whether the just man wants, and claims c he deserves, to get the better of the unjust and not of the just man?"

"He does," he said.

"And what about the unjust man? Does he claim he deserves to get the better of the just man and the just action?"

"How could it be otherwise," he said, "since he claims he deserves to get the better of everyone?"

"Then will the unjust man also get the better of the unjust human being and action, and will he struggle to take most of all for himself?"

"That's it."

"Let us say it, then, as follows," I said, "the just man does not get the better of what is like but of what is unlike, while the unjust man gets the better of like and unlike?"   d

"What you said is very good," he said.

"And," I said, "is the unjust man both prudent and good, while the just man is neither?"

"That's good too," he said.

"Then," I said, "is the unjust man also like the prudent and the good, while the just man is not like them?"

"How," he said, "could he not be like such men, since he is such as they, while the other is not like them."

"Fine. Then is each of them such as those to whom he is like?"

"What else could they be?" he said.

e   "All right, Thrasymachus. Do you say that one man is musical and that another is unmusical?"

"I do."

"Which is prudent and which thoughtless?"

"Surely the musical man is prudent and the unmusical man thoughtless."

"Then, in the things in which he is prudent, is he also good, and in those in which he is thoughtless, bad?"

"Yes."

50a   "And what about a medical man? Is it not the same with him?"

"It is the same."

"Then, you best of men, is any musical man who is tuning a lyre in your opinion willing to get the better of another musical man in tightening and relaxing the strings, or does he claim he deserves more?"

"Not in my opinion."

"But the better of the unmusical man?"

"Necessarily," he said.

"And what about a medical man? On questions of food and drink, would he want to get the better of a medical man or a medical action?"

"Surely not."

"But the better of what is not medical?"

"Yes."

"Now, for every kind of knowledge and lack of knowledge, see if in your opinion any man at all who knows chooses voluntarily to say or do more than another man who knows, and not the same as the man who is like himself in the same action."

b   "Perhaps," he said, "it is necessarily so."

"And what about the ignorant man? Would he not get the better of both the man who knows and the man who does not?"

"Perhaps."

"The man who knows is wise?"

"I say so."

"And the wise man is good?"

"I say so."

"Then the man who is both good and wise will not want to get the better of the like, but of the unlike and opposite?"

"It seems so," he said.

"But the bad and unlearned will want to get the better of both the like and the opposite?"

"It looks like it."

"Then, Thrasymachus," I said, "does our unjust man get the better of both like and unlike? Weren't you saying that?"

"I was," he said.

"And the just man will not get the better of c like but of unlike?"

"Yes."

"Then," I said, "the just man is like the wise and good, but the unjust man like the bad and unlearned."

"I'm afraid so."

"But we were also agreed that each is such as the one he is like."

"We were."

"Then the just man has revealed himself to us as good and wise, and the unjust man unlearned and bad."

Now, Thrasymachus did not agree to all of this so easily as I tell it now, but he dragged his feet and resisted, and he produced a won- d derful quantity of sweat, for it was summer. And then I saw what I had not yet seen before—Thrasymachus blushing. At all events, when we had come to complete agreement about justice being virtue and wisdom, and injustice both vice and lack of learning, I said, "All right, let that be settled for us." . . .

Book IV

[Socrates:] . . . "So then, son of Ariston," I said, "your city would now be founded. In the next place, get yourself an adequate light 427d somewhere; and look yourself—and call in your brother and Polemarchus and the others—whether we can somehow see where the justice might be and where the injustice, in what they differ from one another, and which the man who's going to be happy must possess, whether it escapes the notice of all gods and humans or not."

"You're talking nonsense," said Glaucon. "You promised you would look for it because e it's not holy for you not to bring help to justice in every way in your power."

"What you remind me of is true," I said, "and though I must do so, you too have to join in."

"We'll do so," he said.

"Now, then," I said, "I hope I'll find it in this way. I suppose our city—if, that is, it has been correctly founded, perfectly good."

"Necessarily," he said.

"Plainly, then, it's wise, courageous, moderate and just."

"Plainly."

"Isn't it the case that whichever of them we happen to find will leave as the remainder what hasn't been found?"

428a "Of course."

"Therefore, just as with any other four things, if we were seeking any one of them in something or other and recognized it first, that would be enough for us; but if we recognized the other three first, this would also suffice for the recognition of the thing looked for. For plainly it couldn't be anything but what's left over."

"What you say is correct," he said.

"With these things too, since they happen to be four, mustn't we look for them in the same way?"

"Plainly."

"Well, it's wisdom, in my opinion, which
b first comes plainly to light in it. And something about it looks strange."

"What?" he said.

"The city we described is really wise, in my opinion. That's because it's of good counsel, isn't it?"

"Yes."

"And further, this very thing, good counsel, is plainly a kind of knowledge. For it's surely not by lack of learning, but by knowledge, that men counsel well."

"Plainly."

"But, on the other hand, there's much knowledge of all sorts in the city."

"Of course."

"Then, is it thanks to the carpenters' knowledge that the city must be called wise and of good counsel?"

"Not at all," he said, "thanks to that it's
c called skilled in carpentry."

"Then, it's not thanks to the knowledge that counsels about how wooden implements would be best that a city must be called wise."

"Surely not."

"And what about this? Is it thanks to the knowledge of bronze implements or any other knowledge of such things?"

"Not to any knowledge of the sort," he said.

"And not to the knowledge about the production of the crop from the earth; for that, rather, it is called skilled in farming."

"That's my opinion."

"What about this?" I said. "Is there in the city we just founded a kind of knowledge belonging to some of the citizens that counsels not about the affairs connected with some d particular thing in the city, but about how the city as a whole would best deal with itself and the other cities?"

"There is indeed."

"What and in whom is it?" I said.

"It's the guardian's skill," he said, "and it's in those rulers whom we just now named perfect guardians."

"Thanks to this knowledge, what do you call the city?"

"Of good counsel," he said, "and really wise."

"Then, do you suppose," I said, "that there will be more smiths in our city than these e true guardians?"

"Far more smiths," he said.

"Among those," I said, "who receive a special name for possessing some kind of knowledge, wouldn't the guardians be the fewest of all in number?"

"By far."

"It is, therefore, from the smallest group and part of itself and the knowledge in it, from the supervising and ruling part, that a city founded according to nature would be wise as a whole. And this class, which properly has a share in that knowledge which 429a alone among the various kinds of knowledge ought to be called wisdom, has, as it seems, the fewest members by nature."

"What you say," he said, "is very true."

"So we've found—I don't know how—this one of the four, both it and where its seat in the city is."

"In my opinion, at least," he said, "it has been satisfactorily discovered."

"And, next, courage, both itself as well as where it's situated in the city—that courage thanks to which the city must be called courageous—isn't very hard to see."

"How's that?"

b "Who," I said, "would say a city is cowardly or courageous while looking to any part other than the one that defends it and takes the field on its behalf?"

"There's no one," he said, "who would look to anything else."

"I don't suppose," I said, "that whether the other men in it are cowardly or courageous would be decisive for its being this or that."

"No, it wouldn't."

"So a city is also courageous by a part of itc self, thanks to that part's having in it a power that through everything will preserve the opinion about which things are terrible—that they are the same ones and of the same sort as those the lawgiver transmitted in the education. Or don't you call that courage?"

"I didn't quite understand what you said," he said. "Say it again."

"I mean," I said, "that courage is a certain kind of preserving."

"Just what sort of preserving?"

"The preserving of the opinion produced by law through education about what—and what sort of thing—is terrible. And by preserving through everything I meant preserving that opinion and not casting it out in pains and pleasures and desires and fears. If d you wish I'm willing to compare it to what I think it's like."

"But I do wish."

"Don't you know," I said, "that the dyers, when they want to dye wool purple, first choose from all the colors the single nature belonging to white things; then they prepare it beforehand and care for it with no little preparation so that it will most receive the color; and it is only then that they dye? And if e a thing is dyed in this way, it becomes colorfast, and washing either without lyes or with lyes can't take away its color. But those things that are not so dyed—whether one dyes other colors or this one without the preparatory care—you know what they become like."

"I do know," he said, "that they're washed out and ridiculous."

"Hence," I said, "take it that we too were, to the extent of our power, doing something similar when we selected the soldiers and ed- 430a ucated them in music and gymnastic. Don't think we devised all that for any other purpose than that—persuaded by the laws—they should receive them from us in the finest possible way like a dye, so that their opinion about what's terrible and about everything else would be color-fast because they had gotten the proper nature and rearing, and their dye could not be washed out by those lyes so terribly effective at scouring, pleasure—more terribly effective for this than any Chalestrean soda[1] and alkali; and b pain, fear, and desire—worse than any other lye. This kind of power and preservation, through everything, of the right and lawful opinion about what is terrible and what is not, I call courage; and so I set it down, unless you say something else."

"But I don't say anything else," he said. "For, in my opinion, you regard the right opinion about these same things that comes to be without education—that found in beasts and slaves—as not at all lawful and call it something other than courage."

"What you say," I said, "is very true." c

"Well, then, I accept this as courage."

"Yes, do accept it, but as political courage," I said, "and you'd be right in accepting it. Later, if you want, we'll give it a still finer treatment. At the moment we weren't looking for it, but for justice. For that search, I suppose, this is sufficient."

"What you say is fine," he said.

"Well, now," I said, "there are still two left that must be seen in the city, moderation and d that for the sake of which we are making the whole search, justice."

"Most certainly."

"How could we find justice so we won't have to bother about moderation any further?"

"I for my part don't know," he said, "nor would I want it to come to light before, if we aren't going to consider moderation any further. If you want to gratify me, consider this before the other."

"But I do want to," I said, "so as not to do e an injustice."

"Then consider it," he said.

"It must be considered," I said. "Seen from here, it's more like a kind of accord and harmony than the previous ones."

"How?"

"Moderation," I said, "is surely a certain kind of order and mastery of certain kinds of pleasures and desires, as men say when they use—I don't know in what way—the phrase 'stronger than himself'; and some other phrases of the sort are used that are, as it were, its tracks. Isn't that so?"

"Most surely," he said.

"Isn't the phrase 'stronger than himself' ridiculous though? For, of course, the one who's stronger than himself would also be weaker than himself, and the weaker stron431a ger. The same 'himself' is referred to in all of them."

"Of course it is."

"But," I said, "this speech looks to me as if it wants to say that, concerning the soul, in the same human being there is something better and something worse. The phrase 'stronger than himself' is used when that which is better by nature is master over that which is worse. At least it's praise. And when, from bad training or some association, the smaller and better part is mastered by the inb ferior multitude, then this, as though it were a reproach, is blamed and the man in this condition is called weaker than himself and licentious."

"Yes," he said, "that's likely."

"Now, then," I said, "take a glance at our young city, and you'll find one of these conditions in it. For you'll say that it's justly designated stronger than itself, if that in which the better rules over the worse must be called moderate and 'stronger than itself.' "

"Well, I am glancing at it," he said, "and what you say is true."

"And, further, one would find many diverse desires, pleasures, and pains, espec cially in children, women, domestics, and in those who are called free among the common many."

"Most certainly."

"But the simple and moderate desires, pleasures and pains, those led by calculation accompanied by intelligence and right opinion, you will come upon in few, and those the

ones born with the best natures and best educated."

"True," he said.

"Don't you see that all these are in your city too, and that there the desires in the common many are mastered by the desires d and the prudence in the more decent few?"

"I do," he said.

"If, therefore, any city ought to be designated stronger than pleasures, desires, and itself, then this one must be so called."

"That's entirely certain," he said.

"And then moderate in all these respects too?"

"Very much so," he said.

"And, moreover, if there is any city in which the rulers and the ruled have the same e opinion about who should rule, then it's this one. Or doesn't it seem so?"

"Very much so indeed," he said.

"In which of the citizens will you say the moderation resides, when they are in this condition? In the rulers or the ruled?"

"In both, surely," he said.

"You see," I said, "we divined pretty accurately a while ago that moderation is like a kind of harmony."

"Why so?"

"Because it's unlike courage and wisdom, each of which resides in a part, the one mak- 432a ing the city wise and the other courageous. Moderation doesn't work that way, but actually stretches throughout the whole, from top to bottom of the entire scale, making the weaker, the stronger and those in the middle—whether you wish to view them as such in terms of prudence, or, if you wish, in terms of strength, or multitude, money or anything else whatsoever of the sort—sing the same chant together. So we would quite rightly claim that this unanimity is moderation, an accord of worse and better, according to nature, as to which must rule in the city and in each one."

"I am," he said, "very much of the same b opinion."

"All right," I said. "Three of them have been spied out in our city, at least sufficiently to form some opinion. Now what would be the remaining form thanks to which the city would further partake in virtue? For, plainly, this is justice."

"Plainly."

"So then, Glaucon, we must, like hunters, now station ourselves in a circle around the thicket and pay attention so that justice doesn't slip through somewhere and disappear into obscurity. Clearly it's somewhere c hereabouts. Look to it and make every effort to catch sight of it; you might somehow see it before me and could tell me."

"If only I could," he said. "However, if you use me as a follower and a man able to see what's shown him, you'll be making quite sensible use of me."

"Follow," I said, "and pray with me."

"I'll do that," he said, "just lead."

"The place really appears to be hard going and steeped in shadows," I said. "At least it's dark and hard to search out. But, all the same, we've got to go on."

d "Yes," he said, "we've got to go on."

And I caught sight of it and said, "Here! Here! Glaucon. Maybe we've come upon a track; and, in my opinion, it will hardly get away from us."

"That's good news you report," he said.

"My, my," I said, "that was a stupid state we were in."

"How's that?"

"It appears, you blessed man, that it's been rolling around at our feet from the beginning and we couldn't see it after all, but were quite ridiculous. As men holding something in e their hand sometimes seek what they're holding, we too didn't look at it but turned our gaze somewhere far off, which is also perhaps just the reason it escaped our notice."

"How do you mean?" he said.

"It's this way," I said. "In my opinion, we have been saying and hearing it all along without learning from ourselves that we were in a way saying it."

"A long prelude," he said, "for one who desires to hear."

433a "Listen whether after all I make any sense," I said. "That rule we set down at the beginning as to what must be done in everything when we were founding the city—this, or a certain form of it, is, in my opinion, justice. Surely we set down and often said, if you remember, that each one must practice one of the functions in the city, that one for which his nature made him naturally most fit."

"Yes, we were saying that."

"And further, that justice is the minding of one's own business and not being a busybody, this we have both heard from many others and have often said ourselves." b

"Yes, we have."

"Well, then, my friend," I said, "this—the practice of minding one's own business—when it comes into being in a certain way, is probably justice. Do you know how I infer this?"

"No," he said, "tell me."

"In my opinion," I said, "after having considered moderation, courage, and prudence, this is what's left over in the city; it provided the power by which all these others came into being; and, once having come into being, it provides them with preservation as long as it's in the city. And yet we were saying that justice would be what's left over from c the three if we found them." . . .

Book V

[Socrates:] . . . "So, next, as it seems, we must try to seek out and demonstrate what is badly done in cities today, and thereby keeps them from being governed in this way, and with what smallest change—preferably one, if not, two, and, if not, the fewest in number and the smallest in power—a city would come to this manner of regime."

[Glaucon:] "That's entirely certain," he 473c said.

"Well, then," I said, "with one change—not, however, a small or an easy one, but possible—we can, in my opinion, show that it would be transformed."

"What change?" he said.

"Well here I am," I said, "coming to what we likened to the biggest wave. But it shall be said regardless, even if, exactly like a gurgling wave, it's going to drown me in laughter and ill repute. Consider what I am going to say."

"Speak," he said.

"Unless," I said, "the philosophers rule as kings or those now called kings and chiefs d genuinely and adequately philosophize, and political power and philosophy coincide in

the same place, while the many natures now making their way to either apart from the other are by necessity excluded, there is no rest from ills for the cities, my dear Glaucon, nor I think for human kind, nor will the re-
e gime we have now described in speech ever come forth from nature, insofar as possible, and see the light of the sun. This is what for so long was causing my hesitation to speak: seeing how very paradoxical it would be to say. For it is hard to see that in no other city would there be private or public happiness."

And he said, "Socrates, what a phrase and argument you have let burst out. Now that it's said, you can believe that very many men,
474a and not ordinary ones, will on the spot throw off their clothes, and stripped for action, taking hold of whatever weapon falls under the hand of each, run full speed at you to do wonderful deeds. If you don't defend yourself with speech and get away, you'll really pay the penalty in scorn."

"Isn't it you," I said, "that's responsible for this happening to me?"

"And it's a fine thing I'm doing," he said. "But no, I won't betray you, and I'll defend you with what I can. I can provide good will and encouragement; and perhaps I would answer you more suitably than another. And
b so, with the assurance of such support, try to show the disbelievers that it is as *you* say."

"It must be tried," I said, "especially since you offer so great an alliance. It's necessary, in my opinion, if we are somehow going to get away from the men you speak of, to distinguish for them whom we mean when we dare to assert the philosophers must rule. Thus, when they have come plainly to light,
c one will be able to defend oneself, showing that it is by nature fitting for them both to engage in philosophy and to lead a city, and for the rest not to engage in philosophy and to follow the leader."

"It would be high time," he said, "to distinguish them."

"Come, now, follow me here, if we are somehow or other to set it forth adequately."

"Lead," he said.

"Will you need to be reminded," I said, "or do you remember that when we say a man loves something, if it is rightly said of him, he mustn't show a love for one part of it and not for another, but must cherish all of it?"

"I need reminding, as it seems," he said. d "For I scarcely understand."

"It was proper for another, Glaucon, to say what you're saying," I said. "But it's not proper for an erotic man to forget that all boys in the bloom of youth in one way or another put their sting in an erotic lover of boys and arouse him; all seem worthy of attention and delight. Or don't you people behave that way with the fair? You praise the boy with a snub nose by calling him 'cute'; the hook-nose of another you say is 'kingly'; and the e boy between these two is 'well proportioned'; the dark look 'manly'; and the white are 'children of gods.' And as for the 'honey-colored,' do you suppose their very name is the work of anyone other than a lover who renders sallowness endearing and easily puts up with it if it accompanies the bloom of youth? And, in a word, you people take advantage of every excuse and employ any expression so as to reject none of those who glow with the 475a bloom of youth."

"If you want to point to me while you speak about what erotic men do," he said, "I agree for the sake of the argument."

"And what about this?" I said. "Don't you see wine-lovers doing the same thing? Do they delight in every kind of wine, and on every pretext?"

"Indeed, they do."

"And further, I suppose you see that lovers of honor, if they can't become generals, are lieutenants, and if they can't be honored by greater and more august men, are content to b be honored by lesser and more ordinary men because they are desirers of honor as a whole."

"That's certainly the case."

"Then affirm this or deny it: when we say a man is a desirer of something, will we assert that he desires all of that form, or one part of it and not another?"

"All," he said.

"Won't we also then assert that the philosopher is a desirer of wisdom, not of one part and not another, but of all of it?"

"True."

"We'll deny, therefore, that the one who's finicky about his learning, especially when c he's young and doesn't yet have an account of what's useful and not, is a lover of learning or a philosopher, just as we say that the man who's finicky about his food isn't hungry, doesn't desire food, and isn't a lover of food but a bad eater."

"And we'll be right in denying it."

"But the one who is willing to taste every kind of learning with gusto, and who approaches learning with delight, and is insatiable, we shall justly assert to be a philosopher, won't we?"

d And Glaucon said, "Then you'll have many strange ones. For all the lovers of sights are in my opinion what they are because they enjoy learning; and the lovers of hearing would be some of the strangest to include among philosophers, those who would never be willing to go voluntarily to a discussion and such occupations but who—just as though they had hired out their ears for hearing—run around to every chorus at the Dionysia, missing none in the cities or the villages. We will say that all these men and other learners of such things and the petty arts are philosophers?"

"Not at all," I said, "but they are like philosophers."

"Who do you say are the true ones?" he said. "The lovers of the sight of the truth," I said.

"And that's right," he said. "But how do you mean it?"

"It wouldn't be at all easy to tell someone else. But you, I suppose, will grant me this."

"What?"

"Since fair is the opposite of ugly, they are two."

76a "Of course."

"Since they are two, isn't each also one?"

"That is so as well."

"The same argument also applies then to justice and injustice, good and bad, and all the forms; each is itself one, but, by showing themselves everywhere in a community with actions, bodies, and one another, each looks like many."

"What you say," he said, "is right."

"Well, now," I said, "this is how I separate them out. On one side I put those of whom you were just speaking, the lovers of sights, the lovers of arts and the practical men; on the other, those whom the argument concerns, whom alone one could rightly call b philosophers."

"How do you mean?" he said.

"The lovers of hearing and the lovers of sights, on the one hand," I said, "surely delight in fair sounds and colors and shapes and all that craft makes from such things, but their thought is unable to see and delight in the nature of the fair itself."

"That," he said, "is certainly so."

"Wouldn't, on the other hand, those who are able to approach the fair itself and see it by itself be rare?"

"Indeed they would." . . . c

Book VII

[Socrates:] "Next, then," I said, "make an 514a image of our nature in its education and want of education, likening it to a condition of the following kind. See human beings as though they were in an underground cave-like dwelling with its entrance, a long one, open to the light across the whole width of the cave. They are in it from childhood with their legs and necks in bonds so that they are fixed, seeing only in front of them, unable because of the bond to turn their heads all the b way around. Their light is from a fire burning far above and behind them. Between the fire and the prisoners there is a road above, along which is a wall, built like the partitions puppet-handlers set in front of the human beings and over which they show the puppets."

[Glaucon:] "I see," he said.

"Then also see along this wall human beings carrying all sorts of artifacts, which project above the wall, and statues of men and c other animals wrought from stone, wood, and, every kind of material; as is to be ex- 515a pected, some of the carriers utter sounds while others are silent."

"It's a strange image," he said, "and strange prisoners you're telling of."

"They're like us," I said. "For in the first place, do you suppose such men would have seen anything of themselves and one another other than the shadows cast by the fire on the side of the cave facing them?"

"How could they," he said, "if they had
b been compelled to keep their heads motionless throughout life?"

"And what about the things that are carried by? Isn't it the same with them?"

"Of course."

"If they were able to discuss things with one another, don't you believe they would hold that they are naming these things going by before them that they see?"

"Necessarily."

"And what if the prison also had an echo from the side facing them? Whenever one of the men passing by happens to utter a sound, do you suppose they would believe that anything other than the passing shadow was uttering the sound?"

No, by Zeus," he said. "I don't."

c "Then most certainly," I said, "such men would hold that the truth is nothing other than the shadows of artificial things."

"Most necessarily," he said.

"Now consider," I said, "what their release and healing from bonds and folly would be like if something of this sort were by nature to happen to them. Take a man who is released and suddenly compelled to stand up, to turn his neck around, to walk and look up toward the light; and who, moreover, in doing all this is in pain and, because he is dazzled, is unable to make out those things
d whose shadows he saw before. What do you suppose he'd say if someone were to tell him that before he saw silly nothings, while now, because he is somewhat nearer to what *is* and more turned toward beings, he sees more correctly; and, in particular, showing him each of the things that pass by, were to compel the man to answer his questions about what they are? Don't you suppose he'd be at a loss and believe that what was seen before is truer than what is now shown?"

"Yes," he said, "by far."

e "And, if he compelled him to look at the light itself, would his eyes hurt and would he flee, turning away to those things that he is able to make out and hold them to be really clearer than what is being shown?"

"So he would," he said.

"And if," I said, "someone dragged him away from there by force along the rough, steep, upward way and didn't let him go be-

fore he had dragged him out into the light of the sun, wouldn't he be distressed and annoyed at being so dragged? And when he 516a came to the light, wouldn't he have his eyes full of its beam and be unable to see even one of the things now said to be true?"

"No, he wouldn't," he said, "at least not right away."

"Then I suppose he'd have to get accustomed, if he were going to see what's up above. At first he'd most easily make out the shadows; and after that the phantoms of the human beings and the other things in water; and, later, the things themselves. And from there he could turn to beholding the things in heaven and heaven itself, more easily at night—looking at the light of the stars and b the moon—than by day—looking at the sun and sunlight."

"Of course."

"Then finally I suppose he would be able to make out the sun—not its appearances in water or some alien place, but the sun itself by itself in its own region—and see what it's like."

"Necessarily," he said.

"And after that he would already be in a position to conclude about it that this is the source of the seasons and the years, and is the steward of all things in the visible place, c and is in a certain way the cause of all those things he and his companions had been seeing."

"It's plain," he said, "that this would be his next step."

"What then? When he recalled his first home and the wisdom there, and his fellow prisoners in that time, don't you suppose he would consider himself happy for the change and pity the others?"

"Quite so."

"And if in that time there were among them any honors, praises, and prizes for the man who is sharpest at making out the things that go by, and most remembers which of them are accustomed to pass before, which after, and which at the same time d as others, and who is thereby most able to divine what is going to come, in your opinion would be desirous of them and envy those who are honored and hold power among these men? Or, rather, would he be affected as Homer says and want very much 'to be on the soil, a serf to another man, to a portionless man,' and to undergo anything whatsoever rather than to opine those things and live that way?"

e "Yes," he said, "I suppose he would prefer to undergo everything rather than live that way."

"Now reflect on this too," I said. "If such a man were to come down again and sit in the same seat, on coming suddenly from the sun wouldn't his eyes get infected with darkness?"

"Very much so," he said.

"And if he once more had to compete with those perpetual prisoners in forming judgments about those shadows while his vision
17a was still dim, before his eyes had recovered, and if the time needed for getting accustomed were not at all short, wouldn't he be the source of laughter, and wouldn't it be said of him that he went up and came back with his eyes corrupted, and that it's not even worth trying to go up? And if they were somehow able to get their hands on and kill the man who attempts to release and lead up, wouldn't they kill him?"

"No doubt about it," he said.

"Well, then, my dear Glaucon," I said,
b "this image as a whole must be connected with what was said before. Liken the domain revealed through sight to the prison home, and the light of the fire in it to the sun's power; and, in applying the going up and the seeing of what's above to the soul's journey up to the intelligible place, you'll not mistake my expectation, since you desire to hear it. A god doubtless knows if it happens to be true. At all events, this is the way the phenomena look to me: in the knowable the last thing to
c be seen, and that with considerable effort, is the *idea* of the good; but once seen, it must be concluded that this is in fact the cause of all that is right and fair in everything—in the visible it gave birth to light and its sovereign; in the intelligible, itself sovereign, it provided truth and intelligence—and that the man who is going to act prudently in private or in public must see it."

"I, too, join you in supposing that," he said, "at least in the way I can."

"Come, then," I said, "and join me in supposing this, too, and don't be surprised that the men who get to that point aren't willing to mind the business of human beings, but rather that their souls are always eager to d spend their time above. Surely that's likely, if indeed this, too, follows the image of which I told before."

"Of course it's likely," he said.

"And what about this? Do you suppose it is anything surprising," I said, "if a man, come from acts of divine contemplation to the human things, is graceless and looks quite ridiculous when—with his sight still dim and before he has gotten sufficiently accustomed to the surrounding darkness—he is compelled in courts or elsewhere to contest about the shadows of the just or the representations of which they are the shadows, e and to dispute about the way these things are understood by men who have never seen justice itself?"

"It's not at all surprising," he said.

"But if a man were intelligent," I said, "he 518a would remember that there are two kinds of disturbances of the eyes, stemming from two sources—when they have been transferred from light to darkness and when they have been transferred from darkness to light. And if he held that these same things happen to a soul too, whenever he saw one that is confused and unable to make anything out, he wouldn't laugh without reasoning but would go on to consider whether, come from a brighter life, it is in darkness for want of being accustomed, or whether, going from greater lack of learning to greater brightness, it is dazzled by the greater brilliance. And then he would deem the first soul happy b for its condition and its life, while he would pity the second. And, if he wanted to laugh at the second soul, his laughing in this case would make him less ridiculous himself than would his laughing at the soul which has come from above out of the light."

"What you say is quite sensible," he said.

"Then, if this is true," I said, "we must hold the following about these things: education is not what the professions of certain men assert it to be. They presumably assert that they put into the soul knowledge that isn't in

it, as though they were putting sight into
c blind eyes."

"Yes," he said, "they do indeed assert that."

"But the present argument, on the other hand," I said, "indicates that this power is in the soul of each, and that the instrument with which each learns—just as an eye is not able to turn toward the light from the dark without the whole body—must be turned around from that which *is coming into being* together with the whole soul until it is able to endure looking at that which *is* and the brightest part of that which *is*. And we affirm
d that this is the good, don't we?"

"Yes."

"There would, therefore," I said, "be an art of this turning around, concerned with the way in which this power can most easily and efficiently be turned around, not an art of producing sight in it. Rather, this art takes as given that sight is there, but not rightly turned nor looking at what it ought to look at, and accomplishes this object."

"So it seems," he said.

"Therefore, the other virtues of a soul, as they are called, are probably somewhat close to those of the body. For they are really not there beforehand and are later produced by
e habits and exercises, while the virtue of exercising prudence is more than anything somehow more divine, it seems; it never loses its power, but according to the way it is turned, it becomes useful and helpful or, again, useless and harmful. Or haven't you
519a yet reflected about the men who are said to be vicious but wise, how shrewdly their petty soul sees and how sharply it distinguishes those things toward which it is turned, showing that it doesn't have poor vision although it is compelled to serve vice; so that the sharper it sees, the more evil it accomplishes?"

"Most certainly," he said.

"However," I said, "if this part of such a nature were trimmed in earliest childhood and its ties of kinship with becoming were
b cut off—like leaden weights, which eating and such pleasures as well as their refinements naturally attach to the soul and turn its vision downward—if, I say, it were rid of them and turned around toward the true

things, this same part of the same human beings would also see them most sharply, just as it does those things toward which it now is turned."

"It's likely," he said.

"And what about this? Isn't it likely," I said, "and necessary, as a consequence of what was said before, that those who are without education and experience of truth would never be adequate stewards of a city, c nor would those who have been allowed to spend their time in education continuously to the end—the former because they don't have any single goal in life at which they must aim in doing everything they do in private or in public, the latter because they won't be willing to act, believing they have emigrated to a colony on the Isles of the Blessed[2] while they are still alive?"

"True," he said.

"Then our job as founders," I said, "is to compel the best natures to go to the study which we were saying before is the greatest, to see the good and to go up that ascent; and, d when they have gone up and seen sufficiently, not to permit them what is now permitted."

"What's that?"

"To remain there," I said, "and not be willing to go down again among those prisoners or share their labors and honors, whether they be slighter or more serious."

"What?" he said. "Are we to do them an injustice, and make them live a worse life when a better is possible for them?"

"My friend, you have again forgotten," I e said, "that it's not the concern of law that any one class in the city fare exceptionally well, but it contrives to bring this about for the whole city, harmonizing the citizens by persuasion and compulsion, making them share with one another the benefit that each class is able to bring to the commonwealth. 520a And it produces such men in the city not in order to let them turn whichever way each wants, but in order that it may use them in binding the city together."

"That's true," he said. "I did forget."

"Well, then, Glaucon," I said, "consider that we won't be doing injustice to the philosophers who come to be among us, but rather that we will say just things to them while

compelling them besides to care for and guard the others. We'll say that when such
b men come to be in the other cities it is fitting for them not to participate in the labors of those cities. For they grow up spontaneously against the will of the regime in each; and a nature that grows by itself and doesn't owe its rearing to anyone has justice on its side when it is not eager to pay off the price of rearing to anyone. 'But you we have begotten for yourselves and for the rest of the city like leaders and kings in hives; you have been better and more perfectly educated and are more able to participate in both lives. So you
c must go down, each in his turn, into the common dwelling of the others and get habituated along with them to seeing the dark things. And, in getting habituated to it, you will see ten thousand times better than the men there, and you'll know what each of the phantoms is, and of what it is a phantom, because you have seen the truth about fair, just, and good things. And thus, the city will be governed by us and by you in a state of waking, not in a dream as the many cities nowadays are governed by men who fight over shadows with one another and form factions for the sake of ruling, as though it were some great good. But the truth is surely this:
d that city in which those who are going to rule are least eager to rule is necessarily governed in the way that is best and freest from faction, while the one that gets the opposite kind of rulers is governed in the opposite way.' "

"Most certainly," he said.

"Do you suppose our pupils will disobey us when they hear this and be unwilling to join in the labors of the city, each in his turn, while living the greater part of the time with one another in the pure region?"
e "Impossible," he said. "For surely we shall be laying just injunctions on just men. However, each of them will certainly approach ruling as a necessary thing—which is the opposite of what is done by those who now rule in every city."

"That's the way it is, my comrade," I said. "If you discover a life better than ruling for 521a those who are going to rule, it is possible that your well-governed city will come into being. For here alone will the really rich rule, rich not in gold but in those riches required by the happy man, rich in a good and prudent life. But if beggars, men hungering for want of private goods, go to public affairs supposing that in them they must seize the good, it isn't possible. When ruling becomes a thing fought over, such a war—a domestic war, one within the family—destroys these men themselves and the rest of the city as well."

"That's very true," he said.

"Have you," I said, "any other life that de- b spises political offices other than that of true philosophy?"

"No, by Zeus," he said. "I don't."

"But men who aren't lovers of ruling must go to it; otherwise rival lovers will fight."

"Of course."

"Who else will you compel to go to the guarding of the city than the men who are most prudent in those things through which a city is best governed, and who have other honors and a better life than the political life?"

"No one else," he said. ⋮ . . .

Notes

1. Chalestra was a town on the Thermaic Gulf in Macedonia. In a nearby lake there was carbonate of soda used in washing [Bloom].

2. A happy place where good men live forever. In some accounts they went there before dying, in others afterward [Bloom].

Adapted from: Plato, *The Republic of Plato* (2nd Ed.), translated by Allan Bloom, pp. 23–39, 105–111, 153–156, 193–200. Copyright © 1968 by Allan Bloom. Reprinted by permission of Perseus Book Group. ✦

6
The *Republic* and the 'Limits of Politics'

Dale Hall

I

Professors Leo Strauss and Allan Bloom have offered a radical, challenging and new interpretation of Plato's *Republic*.[1] Emphasizing the crucial importance of certain passages referring to the philosopher's return to the Cave and reconsidering the general character of Plato's political argument, they question many of our most basic assumptions about Plato's notion of philosophical politics. They turn our attention to the problem of clarifying his overall purpose by offering a startling account of his intentions. They both identify the relation between the *kallipolis* [fair or beautiful city] which Socrates depicts and existing, ordinary *poleis* [cities] as crucial, and they are sure that Plato was preoccupied with the possibility of the good *polis* coming into being. They conclude that Plato is finally pessimistic about the prospects for its realisation, that he presents it as an ideal remote from actual human endeavour. Apparently, the *kallipolis* is unrealisable and unrealistic. They agree that the prospect of philosophical politics is renounced in the *Republic*, and that such a political order is not only impossible but, according to Plato, contrary to nature. Strauss claims that "the *Republic* conveys the broadest and deepest analysis of political idealism ever made."[2] The *Republic*'s "claim that the tension between philosophy and the city would be overcome if the philosophers became kings"[3] is only apparent, for, in fact, Plato presents "the most magnificent cure

ever devised for every form of political ambition."[4] In this, as in so many other of his conclusions, Bloom is substantially influenced by Strauss. He agrees with Strauss' superlatives: "Political idealism is the most destructive of human passions" and the *Republic* is "the greatest critique of political idealism ever written."[5] He concludes that the "extreme spirit of reform or revolution loses its ground if . . . the infinite longing for justice on earth is merely a dream or a prayer."[6] "The Republic serves to moderate the extreme passion for justice by showing the limits of what can be demanded and expected of the city."[7] Instead of an optimistic argument revealing a definitive political order, they find a pessimistic meditation upon the "limits of politics."[8] Plato discloses the "the limits of politics" by revealing, first, that the *kallipolis* is an order contrary to human nature, because it " 'abstracts' from the body,"[9] and second, that the philosopher is not naturally a political ruler. We shall examine both claims, but the latter is the more important. According to Strauss and Bloom, because it is contrary to the philosophers' nature that they should rule, the *Republic*'s requirement that they be compelled to return to the Cave and rule represents the utmost perversion of nature by art. Apparently, even within the *kallipolis* there exists an irreconcilable opposition between the good of the individual and the good of the whole community. Because the individual realises himself most perfectly in philosophy, it is a diminution of his *eudaimonia* [happiness] and contrary to his nature for the philosopher to be compelled to leave the Sunlight and rule for the common good.

Such an account is startling, for we are accustomed to taking Socrates seriously. He does recommend that philosophers should rule; he says that human well-being is achievable only through the union of philosophy and politics; he presents the *kallipolis* as the natural political order and interprets existing, corrupt *poleis* as disordered perversions of the ideal. For Strauss and Bloom the *Republic* must be consummately ironic, as an instance of Socrates appearing to say one thing, in recommending the *kallipolis* as natural, but actually meaning another. Socrates' meaning must be reversed, for the *Republic* is really a "Modest Proposal," proposing ironically a solution to our evils that no rational man would pursue. . . . [A]lthough Strauss and Bloom find Plato ironic in covertly disclosing the unnaturalness of the *politeia* that Socrates appears to advocate, they . . . offer no extended account of his irony. Strauss just says that we should not assume that Socrates is Plato's spokesman, for to speak through the mouth of a man notorious for his irony is "tantamount to not asserting anything."[10] Bloom argues only that to neglect man's physical aspect, "to forget the other side of man—to neglect the irony of Socrates' proposals—is . . . a fatal error. The cosmopolitan communistic society of egalitarian man is a distortion of man and the city which is more terrible than barbarism . . . a society is constituted which satisfies neither body nor soul."[11]

II

To consider their claim that the *Republic* is somehow wholly ironic and discloses the limits of politics we must distinguish three elements in the interpretations of Strauss and Bloom, although they do not separate them clearly. Both of them claim that the earlier parts of Book V have a comic character, that the *kallipolis* of Socrates' construction is unnatural, and that the activity of political ruling is contrary to the philosopher's nature. We shall discuss the first two of these claims briefly here and then concentrate on the third in the next section.

They find Book V comic, particularly in its discussion of communal life and the equality of women. For Strauss, it is "akin to Aristophanes' *Assembly of Women*," and the equality of the sexes is presented as "laughable."[12] For Bloom, Plato's comedy is "more fantastic, more innovative, more comic and more profound than any work of Aristophanes."[13] So both of them relate Book V to the *Ecclesiazusae* [comedy by Aristophanes, 391 B.C.E.], but neither of them explains or examines the relationship. Quite uncritically they just assume that Plato was trying to outdo Aristophanes in a comic satire of certain radical contemporary

ideas, presupposing that Plato's purpose was in common with that of the dramatist. They refer neither to Barker (who is sure that "Plato is seeking to meet the current satire on communism, including that of Aristophanes")[14] nor to the excellent discussion of Adam, who finds that Plato's purpose was far from comic or satiric.[15] Adam writes that Plato was probably dissatisfied with the comedian's travesty of views with which he (Plato) had no little sympathy, and that he touches, with serious purposes, on nearly all the proposals which Aristophanes had tried to make ridiculous.[16] Adam agrees that Plato probably had Aristophanes' satire in mind, but gives no support at all to the speculative claim that Plato's intention was also satiric. Clearly, we should not assimilate Plato's intentions to Aristophanes' just on the basis of certain (superficial) resemblances.[17] Strauss and Bloom neglect that for Aristophanes' satire of such social arrangements to have had point, others must have recommended them quite seriously. They are too ready to interpret the text according to their own responses, forgetting that we are most susceptible mistakenly to call an author comic or ironic when his beliefs and assumptions differ most from our own.[18] They find comic Plato's comparisons with animals, his proposals for selective breeding and for exposure of inferior *phylakes* [guardians], but these ideas were not necessarily unacceptable or ridiculous to a fourth-century Greek.[19] Many Greeks felt that Spartan experience vindicated such arrangements. Similarly, the equality of women and the community of women and children were familiar subjects of speculation and report.[20] There are none of the familiar signs of irony or comedy in Plato's discussion of equality: Socrates does not appeal to absurd premises, nor reason fallaciously, nor contradict himself, and the seriousness of the discussions of Book V is further attested by their coherence with Plato's account of justice in the *Republic*.[21] Clearly, because Strauss and Bloom find the *kallipolis* a fantastic and uncongenial moral and social order, they just assume that Plato could not have meant what he said. Their approach is anachronistic and unhistorical, and it fails to provide any criterion by which we can identify Plato's irony. For example, if they doubt his commitment to the community of women and children, why do they not suspect his seriousness with respect to the theory of forms—for Plato intends the ideal social order to cohere with his psychology and metaphysics?

Strauss has two main grounds for asserting that the *kallipolis* is contrary to nature: first, it disregards the realities of human nature (it " 'abstracts' from the body")[22], and, second, it cannot perfectly embody the form of justice.[23] Like Strauss, Bloom pays most attention to the first of these, also finding an opposition between the *eros* of the body and the requirements and practices of the *kallipolis*. Only through the "depreciation of *eros* can the city come into its own,"[24] for, in abolishing privacy, regulating man's sexual *eros* and allowing women to perform the same functions as men, the *kallipolis* ignores propensities basic to human nature.[25] According to Strauss and Bloom, Plato's regulations impose unnatural arrangements and practices on the *phylakes*.[26] However, they offer no evidence for such conclusions, and they quite neglect all possible historical and anthropological comparisons. For example, Bloom is sure that, "as a political proposal the public nakedness of men and women is nonsense," although men can go naked together, "because it is relatively easy to desexualise their relations."[27] What of Greek homosexuality? And if the regulation of both sexes' public nudity is nonsense, what would Bloom say of Xenophon, who insists that Sparta did just that and avoided licentiousness?[28] Once more, plausible comparisons of Plato's ideas with contemporary practices are ignored, so that, set in an ahistorical limbo, the *kallipolis* appears comic or unnatural. Strauss' subsidiary reason for calling the *kallipolis* unnatural is no more satisfactory. He argues that the just *polis* cannot manifest the form of justice perfectly, for real justice is not capable of coming into being.[29] Because forms are incorporeal, even the most perfect *polis* must fall short of their perfection.[30] Although true, this is more than a little misleading, for there is no suggestion in Plato that the *kallipolis* is merely

conventional or contrary to nature. Although the just *polis* only approximates the forms, it is the most natural association possible for man. Only in the *kallipolis* do social life and men's *psychai* [souls] manifest the natural order that is well-being. Only there are the forms made immanent, only through philosophic rule does the political order assume its greatest reality and intelligibility. The forms are in nature (*en tei physei*), and so is the *kallipolis* because it is modeled upon them. Strauss' interpretation neglects the relationship of participation between the physical world and the forms, and so he distorts Plato's political argument. On Strauss' reading, human beings are unnatural, for being corporeal.

Socrates is explicit that his *polis* is natural. It is based on no reluctant agreement, but on man's most basic needs; the most primitive relationships represent a division of labour based on *physis* [nature] (370a–c. Cf. 374e); the duality of the dispositions of the *phylakes* is not unnatural (375e), and even the introduction of the rulers complements *physis*, for they are those *phylakes* whose natures are properly harmonized by music and gymnastics (412a). No element of the *kallipolis* is antipathetic to nature, and Socrates reveals that political justice is the natural ordering principle, the division of labour, now more adequately understood to take account of all men's natural differences. In identifying the other excellences, Socrates presupposes that his is the natural *polis* (428e–429a). The same theme continues in Book V, where we are clearly told that all the regulations about women and children are natural (453b, 456b, and 466d). There Socrates introduces the notion of philosophic rule as the precondition for the growth of the only natural political order, for unless philosophy and politics unite, "there is no rest from ills for cities, nor will the regime we have described in speech ever come forth from nature" (473d–e). We learn that the philosopher is he who is fitted by nature both to practice philosophy and to lead the *polis* (474b–c).

III

It is the third aspect of Strauss' and Bloom's case that we must discuss in more detail, namely, their claim that although Plato postulates an harmony of philosophy and politics, his meaning is actually far from straightforward. Properly understood, the *kallipolis* is unnatural, because ruling is an unnatural activity for the philosopher. Their argument depends upon finding two separate senses of justice within the *Republic*. In relation to the individual, there is justice understood as an internal hierarchical harmony of reason, spirit, and appetite within the *psyche*, and there is justice as a quality of actions.[31] It is convenient to refer to the first of these kinds of justice as "platonic justice," a phrase taken from an influential article by Sachs[32]. . . . For Strauss, only the philosopher is platonically just, for only he can perfectly harmonise his *psyche* according to the pattern of the forms.[33] But everyone can be just in the second sense; they can observe what Strauss sometimes calls "civic virtue"[34] and what we shall call (like Sachs) "vulgar justice." Vulgar justice is the quality of our actions realised in service to the *polis* and in our relations with others when we fulfil our obligations and observe the conventional rules of moral conduct. . . . Strauss and Bloom believe that because Plato does not connect vulgar with platonic justice (and so with *eudaimonia*) he fails to show (a) that platonically just men will naturally serve the *polis* and (b) that a life of service to the *polis* (even of fulfilling one's function in the *kallipolis*) constitutes human well-being.[35] Strauss emphasises only the first of these, but Bloom mentions both. He says, "The question is whether . . . devotion to the common good leads to the health of the soul or whether the man with an healthy soul is devoted to the common good."[36] By separating the two senses of justice, . . . Strauss and Bloom infer that men have no good reason for being good citizens; and . . . reason . . . that because the *kallipolis* requires that philosophers serve the common good by accepting the unwelcome burdens of ruling, it follows that even the just *polis* is unnatural.[37]

Although they require that both a and b be satisfied, Strauss and Bloom emphasise a, making b subsidiary. This subordinate aspect of their case, that Plato must show that those who serve the *polis* necessarily enjoy platonic justice, can be dismissed immediately. Contrary to their claim, Plato does not need to show that a life of vulgar justice entails platonic justice. His argument is not impugned by any failure to show that all those whose actions are merely unexceptionable have psychic harmony, for they may be so through fear, or from cynical calculation of likely future advantage. Vulgar justice implies platonic justice only when a man has a settled and sincere disposition to behave justly. In corrupt *poleis* only exceptional men have such dispositions, but in the *kallipolis*, where the philosopher's subjects enjoy the right musical and gymnastic *paideia* [education] such a disposition is characteristic. There the subjects enjoy a measure of psychic harmony, based on right belief, guaranteed by the philosopher's knowledge.[38] Through their participation in the *kallipolis* their spirited and appetitive elements are disciplined and their reason is guided by the ruler's knowledge.

Clearly, then, the crucial question is that referred to as a above, whether the possession of platonic justice will make a man vulgarly just, "whether the man with an healthy soul is devoted to the common good." According to Strauss and Bloom, Plato reveals that the platonically just philosopher does not naturally rule. Apparently, the excellence appropriate to philosophy is distinct from the excellence required for ruling, and the philosopher has no reason to sacrifice his private good, consisting in theoretical contemplation, for the sake of the common good, which consists in his undertaking the practical activity of ruling. They believe that, by emphasizing the opposition of individual and common goods, Plato disclosed the "limits of politics" and revealed the "nature and problems of politics."[39] The central question of the *Republic* is, "Can there be a regime whose laws are such as to serve the common good while allowing each of its members to reach his natural perfection?"[40] When Plato introduces the rulers, Bloom's commentary asks, "Is the wise man, who makes full use of the powers of his reason, the same as the prudent statesman?" And by the end of Book VII, Bloom says, it has become "manifest that the life of reason has a character of its own" and that the *polis* cannot "comprehend the highest activity of man."[41] It cannot "comprehend" the highest theoretical excellence because it demands an inferior practical service, requiring that the philosopher abandon contemplation for ruling. The *kallipolis'* very existence depends upon the most perfect human type sacrificing his excellence and *eudaimonia*.[42] Men can live well in the Cave only if philosophers abandon their odyssey and return from the sunlight to an inferior world and activity. Their reluctance to return, and Socrates' insistence that they must be compelled, intimates the unnatural character of the *kallipolis*, which "abuses and misuses the best men."[43] There is a fundamental opposition between the philosophic *eros*, which aspires to know the forms, and the requirements of any political order.[44] The relation of politics and philosophy is only an "alleged harmony," postulated to reveal an actual opposition.[45] So, instead of recommending that philosophers should rule, Plato reveals that they are not naturally political rulers; instead of approving the *kallipolis*, he discloses that its most fundamental postulate is contrary to nature. And so the *Republic* appears as an indictment of idealism and utopianism, by revealing the "limits of politics."

We shall suggest that this account of the *Republic's* philosophical politics is mistaken, by arguing that (1) Strauss and Bloom misinterpret the reference to the philosophers being compelled to return to the Cave and rule; (2) that they divorce theoretical and practical wisdom in a manner quite foreign to Plato; (3) that the philosopher's well-being does not consist exclusively in reflection in the theoretical mode; (4) that the platonically just individual with an harmonious *psyche* will act for the good of others; (5) that the philosopher's goodness is most perfectly realised when he rules politically; (6) that Strauss and Bloom misunderstand Plato's account of "politics" within the *kallipolis*;

and (7) that they are unsympathetic to his notion of *eudaimonia*.

1. To maintain their account, Strauss and Bloom must dismiss traditional interpretations of the *Republic*, according to which there exists no opposition between philosophy and politics because the philosopher's excellence is precisely that excellence which qualifies him and equips him to rule. They do dismiss such orthodox interpretations, on the basis of Plato's references to the philosopher's reluctance to rule.[46] Strauss emphasises the important passage (519c–520d) in which Socrates declares that philosophers must be compelled to rule in the *kallipolis*. Socrates insists that:

> Our job as founders is to compel the best natures to go to the study which we were saying before is the greatest, to see the good and to go up that ascent; and, when they have gone up and seen sufficiently, not to permit them . . . to remain there and not be willing to go down again among the prisoners to share their labours. . . . It's not the concern of law that any one class in the city fare exceptionally well, but it contrives to bring this about for the whole city. . . . And it produces such men in the city not in order to let them turn whichever way each wants, but in order that it may use them in binding the city together. . . . We won't be doing injustice to the philosophers who come to be among us. . . . We will say just things to them, while compelling them besides to care for and guard the others. We'll say that . . . "You we have begotten for yourselves and for the rest of the city, like leaders and kings in hives; you have been better and more perfectly educated and are more able to participate in both lives. So you must go down."

Other passages have a similar character, using the language of constraint and necessity (499b–c, 500d 4–5, 539e 2–3, and 540a) or referring to the philosophers' reluctance to rule (520c–521b and 540b), and they are held to support the conclusion that within the *kallipolis* the best men are misused.[47] However, we should not conclude that Plato uses the notion of compulsion (*anagkaxo*) to indicate that the required undertaking is contrary to nature, for there are at least two important instances (one in the passage above) where he refers to compulsion when it is perfectly clear that the relevant action is not unnatural. As founders, Socrates says, they must "compel the best natures" to undertake the study culminating in the apprehension of the Good (519c), at 540a he declares that the philosophers must be compelled to look toward the Good itself, and the Cave suggests that the philosophic odyssey is arduous. Strauss and Bloom do not explain these passages; but, if we were to follow their inference from the language of compulsion, we would conclude that the philosophic education perverts man's natural inclinations! Clearly, in being compelled to undertake the highest studies the philosophers are "forced to be free," and so, although Plato writes of them being compelled to rule, it remains at least possible that political rule is not a perversion, but a completion of the philosophic experience. We should consider seriously the possibility that ruling represents the fulfillment of the philosophic nature because it constitutes, to the greatest degree possible, the natural rule of reason over spirit and appetite. Viewed in this light, ruling provides the philosopher with the opportunity of overcoming his awareness of the disparity between the physical and ideal realms, for the philosopher ruler models the social order according to the harmony of the forms (501a–c).

2. Bloom, particularly, appears to read Plato through Aristotle, for he finds in the former the latter's separation of theoretical and practical wisdom. He assumes that the exercise of practical wisdom is unrelated to the theoretical wisdom of the forms, and that *eudaimonia* consists exclusively in the practice of theoretical contemplation. . . .[48] These two elements in the interpretation of Strauss and Bloom are distinct, for the distinction between platonic and vulgar justice is compatible with no separation between the two modes of reason. The exercise of practical reason is compatible with either vulgar justice or injustice, and platonic justice cannot be defined simply as the theoretical contemplation of the forms, for it involves the harmony of the whole *psyche*. So we must examine these two distinctions sep-

arately, taking first that aspect which is peculiar to Strauss and Bloom.

Strauss and Bloom do not acknowledge that the separation of the practical and theoretical faculties of reason is quite foreign to Plato. Throughout the *Republic* Plato insists on the relation between the intelligible and sensible "worlds," and he does not suggest that the philosopher apprehends an order entirely unrelated to the physical world. Sensible experience is contradictory, uncertain, and impermanent; particulars are poor copies of the forms, and the philosopher is acutely aware of the disparity between the phenomenal and ideal worlds; but the forms are not altogether removed from the particulars of ordinary experience. When perfected, the philosopher's understanding consists not just in contemplating the forms, but in resolving all levels of experience as he recognises the interconnectedness of the intelligible and sensible orders. . . . For Plato, philosophic knowledge is not only a mystic state, but a disciplined recognition that the world is "knowable" and the realisation that all the elements of our experiences are reconcilable in a more complete understanding. The Good is not an object of aesthetic contemplation, or not only that, but the principle of intelligibility by which the philosopher understands how the world is conformed to reason. . . .

Because he asserts the relation of the intelligible and sensible orders, Plato makes no separation of theoretical and practical wisdom. Bloom is reluctant to admit that the knowledge of the forms could authorise practical moral judgements, but that is a most un-Platonic assumption. The belief that the forms are irrelevant to the practical mode might be cogent, given *our* conception of reason, but Plato's conception is distinctive, and to neglect it is to make nonsense of the *Republic's* structure. In terms of the forms and the image of the *kallipolis*, where the nonphilosophers enjoy *arete* based on right belief inculcated by the philosopher-rulers, Plato resolves the Socratic paradoxes that virtue is knowledge and all virtue is one. Knowledge of the forms is the essential qualification for ruling, and when Adeimantus objects that philosophers would be useless

(487d), Socrates replies that such is the case only when the public affairs of men are disordered (488a–489c). The forms are the paradigms for the philosopher's ordering of the social world (484c–d, 500d, and 501b). Because Plato sees the physical world as a copy of perfection, there is enough order and goodness in it to sustain the efforts of the philosopher to improve it when once he comes to rule. He does not suggest that philosophizing and ruling are unrelated functions, and he represents the rule of philosophers as the fulfilment of the division of labour principle in the *polis*.

3. However, Strauss and Bloom might allow that Plato separates neither the sensible and intelligible orders nor practical and theoretical wisdom, but still maintain that the philosopher's fullest happiness consists exclusively in reflection in the theoretical mode. . . . Having argued that Plato does not separate the two modes of reason, we must now show that the *Republic*'s argument is distorted by the assumption that *eudaimonia* can consist exclusively in theoretical wisdom. Now, Plato's account of reason in the *psyche* should make us question such an interpretation, for reason does its own natural function when it decides what is good and bad for the whole *psyche* (441e). Reason's function is to order the *psyche*, for the *psyche* is not just, and so is not *eudaimon*, *only* by virtue of an activity of the reasoning part. When Plato develops his account of reason in man he does not separate its activity of theorising from its role of creating order, and we learn nothing later which contradicts the earlier account that the *psyche* is just and *eudaimon* only when each part does its own with respect to ruling and being ruled (441e–442c, 443b–444a). Plato treats reason's aspiration to know as a kind of desire (589d 6–8), but he does not separate that desire from the inclination to rule. Indeed, each part of the *psyche* seems to possess a natural inclination to impose its own distinctive character on the functioning of the whole *psyche*. Plato does not suggest that it is contrary to the nature of philosophically trained reason to rule in the *psyche*, for reason's inclination is to harmonise it, according to reason's own order. Only reason has

the well-being of the whole as its conscious objective, and its function is to promote platonic justice, which is the harmony of the whole *psyche*. In the platonically just man, reason exercises control at such a fundamental level that the other elements are reconciled to their subordination and concur easily.

4. Because Plato interprets the *psyche* as a union of potentially contending elements, the comparison with the *polis* becomes plausible and important. He made no distinction of kind between reason's rule in the *psyche* and its rule in the *polis* through the political preeminence of the philosophers. There is no disjunction between the functioning of reason at the level of the individual *psyche* and its operation politically, for in the two contexts its role is the same: to harmonise spirit and appetite to good functioning under its own rule. It is difficult to see why philosophic reason's rule in the *polis* is unnatural if its role within the individual *psyche* is not so characterised. To defend their case, Strauss and Bloom . . . must distinguish in kind between the "private" and "social" action of reason. Strauss and Bloom attempt this by combining the disjunction between platonic and vulgar justice with their alleged disjunction between theoretical and practical reason. Because they can see no connection between the philosopher's platonic justice and his performing vulgarly just action for the good of others, they assume that he is not naturally a political ruler. Believing that his theoretical activity is unrelated to any practical life and believing that the philosopher's *eudaimonia* consists exclusively in theorising and the possession of an ordered *psyche*, Strauss and Bloom can see no reason to accept that he will be concerned with action for the good of others. Apparently, Plato fails to connect the internal justness of the philosopher with his public role as ruler because platonic justice is a self-centred condition. To answer such a case we must consider whether Plato fails to connect platonic and vulgar justice in general terms before examining the case of the philosopher-ruler in particular.

Plato states explicitly that platonically just men will observe conventional norms

(422e–443b), and . . . that the rule of reason in the *psyche* expresses itself in just action. Platonic justice is plausibly understood as the efficient cause of just action, for reason not only apprehends, but aspires to the Good, which includes the form of justice as a universal and not private good. Reason's concern is that the good should be exemplified everywhere. Reason "does its own" only when it makes correct moral judgements, and the platonically just man acts rightly because the sources of his wrongdoing—appetite and spirit—are disciplined and subordinated. The two justices are connected not only because psychic harmony is the efficient cause of just action, but because that harmony is the *telos*, or final cause, of such action. By so understanding platonic justice, Plato introduces a "revisionist" account of ordinary moral conduct: those actions are called just which create and preserve internal harmony, and unjust actions are those which unleash spirit and appetite (443d6–44a2 and 588e–592a). Yet he revises and does not reject altogether ordinary rules of conduct, for their observance contributes to the creation of an harmonious *psyche* (589c–590a). Because that harmony consists in the excellence of the whole *psyche*, it cannot be realised by theoretical reason in isolation. To integrate and harmonise appetite and spirit within a complete life, reason must operate in the practical mode. Obviously, spirit and appetite cannot join with reason in understanding the forms, so they function within the harmony of a whole *psyche* only through the practice of right conduct; like wild beasts, appetite and spirit are disciplined only by being repeatedly trained. Therefore, the philosopher acts naturally for the good of others, perfecting his own nature in so doing.

5. However, Strauss and Bloom might still argue that, although the philosopher will act justly for the good of others, ruling remains an altogether different kind of activity, with a final cause other than the psychic harmony of the philosopher. They might deny that ruling is included within the concept of vulgar justice. To say that a philosopher must act justly is not, it could be argued, the same as saying that a philosopher must rule. The dif-

ficulty about such a reply is that it neglects essential aspects of Plato's metaphysics. If we understand his account of reason properly, we shall see that the philosopher's platonically just *psyche* naturally acts justly, and rules, in order to reproduce its own harmony in other subjects. Reason's final cause is the platonic justice of its own and other men's *psychai*, and the philosopher's reason is impartial between its own and their *psychai* as potential spheres of justice. That Plato did consider reason to be impartial in exactly this way is evident from the formal properties that he attributes to its operation in the theoretical mode. In theorising, when it considers the sensible world as an imperfect manifestation of the forms' order, reason is impartial between particulars, as it reflects on the forms in which they share. Certain particulars (say actions) will be better or worse exemplifications of a form (like justice), but the degree of their participation in the form is the only ground for reason's differentiation. For reason there is no "material" difference between particulars, excepting the degrees of their resemblances of the forms. Now, because theoretical and practical reason are the two aspects of the same power or faculty, we can generalize from reason's procedure in the theoretical mode to its operation in the practical. Because in the practical mode reason functions in the same way, it seeks naturally to reproduce platonic justice equally in any of the particular *psychai* that fall within the scope of its action. Just as in the theoretical mode reason's purpose of apprehending the forms is identical in relation to all the particulars of the sensible world, so, in the practical mode, its purpose of recreating the order of the forms is the same in all similar cases. Given the nature of reason, as the element that aspires to the imposition of its own rule and which looks to the good of the whole, and given its manner of operation in the theoretical mode, there is no ground for restricting its natural function of ruling to any one *psyche* rather than another. . . . Because the philsopher's reason naturally creates the psychic harmony that is based on the forms, its natural role extends potentially to all *psychai* in which order can be created. There is no principle by which the philosopher's reason can be restricted to self-centred operation. Political ruling, then, appears as the natural realisation of reason's function.

6. This conclusion, which arises from Plato's distinctive understanding of reason and the unity of the *psyche*, assumes an enhanced intelligibility if we remember his conception of philosophic rule. Some commentators have found this so singular that they have denied altogether its *political* character.[49] For Wolin, Plato's philosophic rule is nonpolitical because it involves the implementation of a definitive order and the elimination from public life of such features as disagreement, conflict, conciliation, competition, and persuasion—all, or some of which, many modern commentators take as constitutive features of "politics." If politics is so understood, then the activity of ruling can certainly appear foreign to the philosopher's nature. Because Strauss and Bloom implicitly understand politics in such political scientist terms and because they do not recognize how distinctive is Plato's account of political rule, they are inclined to separate sharply the philosopher's contemplation of the forms from his activity of ruling. The harmony of the forms appears so remote from the practices constitutive of politics that philosophical politics appears an unnatural combination, perverting the philosopher's nature. . . .

The *Republic* reveals that competition, conflict, and so on are features of politics only in corrupt *poleis*, which are perversions of the proper political order. Plato does not consider ideal political rule as foreign to the philosopher's nature, because his ruler neither arbitrates nor participates in contingent divisions of opinion. His rulers are not even primarily legislators, but guardians of the right *paideia*, from which so much follows.[50] Their purpose is to preserve those educational arrangements and divisions of social function that make their subjects as far as possible good by developing the harmony of their *psychai*. Their subjects' lives and *psychai* are ordered according to the direction of philosophic reason, which makes each man's psyche a unity and combines them all in a further whole that is the *kallipolis*. Benefiting from the right education and observing their social function faithfully, the subjects enjoy a measure of platonic justice. When politics is understood in this way, then there is nothing more appropriate than that philosophers should rule, for that activity consists in modeling the moral and social whole according to the harmony of the forms. Reason realises its own nature most perfectly by creating the natural harmony of appetite, spirit, and reason within the political whole. Ruling is the natural extension of reason's role within the *psyche*.

7. The standpoint just developed makes intelligible Socrates' statement that, for the philosophers, "it is by nature fitting for them both to engage in philosophy and to lead the city" (474c). He is explicit that the philosopher who retires from public life, in corrupt *poleis*, does not realize himself perfectly. In the *kallipolis*, the philosopher will "grow more and save the common things along with the private" (497a). So what of the references to their reluctance to rule? Does Plato imply that ruling is a diminution of their *eudaimonia?* No, for the references mean only that the philosophers see before them, on a larger and more difficult scale in the public world, the task they have already accomplished within their own *psychai*—namely, the ordering of spirit and appetite. That they are individually reluctant to accept the task does not imply that it is not their appropriate role, for Plato presents the rule of reason as the primary and natural imperative. Any refusal to rule would be an artificial restriction upon the sphere of reason and cannot be defended in terms of the philosophers' personal happiness. Plato, clearly, does not define *eudaimonia* in terms of felt satisfaction, but as the natural harmony of reason, spirit, and appetite, and the *personal* happiness of the philosophers is not his primary desideratum. As we have already maintained, there is no personal identity logically prior to the elements of the *psyche*, which "possesses" them and whose felt happiness varies according to how they are ordered. We misunderstand Plato's notion of *eudaimonia* grossly if we conceive it in terms of the effect of platonic justice on some agent possessing

reason, spirit, and appetite. The idea of rational order in the *psyche* is prior to the idea of agent, for the agent's identity consists in that rational order. Within the individual and the moral and social whole, *eudaimonia* consists in the harmony of reason, spirit, and appetite. So the philosophers' reluctance to rule cannot be justified in terms of their private happiness, because *eudaimonia*, when properly understood, is not a personal condition dividing one man from his fellows, but an impersonal or transpersonal rational ordering, in which, ideally, men are combined. Socrates' insistence that he and his interlocutors consider the *eudaimonia* of the whole *polis* is perfectly intelligible, and to reply that a *polis* cannot be *eudaimon* as a man can be betrays a misunderstanding. Socrates leads his listeners away from the notion of happiness as private satisfaction to the idea of *eudaimonia* as transpersonal rational harmony. When the philosophers realise that ultimately there is no incompatibility between their fulfillment and their political role in the *kallipolis*, then, ruling, they combine perfectly with their subjects and achieve their fullest growth.

So the *Republic* does not disclose the "limits of politics" by revealing that the philosopher's life of service to the *polis* is incompatible with his self-realisation. The individual and common goods are not opposed, and, within the *kallipolis*, the philosophic nature is not divorced by its excellence from the rest of the community, for rational order must be realised in both. If they resist the offer to rule, the philosophers act contrary to nature. Quite appropriately, then, Plato says they must be compelled. When we realise that the *Republic* does not disclose the "limits of politics" but represents a truly ideal political order, then we shall understand Plato's intentions more adequately.

Notes

1. L. Strauss, *The City and Man* (Chicago, 1964) and A. Bloom, *The Republic of Plato*, translated, with notes and an "Interpretive Essay," (New York, 1968). Strauss has written about Plato in several works over many years. However, *The City and Man* provides the most developed version of his views and, because we are concerned with the cogency of his interpretation, not with its genesis, and because his account remained stable in essentials, it is to this work that we shall restrict ourselves. Bloom's account derives from that of Strauss. To be sure of being fair to them, our quotations from the *Republic* are taken from Bloom's excellent translation.

2. Strauss, *The City and Man*, p. 127.

3. Ibid., p. 112.

4. Ibid., p. 65.

5. Bloom, *Republic*, p. 410.

6. Ibid., p. 409.

7. Ibid., p. 410. Cf. pp. 343 and 408, and Strauss, *The City and Man*, p. 138.

8. Strauss, *The City and Man*, p. 138, and Bloom, *Republic*, p. 408.

9. Strauss, *The City and Man*, pp. 116–117 and 138, and Bloom, *Republic*, pp. 382–289.

10. Strauss, *The City and Man*, pp. 50–51.

11. Bloom, *Republic*, p. 411.

12. Strauss, *The City and Man*, pp. 61 and 116.

13. Bloom, *Republic*, p. 380.

14. E. Barker, *Greek Political Theory* (reprinted London, 1964), p. 242, n. 1.

15. J. Adam, *The Republic of Plato* (Cambridge, 1902, 2 Vols.), I, pp. 345–355.

16. Ibid., p. 355.

17. Cf. H. D. Rankin, *Plato and the Individual* (London, 1964), p. 93.

18. Cf. W. C. Booth, *A Rhetoric of Irony* (Chicago and London, 1974), p. 81.

19. Cf. Rankin, *Plato and the Individual*, chs. II and V.

20. Cf. E. Barker, *Greek Political Theory*, pp. 252–253 and Rankin, *Plato and the Individual*, p. 92. And see, too, Herodotus, *Histories*, IV, 104, 116, 180.

21. For a discussion of this coherence see Barker, *Greek Political Theory*, pp. 242–276.

22. Strauss, *The City and Man*, pp. 115–117 and 138. Cf. Bloom, *Republic*, pp. 382–389.

23. Ibid., pp. 118–120.

24. Ibid., p. 111.

25. Ibid., pp. 116–117. Cf. Bloom, *Republic*, pp. 364, 375, 382, and 386.

26. Strauss, *The City and Man*, p. 127 and Bloom, *Republic*, p. 411.

27. Bloom, *Republic*, p. 382.

28. Xenophon, *The Constitution of the Lacedaemonians*.

29. Strauss, *The City and Man*, pp. 118–121.

30. Ibid., p. 118.

31. Ibid., pp. 109–110, 115, and cf. Bloom, *Republic,* pp. 374 and 378.

32. D. Sachs, "A Fallacy in Plato's Republic," *Philosophical Review,* LXXII (1963), 141–158. Reprinted in A. Sesonske (ed.), *Plato's Republic: Interpretation and Criticism,* pp. 66–81 and in G. Vlastos (ed.), *Plato II: Ethics, Politics and Philosophy.* . . .

33. Strauss, *The City and Man,* p. 127.

34. Ibid., p. 97.

35. Ibid.; pp. 127–128.

36. Bloom, *Republic,* p. 337 and cf. pp. 373–374 and 378.

37. Ibid., pp. 343–344, 373–374, 378, 380, 407–408, and 411. And cf. Strauss, *The City and Man,* p. 127.

38. Cf. the too-much ignored passage at *Republic* 588b–591a.

39. Bloom, *Republic* p. 343. Cf. pp. 408 and 410, and the important closing words of Strauss' essay, *The City and Man,* p. 138.

40. Bloom, *Republic,* p. 343 and cf. pp. 373–374.

41. Ibid., pp. 378 and 407–408.

42. Ibid., pp. 380, 407 and 410.

43. Ibid., p. 410. . . .

44. Strauss, *The City and Man,* pp. 111–112, 115, 125, 133, and 138.

45. Bloom, *Republic,* p. 309.

46. Ibid., pp. 407–408 and Strauss, *The City and Man,* pp. 124–125.

47. Bloom, *Republic,* p. 410.

48. Ibid., p. 407.

49. See: S. Wolin, *Politics and Vision* (Boston, 1960), ch. 2. . . .

50. Plato argues this explicitly at 425b–427a. Cf. 412a.

7
Response to Hall

Allan Bloom

> [Plato in the *Republic*] sought and
> made a city more to be prayed for than
> hoped for . . . not such that it can possibly
> be but one in which it is possible to see
> the meaning [*ratio*] of political things.
>
> Cicero, *Republic* II 52

I am grateful to Professor Hall for a number of reasons, especially for the seriousness with which he has taken my interpretation of the *Republic*. That he disagrees with it is secondary. We do agree on the fundamental thing: it is of utmost importance to understand Plato.

The issues raised by Hall are enormous, and an adequate response to his arguments would require volumes, but what we really disagree about is how to read Plato. He asserts that I read my prejudices into the text. I respond that he does not pay sufficient attention to the text. In looking at a few of his central criticisms, I shall attempt to prove my contention and show the characteristic errors of his approach to the Platonic dialogue.

I

In the first place, Hall presupposes that he knows the Platonic teaching and reads his understanding of it into the text. Arguing against my contention that the best regime of the *Republic* is not a serious proposal, he tells us, "Socrates is explicit that his *polis* is natural." I search in vain for Socrates' statement to that effect. Indeed, I know of no assertion anywhere in the Platonic corpus that the city is natural or that man is by nature a political animal. Whatever the *ideas* may be—and they are the highest and most elusive theme to which we must ascend very carefully and slowly from the commonly

sensed particulars—there is not the slightest indication that there is an *idea* of the city or of the best city, as there is said to be an *idea* of the beautiful or an *idea* of the just. What the omission means is debatable, but one must begin by recognizing that it is so. Obviously, from the point of view of the *ideas*, the naturalness of the city must have a status very different from that of, for example, man. The *kallipolis* cannot participate in an *idea* which is not. While there are many men and an *idea* of man, the city does not exist as a particular or as a universal; it is neither sensed nor intellected.

Careful observation of what the text says about this question of naturalness would have helped Hall. In his discussion of the three waves of paradox in Book V, Socrates says (a) the same education and way of life for women as for men is possible because it is natural (456b–c); (b) the community of women and children is not against nature (466d)—however, now Socrates shifts the criterion of possibility from naturalness to coming into being (many things which are not natural, and even against nature, can come into being); (c) the coincidence of philosophy and rule is just that, coincidence or chance (473c–d). All the attention is given to the possibility of that highly improbable coincidence. Cities, let alone the best city, do not come into being as do plants and animals. Some men are by nature fit both to philosophize and to rule in the city, but it is not said that it is natural that they do so. If they actually do both, the cause is art, human making, not nature. If I were to use against Hall the methods he uses against me, I would say that, with respect to the naturalness of the city, he has read Aristotle's *Politics*, not Plato's *Republic*. He does not see that the city is more problematic for Plato than for Aristotle.

Just as Hall reads in, he reads out. In trying to argue that for Plato there is no significant distinction between the theoretical and the practical life, he says that Plato "does not suggest that philosophizing and ruling are unrelated functions." Compare that to the text: "each of [the philosophers] will go to ruling as a necessary as opposed to a good thing . . . if you discover a life better than ruling for those who are going to rule, it is possible that your well-governed city will come into being. . . . Have you another life that despises political offices other than that of true philosophy? . . . But men who aren't lovers of ruling [they love something other: wisdom] must go to it" (521a–b). The philosophers won't be willing to act [engage in *praxis*] (519c). There could be no more radical distinction made between the practical and theoretical lives than that drawn in Books V–VII and IX of the Republic (cf. especially 476a–b). The separateness of the forms is strongly asserted, as are the possibilities of a reason using only forms without admixture of the senses and a life lived in contemplation of the forms purely. This latter life is the best life, the only good life. It is precisely the difference between it and the life of ruling that is the artifice that is supposed to make the city work. Deed and speech are also radically distinguished, and the latter is said to be absolutely superior.[1] I really find it hard to imagine how Hall is able to say the things he does in the face of the evidence to the contrary. I challenge him to find a single statement in the *Republic* that indicates that the philosophic life requires ruling or that the activity of ruling in any way contributes to philosophizing.[2] What is striking about the *Republic* is the distance Socrates puts between the theoretical and practical lives, a distance belied by things he says elsewhere and by his own life. But that is what he does here, and, as Hall says, "we are accustomed to taking Socrates seriously." There is simply not a scintilla of proof that the making, painting, or "creating" activity of the founders of the city is a part of the philosopher's life as such. Hall piles abstraction on abstraction, unrelated to the text, in order to construct a case for the sameness of the two lives, but he has no evidence. The most striking aspect of the last half of his paper is its almost entirely personal character and almost total absence of reference to text. It is true, as he says, that the potential philosophers must be compelled to leave the cave as well as return to it. But once out, they recognize how good it is to be out. They never see a reason to go back, and compelling them to go back is said to be good for the city, not the philoso-

phers. If they thought it good to go back, they would not be good rulers. It is only by going out that they became aware that the *kallipolis* is a cave, nay Hades, and to be in it is as to be a shade (516d; 521c; cf. 386c). In the midst of his complex prestidigitatory activity, Hall announces that it is because I am a modern political scientist that I cannot see that Platonic ruling is really philosophizing. I would like to accept that testimonial to impress some of my colleagues who have their doubts about the genuineness of my credentials as a political scientist, but unfortunately the explanation does not work. Again, one must look at the text. Rulers, in the best city, provide for food, clothing, and shelter, and they lead the soldiers to war. Above all, Hall forgets the reasons the philosophers are invoked: they are primarily matchmakers or eugenicists who have to spend a great deal of time and subtlety on devising "throngs of lies and deceptions" designed to get the right people to have sexual intercourse with one another (458d–460b). Is that a philosophic activity?

Displaying the same tendency to neglect what is really in the text, Hall spins a subtle web of reasonings about a Platonic notion of happiness which is frankly beyond my comprehension, a notion evidently intended to overcome the tensions between philosophy and ruling. In this context he insists that "Plato, clearly, does not define *eudaimonia* in terms of felt satisfaction . . . and the personal happiness of the philosophers is not his primary desideratum." Now, the culmination of the whole dialogue—the judgment concerning the happiness of the unjust man versus that of the just man, which was demanded by Glaucon at the beginning of the dialogue and was its explicit motive—concerns, if I understand what Hall means by *personal* happiness, the personal happiness of the philosopher (576b–588a). The terms of the comparison have been quietly changed during the course of the dialogue from the unjust man versus the just man to the tyrant versus the philosopher. Three tests are made, all three of which are won by the philosopher. The first test is self-sufficiency: the philosopher can get the good things he desires without needing or depending on other men while the tyrant lives in fear and is full of unsatisfiable desires because of his dependency on men. The other two tests prove that the philosopher is the expert *par excellence* in pleasure and that he experiences the purest and most intense pleasures. Socrates calculates that the philosopher's life is 729 times more pleasant than the tyrant's. Is this not "felt satisfaction" of a wholly personal kind? Philosophy is presented as choiceworthy on the ground that it provides permanently accessible pleasures for the individual, and the philosopher here is not presented as ruling or in any way concerned with the city.

In addition to making Plato answer his own questions rather than discovering what Plato's questions are and distorting the phenomena by casting a gray web of abstraction around them rather than letting them come to light in their fullness and complexity, Hall moralizes, not open to the possibility that justice is not preached in the *Republic* but rather questioned and investigated. For example, so sure is he that benefiting one's fellow man is an imperative of Plato's thought that he does not take note of the fact that the city has no concern for other cities and is even willing to harm and stir up factions in them, supporting the inferior elements, solely to keep them from threatening it. Best would be isolation, and next best is crippling one's neighbor; never would it try to improve them (422a–423a). Since the soul is said to be like the city, would not it, too, be concerned only with itself? The vulgar standards of just conduct to which the well-ordered soul is said to conform are all negative—things it does not do, such as stealing, lying, and committing adultery (442e–443a). As was indicated early on, Socrates' just man does no harm; he is not said to do good, to be a benefactor (335d). And the reason why the well-ordered soul does not do harm becomes clear when it is revealed to be the philosophic soul. The philosopher's abstinences are not due to good will, a Kantian "settled and sincere disposition to behave justly," but to a lack of caring for the vulgar things on which the vulgar standards are founded. His passionate love of wisdom makes him indifferent to, for example, money (485d–486b). This is no more praiseworthy than a eu-

nuch's abstinence from rape. There is no "moral" motive involved.[3] It escapes Hall that of the three classes in the city, two have no concern for the common good at all—the artisans are in it for gain or out of fear, and the philosophers are there because they are compelled to be—while the dedicated class, the warriors, are dedicated only because they believe in a lie and are deprived of any possibility of privacy. There is, on the evidence of the *Republic*, no enlightened, nonillusionary love of the common good. The virtues of the warriors are finally said to belong more to the body than to the soul, to be mere habits (518d–e). The only authentic virtue is that of the mind contemplating its proper objects. It is not I who Aristotelianize. The *Republic* is not the *Ethics*; there are no moral virtues in it.

I have chosen to mention these points because they help to illustrate what is required to read a Platonic dialogue; and Plato intended to make the requirements for reading him identical to those for philosophizing; his little world is the preparation for the big world. In fine, what is needed is an openness to things as they appear unaided by the abstractions which so impoverish things that they can no longer cause surprise or wonder and a freedom from a moralism which forbids us to see what in nature defies convention and refuses to console us in our hopes and fears.

II

My difference with Hall can be summarized by saying that he does not take the form of the dialogue seriously, that he does not begin where it fairly cries out for us to begin, with the story or the drama, with those pictures of life on the basis of which we might generalize about life and which are so much more accessible to us than are "Plato's metaphysics" or the *ideas*. If I may be permitted an Aristotelian expression, but one which is of Platonic inspiration, we must begin from the things which are first according to us in order to ascend to the things which are first according to nature. We must talk about shoemakers and pilots and dogs and such things, the Socratic themes so despised by his less wise interlocutors. I can appreciate Hall's opinion that there is something mad in the assertion that a work of political philosophy which argues that philosophers should be kings actually means that philosophers should not be kings. But if we were to suppose for a moment that this is not precisely a book of political philosophy, at least such as we know books of political philosophy to be, but is a drama at one moment of which one of the characters makes an unusual proposal that is designed to affect the action, as are so many speeches in dramas, then the paradoxical character of my interpretation disappears. The tale would go roughly as follows. Socrates visits the Piraeus in the company of a young man whom, according to Xenophon, he is trying to cure of excessive political ambition as a favor to his brother, Plato (Mem. III, vi). There they meet a group of men among whom is a famous intellectual who argues that justice is abiding by laws set down in the interest of the rulers. It is, therefore, in one's interest to be ruler or, put otherwise, to be a tyrant. Glaucon, evidently motivated by more than idle curiosity, asks Socrates to show him that justice (understood as concern for equality or law-abidingness) is a good outweighing all the obvious good things (pleasures and honors) which tyranny (understood as the peak of injustice) can procure. Socrates never precisely shows Glaucon that justice as Glaucon conceives it is good. Rather, in the course of founding a city and, thus, learning the nature of justice, Socrates introduces, as a political necessity, the philosophers. Glaucon learns that to be a ruler in the city he has founded he must be a philosopher. Then, when he is shown what philosophy is, he learns that it is the best life and is essentially independent of political life. From the point of view of philosophy—which Glaucon had not considered and, thus, had not considered as a good thing—the city looks like a cave or a prison. The movement from rulers simply to philosophic rulers is a stage in Glaucon's liberation from the desire to rule. The dialogue has the character of an ascent, like the ascent from the cave to the region of the *ideas*. At the peak of that ascent Socrates reveals himself to be the happy man. He does not persuade Glaucon that he should not pursue his own good. He only makes him aware of goods to which the tyrant cannot attain and the pursuit of which takes away the temptation to meddle in politics and, hence, to be unjust as a tyrant is unjust. At the end of the comparison between the tyrant's and the philosopher's lives, close to the end of his education, Glaucon recognizes that the philosopher's city exists only in speech, and that no longer disturbs him. Socrates tells him it makes no difference whether it exists, for it can exist in the soul and that is enough (592a–b). A man can be happy being a good citizen of the city of philosophy without its existing. Timocrats and timocratic cities exist; democrats and democratic cities exist; tyrants and tyrannical cities exist; but, although there are no philosophical cities, philosophers exist. The tyrannical man who does not rule a city is not fully a tyrant (578b–c); the philosopher is a philosopher whether or not he is a king in a city. And there is, at this final stage, no suggestion that Glaucon should work to establish this city or that he should even long for its establishment. Glaucon has moved from the desire to be a ruler to the desire to be a ruler-philosopher to the desire to be a philosopher. The conceit of philosopher-kings was the crucial stage in his conversion. In the last word of the *Republic*, Odysseus—the archetype of the wise man—cured of love of honor or ambition and, having seen all the human possibilities, chooses the life of a private man who minds his own business. The *Republic*, while demonstrating Socrates' concern for justice, culminates in providing a foundation not for justice but for moderation.

Hall rightly concentrates on the statement that "unless philosophers rule as kings or those now called kings . . . philosophize . . . there is no rest from ills for the cities." That there will be no rest from ills for the cities is the teaching of the *Republic*, and this is what distinguishes ancient from modern philosophical politics. Socrates, moreover, does not suggest that there are ills of philosophy that would be cured by the union of wisdom and politics. The proposal is for the sake of the city, and not the philosopher. The distinction made in the discussion with Thrasymachus between justice as devotion to a community (be it a band of thieves), which is only necessary, a means to an end (351c–d; 352c–d), and justice as perfection of the soul, which is good in itself (352d–354a), persists throughout. The philosophers' service to the community is necessary, while their life of contemplation on the Isles of the Blessed is good (540b). The two senses of justice are never resolved into a single coherent one.

Hall's failure to read the dialogue as a dialogue, his unawareness of its movement, causes him to give undue weight to isolated phrases or passages torn from their contexts. His greatest error is to take the discussion of *logismos*—calculation or deliberation—in Book IV as providing a definition of the "natural function" (both words are Hall's, not Plato's) of reason rather than as a provisional statement corresponding to the incomplete stage of the argument and of the interlocutors' awareness. Following the parallel of the rulers in the city, who deliberate about the affairs of the city, reason first comes to light in the *Republic* as the element of the soul which calculates about the desires, deciding which should and which should not be indulged. This description is a consequence of the analogy between city and soul which is being pursued in the discussion. What has first been determined about the city is applied to the soul (although Socrates points out that the discussion is inadequate, 435c–d). What we get in Book IV is a plausible account of reason's activity in the affairs of daily life, an activity akin to that of rulers who deliberate about public affairs, one that supports the view that man and city are in perfect harmony. But after the emergence of philosophy in Book V, a totally different account of the rational part of the soul is given, one which shows that the parallel between city and soul breaks down. The highest reaches of the soul are said to long only to *see* what *is* (437c–487a; 509c–511e; 514a–518b; 532a–534d). Deliberation or calculation (*logismos*), which was the only attribute of the rational part of the soul given in Book IV, is no longer even mentioned. The opposition between desire and calculation which was the defining characteristic of calculation in the earlier passage is overcome and philosophy is described as a form of *eros* (485c; 499b). The contemplative activity of the soul is simply something entirely different from the deliberative activity of a ruling class in a city (533b). Such contemplation is alien to the rulers' ends, and as a body they possess no organ for it. What the soul really is is both a revelation and a surprise in Book V, and its almost accidental discovery changes everything. The philosophic part of the soul has no use for action, and deliberation is not part of its function (527d–528e); it does not calculate. One must look to the difference between *logismos* and *nous* to appreciate the significance of this development. *Logismos* is for action; *nous* is for itself. The rulers of the city are highest because they are most useful to the city and its nonphilosophic ends. Reason in the soul is highest because it is the end of man and should be the end of the city. Unless ones reads the *Republic* as a drama, one does not see that it has a reversal and a discovery, that there is a peripety. Platonic books are closer in form to dramas than to treatises.

III

I have put off until the end discussion of what is only a subsidiary part of Hall's criticism—what he says about Plato's relation to Aristophanes. But this issue seems to me central to our differences. The elusive texture of Platonic thought—so different from our own—can, I believe, only be approached when one becomes aware of its peculiar combination of what we take to be poetry and philosophy. Or, put otherwise, Platonic philosophy is poetic, not merely stylistically but at its intellectual core, not because Plato is not fully dedicated to reason, but because poetry points to problems for reason that unpoetic earlier and later philosophy do not see and because poetic imagination properly understood is part of reason. The Socrates of the *Clouds*—an account of the early Socrates substantially confirmed by the Platonic Socrates (*Phaedo* 96a ff.)—was unpoetic, and this had something to do with his incapacity to understand political things. The Platonic Socrates can in some sense be understood as a response to the Aristophanic Socrates, or, more strongly stated, Socrates may have learned something from Aristophanes. The *Republic*, in one of its guises, is the proof that philosophers are not unpolitical (and it must not be forgotten that, according to all serious testimony, in particular that of Aristotle and Cicero, there was no political philosophy prior to Socrates), that they know the political things best and are most necessary for politics. Socrates, who in the *Clouds* stands aside, is neutral, in the dispute between the just and the unjust speeches, in the *Republic*—in a reference which is clearly to Aristophanes—presents himself as an unconditional partner of the just speech (*Clouds*, 896–7; *Republic*, 368b–c). And in the *Symposium* Aristophanes is Socrates' only serious competitor in the contest for the best praise of *eros*: only these two have some inkling of what *eros* really is. Socrates the philosopher shows that his valid interlocutor is Aristophanes the comic poet, and that he is Aristophanes' superior in politics and erotics. Until we can take Aristophanes seriously and Plato comically we shall not understand either. It is only our stiff pedantry that causes us to ignore Plato's countless allusions to Aristophanes. For us academics they simply cannot be important. Professor Plato must talk only to his fellow professors. My response is that we must look where Plato tells us to look and not where we think we should look.

Now Hall says he sees nothing funny in Book V. My assertion that there is something ridiculous about the two sexes exercising naked together is tossed off lightly by Hall by reference to a passage in Xenophon which does not exist. Hall really means Plutarch, and a glance at the appropriate passage will prove to him that boys and girls in Sparta did not exercise naked together. He, further, fails to understand me. I know that there was homosexuality in Greece. What I meant is that a legislator can consistently forbid homosexual relations and condemn the attractions connected with them (as did the Athenian and Spartan legislators), but he cannot do the same for heterosexual relations. Socrates explicitly says that those who exercise naked together, because they do so, will be sexually drawn to one another (458c–d).

Senses of humor, I am aware, do differ, but imagination suggests that the external signs of those attractions on the playing fields might provide some inspiration for tasteless wits.

Similarly, Hall says that Socrates does not appeal to absurd premises in Book V. I do not think it is just my ethnocentrism which gives me the impression that it is absurd for Socrates to found his argument on the assertion that the difference between male and female is no more to be taken into account than the one between bald men and men with hair.

But, to speak meaningfully about the *Republic*'s debt to the *Ecclesiazusae*, we must say a few words about the meaning of that play. . . .

Hall tells us that "for Aristophanes' satire of such social arrangements to have had point, others must have recommended them quite seriously." On the basis of such reasoning we would be forced to say that someone must have seriously proposed that the birds be made gods or that a dung beetle be used to get to heaven and bring back Peace for Aristophanes to have invented such conceits. Why should these schemes not have been among the imaginative poetic novelties on which Aristophanes prided himself? Surely the hilarious schemes which animate every comedy of Aristophanes ridicule, or show the ridiculous aspect of, something important. But the explicit project of the heroes does not reveal the intended object; it must be sought in an understanding of the effect of the play as a whole. In the *Ecclesiazusae*, the point is really quite clear: Aristophanes extends the principle of Athenian democracy to the extreme and shows that it is absurd, and thereby shows the limits, or the problem, of that regime. Athens is ridiculed, not some anonymous political projector. The Athenians want equality or to abolish the distinction between rich and poor, have and have-not. Athens is in trouble, and it is popularly thought that salvation can be achieved only by reforms which realize the goals of its popular regime. New rulers, women, propose communism, the utter destruction of privacy, in order to insure dedication to the common good and allow all to share equally in all good things, in order to make the city one. This will be a city which comprehends everything and satisfies all human longings. Praxagora's reform is subjected to searching criticism in two great scenes: (a) Chremes in good faith gives all his property to the city when it is perfectly clear that other men will not. He appears as a decent fool because the roots of private property go too deep to be torn out. Hence, inequality and selfishness would seem to be necessary concomitants of any political order. (b) A beautiful young man is forced to have sexual intercourse with a succession of ugly old hags. This is the application of the most radical, but also most necessary, reform connected with communism. What seems to be most private and most unequal by nature must become subject to the public sector, or there will be have-nots in the most extreme and important sense, and the young and the beautiful will have profound reservations in their commitment to civil society. This powerful and unsurpassedly ugly scene lays bare the absurdity of trying to make politics total, of trying to make an equal distribution of all that is rare, special, and splendid, of allowing nothing to escape or transcend the political order. It reveals the tension between *physis* and *nomos*, nature and civil society. By hypothesizing a perfect social union, Aristophanes lets his audience see for itself that it would be a hell, that some things must remain private and that men must accept the inconsistencies of a community which leaves much to privacy. The actualization of the Athenian goal is not to be desired.

Socrates adopts the premise of the *Ecclesiazusae*: for there to be a community, everything must be made public; above all there must be a community of women and children. In a passage that is all but a direct quote from the *Ecclesiazusae* (461c–d; *Ecclesiazusae,* 634–9), Glaucon asks how the citizens would recognize their close kin, to which Socrates responds, as did Praxagora, that they will not. Neither of these great reformers is worried about incest, the prohibition against which is most sacred and seems to be the backbone of both family and city. Their reform is far-reaching indeed.

But this defiance of *nomos* in Plato's picture does not turn out to be ugly or ridicu-

lous, and we should therefore conclude that Plato thought Aristophanes to be wrong about the intransigent character of *nomos,* the impossibility of perfect communism and the transpolitical nature of *eros.* Aristophanes' hostility to philosophy made him miss the crucial point: philosophers, those consummate liars, could make it all work. Because he did not understand philosophy Aristophanes thought the political problem to be insoluble. The focus of the issue for both Praxagora and Socrates is sexual affairs, and Socrates acts as though he can handle them as Praxagora could not. Useless philosophy proves to be most useful. Socrates as the replacement for Praxagora to turn failure into success is the Platonic improvement on Aristophanes' female drama.

Now it must be noted that Socrates is not introducing some grave, ponderous scholar as ruler. Philosophers as types were as yet essentially unknown and hardly respectable. The public model of the philosopher is that silly little fellow in the basket who makes shoes for gnats in the *Clouds.* Socrates dares to say that he is the perfect ruler. The comedy consists partly in Socrates' bringing together two of Aristophanes' plays, the *Clouds* and the *Ecclesiazusae,* using the ridiculous character of the one to solve the ridiculous problem of the other. The philosophers will see to it that the beautiful sleep with the ugly for the public good and do so without disorder or dissatisfaction.

So all is well. But now Socrates adds his scene, akin to those of Aristophanes. We get a glimpse of the relation of the philosopher to the multitude. Socrates follows Aristophanes' procedure. He makes the proposal and then lets his audience see it in action, letting them judge its actualization for themselves. Socrates uses the same language about the philosopher's relation to the multitude that one of the old hags uses to the beautiful young man: their intercourse is a Diomedean necessity (*Ecclesiazusae,* 1028–1029; *Republic,* 493c–494a). The multitude can never know or properly use the beautiful, but it will make the beautiful slave. Aristophanes' comic scene is repeated on a higher level. The impossible and undesirable thing is the forced intercourse of philosophy and the city. The city, which once looked beautiful, has become ugly, and it compels what has now come to light as the truly beautiful. Hag is to boy as city is to philosopher. The privileged *eros* is philosophic *eros*. The differences between Aristophanes and Socrates have to do with the old war between philosophy and poetry, and here we can do no more than mention it and point out that it is what we must study. They agree about the limits of the city with respect to the highest things. Socrates uses Aristophanes' mad conceits to highlight both of these points. The political result of the inquiry of the *Republic* is revealed in the *Laws*, Plato's discussion of an actualizable regime. There the fundamental compromise is made: private property is accepted. It follows immediately that gentlemen, not philosophers, rule, that women are educated differently and lead very different lives from men, and that the family is retained. . . .

Now, what precedes is nothing but a series of hints. An adequate articulation of the issues involved in Socrates' playful competition with Aristophanes is the work of a lifetime. The real questions will only come to light by looking at the texts in full consciousness that we do not now know what the real questions are, let alone the answers to them. Plato's way is to think about the seemingly trivial or outrageous proposals of a Praxagora. We must imitate that way if we are to understand not only ancient thought but the permanent human problems, problems no longer quite visible to us.

Conclusion

My differences with Hall come down to whether philosopher-king is a compound formula, joining two distinct activities and, thus, violating the rule of justice, one man–one job, as I insist, or whether philosopher and king are two words for the same thing, as Hall insists. I believe Hall produces no evidence for his belief. Socrates' irony, which he claims I invoke as a *deus ex machina*, is to be found in the relation of his speeches to his deeds and his treatment of his various companions. It is present to every eye, and only by looking the other way can the problems I

say need explaining be ignored or denied. As I pondered what separates me from Hall, I came to the conclusion that he misunderstands how political I take Socrates to be and how much attention I think he paid to particulars (as opposed to ideas). In other words, he does not pay attention to what I say about the cave or to the cave itself. The philosopher, of course, begins, as do all men, in the cave; and, to go Hall one better, he pays the strictest attention not only to particular or individual things but to their shadows. But the difference between him and other men is that he learns that they are only shadows—shadows which give us access to the truth—whereas they believe the shadows are the real things and are passionately committed to that belief. That is what cave-dwelling means. The cave must always remain cave, so the philosopher is the enemy of the prisoners since he cannot take the nonphilosopher's most cherished beliefs seriously. Similarly, Socrates does care for other men, but only to the extent that they, too, are capable of philosophy, which only a few are. This is an essential and qualitative difference, one that cannot be bridged and that causes fundamental differences of interest. Only they are capable of true virtue (518b–519b). To the extent that the philosopher turns some men to the light, he robs the cave-dwellers of allies. It is not because he lives in the sun, out of the cave, that I say the philosopher is at tension with the city; his problem is due precisely to the fact that he is in it, but in a way different from that of other men. This, however, should be the theme for an ongoing discussion. I only hope that it is clear that Hall's criticism has not settled the issue.

Notes

1. 471e–473b; 475d–480a; 510a–511d; 514a–519c; 532a–b; 540a–b. Plato surely makes a distinction between the practical and theoretical lives. Hall only introduces a red herring when he says I took the distinction from Aristotle. There is a difference between them concerning the distinction between *phronesis* and *sophia*, but that is irrelevant here. Everything I said was based on Plato. Hall, on the other hand, comes dangerously close to say-

ing that knowing is making, a view to be found only in modern thought.

2. The statement at 497a, an intermediary stage in the discussion of philosophy and the city, need mean nothing more than that the philosopher would find more encouragement in such a city than elsewhere. Cf. 528b–c.

3. At 487a justice appears in the list of virtues belonging to the philosopher. By 536a it has dropped out.

Reprinted from: Allan Bloom, "Response to Hall." In *Political Theory* 5:3, pp. 315–330. Copyright © 1977. Reprinted by permission of Sage Publications. ✦

Aristotle

Aristotle is probably best known for his assertion that man is the *"zoon politikon,"* the political animal. This phrase is especially useful in characterizing Aristotle's work since it represents many facets of his thought. First, it reflects his interest in nature. Aristotle's father was a physician and, no doubt, imparted a love for natural science to his son. Aristotle spent several years away from Athens studying various animal species, especially marine life. This interest in biological studies contributed to Aristotle's reliance on nature as a standard for judging the function and virtue of a thing. The nature of a thing can be understood on the basis of the functions it performs when it reaches a mature state. This is the "final factor," or teleological end of which Aristotle often speaks. For example, we might say the *"telos"* of an acorn is becoming a mighty oak. Humans, too, can be understood by virtue of that natural function which, when fully developed, distinguishes us from all other beings. Reason is that function. It is, as Aristotle puts it, the "best thing in us." Reason places humans above all other creatures and provides us with the opportunity to order our own lives and our political communities. But reason can only flourish in political communities where there is time for reflection and opportunity for discourse. Thus, only in the city where politics is a necessary component of life can man be fully human (i.e., exercise his highest faculty).

Secondly, the phrase "man is a political animal" reflects Aristotle's interest in the practical. Unlike his tutor, Plato, Aristotle did not believe in the priority of abstract forms. Rather, the material world provides the objects appropriate for scientific study. Understanding arises from the study of common aspects of particular elements, not from contemplation of abstract ideas. Politics is especially practical since it deals with bringing harmony and order to the city from the actions of diverse individuals. For Aristotle, not all are capable of performing the same functions in the state. As we will see, Aristotle uses differences in the capacity for reason to differentiate between the proper function of men and women, masters and slaves. In a practical sense, then, man is political because he apportions political duties on the basis of capacity to reason in the interest of assuring social harmony.

Aristotle was born in 384 B.C.E. in the northern Greek city of Stagira, bordering provinces under Macedonian control. His parents were quite comfortable economically and socially. His father, Nicomachus, was a physician in the service of royalty and, no doubt, inspired his son's interest in biology. Upon the death of his parents when he was still a boy, Aristotle was made a ward of a relative by the name of Proxenus. When he was 18, Aristotle entered Plato's Academy where he studied and taught for approximately 20 years, until Plato's death. There is still speculation over why Aristotle left Athens at this point. Some say he was disgruntled over not being named Plato's successor at the Academy. For whatever reason, he moved to Assos where he married a woman named Pythias. His wife bore him a daughter but died shortly after their return to Athens. He later entered into a relationship with a woman named Herpyllis and had a son by her, Nicomachus. In 343–2, Philip of Macedon invited Aristotle to tutor his son. During this period, Aristotle renewed his interest in politics, collecting and studying constitutions from around the world. Little is known about Aristotle's political influence over his pupil, who was to become known as Alexander the Great. Soon after the death of Philip, Aristotle returned to Athens and began his own school, the Lyceum. There he worked productively for 12 or 13 years, producing most of the works that survive to this day in the form of lecture notes. Aristotle left Athens after the death of Alexander. This was a time when anti-Macedonian feeling swept through Greece and Aristotle, who was associated with the Macedonian ruler, became the subject of attack and unfounded charges, including that of impiety—the same charge which resulted in the death of Socrates. He died in Chalcis one year later at the age of 62 or 63. We know from his will that he left his estate to his family, but one especially noteworthy item, given his defense of slavery, was that he provided for the gradual emancipation of several of his slaves, an act which clearly set him apart from his contemporaries.

Nicomachean Ethics and the *Politics*

Aristotle spoke about two kinds of wisdom: theoretical and practical. Theoretical wisdom deals with universal truths and is revealed in studies of philosophy. Practical wisdom deals with those things subject to change; it involves deliberation about means for attaining ends judged to be good. Among the studies belonging to the realm of practical knowledge are ethics and politics. These two subject matters were considered closely related, a contention which is not easily understood in an age of political scandals and corruption. In fact, at the end of the *Ethics*, Aristotle turns his attention to political constitutions as a way of completing "to the best of our ability our philosophy of human nature." Ethics is a prelude to politics; politics completes the study of ethics.

Aristotle's *Nicomachean Ethics*, named after his son, who is supposed to have edited his notes, explores human happiness. According to Aristotle, happiness depends on a number of external factors (including health and some minimal standard of living) and on internal habits or virtues that keep us from pursuing too much or too little of a good thing. Happiness is not a subjective state which differs from individual to individual, but an objective state of personal well-being. For Aristotle, happiness depends on finding the mean in our actions between the extremes of excess and deficiency. For example, courage is considered a mean between the extremes of foolish bravado and cowardice. No citizen can be happy, reasons Aristotle, unless he acquires a level of courage commensurate with his abilities. Justice is one of the virtues Aristotle describes, though it is special in that it exhibits aspects of all the other virtues as applied in our dealings with our neighbors.

Surprisingly for the modern reader not familiar with Aristotle, we are told that the subject of human happiness is one which political rulers must study since it is their job to bring about regimes that contribute to the happiness of citizens. The "end" or goal of the city is to lead men to the good life, not mere life. In the selection below from Book I, Aristotle explores the notion of happiness and the place political science plays as the "master art" in bringing about happiness in the city.

The *Politics* is a wide-ranging volume containing discussions about the nature and origin of the state, class relationships, various forms of government, a theory of regime change, and a discussion of ideal and actual forms of government. In the first Book, Aristotle speaks of the state as the perfection of earlier forms of association; i.e., the state is the end toward which these earlier associations lead. Not all in the state can perform the same functions, however. In a set of passages that continue to inspire controversy, Aristotle cites the reasons he believes women and slaves must hold lower political status than male citizens.

In the selection from Book III, Aristotle discusses the various forms of government and the place of the multitude within the state. As will be shown, he identifies three pure types of regime and three "perverted" forms, with the distinction between these two categories centering around dedication to the common versus individual good. In the selection from Book IV, Aristotle discusses the broad outlines of the best practicable constitution for most states.

Commentaries

Scholars have long argued over the meaning of the term "natural" in Aristotle's works.

Particularly because of his teleological approach, it is often difficult to distinguish which relationships Aristotle believes spring from innate attributes and which he believes are the result of nurture in the political community toward our proper ends or goals. This is particularly important in relation to Aristotle's views on women and slaves. Cary J. Nederman assesses the meaning of Aristotle's construction of humans as political animals, arguing that both nature and nurture are involved. Innate human potentiality, including the potential for living in societies, needs to be nurtured by education in the *polis*.

Mary Nichols examines Aristotle's distinctive treatment of men and women. Despite what on the surface appears to be a simple affirmation of male dominance, Nichols suggests that Aristotle questions this social arrangement. He identifies complementary attributes ascribed to each sex and prescribes a role for friendship as a necessary ingredient for combining these attributes within the healthy individual. Nichols's essay suggests the relevance of Aristotle's work in the ongoing debate about sexual differences.

Web Sources

http://www.utm.edu/research/iep/a/aristotl.htm
The Internet Encyclopedia of Philosophy. This site provides a useful overview of the life and major works of Aristotle, including his *Ethics* and *Politics*.

http://www.swan.ac.uk/poli/texts/aristotle/aripola.htm
Aristotle's Politics. Full text of the Benjamin Jowett translation.

http://www.constitution.org/ari/ethic_00.htm
Aristotle's Nicomachean Ethics. Full text of the W.D. Ross translation.

http://www.philosophypages.com/hy/index.htm
History of Western Philosophy Page. Includes a list of major contributors to the Western tradition as well as links to complete texts, commentary, a dictionary of terms, and a study guide.

http://members.tripod.com/batesca/natlaw.htm
The Natural Law/Natural Right Page. Forum for the discussion of the natural right and natural law tradition in Western political thought to which Aristotle is a contributor.

Class Activities and Discussion Items

1. What does Aristotle mean by "happiness" and the "good life"? What role do these concepts play in his political theory?

2. Discuss the role of ethics in contemporary politics. To what extent is virtue an important attribute in politics? To what extent does discussion of virtue in politics improve political discourse or deteriorate into disputes over irreconcilable religious values?

3. Compare Aristotle's claims about the "naturalness" of political relations to contemporary theories in biology and ethology asserting innate propensities toward sociality and conflict. The works of Edward O. Wilson and Larry Arnhart (see Further Reading below) would be appropriate sources for reviews of such theories.

4. Aristotle makes the case that a substantial middle class provides stability for a political community. Utilizing information from statistical abstracts and world almanacs, compare rates of violence and political upheaval in third world countries with wide disparities between rich and poor. On the basis of your research, assess the validity of Aristotle's claim.

5. Aristotle says that "some are slaves everywhere, others nowhere." What does he mean by this distinction? Would Aristotle have condoned the type of slavery practiced in the United States? Why or why not? If Aristotle would not have condoned U.S. slavery, then what kind of slavery does he intend to justify? Assess the validity of his claims. (See the entries for Bentley and Goodey in Further Reading below.)

6. Aristotle seems to ascribe a subservient role to women in the political community. On what grounds does he justify his position? How much of his claim is based on "natural" differences between

men and women? How much is based on differences based on the conventions of his day? How does Aristotle's ascription of sexual differences relate to debates between "equity" feminists (e.g., Sommers) who hold that there are no significant natural differences between men and women and "difference" feminists (e.g., Gilligan) who hold that there are consequential differences between the way men and women relate to each other and to the political world around them?

Further Reading

Arnhart, Larry. 1998. *Darwinian Natural Right: The Biological Ethics of Human Nature.* Albany, New York: State University of New York Press. Arnhart argues that recent biological claims regarding the biological basis of human ethics revitalizes Aristotle's teachings regarding the political community.

Bentley, Russell. 1999. "Loving Freedom: Aristotle on Slavery and the Good Life." *Political Studies* 47 (1): 100–113. Bentley attempts to show that Aristotle's natural slaves are not intellectually deficient in the way normally assumed, but are lacking an emotional faculty, "*thymos*," which Aristotle connects to actual enslavement through its power to generate a love of freedom.

Freeland, Cynthia, ed. 1998. *Feminist Interpretations of Aristotle.* University Park, PA: Penn State University Press. Collection of essays assessing the Aristotolean legacy for women.

Goodey, C. F. 1999. "Politics, Nature and Necessity: Were Aristotle's Slaves Feeble-Minded?" *Political Theory* 27 (2): 203–224. Goodey discusses Aristotle's claim that, in some cases, slavery is natural.

Jiang, Xinyan. 2000. "What Kind of Knowledge Does a Weak-Willed Person Have? A Comparative Study of Aristotle and the Ch'Eng-Chu School." *Philosophy East and West* 50 (2): 242–253. This comparative study argues that both Aristotle and the Ch'eng-Chu School believe that practical knowledge presupposes repeatedly acting on that knowledge, and thus a weak-willed person's knowledge cannot be overcome by purely cognitive training.

Lord, C. 1987. "Aristotle." In L. Strauss and J. Cropsey, eds. *History of Political Philosophy.* Chicago: University of Chicago Press. Essay on Aristotle's contributions to Western thought from a Straussian perspective.

Smith, Thomas W. 1999. "Aristotle on the Conditions for and Limits of the Common Good." *American Political Science Review* 93 (3): 625–636. Smith argues that contemporary debates over liberal political theory should encourage renewed investigation of the common good, specifically the idea that the common good requires a reorientation away from external goods and towards activities that do not diminish in the sharing. See also Terchek, Ronald J. and David K. Moore. 2000. "Recovering the Political Aristotle: A Critical Response to Smith." *American Political Science Review* 94 (4): 905–911.

Sommers, Christina Hoff. 1994. *Who Stole Feminism? How Women Have Betrayed Women.* New York: Simon & Schuster. Critiques difference feminism from the perspective of an equity feminist. Useful in analyzing Aristotle's relevance regarding sexual differentiation.

Voegelin, Eric. 1957. *Plato and Aristotle.* Baton Rouge: Louisiana State University Press. A review of the classic authors from the perspective of a thinker who admired the attempt to blend transcendental values with an appreciation of human frailties.

Wilson, E.O. 1978. *On Human Nature.* Cambridge, MA: Harvard University Press. Pioneering statement regarding the biological basis of ethical behavior. ✦

8
Excerpts from *Nicomachean Ethics*

Aristotle

Book I

Chapter 1

1094ᵃ Every art and every inquiry, and similarly every action and pursuit, is thought to aim at some good; and for this reason the good has rightly been declared to be that at which all things aim. But a certain difference is found among ends; some are activities, others are products apart from the activities that produce them. Where there are ends apart from the actions, it is the nature of the products to be better than the activities. Now, as there are many actions, arts, and sciences, their ends also are many; the end of the medical art is health, that of shipbuilding a vessel, that of strategy victory, that of economics wealth. But where such arts fall under a single capacity—as bridle-making and the other arts concerned with the equipment of horses fall under the art of riding, and this and every military action under strategy, in the same way other arts fall under yet others—in all of these the ends of the master arts are to be preferred to all the subordinate ends; for it is for the sake of the former that the latter are pursued. It makes no difference whether the activities themselves are the ends of the actions, or something else apart from the activities, as in the case of the sciences just mentioned.

Chapter 2

If, then, there is some end of the things we do, which we desire for its own sake (everything else being desired for the sake of this), and if we do not choose everything for the sake of something else (for at that rate the process would go on to infinity, so that our desire would be empty and vain), clearly this must be the good and the chief good. Will not the knowledge of it, then, have a great influence on life? Shall we not, like archers who have a mark to aim at, be more likely to hit upon what is right? If so, we must try, in outline at least, to determine what it is, and of which of the sciences or capacities it is the object. It would seem to belong to the most authoritative art and that which is most truly the master art. And politics appears to be of this nature; for it is this that ordains which of the sciences should be studied in a state, and which each class of citizens 1094ᵇ should learn and up to what point they should learn them; and we see even the most highly esteemed of capacities to fall under this, e.g. strategy, economics, rhetoric; now, since politics uses the rest of the sciences, and since, again, it legislates as to what we are to do and what we are to abstain from, the end of this science must include those of the others, so that this end must be the good for man. For even if the end is the same for a single man and for a state, that of the state seems at all events something greater and more complete whether to attain or to preserve; though it is worth while to attain the end merely for one man, it is finer and more godlike to attain it for a nation or for city-states. These, then, are the ends at which our inquiry aims, since it is political science, in one sense of that term.

Chapter 3

Our discussion will be adequate if it has as much clearness as the subject-matter admits of, for precision is not to be sought for alike in all discussions, any more than in all the products of the crafts. Now fine and just actions, which political science investigates, admit of much variety and fluctuation of opinion, so that they may be thought to exist only by convention, and not by nature. And goods also give rise to a similar fluctuation because they bring harm to many people; for before now men

have been undone by reason of their wealth,
20 and others by reason of their courage. We
must be content, then, in speaking of such
subjects and with such premises to indicate
the truth roughly and in outline, and in
speaking about things which are only for the
most part true and with premises of the
same kind to reach conclusions that are no
better. In the same spirit, therefore, should
25 each type of statement be *received;* for it is
the mark of an educated man to look for precision in each class of things just so far as the
nature of the subject admits; it is evidently
equally foolish to accept probable reasoning
from a mathematician and to demand from
a rhetorician scientific proofs.

Now each man judges well the things he
knows, and of these he is a good judge. And
)95ᵃ so the man who has been educated in a subject is a good judge of that subject, and the
man who has received an all-round education is a good judge in general. Hence a
young man is not a proper hearer of lectures
on political science; for he is inexperienced
in the actions that occur in life, but its discussions start from these and are about
these; and, further, since he tends to follow
his passions, his study will be vain and unprofitable, because the end aimed at is not
5 knowledge but action. And it makes no difference whether he is young in years or
youthful in character; the defect does not depend on time, but on his living, and pursuing
each successive object, as passion directs.
For to such persons, as to the incontinent,
knowledge brings no profit; but to those who
10 desire and act in accordance with a rational
principle knowledge about such matters will
be of great benefit.

These remarks about the student, the sort
of treatment to be expected, and the purpose
of the inquiry, may be taken as our preface. . . .

Chapter 7

Let us again return to the good we are
15 seeking, and ask what it can be. It seems different in different actions and arts; it is different in medicine, in strategy, and in the
other arts likewise. What then is the good of
each? Surely that for whose sake everything
20 else is done. In medicine this is health, in

strategy victory, in architecture a house,
in any other sphere something else, and in
every action and pursuit the end; for it is
for the sake of this that all men do whatever else they do. Therefore, if there is an
end for all that we do, this will be the good
achievable by action, and if there are
more than one, these will be the goods
achievable by action.

So the argument has by a different
course reached the same point; but we
must try to state this even more clearly.
Since there are evidently more than one
end, and we choose some of these (e.g. 25
wealth, flutes, and in general instruments) for the sake of something else,
clearly not all ends are final ends; but the
chief good is evidently something final.
Therefore, if there is only one final end,
this will be what we are seeking, and if
there are more than one, the most final of
these will be what we are seeking. Now we
call that which is in itself worthy of pur- 30
suit more final than that which is worthy
of pursuit for the sake of something else,
and that which is never desirable for the
sake of something else more final than the
things that are desirable both in themselves and for the sake of that other thing,
and therefore we call final without qualification that which is always desirable in
itself and never for the sake of something
else.

Now such a thing happiness, above all
else, is held to be; for this we choose always for itself and never for the sake of
something else, but honour, pleasure, rea- 1097ᵇ
son, and every virtue we choose indeed
for themselves (for if nothing resulted
from them we should still choose each of
them), but we choose them also for the 5
sake of happiness, judging that by means
of them we shall be happy. Happiness, on
the other hand, no one chooses for the
sake of these, nor, in general, for anything
other than itself.

From the point of view of self-sufficiency the same result seems to follow; for
the final good is thought to be self-sufficient. Now by self-sufficient we do not
mean that which is sufficient for a man by 10
himself, for one who lives a solitary life,

but also for parents, children, wife, and in general for his friends and fellow citizens, since man is born for citizenship. But some limit must be set to this; for if we extend our requirement to ancestors and descendants and friends' friends we are in for an infinite series. Let us examine this question, however, on another
15 occasion; the self-sufficient we now define as that which when isolated makes life desirable and lacking in nothing; and such we think happiness to be; and further we think it most desirable of all things, without being counted as one good thing among others—if it were so counted it would clearly be made more desirable by the addition of even the
20 least of goods; for that which is added becomes an excess of goods, and of goods the greater is always more desirable. Happiness, then, is something final and self-sufficient, and is the end of action.

Presumably, however, to say that happiness is the chief good seems a plati-
25 tude, and a clearer account of what it is is still desired. This might perhaps be given, if we could first ascertain the function of man. For just as for a flute-player, a sculptor, or an artist, and, in general, for all things that have a function or activity, the good and the 'well' is thought to reside in the function, so would it seem to be for man, if he has a
30 function. Have the carpenter, then, and the tanner certain functions or activities, and has man none? Is he born without a function? Or as eye, hand, foot, and in general each of the parts evidently has a function, may one lay it down that man similarly has a function apart from all these? What then can this be? Life seems to be common even to plants, but we are
1098^a seeking what is peculiar to man. Let us exclude, therefore, the life of nutrition and growth. Next there would be a life of perception, but *it* also seems to be common even to the horse, the ox, and every animal. There remains, then, an active life of the element that has a rational principle; of this, one part has such a principle in the sense of being obedient

to one, the other in the sense of possessing 5 one and exercising thought. And, as 'life of the rational element' also has two meanings, we must state that life in the sense of activity is what we mean; for this seems to be the more proper sense of the term. Now if the function of man is an activity of soul which follows or implies a rational principle, and if we say 'so-and-so' and 'a good so-and-so' have a function which is the same in kind, e.g. a lyre, and a good lyre-player, and so without qualification in all cases, eminence in respect of goodness being added to the name of the function (for the function of a 10 lyre-player is to play the lyre, and that of a good lyre-player is to do so well): if this is the case, [and we state the function of man to be a certain kind of life, and this to be an activity or actions of the soul implying a rational principle, and the function of a good man to be the good and noble performance of these, and if any action is well performed when it is performed in accordance with the appropri- 15 ate excellence: if this is the case,] human good turns out to be activity of soul in accordance with virtue, and if there are more than one virtue, in accordance with the best and most complete.

But we must add 'in a complete life.' For one swallow does not make a summer, nor does one day; and so too one day, or a short time, does not make a man blessed and happy.

Let this serve as an outline of the good; for we must presumably first sketch it roughly, and then later fill in the details. But it would 20 seem that any one is capable of carrying on and articulating what has once been well outlined, and that time is a good discoverer or partner in such a work; to which facts the advances of the arts are due; for any one can add what is lacking. And we must also remember what has been said before, and not look for precision in all things alike, but in 25 each class of things such precision as accords with the subject-matter, and so much as is appropriate to the inquiry. For a carpenter and a geometer investigate the right angle in different ways; the former does so in so far as the right angle is useful for his work, while the latter inquires what it is or what sort of thing it is; for he is a spectator of the truth. We must act in the same way, then, in all other matters as well, that our main task may not be subordinated to minor questions. Nor must we demand the cause in all matters alike; it is enough in 98ᵇ some cases that the *fact* be well established, as in the case of the first principles; the fact is the primary thing or first principle. Now of first principles we see some by induction, some by perception, some by a certain habituation, and others too in other ways.

But each set of principles we must try to investigate in the natural way, and we must take pains to state them definitely, since they have a great influence on what follows. For the beginning is thought to be 5 more than half of the whole, and many of the questions we ask are cleared up by it.

Adapted from: Aristotle, *Nicomachean Ethics*, translated by W. D. Ross, pp. 346–348, 354–357. Originally published by Oxford University Press, 1925. ✦

9
Excerpts from the *Politics*

Aristotle

Book One

Every state is a community of some kind, and every community is established with a view to some good; for mankind always act in order to obtain that which they think good. But, if all communities aim at some good, the state or political community, which is the highest of all, and which embraces all the rest, aims at good in a greater degree than any other, and at the highest good.

Some people think that the qualifications of a statesman, king, householder, and master are the same, and that they differ, not in kind, but only in the number of their subjects. For example, the ruler over a few is called a master; over more, the manager of a household; over a still larger number, a statesman or king, as if there were no difference between a great household and a small state. The distinction which is made between the king and the statesman is as follows: When the government is personal, the ruler is a king; when, according to the rules of the political science, the citizens rule and are ruled in turn, then he is called a statesman.

But all this is a mistake; for governments differ in kind, as will be evident to any one who considers the matter according to the method which has hitherto guided us. As in other departments of science, so in politics, the compound should always be resolved into the simple elements or least parts of the whole. We must therefore look at the elements of which the state is composed, in order that we may see in what the different kinds of rule differ from one another, and whether any scientific result can be attained about each one of them.

II

He who thus considers things in their first growth and origin, whether a state or anything else, will obtain the clearest view of them. In the first place there must be a union of those who cannot exist without each other; namely, of male and female, that the race may continue (and this is a union which is formed, not of deliberate purpose, but because, in common with other animals and with plants, mankind have a natural desire to leave behind them an image of themselves), and of natural ruler and subject, that both may be preserved. For that which can foresee by the exercise of mind is by nature intended to be lord and master, and that which can with its body give effect to such foresight is a subject, and by nature a slave; hence master and slave have the same interest. Now nature has distinguished between the female and the slave. For she is not niggardly, like the smith who fashions the Delphian knife for many uses; she makes each thing for a single use, and every instrument is best made when intended for one and not for many uses. But among barbarians no distinction is made between women and slaves, because there is no natural ruler among them: they are a community of slaves, male and female. Wherefore the poets say,

It is meet that Hellenes should rule over barbarians;

as if they thought that the barbarian and the slave were by nature one.

Out of these two relationships between man and woman, master and slave, the first thing to arise is the family, and Hesiod is right when he says,

First house and wife and an ox for the plough,

for the ox is the poor man's slave. The family is the association established by nature for the supply of men's everyday wants, and the members of it are called by Charondas 'companions of the cupboard,' and by Epimenides the Cretan, 'companions of the manger'

But when several families are united, and the association aims at something more than the supply of daily needs, the first society to be formed is the village. And the most natural form of the village appears to be that of a colony from the family, composed of the children and grandchildren, who are said to be suckled 'with the same milk.' And this is the reason why Hellenic states were originally governed by kings; because the Hellenes were under royal rule before they came together, as the barbarians still are. Every family is ruled by the eldest, and therefore in the colonies of the family the kingly form of government prevailed because they were of the same blood. As Homer says:

Each one gives law to his children and to his wives.

For they lived dispersedly, as was the manner in ancient times. Wherefore men say that the Gods have a king, because they themselves either are or were in ancient times under the rule of a king. For they imagine, not only the forms of the Gods, but their ways of life to be like their own.

When several villages are united in a single complete community, large enough to be nearly or quite self-suffing, the state comes into existence, originating in the bare needs of life, and continuing in existence for the sake of a good life. And therefore, if the earlier forms of society are natural, so is the state, for it is the end of them, and the nature of a thing is its end. For what each thing is when fully developed, we call its nature, whether we are speaking of a man, a horse, or a family. Besides, the final cause and end of a thing is the best, and to be self-suffing is the end and the best.

Hence it is evident that the state is a creation of nature, and that man is by nature a political animal. And he who by nature and not by mere accident is without a state, is either a bad man or above humanity; he is like the

Tribeless, lawless, heartless one,

whom Homer denounces—the natural outcast is forthwith a lover of war; he may be compared to an isolated piece at draughts.

Now, that man is more of a political animal than bees or any other gregarious animals is evident. Nature, as we often say, makes nothing in vain, and man is the only animal whom she has endowed with the gift of speech. And whereas mere voice is but an indication of pleasure or pain, and is therefore found in other animals (for their nature attains to the perception of pleasure and pain and the intimation of them to one another, and no further), the power of speech is intended to set forth the expedient and inexpedient, and therefore likewise the just and the unjust. And it is a characteristic of man that he alone has any sense of good and evil, of just and unjust, and the like, and the association of living beings who have this sense makes a family and a state.

Further, the state is by nature clearly prior to the family and to the individual, since the whole is of necessity prior to the part; for example, if the whole body be destroyed, there will be no foot or hand, except in an equivocal sense, as we might speak of a stone hand; for when destroyed the hand will be no better than that. But things are defined by their working and power; and we ought not to say that they are the same when they no longer have their proper quality, but only that they have the same name. The proof that the state is a creation of nature and prior to the individual is that the individual, when isolated, is not self-suffing; and therefore he is like a part in relation to the whole. But he who is unable to live in society, or who has no need because he is sufficient for himself, must be either a beast or a god: he is no part of a state. A social instinct is implanted in all men by nature, and yet he who first founded the state was the greatest of benefactors. For man, when perfected, is the best of animals, but, when separated from law and justice, he is the worst of all; since armed injustice is the more dangerous, and he is equipped at birth with arms, meant to be used by intelligence and virtue, which he may use for the worst ends. Wherefore, if he have not virtue, he is the most unholy and the most savage of animals, and the most full of lust and gluttony. But justice is the bond of men in states, for the administration of justice, which is the determination of what is just, is the principle of order in political society.

III

Seeing then that the state is made up of households, before speaking of the state we must speak of the management of the household. The parts of household management correspond to the persons who compose the household, and a complete household consists of slaves and freemen. Now we should begin by examining everything in its fewest possible elements; and the first and fewest possible parts of a family are master and slave, husband and wife, father and children. We have therefore to consider what each of these three relations is and ought to be: I mean the relation of master and servant, the marriage relation (the conjunction of man and wife has no name of its own), and thirdly, the procreative relation (this also has no proper name). And there is another element of a household, the so-called art of getting wealth, which, according to some, is identical with household management, according to others, a principal part of it; the nature of this art will also have to be considered by us.

Let us first speak of master and slave, looking to the needs of practical life and also seeking to attain some better theory of their relation than exists at present. For some are of opinion that the rule of a master is a science, and that the management of a household, and the mastership of slaves, and the political and royal rule, as I was saying at the outset, are all the same. Others affirm that the rule of a master over slaves is contrary to nature, and that the distinction between slave and freeman exists by law only, and not by nature; and being an interference with nature is therefore unjust.

IV

Property is a part of the household, and the art of acquiring property is a part of the art of managing the household; for no man can live well, or indeed live at all, unless he be provided with necessaries. And as in the arts which have a definite sphere the workers must have their own proper instruments for the accomplishment of their work, so it is in the management of a household. Now instruments are of various sorts; some are living, others lifeless; in the rudder, the pilot of a ship has a lifeless, in the look-out man, a living instrument; for in the arts the servant is a kind of instrument. Thus, too, a possession is an instrument for maintaining life. And so, in the arrangement of the family, a slave is a living possession, and property a number of such instruments; and the servant is himself an instrument which takes precedence of all other instruments. For if every instrument could accomplish its own work, obeying or anticipating the will of others, like the statues of Daedalus, or the tripods of Hephaestus, which, says the poet,

of their own accord entered the assembly of the Gods;

if, in like manner, the shuttle would weave and the plectrum touch the lyre without a hand to guide them, chief workmen would not want servants, nor masters slaves. Here, however, another distinction must be drawn; the instruments commonly so called are instruments of production, whilst a possession is an instrument of action. The shuttle, for example, is not only of use; but something else is made by it, whereas of a garment or of a bed there is only the use. Further, as production and action are different in kind, and both require instruments, the instruments which they employ must likewise differ in kind. But life is action and not production, and therefore the slave is the minister of action. Again, a possession is spoken of as a part is spoken of; for the part is not only a part of something else, but wholly belongs to it; and this is also true of a possession. The master is only the master of the slave; he does not belong to him, whereas the slave is not only the slave of his master, but wholly belongs to him. Hence we see what is the nature and office of a slave; he who is by nature not his own but another's man, is by nature a slave; and he may be said to be another's man who, being a human being, is also a possession. And a possession may be defined as an instrument of action, separable from the possessor.

V

But is there any one thus intended by nature to be a slave, and for whom such a condition is expedient and right, or rather is not all slavery a violation of nature?

There is no difficulty in answering this question, on grounds both of reason and of fact. For that some should rule and others be ruled is a thing not only necessary, but expedient; from the hour of their birth, some are marked out for subjection, others for rule.

And there are many kinds both of rulers and subjects (and that rule is the better which is exercised over better subjects—for example, to rule over men is better than to rule over wild beasts; for the work is better which is executed by better workmen, and where one man rules and another is ruled, they may be said to have a work); for in all things which form a composite whole and which are made up of parts, whether continuous or discrete, a distinction between the ruling and the subject element comes to light. Such a duality exists in living creatures, but not in them only; it originates in the constitution of the universe; even in things which have no life there is a ruling principle, as in a musical mode. But we are wandering from the subject. We will therefore restrict ourselves to the living creature, which, in the first place, consists of soul and body: and of these two, the one is by nature the ruler, and the other the subject. But then we must look for the intentions of nature in things which retain their nature, and not in things which are corrupted. And therefore we must study the man who is in the most perfect state both of body and soul, for in him we shall see the true relation of the two; although in bad or corrupted natures the body will often appear to rule over the soul, because they are in an evil and unnatural condition. At all events we may firstly observe in living creatures both a despotical and a constitutional rule; for the soul rules the body with a despotical rule, whereas the intellect rules the appetites with a constitutional and royal rule. And it is clear that the rule of the soul over the body, and of the mind and the rational element over the passionate, is natural and expedient; whereas the equality of the two or the rule of the inferior is always hurtful. The same holds good of animals in relation to men; for tame animals have a better nature than wild, and all tame animals are better off when they are ruled by man; for then they are preserved. Again, the male is by nature superior, and the female inferior; and the one rules, and the other is ruled; this principle, of necessity, extends to all mankind.

Where then there is such a difference as that between soul and body, or between men and animals (as in the case of those whose business is to use their body, and who can do nothing better), the lower sort are by nature slaves, and it is better for them as for all inferiors that they should be under the rule of a master. For he who can be, and therefore is, another's and he who participates in rational principle enough to apprehend, but not to have, such a principle, is a slave by nature. Whereas the lower animals cannot even apprehend a principle; they obey their instincts. And indeed the use made of slaves and of tame animals is not very different; for both with their bodies minister to the needs of life. Nature would like to distinguish between the bodies of freemen and slaves, making the one strong for servile labor, the other upright, and although useless for such services, useful for political life in the arts both of war and peace. But the opposite often happens—that some have the souls and others have the bodies of freemen. And doubtless if men differed from one another in the mere forms of their bodies as much as the statues of the Gods do from men, all would acknowledge that the inferior class should be slaves of the superior. And if this is true of the body, how much more just that a similar distinction should exist in the soul? But the beauty of the body is seen, whereas the beauty of the soul is not seen. It is clear, then, that some men are by nature free, and others slaves, and that for these latter slavery is both expedient and right.

VI

But that those who take the opposite view have in a certain way right on their side, may be easily seen. For the words slavery and slave are used in two senses. There is a slave or slavery by law as well as by nature. The law of which I speak is a sort of convention—the law by which whatever is taken in war is supposed to belong to the victors. But this right many jurists impeach, as they would an orator who brought forward an unconstitutional measure: they detest the notion that, because one man has the power of doing violence and is superior in brute strength, another shall be his slave and subject. Even among philosophers there is a difference of opinion. The origin of the dispute, and what makes the views invade each other's territory, is as follows: in some sense virtue, when furnished with means, has actually the greatest power of exercising force; and as superior power is only found where there is superior excellence of some kind, power seems to imply virtue, and the dispute to be simply one about justice (for it is due to one party identifying justice with goodwill while the other identifies it with the mere rule of the stronger). If these views are thus set out separately, the other views have no force or plausibility against the view that the superior in virtue ought to rule, or be master. Others, clinging, as they think, simply to a principle of justice (for law and custom are a sort of justice), assume that slavery in accordance with the custom of war is justified by law, but at the same moment they deny this. For what if the cause of the war be unjust? And again, no one would ever say he is a slave who is unworthy to be a slave. Were this the case, men of the highest rank would be slaves and the children of slaves if they or their parents chance to have been taken captive and sold. Wherefore Hellenes do not like to call Hellenes slaves, but confine the term to barbarians. Yet, in using this language, they really mean the natural slave of whom we spoke at first; for it must be admitted that some are slaves everywhere, others nowhere. The same principle applies to nobility. Hellenes regard themselves as noble everywhere, and not only in their own country, but they deem the barbarians noble only when at home, thereby implying that there are two sorts of nobility and freedom, the one absolute, the other relative. The Helen of Theodectes says:

Who would presume to call me servant who am on both sides sprung from the stem of the Gods?

What does this mean but that they distinguish freedom and slavery, noble and humble birth, by the two principles of good and evil? They think that as men and animals beget men and animals, so from good men a good man springs. But this is what nature, though she may intend it, cannot always accomplish.

We see then that there is some foundation for this difference of opinion, and that all are not either slaves by nature or freemen by nature, and also that there is in some cases a marked distinction between the two classes, rendering it expedient and right for the one to be slaves and the others to be masters: the one practicing obedience, the others exercising the authority and lordship which nature intended them to have. The abuse of this authority is injurious to both; for the interests of part and whole, of body and soul, are the same, and the slave is a part of the master, a living but separated part of his bodily frame. Hence, where the relation of master and slave between them is natural they are friends and have a common interest, but where it rests merely on law and force the reverse is true. . . .

XII

Of household management we have seen that there are three parts—one is the rule of a master over slaves, which has been discussed already, another of a father, and the third of a husband. A husband and father, we saw, rules over wife and children, both free, but the rule differs, the rule over his children being a royal, over his wife a constitutional rule. For although there may be exceptions to the order of nature, the male is by nature fitter for command than the female, just as the elder and full-grown is superior to the younger and more immature. But in most constitutional states the citizens rule and are ruled by turns, for the idea of a constitutional state implies that the natures of the citizens are equal, and do not differ at all. Nevertheless, when one rules and the other is ruled we endeavor to create a difference of outward forms and names and titles of respect, which may be illustrated by the saying of Amasis about his foot-pan. The relation of the male to the female is of this kind, but there the inequality is permanent. The rule of a father over his children is royal, for he rules by virtue both of love and of the respect due to age, exercising a kind of royal power. And therefore Homer has appropriately called Zeus "father of Gods and men," because he is the king of them all. For a king is the natural superior of his subjects, but he should be of the same kin or kind with them, and such is the relation of elder and younger, of father and son.

XIII

Thus it is clear that household management attends more to men than to the acquisition of inanimate things, and to human excellence more than to the excellence of property which we call wealth, and to the virtue of freemen more than to the virtue of slaves. A question may indeed be raised, whether there is any excellence at all in a slave beyond and higher than merely instrumental and ministerial qualities—whether he can have the virtues of temperance, courage, justice, and the like; or whether slaves possess only bodily and ministerial qualities. And, whichever way we answer the question, a difficulty arises; for, if they have virtue, in what will they differ from freemen? On the other hand, since they are men and share in rational principle, it seems absurd to say that they have no virtue. A similar question may be raised about women and children, whether they too have virtues: ought a woman to be temperate and brave and just, and is a child to be called temperate, and intemperate, or not? So in general we may ask about the natural ruler, and the natural subject, whether they have the same or different virtues. For if a noble nature is equally required in both, why should one of them always rule, and the other always be ruled? Nor can we say that this is a question of degree, for the difference between ruler and subject is a difference of kind, which the difference of more and less never is. Yet how strange is the supposition that the one ought, and that the other ought not, to have virtue! For if the ruler is intemperate and unjust, how can he rule well? If the subject, how can he obey well? If he be licentious and cowardly, he will certainly not do his duty. It is evident, therefore, that both of them must have a share of virtue, but varying as natural subjects also vary among themselves. Here the very constitution of the soul has shown us the way; in it one part naturally rules, and the other is subject, and the virtue of the ruler we maintain to be different from that of the subject; the one being the virtue of the rational, and the other of the irrational part. Now, it is obvious that the same principle applies generally, and therefore almost all things rule and are ruled according to nature. But the kind of rule differs; the freeman rules over the slave after another manner from that in which the male rules over the female, or the man over the child; although the parts of the soul are present in all of them, they are present in different degrees. For the slave has no deliberative faculty at all; the woman has, but it is without authority, and the child has, but it is immature. So it must necessarily be supposed to be with the moral virtues also; all should partake of them, but only in such manner and degree as is required by each for the fulfillment of his duty. Hence the ruler ought to have moral virtue in perfection, for his function, taken absolutely, demands a master artificer, and rational principle is such an artificer; the subjects, on the other hand, require only that measure of virtue which is proper to each of them. Clearly, then, moral virtue belongs to all of them; but the temperance of a man and of a woman, or the courage and justice of a man and of a woman, are not, as Socrates maintained, the same; the courage of a man is shown in commanding, of a woman in obeying. And this holds of all other virtues, as will be more clearly seen if we look at them in detail, for those who say generally that virtue consists in a good disposition of the soul, or in doing rightly, or the like, only deceive themselves. Far better than such definitions is their mode of speaking, who, like Gorgias, enumerate the virtues. All classes must be deemed to have their special attributes; as the poet says of women,

Silence is a woman's glory,

but this is not equally the glory of man. The child is imperfect, and therefore obviously his virtue is not relative to himself alone, but to the perfect man and to his teacher, and in like manner the virtue of the slave is relative to a master. Now we determined that a slave is useful for the wants of life, and therefore he will obviously require only so much virtue as will prevent him from failing in his duty through cowardice or lack of self-control. Some one will ask whether, if what we are saying is true, virtue will not be required also in the artisans, for they often fail in their work through the lack of self control? But is there not a great difference in the two cases? For the slave shares in his master's life; the artisan is less closely connected with him, and only attains excellence in proportion as he becomes a slave. The meaner sort of mechanic has a special and separate slavery; and whereas the slave exists by nature, not so the shoemaker or other artisan. It is manifest, then, that the master ought to be the source of such excellence in the slave, and not a mere possessor of the art of mastership which trains the slave in his duties. Wherefore they are mistaken who forbid us to converse with slaves and say that we should employ command only, for slaves stand even more in need of admonition than children.

So much for this subject; the relations of husband and wife, parent and child, their several virtues, what in their intercourse with one another is good, and what is evil, and how we may pursue the good and escape the evil, will have to be discussed when we speak of the different forms of government. For, inasmuch as every family is a part of a state, and these relationships are the parts of a family, and the virtue of the part must have regard to the virtue of the whole, women and children must be trained by education with an eye to the constitution, if the virtues of either of them are supposed to make any difference in the virtues of the state. And they must make a difference: for the children grow up to be citizens, and half the free persons in a state are women.

Of these matters, enough has been said; of what remains, let us speak at another time. Regarding, then, our present inquiry as complete, we will make a new beginning. And, first, let us examine the various theories of a perfect state. . . .

Book Three

VII

Having determined these points [regarding citizenship and types of rule], we have next to consider how many forms of government there are, and what they are; and in the first place what are the true forms, for when they are determined the perversions of them will at once be apparent. The words constitution and government have the same meaning, and the government, which is the supreme authority in states, must be in the hands of one, or of a few, or of the many. The true forms of government, therefore, are those in which the one, or the few, or the many, govern with a view to the common interest; but governments which rule with a view to the private interest, whether of the one, or of the few, or of the many, are perversions. For the members of a state, if they are truly citizens, ought to participate in its advantages. Of forms of government in which one rules, we call that which regards the common interests, kingship or royalty; that in which more than one, but not many, rule, aristocracy; and it is so called, either because the rulers are the best men, or because they have at heart the best interests of the state and of the citizens. But when the citizens at large administer the state for the common interest, the government is called by the generic name—a constitution. And there is a reason for this use of language. One man or a few may excel in virtue; but as the number increases it becomes more difficult for them to attain perfection in every kind of virtue, though they may in military virtue, for this is found in the masses. Hence in a constitutional government the fighting-men have the supreme power, and those who possess arms are the citizens.

Of the above-mentioned forms, the perversions are as follows: of royalty, tyranny; of aristocracy, oligarchy; of constitutional government, democracy. For tyranny is a kind of monarchy which has in view the interest of the monarch only; oligarchy has in view the interest of the wealthy; democracy, of the needy: none of them the common good of all.

VIII

But there are difficulties about these forms of government, and it will therefore be necessary to state a little more at length the nature of each of them. For he who would make a philosophical study of the various sciences, and does not regard practice only, ought not to overlook or omit anything, but to set forth the truth in every particular. Tyranny, as I was saying, is monarchy exercising the rule of a master over the political society; oligarchy is when men of property have the government in their hands; democracy, the opposite, when the indigent, and not the men of property, are the rulers. And here arises the first of our difficulties, and it relates to the distinction drawn. For democracy is said to be the government of the many. But what if the many are men of property and have the power in their hands? In like manner oligarchy is said to be the government of the few; but what if the poor are fewer than the rich, and have the power in their hands because they are stronger? In these cases the distinction which we have drawn between these different forms of government would no longer hold good.

Suppose, once more, that we add wealth to the few and poverty to the many, and name the governments according—an oligarchy is said to be that in which the few and the wealthy, and a democracy that in which the many and the poor are the rulers—there will still be a difficulty. For, if the only forms of government are the ones already mentioned, how shall we describe those other governments also just mentioned by us, in which the rich are the more numerous and the poor are the fewer, and both govern in their respective states?

The argument seems to show that, whether in oligarchies or in democracies, the number of the governing body, whether the greater number, as in a democracy, or the smaller number, as in an oligarchy, is an accident due to the fact that the rich everywhere are few, and the poor numerous. But if so, there is a misapprehension of the causes of the difference between them. For the real difference between democracy and oligarchy is poverty and wealth. Wherever men rule by reason of their wealth, whether they be few or many, that is an oligarchy, and where the poor rule, that is a democracy. But as a fact the rich are few and the poor many; for few are well-to-do, whereas freedom is enjoyed by all, and wealth and freedom are the grounds on which the oligarchical and democratical parties respectively claim power in the state. . . .

XI

. . . The principle that the multitude ought to be supreme rather than the few best is one that is maintained, and, though not free from difficulty, yet seems to contain an element of truth. For the many, of whom each individual is but an ordinary person, when they meet together may very likely be better than the few good, if regarded not individually but collectively, just as a feast to which many contribute is better than a dinner provided out of a single purse. For each individual among the many has a share of virtue and prudence, and when they meet together, they become in a manner one man, who has many feet, and hands, and senses; that is a figure of their mind and disposition. Hence the many are better judges than a single man of music and poetry; for some understand one part, and some another, and among them they understand the whole. There is a similar combination of qualities in good men, who differ from any individual of the many, as the beautiful are said to differ from those who are not beautiful, and works of art from realities, because in them the scattered elements are combined, although, if taken separately, the eye of one person or some other feature in another person would be fairer than in the picture. Whether this principle can apply to every democracy, and to all bodies of men, is not clear. Or rather, by heaven, in some cases it is impossible of application; for the argument would equally hold about brutes; and wherein, it will be asked, do some men differ from brutes? But there may be bodies of men about whom our statement is nevertheless true. And if so, the difficulty which has been already raised, and also another which is akin to it—viz., what power should be assigned to the mass of freemen and citizens, who are not rich and have no personal merit—are both solved. There is still a danger in allowing them to share the great offices of state, for their folly will lead them into error, and their dishonesty into crime. But there is a danger also in not letting them share, for a state in which many poor men are excluded from office will necessarily be full of enemies. The only way of escape is to assign to them some deliberative and judicial functions. For this reason Solon and certain other legislators give them the power of electing to offices, and of calling the magistrates to account, but they do not allow them to hold office singly. When they meet together their perceptions are quite good enough, and combined with the better class they are useful to the state (just as impure food when mixed with what is pure sometimes makes the entire mass more wholesome than a small quantity of the pure would be), but each individual, left to himself, forms an imperfect judgment. On the other hand, the popular form of government involves certain difficulties. In the first place, it might be objected that he who can judge of the healing of a sick man would be one who could himself heal his disease, and make him whole—that is, in other words, the physician; and so in all professions and arts. As, then, the physician ought to be called to account by physicians, so ought men in general to be called to account by their peers. But physicians are of three kinds: there is the ordinary practitioner, and there is the physician of the higher class, and thirdly the intelligent man who has studied the art: in all arts there is such a class; and we attribute the power of judging to them quite as much as to professors of the art. Secondly, does not the same principle apply to elections? For a right election can only be made by those who have knowledge; those who know geometry, for example, will choose a geometrician rightly, and those who know how to steer, a pilot; and, even if there be some occupations and arts in which private persons share in the ability to choose, they certainly cannot choose better than those who know. So that, according to this argument, neither the election of magistrates, nor the calling of them to account, should be entrusted to the many. Yet possibly these objections are to a great extent met by our old answer, that if the peo-

ple are not utterly degraded, although individually they may be worse judges than those who have special knowledge—as a body they are as good or better. Moreover, there are some arts whose products are not judged of solely, or best, by the artists themselves, namely those arts whose products are recognized even by those who do not possess the art; for example, the knowledge of the house is not limited to the builder only; the user, or, in other words, the master, of the house will be even a better judge than the builder, just as the pilot will judge better of a rudder than the carpenter, and the guest will judge better of a feast than the cook.

This difficulty seems now to be sufficiently answered, but there is another akin to it. That inferior persons should have authority in greater matters than the good would appear to be a strange thing, yet the election and calling to account of the magistrates is the greatest of all. And these, as I was saying, are functions which in some states are assigned to the people, for the assembly is supreme in all such matters. Yet persons of any age, and having but a small property qualification, sit in the assembly and deliberate and judge, although for the great officers of state, such as treasurers and generals, a high qualification is required. This difficulty may be solved in the same manner as the preceding, and the present practice of democracies may be really defensible. For the power does not reside in the dicast, or senator, or ecclesiast, but in the court, and the senate, and the assembly, of which individual senators, or ecclesiasts, or dicasts, are only parts or members. And for this reason the many may claim to have a higher authority than the few; for the people, and the senate, and the courts consist of many persons, and their property collectively is greater than the property of one or of a few individuals holding great offices. But enough of this.

The discussion of the first question shows nothing so clearly as that laws, when good, should be supreme; and that the magistrate or magistrates should regulate those matters only on which the laws are unable to speak with precision owing to the difficulty of any general principle embracing all particulars. But what are good laws has not yet been clearly explained; the old difficulty remains. The goodness or badness, justice or injustice, of laws varies of necessity with the constitutions of states. This, however, is clear, that the laws must be adapted to the constitutions. But if so, true forms of government will of necessity have just laws, and perverted forms of government will have unjust laws. . . .

Book Four

XI

We have now to inquire what is the best constitution for most states, and the best life for most men, neither assuming a standard of virtue which is above ordinary persons, nor an education which is exceptionally favored by nature and circumstances, nor yet an ideal state which is an aspiration only, but having regard to the life in which the majority are able to share, and to the form of government which states in general can attain. As to those aristocracies, as they are called, of which we were just now speaking, they either lie beyond the possibilities of the greater number of states, or they approximate to the so-called constitutional government, and therefore need no separate discussion. And in fact the conclusion at which we arrive respecting all these forms rests upon the same grounds. For if what was said in the *Ethics* is true, that the happy life is the life according to virtue lived without impediment, and that virtue is a mean, then the life which is in a mean, and in a mean attainable by every one, must be the best. And the same principles of virtue and vice are characteristic of cities and of constitutions; for the constitution is in a figure the life of the city.

Now in all states there are three elements: one class is very rich, another very poor, and a third in a mean. It is admitted that moderation and the mean are best, and therefore it will clearly be best to possess the gifts of fortune in moderation; for in that condition of life men are most ready to follow rational principle. But he who greatly excels in beauty, strength, birth, or wealth, or on the other hand who is very poor, or very weak, or very much disgraced, finds it difficult to follow rational principle. Of these two the one

sort grow into violent and great criminals, the others into rogues and petty rascals. And two sorts of offenses correspond to them, the one committed from violence, the other from roguery. Again, the middle class is least likely to shrink from rule, or to be over-ambitious for it; both of which are injuries to the state. Again, those who have too much of the goods of fortune, strength, wealth, friends, and the like, are neither willing nor able to submit to authority. The evil begins at home; for when they are boys, by reason of the luxury in which they are brought up, they never learn, even at school, the habit of obedience. On the other hand, the very poor, who are in the opposite extreme, are too degraded. So that the one class cannot obey, and can only rule despotically; the other knows not how to command and must be ruled like slaves. Thus arises a city, not of freemen, but of masters and slaves, the one despising, the other envying; and nothing can be more fatal to friendship and good fellowship in states than this: for good fellowship springs from friendship; when men are at enmity with one another, they would rather not even share the same path. But a city ought to be composed, as far as possible, of equals and similars; and these are generally the middle classes. Wherefore the city which is composed of middle-class citizens is necessarily best constituted in respect of the elements of which we say the fabric of the state naturally consists. And this is the class of citizens which is most secure in a state, for they do not, like the poor, covet their neighbors' goods; nor do others covet theirs, as the poor covet the goods of the rich; and as they neither plot against others, nor are themselves plotted against, they pass through life safely. Wisely then did Phocylides pray—"Many things are best in the mean; I desire to be of a middle condition in my city."

Thus it is manifest that the best political community is formed by citizens of the middle class, and that those states are likely to be well-administered in which the middle class is large, and stronger if possible than both the other classes, or at any rate than either singly; for the addition of the middle class turns the scale, and prevents either of the extremes from being dominant. Great then is the good fortune of a state in which the citizens have a moderate and sufficient property; for where some possess much, and the others nothing, there may arise an extreme democracy, or a pure oligarchy; or a tyranny may grow out of either extreme—either out of the most rampant democracy, or out of an oligarchy; but it is not so likely to arise out of the middle constitutions and those akin to them. I will explain the reason of this hereafter, when I speak of the revolutions of states. The mean condition of states is clearly best, for no other is free from faction; and where the middle class is large, there are least likely to be factions and dissensions. For a similar reason large states are less liable to faction than small ones, because in them the middle class is large; whereas in small states it is easy to divide all the citizens into two classes who are either rich or poor, and to leave nothing in the middle. And democracies are safer and more permanent than oligarchies, because they have a middle class which is more numerous and has a greater share in the government; for when there is no middle class, and the poor greatly exceed in number, troubles arise, and the state soon comes to an end. A proof of the superiority of the middle class is that the best legislators have been of a middle condition; for example, Solon, as his own verses testify; and Lycurgus, for he was not a king; and Charondas, and almost all legislators. . . .

Adapted from: Aristotle, *Politics*, translated by Benjamin Jowett, pp. 5–15, 26–30, 91–93, 97–100, 138–141. Originally published by Oxford University Press, 1921. ✦

10
The Puzzle of the Political Animal

Nature and Artifice in Aristotle's Political Theory

Cary J. Nederman

I

There is perhaps no doctrine so closely associated with Aristotle's political philosophy as the claim of *Politics* 1253a1–3 that "man is a political animal" (*zo͞on politikon*), in conjunction with [the] statement at 1252b30 that the polis or political community exists by nature. From the Latin Middle Ages to the late twentieth century, Aristotelians of many different orientations have been able to agree at least on the naturalness of political life to human existence.[1] But in very recent years, some scholars have questioned Aristotle's formulation and defense of the political naturalist thesis. There are various sources for this dissatisfaction: apparent contradictions between the *Politics* and other of Aristotle's authentic writings, as well as ostensive inconsistencies within the position as stated in the *Politics* itself.[2]

As a rule, contemporary studies of Aristotle's political naturalism have eventually concluded that his position is philosophically coherent, requiring only more careful interpretation to illuminate its internal consistency. By contrast, David Keyt in a stimulating and controversial 1987 essay has declared frankly that "there is a blunder at the very root of Aristotle's political philosophy," arising from his very assertion of the political nature of man.[3] Specifically, this "blunder" stems from the alleged irreconcilability of two facets of Aristotelian teaching. On the one hand, Aristotle repeatedly insists that

the formation and perpetuation of the polis depends upon the education of citizens by a lawgiver or statesman as well as by the laws themselves. Hence, it would seem that the "art" of ruling implies that the polis itself is an artifice. On the other hand, Aristotle in *Physics* 192b9–193b21 quite clearly delineates what it is for an entity to be natural: that which is natural has within itself its own source of change, that is, motion or growth. He explicitly contrasts "nature" with "artifice" in this connection: the cause of alteration in artificial things is characteristically external to them. Thus, to determine whether an entity or phenomenon is natural or artificial, we must discover the location of its principle of change. Since it appears that the polis, as a creation of the instruction and practical wisdom of its leaders, has its source of motion or growth outside of its citizens, Keyt concludes that men cannot be political animals and the polis is not itself natural.[4] This is the core of Aristotle's supposed blunder.

Keyt is not, of course, the first scholar to notice this contradiction. But earlier generations usually explained it away by understanding Aristotle to posit a latent human impulse which requires active stimulation from an external human source to be realized and acted upon.[5] In my view, Keyt is quite correct to reject this interpretation as inadequate: it defers but does not solve the apparent conflict between nature and artifice.[6] To make a plausible case for the traditional reading, it would be necessary to argue that Aristotle had weakened in the *Politics* the teleological conception of nature that he proposed in his other writings. There is no convincing evidence that he altered his formulation; and given the systematic character of his basic principles throughout his corpus, it would seem an unlikely conclusion to draw.

Not surprisingly, Keyt's terse dismissal of Aristotle's political naturalism has evoked a storm of hostile response.[7] For example, Fred Miller, Jr., has argued that Keyt's position fails to take into account the depth and scope of Aristotelian teleology. Miller says that Keyt has identified "only an apparent inconsistency. According to Aristotle's teleology, . . . the development of the polis . . . require[s] the cooperative contribution of both nature and human beings. Granted his teleological framework, his account is coherent and plausible."[8] But, as Joseph Chan has pointed out, Miller's defense of Aristotle ultimately plays into precisely the contradiction alleged by Keyt: "I cannot see how the approach can resist the conclusion that the polis is therefore partly natural and partly conventional, a conclusion that does not fit the conceptual categories in Aristotle's *Physics* and would certainly be regarded by Aristotle as an incorrect description of the nature of the polis."[9] Chan himself proposes an alternate, "multiple-level" way of rescuing Aristotle. In his view, we ought to distinguish between the so-called type-characteristic of the polis and the form of the polis.[10] The first denotes those essential features which all poleis in general share, such as some constitutional structure; the second pertains to the particular constitution and laws which a given polis (say, Athens as contrasted with Crete) adopts. Chan asserts Aristotle must have regarded the "type-characteristic" of the polis—those features which make a polis a polis—as natural, arising from a principle internal to man. By contrast, the specific organization of any given polis is a matter of artifice, of practical wisdom and statesmanship. Hence, the polis can be said, without contradiction, to be natural in one sense (or at one level) but artificial in another way.

Chan's suggestion is intriguing, but he admits that it also depends upon "a distinction . . . not explicitly made by Aristotle."[11] Chan may have found a possible solution to the dilemma of Aristotle's political naturalism, but it does not seem to be a solution that Aristotle himself offered or would have recognized as such. And Miller is certainly correct in thinking that we should not assume without some compelling evidence that Aristotle was unaware of the premises and implications of his own arguments.[12] So I would propose that before we accept an "external" interpretation such as Chan's—that is, one which is consistent with Aristotle's argument but not derived directly from or warranted by Aristotelian texts—we attempt once again to find a satisfactory reading from within the Aristotelian corpus. In particular, there has been surprisingly little attempt to figure out how the Aristotelian notion of nature (as distinct from artifice) applies to human nature. What does it mean to say that human beings are the source of their own change? Does the answer to this question have any impact on our understanding of the political nature of mankind and of the consequent naturalness of the polis? In exploring these questions, I propose to draw upon segments of the Aristotelian corpus that have hitherto been largely ignored by contributors to this debate, including the *De anima*, the *De motu animalium*, and the two versions of the *Ethics*.

In schematic form, the article will argue in the following manner. The natural principle of change characteristic of human beings is their voluntary choice; it is because people choose that their motion can be traced back to them. As humans, we are moved to act (that is, we choose or exercise practical intellect) in accordance with our *hexeis*, that is, the dispositions of our soul acquired through training and practice. Hence, it is necessary for people to receive a moral education in order for them to live in accordance with their own natural principle. Voluntary choice is a defining mark of human (as opposed to organic nonhuman) nature; but choosing means that we choose on the basis of learned qualities, which compose our moral character. In turn, it is the provision of this education which Aristotle regards to be the central purpose of the lawgiver and the statesman, as well as the constitution and laws. Hence, in relation to the soul, the polis is not at all artificial or external to the process by which human beings are moved; therefore, the polis is natural to man, and men are political animals. It is perhaps with this in mind that Aristotle holds the polis to exist for the sake not merely of living, but of living well (*Pol.* 1280a32). For only in the polis may men live a fully moral life, because the polis alone (through its leaders and laws) provides the education requisite for choosing as human beings choose, that is, choosing well.

II

At *Physics* 192b13–19, Aristotle states unequivocally what it means for something to be natural. An object that exists by nature, he says, "has in itself a source of motion and of rest in respect of place or of increase and diminution or of alteration."[13] In Aristotle's view, it is the first of these—locomotion (*kinesis*) or movement in respect of place—that distinguishes animals from the rest of nature, even organic nature: plants, for example, have the power of growth (increase and diminution) but not locomotion. As he remarks at *Physics* 253114–15, "We say that the animal itself originates not all of its motions, but its locomotion." Locomotion is "always for the sake of something," that is, it always aims at a goal or a result outside of itself (*De an.* 432b16).

Aristotle's analysis of locomotion may be characterized roughly as follows. The end or object of locomotion, that for the sake of which the animal moves, originates with desire (*orexis*).[14] The object of desire serves as a kind of unmoved mover for the animal. The object or end stimulates desire, and it is apprehended by sense-perception, imagination or thought, that is, the intellect (*nous*). The animal is thereby impelled to move (*De motu* 701a29–701b1). Since desire plays an integral role in the process, and the animal is not physically compelled to move by some external force, the animal may be said to "move itself" or "originate its motion."[15] This is the sense in which locomotion is natural to animals: through the desiring and intellective faculties of the soul, the animal is endowed with agency, that is, the ability to move itself in accordance with and in relation to a desired object.

Human locomotion is a subspecies of this general account of animal self-movement. Aristotle contends that *nous* in lower animals is confined to the realms of perception and imagination (*De an.* 429a1–9). Thus, lower animals "think" only figuratively; to talk about "thought" in animals, we must "take the imagination as a kind of thinking. . . . In other animals, although there is neither thought nor rationality, there is imagination" (*De an.* 433a10, 11–12). By contrast, the human intellect encompasses thought and reason as well as perception and imagination, and is thus *nous* in its full and proper sense.[16] What especially characterizes uniquely human action (as distinct perhaps from acts performed by human beings in an beastlike way) is that it occurs on the basis of knowledge, as the result of a rational process. According to *De anima* 433a13–16, in human beings,

> both intellect and desire produce movement in respect of place, but [only] intellect which reasons for the sake of something and is practical; and it differs from contemplative intellect in respect of end. Every desire too is for the sake of something; for the object of desire is the starting point (*arche*) for the practical intellect, and the final step is the starting point for action (*praxis*).

It is clear that this passage is meant to pertain specifically to human action, since Aristotle is careful to distinguish between the kind of intellect that produces movement (i.e., the practical intellect) and that which does not directly command "avoidance or pursuit" (*De an.* 432b26–35), namely, the speculative or theoretical intellect, which is self-sufficient. Since Aristotle would not doubt that human beings alone among animals are capable of theoretical wisdom, it only makes sense to draw such a distinction in the case of human intellect.

Thus, Aristotle apparently regards the practical intellect as a unique possession of human beings. Distinctive among all animals, human beings calculate rationally the best means to achieve the ends they desire. It is in this sense that human beings may trace their acts back to themselves: they reason from their object of desire backwards to their present condition and then forward again to the act(s) that will realize their desired goal. The practical intellect, with thought as its crown, functions as the bridge between desire and action. Since such a calculative element is utterly lacking in other, nonrational animals, the practical intellect singles out human self-movement as a special case within the animal kingdom.

Aristotle's account of human action in the *Nicomachean Ethics* is in its essentials consistent with his presentation of human loco-motion elsewhere in his corpus. In a manner reminiscent of *De anima* 433a15–16, Aris-totle states at *Nicomachean Ethics* 1113b17–19 that "man is a moving principle (*arche*) or begetter of his actions as of his children." Specifically, human action (or at least the ac-tion of the *enkrates*, the continent person who is able to resist the irrational form of de-sire, *epithumia* or wanting)[17] is regarded by Aristotle to be the result of rational desire or deliberation (*boulesis*) combined with the exercise of practical intellect, especially thought. Indeed, it is in this sense that he considers human action, unlike the motion of other animals, to be both voluntary (*hekousion*) and chosen or purposive (*prohairetike*).

We speak of actions as "voluntary," Aris-totle says, when we can assign praise or blame to them (*NE* 1109b31–33).[18] We do not praise or blame a person when he is not the cause of his own actions, that is, when they are "done under compulsion or through ignorance" (*NE* 1111a22). By contrast, "if it is clear that a man is the author of his own actions, and if we are unable to trace our conduct back to any other origins than those within ourselves, then actions of which the origins are within us, themselves depend on us and are voluntary" (*NE* 1113b19–21). What Aristotle terms "voluntary" acts in the *Nicomachean Ethics* are precisely those ac-tions which arise "naturally," that is, as the result of a principle of movement that lays within the agent.[19] When we talk about human beings specifically as having within themselves "a source of motion," we are re-ferring to the realm of their voluntary ac-tions.

Most voluntary human conduct is charac-terized by Aristotle as the result of choice (*prohairesis*). I say "most" because Aristotle refuses to discount actions done in anger or another passion as involuntary (*NE* 1111a24–1111b3), but they are also not cho-sen (*NE* 1111b18–20). Choice encompasses a narrower band of conduct than volition, since Aristotle says that the actions of chil-dren and even animals may be counted as voluntary even though they are unchosen (*NE* 1111b12–13; *EE* 1226b21–23). Choice,

we may say, is the typically or essentially human mode of voluntary action. *Prohairesis* partakes of both desire and prac-tical intellect, but it cannot be reduced to ei-ther. Rather, *prohairesis* is the way in which human beings typically initiate action on the basis of *orexis* (specifically, wish) and *nous* (in particular, thought). Aristotle says, "Choice may be called either intellect related to desire or desire related to intellect; and man, as the moving principle (*arche*) of ac-tion, is a union of desire and intellect" (*NE* 1139b5–6). Expressed schematically, Aris-totle explains human action as follows:

1. An agent desires (wishes for) an ulti-mate end, which is always a good.

2. The agent reasons (practically) about the chain of actions (A, A', A" . . .) that will serve as the means to the end.

3. The agent chooses that action A which is "closest to him," that is, which he can carry out immediately and which is the practical "object of deliberation (*boulesis*) and choice."

4. The agent performs A.

Hence, *prohairesis* is the outcome of desire and intellect acting together in order to achieve an end. As Aristotle remarks, "A man stops enquiring how he is to act as soon as he has carried back the moving principle (*arche*) of action to himself, and to the domi-nant part of himself. It is that part which chooses." (*NE* 1113a4–7). Choice in a sense signifies the recognition that man is his own rational moving principle, that the origin of human action lies within the human soul it-self. Chosen action is natural to human be-ings.

It is noteworthy that the object of deliber-ation and choice is always the means to an end, not the end itself. Specifically, the end for the sake of which we wish and choose, Ar-istotle contends, is always a good. He stipu-lates near the beginning of the *Nicomachean Ethics* that "if therefore among the ends at which our actions aim there be one which we wish for its own sake, while we wish the oth-ers only for the sake of this, . . . it is clear that the one ultimate end must be a good and in-deed the best" (*NE* 1094b19–22). All human conduct must be conducive to the good, and that whatever intermediary objects are desired, they must be ordered towards the final good. Hence, *prohairesis* is choice in accordance with some good.

But if this is the case, why do people choose actions that are evil? In other words, how is bad conduct possible if all people wish for and choose the good? Aristotle's answer is important. Although he believes that the "true" goods (and good) are the same for all men, he claims that the good will appear differently to each person: "We should say that what is wished for in the true and unqualified sense is the good, but that what appears good to each person is wished for by him" (*NE* 1113a24–25). Stated simply, people who do evil think that they are doing good, because they are doing the good as they perceive it. The problem is that they are mistaken about the true or real good. The source of this mistake is their moral character:

> Specific things are noble and pleasant corresponding to each type of disposition (*hexis*), and perhaps what chiefly distinguishes the good man is that he sees the truth in each kind, being himself as it were the standard and measure of the noble and the pleasant. It appears to be pleasure that misleads the mass of mankind; for it seems to them to be a good, which it is not, as they choose what is pleasant as good and shun pain as evil. (*NE* 1113a31–1113b2)

We choose in accordance with a conception of the good that derives from the moral traits we have acquired. When someone's characteristics are ill-formed (because, say, they stem from an equation of the pleasant with the good), that person will do evil while believing it to be good. Evil as well as good deeds arise from a source or moving principle within the individual, and hence are both voluntary and chosen; virtue and vice both depend upon us (*NE* 1113b3–21).

III

Aristotle's ability to sustain the position that human beings always wish for the good, but that the good appears differently to different people according to their moral qualities, depends crucially upon his account of moral education. He argues that virtue itself must never be confused with mere morally correct action. To be virtuous, Aristotle asserts, is not merely to do what is good, but to do so as the result of a well-formed moral character or set of moral habits (*ethos*) (*NE* 1103a17–24). In other words, morally significant actions are rooted in more permanent principles or traits which regulate the behavior of the agent, so that deliberation and choice are always in accordance with the character of the agent who deliberates and chooses. Without the doctrine of ethos, Aristotle could never claim that "the good man judges everything correctly," since "what chiefly distinguishes the good man is that he sees the truth of each matter" (*NE* 1113a29–30, 32–33). The good man is so thoroughly imbued with virtue, Aristotle maintains, that he may be regarded as the "standard and measure" against which all conduct ought to be gauged.

Yet regardless of the permanence and stability Aristotle attributes to *ethos*, Aristotle does not wish to claim that moral traits are inbred. We are born with only a capacity (*dynamis*) to be good or evil. The capacity must still be actualized by the process of moral education (*NE* 1103a24–31). Thus, virtue cannot merely be described as a capacity to act in accordance with goodness, since *dynamis* is by definition outside of our control and hence something for which we cannot be held responsible (*NE* 1106a7–14). On the same grounds, Aristotle insists at *Topics* 160b20 that the conduct "which a bad character (*ethous*) would prefer" ought to be shunned and avoided. It is the character of the agent that constitutes the real concern of ethical evaluation. Thus, Aristotle posits a firm distinction between evil actions and evil men: "Even God and the good man are capable of doing bad deeds, but God and such men are not of that type; for the wicked are always so called because of their deliberate choice of evil" (*Top.* 126a24–26). Men always retain the capacity for evil, in the sense that they are capable of committing vicious acts. But those actions that can legitimately be praised or blamed arise from the acquired moral traits of the agent. *Topics* 145b36–146a3 accordingly argues against the ethical significance of *dynamis:* "A just man is he who deliberately chooses to distribute what is equal rather than he who has a capacity (*dynamenon*) for doing so. Justice could not be a capacity for distributing what is equal, for then a man would be most just who has the greatest capacity for distributing what is equal." Virtue must be something active rather than passive, a feature of what we do, but still in such a fashion that it is an ingrained characteristic. Moral choice, in other words, is necessarily rooted in firm traits which are demonstrably the products of our own activity.

Aristotle's ability to defend this view depends upon his definition of virtue as a *hexis* of the soul. As a general concept in Aristotelian philosophy, *hexis* denotes a type of quality, that is, a way in which a qualitative property may be ascribed to a subject or substance. Specifically, *hexis* is the term employed by Aristotle to denote those qualities which become so firmly rooted in that which they qualify that are difficult (if not impossible) to alter. He says in *Categories* that *hexis* differs from other qualities "in being more long lasting and stable" (*Cat.* 8b28), so that should some property eventually "become through length of time part of man's nature and irremediable or hard to change, one would perhaps call this a *hexis*" (*Cat.* 9a2–4). When we "hold of the virtues, justice and temperance and the like" that they are *hexeis*, then, we mean to convey that they are "not easily changed or dislodged" (*Cat.* 8b33–35). The goodness of the virtuous man is relatively permanent: its status as *hexis* ensures that virtue will last over time and will thus provide a stable foundation for moral choice. Yet the *Categories* is quick to emphasize that *hexis* cannot be assimilated to a capacity. Rather, *hexeis* must be acquired through a lengthy and difficult process of moral education typified by the gradual inculcation of goodness through practice and experience (*Cat.* 13a23–31).

This position is elaborated in the *Nicomachean Ethics*, where Aristotle maintains that "*hexis* is the genus of virtue" (*NE* 1106a14) and "the virtues are *hexeis*" (*NE* 1143b24–25) in order to convey that moral action arises from a character which is "something permanent and not easily subject to change" (*NE* 1100b3–4). The appeal to *hexis* works from the psychological premise that the virtues are acquired by exposure to and practice of virtuous conduct; performing virtuous acts so as to ingrain a course of action constitutes the basis for a correct moral education (*NE* 1103a1–33, 1103b1–3). For evolving the right moral habits, and becoming good thereby, is a matter of molding one's *hexeis*, since "*hexeis* develop from corresponding activities" and "the quality of our *hexeis* depends upon what we do" (*NE* 1103b22–24). The regular practice of morally significant actions forms our ethical dispositions, with the eventual consequence that sufficient training yields "a firm and unchangeable character" (*NE* 1105a35–b1). In turn, a man whose *hexeis* are inclined towards good conduct will choose what is virtuous constantly and consistently, as a matter of policy (*NE* 1105b5–9). The *hexeis* he has developed will, in effect, prohibit him from the commission of uncharacteristic acts on purpose. This last qualification is important. Aristotle would not deny, of course, that a good man might occasionally commit an evil action. There are various sorts of reasons why he might do so, such as ignorance, faulty cognition, and the like. Aristotle's point, instead, is that the bad act committed by the good man can never have been done deliberately, that is, on the basis of choice in conformity with his *hexis*. Only the individual whose moral habits are ill-formed truly does evil, since his bad acts issue from the application of his vicious character to the process of ethical decision-making. Virtue and vice cannot be ascribed in isolation from the qualities of the people who perform moral action.

Since we speak of action as natural (i.e., as having an internal moving principle) to man when it is chosen, and since choice as Aristotle conceives it occurs in accordance with a fixed character, it is impossible for anyone to be regarded as the source of his own actions if he has not developed moral *hexeis*. Indeed, it is for precisely this reason that we would not consider a child to be the author of his own conduct: he has not acquired the moral traits necessary for the possession of a stable conception of the good in accordance with which he might choose. Aristotle indirectly confirms the importance of *hexis* for the "naturalness" of human action in the *Nicomachean Ethics* when he distinguishes works of virtue from works of art. The product of artifice, he says, stands on its own, separate and distinct from its creator, since its creator is external to it (*NE* 1105a26–29). Nothing is detracted from the artifice if it were to have been produced by accident or at the prompting of some person other than its creator (*NE* 1105a21–25). By contrast, virtuous actions are not truly virtuous "if they themselves are of a certain sort, but only if the agent also is in a certain state of mind when he does them: he must act with knowledge; he must choose the act and choose it for its own sake; and the act must spring from fixed and permanent dispositions" (*NE* 1105a31–35). In the case of art, the most that will be required is knowledge, whereas knowledge is really quite secondary for moral conduct. The basis for this view is evidently Aristotle's claim that virtue and vice, as matters of volition, spring from within the individual; even though they are not inborn, they are natural to man in a way that artifice is not.

Aristotle's position on moral character in the *Ethics* suggests that the equation (embraced by Keyt and apparently accepted by his critics) of his distinction between "nature" and "artifice" with a distinction between "nature" and "nurture" is fundamentally misguided. Stated simply, those (voluntary) actions which are most natural to man arise as the result of moral dispositions acquired and fashioned through training and practical activity. These actions are natural because their source ultimately lies within man: Aristotle takes the view that, in the case of voluntary and chosen action, we are responsible for them, at least in part because we are responsible for the formation of our characters.[20] An "unnatural" human action, one that is involuntary and (for the most part) unchosen, is precisely that action for which we cannot be held responsible. It is "artificial" to the agent exactly because it is

not matter of choice; it is external to his control and volition. The distinction which Aristotle seeks to uphold is not a simple-minded one which differentiates "inborn" from "acquired" qualities or traits. Instead, it is a far more sophisticated division between those actions which spring from the characteristic state of mind (whatever their source) of the agent and those movements which are accidental or externally caused. No one can be said to be author of his own actions if such a state of mind is not present; they are not his own acts, that is, natural to him.

IV

None of this yet explains, however, what Aristotle means by the claims that man is a political animal and that the polis exists by nature. We may arrive at a satisfactory answer to our dilemma by examining his account of the connection between ethics and politics.[21] Aristotle asserts near the beginning of the *Nicomachean Ethics* that the "master science of the good"—the field of study which ultimately governs the quest for the good life—is the "science of politics" (*NE* 1094a30). He reasons that

> Inasmuch as the other sciences are employed by this one, and as it moreover lays down laws as to what people shall do and what they shall refrain from doing, the end of this science must include the ends of all the others. Therefore, the good of man must be the end of the science of politics. For even though the good is the same for the individual and the polis, still the good of the polis is manifestly a greater and more perfect good, both to attain and to preserve. (*NE* 1094b4–7)

Since voluntary human action aims at the good, or occurs in relation to a conception of the good, the realm of politics and the study of political science are necessary for the realization of the good, according to Aristotle.[22] For the good is more fully realized in a communal than in a solitary setting; and political science yields the knowledge which makes it possible to distinguish true from apparent goods.

Why should this be so? Recall some of the basic principles of Aristotle's moral psychology. For a man's actions to lie (in Aristotle's sense) "inside himself," he must have acquired a firm and stable character, which differs from both *dynamis* and speculative knowledge. Moreover, for that character to be truly good (that is, for it to direct him to honorable rather than merely pleasant deeds), the individual must be taught to perform actions in the way that a good and honorable man would do them. It remains, however, to establish the best means to "secure that the character shall have from the outset an affinity for virtue, loving what is noble and hating what is base" (*NE* 1179b30–31). Assuring constancy of character is a twofold affair: "in order to be good, a man must have been properly educated and trained, and must subsequently continue to follow virtuous ways of living and to do nothing base whether voluntarily or involuntarily" (*NE* 1190a15–17). Not only is early instruction absolutely necessary to inculcate character, but there must be some means of regulating later action in order to test and reinforce that character (*NE* 1180a1–3).[23] What is needed, in other words, is an all-encompassing system of fashioning and measuring the moral dispositions of individuals.

Aristotle is not convinced that private individuals are up to this task. Although he admits that the training of *hexeis* often falls to those persons most closely associated with a given individual—parents and other relatives, teachers, and friends—he regards this as an unsatisfactory arrangement. The major reason for the failure of private training is its unreliability. He points out that "it is difficult to obtain a right education from youth up," because "to live temperately and hardily is not pleasant to most men, especially when young" (*NE* 1179b31–32, 33–34). Aristotle believes that nothing short of compulsion or fear can steer most men away from the pleasant and towards the honorable (*NE* 11779b4–20). But compulsion does not pertain to the private realm: "Paternal authority does not have the power to compel obedience, nor indeed generally speaking has the authority of any individual" (*NE* 1180a19–21). Of course, good men should

try to incite and inspire others to virtue, but Aristotle is clearly pessimistic about the chances of success (*NE* 1180a30–33).

Aristotle's preferred method—indeed, he seems to think the only secure and reliable method—of shaping the character required by individuals to act virtuously entails a communal program of education. In the *Nicomachean Ethics*, he appeals to the instructional and disciplinary power of the law: the law, unlike mere domestic authority, measures human beings according to wise principles which are supported by the force of compulsion. Consequently, law constitutes a surer and more permanent standard for the inculcation of moral character in youth and the encouragement of virtuous action in maturity:

> The nurture and exercises of the young should be regulated by law, since temperance and hardiness will not be painful when they have become habitual. . . . We shall need laws to regulate the discipline of adults as well, and in fact the whole of the people generally; for the many are more amenable to compulsion and punishment than to reason and moral ideals. . . . [Goodness] will be secured if men's lives are regulated by a certain intelligence and by a right system invested with adequate sanctions. (*NE* 1179b33–35, 1180a3–5, 18–19)

The advantages afforded by the law are evident. Not only does law carry with it the weight of community authority (and, by inference, coercive power), but it is impersonal and thus not susceptible to the resentment that attaches to individuals (*NE* 1180a22–24). The law's commands have precisely the practical aim (of condoning and forbidding specific conduct consistent with virtue) that constitutes the end of moral science.

Consequently, no lawgiver or statesman can expect to be successful or effective in performing his tasks if he has not first mastered political or legislative science. It is this science which teaches how to translate the good for man into a set of public standards and to apply these standards to the shaping of character. The inculcation of human goodness cannot be achieved except by those qualified in the science of legislation. This is true not only for the polis, but even for *ad hoc* educators who seek to teach virtue to family and friends: they, too, must have grasped the principles of political science if they are to be successful (*NE* 1180a33–34). The legislator and his science are not external to the process by which human beings achieve the good—his is not the work of artifice—but instead law-giving and statesmanship are integral to the process of character formation which is necessary for persons to act voluntarily, that is, as rational beings who are self-propelled in virtue of their practical intellects. The polis makes possible the fashioning of a stable moral identity on the basis of which human beings choose. If the polis is governed by one of the well-ordered constitutions, then its citizens will receive an education in genuine goodness, since the laws of such a polis will promote (indeed, demand) virtuous conduct. If the polis has a perverted constitution, then its laws will permit citizens to indulge their pleasures in the name of rectitude, and the good which appears to citizens in accordance with their characters will be merely apparent. Thus, a well-ordered constitution is an absolute prerequisite for widespread virtue; and inasmuch as Aristotle regards virtue to be necessary for human happiness, it matters a great deal about the kind of constitutional arrangements through which the polis is organized. The quality of the good which human beings seek, and hence the very possibility of happiness, rest on the type of polis in which one is raised and lives.

The importance of political life to the moral and psychological well-being of mankind is emphasized not only in Book 10 of the *Nicomachean Ethics*, but also in his discussion of the ideal polis in the seventh and eighth books of the *Politics*. The central principle of Aristotle's optimal constitutional system is that "the good is identical for the individual and the community; and it is the good which the legislator ought to instill in the minds of his citizens" (Pol. 1333b36–38). This is to be done by reference to endowment, habituation and reason. By definition, little can be done to alter factors such as intellect and spirit. Rather, by discussing en-

dowment, Aristotle merely seeks to explain why some races (specifically, the Greeks) are especially well-suited to create virtuous constitutional systems: "The sort of people which a legislator can easily guide into the way of goodness is one with a natural endowment that combines intelligence and spirit" (*Pol.* 1327b36–38). At best, birth is a necessary condition for the realization of an ideal polis, but it can never be sufficient. Likewise, the teaching of rational understanding constitutes a higher function of the human soul than does the inculcation of dispositions to act; yet the exercise of reason only becomes possible once a firmly rooted character has been established. As Aristotle states, "The exercise of rational principle and thought is the ultimate end of man's nature. It is therefore with a view to the exercise of these faculties that we should regulate from the outset the birth and the training of the *hexeis* of our citizens" (*Pol.* 1334b15–17). In other words, the best constitution shapes the character of citizens in such a fashion that its practical inculcation will ultimately lead to their recognition of the rational foundations which underlie virtue and knowledge. Reason is the goal, but it may only be achieved once those persons with the most appropriate endowments have been drilled in the proper activities which will instill in them virtuous traits of character.

As a consequence, Aristotle places a premium on the training of character as the cornerstone of the ideal city. Consistent with the *Ethics*, he thinks that birth ordinarily generates only basic capacities and that most people are not able to learn the practical skills of virtuous conduct solely or initially by grasping their basis in reason. Consequently, the primary concern of the legislator is to oversee the education of all those qualified for citizenship (which excludes, of course, the vast body of those people occupied with "banausic" arts requiring physical labor, as well as women, slaves and foreigners). By introducing a rigorous system of public education, which he starts to detail in the incomplete eighth book of the *Politics*, Aristotle believes that it will be possible for men to be "trained and habituated" in the dispositions required "before they can practice virtue," which is the appropriate common end of the polis (*Pol.* 1337a19–23). Thus, just as in the *Ethics*, the practice of good acts (now through a systematic, publicly mandated curriculum) yields the civic character required for the implementation of an optimal constitutional system whose perpetuation is assured by the reinforcement of one's firm moral dispositions through the regular opportunities afforded to practice civic virtue.

V

We are now in a position to appreciate the consistency and coherence of Aristotle's political naturalism. For Aristotle to claim that man is a political animal is to say that human choice in accordance with the good (and perhaps more importantly, that good which is truly so and thus productive of happiness) requires political life under law and the skills of statesmen steeped in legislative science. Since voluntary choice constitutes the "Moving principle" of distinctively human action (*praxis*), arising from the exercise of the practical intellect in accordance with rational desire, the moral education provided uniquely within political associations is natural to mankind, in the sense that it is internal to the unique way in which human beings move in respect of place. Aristotle's psychology seems to lead him to adopt the view that human beings cannot be fully moral (hence, rationally self-moving and responsible) agents except when they are raised and ruled within the confines of the polis and its laws. If we draw this conclusion, it may become possible to extend our understanding of other important claims made by Aristotle in the *Politics*, such as his view of so-called natural slavery (natural slaves being those creatures who are not self-moving in the special human sense precisely insofar as they cannot live as political animals).[24]

In turn, since the very purpose of the polis is to provide those laws necessary for citizens to live well (i.e., in accordance with the good), the polis itself exists by nature. Certainly, this claim is true in the "teleological" sense of "natural existence" identified by Fred Miller, namely, that "all things which come to be for the sake of something" (for example, bird's nests and spider's webs) are said by Aristotle to "exist by nature."[25] The polis, likewise, because it exists for the sake of the kind of "natural" self-movement distinctive of human beings through their choice, can be said to exist by nature in this sense. Aristotle indeed corroborates this at *Politics* 1281a3–4 when he remarks that "political society exists for the sake of noble actions, not merely for common life." Political life is something without which human beings would not be able to live according to their natures; hence, the polis is natural.

But it may additionally be possible to argue for a stronger reading of the natural existence of the polis, in precisely the sense (ridiculed by Keyt) of what Miller terms the "internal-cause interpretation," according to which the polis itself is a natural entity that possesses its own source of movement.[26] The objection to interpreting the polis in this way stems from Aristotle's repeated references to the craft or artisan functions of the lawgiver and the statesman.[27] The polis allegedly cannot develop according to its own, inner principle when it is in effect fabricated (like an artifact) by an "external" force. But this is to misconceive the roles of legislator and statesman. The polis develops "naturally" because citizens individually and jointly seek the good life and the happiness which is conferred thereby. Aristotle insists that neither geographic proximity nor intermarriage nor commercial exchange are sufficient to explain the polis (*Pol.* 1280a34–1280b4, 1280b1435). Rather, he asserts, "Men, even when they do not require one another's help, desire to live together. . . . The good life then is the chief aim, both of individuals and of the collective whole" (*Pol.* 1278b20–22, 23–24). Legislators and statesmen simply facilitate the process by which this aim—which human beings recognize to be a proper object of desire and choice—is realized for citizens.

The lawgiver and the statesman are thereby comparable to the farmer who plants seeds and nourishes them with water and fertilizer until they achieve their full growth. The farmer clearly does not create the seed nor is the mature plant that arises from his tending in any sense artificial. Rather, the farmer provides conditions conducive to the best and most effective growth of the seeds he plants. Likewise, the lawgiver plants the constitution and laws in a manner gauged to promote the well-being and moral goodness of citizens; the statesman applies and extends the laws so as to realize the polis' ultimate end. Their activities do not make the polis an artificial object, since the polis would arise in any case just because it is an object of human desire and choice. The legislator and the statesman simply apply their practical wisdom to the aim of ensuring that the polis which emerges will be successful in achieving that goal of goodness which is the "moving principle" of the members of all political associations.[28]

Notes

1. The history of the doctrine, and the "unity" of the Aristotelian tradition, are matters that have not received adequate treatment from intellectual historians. For an interesting attempt to analyze the dimensions of recent "neo-Aristotelianism," including the use of political naturalism, see John R. Wallach, "Contemporary Aristotelianism," *Political Theory* 20 (November 1992): 613–41. Acceptance of Aristotle's formulation of the naturalist thesis is ordinarily taken as a token of medieval Aristotelianism. See J. H. Burns, ed., *The Cambridge History of Medieval Political Thought* (Cambridge: Cambridge University Press, 1988), pp. 360–61 and 527–31. Even such unlikely modern figures as John Locke, *Two Treatises of Civil Government*, II. 15 show a fondness for the teaching that "we are naturally induced to seek Communion and Fellowship with others."

2. Among those who raise this problem (if only to resolve it) are: Richard G. Mulgan, "Aristotle's Doctrine that Man is a Political Animal," *Hermes* 102 (1974): 438–45; Wolfgang Kullmann, "Der Mensch als politisches Lebenwesen bei Aristoteles," *Hermes* 108 (1980): 419–43 (translated in *A Companion to Aristotle's Politics*, ed. D. Keyt and F. D. Miller, Jr. [Oxford: Blackwell, 1991], pp. 94–117); Wayne Ambler, "Aristotle's Understanding of the Naturalness of the City," *Review of Politics* 47 (1985), 163–85; Pierre Pellegrin, "Naturalité, excellence, diversité: Politique et biologie chez Aristote," in *Aristoteles'*

"Politik," ed. G. Patzig (Göttingen: Vanderhoeck and Reprecht, 1990), pp. 124–51; John M. Cooper, "Political Animals and Civic Friendship," in Patzig, *Aristoteles' "Politik,"* pp. 220–41.

3. David Keyt, "Three Basic Theorems in Aristotle's *Politics*," in Keyt and Miller, *A Companion to Aristotle's Politics*, p. 118; this is a revised version of an essay entitled "Three Fundamental Theorems in Aristotle's *Politics*," originally published in *Phronesis* 32 (1987): 54–79.

4. Keyt, "Three Basic Theorems in Aristotle's *Politics*," p. 140.

5. Keyt singles out A. C. Bradley and Ernest Barker as proponents of this view (*ibid.*, pp. 199–20). But the tradition for this reading is very old; Thomas Aquinas in his commentary on the *Politics* already adopted essentially the same interpretation. See Burns, *Cambridge History of Medieval Political Thought*, p. 527.

6. I do not mean to argue that this position is philosophically indefensible in any version whatsoever; on a weaker, less-teleological view of history, such as is adopted by Cicero and some medieval Ciceronians, artifice and nature can be seen as compatible and mutually reinforcing. See Neal Wood, *Cicero's Social and Political Thought: An Introduction* (Berkeley: University of California Press, 1988), pp. 70–104; also Cary J. Nederman, "Nature, Sin and the Origins of Society: The Ciceronian Tradition in Medieval Political Thought," *Journal of the History of Ideas* 49 (1988): 3–26 and "The Union of Wisdom and Eloquence Before the Renaissance: The Ciceronian Orator in Medieval Thought," *Journal of Medieval History* 18 (1992): 75–95.

7. In addition to what follows, there are several unpublished replies to Keyt of which I am aware, including those by Ronald Polansky, "What Aristotle Means by the Naturalness of the Polis" and David Depew, "Does Aristotle's Philosophy Rest on a Contradiction?" (read to the Society for Ancient Greek Philosophy in 1989) and "Political Animals."

8. Fred D. Miller, Jr., "Aristotle's Political Naturalism," *Apieron* 22 (December 1989): 216.

9. Joseph Chan, "Does Aristotle's Political Theory Rest on a 'Blunder'?" *History of Political Thought* 13 (Summer 1992): 201.

10. *Ibid.*, pp. 196–97.

11. *Ibid.*, p. 196.

12. Miller, "Aristotle's Political Naturalism," p. 211.

13. Translations are based on the Greek text of Aristotle found in the Loeb Classical Library editions; translations are my own, unless otherwise noted, although I have consulted standard English renderings.

14. A detailed examination of *orexis* has been given by Henry S. Richardson, "Desire and Good in *De Anima,*" in *Essays on Aristotle's* De anima, ed. M. C. Nussbaum and A. O. Rorty (Oxford: Clarencleon Press, 1992), pp. 381–99.

15. See David J. Furley, "Self-Movers," in *Essays on Aristotle's Ethics*, ed. A. O. Rorty (Berkeley: University of California Press, 1980), pp. 55–67.

16. The nature of thought in relation to the other elements of *nous* is analyzed by Charles H. Kahn, "Aristotle on Thinking," in Nussbaum and Rorty, *Essays on Aristotle's* De anima, pp. 359–79.

17. *Akrasia* (usually translated as "incontinence" or "weakness of will") counts as a special case for Aristotle, which he takes up at length in the seventh book of *NE*. For an appraisal of the problems posed by the weak-willed character (whom, in any case, Aristotle regards as a relatively rare aberration), see David Wiggins, "Weakness of Will, Commensurability and the Objects of Deliberation and Desire" and Amélie O. Rorty, "Akrasia and Pleasure: *Nicomachean Ethics* Book 7," in Rorty, *Essays on Aristotle's Ethics*, pp. 241–84.

18. On the whole issue of *hekon* in Aristotelian ethics, see Frederick A. Siegler, "Voluntary and Involuntary," *The Monist* 52 (April 1968): 268–87.

19. This demonstrates the importance of the practical intellect: for the moving principle to be in the agent, the agent must know accurately the particular circumstances of his action (*NE* 1111a23–24). In some sense, the agent must know what he is doing. If I sleep with a married woman not knowing that she is married, I may (depending on whether I regret my conduct) be excused and my conduct regarded as involuntarily. However, if I sleep with a married woman knowing that she is married, but not knowing that adultery is wrong, my action is voluntary and hence worthy of blame, according to *NE* 1110b18–35.

20. See William Bondeson, "Aristotle on Responsibility for One's Character and the Possibility of Character Change," *Phronesis* 19 (1974): 59–65.

21. This subject has been a topic of intense discussion in its own right, which cannot directly concern us here. See Sanford Cashdollar, "Aristotle's Politics of Morals," *Journal of the History of Philosophy* 11 (April 1973): 145–60; Richard Bodéüs, *Le philosophie et la cité: 'Recherches sur les rapports entre morale et politique dans la pensée d'Aristote* (Paris: Les Belles Lettres, 1982) (English trans.: *The Political Dimensions of Aristotle's Ethics,* trans. J. Garrett [Albany: SUNY Press, 1993]); P. A. VanderWendt, "The Political Intention of Aristotle's Moral Philosophy," *Ancient Philosophy* 5 (Spring 1985): 77–89; Aristide Tessitore, "Making the City Safe for Philosophy," *American Political Science Review* 84 (1991):1251–62.

22. On the Aristotelian conception of the good, and its relation to political life, see Richard Kraut, *Aristotle on the Human Good* (Princeton: Princeton University Press, 1989), esp. chaps. 1 and 6; Terence Irwin, "The Good of Political Activity," in Patzig, *Aristoteles' "Politik,"* pp. 73–98; and Marcia L. Homiak, "Politics as Soul-Making: Aristotle on Becoming Good," *Philosophia* 20 July 1990): 167–93.

23. The need for reinforcement presumably exists on the grounds that dispositions not occasionally acted upon may eventually atrophy.

24. Aristotle in effect states this position at *Pol.* 1280a31–34: "The polis was formed not only for the sake of life but for the sake of the good life (for otherwise a collection of slaves or lower animals could form a polis, yet this could not be, since slaves and animals have no share in happiness or a life according to choice)." I cannot defend my interpretation of natural slavery here, but it would certainly diverge from the range of views currently on display. Two differing understandings of the doctrine may be found in Nicholas D. Smith, "Aristotle's Theory of Natural Slavery," in Keyt and Miller, *A Companion to Aristotle's Politics,* pp. 142–55 and Wayne Ambler, "Aristotle on Nature and Politics: The Case of Slavery," *Political Theory* 15 (August 1987): 390–410.

25. Miller, "Aristotle's Political Naturalism," p. 211.

26. *Ibid.,* pp. 207–208.

27. These texts are collated by Keyt, "Three Basic Theorems in Aristotle's *Politics,*" p. 119 and notes 3–5.

28. An earlier version of this paper was presented to the 1993 Annual Meeting of the Southern Political Science Association, Savannah, Georgia. The author wishes to thank Timothy

Duvall, Arlen Feldwick, George Klosko and an anonymous reader for this *Review* for their suggestions and aid. Many ideas incorporated into this paper were first visited in discussions with Bonnie Kent which occurred nearly twenty years ago.

11
An Ancient Framework for a New—and Old— Feminism

Mary P. Nichols

There seems to be little in ancient thought to warm the feminist's heart. There were, of course, the heroines of Aristophanes' plays who assert the rights of women, but Aristophanes after all wrote comedies, and so he seems to treat the heroism of women as a joke. Although there is much that is serious in his comedies, which, Saxonhouse argues, force us to think about the place of public and private in a community, "the political women of ancient comedy are not about to step off the stage and march over to the assemblies where they will make demands of their political leaders."[1] Plato, for his part, did include the equality of sexes in the city described in the *Republic*, but he may not have considered that city politically viable;[2] at any rate, he deviated from the *Republic*'s views on women in later works such as the *Laws*.[3] And Aristotle, from the point of view of feminists, is the worst ancient of them all, appearing to believe that women should be ruled by their husbands because they do not possess the full human capacity to reason (*Politics* [*Pol.*] 1254b12–14, 1260a9, 12–14).[4] It is no wonder that Susan M. Okin, in her *Women in Western Political Thought*, treats Aristotle as the archvillain of the history of philosophy, who "relegates woman to an altogether subhuman position."[5]

Modern scholars typically interpret Aristotle as a defender of the social status quo who elaborated views of nature that support the institutions of his own society, with its hierarchy of masters and slaves, men and women.[6] In examining Aristotle's view of women, however, we should remember that Aristotle is addressing a society that by and large believed in the inferiority of women to men and restricted women's sphere to the home. Aristotle proceeds cautiously in contradicting the major prejudices of his day, but he does contradict them.[7] He is an ironist who makes his points in complex and subtle ways.[8] Unaware of the ironical dimensions of Aristotle's text, and certain that Aristotle is merely the product of his age, many scholars do not heed carefully enough what Aristotle says.[9] Although he says, for example, that the relation of male to female is by nature that of ruler to ruled (1254b14), he also says that nature does not *often* fulfill its intention (*Pol.* 1254b27–33; 1255b1–3). Is nature's intention fulfilled in the case of men and women any more than in other cases Aristotle mentions? By means of these references to nature's failures, Aristotle suggests that nature does not often provide the human materials necessary for male dominance of women to be just. What, then, does he think is nature's intention?[10] Could we have read society's prejudices back into nature?

Aristotle distances himself from simple patriarchy even further when he maintains that men should rule women politically rather than despotically (*Pol.* 1259b1). He defines political rule, which he says is appropriate to free and equal beings, as a sharing in ruling and being ruled (e.g., *Pol.* 1259b4–6; 1261b2–5; 1279a8–10).[11] Freedom and equality for Aristotle result not in abstract individualism but rather in sharing. Although he does not conceive of men and women taking turns ruling in the family as citizens might in elected office (*Pol.* 1259b2), by defining the relation between men and women as political, Aristotle insists that women have a part in ruling. He could not be more specific about their part presumably because it depends on their particular capacities and circumstances. Since political rule is appropriate to men and women, if men do not share rule with women, they are acting despotically and unjustly. Aristotle even attributes the despotic rule of men over women to barbarians (*Pol.* 1252b4–5).

That Aristotle questions male dominance is confirmed by the ironic parallel he draws between male rule and the preeminence of Amasis's footpan (*Pol.* 1259b8–9). Aristotle here refers to the story of Amasis, a slave who became king of Egypt. Once king, he melted down his golden footpan and made it into a god for his subjects to worship. Amasis used the transformation of his footpan as a symbol for his own rise to kingship.[12] What has no special preeminence by nature comes to assume authority—a footpan becomes a god, a slave becomes a king, and, if we may follow through on Aristotle's analogy, a man becomes ruler over his wife. Male insistence on authority over women, Aristotle suggests, resembles Amasis's claim that his footpan is a god.

There is nevertheless a parallel between Amasis's re-forming his golden footpan and humanity's political development. According to Aristotle, political communities that have come into being for the sake of life can, through human choice and activity, continue to exist for the sake of the good life (*Pol.* 12521b29–30). Statesmen in their cities give new forms and ends to what has already come into being, providing opportunities for human beings to exercise their natural capacities as rational and political animals (see, e.g., *Pol.* 1253a30 and 1289a1–7). Amasis too transforms the given, endowing it with new form and purpose. But in this case, the new form and the new end hinder, rather than encourage, rational, political activity. By referring to Amasis, Aristotle points to the danger that politics—and the male's relation to the female—could change into despotism.

Moreover, by referring to the story of Amasis in the context of male-female relations, Aristotle recalls the account that he himself presents in his biological writings of the male's relation to the female. Aristotle explains that in the generation of offspring the male provides the form, the female the matter, for only the male provides sufficient heat for the transfer of form to matter (*Generation of Animals* [*GA*] 765b10 ff.; 766a30 ff.). In melting down his footpan and giving it new form, Amasis is like the male who begets—both generate heat to give form to

matter. There is something questionable, even false, however, about Amasis's re-formation of the footpan, for he induces his people to worship as a god what is only an image of a god. It has more in common with despotic rule than with political rule. Perhaps some male foundings and refoundings come, as does Amasis's, at the cost of their community's worshiping false gods of various kinds.

At the same time, however, the story of Amasis indicates the importance of the material to the form. It is presumably the golden character of the footpan that permits Amasis to transform it into a god. This is what justifies Aristotle's speaking of the material as a cause. As Daryl Tress explains in the case of the generation of life, the capacity to generate is "a potential that can only be exercised in concert with specialized material which itself has a potential capacity to be formed as a particular kind of creature."[13] Male and female contributions are potentials that together actualize to produce offspring.[14] Even in Aristotle's biological account of the male's contribution of form and the female's of matter, then, there is necessarily a shared or "political" rule (*arche*). This is why Aristotle explains both male and female as "ruling principles" or "origins" (*archai*) of generation although they make different contributions (*GA* 716a14). If their contributions were identical, there would be no reason one alone could not be the cause of generation. The difference between the sexes therefore points to their lack of self-sufficiency.[15]

Similarly, political rule is based not only on the equality that makes shared rule just, it is based as well on the differences among members of the community. The political community needs different kinds of contributions, and no one individual can adequately provide them (*Pol.* 1279b41–81a8). Rule therefore must be shared. As Aristotle said in response to the communism of the *Republic*, political communities are composed not merely of many human beings, but of human beings differing in kind (*Pol.* 1261a22–24). Again, difference indicates our lack of self-sufficiency, our need for others. Just as equality does not result for Aristotle in a generic universalism, neither does difference result in separate, unconnected entities. Both equality and difference lead to sharing. While equality makes sharing just, difference makes it advantageous.

An Aristotelian approach to feminism is based on this formulation about equality and difference. Aristotle distinguishes maleness and femaleness as something more fundamental than accidental attributes like eye or hair color (GA 716b3–13).[16] Aristotle's implicit objection to Socrates' treatment of gender in the *Republic* as being as inessential as baldness (see *Rep.* 453c–456b, esp. 454c) is also an objection to the generic individuals of liberal theory. The difference between male and female, however, is not a bar to common humanity. Men and women possess the same essence; they belong to the same species (*Metaphysics* 1058a30–32, b29–31; GA 730b34–35). Maleness and femaleness, then, seem to be some middle ground for Aristotle between essence and accident; thus he can say that "things are alive that have in them *a share* of the male and the female" (*GA* 732a12; emphasis mine). However Aristotle conceived the differences between male and female, individual men and women share male and female traits, just as they share in ruling and being ruled, if in different degrees and forms. As we shall see, Aristotle attributes a kind of courage (*andreia*), a virtue that could be translated as "manliness," to women.[17] And when he speaks of the human ability to share suffering and sorrow, as we shall see, he refers not to men and women but to "manly types" (*androdeis*) and to "womanly types [*gynaia*] and men who are like them" (*Nicomachean Ethics* [*NE*] 1171b7–11). Aristotle gives us several hints as to how he views those differences between male and female that men and women share.

In writing about the different activities of men and women in the family, for example, Aristotle states that while the man acquires, the woman preserves (*Pol.* 1277b25). To acquire is to make something alien one's own or to expand one's own to embrace something new. It requires moving beyond what is given, perhaps initiating change or generating new forms. To preserve, on the other hand, is to protect the given, to nurture. Aris-

totle observes in the *History of Animals* that whereas the male is more spirited than the female, the female is more thoughtful concerning the nurture of offspring (*History of Animals* [*HA*] 608a35–b2). Similarly, Aristotle says in the *Politics* that there is a courage of rule and a courage of service (*Pol.* 1260a14–24). The different kinds of courage, however, do not necessarily mean that men should have the courage to rule women and women the courage to serve men. The Greek word for "rule" also means "to initiate" or "to begin." To begin is to rule, because the beginning provides the direction and the purpose. The man's courage lies in his going beyond what he possesses or what he is, even in risking it, for the sake of bringing something new into being. A woman's courage, on the other hand, is manifest in serving, whether another human being or some undertaking or project. Such courage lies in protecting and nurturing, even at the risk of oneself and one's new visions or goals that seem to hold more promise. The courage of service is no less a part of human flourishing than the courage of rule. Both are necessary, and each has a share in the other.

Some virtues, Aristotle says, are appropriate to women, others to men. He illustrates this by quoting a line by the Greek hero, Ajax, from Sophocles' play of that name. Ajax says to his wife Tecmessa that "silence gives grace to women" (*Ajax* 293). But the context of the play gives Aristotle's quotation of Ajax an ironic cast. Ajax, driven mad by one of the gods, mistakes a herd of beasts for his enemies and slaughters them. When Tecmessa questions him, he dismisses her with the words that Aristotle quotes. Had Ajax stopped to give an account of himself to his wife, he would have at least delayed the senseless slaughter that later shamed him into taking his life. It is a madman, Aristotle implies by quoting Ajax, who dismisses the speech of a woman. When Aristotle notes that a woman's deliberative element is without authority (*Pol.* 1260a12–14), perhaps he is ironically pointing to the fact that her deliberative element is without authority among men, just as Tecmessa's held no authority for Ajax when he silenced her and foreclosed the possibility of deliberation.[18]

In what way, then, does the story of Ajax and Tecmessa illustrate the different virtues appropriate to men and women? When Tecmessa senses that her husband is going to kill himself, she tries to prevent his suicide, but she arrives too late. Through her attempt to prevent his death and her grief when she finds his body, she affirms the goodness of life. Ajax's suicide, on the other hand, reveals that for him life is not worth living at all costs. He can distance himself from his own life and reject it if he does not perceive it as good. These differences complement each other. The woman encourages a respect for one's own, a respect for the given, a respect necessary for acquiring and ruling, insofar as it must build on what is given. She teaches that life itself is good, not merely its activities. The man, on the other hand, encourages going beyond the given, bringing something new into being, something necessary if nurturing is to be successful, since nurturing fosters change when it fosters growth. Men teach the extent to which the goodness of life is due to human activity. Each needs the other and must share in the other in order to be happy. The interaction between the two sustains life.

In the *Nicomachean Ethics* Aristotle discusses the relations between friends in good fortune and in bad. Because "it is noble to do good deeds" and "ignoble to be eager to receive benefits" (*NE* 1171a17, 25–26), the noble friend who prospers wants to share his good fortune with his friend, while he hesitates to share his suffering, for he wants to give pleasure and not pain. He understands that it is nobler to give than to receive. His friend, on the other hand, if he also understands this, shrinks from receiving benefits from his friend but is eager to help when his friend is in need (*NE* 1171a34–b28). As long as friends strive for noble self-sufficiency, their noble desires lead to an impasse between them. Yet Aristotle finds a difference between how "manly types" and "womanly types and men who are like them" act in such situations. In particular, the former will not allow others to grieve with them, for they are not given to grief themselves, while the latter like others to grieve with them and love them as friends. They are therefore able to share

their suffering with their friends; presumably they would also be able to share their friends' good fortune with them. Although women and men who are like them avoid the impasse between friends that he describes, Aristotle says merely that "one should imitate the better in all things" (*NE* 1171b7–13). Imitation is a way to change, to improve; since we are educable in this way human nature is open to change. One can learn from the other and acquire what is characteristic of the other.[19]

Aristotle does not indicate who is the better, possibly because he does not want to criticize unduly the striving for nobility that is a sign of human independence and freedom. While manly types manifest a noble independence, they must also learn to share sorrow. The sign of freedom may not be a willingness simply to give but also to allow one's friend to give. It may be nobler to give than to receive, but it is more difficult to receive than to give, at least for the noblest. Thus, only if we understand and appreciate nobility can our receiving manifest our freedom. It is in this way that the male and the female are the sources or principles (*archai*) not only of generation but also of a reconciliation between independence and need, equality and difference, individualism and community.

Notes

1. Arlene W. Saxonhouse. 1996. "Political Woman: Ancient Comedies and Modern Dilemmas." In Pamela Grande Jensen, ed., *Finding a New Feminism: Rethinking the Woman Question for Liberal Democracy.* Lanham, MD: Rowman and Littlefiend, p. 167.

2. Leo Strauss. 1964. *The City and Man.* Chicago: Rand McNally. E.g., 116–17, 125–127.

3. See the discussion by Okin in Susan Moller Okin. 1979. *Women in Western Political Thought.* Princeton, NJ: Princeton University Press, pp. 44–50.

4. Unless otherwise noted, citations in parentheses are to Aristotle, *The Politics,* trans. by Carnes Lord. 1985. Chicago: University of Chicago Press.

5. Okin, *Women,* p. 235.

6. See, for example, Okin, *Women,* pp. 73–76.

7. Addressing the position that Aristotle is merely a defender of the opinions and institutions of his day, Stephen G. Salkever points out that "according to Aristotle, most of the so-called cities have no definite goal whatever, while the most coherent of them (especially Sparta) make the typically Greek error of thinking that the purpose of political life is ruling over outsiders, or war, rather than political development. Strictly speaking, there are no real polities either in Greece, or elsewhere. This is hardly theodicy, or ideological mirroring of Greek opinion." Stephen G. Salkever, *Finding the Mean: Theory and Practice in Aristotelian Political Philosophy* (Princeton, NJ: Princeton University Press, 1990), 181.

8. Salkever gives an example of Aristotle's "rhetorical evocation of the 'barbarians' as a device for loosing the Greeks from their prejudices." Salkever, *Finding the Mean*, 184 n.50; and Saxonhouse, *Women*, 72–76.

9. For fuller discussion of Aristotle's treatment of women in the *Politics*, see Mary P. Nichols. 1992. *Citizens and Statesmen: A study of Aristotle's Politics*. Savage, MD: Rowman and Littlefield, pp. 28–35; Saxonhouse, *Women*, pp. 68–91; Judith A. Swanson. 1992. *The Public and the Private in Aristotle's Political Philosophy*. Ithaca, New York: Cornell University Press; and Harold L. Levy. 1990. "Does Aristotle Exclude Women from Politics?" *Review of Politics* 52 (3), 397–416.

10. See also Saxonhouse, *Women*, p. 71.

11. See the discussion of political rule in Nichols, *Citizens and Statesemen*, 5–6 and 29–30.

12. Herodotus, 2.171.

13. Daryl Tress. 1992. "The Metaphysical Science of Aristotle's Generation of Animals and Its Feminist Critics." *Review of Metaphysics* 46 (2), pp. 321 m. 25. In her excellent article, Tress emphasizes the importance of matter, the contribution of the female, as a cause of generation. "Aristotle's feminist critics," she argues, "fail to appreciate the importance of the material cause in Aristotle's metaphysics" and "[read] 'matter' in a post-seventeenth-century sense."

14. Similarly, Aristotle considers movers and moved as potentials whose "actualization coincides." *Physics* 202a19. See Tress, "Metaphysical Science," 332–33; and Jonathan Lear. 1988. *Aristotle: The Desire to Understand*. Cambridge: Cambridge University Press, pp.59–65.

15. Tress, "Metaphysical Science," p. 324.

16. Tress, "Metaphysical Science," p. 315 n. 15. That something more fundamental Aristotle calls an *arche*, a source, origin, or ruling principle. A.L. Peck explains this usage in the *Generation of Animals* as a "a source or starting point upon which other things depend." See the preface to *Generation of Animals*, trans. A.L. Peck. 1979. Cambridge: Harvard University Press, xiv. Peck sees "little difficulty about this term."

17. Even in the animal kingdom, Aristotle found some females sharing male traits. In the *History of Animals*, he notes that female bears and leopards are more "manly" or "courageous" than the males of their species. Aristotle, *History of Animals*, 680a21–b18.

18. For a discussion of Aristole's reference to woman's deliberative element, see Saxonhouse, *Women*, 74 and Nichols, *Citizens and Statesmen*, 31–32.

19. Consider in this context the educative role performed by the Argentinean Mothers of the Plaza de Mayo, as described by Jean Bethke Elshtain in "The Mothers of the Disappeared: An Encounter with Antigone's Daughters" in Pamela Grande Jensen, ed. *Finding a New Feminisnm: Rethinking the Woman Question for Liberal Democracy*. Lanham, MD: Rowman and Littlefield, pp. 129–148. Living under a tyrannical regime that "disappeared" their children and having at first "lived an atomized life of grief," they "found strength and political identity by deprivatizing their mourning" (p. 140). According to Elshtain, the mothers' language of human rights "gave political form and shape to their disobedience, linking them to an international network of associations." But such rights talk, she argues, did not become a "vehicle for entitlements"; underlying their appeal to universal human rights was a more ancient maternal language of "mourning and loss" (p. 141).

Adapted from: Mary P. Nichols, "Toward a Feminism for Liberal Democracy." In *Finding a New Feminism: Rethinking the Woman Question for Liberal Democracy*, pp. 176–181, 188–192. Edited by Pamela Grande Jensen. Copyright © 1996 by Rowman and Littlefield. Reprinted by permission of Rowman and Littlefield Publishers. ✦

Part II

The Age of Empire—Civil and Religious

The Hellenistic Age

With the Macedonian conquest of the Greek peninsula by Aristotle's pupil, Alexander the Great, the political and philosophic landscape of the Western world began to change dramatically. The politics of the city-state gave way to the requirements of empire. The unity of philosophic and political discourse exemplified by the teachings of Plato and Aristotle became fragmented and gave rise to divergent schools.

In the era of the city-state, political participation (at least by those granted rights of citizenship) was utilized to forge an intimate connection between the good of the individual and the good of the *polis*. Service to community insured individual security and continuance of the lifestyle that distinguished one's own community from that of the "barbarian." Alexander's reign brought an end to the small coherent community and replaced it with the empire, a far-ranging confluence of distinct races, ethnicities, customs, traditions, and languages under the command of a single ruler. Nevertheless, because members of the Greek aristocracy served as local administrators for Macedonian rulers,

Greek culture continued to spread throughout the empire as far West as Italy and as far East as India during the period from 320 to 30 B.C.E. known as the Hellenistic Age. Macedonian hegemony came to an end, however, with the weakening of internal political cohesion and the rise of rival empire builders, most notably the powerful Roman state. Soon Rome would stretch her borders beyond Egypt, and Macedonian power would end.

As political rule became more global, political thought became more diverse and fractured. Portions of Socratic, Platonic, and Aristotelian thought were separated from the rest of the teachings of the masters and used to construct new edifices. At least three major schools of political thought claiming, in part, the mantle of the ancients characterized the Hellenistic world: Epicureanism, skepticism, and stoicism.

Epicureanism

Followers of Epicurus (341–270 B.C.E.) believed that physical events were random and lacked inherent meaning. Nature, therefore, could not serve as a model for human behavior or ethics as Aristotle held. Instead, the most humans could expect was to live a pleasant and peaceful life by enjoying its pleasures. For those who were capable, intellectual pleasures were preferred but only because they allowed for greater self-sufficiency and less often produced conflict over the scarce material resources that were the source of pleasure for the masses. To avoid such conflict, the Epicureans preached discipline over the appetites. This was an individualistic philosophy that did not produce profound political theory. As James Wiser describes their worldview:

> Society is not natural. Rather, it is the result of a contract among individuals who agree to set up certain rules of conduct so that each person may be insured against the infliction of pain and the intrusion of worldly forces. Justice therefore is simply a matter of convention, and the laws are to obeyed only inasmuch as they allow for public order and personal security. Consequently, in all instances political values were reduced to a calculation which began with the primacy of personal, individual needs.[1]

Skepticism

While the term skepticism connotes a distrustful attitude toward knowledge that characterizes some thinkers in almost any era, the skeptic school is thought to have arisen with the teachings of Pyrrho in the 4th century B.C.E. Pyrrho attacked theories that sought to demonstrate an objective reality independent of sense perception. The senses only reveal what appears to be and cannot be used to guarantee existence of the object itself. While we cannot know for sure the reality of objects in the world, we can make valid statements regarding our own perceptions. This means we must suspend judgment about things as they are in the world. This suspension applies equally to morality: we cannot say what is good or bad outside of one's own perceptions on these matters. Later academic skeptics like Arcesilaus, who headed the Greek Academy in about 265 B.C.E., and Carnaedes, one of three Greek philosophers chosen to represent Athens in Rome in 155 B.C.E., sought to bring greater subtlety and power to skepticism by establishing principles meant to distinguish more and less reliable sensations and judgments in the evaluation of arguments.[2] Still, suspension of judgment and trusting only one's own perceptions do not provide a solid foundation for the political community. Instead, they give rise to self-reliance and produce a politics of self-interest that is characterized by the arguments toward justice that Cicero attributes to Carnaedes in his *Republic*, as we shall see.

Stoicism

The stoic school is generally traced to the ideas of Zeno (c. 336 B.C.E.), Chrysippus (c. 279–206 B.C.E.) and Panaetius (c. 180 B.C.E.). Zeno is credited with tying human existence to an ordered state of nature. Chrysippus gave voice to the notion of equality and universal law. Panaetius brought the stoic ideal to Rome and developed more systematically its central ideas: man is a rational creature at home in a knowable, rational universe; since all men share a measure of reason, they are equal; and duty as virtue allows man to rise above pain and despair to achieve self-sufficiency.[3] In such a universe, law, both natural and human, orders our existence. The stoic ideal informed the politics of Rome at home before its decline by attention to the careful balancing of the interests of equal individuals under law through the use of a mixed constitution. Stoicism was expanded by thinkers like Polybius (c. 204 B.C.E.), Seneca (3 B.C.E.–65 C.E.), Epictetus (c. 60 C.E.) and Cicero, whose work we will encounter below.

One important, if as yet opaque, element of their thought is the notion of *natural law*, one which is universal and knowable by all men and which serves as a guide for human law. In the face of this idea, it became increasingly difficult for Rome to maintain two types of law—*jus civile*, the code for Roman citizens, and *jus gentium*, law for foreign subjects. The philosophic tension caused by the existence of different applications of law was eventually relieved in 212 C.E. when the Edict of Caracalla abolished the dual code. The concept of natural law would find religious foundation as the empire of Rome yielded to the empire of Christendom.

The Beginning of the Christian Era

Through concerted expansion, the Roman Empire eventually came to dominate Europe, North Africa, and the Middle East. Though it created unique institutions, the political thought embraced by the leaders of Rome was largely derivative of the Greek sources upon which it relied. Cicero's adaptation of Platonic philosophy thus remained a primary influence for anyone seeking to understand the forms of government, the nature of justice, or the role of the political leader. Nonetheless, in the 1st century C.E., the culture of the classical world was soon challenged by another force—Christianity.

When Christianity first spread throughout the Empire, the challenges it presented were less political than spiritual or intellectual. Though Jesus and his followers had initially been seen as a group of rebels, the practical views of Christian teaching actually counseled obedience. Rather than a political theory, Christianity offered people a new interpretation of their place in the cosmos; it told a new story—one of creation, fall, pilgrimage, and salvation. It provided people with a strong sense of community, and encouraged a new morality of asceticism and fairness. Within a century or two, the old Roman ways with their pagan culture began to give way. The Emperor Diocletian, who ruled from 284 to 305, sought to revive ancestral religion through a forceful persecution of Christians, but by 313, Constantine decreed that religious tolerance would be the official policy of the Empire. Constantine later presided over the Council at Nicea that set forth the church's basic creed, and in 380, the Emperor Theodosius formally declared Christianity to be the official religion of the Empire. Not long after, though, the empire split into Western and Eastern portions.

The political uncertainties of the late empire were matched by theological disputes among believers. "Side by side with state persecution and the criticisms of non-Christians, the church found itself beset by heresies within the fold resulting from the tendency of pagan converts to try Christian ideas on for size and to tailor them to fit pagan assumptions, whether religious or philosophical."[4] St. Augustine, whose thought we will encounter later, thus plays an important role not only in clarifying Christian beliefs, but also in making the transition from classical to Christian culture. Classically educated himself, he soon turned his intellectual prowess to elaborating and defending Christian theology. Inspired by Neoplatonist thinkers such as Plotinus (c. 205–270), Augustine and the other leaders of the early Church laid the groundwork for Christian political thought just as Rome fell and the Middle Ages began.

The Middle Ages

The medieval period in Europe lasted from the 5th to the 15th century. Later Europeans called it the Dark Ages, but it was actually a time of substantial innovation. During this period, thinkers found their way from a classical to a Christian understanding of the world. Indeed, as the historian B.B. Price has noted, the period we know as the Middle Ages "can be characterized as one with a unifying and forceful set of Christian ideas about moral and intellectual conduct"—the very areas "which were considered to be the foundation of all human activity."[5]

The reliance of Christian thinkers upon the philosophy of Plato soon gave way to an interest in Aristotle, whose works on logic were translated into Latin by Boethius (c. 480–526), a Roman scholar and statesman. Although predominantly a Platonist, Boethius became very influential for medieval Christian thinkers not only through his translations and interpretations of Aristotle, but primarily through his own work, the *Consolation of Philosophy*. Like many other medieval theorists, Augustine and Boethius wrote in Latin and dealt with the philosophical aspects of theology—for example, the problem of evil, the nature of the divine, and the relationship between the secular and the spiritual. Throughout the Middle Ages, then, scholars made repeated efforts to reconcile pagan philosophy with Christian theology.

Beginning in the 12th century, just as the church was becoming more centralized, European intellectual life became localized within the universities of such cities as Bologna and Paris. The tradition of thought present in those institutions has been labeled scholasticism. Long associated with minute quarrels over equally minute matters, scholasticism was in fact a systematic way of thinking rooted in Aristotelian logic. "Scholasticism was essentially a movement which attempted a methodological and philosophical demonstration of Christian theology as inherently rational and consistent."[6] Through lectures, discussions, and formal disputations, the scholastics commented on classic texts in order to reconcile the insights of Christianity with those of pagan philosophy. Peter Abelard's *Sic et Non* (1120) was a prime example of the scholastic effort to criticize and reconcile conflicting authorities on theological and philosophical matters. By the 13th century, increased contact with the Arab world brought a wide range of Aristotle's works to the attention of Latin scholars, and thus, the scholastics' efforts culminated in the systematic theology of Thomas Aquinas.

With outlooks shaped by a combination of classical philosophy, Christian theology, and feudal realities, "political theorists in the Middle Ages were usually most concerned to adopt the lessons of ancient writings to more immediate circumstances and problems."[7] As such, it is difficult to summarize the character of their thinking about political life. Nonetheless, one can identify a number of themes that appear fairly frequently in medieval political thought.

First, there is the theme of social order. Emerging from a society shaped by a complex network of loyalties, it is not surprising that medieval thought often concerned the peculiar roles given to particular classes or estates. Analogous to the "chain of being" in the physical world, medieval thinkers spent time contemplating the hierarchies embedded within the social and political world. Each level owed obedience to those above and some measure of care for those below, but more importantly, each level had its precise role to play—as can be seen in the metaphor of the "body politic" employed by John of Salisbury (1120–1180) and others.

Thinking about order quite easily led to thinking about the guarantors of that order, namely monarchs. Again, following the idea of the chain of being, kingship was presumed to be the natural, even divine, form of rule. Only a monarch could bring about the sort of peace one could expect in this world. Even so, feudal monarchy was essentially a limited monarchy, for "the king, as suzerain, is bound to each of his vassals by a feudal contract specifying reciprocal rights and duties."[8] Political protection and land were thus exchanged for loyalty and military service. From the time of John of Salisbury on, medieval thinkers frequently drew a distinction between a king and a tyrant, between one whose rule was based on law and one who ruled by force. Only the latter could be disobeyed, even murdered, with relative impunity.

With law as the central criterion for determining whether a ruler was a king or a tyrant, political thought in the Middle Ages naturally turned its attention to the concept of law. The *Summa Theologica* of Aquinas, as we will note later, presents an extensive discussion in which four specific categories of law are described and analyzed. Rooting political power in law, and limiting its exercise by law, was also the task of such theorists as Dante Alighieri (1263–1321) and Marsiglio of Padua (c. 1275–1342). Beyond this focus on law, medieval political thinkers also focused on understanding the character of the ruler—how the prince should be educated, what personal qualities and skills the prince should possess, what orientation the prince should take toward his counselors and his people. This "mirror for princes" genre became fairly standard fare for writers throughout the latter Middle Ages. We will encounter two contrasting uses of it later though, in the works of both Christine de Pizan and Niccolò Machiavelli.

Finally, it is important to note the importance of the concept of authority to political thinking in the Middle Ages. Despite an increasingly centralized Catholic Church and a Europe mostly run by the Holy Roman Empire, authority was for the most part divided.

Church and state, religious and secular authorities, coexisted and competed with one another amid the overlapping networks of obligations that marked feudal relations. While many theologians initially believed that the state could be used to achieve religious aims—some earthly incarnation of divine peace and justice, for example—others began to acknowledge the possibility of conflict between church and state. With the Investiture Controversy sparked by a conflict between Pope Gregory VII and Emperor Henry IV in 1075, medieval thinkers developed the doctrine of the "two swords." Both spiritual and temporal power was granted by God to the pope, who then delegated the latter to the emperor; however, any emperor who failed to rule wisely or justly could not only be excommunicated by the pope, he could even be deposed.

As the Middle Ages progressed, then, Western politics was shaped by this tension between temporal and spiritual authority, *regnum* and *sacerdotum*. Eventually, on the cusp of the modern era, *regnum* gained a measure of independence. This development was liberating in two senses: "For in freeing the offices of the Church from the direct control of princes, the secular rulers had also succeeded in liberating themselves from immediate responsibility for religious and ecclesiastical affairs."[9]

Notes

1. James L. Wiser, *Political Philosophy: History of the Search for Order* (Englewood Cliffs, NJ: Prentice Hall, 1983), 71.

2. A. A. Long, *Hellenistic Philosophy: Stoics, Epicureans, Sceptics* (London: Duckworth, 1974), 75–106.

3. Lee Cameron McDonald, *Western Political Theory: Part I, Ancient and Medieval* (New York: Harcourt, Brace, Jovanovich, 1968), 73.

4. Marcia L. Colish, *Medieval Foundations of the Western Intellectual Tradition 400–1400* (New Haven, CT: Yale University Press, 1997), 6.

5. B.B. Price, *Medieval Thought: An Introduction* (Oxford: Blackwell, 1992.) vii.

6. Price, *Medieval Thought,* 120.

7. Cary J. Nederman and Kate Langdon Forhan, *Readings in Medieval Political Theory, 1100–1400* (Indianapolis: Hackett, 2000), 3.

8. Colish, *Medieval Foundations of the Western Intellectual Tradition,* 345.

9. Nederman and Forhan, *Readings in Medieval Political Theory,* 16.

References

Colish, Marcia L. 1997. *Medieval Foundations of the Western Intellectual Tradition 400–1400.* New Haven, CT: Yale University Press.

Klosko, George. 1994. *History of Political Theory: An Introduction, Volume 1: Ancient and Medieval Political Theory.* Fort Worth, TX: Harcourt Brace.

Long, A. A. 1974. *Hellenistic Philosophy: Stoics, Epicureans, Sceptics.* London: Duckworth.

McDonald, Lee Cameron. 1968. *Western Political Theory: Part I, Ancient and Medieval.* New York: Harcourt, Brace, Jovanovich.

Nederman, Cary J., and Kate Langdon Forhan. 2000. *Readings in Medieval Political Theory 1100–1400.* Indianapolis: Hackett.

ORB: The Online Reference Book for Medieval Studies http://orb.rhodes.edu/.

Price, B.B. 1992. *Medieval Thought: An Introduction.* Oxford: Blackwell.

Wiser, James L. 1983. *Political Philosophy: History of the Search for Order.* Englewood Cliffs, N.J.: Prentice Hall. ✦

Marcus Tullius Cicero

For Plato, the philosopher would be content to live in the shadows of the city contemplating the forms and taking part in government only as a last resort. For Cicero, philosophy is not complete without practical application in the service of the state; and, besides, the philosopher owes the city wisdom in return for the opportunities the city has provided:

> For the conditions upon which our country bore and reared us were not that she should expect no maintenance at our hands, or that she should merely serve our convenience and supply us with a safe retreat for our idleness and an undisturbed place for our repose. Her terms were rather that she herself should claim for her own advantage the greater share of our most important powers of mind, ability and wisdom; and that, in return, she should give us for our private needs only so much as she might find superfluous. (*On the Commonwealth*, Bk. I, Sec. IV)

For Plato, the city exists for the sake of the philosopher, so to speak; for Cicero, the philosopher must serve the city.

The role of philosophy is not the only point about which Plato and Cicero disagree. For Plato, for example, virtue in the form of moderation, courage, and wisdom is largely a mater of private taste and demeanor. Even justice is a matter of "minding one's own business." While Cicero does not completely abandon the notion of virtue as a private good, it is a much more public affair characterized by participation, service, and duty to the state. Plato extolled the man of thought; Cicero, the man of action. Yet, these differences should not overshadow important similarities between the two thinkers. Two of Cicero's most important works, *On the Commonwealth* (*De Republica*) and the *Laws* (*De Legibus*), were patterned directly on Plato's works, down to the dialogue form and many of the dramatic devices employed. Cicero studied the classic philosophers in Athens and had a deep appreciation for their work, upon which he saw himself building. Correctly, Cicero is not portrayed by historians as a major philosopher in his own right. Rather, he was a statesman who appreciated the contributions philosophy—especially those elements of Hellenistic thought from which he borrowed—could make to governing. Yet, as an advocate of the mixed constitution and for a type of statesmanship that blends philosophic wisdom and duty, his legacy is secure.

Cicero was born in 106 B.C.E. in the town of Arpinum between Rome and Naples. He was tutored in the classics and prepared for a career in law, serving as an advocate of the court while he was in his 20s. He left Rome to study philosophy and rhetoric abroad in Athens and Rhodes. Upon his return, he married well and began his political career, first with minor offices but quickly moving up to the senate. His most famous official act was to sponsor a virtual state of martial law in response to an insurrectional conspiracy led by Catiline, a popular plebeian leader. When Catiline's followers were summarily executed, Cicero was hailed by some and reviled by others for violating the rights of Roman citizens. His political fortunes declined shortly after this episode although he continued to serve as court advocate. Beginning in about 55 B.C.E., Cicero set about writing his philosophical tracts. This coincided with a period of disillusionment and depression brought about in part by personal tragedy, the death of his daughter, and in part by his concern over the decaying state of Roman politics characterized by treachery and personal ambition.[1] Allying with Caesar in the latter's dispute with Pompey, Cicero himself became the target of attack in the wake of Caesar's death. He was put to death by the followers of Antonius, Caesar's murderer, in 43 B.C.E., his head and hand placed on a post for public display in the Forum. Cicero's major regret was that Rome had lost sight of the greatness of her institutions and the soundness of her mixed constitution.

On the Commonwealth

Much like Plato's *Republic*, Cicero's *Commonwealth* is in the form of a dialogue among friends who meet over the course of a holiday to discuss politics and justice. Several of the characters in the drama are sometimes referred to as the Scipionic Circle, after Publius Cornelius Scipio Africanus Minor, a distinguished Roman general and statesman with an appreciation for Greek philosophy. Scipio gathered with notable thinkers of his day, including the poet Terence and the historian Polybius, to discuss literature, philosophy, and politics. Others in the dialogue include Gaius Lelius, a statesman and veteran of the Third Punic War; Lucius Furius Philus, consul and orator; the legal scholar Manius Manilius; and Quintus Aelius Tubero, tribune of the plebs and student of Panaetius, the Stoic philosopher.

The text of this work is extremely fragmented, with large sections missing. The most authoritative manuscript is the Vatican Palimpsest consisting of 150 leaves probably dating to the 4th or 5th century C.E. and overwritten by commentators, including Vatican librarian Angelo Mai and Saint Augustine, whose efforts preserved some of its basic sense if not the exact wording. Following the work of the translators, George Sabine and Stanley Barney Smith, material in normal type represents Cicero's own words; italics represent the work of various translators and commentators to recover the sense of the original missing work; and brackets are used to complete meaning or add clarity where the original is missing.

Five excerpts are presented. In the first, Cicero confronts the question of the philosopher's duty to the city. This initial discussion presents a sharp contrast to the views of both Plato and the Epicureans, whose position

Cicero attacked. Yet, because the matter is taken up at later points in the work, this statement should be considered provisional.

The second excerpt finds the interlocutors discussing the nature of the commonwealth. Of particular importance is Scipio's definition of the commonwealth as "a people's affair," a definition upon which Saint Augustine would build generations later. Humans are depicted as naturally social beings, making the political society an organic entity and not simply a contrivance. Scipio voices support for the mixed regime, one which blends the interests of all parties and achieves harmony, much as did the early institutions of Rome. Yet, as Scipio indicates, while this may be the best *practicable* regime, it may not be the best from an ideal perspective.

The third and fourth excerpts present Cicero's classic statement on natural law. In the third reading Philus echoes the views of the skeptic Carnaedes in attacking the natural foundation of law, asserting that laws are relative conventions serving the interests of those who rule. In the fourth excerpt, Laelius defends justice as a universal attribute informed by reason and accessible to all rational creatures. This formulation would be fortified by Medieval Christian scholars. The importance of this perspective in providing a potential basis for challenging the decisions of actual political leaders and the wars they fight in the name of the state cannot be overemphasized.

Finally, in excerpt five, the interlocutors discuss the characteristics of the good ruler. Here Scipio downplays the role of abstract knowledge as an end in itself and asserts the practical nature of the ruler's art, including the importance of glory as a motivating force. One should contrast these characteristics with those advanced by Plato when he presents his first choice for political rule.

Commentaries

We have seen how important was the mixed regime to Cicero, particularly as it applied to Rome in an earlier time when her institutions were healthy. Neal Wood discusses the specific features of Cicero's ideal mixed regime and finds that the harmony and balance of interests he sought came at the expense of the lower classes. Cicero, Wood reveals, extolled a form of government that guaranteed aristocratic rule despite a philosophic veneer of equality. Walter Nicgorski, by contrast, warns us not to focus on the particular elements of Cicero's mixed regime. He asserts that Cicero's position on mixed rule was not only ambiguous but took a back seat to his interest in the elements of statesmanship required to harmonize the political community despite its institutional or class structure. Cicero's great contribution, says Nicgorki, was to render the details of the best regime less important than the qualities of statesmanship.

Note

1. Lee Cameron McDonald, *Western Political Theory: Part I, Ancient and Medieval* (New York: Harcourt, Brace, Jovanovich, 1968), 83.

Web Sources

http://www.utm.edu/research/iep/c/cicero.htm
Internet Encyclopedia of Philosophy: Cicero. Accessible source for an overview of Cicero's life, times, and works.

http://www.utexas.edu/depts/classics/documents/Cic.html
The Cicero Homepage. Offers links to original texts, biographical and bibliographic material as well as images of the Roman orator and statesman.

http://members.tripod.com/~batesca/natlaw.htm
The Natural Law/Natural Right Page. Explores Cicero's work in relation to the development of natural law doctrine prior to and after the work of the Roman theorist.

Class Activities and Discussion Questions

1. Discuss the role played by the concept of duty in Cicero's political thought.

2. For Cicero, what is the nature of the best regime? How do his ideas on the best regime compare with those of other theorists?

3. Compare and contrast the views of Cicero and other theorists on the causes and consequences of tyranny. What, if anything, should people do if a ruler becomes tyrannical?

4. In one fashion or another, Plato, Aristotle and Cicero all speak of "virtue." What does each of them mean by the concept? Who has better understanding of it? Why?

5. Compare and contrast the idea of natural law with conventional law. Is the concept of unjust law of relevance in today's society?

6. How would you use Cicero's notion of natural law in registering a complaint against what you believe is an "unjust war"?

Further Reading

George, Robert P. 1992. *Natural Law Theory: Contemporary Essays.* New York: Oxford University Press. Review of the idea of natural law espoused in the writings of Cicero and its continuing relevance.

Habict, Christian. 1990. *Cicero, the Politician.* Baltimore, MD: Johns Hopkins Press. Reviews the public life and ideas of Cicero.

Holton, James E. 1987. "Marcus Tullius Cicero." In *History of Political Philosophy*, Third Edition. Leo Strauss and Joseph Cropsey, eds. Chicago: University of Chicago Press. Primarily an exploration of the *Commonwealth* and *Laws* from a Straussian perspective.

Pangle, Thomas L. and Peter J. Ahrensdorf. 1999. *Justice Among Nations: On the Moral Basis of Power.* Lawrence, KS: University of Kansas Press. Cicero's ideas are explored within the context of forging a moral basis for relations among nations.

Sabine, George and Stanley Barney Smith. 1981. "Introduction." In *On the Commonwealth.* Indianapolis: Bobbs-Merrill. This excellent introduction to the definitive text discusses Hellenistic influences upon Cicero as well as his influence on others.

Starr, Chester G. 1971. *The Ancient Romans.* New York: Oxford University Press. A good overview of Roman life, culture, and politics.

Tacitus, Cornelius. [1997]. *The Histories.* Translated by W. H. Fyfe with an introduction by D. S. Levene. New York: Oxford University Press. The famous historian traces the events of 69 C.E. when the Roman Empire was torn apart by conflicts that presaged its continuing decline. ✦

12
Excerpts from *On the Commonwealth*

Marcus Tullius Cicero

Book I

I. [Without a sense of public duty, Manius Curius, Gaius Fabricius, and Tiberius Coruncanius] would not have freed [Italy] from the attack [of Pyrrhus.[1]] Without this feeling Gaius Duelius, Aulus Atilius, and Lucius Metellus would not have banished the fear of Carthage.[2] Without it, the two Scipios would not have quenched with their own blood the rising fire of the Second Punic War; nor, when fresh fuel had been added to the flames, would Quintus Maximus have stayed its violence, nor Marcus Marcellus have stamped it out. Without it, Publius Scipio Africanus would not have snatched the brand of war from before the city's gates, and hurled it within the enemy's walls.

Now take the case of Marcus Cato,[3] who serves as the model of an active and virtuous life for all of us whose interests, like his, are political. Unknown and without an inherited tradition of public service, he might surely have enjoyed himself in quiet repose at Tusculum, a healthful and convenient place. But he was a fool, as your philosophical friends believe,[4] because he chose to ride the storms and tempests of public life until advanced age, rather than to live a life of ease amid the calm and restfulness of Tusculum.

I pass by countless men who have individually contributed their share to the safety of the state; and others, whose lives are too nearly[5] contemporaneous, I do not mention for fear that someone may complain that he or one of his family has been slighted. I content myself with this one assertion: The need and love for noble actions, which nature has given to men that they may defend the common weal, are so compelling that they have overcome all the enticements of pleasure and of ease.

II. But merely to possess virtue as you would an art is not enough, unless you apply it. For an art, even if unused, can still be retained in the form of theoretical knowledge, but virtue depends entirely upon its use. And its highest use is the government of a state and the actual performance, not the mere discussion, of those deeds which your philosophers rehearse in their secluded retreats. For, even when philosophers express just and sincere sentiments about these matters, they merely state in words what has been actually realized and put into effect by those statesmen who have given states their laws. From whom, we may ask, comes our sense of moral obligation and our reverence toward the gods? From whom do we derive that law which is common to all peoples, or that to which we apply the term civil?[6] From whom comes our feeling for justice, for honor, for fair dealing? Whence our sense of shame, our self-control, our avoidance of what is base, our craving for a name and reputation? From whom is derived our courage in the face of toil and danger? Assuredly, from those statesmen who have developed these qualities by education and have embedded some of them in custom and have enforced others by the provisions of their laws. Xenocrates,[7] one of the most distinguished of philosophers, was once asked, so the story goes, what his pupils gained from his instruction. He replied that of their own free will they would perform the duties they would be forced to do by the laws.

A statesman, therefore, who by his authority and by the punishments which his laws impose obliges all men to adopt that course which only a mere handful can be persuaded to adopt by the arguments of philosophers, should be held in even greater esteem than the teachers who make these virtues the subject of their discussions. For what argument of your philosophers is so carefully wrought out that it should be preferred to a state firmly established under public law and custom? Cities "mighty and imperial," to quote Ennius,[8] ought, in my opinion, to be considered superior to hamlets and outposts. Similarly, those who by their advice and influence rule such cities must, I feel, be assigned a far higher place in respect to wisdom itself than those who take no part in any public duty. Since, therefore, we are powerfully moved to increase the resources of the human race, since we desire through our planning and toiling to render life safer and richer, and since we are spurred on to this agreeable task by nature herself, let us persevere in that course which has ever been chosen by the best of men, and let us not heed the trumpets which sound retreat and would recall even the soldiers who have already advanced.

III. Against these conclusions, clear and indisputable though they be, those who take the opposite view urge, first, the toil which must be borne if the commonwealth is to be defended. But in truth this is a light burden for an alert and active man, and one which he must scorn to consider, not only when engaged in affairs of such pith and moment, but even when engaged in unimportant interests or duties or mere matters of business. Moreover, these objectors cite the grave risks involved in a political career. They hold up the base fear of death before the eyes of brave men, although brave men usually find it more pitiable to be worn out by the natural infirmities of age than to have the opportunity of surrendering for their country, as they prefer, the life which in any case they must surrender to nature.

And yet it is upon this point that our critics think themselves resourceful and adroit, for they string together the misfortunes of distinguished men and the injuries that have been heaped upon them by ungrateful states. Of these they enumerate the well-known instances to be found in Greek history: the victorious Miltiades,[9] conqueror of the Persians, with the wounds not yet healed which he received facing the enemy in a glorious victory, yielding up in an Athenian prison the life which he had saved from the weapons of the enemy; and Themistocles,[10] banished from the country which he had set free, fleeing in terror, not to the harbors of Greece

which he had saved, but to the harbors of Persia which he had humbled!

Nor is it only among the Athenians that we find instances of fickleness and inhumanity towards distinguished citizens,[11] but though these traits of character had their origin at Athens and were frequently manifested there, they have infected, so the critics say, our own stable commonwealth. They cite, for example, the exile of Camillus,[12] or the downfall of Ahala,[13] or the unpopularity of Nasica,[14] or the banishment of Laenas,[15] or the conviction of Opimius,[16] or the exile of Metellus,[17] or the disaster of Gaius Marius and the murder of the chief men of the state,[18] or the ruin of many of them which followed shortly after.[19] Already, indeed, they add my name to the list; and, I suppose, it is because they think that my foresight and the dangers I incurred have kept for them their life of ease, that they bewail my misfortunes more deeply and more affectionately. And yet, when those very men cross the sea for purposes of education and travel, I can hardly say why [they are surprised that I brave the greatest perils for my country's sake. . . .]

(The last leaf of the third quaternion is missing)

IV. . . . [S]ince, at the close of my consulate, I had taken an oath before the people that [the state] was safe [because of my efforts]—and the Roman people put the same value upon my services[20]—I might easily have set off [the pride of this achievement] against the anxiety and suffering which all my injuries entailed. And yet my misfortunes carried more of honor than of hardship, less of humiliation than of fame. For the happiness which I reaped because good men regretted my exile was greater than my sorrow because bad men rejoiced at it. But even if the result had been different from what I have said, how could I have complained? In view of my great deeds, nothing indeed had happened to me which I had not foreseen, nothing worse than I had anticipated. I was free, to a greater extent than other men, to derive enjoyment from a quiet life because of the delightful variety of the studies which I had followed from boyhood; and if some unusual disaster were to visit all men, I should have suffered no exceptional fate beyond that which came to all. Nevertheless, that I might save my fellow citizens, I was not the man to shrink from facing the wildest storms—nay, even the thunderbolts themselves—or to hesitate in securing at my own peril a peace which all might share. For the conditions upon which our country bore and reared us were not that she should expect no maintenance at our hands, or that she should merely serve our convenience and supply us with a safe retreat for our idleness and an undisturbed place for our repose. Her terms were rather that she herself should claim for her own advantage the greater share of our most important powers of mind, ability, and wisdom; and that, in return, she should give us for our private needs only so much as she might find superfluous.

V. To the evasions by which men would fain excuse themselves from public duties in order to enjoy retirement more comfortably, we must by no means give ear. It is asserted, for example, that political life attracts in general utterly worthless men, to be compared with whom is disgusting and to contend with whom, especially when the mob is aroused, is deplorable and dangerous. Therefore, it is said, a wise men does not grasp the reins of government since he cannot restrain the mad lunges of the untamed rabble, nor does a free man strive against vile and savage opponents, or submit to the lash of insult, or suffer injuries that a wise man should not bear. As if a good and brave and fair-minded man could find a more honorable reason for entering public life than the desire to avoid the rule of scoundrels or to prevent them from rending the commonwealth, while he himself, though eager to aid, looks impotently on![21]

VI. And who, moreover, can approve of the exception that they make when they say that the wise man will not assume a role in political life except under the compulsion of circumstances? As if a greater compulsion could come to any man than came to me! And yet what could I have done in that emergency had I not then been consul? And how could I have been consul if I had not from early youth persisted in that course of life by which, though born in the equestrian order, I finally attained the highest position in the state?[22] You cannot aid the state at a moment's notice or when you wish, although she is faced with great danger, unless you are in a position to do so. It has always seemed especially strange to me in the discourses of the learned, that men who admit that they cannot pilot the ship when the sea is calm, because they have never learned how nor troubled about such knowledge, nevertheless declare that they will take the helm when the waves are highest.[23] Your philosophers, indeed, assert openly—and they even pride themselves not a little upon it—that they have not learned, nor do they teach, anything about the principles either of founding or preserving the state. According to them, such knowledge should be the province, not of scholars and philosophers, but of practical politicians. How, then, is it becoming for them to proffer their aid to the commonwealth only under the pressure of necessity, although they do not know how to perform the far easier task of ruling the state when no emergency confronts it? But even if we grant that the philosopher of his own accord does not generally condescend to deal with affairs of state, though he does not refuse the duty if circumstances make it necessary, nevertheless I should feel that the philosopher ought by no means to neglect the science of politics, since he should be forearmed with all the weapons which he may sometime be obliged to use.

VII. I have spoken thus at length because in the present work I have projected and undertaken a discussion of the commonwealth. That it might not be in vain, I had first to banish the reluctance that is felt toward entering politics. But if there still are any who are influenced by the prestige of philosophers, I would have them give earnest attention for a moment to thinkers whose influence and renown have great weight with the learned. These thinkers, even though not actually holding public office, have investigated and treated many problems of the state; and I accordingly feel that they have performed some public function. I notice that nearly all of those whom the Greeks called the Seven Sages[24] passed their lives in the midst of public affairs. There is, indeed, nothing in which human excellence can more nearly approximate the divine than in the foundation of new states or in the preservation of states already founded.

VIII. Now it has been my good fortune not only to have performed some memorable service in the course of my public career, but also to have attained a degree of skill in the exposition of political theory.[25] Both as a result of experience, therefore, and also because of my zeal for learning and teaching, I became an authority on matters touching the state. The scholars of the past, on the other hand, had been either acute in argument but without any record of achievement, or they had been commendable for their conduct of public office but without skill in presenting their arguments.

In fact, however, I am not obliged to develop a theory of politics, which is either new or of my own devising. On the contrary, I have only to reconstruct from memory a discussion held by the wisest and most famous men of a certain period of our history, and repeated to us by Publius Rutilius Rufus,[26] while we were once spending several days together in Smyrna during your youth. In this discussion practically nothing, I believe, has been omitted which might concern in any important way the theory of politics. . . .

LAELIUS: . . . Although the studies pursued by the Greeks give you such pleasure, there are others, of a more liberal character and of a more extended application, which we can bring to bear either upon our private business or even upon the commonwealth itself. In truth, the value of these more speculative studies that you are interested in—if, indeed, they have any value at all—lies in the fact that they sharpen somewhat the minds of the young, and, as we may say, stimulate them to a greater facility in learning more important matters.

XIX. TUBERO: I agree with you, Laelius, but I ask you: What are the subjects that you deem more important?

LAELIUS: I shall express my views—rest assured of that and perhaps I shall earn your contempt by doing so. For while you are asking Scipio questions about what happens in the heavens, I feel that these practical matters immediately before our eyes are a more worthy object of investigation. Why, indeed, does Tubero, the grandson of Lucius Paulus and the nephew of Africanus here, a member of Rome's most distinguished family and a citizen of so glorious a commonwealth—why, I repeat, does such a man inquire how two suns could have appeared in the sky, and does not rather ask why there are two senates in one commonwealth and now practically two peoples? For, as you see, the death of Tiberius Gracchus and, even before then, his entire conception of the tribunate divided one people into two factions.[27] The critics and slanderous foes of Scipio continue the disturbance which Publius Crassus and Appius Claudius began; and now, even though these two are dead, they still control that second party in the senate which Metellus and Publius Mucius induce to desert Scipio and his followers. The allies and the Latin League have been aroused. Our treaties have been broken. Every day the agrarian commission is treacherously devising some new and revolutionary measure. Loyal citizens are harassed. And yet, the factious element does not allow our friend Scipio to relieve this dangerous condition of the state, although he is the only one who can do so. Therefore, my young friends, if you will take my advice, do not trouble yourselves about this second sun. For it is a matter of indifference whether its existence be impossible or whether we suppose that it really exists, as appears to be the case, so long as it does not cause us trouble. Either we can know nothing of such matters or even if we fully understand them, we cannot thereby become either better or happier men. On the other hand, we can bring about the union of senate and people, and our condition is serious unless we do so. We know that such union does not exist now, and we see that, if it were realized, we should live both better and happier lives.

XX. MUCIUS: What studies do you think we should master, Laelius, in order to bring about the end that you desire?

LAELIUS: Assuredly, such subjects as would make us useful to the state. For service to the state I consider the most glorious function of the wise and the chief mark or duty of the good. Accordingly, in order that we may spend this holiday in discussions conducive to the highest interests of our country, let us request Scipio to explain what he regards as the best form of constitution for the state. After that we shall conduct other inquiries. When these are answered, I hope that we shall immediately arrive at the discussion of our present political situation, and explain the meaning of the perils that are now upon us.

XXI. When Philus and Manilius and Mummius had expressed their hearty approval. . . .

(The fourth leaf of the eighth quaternion is missing)

There is no pattern to which we prefer to compare the commonwealth.[28]

Therefore, if you please, bring down your conversation from the remote heavens to these nearer topics of earth.[29]

LAELIUS: . . . I desired [you to discuss this question], not only because it was fitting that the state should be discussed preferably by its leading citizen, but also because I recalled that in your frequent discussions with Panaetius and Polybius[30]—the two Greeks most thoroughly versed in political science—you assembled much evidence for the view which you set forth, that by far the best form of constitution was the one bequeathed us by our ancestors. You are accordingly more at home in this subject than any one else; and so, if you will expound your views of the commonwealth—let me speak for my friends here as well as for myself—you will confer a favor upon all of us.

XXII. SCIPIO: I cannot indeed say that there is any subject to which I habitually devote more ardent or earnest thought than the very one which you, Laelius, propose. Now I observe that every workman, at least if he is a master workman, makes it the object of all his thoughts, deliberations, and efforts to improve his skill in his special craft. Since my sole duty, which I inherit from parents and ancestors, has been the watchful supervision and performance of public tasks, should I not confess that I was less energetic than a mere craftsman if I did not bestow on

the greatest of professions as much effort as artizans devote to their petty tasks?[31] But I am not satisfied with the literature on this subject which the greatest and wisest men of Greece have left us, nor am I bold enough to prefer my own conclusions to theirs. I ask, therefore, that when you hear my arguments you will bear this in mind: that I am neither wholly ignorant of Greek researches nor minded to accord them preference over our own authors, especially in the field of politics; that I am, rather, simply a typical Roman citizen who, because of a father's care, received a liberal education, who has been fired from boyhood with the love of learning, but who nevertheless has gained a far wider training from experience and a father's precepts than he has derived from the study of books.

XXIII. PHILUS: Assuredly, Scipio, I am convinced that no one has excelled you in native ability, while in the practical knowledge derived from the holding of high public office you are without an equal. The wide range of interests which has ever been yours we all know. If, then, as you say, you have applied your mind also to the science or art of politics, as we may call it, I am extremely indebted to Laelius. For I expect that your words will be much more fruitful than the whole body of Greek political speculation.

SCIPIO: Great, indeed, is the anticipation you arouse with reference to my discourse. And that is the heaviest burden which can be placed on anyone who is to discuss a serious subject.

PHILUS: However great our hopes may be, you will surpass them, as you always do. For there is no danger that, when you discuss the commonwealth, you will fail in effective presentation.

XXIV. SCIPIO: I shall do what you wish to the best of my ability and shall proceed immediately to the discussion. First, however, I must lay down one rule which, I believe, should guide all men in any discussion aimed to remove error: namely, that, if they agree to discuss a certain subject, that subject shall be first defined. Only if the definition meets with approval will it be proper for us to embark upon our discussion. For assuredly the nature of the subject can never be understood unless we first comprehend what it is. Since, therefore, the commonwealth forms the subject of our inquiry, let us first consider its precise definition.

After Laelius had expressed his approval, Scipio continued: In spite of what I have said, in the analysis of a thing so well-known and obvious as the state, I shall not go back to its primal constituents. I shall not, for example, follow the usual custom of scholars in this field, and begin with the first union of male and female, with the propagation of offspring, and with the family relationships that ensue.[32] Nor shall I define too frequently what each term means and in how many ways it is used. Since I am speaking before experienced men who, at home and abroad, have played an honorable part in the greatest of states, I shall not commit the fault of making the subject of my discourse obvious, while the discussion itself is obscure. The task, indeed, which I have undertaken is not to elaborate like a schoolmaster every detail of the topic; nor do I bind myself to cover the entire field in my treatment and leave no gaps at all.

LAELIUS: For my part, I am looking forward to the very type of discussion which you promise.

XXV. SCIPIO: The commonwealth, then, is the people's affair; and the people is not every group of men associated in any manner, but is the coming together of a considerable number of men who are united by a common agreement about law and rights and by the desire to participate in mutual advantages.[33] The original cause of this coming together is not so much weakness as a kind of social instinct natural to man. For the human kind is not solitary nor do its members live lives of isolated roving; but it is so constituted that, even if it possessed the greatest plenty of material comforts, [it would nevertheless be impelled by its nature to live in social groups. . . .]

(The second leaf of the ninth quaternion is missing)

For what is the commonwealth except the people's affair?[34] *Hence, it is a common affair, that is, an affair belonging to a state. And what is a state except a considerable number of men brought together in a certain bond of harmony? The view that we meet in the Roman authors is as follows:* In a short time a scattered and wandering aggregate of men became a state through harmony.

—Augustine: *epist.* 138. 10; *CSEL.* 44, p. 135. 8.

Scholars have not attributed the founding of cities to a single first principle.[35] *For some hold that, when men first sprang up from the soil, they lived a roving life in the forests and plains, and were united by no bonds either of speech or of law, but made their beds in the leaves and grass and had caves and crevices in the rocks for houses, and were a prey to the more powerful wild beasts and animals. Later, they say, those men who had been torn by wild beasts or had seen their comrades torn, and had made their escape, were driven by consciousness of their danger to ally themselves with other men. From them they sought aid, at first making their wants known by signs and gestures. Afterwards they experimented with the beginnings of speech and, by giving names to things, gradually developed a system of language. These scholars believe, further, that, when men perceived that even in large numbers they needed to be protected against animals, they began to build towns, either with a view to making themselves safe at night, or for the purpose of warding off the attacks of animals, not by fighting them, hand to hand, but by interposing barriers for their own protection. . . . To other scholars, on the other hand, these views have appeared little better than madness, as in fact they were. These scholars held that the reason why men came together in groups is not to be found in the depredations of wild beasts, but rather in the social nature of mankind. Consequently, they said, men formed societies because it is their nature to shun solititde and to seek the relationships of social intercourse.*

—Lactantius: *inst.* 6. 10. 13–15; 18.

XXVI. SCIPIO: . . . [These gregarious impulses] are, so to speak, the seeds [of social virtues]; nor can any other source be found for the remaining virtues or, indeed, for the commonwealth itself. Such groups, therefore, brought into being for the reason I have mentioned, first settled themselves in a fixed abode that they might have dwellings. And when they had fortified this abode, either by taking advantage of the natural features of the land or by building artificial works, they called such a group of buildings, with the places set aside for shrines and for common use, either a town or a city. Consequently, every people, which is a number of men united in the way I have explained, every state, which is an organization of the people, every commonwealth, which, as I have said, is the people's affair, needs to be ruled by some sort of deliberating authority in order that it may endure. This authority, in the first place, must always be relative to the peculiar grounds which have brought the particular state into being.[36] It must, in the second place, be delegated either to a single man, or to certain selected persons, or it must be retained by all the members of the group.

When, therefore, the supreme power is in the hands of one man, we call that man a king and that form of government a monarchy. When it is in the hands of certain selected persons, the state is said to be ruled by the will of an aristocracy. And a state is democratic—for that is the term used—when all authority is in the hands of the people themselves.[37] Any one of these three forms of government, while not, of course, perfect nor in my judgment the best, is nevertheless a passable form of government, if the bond holds which originally united its members in the social order of the commonwealth; and one may be better than another.[38] For either a just and wise king, or an aristocracy of leading citizens, or even the people themselves—though this last is the least desirable form of the three—appears capable of carrying on a stable government so long as injustice and greed have not crept into the state.

XXVII. Nevertheless, in a monarchy all except the king are too much excluded from the protection of the law and from participation in deliberative functions, though these rights belong to the whole people. In a government dominated by an aristocracy the mass of the people have hardly any share in freedom, since they have no part in common deliberative and executive powers. And when the state is governed by the people, even though they be just and self-disciplined, yet their very equality is inequitable in that it does not recognize degrees of merit.[39] Therefore, even if Cyrus[40] the Persian was a perfectly just and wise king, nevertheless the condition of the commons—that is, the commonwealth, as I have said above—does not seem to have been one which we should particularly covet, since it was subject to the caprice of a single man. Similarly, even if our clients, the Massilians,[41] are governed with the greatest justice by their oligarchy of nobles, still in a people so situated there exists something like slavery. And even if the Athenians at certain periods after the fall of the Areopagus conducted all public business through enactments and decrees of the people, still their state did not preserve its glory, since it failed to regard differences of worth.[42]

XXVIII. I am speaking of the three types of government, not as they are when they have become disordered and deranged, but as they are when they maintain their true character. In this condition, each type is subject, first, to the defects which I have mentioned, and in addition has other faults likely to be fatal to its permanence. For each of these types of commonwealth has a tendency to slip headlong into that form of evil government which is most closely related to it.[43] Take, for example, a king at his best, a Cyrus, who was an endurable or, if you like, even a lovable ruler. Nevertheless, his character may change, for there lurks in him the utterly inhuman Phalaris into whose likeness arbitrary power in the hands of one man readily and easily degenerates.[44] Furthermore, the government of the Massilian state by a few chief men is closely approximated by the oligarchical conspiracy of the Thirty Tyrants which once ruled Athens.[45] And finally, at Athens the Athenians themselves—to seek no other [authority—admit] that the absolute power of the people degenerated into the irresponsible madness of a mob. . . .

(The seventh leaf of the ninth quaternion is missing)

XXIX. SCIPIO: . . . a veritable scoundrel [comes to the front;] and from this condition of the state there may arise an aristocracy or a tyrannical government by a party or a monarchy or, quite frequently, even a democracy.[46] And likewise it often happens that from this last type there grows up one of those forms of state which I have noted before. For there is a remarkable rotation and, if I may say so, cycle of changes in the life of states. It is the business of a philosopher to understand the order in which these changes occur; but to foresee impending modifications, and at the same time to pilot the state, to direct its course, and to keep it under control, is the part of a great statesman and a man of all but godlike powers.[47] There is, accordingly, a fourth kind of commonwealth which, in my opinion, should receive the highest approval, since it is formed by the combination, in due measure, of the three forms of state which I described as original.[48]

XXX. LAELIUS: I know, Africanus, that you prefer this composite type of state, for I have often heard you say so. But still, if there is no objection, I should like to know which of the three unmixed kinds of state you consider the best. For it will be of some use to know. . . .

(The first leaf of the tenth quaternion is missing)

XXXI. SCIPIO: . . . and every state varies according to the character and inclination of its sovereign.[49] Consequently, no state except one in which the people have supreme power provides a habitation for liberty, than which surely nothing can be sweeter. But if liberty is not equally enjoyed by all the citizens, it is not liberty at all.[50] And yet, how can all citizens have an equal share in liberty—I pass over the citizens in a monarchy, for there, of course, the subjection of the people is neither concealed nor questionable—but even in those states in which all men are nominally free? They do, of course, cast their votes; they elect the civil and military officials; their suffrages are solicited for purposes of election and legislation. Nevertheless, the powers which they bestow they would have to bestow, even against their will; and they do not possess the powers which others seek to obtain from them. For they have no share in military commands, or in advisory councils, or in special jury panels.[51] These offices are in fact reserved to men of ancient family or to men of wealth. But in a free people, as at Rhodes or at Athens, there is no citizen who [is not eligible to all the offices of state].[52] . . .

(The third leaf of the tenth quaternion is missing)

XXXII. SCIPIO: [The advocates of democracy] affirm that [when] one man or a few men become wealthier and more powerful than the other citizens, their pride and arrogance give rise [to special privileges], because the inactive and the weak give way and submit to the pretensions of the rich.[53] So long, however, as the people actually retain their power, these thinkers hold that no form of government is better, more liberal, or more prosperous, since the people have control over legislation, the administration of justice, the making of war and peace, the concluding of treaties, and over the civil status and property of each individual citizen.[54] This, according to their view, is the only form of government which can properly be called a commonwealth, that is, the people's affair; and therefore, while there are many instances where the people's affair is freed from the yoke of kings and patricians, there is none of a free people's demanding a king or an aristocratic form of government. They assert, moreover, that it is not right for democracy in general to be condemned because an uncontrolled populace has defects; that, so long as a people is harmonious and subordinates everything to its safety and freedom, there is no form of government less subject to revolution or more stable; and that the kind of state in which harmony is most easily attained is one in which the interests of all the citizens are the same.[55] Dissension, as they hold, arises from diversity of interests, whenever the well-being of some is contrary to the well-being of others. Consequently, when the government was in the hands of aristocrats, the form of the state has never remained stable. Still less has this been the case with monarchies, for, in Ennius' words,

In a kingdom there is no sacred fellowship or trust.

Since, then, law is the bond that holds political society together[56] and since equality of rights is a part of law, by what principle of right can an association of citizens be held together, when the status of these citizens is not equal? For, if it is not thought desirable that property should be equally distributed,[57] and if the natural capacities of all men cannot possibly be equal, yet certainly all who are citizens of the same commonwealth ought to enjoy equal rights in their mutual relations. What, indeed, is a state, if it is not an association of citizens united by law?[58] . . .

(The sixth leaf of the tenth quaternion is missing)

XXXIII. SCIPIO: . . . in fact, [the advocates of democracy] do not think that the other forms of government deserve even the names by which they would be called. Why, indeed, should I apply the word king—a name which belongs properly to Jupiter the Most High—to a human being who is greedy for lordship and exclusive dominion and who is the slave-driver of an oppressed people? Should I not rather call him a tyrant? For mercy is as possible in a tyrant as cruelty in a king.[59] Accordingly, the only concern of the people is whether they are the slaves of a kindly or of a harsh master, since under this form of government they are inevitably the slaves of someone. Moreover, how was it that, at the time when Spartan political institutions were supposedly at their best, this famous people contrived to have only good and just kings, although they had to take as king anyone who happened to be born of the royal family? And as for aristocrats, who can tolerate those who have assumed this title not as the result of popular grant but as the result of their own election? What, I ask, is the criterion by which your aristocrat is judged? Is it learning, or culture, or scholarly tastes, as I hear? When. . . .

(The eighth leaf of the tenth, and the first leaf of the eleventh quaternion are missing)

XXXIV. SCIPIO: . . . if a state [chooses its rulers] at haphazard, it will be overthrown as quickly as a ship will founder if its pilot is chosen by lot from among the passengers.[60] But if a free people chooses those to whose guidance it will submit itself, and if it chooses for this purpose all its best citizens—provided, of course, that the people wish to be secure—surely, then, the safety of the state has been founded upon the wisdom of its ablest members. This is particularly true since nature has contrived to make the men who are superior in courage and ability rule over the weak, and the weak willing to submit themselves to the best.[61] This perfect relationship between men has been overthrown, according to the partisans of aristocracy, by the false notions that prevail about human excellence. For, as few men possess excellence, so few are able to recognize and judge it. Thus, being ignorant of its nature, the masses suppose that men of wealth, influence, and important family connections are the best. When, as a result of this error on the part of the commons, the wealth rather than the excellence of a few men has come to control the state, these leaders cling stubbornly to the title of aristocrats, utterly lacking though they may be in the substance of excellence. For riches and reputation and power, if devoid of wisdom and of moderation in conduct and in the exercise of authority, are characterized by shamelessness and insufferable arrogance. There is, indeed, no uglier kind of state than one in which the richest men are thought to be the best.[62]

On the other hand, when excellence governs the commonwealth, what can be more glorious? For then he who rules over others is not himself the slave of any base desire; the requirements which he lays upon his fellow-citizens he has fulfilled himself; he does not impose upon the people laws which he does not himself obey;[63] he holds up his own life before his fellow-citizens as the law by which they may guide their lives. If one such man were able to accomplish effectively all the business of the state, there would be no need for others; and if the body of citizens could always discover this perfect ruler and agree in regard to him, no one would demand specially chosen leaders. The difficulty of determining policy wisely has caused the transfer of authority from the king to several persons;

and, conversely, the ignorance and reckless-ness of the commons have caused it to pass from the many to the few. Thus, between the weakness inherent in a single ruler and the recklessness inherent in the many, aristoc-racy has come to hold a middle place. Noth-ing, in fact, can be more perfectly balanced; and as long as an aristocracy guards the state, the people are necessarily in the happi-est condition, since they are free from all care and anxiety. Their ease has been put into the safe-keeping of others, who must protect it and take care that nothing arises to make the people believe that their interests are being neglected by their leaders.

Now the equal rights of which democra-cies are so fond cannot be maintained. In-deed, no matter how free and untrammeled popular governments may be, they are still exceptionally prone to confer many favors on many men, and show decided preferences in the matter of individuals and in the matter of high rank. And what is called equality is, in reality, extremely unequal. For when the same importance is attached to the high and the low—and in every community these two classes necessarily exist—that very equality is most unequal. Such a condition cannot arise in states that are governed by aristocra-cies.

Arguments of much this character, Laelius, and others of the same kind, are usually put forward by those who praise most highly the aristocratic form of govern-ment.

XXXV. LAELIUS: But of the three simple forms of state, Scipio, which do you espe-cially approve?

SCIPIO: You frame your question well when you ask, "Which of the three" I espe-cially approve, because I do not approve any one of them considered separately and by it-self. I prefer rather the mixed form, which is a combination of all three, to any one taken by itself. Still, if I had to express preference for one of the unmixed forms, I should choose monarchy [[64]and accord it first place. In this kind of state] we find that the king is described as if he were a father, planning for his subjects as if they were his children, and zealously protecting them [but never reduc-ing them to subjection. Thus it is much

better for the weak and ignorant] to be guarded by the care of one man, who is at once the strongest and the best man in the state. There are, to be sure, the aristocrats, who claim that they do this better than the king, and assert that there would be greater wisdom in a number of men than in one, and withal the same justice and good faith. Finally, the people themselves declare loudly that they do not wish to obey either one man or several. Nothing, they say, is sweeter than freedom, even to wild beasts; and no citizen possesses freedom when he is subject either to a king or to an aristocracy.

Thus I prefer monarchy for the love which the king bears to his subjects; aristocracy for its wisdom in counsel; and democracy for its freedom. When I compare them, I find it hard to decide which feature we desire the most. . . .

Book III

PHILUS: Very well, then, I shall comply with your request and knowingly defile my-self. Men who hunt gold do not think that they should spare themselves trouble; and we who seek justice, a thing much more pre-cious than all the gold in the world, surely ought not to shun any inconvenience.[65] As the arguments which I shall use are an-other's, I would that I might speak with the mouth of another. But as matters stand, I, Lucius Furius Philus, must set forth the ar-guments by which Carneades,[66] who was a Greek and accustomed to propound any view that suited his purpose, [attempted to overthrow justice].

(The first two leaves of the twenty-ninth quaternion are missing)

[I advance these views merely] that you may controvert the arguments of Carneades, who frequently uses clever quibbles to make sport of worthy topics.[67]

VI. *Carneades was a philosopher of the Academy. Anyone who does not know his force in argument, his eloquence, and his shrewdness will understand them from the commendation given him by Cicero and Lucilius. For the latter represents Neptune as discussing a difficult question and as showing that the matter cannot be explained,*

> *Not even if Hades should send back Carneades himself.*[68]

It was Carneades whom the Athenians sent to Rome on an embassy[69] *and who discoursed eloquently on justice in the hearing of Galba and Cato the Censor, the most important orators of the age. But the next day Carneades refuted his former arguments and overthrew justice, which he had eulogized the day before. His performance was somewhat beneath the dignity of a philosopher, whose views should be fixed and unvarying. It was rather a kind of rhetorical exercise in arguing on both sides of a question*[70]*—a practice he regularly followed in order to refute other speakers, no matter what views they supported. His refutation of justice is reproduced in Cicero's work by Lucius Furius Philus. Cicero's purpose in his discussion of the state, as I suppose, was to include a defense and eulogy of justice, which he regarded as a necessary element in government. Carneades, on the other hand, because he wished to refute Plato and Aristotle, who were the champions of justice, brought together in his first speech all the arguments which they used in support of it. His purpose was to be in a position to overthrow justice [in his second speech], and as a matter of fact he did it.*[71]

—Lactantius: *inst. 5. 14. 3–5.*

VII. *Many philosophers, but especially Plato and Aristotle, have had much to say about justice. It was this virtue which they esteemed and praised most highly, because it gives to every man his own and preserves fair dealing in all human relationships. And while all other virtues are, so to speak, silent and self-centered, justice is the only one, they said, which does not exist for itself alone and is not secret, but exerts its influence wholly abroad and tends to do good and thus to benefit the greatest possible number of persons. As if, in truth, justice were required only of judges and those in authority, and not of all men! For there is in fact no man, not even the humblest beggar, who is not concerned with justice. But because Plato and Aristotle did not understand the nature of justice, or its source, or its*

function, they attributed to a few that supreme virtue which is the common good of all mankind. Moreover, they said that justice seeks no selfish advantage but considers solely the interests of others. Quite reasonably, therefore, Carneades, who was a man of great ability and shrewdness, came forward to refute their arguments and overturn a view of justice which was without firm foundation. He was led to do this, not because he believed that justice deserved to be assailed, but in order to show that the defenders of justice urged nothing in its behalf that was indisputable or well proved.

—Lactantius: *epit 50 (55). 5–8.*

Justice turns its gaze abroad; it is wholly directed toward interests outside the individual and rises above selfish considerations.[72]

This virtue more than any other devotes and dedicates itself to the interests of others.[73]

VIII. PHILUS: [In the *Republic* Plato formulated an ideal commonwealth in order to] discover justice and defend it, while [Aristotle][74] devoted four good-sized books to justice itself. From Chrysippus[75] I expected nothing significant or elevating, for it was characteristic of him to investigate all questions rather by examining the meanings of words than by weighing the facts at issue. It was the task of Plato and Aristotle, the princes of philosophy, to awaken justice and raise her from her lowly place to that divine throne only a little below philosophy itself. For justice—assuming that it exists—is the only virtue pre-eminently unselfish and generous, and [only a man who is inspired by justice] prefers the interests of all men to his own and is born to serve others rather than himself.[76] Certainly Plato and Aristotle did not lack the inclination to extol justice, for this was the only motive or design that prompted them to write about it at all; nor were they lacking in genius, for in this they excelled all men. And yet their inclination and resources were defeated by the weakness of their cause. For the justice which forms the object of our investigation pertains to society but not at all to nature.[77] If it were a part of nature, justice and injustice, like heat and cold or bitterness and sweetness, would be the same for all men.

IX. Suppose now that we could ride in Pacuvius' chariot drawn by winged serpents[78] and, looking down, could survey the many races and cities of men. We should perceive, first, that the Egyptians, though they retain an unexampled simplicity of life and possess written records covering the events of many ages, nevertheless regard a bull as a god and call him Apis. We should perceive also that they have enrolled among the gods many other strange monsters and beasts of every kind. If we should pass next to Greece, we should observe there, as at Rome, splendid temples dedicated to gods in human form. This practice the Persians regarded as impious and it is said that Xerxes ordered the Athenian temples to be burned solely because he thought it wicked for gods to be shut in and confined by walls, when their home is this entire world.[79] And yet, somewhat later, Philip planned a war against the Persians and Alexander carried it out, alleging as their motive the desire to avenge the shrines of Greece. Moreover, the Greeks thought that their temples should not even be rebuilt, in order that posterity might have eternally before its eyes a reminder of the crimes committed by the Persians.[80] How many peoples have there been, like the Taurians on the shores of the Euxine Sea, like the Egyptian King Busiris, and like the Gauls and the Carthaginians, who have thought that it was right and pleasing in the sight of the immortal gods to offer human sacrifices![81]

Manners of life are in fact so diverse that the Cretans and Aetolians consider brigandage an honorable calling,[82] and the Lacedaemonians asserted that they owned all the territories which they could touch with the dart.[83] The Athenians even had the custom of taking public oath that every land which bore grain or the olive belonged to them.[84] The Gauls hold it to be ignominious to raise grain by their own labor; hence they go forth in armed bands and appropriate the grain in other men's fields.[85] We Romans are strongly moved by considerations of justice, and yet, in order that the products of our own vineyards and olive groves may bring us a larger return, we do not permit the races beyond the Alps to plant the vine and the olive.[86] In this policy we are said to act prudently but not justly. From this fact you may perceive that justice and wisdom are not identical. Finally, Lycurgus, who devised excellent statutes and a notably just code of laws, made the common people cultivate the lands of the wealthy, just as though they were slaves.[87]

X. Now if I cared to enumerate the different kinds of laws, institutions, customs, and practices, I might show not only that they differ in different races, but that even in a single city—our own, for example—they have undergone a thousand changes. Thus our friend Manilius here, in his capacity of jurisconsult, advises those who ask his opinion that the law governing legacies and inheritances by women is different now from what it was when he gave his opinion as a younger man, before the Voconian Law[88] was passed. This is a statute enacted in the interests of men but fraught with injustice toward women. For why should a woman not have money [on the same terms as a man]? Why may a Vestal bequeath property and her mother not?[89] Or again, granting that the amount of property which a woman can receive must be limited, why should the daughter of Publius Crassus, if she be his only child, be permitted to inherit a hundred million sesterces without violating the law, while my daughter cannot inherit three million? . . .

(The seventh leaf of the twenty-ninth quaternion is missing)

XI. PHILUS: [If justice were natural, then nature] would have laid down our laws; all peoples would be subject to the same laws; and the same people would not be subject to different laws at different times. Now I put the question to you:[90] If it be the duty of a just man and a good citizen to obey the laws, what laws should he obey? Shall he obey any laws that happen to prevail? But surely rectitude does not admit of inconsistency, and nature does not permit different standards of conduct. Laws, therefore, are obeyed because of the penalties they inflict and not because of our sense of justice. Consequently, the law has no sanction in nature. It follows, then, that men are not just by nature. Or do they mean that, while there is diversity in human legislation, good men follow true justice rather than that which is merely thought to be just?[91] For rendering unto everything its deserts is said to be the mark of a good and just man. But in the first place, then, what shall we render to dumb animals? Thus, Pythagoras and Empedocles, men of no ordinary attainments but scholars of the first rank, assert that there is a single legal status belonging to all living creatures.[92] They proclaim, moreover, that everlasting punishment awaits those who have wronged anything that lives. It is a crime, accordingly, to injure an animal, and he who presumes to commit this offense. . . .[93]

(Of the next eighty leaves, composing quaternions thirty to thirty-nine, all but four are missing and these four cannot be precisely placed)

XXI. PHILUS: I should not feel it burdensome [to continue the subject], Laelius, if I did not think that our friends here wished that you too should take some part in this discussion of ours, and if I myself did not desire it also, especially since you said yesterday that you would have even more to say than we should care to hear. But, of course, that is impossible, and we all beg you not to disappoint us.[94]

LAELIUS: But our youth ought not to listen to [Carneades] at all. For in fact, if he meant what he says, he is a scoundrel; if he believed otherwise, as I prefer to think, his discourse is nevertheless monstrous.[95]

XXII. LAELIUS: There is in fact a true law[96]—namely, right reason—which is in accordance with nature, applies to all men, and is unchangeable and eternal. By its commands this law summons men to the performance of their duties; by its prohibitions it restrains them from doing wrong. Its commands and prohibitions always influence good men, but are without effect upon the bad. To invalidate this law by human legislation is never morally right, nor is it permissible ever to restrict its operation, and to annul it wholly is impossible. Neither the senate[97] nor the people can absolve us from our obli-

gation to obey this law, and it requires no Sextus Aelius[98] to expound and interpret it. It will not lay down one rule at Rome and another at Athens, nor will it be one rule today and another tomorrow. But there will be one law, eternal and unchangeable binding at all times upon all peoples; and there will be, as it were, one common master and ruler of men, namely God, who is the author of this law, its interpreter, and its sponsor. The man who will not obey it will abandon his better self, and in denying the true nature of a man, will thereby suffer the severest of penalties, though he has escaped all the other consequences which men call punishment.[99]

XXIII. *I know that in Cicero's work on the Commonwealth—in the third book, unless I am mistaken—there is a discussion of the proposition that* no war is undertaken by a well-conducted state except in defense of its honor or for its security.[100] *What he means by security, or what he would have his reader understand by a state that is secure, he shows in another passage:* From those penalties of which even the stupidest men are sensible— such as destitution, exile, chains, and stripes—private individuals often escape by adopting the proffered alternative of a speedy death. But for states death is itself a punishment, though for individual men it seems to be a deliverance from punishment. For the state ought to be so organized that it will endure forever. Hence, death is not a natural end for the commonwealth as it is for a human being, whose death is not only necessary but frequently even desirable. But when a state is destroyed and wiped out and annihilated, it is somewhat as if—to compare small things with great—this whole world should perish and collapse.[101]

There are four kinds of wars, the lawful, the unlawful, civil wars, and foreign wars. A lawful war is one which is formally declared and which is waged either to secure restitution of property for which a claim has been made, or to repel an invader. An unlawful war is one that is begun from a mad impulse and without a legitimate cause. Of this kind of war Cicero says in his work on the Commonwealth: Wars are unlawful which are undertaken without a reason. For no war can be justly waged except for the purpose of redressing an injury or of driving out an invader. *And a little farther on Cicero adds:* No war is held to be lawful unless it is officially announced, unless it is declared, and unless a formal claim for satisfaction has been made.[102]

Our people, on the other hand, were by this time masters of the whole world because they defended their allies.[103] . . .

Book V

I. *The Roman state, being in the condition which Sallust describes, could not properly be represented as a "corrupt and depraved" form of government, as Sallust calls it.[104] In fact, it was not a commonwealth at all, if we accept the theory set forth in [Cicero's] dialogue on the Commonwealth, in which the speakers were the great statesmen [of the Gracchan age]. Indeed, at the opening of Book V, Cicero himself, speaking not in the character of Scipio or of anyone else but in his own person, first quotes the verse of Ennius wherein the poet had declared that*

> By ancient customs and by men the Roman state endures,

and then adds, this is indeed a verse which, by its brevity and truth, makes me feel that Ennius spoke as if he were an oracle. For neither distinguished men without a state thus endowed with a high standard of conduct, nor a high standard of conduct without distinguished men in positions of authority, could have either established or long maintained so great a commonwealth as ours and one of such extent and dominion. Before our time, therefore, our inherited standards themselves brought forward distinguished men, and eminent men cherished the ways and customs of our ancestors. But our own generation, after inheriting the commonwealth as if it were a painting, of unique excellence but fading with age, has not only failed to restore its original hues, but has not even troubled to preserve its outline and the last vestiges of its features. What, I ask, is left of those ancient customs by which, as Ennius said, the Roman state endures? We see them so out of fashion and forgotten that they are no longer even known, much less cherished. And

what shall I say of men? It is indeed the lack of distinguished men that has caused these rules of living to perish. This is an evil for which we must not only render an account, but which we must even answer for as if we were defendants on a capital charge. For it is by our defects of character and not by accident that we long since lost the substance of the commonwealth, though we still retain its name.

—Augustine: *de civ.* 2. 21.

II. MANILIUS ?[105]: [They felt that there was no task of government more] becoming to a king than the pronouncement of justice; this included the interpretation of the law, which private citizens habitually sought from their kings.[106] For this reason lands, fields, and broad and fertile grazing places were set apart for the kings, to be cultivated without toil or labor on their part. In this way, therefore, it was intended that no concern for their private affairs should distract them from public interests. In fact, there was not a single arbitrator or judge in private station, and all legal business was transacted in the royal courts. I, at least, feel that Numa in particular followed the ancient custom of the kings of Greece. For our other kings, though they concerned themselves also with the duty of administering justice, mainly waged wars and developed the laws of war. But the long peace of Numa's reign was the mother of law and religious observance in our city. Numa also drew up statutes which, as you know, are still extant.[107] Now legislation is the special function of the statesman, whose character we are considering. . . .

(Either two or four leaves are missing)

III. . . . but, nevertheless, as the wise owner of an estate needs experience in cultivation, building, and calculation. . . .[108]

SCIPIO: [If the overseer of an estate is interested] in knowing the nature of roots and seeds, it will not displease you, will it?[109]

MANILIUS: Not at all, if any need for it shall arise.

SCIPIO: But you do not think, do you, that such an interest belongs properly to an overseer?

MANILIUS: By no means, since very frequently his duties have nothing to do with tilling the soil.

SCIPIO: Very well, then, as an overseer understands the nature of the soil and a steward knows how to write, but as both of them turn away from the delight in knowledge to the performance of useful tasks, so our governor, though of course he will be interested in understanding the provisions of the law and will undoubtedly perceive the sources from which they spring, will not permit his duties as a jurisconsult, his researches, and his writings to prevent him from being, as we may say, the steward of the commonwealth and in some sense its overseer. In the law of nature he must be perfectly versed, for without this no man can be just. In the civil law he must not be unversed, but in the latter field his knowledge should resemble the pilot's knowledge of astronomy or the doctor's of natural philosophy, which these men adapt to their own uses but never allow to be an obstacle in their own profession.[110] Now our statesman will perceive this. . . .

(The number of missing leaves cannot be determined)

IV. SCIPIO: . . . in states where the best citizens desire renown and glory, they shun disgrace and shame.[111] Fear of the punishment that is prescribed by law does not move them so deeply as the feeling of shame which nature has implanted in man in the form of a fear of deserved reproach. This feeling the wise governor has strengthened by his guidance of public opinion and has brought to a state of great effectiveness by custom and education, in order that shame, no less than fear, might restrain the citizens from wrong doing. The same idea applies, of course, to the love of praise, and might have been expanded and developed in more detail.

V. As regards private life and the practice of everyday living this plan has been further elaborated by giving a legal sanction to marriage,[112] by describing children [born in wedlock] as legitimate, and by declaring holy the shrines of the Penates and domestic Lares,[113] to the end that all citizens might enjoy both common and private advantages.

Thus it was intended that a good life should be impossible except in a good state and that nothing might be more conducive to happiness than a well-organized government.[114] For this reason it always seems very strange to me . . . what [form of training] is so powerful. . . .

(The end of the palimpsest)

VI. SCIPIO: A pilot's aim is a successful voyage; a doctor's, health; a general's, victory. Similarly, the goal set before the ideal ruler of the commonwealth is the happiness of his citizens;[115] and he strives to make them secure in their resources, rich in wealth, great in renown, distinguished in virtue. This is the task—the greatest and noblest in human life—that I would have the governor carry through to completion.[116]

And do you not recall the passage even in [pagan] literature which praises the governor of a state who considers, not the whim, but the advantage of his people?[117]

—Augustine: *epist.* 104. 7; *CSEL.* 34. 587. 24.

VII. *Hence, even Cicero, in the same work on the Commonwealth, could not conceal the fact [that the love of glory, though itself a vice, may yet restrain men from worse vices].*[118] *For, speaking about the education of a chief of the state, he says that such a man must be* nurtured by glory, *and then he declares that* his ancestors performed many extraordinary and brilliant deeds because of their love for glory.

—Augustine: *de civ.* 5. 13.

The chief of the state must be nurtured by glory; and the commonwealth endures only so long as all men accord honor to their chief.[119]

Then we should be permitted to seek the character of a great man in excellence, activity, and energy, except in those cases where a nature too passionate and wild has in some way [led him astray].[120]

This virtue is called courage; it includes the quality of high-mindedness and a lofty scorn of death and pain.[121]

Notes

1. Seventeen leaves (thirty-four pages) of the palimpsest are lost at the beginning. Our reconstruction of the first sentence, which we adopt from Mai, is based on *Tusc.* 1. 37. 89 ff. and *parad.* 1. 2. 12.

2. These were generals in the First Punic War.

3. Marcus Porcius Cato the Censor (234–149 B.C.), the famous model of ancient Roman austerity and the persistent foe of Greek learning and manners, was for some thirty-five years the most influential man in Rome. He also composed the earliest history of Rome in Latin, the *Origines,* cited by Cicero (*de rep.* 2. 1, below).

4. *Ut isti putant.* Cicero's introduction was probably addressed to his brother Quintus. The reference is clearly to the philosophy of Epicurus, according to whom, "The wise man will play no part in politics" (Diog. L. 10. 119; cf. Cic. *ad fam.* 7. 12. 2; *de rep.* 1. 6, below; *de leg.* 1. 13. 39).

5. With Mai, we read *haut* before *procul.* The text is corrupt.

6. On the meaning of *ius gentium* and *ius civile* see Gaius: *inst.,* ed. Poste (1904), 1. 1, and commentary.

7. Xenocrates of Chalcedon was the head of the Academy second after Plato, i. e., from 339 to 314 B.C.

8. For Ennius (239–169 B.C.), the first important figure in Latin literature and the friend of Cato the Censor and Scipio Africanus the Elder, see Schanz: *Gesch. d. röm. Lit.* 1. 1 (1907), pp. 109 ff.

9. For Miltiades, commander of the Greek forces at Marathon, see Kirchner: *Prosopographia Attica* (1903), no. 10212.

10. For Themistocles, the most brilliant and versatile politician of the first quarter of the fifth century B.C., see references in Kirchner: *Prosopographia Attica* (1901), no. 6669.

11. Such examples as the ostracism of Aristides, and the execution of the generals after Arginusae in 406 B.C. (Cic. *de rep.* 4. 8, below), of Socrates in 399 B.C., and of Phocion in 318 B.C. (Ferguson: *Hellenistic Athens,* 1911, pp. 32 ff.) give weight to the judgment which Polybius (6. 44. 3) pronounced upon Athens: "The Athenian *demos* at all times resembles a ship without a pilot."

12. According to tradition, he conquered Veii, suffered exile, and was recalled to defend Rome against the Gauls.

13. Gaius Servilius Ahala was exiled for his summary execution of Spurius Maelius. See Cic. *pro domo,* 32 86; *in Cat.* 1. 1. 3.

14. For Publius Cornelius Scipio Nasica, leader of the senatorial mob that killed Tiberius Gracchus, see Greenidge: *History of Rome,* 1 (1904), pp. 141 ff.

15. Publius Popilius Laenas, consul in 132 B.C., member of the special commission to try the followers of Tiberius Gracchus, was exiled as the result of a law passed in 123; see Greenidge: *op. cit.* pp. 146; 199 ff.

16. Lucius Opimius, consul in 121 B.C., crushed the movement led by Gaius Gracchus. Twelve years later he was condemned by the Mamilian Commission, ostensibly for his part in the Jugurthine War; see Greenidge: *op. cit.* pp. 248 ff.; 378.

17. For Quintus Caecillus Metellus Numidicus, a general who fought Jugurtha, exiled because he refused to support the agrarian law of Saturninus, see Greenidge: *op. cit.* ch. 7; Heitland: *Roman Republic* (1909), sect. 813.

18. We read *et* before *principum.* For Marius see Heitland: *op. cit.,* Book 6, *passim,* esp. ch. 40 and sect. 858 ff.

19. This apparently refers to the proscriptions of Sulla on his return from Asia in 83–82 B.C.; see Heitland: *op. cit.* ch. 7.

20. Cicero refers to the speech which he attempted to deliver when he retired from the consulate. It was the custom for the retiring consuls to take public oath that they had not violated the laws. When Cicero tried to comply with the custom, he was prevented by the tribune Metellus Nepos, who asserted that Cicero had acted illegally in inflicting summary punishment upon the Catilinarian conspirators. Accordingly, Cicero modified the customary oath as indicated in the text, and declared that by his action in connection with the conspiracy of Catiline (63 B.C.) the state was saved. See Cic. *in Pis.* 3. 6 ff.; *ad fam.* 5. 2. 7 ff.; Heitland: *op. cit.* sect. 1044.

21. Cf. Plato: *Republic,* 347 b ff.

22. The higher offices in Rome were limited in practice, though not in theory, to the *nobiles,* that is, members of families whose ancestors had held such offices; see Mommsen: *Röm. Staatsrecht,* 3. 1 (1887), pp. 458 ff. Cicero was a *novus homo,* one of the exceptional men who attained high office without being born in the privileged class.

23. Cf. Plato: *Republic,* 488 a ff.

24. The Seven Sages lived in the sixth century B.C. and, as the list is generally given, included Solon of Athens, Periander of Corinth, Chilon of Sparta, Pittacus of Mitylene, Bias of Priene, Thales of Miletus, and Cleobulus of Lindus. See Bury: *History of Greece* (1916), p. 321; Beloch: *Gr. Gesch.* 1. 1 (1924), p. 427; 1. 2 (1913), pp. 352 ff.

25. The text of this paragraph is corrupt, an entire clause having been lost; the English is accordingly a paraphrase rather than a translation. Cicero clearly intends to present the combination of scholarly interests and political experience as his chief qualification as a writer on political philosophy; see Cic. *de leg.* 3. 6. 14. Since, so far as we know, he had not previously published any work on the subject, the "skill in the exposition of political theory," to which he refers, must have been gained from his studies and his duties as a jurisconsult, and displayed by the occasional insertion of political ideas into his speeches; see e. g., *pro Cluent.* 53. 146. Cicero (*de leg. loc. cit.*) mentions Demetrius of Phalerum as the only one beside himself who has combined the theoretical with the practical side of politics.

26. See the account of the persons of the dialogue in the "Introduction," Cicero, *On the Commonwealth* (trans. by George Sabine and Stanley Barney Smith), Indianapolis: Bobbs-Merrill, 1976, p. 6.

27. For Gracchus' conception of the tribunate see Greenidge: *A History of Rome*, 1 (1904), pp. 132 ff. The persons mentioned in the following sentences, with the exception of Metellus, were attached to the party of Tiberius. Metellus was at odds with Scipio over some personal matter. Laelius gives the conservative interpretation of Gracchus' reform.

28. Diomedes: *gram. Lat.*, ed. Keil, 1, p. 365, 20.

29. Nonius, p. 85. 18; p. 289. 8.

30. On Panaetius and Polybius and their relation to the Scipionic Circle, see the "Introduction," Cicero, *On the Commonwealth* (trans. by George Sabine and Stanley Barney Smith), Indianapolis: Bobbs-Merrill, 1976, pp. 27 ff.

31. This passage should be compared with Aristotle; *Nic. Eth.* 1094 a 26 ff.; *Politics*, 1282 b 14 ff.; *Mag. mor.* 1182 a 32 ff.

32. This may refer to Aristotle: *Politics*, 1252 a 24 ff. (see Newman: *The Politics of Aristotle*, 1, 1887, p. 34), or it may refer to some Stoic work on the state; cf. Cic. *de off.* 1. 17.53 ff. The Stoics explained human conduct by an instinct of self-preservation, which included the appetite which brings the sexes together and the love of offspring; see Cic. *de off.* 1. 4. 11; *de fin.* 3. 19. 62; Polybius: 6. 6. 2. The complaint of verbalism made below was very often directed against the Stoic Chrysippus; see Cic. *de rep.* 3. 8, below.

33. See the "Introduction," Cicero, *On the Commonwealth* (trans. by George Sabine and Stanley Barney Smith), Indianapolis: Bobbs-Merrill, 1976, pp. 51 ff.

34. We have translated the context from Augustine, which Ziegler prints in the apparatus criticus.

35. The first part of this section from Lactantius is clearly derived from Lucretius (5. 805–1116, *passim*). Mai supposed that Cicero discussed different views of the origin of the state, and Ziegler hesitatingly retains the passage. The contrast is between the Stoic and Epicurean theories.

36. This sentence suggests Aristotle's statement that even the founder of an ideal state is dependent upon the materials at his disposal, such as the location of his city, the number and character of his people, and the resources of the country; see *Politics*, 1325 b 40 ff.

37. With this classification of states compare Herodotus: 3. 80. 3–6; Thucydides: 2. 37. 1; 6. 39. 1; Plato: *Republic*, 545 b ff.; *Statesman*, 291 d ff.; Aristotle: *Politics*, 1279 , 22 ff.; *Rhetoric*, 1365 b 31 ff.; Polybius: 6. 4. 2 ff.; Tacitus: *ann.* 4. 33.

38. The Latin text of this last clause is corrupt.

39. A reference to proportional as against absolute equality. The distinction depends on Plato's definition of justice as the performance of function (*Republic*, 433 b), and the principle is clearly stated in the *Laws*, 757 a ff. See also Isocrates (3. 14): "The essence of justice is . . . that unequals should not receive equal treatment. But that individuals should both act and be honored in accordance with their merits." The theory of proportional equality is developed by Aristotle especially. See *Nic. Eth.* 1131 a 10 ff.; *Politics*, 1280 a 7 ff.; 1301 b 29 ff.; 1318 a 10 ff. When developed as a legal conception, proportional justice becomes the Roman principle *ius suum cuique tribuere.*

40. Cyrus the Great ruled from 558 to 529 B.C. The endearing personality which Cicero attributed to him perhaps originated in Xenophon's biographical romance, the *Cyropaedeia*, the unhistorical character of which is noted in *ad Q. fr.* 1. 1. 8. 23. Plato (*Laws*, 694

a) says that under the rule of Cyrus the Persians were free.

41. See Strabo: 179 c and d, where we read: "The Massiliotes are governed by an aristocracy which is more orderly than any other. They have created a council of six hundred members who are called *timouchoi* (honor-holders) and who are invested with the honor of their office for life. The assembly is directed by fifteen men whose duty is the administration of current business; and the three who have most power preside over the fifteen. No *timouchos*, however, may become one of these three unless he has children and unless his ancestors have been citizens for three generations." See Gilbert: *Gr. Staatsalt.* 2 (1885). pp. 259 ff.; E. Meyer: *Gesch. des Alt.* 3 (1915), pp. 670 ff.; Busolt: *Gr. Staatskunde*, 1 (1920), pp. 357 ff.

42. In 462–1 B.C. the democratic party, under the leadership of Ephialtes and Pericles, took from the Areopagus all its significant powers. The aristocratic tradition of Athenian history represents the epoch before the fall of the Areopagus as the golden age of Athens; see Isocrates: 7. 20 ff.; Plato: *Gorgias*, 515 e; Aristotle: *Const. of the Athenians*, 29. 3; Ferguson: *Hellenistic Athens* (1911), pp. 419 ff.

43. See Polybius (6. 4. 8), where he mentions the natural tendency of monarchy to change to the related evil form of government, or tyranny; of aristocracy to lapse to oligarchy; and of democracy to decline into ochlocracy. On the cycle of constitutions see Cic. *de rep.* 1. 42, below, and note: also "Introduction," Cicero, *On the Commonwealth* (trans. by George Sabine and Stanley Barney Smith), Indianapolis: Bobbs-Merrill, 1976, pp. 57 ff.

44. Phalaris, the tyrant of Agrigentum (sixth century B.C.), was noted in antiquity as the inventor of a hollow bronze bull into which his enemies were put and roasted to death. See Cic. *de div.* (ed. Pease), 1. 23. 46; *de rep.* 3. 30, below; Grote: *History of Greece* (ed. Murray, 1870), 4, pp. 305 ff.; Beloch: *Gr. Gesch.* 1. 1 (1924), p. 360.

45. The regime of the Thirty Tyrants and of the Ten Commissioners who followed them occurred in 404–3 B.C., and was set up by Lysander. The arbitrary character of their rule, as indicated by Aristotle (*Const. of the Athenians*, 35. 4; 36. 2, ed. Sandys, 1912, where the notes give many other references), justifies Cicero's description of their rule as *consensus et factio*. See E. Meyer: *Gesch. des Alt.* 5 (1902), pp. 18 ff.

46. The lacuna which precedes this sentence prevents us from understanding with certainty the relation which the sentence bears to Cicero's theory of constitutional cycles. It would appear that the "scoundrel" (*taeterrimus*) refers to the tyrant; and that the "tyrannical government by a party" refers to the Thirty Tyrants mentioned at the end of the preceding chapter.

47. Cf. Aristotle: *Politics*, 1308 a 33 ff.; Polybius: 38. 21. 3.

48. The *locus classicus* on the composite type of state is Polybius: 6. 3. 7 ff.; see also Aristotle: *Politics*, 1265 b 33 ff.; Newman: *The Politics of Aristotle* 2 (1887), p. xiii; esp. *Cambridge Ancient History*, 6 (1.927), pp. 532 ff.

49. With this compare Aristotle's statement that a constitution is an arrangement of magistracies, especially the highest (*Politics*, 1278 b 9 ff.). Following the question put by Laelius at the end of the preceding chapter, Scipio states the arguments in favor of each of the unmixed kinds of state, beginning with democracy.

50. See Cic. *de rep.* 2. 23 (end) below, and note.

51. Cicero apparently refers to the fact that at Rome the possession of *nobilitas* (see note 22 on ch. 6, above) was usually necessary if a man aspired to important political offices or to a military career.

52. If our reconstruction of the meaning of the sentence be correct, Cicero's statement is accurate, generally speaking, for Athens, though there were some exceptions. On Rhodes cf. Cic. *de rep.* 3. 35, below, and for a general treatment of the Rhodian constitution see Gilbert: *Gr. Staatsalt.* 2 (1885), pp. 174 ff. Aristotle mentions the eligibility of all citizens to magistracies and to jury service as typical of democracy, and election by all or by lot as the democratic mode of filling offices: see *Politics*, 1300 a 31 ff.; 1301 a 11 ff.

53. For Aristotle also the fundamental difference between democracy and oligarchy lies not in the number of rulers but in the contrary interests of the rich and poor; see *Politics*, 1279 b 11 ff.

54. See Polybius: 6. 14. 3 ff., where the author, in enumerating the democratic elements of the tripartite Roman constitution, mentions among the powers of the people those here described as characteristic of democracy.

55. Compare Plato: *Republic*, 461 e ff.

56. See Aristotle's argument (*Politics,* 1286 a 7 ff.) that law should be supreme in the state; also *op. cit.* 1292 a 32; 1295 a 14 ff.

57. See Aristotle's criticism of various plans for equalizing property: *Politics,* 1266 a 37, ff.; also Cic. *de off.* 2. 21. 73. For Aristotle also legislation implies the equality in birth and power of those who are to be subject to the law; see *Politics,* 1284 a 11 ff.

58. Since a lacuna immediately follows the word *civium,* it is impossible to tell whether the sentence ends with that word; and indeed *civium* may belong to the following sentence which has been lost. For the idea see Cic. *de rep.* 1. 2; 25, above; 6. 13, below; *parad.* 4. 1. 27 ff.

59. We follow the manuscript and translate *rex.*

60. In the lacuna Cicero passes to the arguments for aristocracy. The reference in the first sentence following the lacuna is to election by lot and to Socrates' criticism of it, This criticism, which is mentioned in Xenophon (*Mem.* 1. 2. 9), was probably one of the grounds for the prosecution of Socrates. Until the end of the fourth century B.C., all Athenian magistrates were chosen by this method, with the exception of military commanders, certain financial officials, and a few others. See Gilbert: *Gr. Staatsalt.* 1 (1893), p. 240; Schoemann: *Gr. Alt.* 1 (1897), p. 432; Busolt: *Gr. Staatskunde,* 2 (1926), p. 1064; Headlam: *Election by Lot in Athens* (1891), *passim.* In fact, election by lot was so universal in popular governments of the Greek world that it was often regarded as the criterion of democracy. See Herod. 3. 80; Pseud. Xen. *Ath. pol.* 1. 2; Plato: *Republic,* 557 a; Aristotle: *Rhetoric,* 1365 b 32; *Politics,* 1317 b 17 ff.; Busolt: *Gr. Staatskunde,* 1 (1920), p. 420.

61. The natural superiority of the wise is the foundation of Plato's theory of government, and the principle is stated in the *Laws* (690 a ff.). For Aristotle also the rule of reason is natural; see *Politics,* 1252 a 30 ff.; 1254 b 2 ff., where this is made the basis of his famous defense of slavery; 1293 b 38 ff. The inferior, whether in nature or in art, exists always for the sake of the better; see *ibid.* 1333 a 21. A similar type of reasoning appears in Cic. *de rep.* 3. 24 and 25. below, where it apparently has Cicero's approval, in spite of the discrepancy with his own theory of natural equality.

62. It is to be noted, however, that Cicero's solution of the practical problem of giving the best men a controlling power in the state is a property qualification for the suffrage; see his account and apparent approval of the Servian constitution in *de rep.* 2. 22, below. In this respect he is at one with Aristotle, whose best practicable state is one ruled by the middle class; see *Politics,* 1295 b 1 ff.; also Plato's second-best state in the *Laws,* 744 b ff.; 756 b ff.

63. The view that a ruler is bound to respect law passed into the *corpus iuris civilis:* "Our authority depends upon the authority of law. And in fact, to subject the imperial authority to law is a greater thing than empire" (*cod.* 1. 14. 4; cf. 6. 23. 3). As a qualification of the principle that the emperor is *legibus solutus,* the doctrine became an important element in the political theory of the Roman lawyers, and it exerted a profound influence upon mediaeval political theory. See Carlyle: *Mediaeval Political Theory,* 3 (1915), pp. 38 ff.; 137 ff.

64. The Vatican manuscript is mutilated at this point; we base our translation on Mai's supplement.

65. This closely parallels Plato: *Republic,* 336 e.

66. On the philosophy of Carneades, and especially its influence upon Stoicism in the period to which Cicero attributes his dialogue, see "Introduction," Cicero, *On the Commonwealth* (trans. by George Sabine and Stanley Barney Smith), Indianapolis: Bobbs-Merrill, 1976, p. 26 ff.

67. Nonius, p. 263. 8.

68. Lucilius (ed. Marx): 1. 3 1. Cicero (*de or.* 1. 11. 45) says of Carneades that, according to report, he was "the shrewdest and most eloquent of all speakers"; cf. *ibid.* 2. 38. 161; 3. 18. 68; Polybius: 12. 26 c; 33. 2. Admiration of his eloquence and logical power was universal among the ancients; many references will be found in Zeller: *Phil. d. Griech.* 3. 1 (1923), P. 517, n. 3.

69. This embassy, consisting of Carneades, the Stoic Diogenes, and the Peripatetic Critolaus, came to Rome in 156–5 B.C. to obtain the release of Athens from a fine imposed for attempting to seize the town of Oropos. The embassy has generally been regarded by both ancient and modern writers as a landmark in the process of introducing Greek education at Rome; see Ferguson: *Hellenistic Athens* (1911), ch. 8, especially pp. 325 ff.; 333 ff.

70. This was a common practice of skeptical philosophers and part of the device by which they sought to show the uncertainty of all knowledge. Cicero frequently refers to it as characteristic of the critical method of the Academy; see *acad. prior.* (ed. Reid), note to 2.

3. 7; *de div.* 2. 72. 150, with Pease's commentary, where references to other passages in Cicero will be found.

71. This and the following extract are colored by the views of Lactantius himself. He is following the text, "The wisdom of this world is foolishness with God." Hence philosophy without revelation is "empty and false" (*inst.* 3. 2) and the virtues, without the rewards and punishments of a future life, are "the most useless and stupid things in human existence" (*ibid.* 5. 19).

72. Nonius, p. 373. 30.

73. Nonius, p. 299. 30.

74. The passages from Lactantius in the two preceding chapters make it clear that the reference is to Plato and Aristotle. For Plato's object in constructing an ideal state see *Republic*, 368 c ff. Aristotle's work on justice was one of his earlier writings, probably in dialogue form; see Zeller: *Phil. d. Griech.* 2. 2 (1921), p. 58, n. 3. The extant fragments are in Rose: *Arist. fragmenta* (1886), pp. 86 ff.

75. The charge of verbalism was universally brought against Chrysippus in antiquity. For references see Zeller: *Phil. d. Griech.* 3. 1 (1023), p. 44, n. 1, and the testimonia on his life and writings in von Arnim: *Stoicorum veterum fragmenta*, 2 (1923), pp. 1 ff. Chrysippus was the author of a work on justice, the extant fragments of which. so far as they can be assigned to this work, are listed by von Arnim: *ibid.* 3 (1923), p. 195.

76. This view of justice is assigned to Plato, perhaps on the strength of his contention that doing injury, even to enemies, can never be just (*Republic*, 335 b ff.). The definition of justice as rendering to every man his own is not Platonic but Stoic. See the references in von Arnim: *Stoicorum veterum fragmenta*, 4 (1924), Index, s. v. *dikaiosune*. This definition developed no doubt from the conception of proportional justice in Plato and Aristotle; see note to *de rep.* 1. 27, above.

77. On the distinction of nature and convention, see "Introduction," Cicero, *On the Commonwealth* (trans. by George Sabine and Stanley Barney Smith), Indianapolis: Bobbs-Merrill, 1976, pp. 14 ff.

78. A reference to a chariot used in one of Pacuvius' plays, perhaps, as Mai suggests, one in which Medea was a character. For the idea see Cic. *Tusc.* 1. 45. 108.

79. See Cic. *de leg.* 2. 10. 26; Herodotus: 1. 131; 8. 109; cf. Augustine: *de civ.* 4. 9; 3 1; 6. 10.

80. For the refusal to rebuild the temples see Pausanias: 10. 35.

81. For human sacrifice among the Taurians see Euripides: *Iphigeneia in Tauris*, hypothesis; Pomponius Mela: 2. 1. 11. For King Busiris see Vergil: *georg.* 3. 5. For the Gauls see Caesar: *de bell. Gall.* 6. 16; Diodorus: 5. 31. For the Carthaginians see Plato: *Minos*, 315 b ff.; Diodorus: 20. 14; Augustine: *de civ.* 7. 19.

82. In Polybius (4. 3; 18. 4) the Aetolians are represented as being habitually engaged in brigandage and in the same author (6. 46) a general charge of greed, wrongfully satisfied, is brought against the Cretans.

83. See Plutarch: *apophth. Lac.* 28; *quaest. Rom.* 15.

84. This was a part of the ephebic oath taken by young men on attaining their eighteenth year. See Plutarch: *Alcib.* 15; the phrase does not occur in Lycurgus: *contra Leocr.* 7, where the oath is given; Gilbert: *Gr. Staatsalt.* 1 (1893), pp. 347 ff.; Schoemann: *Gr. Alt.* 1 (1897), p. 379; Busolt: *Gr. Staatskunde*, 2 (1926), p. 1190.

85. See Diodorus: 5. 32.

86. In the era preceding the Gracchi, due in part to incessant warfare, there had been a general increase of pasture land worked by slaves at the expense of tilled soil managed by freemen. The dangerous consequences of this economic decline had been realized. One of the measures passed to aid the small farmers of Italy in raising the vine and the olive, products for which that country, or at least parts of it, was admirably adapted, was the law mentioned in the text. See Columella: 3. 3. 11; Greenidge: *History of Rome*, 1 (1904), pp. 79 ff.; 269; Rostovtzeff: *Social and Economic History of the Roman Empire* (1926), p. 22. A similar provision seems to have been in force in the time of Domitian (81–96 A. D.); see Suetonius: *Domit.* 7.

87. For the Helots, who are referred to here, see Gilbert: *Gr. Staatsalt.* 1 (1893), pp. 32 ff.; Busolt: *Gr. Staatskunde*, 2 (1926), pp. 667 ff.

88. The *Lex Voconia* (169 or 168 B.C.), passed with the intention of repressing luxury and immorality among women, forbade a woman to be instituted heiress by a citizen whose property exceeded one hundred thousand sesterces, and also enacted that the amount taken by a legatee (not the heir) should be no more than that taken by the heirs. Thus, a testator with one heir could not make a legacy of more than one-half his property to a woman, or of one-third if he had two heirs, etc. If the

woman were an only child (*filia unica*), as Philus supposes in the case of Crassus' daughter, she might take the whole estate as heiress, if her father died intestate—an uncommon occurrence among the Romans. See Gaius: *inst.* ed. Poste (1904), p. 239; Heitland: *Roman Republic* (1909), sects. 634; 651; Girard: *Manuel de droit romain* (1924), pp. 866 ff.

89. Until the time of Hadrian a woman could not make a will, but the Vestals were an exception; see Buckland: *Textbook of Roman Law* (1921), p. 287.

90. The argument is a dilemma: A just man either obeys the law or renders to everything its deserts. If he obeys the law, which varies from place to place, he cannot follow a universal sense of justice; and if he renders to everything its deserts, he must sometimes go counter to law and usage. On the two definitions of justice see Aristotle: *Nic. Eth.* 1129 a 31 ff.

91. Compare Cic. *de leg.* 1. 18. 48.

92. This is a reference to the transmigration of souls, the only teaching that can be ascribed with certainty to Pythagoras himself; see Burnet: *Early Greek Philosophy*, 1908, pp. 101 ff. For Empedocles see fragments 135–7 in Diels: *Vorsokratiker*, 1 (1912), p. 2–14 ff.; Burnet: *op. cit.* p. 289.

93. This does not represent Cicero's own view; see *de leg.* 1. 8. 26, where animals are said to have been created for man, and among the uses to which they may be put is that of food.

94. Gellius: *noct. Att.* 1. 22. 8. With ch. 20 Philus ends his defense of injustice, and with ch. 21 the presentation of the case for justice is begun by Laelius. See Augustine's summary at the beginning of Book 3.

95. Nonius, p. 323. 18; 324. 15.

96. The definition of true law (*vera lex*) is a Stoic commonplace, going back certainly to Chrysippus and perhaps to Zeno. See "Introduction," Cicero, *On the Commonwealth* (trans. by George Sabine and Stanley Barney Smith), Indianapolis: Bobbs-Merrill, 1976, p. 48, and compare Cic. *de leg.* 1. 6. 18, where he says, "Law is transcendent reason, implanted in nature, commanding what should be done, and forbidding what should not be done." A long list of Stoic parallels will be found in von Arnim: *Stoicorum veterutm fragmenta*, 4 (1924), Index, s. v. *nomos.*

97. While the Roman senate did not possess the right of legislation, it had the power to exempt persons from the operation of the law;

see Greenidge: *Roman Public Life* (1911), pp. 275 ff. During the last century B.C. an attempt was made to deprive the senate of this right and to confer it solely upon the people. As a result of the agitation it was enacted that, when the senate granted such an exemption, there must be present at least two hundred senators; see Bouché-Leclercq: *Manuel des inst. romaines* (1886), pp. 104 ff.

98. For Sextus Aelius see Cic. *de rep.* 1. 18, above, and note.

99. Lactantius: *inst.* 6. 8. 6–9.

100. Cf. Aristotle's view that war is justifiable in three cases: (1) for self-defense; (2) to establish political rule over those who would be benefited thereby; (3) to establish despotic rule over nations that deserve to be enslaved; see *Politics*, 1333 b 38 ff.; also Newman: *Politics of Aristotle*, 1 (1897), pp. 327 ff.

101. Augustine: *de civ.* 22. 6. We have translated the context from Augustine, which Ziegler prints in the apparatus criticus. Laelius clearly undertook to show that the expansion of states, and particularly of Rome, was not necessarily the result of unjust aggression. He adduced the procedure of the Fetial College (see 2. 17, above, and note) as constituting a sort of international law. Philus had asserted (3. 12, above) that it merely gave the color of law to injustice.

102. Isidore: *etym.* 18. 1. 2 ff. Cf. Cic. *de off.* 1. 11. 36. We have combined the two passages given by Ziegler and have added the context in Isidore.

103. Nonius, p. 498. 18. Laelius doubtless argued that Roman expansion had been incidental to a general policy of keeping faith with allies, possibly even that it was a reward of merit, for the Romans had a singular conceit of their own piety. See the extract from Tertullian, ch. 12, above, and the "backward nation" argument in ch. 24, below.

104. Sallust: *Cat.* 5. We translate the context from Augustine, which Ziegler prints in the apparatus criticus. Like the dialogues of the first and second days (the first in Books 1 and 2, the second in Books 3 and 4), the dialogue of the third day (Books 5 and 6) was preceded by an introduction in which Cicero writes in his own person. Augustine's excerpt comes from this introduction. When Cicero wrote (c. 54 B.C.) men felt that the Roman state had declined from its greatest days; see Cic. *in Cat.* 1. 1; Sallust: *Cat.* 5; *Iug.* 41; fr. 12 (ed. Kritz) ; Livy: *praef.* 9 ff. Book 5 of the *Commonwealth* dealt mainly with the character and training

of the great statesman, who might restore the ancient health of his country.

105. Chapters 2–5 include the remaining three leaves of the Vatican palimpsest. The supplement at the beginning of ch. 2 is Mai's. He attributes the speech to Manilius as the representative of the law among the interlocutors; see Cic. *de rep.* 1. 13. above, and "Introduction," Cicero, *On the Commonwealth* (trans. by George Sabine and Stanley Barney Smith), Indianapolis: Bobbs-Merrill, 1976, p.5. Mai's hypothesis is probably correct, that Scipio and Manilius debated the value of a knowledge of law as part of the statesman's equipment, Manilius holding that it was of first importance and Scipio that it was subordinate to his management of public affairs; see *de rep.* 5. 3, below.

106. Manilius urges the example of the ancient kings of Greece and Rome to prove that the statesman is primarily a lawgiver; cf. the origin of monarchy as described by Plato: *Laws*, 681 a ff.; and the duties of the king in the heroic age mentioned by Aristotle: *Politics*, 1285 b 3 ff.

107. Cf. Cic. *de rep.* 2. 14, above.

108. Nonius, p. 497, 23. The analogy of government with the management of an estate occurs in Plato: *Statesman*, 259 c, and is rejected by Aristotle: *Politics*, 1252 a 7 ff.; 1258 a 19; see Newman's note on the last passage. Elsewhere, Cicero calls the magistrate a steward (*vilicus*) of the Roman people (*pro Planc.* 25. 62), but does not pursue the comparison. Logically, Cicero, like Aristotle, ought to hold that political rule is generically different from domestic authority; see *de rep.* 1. 25, above.

109. We translate Mai's supplement. The sense of the passage that follows is not clear but seems to be that knowledge of the civil law is an incidental part of the statesman's equipment, but subordinate to the management of public affairs, as an overseer's knowledge of agriculture is merely part of managing an estate; see the preceding chapter, note 2.

110. In the long account of the general's art given by Polybius (9. 12 ff.) it is stated (ch. 20) that there are certain subsidiary sciences, such as geometry and astronomy, which a general should know, not thoroughly, but in sufficient degree to enable him to conduct his campaigns.

111. Cicero elsewhere attributes great importance to the sense of shame (*verecundia*) as a social virtue; see *de off.* 1. 27. 93 ff. Like Plato (*Laws*, 718 b ff.), he prefers to secure obedience to law by persuasion rather than by force; *see de leg.* 2. 6. 14. Like the Stoics, Cicero regards the elements of all the virtues as innate; and the statesman can impede or assist the growth of these native virtues by appropriate laws and institutions: see Arnold: *Roman Stoicism* (1911), pp. 302 ff.; Hicks: *Stoic and Epicurean* (1910), pp. 77 ff.

112. According to Roman law, marriage was a legal relationship between two qualified persons of opposite sex (see Gaius: *inst.*, ed. Poste, 1904, 1. 56 ff., and commentary), entered into by a form of bilateral contract (*ibid.* p. 47), assumed voluntarily (*dig.* 35. 1. 15), symbolized by a formal escort of the bride to her husband's domicile (*deductio in domum;* see *ibid.* 23. 2. 5; Paulus: *sententiae*, 2. 19. 8; Marquardt: *Privatleben der Römer*, 1886, pp. 53 ff.), marked by *maritalis affectio* (*dig.* 24. 1. 3. 1; 24. 1. 32. 13), assumed to possess a sacred and enduring character (*ibid.* 23. 2. 1), and designed for the propagation of offspring (Justinian: *inst.* 1. 10 pr.; Livy: *epit.* 59; Greenidge: *History of Rome*, 1, 1904, p. 64).

113. By this mention of *iustae nuptiae*, *legitimi liberi*, the Lares, and the Penates, Cicero emphasized the chief elements in Roman family life. It is probable that he contrasted such a system with the communistic theory of Plato. The Penates were deities who presided over the larder; see Fowler: *Religious Experience of the Roman People* (1911), pp. 73 ff.; Wissowa: *Religion und Kultus der Römer* (1912), pp. 161 ff. The Lar—in the plural form, the Lares— was originally the spirit which presided over the plot of land, including the house, occupied by each *familia* and which guarded the productive powers of the land. In the later Roman worship the *Lar familiaris* is essentially a household divinity.

114. See Cic. *de rep.* 4. 3, above, and note; Newman: *Politics of Aristotle*, 1 (1887), p. 63; see also Aristotle: *Politics*, 1264 b 16 ff., where Aristotle, arguing against Plato, declares that in a happy state the citizens must be happy.

115. Cf. the fragment on kingship attributed to Diotogenes the Pythagorean in Stobaeus: *florilegium*, 48. 61, where the following words occur: "The duty of the pilot is to bring his ship safely to port; the task of the charioteer is to keep his chariot upright; the doctor's aim is to cure the sick; and the function of the king or general is to save those who risk their lives in battle."

116. Cic. *ad Att.* 8. 11. 1. On the importance of the statesman's art see Cic. *de rep.* 1. 22, above,

and note. For a discussion of Cicero's conception of the ideal statesman and the role which he should play in the state, see "Introduction," Cicero, *On the Commonwealth* (trans. by George Sabine and Stanley Barney Smith), Indianapolis: Bobbs-Merrill, 1976, pp. 93 ff. It will be sufficient to note here the various passages in which Cicero describes that ruler, whom he calls *rector et gubernator civitatis* (2. 29), *rector* (5. 3; 6. 1; 8; 13), *moderator rei publicae* (5. 6; also introductory sentences of Cic. *ad Att.* 8. 11. 1), *princeps* (5. 7), *gubernator* (2. 29), and, it would appear, simply *civis* either with or without qualification (1. 2; 29; 5. 2; 6. 1)—all of these terms being apparently used as translations of the Greek word *politikos*. According to Richard Heinze ("Ciceros 'Staat' als politische Tendenzschrift," in *Hermes*, 59, 1924, pp. 92 ff.), Cicero coined the terms *rector* and *moderator rei publicae* for that very object.

117. This is a sentence from a letter written by Augustine to Nectarius, a pagan, in which he says that defects of character must be treated solely with an eye to the advantage of the defective person. There is nothing to prove that the sentence was written by Cicero except the words *patriae rectorem*. We do not agree with Ziegler in regarding the words *et ubi . . . laudant* as Cicero's.

118. This fragment and the following have usually been taken to refer to the education of the ideal ruler (*rector rei publicae*). It has been pointed out, however, that the value here set upon glory is in contradiction to the contempt for human fame expressed by Scipio in *de rep.* 1. 17, above, and 6. 21, below. Accordingly, Richard Heinze has conjectured that this fragment refers to the education of the aristocratic class in the state and that it should be transferred to Book 4; see "Ciceros 'Staat' als politische Tendenzschrift," *Hermes*, 59 (1924), p. 77, n. 2, and the reply by R. Reitzenstein, *ibid.* p. 359.

119. Petrus Pictaviensis (Peter of Poitiers): *ad calumn. Bibl. patr. Lugd.* 22, p. 824.

120. Nonius, p. 233. 33. We read, following Lindsay's suggestion, *quaerere daretur* for *quaereretur*. The passage is clearly corrupt.

121. Nonius, p. 201. 29. See *Cic. Tusc.* 2. 18. 43. This quality (*fortitudo*), which is perhaps here mentioned as one of the essential elements of the statesman, Cicero further defines as a rational quality of soul which fearlessly obeys the divine law despite suffering; as the preservation of calm judgment in enduring and repelling sufferings which appear terrible; or as knowledge which maintains unperturbed judgment about experiences which may be horrible or otherwise but which should be disregarded; see *Tusc.* 4.22.50ff.

13
Essentials of the Mixed Constitution

Neal Wood

1. The Doctrine Prior to Cicero

The doctrine of the mixed constitution is one of the most important legacies of ancient political theory to modern times. Not only did it have a decisive impact on the general development of the idea of constitutionalism since the Middle Ages, but also, in the early modern period, especially on the theory of mixed monarchy, the English Classical Republicans, and on Montesquieu and the American founding fathers, who devised and instituted the notion of the separation of powers. Basic to that notion is the historical interpretation of the Roman constitution as a mixture, expounded by Polybius, Cicero, and other writers both ancient and modern. The mixed constitution was thought to combine the merits of the three simple forms of monarchy, aristocracy, and democracy without their defects into a balanced whole that would be resistant, if not entirely immune, to corruption and would impede tyrannical rule.[1] Of the various ancient treatments of the mixed constitution, Cicero's in the *Republic* and *Laws* is perhaps the definitive and clearest one in respect to intention and constitutional operation. Before considering his view of the mixed constitution, however, it may be helpful to summarize briefly some aspects of the "doctrine" as it evolved before Cicero.

The most obvious and fundamental assumption of the doctrine of the mixed constitution is the typology of the three simple constitutions and their degenerate forms.

Herodotus provides the first recorded instance of the typology, which probably had become conventional and was later systematically presented by Plato and Aristotle.[2] Once the classificatory scheme was generally accepted, it was not long before the idea of a mixture of elements of two or all three of the good forms appeared. Thucydides is usually acknowledged to be the first to describe an actual governmental arrangement as a mixture, and both Plato in the *Laws* and Aristotle in the *Politics* briefly discuss various existing constitutions as a combination of three simple forms. Each of the two latter thinkers in their respective works also recommends a mixture in their best practicable or second-best constitutions: Plato's constitution for Magnesia mixes monarchy and democracy; Aristotle's "polity" fuses oligarchy and democracy.[3] The early Stoics prescribed for the best state a blending of the three simple constitutions, or so Diogenes Laertius informs us.[4] Polybius is commonly thought of as the classic theorist of the mixed constitution, because of his detailed analysis of the Roman state as a synthesis of monarchical, aristocratic, and democratic components.[5]

The doctrine is socially and politically conservative, fashioned by and appealing to those of aristocratic values and interests and aimed at securing their own privilege and domination by averting tyranny and paying lip service to democracy. As it developed, the notion of the mixed constitution came to be informed by a number of of basic and closely connected principles. The first, the precept of the mean or "middle way" which shuns excess, can be traced as far back as Solon's poetic utterance that he "stood with a strong shield thrown before the both sorts," the rich and the poor.[6] Theognis's "midst is best in everything" is reflected in such diverse phenomena as the Athenian social ideal of the self-sufficient farmer, neither rich nor poor, and as the philosophic themes of the Delphic *sophrosyne* and the "golden mean."[7] When applied to politics, the idea of the mean and the avoidance of excess gives rise to a psychological assumption that too much power corrupts, or, to paraphrase Acton, all power corrupts and absolute power corrupts absolutely.[8] Hence the power of state officials must be balanced and checked institutionally by an appropriate mixture to prevent them from acting capriciously and irresponsibly. Another fundamental principle is the preference for proportionate over numerical equality.[9] In regard to the distribution of offices, honors, and awards in the state, this signified in practice some combination of the two conceptions of equality or a "mean" between the two. All citizens would be granted a minimal function in government, such as membership in the popular assembly or suffrage, but decisive political power would be a monopoly of the well-born and wealthy. A related principle is the idea that the social unity of the state depends on governmental arrangements that would create balance or harmony of social classes—rich and poor, landlords and peasants. "Balance," of course, in this context, as in the case of the "equality" of the principle of proportionate equality, favors the rich over the poor. Since ancient societies were peasant societies, in the main governed by gentlemanly landed proprietors, a central theme of ancient political thinkers is the problem of constructing a durable modus vivendi between the two classes. This concern with class harmony is associated with a further principle. Untainted by modern notions of the benefits of human progress, the advantages of social change, and the positive value of social and political conflict, the ancients sought an immortal form of constitution, one that would be relatively impervious to the passage of time and generate conditions of lasting unity, order, and stability. In the opinion of ancient theorists, the properly mixed constitution was an ingenious contrivance for the practical implementation of these principles.

The doctrine of the mixed constitution, as it was fashioned in varying ways by the major thinkers before Cicero, was designed for the protection of the propertied status quo and the maintenance of property differentials, and for securing the political domination of the wealthy, while at the same time giving the vast majority of direct economic producers a nominal voice and stake in government. As a kind of middle ground between the extremes of tyranny and democracy, the purpose of the mixed constitution was the obstruction, by complex institutional and legal arrangements, of tyranny from above and tyranny from below. Preservation of the propertied status quo and their continuing political domination could be assured, according to the ancient theorists, by an intricate governmental mechanism that would inhibit, on the one hand, any faction or individual of the landed class from seizing power and ruling despotically; and, on the other hand, any drift of the multitude toward democracy—in their view, synonymous with mob rule—and the eventual emergence of a popular tyrant. This could be accomplished through a hierarchical system of rights and duties allocated to landlords and peasants. The supreme governing function would be reserved for the gentlemanly landed minority, and the majority of peasant producers would be allotted a minimum supportive role. After a development of four centuries, the doctrine of the mixed constitution, in effect, amounted to a conception of autocratic government resorting on occasion to popular approval. Cicero, then, had a rich legacy of ideas, as well as Roman experience, to draw upon for his own notion of the mixed constitution.

2. The Roman Mixture

The second major type of state described and analyzed by Cicero is the mixed constitution that, in the form of the Roman Republic, he judges to be by far the best kind.[10] Cicero rejects the simple constitutions, as we have noted, because of their tendency to degenerate into tyranny, preferring a mixed constitution like the Roman that combines the three simple types into a "moderate and balanced form of government."[11] In such a state there is a supreme or royal element, with power (*potestas*) for the magistrates, authority (*auctoritas*) for the notables, and liberty (*libertas*) for the people.[12] Rights, duties, and functions are balanced in an equitable fashion, with each citizen in his own rank and station. In addition to a true and just equality, a mixed constitution produces great stability, since the causes of its degeneration are held in check by structural constraints. The net result is a harmonious state and a peaceful social order:

> For just as the music of harps and flutes or in the voices of singers a certain harmony of the different tones must be preserved, the interruption or violation of which is intolerable to trained ears, and as this perfect agreement and harmony is produced by the proportionate blending of unlike tones, so also is a state made harmonious by agreement among dissimilar elements, brought about by a fair and reasonable blending together of the upper, middle, and lower classes, just as if they were musical tones. What the musicians call harmony in song is concord in a state, the strongest and best bond of permanent union in any commonwealth; and such concord can never be brought about without the aid of justice.[13]

Throughout his general remarks on the mixed constitution Cicero is thinking of the Roman Republic, with the consuls as the regal power, the senate as the aristocratic power, and the tribunes and popular assemblies as the democratic power. Each checks and balances the other, although the specifics of this arrangement are not spelled out in the detailed fashion of Polybius. But when Cicero identifies the Roman mixture with the best form of state he certainly does not have in mind the Republic of his own day:

> Thus, before our own time, the customs of our ancestors produced excellent men, and eminent men preserved our ancient customs and the institutions of their forefathers. But though the republic, when it came to us, was like a beautiful painting, whose colors, however, were already fading with age, our own time not only has neglected to freshen it by renewing the original colours, but has not even taken the trouble to preserve its configuration and, so to speak, its general outlines. For what is now left of the "ancient customs" on which he [Ennius] said "the commonwealth of Rome" was "founded firm"? They have been, as we see, so completely buried in oblivion that they are not only no longer practiced, but are already unknown. And what shall I say of the men? For the loss of our customs is due to our lack of men, and for this great evil we must not only give an account, but must

even defend ourselves in every way possible, as if we were accused of capital crime. For it is through our own faults, not by any accident, that we retain only the form of the commonwealth, but have long since lost its substance.[14]

Cicero looks back to a golden age in the last century before the Gracchi, whose call for social reform, he thinks, split the Republic into "two parts," the *optimates* and the *populares*, and commenced the troubles that have brought Rome to such a sorry condition. Before this time the Roman constitution followed nature's course, developing over the ages by the wisdom of many eminent individuals and adjusting itself to meet the flux of circumstance.[15] His position is that this sacred ancestral constitution, the apotheosis of *mos maiorum*, safeguarded and advanced by such worthies as Scipio and the other participants in the dialogue of the Republic, has been impeded in its natural growth by the actors and events since those days.

Cicero treats the mixed constitution in the *Republic* and the *Laws*, each of which will be discussed in turn. In the *Republic* he intends to follow Cato's precedent of going back to "the origin of the Roman People," tracing the life history of the Roman state, following the course of nature from its birth through its growth, maturity, and eventual emergence in the ideal form.[16] This recreation of the "constitutional history" of the Roman state and the identification of the acme of its evolution and hence the ideal is the task Cicero sets himself in Book II, which, apart from the first book, is the only nearly complete surviving section of the work. In his constitutional history Cicero hopes to reveal the fundamental political principles for evaluating other states and especially the degenerate structure of rule under which he and his countrymen are living.

The Roman state in its past condition of perfection, according to Cicero, is the ideal because of its mixed nature. He never, however, describes the ideal Roman state simply as a mixture, but, rather, as "moderate and balanced," "well-regulated," a "fair balance," or an "equal mixture."[17] The two characteristics of Cicero's definition of the ideal are absolutely essential. A state can be a mixture and still fall short of the ideal, because of the lack of proper balance of the parts. A mixture of the three simple types of constitution—monarchy, aristocracy, and democracy—is not necessarily a balanced combination. Cicero, then, proposes to identify the balanced quality of the Roman mixture and consequently reveal the essence of the ideal constitution.

In his search for the nature of the balanced mixture of Rome, Cicero begins his constitutional history with the legendary foundation of the city in 753 by Romulus and continues through the reigns of the traditional seven kings, the abolition of the monarchy, and its replacement by an aristocracy, to the middle of the fifth century, when the Twelve Tables are promulgated and the oligarchy of the decemvirs is overthrown. Cicero terminates his story at this point, apparently with the implication that by that time the ideal constitution had been realized and continued at least for two and a half centuries. The details of his recapitulation of the legendary tale of Roman development need not detain us, nor his discussion of the various contributions of Roman heroes to the greatness of the state. But in the search for the meaning of a balanced mixture, a number of his remarks demand attention. By the reign of the sixth king, Servius Tullius (578–535) and before the tyranny of the seventh, Tarquin the Proud (534–510), Cicero writes, the Roman state, like both Sparta and Carthage at the time, is clearly a mixture of monarchy, aristocracy, and democracy. Yet each of the three states is obviously a monarchy, dominated by a king.[18] So while at this early date Rome and others are mixtures, the mixture is not a balanced one, preponderance being given to the monarchical element, and hence the state is still subject to corruption, testified to in Rome by the degeneration of monarchy into tyranny under the seventh king, Tarquin the Proud. After his overthrow in 509 by a conspiracy of nobles led by Junius Brutus, the senate, according to Cicero, dominates the mixture. The consulate is instituted as the "monarchical" element, and while the people are free, they have a minimal political role, senatorial ap-

proval being necessary for all acts of the popular assembly. In comparison to the mixture under the kings ending with Servius Tullius, the mixture is now seemingly more balanced but still imperfect. It is only after the plebians assert their rights with the selection of popular tribunes in 494 to offset the monarchical power of the consulate, and with the abolition of debt bondage, that the mixture of the Roman state approaches perfect balance.[19] The process is a long one, however, the balance of the mixture evidently not being perfected until the publication of The Twelve Tables and, after the mid-fifth century, the overthrow of the oligarchy of the decemvirs.

Clarification of Cicero's conception of a balanced mixture requires still further analysis not only of Book II but also of some of his other views scattered throughout the *Republic*. We are still not in a position to determine precisely what he means by a full or equal balance except that it entails a mixture in which each of the three elements has a role in government. Does this signify that each of the elements possesses a parity of powers? Probably not, given what we know about Cicero's views on numerical equality. An important clue to the resolution of the problem is given in Book II in the comment about the achievement of a balanced mixture by the state when the tribunes of the people are instituted in 494. In that passage he says that fundamental constitutional change cannot be prevented "unless there is in the state a fair [*aequabilis*] balance of rights, duties and functions, so that the magistrates have enough power [*potestatis*], the counsels of the eminent citizens [*in principum consilio*] enough influence [*auctoritas*], and the people [*populo*] enough liberty [*libertatis*]."[20] From this we understand that all the people, the *populus*, including the magistrates and senators, should have *libertas*, largely freedom to vote, but only a portion of the people, the magistrates and senators, will possess power and authority. In other words, a balanced or fair mixture for Cicero is one in which there is no parity of powers among the three elements, but a monopoly of the crucial decision-making functions in the monarchical and aristocratic elements, aided and supported by the popular component. He thinks, moreover, of the monarchical component—the consulate—as fundamentally a creature of the aristocratic senate.

The judgment is confirmed by what Cicero says in different contexts in Book I. There, first in a speech by Scipio, Cicero demands rhetorically whether true liberty in the state can possibly mean the same for all citizens

> even in states where everyone is ostensibly free? I mean states in which the people vote, elect commanders and officials, are canvassed for their votes, and have bills proposed to them, but really grant only what they would have to grant even if they were unwilling to do so, and are asked to give to others what they do not possess themselves. For they have no share in the governing power, in the deliberative function, or in the courts, over which selected judges preside, for those privileges are granted on the basis of birth or wealth.[21]

Here he apparently is thinking of the "well-regulated mixture" of Rome to which he refers,[22] in contrast to the active participation of all citizens in democracies like Rhodes and Athens, which he next mentions. Continuing the discussion somewhat later, he holds that even among free peoples, probably thinking of these same Rhodians and Athenians, distinctions in rank and office are made and special powers are granted to certain individuals. To do otherwise would, he insists, be inequitable: "For when equal honour is given to the highest and the lowest—for men of both types must exist in every nation—then this very 'fairness' is most unfair; but this cannot happen in states ruled by their best citizens."[23]

Although these two passages are meant to be defenses of the simple form of aristocratic constitution, they can be interpreted as expressions of Cicero's own objections to parity and preference for proportionate equality, and his belief that the ideal Roman equal or balanced mixture is one of proportion, not number. In applying this universal precept to a special case, he does not hesitate to state frankly: "And truly in civil dissension, when

the good [*boni*] are worth more than the many [*multi*], I think the citizens should be weighed, not counted."[24] Cicero's conception of the ideal constitution, therefore, can perhaps be interpreted as a balance, like the balance of a scale—the scale of true justice—with the "weightier" minority of wealth and good birth equal to the numerical majority of the poor.

Of particular relevance to the priority given by Cicero to "weight" over "number" in his notion of the "equal balance" of the mixture of the ideal state is the treatment in his constitutional history of the sixth king, Servius Tullius. He is praised for having a "better understanding of the government of a state" than the other kings.[25] Cicero is referring to his division of the citizens into five propertied classes (*classes*), and the separation of the youth from the elders. The division is instituted, Cicero tells us, so that the well-to-do landed proprietors (*locuples*) will have a greater number of votes than the poor in the centuriate assembly. Servius is commended for thus putting into practice a principle that Cicero believes should always prevail in a state, namely, "that the greatest number should not have the greatest power"; by Servius's prudent arrangement the *locuples* would control the assembly, while "a large majority of the citizens would neither be deprived of the suffrage, for that would be tyrannical, nor be given too much power, for that would be dangerous."[26] In his legislation Servius calls the *locuples* money-givers (*assiduos*) because they subvent the expenses of the state, and terms the poor, with little or nothing to offer save themselves and their progeny, child-givers (*proletarios*), deriving *proletarius* from *proles*, children. Cicero concludes that "while no one was deprived of the suffrage, the majority of votes was in the hands of those to whom the highest welfare of the state was the most important,"[27] that is, those with the greatest proprietary interest in the state, the *locuples* who subsidize it.

Cicero, then, certainly grounds his idea of the ideal balanced mixture in the *Republic* on the assumptions and principles of the doctrine of the mixed constitution previously outlined. He endorses the typology of the three simple constitutions and their degenerate forms, denounces excess in all things, and is fearful of the corrupting tendencies of power:

> For just as an excess of power in the hands of the aristocrats results in the overthrow of an aristocracy, so liberty itself reduces a people who possess it in too great degree to servitude. Thus everything which is in excess—when, for instance, either in the weather or in the fields, or in men's bodies, conditions have been too favourable—is usually changed into its opposite; and this is especially true in states, where such excess of liberty either in nations or in individuals turns into an excess of servitude.[28]

Cicero's preference for proportionate equality, expressed by his emphasis on weight instead of number in the equal balance of the ideal mixture, also involves the idea of balancing social classes in one all-embracing harmony, similar to musical harmony of different tones.[29] So this "proportionate blending of unlike tones" is for Cicero the crux of the equal and balanced mixture of the ideal state, one allotting a different role and function to each social class according to its weight and measure, a partnership of unequals, of rich and poor, noble and humble, powerful and powerless. Cicero's objective in prescribing such a harmony is similar to that of the previous theorists of the mixed constitution: the reconciliation of landlord and peasant in order to assure the domination of the former and the compliance of the latter and to withstand any danger of tyrannical rule by either. If his contemporaries would only return to the proportionate balance of social differences constructed by their ancient forebears, Cicero pleads, the Roman state might regain its unity and stability and last forever.[30]

3. Institutions of the Ideal Mixture

Cicero's basic conception of the ideal state in the *Republic*—the ancestral mixed constitution of Rome—is further elucidated in the *Laws*. As we have often seen, he wrote the work to spell out the principal laws and institutions of the ideal mixture, although the dif-

ferences between them and those of the existing Roman constitution are minimal. The Roman constitution has, however, veered from its natural course of development and some of its laws are not true laws in the sense of being just, but the laws of the ideal state will conform to the law of nature. Some of the differences between the ideal and the actual, together with selected portions of his commentary, may be helpful in illuminating his doctrine of the mixed constitution.

Cicero believes that the nature of the ideal state depends essentially on the institutional arrangements for public officials.[31] Chief among them are the senators, and he sees the senate as the core of his recommended system of law and power. The senate should control public policy. The word chosen by Cicero to denote its rule is *dominus*, the "master" of public policy (*publici consilii*).[32] Cicero's choice of *dominus* with its meaning in Roman law of head of the household and owner of property, aptly reflects the paramountcy he accords to the senate in his ideal constitution. The senate of wealthy landed proprietors not only is in effect the master of public policy, but also the "owner" of it, and as a consequence is the "owner" of the state. Citizens should support the supreme role of the senate, dutifully defending and obeying its decisions. Ultimate power (*potestas*) should belong to the people, and authority (*auctoritas*) to the senate, a division, Cicero insists, essential to the preservation of "the moderate and harmonious conditions of the state" (*moderatus et concors civitatis status*)—the balanced mixture.

In acknowledging the ultimate power of the people, Cicero of course, is deferring to the sacred constitutional principle of the sovereign *populus*, and not thinking of the popular exercise of power in the actual management of the daily affairs of the Republic. Because of their crucial role in the constitution, senators "*shall be free from dishonour, and shall be a model for the rest of the citizens.*"[33] Cicero shares the common ancient conviction that corruption begins in the head of the body politic and spreads downward throughout the body, the result of the tendency in human conduct to imitate what we might call authority figures. Hence, senators should always maintain high personal standards and refrain from immoral and illicit conduct.[34] The senate is to consist of ex-magistrates,[35] the definite tendency of that body after the reforms of Sulla; and the censors are empowered to remove any senator for dishonorable conduct.[36] Cicero does not wish to alter in a fundamental way the current distribution of powers between senate and populace, only to establish a firm legal basis for senatorial power and to extend it to a limited degree. So senatorial decrees receive the status of laws, as had long been the case in practice, but not from a strictly legal standpoint. Minor officials, the quaestors, are legally obligated to obey the directives of the senate, the number of praetors being determined by senatorial decree and popular opinion. In times of peril a dictator without consular direction will be appointed for a maximum of six months by the senate. However, the emergency powers of the consuls are evidently to be strengthened without the need of a *senatus consultus ultimum*, the senatorial delegation and confirmation of such extralegal powers, a subject omitted by Cicero.[37]

Two innovations in regard to the popular assemblies are presented. The first is that all presiding magistrates are legally responsible for any violence or undue disturbance occurring in the convocations.[38] The second measure, of a more novel character than the first has to do with voting: a shrewd combination of the current use of the secret ballot with the traditional voice vote.[39] It requires attention because Cicero, in his proposal, quite clearly reveals—perhaps more so than any previous thinker—the essence of the idea of the mixed constitution, and he proves politically more astute than some of his conservative contemporaries. All citizens will have the suffrage, thus guaranteeing their *libertas*. However, Cicero suggests, "let the people have their ballots as a safeguard of their liberty, but with the provision that these ballots are to be shown and voluntarily exhibited to any of our best and most eminent citizens, so that the people may enjoy liberty also in this very privilege of honourably winning the favour of the aristocracy."[40] Secret ballots, Cicero maintains, deprive the aristocracy of its au-

thority by keeping them in ignorance of the true opinions of the voters. He thus hopes to grant "liberty to the people in such a way as to ensure that the aristocracy shall have great authority and the opportunity to use it."[41] Consequently, the people will retain their political freedom, the power of the aristocracy will be preserved, and the dangers of class conflict avoided. While the "appearance of liberty" (*libertatis species*) will be maintained, in actuality the people will be governed by "authority and favour" (*auctoritati aut gratiae*).[42] In other words, the reality of aristocratic power rests on the network of *amicitiae* among the nobility themselves, and on the patron-client relationship between members of the gentlemanly classes and lower orders.

Another device, according to Cicero, that paradoxically tends to keep the people in line is the very institution introduced to enhance their power, the tribunate. He readily admits that the tribunes of the people have in the past been "troublesome," but he feels that some of his friends are misguided in wishing to abolish them, and so he retains them in his ideal constitution.[43] For despite its evils, the people perhaps have less real power under the leadership of the tribunes than without. In fact, contrary to the belief of the people, the power of the tribunes is not equal to that of the senators. While the establishment of the tribunes is a necessary compromise, a sop, Cicero implies, offered by the ancient aristocracy to satisfy the popular clamor for increased participation in government, in reality over the long run, a people organized under the tribunes is less dangerous than without them. Conflict between people and nobility, Cicero seems to suggest, is more restrained and moderate when it is institutionalized, brought out into the open, and regulated by mutually agreed procedures. Hence, liberty through the institution of the tribunes was "granted in such a manner that the people were induced by many excellent provisions to yield to the authority of the nobles [*auctoritati principum cederet*]."[44]

Cicero views the mixed constitution as above all else an ingenious mechanism to maintain the dominance of the large noble landholders in an age of mounting popular demand for more liberty and a greater role in government. However, the question immediately arises as to how he thinks a state with such a complex three-headed government can possibly act as a viable and united whole with solidarity, loyalty, and spirit. What is the basis for the broad social consensus that must be the foundation of aristocratic authority? For one answer we must search behind the formal machinery of government to discover the informal social and political relationships linking and lubricating the system, thereby accounting for the superiority of aristocratic power. One such integrator of the political process and of society as a whole just touched upon is simply taken for granted by Cicero and never explained in any detail. It is the politics of influence and favor arising from *amicitiae* and patronage: the first generates power within the upper classes, the second enables aristocratic power to be exercised over the lower classes.

A second answer is the shaping of popular opinion by the civic religious cult. Cicero, with Plato, Aristotle, and Polybius, is a vigorous advocate of the social utility of religion. Like them, he believes that religion legitimizes the acts of government and induces citizens to be respectful of their institutions and deferential toward their rulers and their policies, thus creating a broad base of support and enduring loyalty. In short, religion is the absolutely crucial foundation of civic education and virtue, and hence of the unity and order of the state. Cicero's reasons for the importance of religion to the state are worth summarizing. First and foremost, religion provides the state with authority, thereby enabling it to command loyalty and obedience from the citizenry.[45] If the state is held to have been founded by the gods and to have acted with the approval of the gods, then all it does possess a divine aura of legitimacy eliciting the respect and wholehearted support of the populace. The state, thus, becomes sacred, and any civic disobedience or act against the state is a matter of sacrilege. Another essential function performed by religion is to foster virtuous conduct, which in turn produces an environment of mutual trust and cooperation. Citizens who come to believe that the gods are ever-watchful, taking note of their individual conduct and observing their transgressions, are more likely to conform carefully to the community's moral prescriptions, especially if these are thought to rest ultimately on divine will. Fear of divine punishment and hope of divine reward help to enforce obligations such as oaths and treaties and to deter crime and the potential criminal. Nor would death be feared if there were a promise of a hereafter where the virtuous would enjoy eternal happiness.[46] Finally, the net social effect of religion is taming and pacifying a people. It lifts them out of savagery and barbarism, and is instrumental in fashioning a harmonious, refined, and civilized way of life.[47] Through religion, a peaceful and orderly society can be established, possessing the morale, vigor, and strength necessary for self-preservation in a hostile world.

In the account of the development of the Roman state in Book II of the *Republic*, Cicero emphasizes the religious innovations of the second king, Numa Pompilius.[48] By creating the "greater auspices," increasing the original number of augurs by two, and appointing five pontiffs to oversee the religious rites and various other religious offices, Numa was responsible for the institution of the Roman civic cult in much the same form in which it continues to exist. His intention was to tame the military passions of the Romans in order to produce a period of peace and consolidation. Cicero concludes that Numa "died after having established the two elements which most conspicuously contribute to the stability of a state—religion and the spirit of tranquility [*dementia*]."[49] In the *Laws*, Cicero affirms that the establishment of religion is even more important than the magistrates in the creation of a commonwealth.[50] It is no accident that in his recommendations for the ideal constitution he begins with a lengthy discourse on religious institutions since he fully realizes their significance for the government he subsequently describes. Toward the end of his life, he reiterates the "conviction that Romulus by his auspices and Numa by his establishment of our ritual laid the foundation of our state."[51]

The system of religion prescribed by Cicero in *Laws*, Book II, for his ideal polity—differing from the Roman state—is practically identical with that of Numa as it evolved. The sacredness of the state will be stressed by the erection of shrines to suggest to the people that the gods dwell among them. An augur himself, Cicero assumes that ideally the priesthood should be a monopoly and instrument of the aristocracy as it was in actual Roman practice.[52] In addition to being in charge of all public rites, priests will attend all private services, because "the people's constant need for the advice and authority of the aristocracy helps to hold the state together."[53] Augurs in the ideal state are to be "the highest and most important authority."[54] The act of every magistrate, in order to be valid, is subject to them, and any disobedience to the augurs is to be penalized by death.[55] From a philosophic perspective, Cicero may express some reservations about divination;[56] nevertheless, he has no doubts about its vital social functions for the state. In the *Republic*, he favors augury and the auspices;[57] and in the *Laws*, he explicitly upholds the art of divination and expresses a conviction of its validity:

> For if we admit that gods exist, and that the universe is ruled by their will, that they are mindful of the human race, and that they have the power to give us indications of future events, then I do not see any reason for denying the existence of divination. . . . Nor indeed would our own Romulus have taken the auspices before founding Rome, nor would the name of Attius Navius have been remembered all these years, had not all these people made many prophecies which were in remarkable agreement with the truth.[58]

Another classic question arises. If the aristocracy through the senate actually governs, how are these custodians themselves to be controlled? In Juvenal's classic query: *Quis custodiet ipsos custodes?* What precautions are to be taken to check their conduct, thereby insuring that in fact they serve as models for the emulation of other citizens? Religion has a vital role in this regard, too. Cicero prescribes simplicity in ritual and wishes to take steps to provide the ancient

beliefs with greater ethical substance. His prohibitions against exorbitant financial outlays for funerals and monuments, monetary contributions for religious purposes, the consecration of useful agricultural land, and soft, licentious music in connection with ceremonies are aimed in part at strengthening the upper classes, curtailing their extravagance, and purifying their morals.[59]

Another significant instrument for the control of the aristocratic custodians of the state, and Cicero's major innovation in the ideal constitution of the *Laws*, is the strengthening and refurbishing of a venerable institution: the censorship.[60] The office should be filled permanently, instead of sporadically, as is the current practice. Two censors would be appointed for five-year terms for the performance of a number of traditional functions. They would categorize all citizens by age, family, and wealth into tribes and other divisions, and enroll recruits into the army. Temples, streets, and aqueducts in the city and the public treasury and state revenues would be under their jurisdiction. The morals of the people and the senators are to be subject to their regulation. In addition, Cicero assigns a number of duties to the censors—the innovative feature of his stipulation—that would have struck his Roman contemporaries as definite oddities. The censors would supervise the texts of all laws with the purpose of determining their authenticity. Above all, in a novel recommendation, he makes the censors Guardians of the Law, *nomophylakes*, in the Greek tradition of Plato, Aristotle, and Demitrius of Phalerum.[61] All governmental acts are to be scrutinized for conformity to the law. On leaving office each magistrate will be required to explain and justify his official conduct to the censors, who in turn will submit a report. If the findings of the censors reveal any legal irregularities or violations, the outgoing magistrate will be liable to state prosecution in a regular court.

Perhaps it is not overstating the case to argue that in the *Republic* and *Laws* the development of the doctrine of the mixed constitution in the ancient world attains its apogee. From Cicero's exposition there can be little doubt as to the basic principles and purpose of the doctrine. It is entirely compatible with an authoritarian, elitist, and inegalitarian political society. It represents a partnership of landlord and peasant, in which the latter is a very junior partner. The mixed constitution is a masterful device for stabilizing and conserving lordly domination, while at the same time pacifying the peasantry and maintaining the solidarity of the state as a whole. But as Cicero fully realizes, no political mechanism can be any better than the men who operate it. The solution to Roman difficulties, he thinks, is the regeneration of its operators, not simply the repair of the constitutional machine. Unless the aristocracy returns to its original harmony and unity, recapturing some of its traditional ancestral vigor and virtue, the constitution can never work as it should. If Cicero the statesman fails to weld the aristocracy into a single, public-spirited phalanx, at least Cicero the educator and philosopher can still cling to the hope of reforming the ways of his peers and, especially, of rejuvenating the noble youth on whom the future operation of the mixed constitution so depends. With the benefit of hindsight, we know that the hope was a vain and forlorn one. The rot had set in too deeply for Cicero to remedy, even with all his powers of persuasion.

Notes

1. Despite the importance of the conception of the mixed constitution, the comprehensive treatise on the subject remains to be written. Of importance are Z. S. Fink, *The Classical Republicans: An Essay in the Recovery of a Pattern of Thought in Seventeenth-Century England* (2d ed. Evanston, Ill.: Northwestern University Press, 1962), chap. 1; Kurt von Fritz, *The Theory of the Mixed Constitution in Antiquity: A Critical Analysis of Polybius' Political Ideas* (New York: Columbia University Press, 1954); Glenn R. Morrow, *Plato's Cretan City: A Historical Interpretation of the "Laws"* (Princeton, N.J.: Princeton University Press, 1960), chaps. 5, 10; G. W. Trompf, *The Idea of Historical Recurrence in Western Thought: From Antiquity to the Reformation* (Berkeley and Los Angeles: University of California Press, 1979), chaps. 1–2; F. W. Walbank, *An Historical Commentary on Polybius* (Oxford: Clarendon Press, 1957), vol. 1; idem, *Polybius* (Berkeley and Los Angeles: University California Press, 1972), chap. 5.
   Also see G. J. D. Aalders, *Political Thought in Hellenistic Times* (Amsterdam: Hakkert, 1975), pp. 105–12; Andrew Lintott, *Violence, Civil Strife and Revolution in the Classical City, 750–330 B.C.* (London: Croom Helm, 1982), chap. 7; G. E. M. de Ste. Croix, *The Class Struggle in the Ancient Greek World: From the Archaic Age to the Arab Conquests* (Ithaca, N.Y.: Cornell University Press, 1981), pp. 74–76; Ellen Meiksins Wood and Neal Wood, *Class, Ideology and Ancient Political Theory: Socrates, Plato, and Aristotle in Social Context* (New York: Oxford University Press, 1978), pp. 237–49.

2. Herodotus, *The Persian Wars* III, 80–82; Plato, *Statesman* 291a–92a, 301a–3b; Aristotle, *Politics*, esp. 1278b–80a.

3. Thucydides, *The Peloponnesian War* VIII, 97; Plato, *Laws* 712b–13a; Aristotle, *Politics* 1269a–73b), 1293a–96b, 1302a, 1318b–19a, 1320b). Plato's specific discussion of the mixed constitution for Magnesia is scattered throughout Books III–VI of the *Laws*.

4. Diogenes Laertius, *Lives of Eminent Philosophers* VII, 131. Zeno, the founder of the school, and its third head, Chrysippus, are mentioned.

5. Polybius's views on the mixed constitution are in *The Histories* VI.

6. Solon, *Elegies* 5; also see 4, and *Iambi* 37 (Loeb Classical Library translation). A useful guide to the question of the "middle way" is Chester G. Starr, *The Economic and Social Growth of Early Greece, 800–500 B.C.* (New York: Oxford University Press, 1977), pp. 124–28, 178–79, 234–35 nn. 18–20.

7. Theognis, *Elegiac Poems* 335; also see 219–20, 331–32 (Loeb Classical Library translation). On the Athenian social ideal see K. J. Dover, *Greek Popular Morality In the Time of Plato and Aristotle* (Oxford: Blackwell, 1974), pp. 112–13, 173.

8. Plato, *Laws* 691c–d, 713c–14a, 875a–d.

9. Plato, *Laws* 757a–e; Aristotle, *Nicomachean Ethics* 1130b–31b; *Politics*, esp. 1280a–81a, 1282b–83a, 1293b–94b, 1301a–2a, 1317b). Also see Neal Wood, *Cicero's Social and Political Thought* (Berkely: University of California Press, 1988), chaps. 4 and 9.

10. Cicero, *Republic* (hereafter *Rep.*) I, 42, 45, 69–70; II, 41–42, 57. In *Rep.* II, 42, Cicero refers to the Roman state with its mixed constitution

as the "most splendid conceivable," and in II, 66, as "the greatest state of all." Cf. Cicero, *De Legibus* (hereafter *Leg.*) II, 23.

11. *Rep.* I, 69.

12. *Rep.* I, 69; 11, 57.

13. *Rep.* II, 69.

14. *Rep.* V, 2.

15. *Rep.* I, 31; II, 2–3, 29–30, 65–66. Nevertheless, as we shall see, Cicero never intends that the Roman state should return to this golden age in any literal constitutional sense, although he believes that his fellow citizens should recapture the virtue and spirit of their forebears. See C. W. Keyes, "Original Elements in Cicero's Ideal Constitution," *American Journal of Philology* 42 (1921): 310, 322–23.

16. *Rep.* II, 3, 30.

17. *Rep.* I, 45, 69; 11, 41, 57, 65, 69.

18. *Rep.* II, 42, 43.

19. *Rep.* II, 56–59.

20. *Rep.* II, 57.

21. *Rep.* I, 47.

22. *Rep.* I, 45.

23. *Rep.* I, 53.

24. *Rep.* VI, 1. Cf *Off.* II, 79.

25. *Rep.* II, 37.

26. *Rep.* II, 39.

27. *Rep.* II, 40.

28. *Rep.* I, 68.

29. *Rep.* II, 69.

30. *Rep.* III, 41.

31. *Leg.* III, 5.

32. *Leg.* III, 28.

33. *Leg.* III, 28.

34. *Leg.* III, 30–32.

35. *Leg.* III, 10, 28. A law of the ideal state.

36. *Leg.* III, 7.

37. *Leg.* III, 6, 8–10.

38. *Leg.* III, 11, 42.

39. *Leg.* III, 10, 33–39.

40. *Leg.* III, 39.

41. *Leg.* III, 38.

42. *Leg.* III, 39.

43. *Leg.* III, 44, and 19–25.

44. *Leg.* III, 25.

45. *Leg.* II, 15–16.

46. Cicero, *The Speech of M. T. Cicero After His Return from the Senate* (hereafter, *Sen.*) 66.

47. *Leg.* II, 36.

48. *Rep.* II, 20–27; V, 3.

49. *Rep.* II, 27.

50. *Leg.* II, 69.

51. Cicero, *De natura deorum libri tres* (hereafter, *N.D.*) III, 5.

52. *Leg.* II, 26, 310.

53. *Leg.* II, 30.

54. *Leg.* II, 31.

55. *Leg.* II, 31, 21.

56. See Neal Wood, *Cicero's Social and Political Thought* (Berkely: University of California Press, 1988), chap. 3 and *Div.* II, 28, 43, 70, 148; *N.D.* II, 60–72; III, 53–60.

57. *Rep.* II, 16–17, 26–27.

58. *Leg.* II, 32–33.

59. *Leg.* II, 19, 22, 24–25, 28, 38–39, 40–41, 45, 59–68.

60. *Leg.* III, 7, 46–47.

61. See Wood and Wood, *Class Ideology,* p. 252.

14
Cicero's Focus

From the Best Regime to the Model Statesman

Walter J. Nicgorski

The question of the best political order is commonly and properly thought to be at the very center of the inquiry known as political philosophy. Its presence is revealed both in efforts at utopian construction and in searches for incontrovertible, if not a priori, principles of justice. That same question of the best regime can be found close to the surface and thus capable of arising in ordinary political disputes and discourse among thoughtful citizens.

Leo Strauss, in his interpretative work on classical political philosophers, has emphasized the citizen perspective as the mark of their approach and initial horizon; he has closely connected that perspective to the question of the best regime, the central concern or "guiding question" of classical political philosophy. Strauss wrote that "it was its direct relation to political life which determined the orientation and scope of classical political philosophy."[1] This meant that "the primary questions of classical political philosophy" and "the terms in which it stated them" were "not specifically philosophic or scientific"; rather, "they were questions that are raised in assemblies, councils, clubs and cabinets, and they were stated in terms intelligible and familiar at least to all sane adults, from everyday experience and everyday usage."[2] These questions and terms are entailed in actual political controversies; such questions are "what group should rule, or what compromise would be the best solution—that is to say, what political order would be the best order." Strauss conceded that though the "immediate concern" of actual controversies is "the best political order for the given political community . . . every answer to that immediate question implies an answer to the universal question of the best political order as such," and thus Strauss spoke of "the natural tendency" of political controversy "to express itself in universal terms."[3]

Strauss's emphasis on these characteristics of classical political philosophy is, to my knowledge, an entirely noncontroversial aspect of his scholarship. Plato's *The Republic,* with its manifest search for and presentation of the best regime or the principles thereof, has been seen—one might say, generation after generation—as not merely the centerpiece and pinnacle of classical political philosophy but as a continuing inspiration to utopian constructions that grow out of the actual political controversies of the day. The reactions to those constructions or to their originator in one sense, namely, Plato, show the reflective citizen's natural tendency to have to confront in the form of a model, utopia or counterutopia, the question of the best regime. Thus witnesses to the centrality of that question and to its significant but natural intrusion into ordinary political disputes are as varied as Machiavelli with his warning against "imagined states and princedoms,"[4] Jefferson with his aversion to Plato, and Karl Popper in his concern over Plato's totalitarianism. Since our actual and immediate political concerns draw us to an encounter with Plato, there is ever the danger that his text might be bent to the cause, either in hostile rejection of Plato or in an effort to appropriate his authority.

Plato's model, it seems, already claimed its central and magisterial role for political philosophy during the ancient period. At least it is reasonable to infer this from its treatment by Aristotle in *The Politics* and its comparable central and formative role in Cicero's major political work, *De Re Publica.* Neither of these legendary students of Plato is entirely deferential—to understate the matter—to his best regime or, more precisely, to their understandings of that best regime proffered in *The Republic.* The task undertaken in this essay is to attend with special care to and to seek to understand Cicero's apparent quarrel with Plato over the

183

model of *The Republic*, a quarrel that seems initially to involve more a challenge to the centrality and importance of the issue of the best regime in a universal sense than a dispute with various details of Plato's city in speech. In Cicero's *De Re Publica* (hereafter cited as *DR*), articulation of the best regime in the nature of things is set aside in favor of depiction of what is taken as the best of actually realized regimes, the Roman republic. Has Cicero thereby sought to dispute in some sense what has been taken to be the very defining core of classical political philosophy, that the question of the best regime, universally understood, is the "guiding" one? In the course of an examination of *DR* with this question in mind, Cicero's "shift of focus" from the best regime to the model statesman comes to our attention.[5]

The essay proceeds first by noticing certain emphatic themes early in *DR* and prior to the raising of the question of the best regime; second, by sketching the problematic, namely, the evidence of Cicero's quarrel in a context of recognition of his thorough-going respect for Plato and of an appreciation of the utility of constructing a guiding model, a utopian best case. Next, the essay turns to observe Cicero's consideration of the best regime question in his *DR* and finds and comments on how his response to the question leads him to a shift from the detailing of a model regime to an emphasis on the model or best statesman. Finally, the essay highlights certain features of Cicero's treatment of the model statesman and reflects on the significance of Cicero's shift and the model statesman in the context of classical political philosophy and in reference to common experience and American political thought. The fragmented state of *DR* enlarges the usual problems of interpretation and more than ordinarily justifies turning occasionally to other works of Cicero to make and sustain the interpretation.

Statesmanship: Greatest Need and Highest Calling

It is useful to begin this close examination of aspects of *DR* by recalling that the work is largely in dialogue form and that the perso-nae of the dialogue are leading statesmen from the second century B.C., including Scipio Africanus Minor and Gaius Laelius whom Cicero admires throughout his works and uses as personae in other works. Scipio's is most often taken as the voice of Cicero in the dialogue, and there are many good reasons for this view.[6] There are also good reasons for caution about a conclusion that Scipio is the exclusive voice of Cicero.[7] The actual dialogue within the work is set during a holiday from the apparently pressing active political responsibilities of the participants.

Cicero, as was generally his practice with other dialogues, appears to have opened each of the six books of *DR* with a preface or introduction (*prooemium*) in which he speaks directly to the reader in his own name. The prefaces in the case of this work are only partially extant. However, there is intact a substantial portion, it appears, of the preface to the first book and, in a sense, to the whole *DR*.

With this introduction to the first book, Cicero steps off in a certain direction and sets a tone for the work that accords well with the dramatic detail of the dialogue. Here, Cicero is found emphasizing that service through political leadership is the greatest necessity and highest calling among men, that governance of the state and thus the realization of such matters as philosophers only talk about is the greatest virtue, and that the well-being of the Roman state has been repeatedly dependent on the response of men of the past to this call to virtue. Neither pleasure nor ease nor philosophy should be allowed to draw the suitably talented from the high service of statesmanship. Cicero's preface focuses attention on leadership of the state and on the basic allurements and arguments that might draw one away from the struggles and difficulties attendant on a life of public leadership. He has done this at some length, he confesses at *DR* 1:12, so that the discussion of the republic (*de republica disputatio*) which is to follow would not seem pointless or in vain (*frustra*).[8] He understands himself to be giving meaning to this discussion to follow (a discussion that initially centers on the best regime) "by removing all hesitations of engaging in politics" (*dubitationem ad rem publicam adeundi*). Thus his openly acknowledged major point in the introduction is to defend inquiries into the state not as philosophically interesting questions but, rather, as justified by their relationship to active participation in political life. It is, in other words, useful and thereby presumably right to make such inquiries and have such conversations. Their utility is related to that greatest utility, that necessary foundation for all good things: political leadership. In fact, and yet within *DR* 1:12, Cicero offers a concession to "those who might be moved by the authority of philosophers"; he observes that those philosophers held in the greatest esteem by the most learned men (all evidence indicates he has in mind at least Plato and Aristotle) have examined politics and written about it and thereby performed a certain political function. Philosophers, in other words, are justified insofar as they contribute to the work of political leadership by illuminating the nature of politics.

As the dialogue actually commences and its various participants are seen arriving, the assembling public leaders struggle some over what their topic should be for this leisurely holiday conversation. By the time they settle, at the suggestion of Laelius, on asking Scipio to speak on the question of the best regime (*optimi status civitatis*), it has been made clear that even the activities of their leisure are to be responsible; that is, these activities must be related to their work as statesmen: They must be, in a sense, useful. Trifling and amusing inquiries should take none of their time, and speculative inquiries that might prove ultimately useful in some way in political or military leadership are clearly to be subordinated to such directly relevant political inquiries as the question of the best regime. Thus when Laelius comes to make his suggestion and the dialogue takes its specific initial focus, he is portrayed saying what one might expect, given Cicero's own introduction, that this topic of the best regime calls forth, above all, conversation of the highest utility (*ad utilissimos rei publicae sermones potissimum*).[9] The knowledge that is sought has the power to make those present better and happier.[10]

The Problematic: The Loving Quarrel with Plato

The first direct indication that Scipio's treatment of the best regime involves a quarrel with its inspiring source, namely, Plato, occurs at the very beginning of his discourse in the first book. Claiming that this topic always gets his concentrated, careful attention and that its pursuit is clearly useful to the conduct of his political responsibilities, Scipio confesses that he is not satisfied with "the writings on this question left by the greatest and wisest men of Greece."[11] He at once, however, shows his great respect for those Greeks by observing that he "hesitates to prefer his own opinions to theirs" and then concludes this segment of his discourse with the following observation:

> So I ask you to bear me in the following light, as one not altogether unknowledgeable of Greek perspectives and not prepared, especially in this manner to give precedence to their views over ours, but as one Roman citizen liberally educated through the care of his father and afire for learning from boyhood, yet having learned much more from experience (*usu*) and the lessons of the home than from books.[12]

Any doubt that the Greek writing which Scipio has in mind is, above all, Plato's *The Republic* can be laid to rest as the second book begins and Scipio undertakes, following Cato as he claims, his account of the Roman regime as the best of actual regimes. "The pursuit of the proposed topic," says Scipio,

> will, however, be easier [*facilius*] if I will have set our polity [*rem publicam*] before you, first in its origins, then in growth and then in maturity and finally in its strong and robust state, than if I will have imagined [*mihi . . . finxero*] some polity as does Socrates in Plato's work.[13]

What could Scipio mean by "easier"? Is his, and apparently Cicero's, discontent with Plato's *The Republic* explained by the fact that Plato's city is simply too intangible, especially for Romans, to provide an effective response to the question what is the best regime? Perhaps this is part of the reason for not being satisfied with this writing of one of the "wisest" of the Greeks. It hardly seems to be the entire reason for the discontent with Plato's city in speech.

There are indications, in one of the more fragmented segments of the text, that certain specific practices and rules concerning sexual relations and common property in Plato's city disturbed Scipio and Cicero just as some specific provisions had provoked Aristotle's dissent in an earlier time.[14] At this very point in Scipio's discourse as he appears to be favorably contrasting Roman ways of upbringing and training young men and potential leaders with those of the Greeks, Laelius is made to notice that Scipio chooses not to contend with "your dear Plato," not even mentioning him in a context in which it seems he too should be a target.[15] Again, the dialogue has drawn attention to the great respect with which Plato is being treated even while an apparently different and un-Platonic approach is taken in discussing the best regime. Thus, whatever the full nature of the quarrel with Plato, it seems to be a loving quarrel. Scipio, perhaps like Cicero and his young interlocutor in the *Tusculan Disputations* (hereafter cited as *TD*), may be more inclined to go wrong with Plato than to be right with his adversaries.[16] Playful though that remark of Cicero's was, Plato's preeminence as a philosopher and as a teacher of Cicero is evident throughout Cicero's writings.[17] R. D. Cumming aptly describes Cicero as *"homo platonicus."*[18]

There is, however, more direct evidence of deference to Plato and even of essential agreement with him in the work presently under our close scrutiny. In the first book, not only does Scipio directly and approvingly quote a lengthy passage from Plato's *Republic* to describe how extreme democracy corrupts into tyranny, but more important, he later explicitly confesses his essential agreement with Plato's political teaching in *The Republic*.[19] This latter passage (*DR* 2:52) is important, indeed critical, not only because of its explicitness on Scipio's agreement with Plato but because it reveals Scipio's and no doubt Cicero's understanding of what Plato intended with his city in speech. The passage was often cited by Leo Strauss as an apparent key to his interpretation of *The Republic*.[20] Scipio is found here observing that Plato sought and created a city "more to be wished for than to be hoped for," a city, as such, "not possible," but one "in which the very rationale [meaning] of political life can be perceived" (*in qua ratio rerum civilium perspici posset*). Contrasting his efforts here with Plato's, Scipio then immediately adds:

> I, however, if only I can find the right words, will so strive , with that very same understanding [*rationibus eisdem*] which he possessed, not in a semblance and imitation of a state [*in umbra et imagine*] but in a large and great polity [*amplissima re publica*], that I may appear to be pointing out, as if with a rod, the cause of every public good and evil.

Plato in *The Republic* is thus taken, above all, to teach an understanding of the nature or rationale of political life (*rationem rerum civilium*), and it is that same understanding that accounts for the critical standards (*rationes easdem*) which Scipio and Cicero employ in *De Re Publica*. Shortly after this very important observation by Scipio and in the course of his relating the rise of the Roman state, he observes "that the very nature of political reality often overcomes reason" (*vincit ipsa rerum publicarum natura saepe rationem*).[21] It appears, then, that a paradox is reached, but by no means an intolerable or unreasonable one, for it seems that part of the very rationale or understanding of political life (*ratio rerum civilium*) is that political life *often* does not follow the way of reason (*rationis*). In this perspective, a rational understanding of politics encompasses that essential dimension of it which is not rational. It will be necessary to return to this perspective in the course of following Scipio's discourse on the best regime.

At this point, it is sufficient to notice that if Scipio and Cicero regard this view of rationality's limits as an important truth about politics and that if they revere Plato and claim he has taught the most important things about politics in *The Republic*, Plato himself, in the absence of any disclaimer in the text, is likely a teacher of this truth. One way to teach it would be to sketch or imagine a perfectly rational city, the city in speech, and then to let appear the incredible gap between such a city and the way human beings are and conduct themselves. This leads to seeing Plato's city as not intended by him as a practicable model for humans as they are known, as a city "more to be wished for than hoped for"; it supports, then, an understanding of Plato's intent in *The Republic* that can be defended, as it was earlier here, from the text of *DR* 2:52 itself. Thus it should not be surprising to find Scipio and Cicero disinclined to challenge or quarrel with Plato over specific institutions and practices of his city in speech. These specifics either are not very important set against the debt to Plato for his illuminating political fundamentals (*rationes*) or, and more likely in the light of what has preceded, they are not intended by Plato as a practicable model to be followed or imitated.

If Plato is so understood by Scipio and Cicero, the problematic posed by the quarrel with him seems to intensify. Why should they be dissatisfied (*DR* 1:33) with Plato's approach to the best regime if it is meant to teach, among other principles, the very limits of rationality in politics, a perspective that they share with Plato, if they have not learned it and other of the most important political truths from him? In what way, then, could Scipio's treatment of the best regime be "easier" (*DR* 2:3) than Plato's? In what way would it be more effective, as implied (*DR* 2:52), for pointing out "the cause of every public good and evil"? Would it really be easier to accomplish what Plato had done with a concrete historical example of a regime? Again, is it the Roman preference for the concrete and tangible that is at issue here? Before a direct effort is made to answer these questions by following Scipio's treatment of the best regime, two other relevant aspects of Cicero's writings need to be noted.

The respect shown Plato and the specific debt to *The Republic* make it wholly inappropriate to see Cicero as one who, according to

Eric Voegelin, "with a sneer dismissed the best polities of the Hellenic philosophers as bodies of no importance by the side of the best polity that was created on the battlefields by the imperatores of Rome."[22] There is, however, evidence that such opinions or similar ones about Greek philosophy were around, if not prevalent, among those Romans who knew anything at all of philosophy and Plato. If the Romans had a historic resistance to philosophy which is evident in a number of ways, including a formal prohibition of philosophers in the century before Cicero, then Plato's "fictitious" city in speech probably played into the hands of those who would deride philosophy as silly, irrelevant, and even at times dangerous. In his *De Oratore* (hereafter cited as *DO*), written in close conjunction with *DR*, Cicero portrays Antonius warning against the influence of philosophical books on the work of the active orator.[23] If such active leaders strictly confine philosophy to a restful holiday, they are, contends Antonius, less apt to find themselves drawing on Plato when their work brings them to speak "on justice and loyalty" (*de justitia et fide*).[24] What's wrong with Plato is that when he wrote on these themes, he "created on his pages a certain novel state [*novam quamdam finxit in libris civitatem*], insofar as what he thought to be the requisites of justice [*usque eo illa, quae dicenda de justitia putabat*] was incompatible with everyday life and the customs of states." Antonius then goes on to suggest that if peoples and states actually implemented Plato's ideas, there would be no free assemblies where oratory might flourish. Clearly, in this perspective, Plato is held responsible for "far out" ideas, and the specifics of his city in speech are taken as proposals meant for implementation. To some, perhaps most Romans, as, in fact, to so many thereafter in Western history, Plato's city seems to function nearly as shorthand or symbol for the irrelevance and the sometimes dangerous irrelevance of the philosophic mind.[25]

Scipio and Cicero, as we have seen, also turn away from Plato's approach to the best regime, but they do so with a different understanding of his intent from that Antonius reveals and with much appreciation for what

Plato has taught. Why they do this may become even more puzzling when another passage in *DO* and through it another theme in Cicero's writings is considered. Cicero uses a model or complete (*perfectum*) orator while eschewing at the same time this approach with regard to the polity or regime. Crassus, the character in *DO* who seems most clearly to have the voice of Cicero himself and whose major discourses dominate the dialogue, defends the great demands which he is making on the orator he sketches there by saying that it is proper to delineate the greatest orator (*summum oratorem*), for whenever one seeks to understand something, one looks to the "pure and perfect" (*absolutam et perfectam*) model.[26] Only, he adds, if one sets before oneself the perfect model will one be able to understand "the essence and nature of a thing" (*vim et naturam rei*).

In a later rhetorical writing, simply titled *Orator,* Cicero returns to the theme of the perfect orator (*summum oratorem*), and speaking directly in his own name and explicitly calling to mind Plato and his "ideas," he claims that by creating (*fingendo*) this orator who likely never was and never will be in the ordinary sense of becoming, he makes with his mind (*cogitatione et mente*) the perfect type (*perfectum genus*).[27] In a reference directly suggesting the opening of book 6 of Plato's *The Republic* where Socrates relates how guardian rulers, like painters who look to a model in mind of the best and truest, make practical decisions in the light of that true model of justice, Cicero compares the idea of the perfect orator to those ideas which Phidias, a great sculptor, and painters hold in mind when they create their imperfect approximations.

Thus Cicero, dissatisfied with Plato's approach to the best regime, seems to turn to that very approach, of constructing the perfect model—the model in speech—in considering the orator. That this orator is the public leader or statesman becomes indubitably evident to the reader of *DO* and *Orator.*[28]

In following Scipio's treatment of the best regime in search of understanding his discontent with Plato's approach, we will find ourselves encountering this perfect orator/ statesman within *DR.* Though obscured by the fragmented condition of *DR,* a "shift in focus" from a Platonic best regime to a Platonic best orator occurs there. In witnessing and understanding the shift in *DR,* one is better able to appreciate not only Cicero's discontent with the Platonic approach to the model city but his emphatic concern with the model statesman.

From the Best Regime to the Model Statesman

Only a sketch or overview can be offered here of the steps in *DR* and primarily in the speeches of Scipio that mark the movement from the posing of the question of the best regime to a focus on the model statesman. As already made clear, the question of the best regime is deflected in the direction of the best of actual regimes, that being the Roman state. In fact, Laelius makes clear as he initially poses the question to Scipio that the question is put to him with awareness that he has been known to deflect it in this way.[29]

This best of actual regimes, Rome, becomes the mediator in the passage of the dialogue from a consideration of the best regime in principle to a consideration of the model statesman. The actual development of this practicable model of Rome exposes a dependence of the model on time and experience; Scipio and Cicero reveal that their primary interest is with the change, the political or regime dynamics, that constitutes the substratum of time and experience. Their concern with fundamental political change is not limited to the largely progressive development illustrated by Rome and considered in some detail in book 2; in fact, what comes to light before that and turns out to dominate *DR* is a concern with degeneration and its patterns and in turn, a concern with stabilization and the balancing and mixing of regimes in the name of that stabilization. The potential change, whatever its form, that time allows and that experience illustrates draws attention to the frequent agent of such change, the possible moderator of it, the hoped for controller of it—who is the leader or statesman (*rector* or *moderator*). The primary quality of that statesman, as was that of the orator considered earlier, is said to be prudence. It is to the statesman and his civil prudence—political science as a practical science—that *DR* directs the reader.

Although Laelius initially called on Scipio as one who looks to Rome, the ancestral regime, as the best regime, Scipio does not, it seems, turn directly to Rome. Rather, he proceeds systematically, as if he were a Greek writing a treatise; he begins by defining a polity in the well-known segment on the meaning of *res publica*, reflects on the origins of the political community in terms of the inclinations and needs of human nature and turns, with an argument that suggests Aristotle's thought and clarity, to say that where there is to be community, there must be governance in the form of a deliberative or legislative power. As that power is placed in the hands of one or a few or all of the citizens, the essential simple regimes are generated, and each of these can be decent and good if the ruling element is just. Despite this possibility, there is a regime better than all of these—a best regime—that Scipio points to and that will turn out to be a judicious mixture of the three simple forms.

As Scipio now turns to show the characteristic strength and weakness of each of the simple regimes and thus shows why no one of them can be the best, he reveals more about his discontent with Plato's city in speech. The simple regimes, even if good and just, are shown to experience corruption, change, and revolution because of their respective defects and because there is at hand no "great citizen and nearly divine man" (*magnus quidam civis et divinus paene vir*) whose knowledge, foresight, and power would allow him to regulate and to keep such changes in his control.[30] Immediately after this observation, Scipio states that he "therefore" turns to the mixed regime as the best regime. Kingship and aristocracy are among the simple regimes, and what Scipio has apparently concluded is that philosopher-kings (that is, either such distinct excellence or politically empowered excellence) are not available to human communities as such have been commonly experienced.[31]

There can be no saving of the simple regimes through divine-like leaders. Thus precisely at this point in the discussion of vari-

ous regimes, Scipio turns away from the Platonic city in speech as the best regime, for he rules out the actuality of the superlatively virtuous individual who is also empowered. In turning to the mixed regime, Scipio turns to a possible model, a practicable model. One might reasonably say that Plato's intention, and so understood by Scipio and Cicero, with the city in speech is to turn the reader in search of just such a practicable model. And that is the direction, we recall, that Aristotle takes and defends as legitimate for political science in his *Politics*.

One might also say that here is a point where reason provides for or encompasses the lack of reason in political life.[32] Scipio has then spoken to the question of the best regime, but it should be no surprise, given the emphasis on the life of the statesman and the requisite insistence on judging all activities in relationship to that life found in Cicero's preface and the early part of the dialogue, that his best regime is a realizable or practical one.[33] Scipio's quarrel with Plato's city in speech has primarily to do with the utility of that approach. In a dialogue where the emphasis from the beginning is on justifying all things in terms of their relationship to the active life of political leadership, it is the practicable best regime that merits attention.

Furthermore, to notice that Scipio has in fact spoken "to the question of the best regime" allows the correction of a common misunderstanding of *DR*, namely, that here Cicero through Scipio offers Rome as his response to the question of the best regime. That best of achievable regimes, the mixed regime, which Scipio explains in book 1, is, we must emphasize, a response in the "universal terms" of which Strauss wrote.[34] One cannot, however, read on in *DR* through book 2 without a sense of assurance that the experience of Rome above all has been instructive in Scipio's discovery of the mixed regime as the best. Thus Rome is reflected in the best regime even before the dialogue's turn in book 2 to exemplify this best regime in Rome and its development. And it should also be noted that the mixed regime's being able to be so substantially instantiated in Rome makes more persuasive its alleged practicability.[35] Rome, however, is never presented as the simply best regime nor as the best practicable regime; rather, it is used as the best exemplification among actual regimes of the best practicable regime.[36] It can properly be said that Cicero in *DR* has replaced Plato's fictive and unreal depiction of the best regime with a specific historical example of the best practicable regime. The utility of what Cicero has done in this step goes well beyond some kind of nod to a Roman preference for the tangible and concrete, for Scipio's Roman exemplification of the best allows him to direct the attention of his fellow statesmen (and Cicero the attention of his readers) at the constitutional form and tradition in which they do their work and at the same time to try to protect, insofar as Rome is but an exemplification, the realm of prudence, thus avoiding the kind of controversies that arose from the very beginning around the specific institutions and customs of Plato's city in speech.[37] Insofar as Rome is for Cicero only the best exemplification of the best practicable regime and Roman development to the mixed regime is as troubled as any human history, Rome too has its defects, and it is wholly consistent with Cicero's overall intent that these would be passed over, or noted but not stressed, in the course of his use of the Roman experience.

The foregoing interpretation of Cicero and Scipio's decisive turn from Plato's city in speech (*DR* 1:45) because of the absence, in the good simple regimes, of an unassailable virtue of a "great citizen and nearly divine man," is supported by Scipio's later contrast of the first Roman tyrant, Tarquinius, with the model statesman (*rectori et gubernatori civitatis*).[38] Explicitly conscious at this point of how Roman experience of tyranny's origin from monarchy differs from Plato's description of its genesis, Scipio chooses to set in contrast to the tyrant not the philosopher-king, as is done so predominantly throughout Plato's *The Republic*, but a type of man whom he characterizes as "good and wise and experienced in matters of public utility and honor." This man is rightly said to be "a guardian and steward of the polity" (*tutor et procurator rei publicae*) as long as he functions as "leader and pilot of the state" (*rector*

et gubernator civitatis). This is the first instance in *DR* where there is a direct mention and a somewhat extensive discussion of that man whom we are calling Cicero's model statesman. He is introduced here in direct contrast to the tyrant, as if to say that we are not to set over against tyranny—the worst of regimes—the rule of the one or few best or virtuous but, rather, the practicable ideal which is the rule by and for the people conducted by statesmen. Since those kind of superior individuals who can save the simple regimes from degradation are not to be found, Scipio and Cicero are apparently interested in another more realizable kind of superiority (consider the examples of Roman history) that can work in and in fact is critical to the success of the mixed regime.[39] The model statesman is a level of human achievement consistent with and necessary to the mixed regime.

In this same passage (*DR* 2:51), Scipio draws emphatic attention to this rector whom, he enjoins his listeners, one must seek to recognize and "who is able to protect the state by his counsel and deeds." This type of man, he adds, must be given much more attention in the remainder of his discourse, and there are indications that this does indeed happen though substantial portions on the model statesman seem to be among the lost parts of original dialogue. Later in book 2, Scipio is shown striving again to deflect attention from a description of the best regime in the nature of things to the founding and preservation of the practicable best regime: that illustrated in the history of Rome.[40] He then introduces the man, to whom he has been pointing and whom he has "long been seeking," as the apparent key to the founding and preservation of cities and to this practicable best regime. This man is here called, at the suggestion of Laelius, the man of prudence (*prudens*).[41] The functions that Scipio then details or suggests for this man make clear that he is one and the same as the rector and gubernator. It is noteworthy that earlier, Scipio observes that the point of his entire discourse and the basis of all political prudence (*caput civilis prudentiae*) is "to understand the course and changes of polities so that when one knows the tendencies of each

polity one might be able beforehand to prevent such developments or meet them in
some way."[42] That Scipio all along has been
most interested in the possession by leaders
of such political prudence sheds new light on
his great interest in Plato manifested in book
1 in a long direct quotation concerning the
degeneration of democracy from *The Republic.* A Plato describing the courses and
changes of regimes is more relevant to the
useful political knowledge that Scipio and
Cicero seek than a Plato detailing the provisions of the city in speech. Scipio has wanted
from the start to bring the discussion around
to the political leader whose prudence,
above all other qualities, is the critical quality in good political practice understood as
moving as best one can to attain or preserve
the practicable best regime. Again, the reason of the prudent man encompasses the less
than reasonable tendencies of political life,
in this case, those ever recurring tendencies
to regime-instability.

At *DR* 2:67, then, Scipio has clearly
brought about the shift in focus which he has
intended all along and which the reader can
see clearly anticipated in the prooemia to
books 1 and 2.[43] Even book 3, which could
properly be called Cicero's book on justice
and which appears to be concerned with the
justice of states, is preceded and, in a sense,
introduced by Scipio's insistence that the
harmony which is justice in that prudent
man's, the rector's, soul is to be the source of
it for the polity as a whole.[44] Here, Scipio
speaks of that single most important duty of
the rector, that which largely encompasses
all others, being that of serving as a moral exemplar. Thus polities depend on just leaders
for their justice; such leaders and their souls
must be at the very center of concern of the
person who seeks useful political knowledge.[45] It seems significant that here (*DR*
2:69) as Scipio specifies the aspects of the
singular duty of being a moral exemplar, he
lists first the need of the statesman "never to
cease from forming and examining himself"
(*ut numquam a se ipso instituendo
contemplandoque discedat*).[46] Thus the
model statesman's very virtue consists partly
in his continual Socratic striving for self-un-
derstanding and moral improvement.

This is no finished incorruptible philosopher-king nor a Stoic perfect wise man of
whom Scipio speaks. It is a model on a more
attainable, human plateau; yet the very in-
completeness, the opening in this model to
self-monitoring and self-improvement, reveals the usefulness of a concept of the
model statesman/orator. The responsibility
of self-improvement that rests on statesmen
and potential statesmen entails the need for
standards of excellence and virtue, for that
concept of the perfect statesman who may
have existed nowhere and to whom Cicero
turned to express such standards.[47] As long
as the perfect model includes the injunction
to self-examination and self-improvement
and as long as the central and most important virtue of this model statesman is prudence, the model has a built-in protection
against a corruptive and smug closure and
against a dangerous stretching of the self toward an unrealistic and inappropriate personal standard. One cannot have too much
prudence.

The model statesman with his characteristic prudence comes to be prior to any specific articulation of a best regime, for not
only must the standard for the wider society
be a practicable one (that is, it must itself
pass the judgment of prudence) if it is to be
good and worthy of pursuit but whatever the
specifics of the best regime at a given time, it
is the statesman who represents the primary
means of attaining this regime. The proximate goal for political improvement would
generally be statesmen with the proper qualities, that is, true statesmen. The same sense
of utility that elevated the life of active political leadership over theoretical inquiry and
that directed attention to a practicable best
regime and to an illustration of it in the form
of the best of achieved regimes leads to a
focus and emphasis on the responsibilities
and qualities of statesmanship. Among the
matters to be learned and reflected on, this is
to have the highest priority. It is this sense of
utility and its implicit priorities which is evidently a central part of the wisdom of those
model statesmen cast in the leading parts in
the discussion of *DR*.

The picture with which Cicero leaves us is
not, however, one where the statesman

stands independent of the surrounding social and political order. The model statesman is neither a god who descends among men nor a fabrication to be made, any more than is the best practicable regime, regardless of the materials at hand. Rather, those men who might be *rectores* are developed from sound customs and laws, and they, in turn, contribute to the defense and making of such laws and customs. They are men who are led initially by their desire for praise and glory to act rightly, but they then come to strengthen and develop those very institutions that nourished them. In Scipio's words, "No one can live well except in a good polity."[48] The mutual interaction and interdependence between outstanding leaders and good institutions is stressed by Scipio and Cicero both before and after the sketch of the development of the Roman regime in book 2, which so clearly manifests this interaction.[49] In Cicero's view, that mutual interaction is the specific manifestation at any given time and in any given statesman's life of the fact that the achievement of a good polity is a collective achievement of many outstanding statesmen who build with the benefit of time and experience. Cato, reports Cicero approvingly,

> taught that there never has existed so great a genius that at any point in time nothing would have eluded him, and that all of human ingenuity collected at a given time is not sufficient to provide that all things would be properly considered without the benefit of experience and the passage of time.[50]

Cicero's statesman is then dependent, for that critical dimension of personal character, on the polity that rears, educates, and protects him, and he is dependent for great political accomplishment on the efforts of those who preceded and those who will follow him.[51]

Despite these truths about the statesman, it is clear that Cicero does not see the statesman as a mere captive and reflection, an epiphenomenon, of his polity's ways, nor does he see the statesman as a personally insignificant moment, instrument, or link in a larger historical process beyond human control. The statesman has a freedom to be responsible and a capacity to choose well in the light of whatever circumstances he faces; he is distinguished as a model statesman by various abilities of leadership and above all by his capacity for prudence and his will to pursue the political good by counsel and deeds. The virtues of the model statesman are constant even as circumstances and regimes vary; they are virtues known to a prephilosophic moral awareness, and it is this awareness that both prevents a statesman from being simply the voice of a tradition and allows him to correct and improve it. The statesman of Cicero is not, however, one who confronts his polity and tradition as a student of philosophy having been enlightened by it. However much moral and political philosophy can clarify, strengthen, and defend the essential understandings of common sense and a prephilosophic moral awareness—and Cicero does insist that this is so and thus that discussions like this one of *DR* are eminently useful—the very moral primacy of political leadership or statesmanship is known before philosophy is known. The need for *true* statesmen follows from common experience with the needs and inclinations of humankind and depends on no more than this and an initial moral awareness of justice and thus of the end of political life.

Conclusion

Cicero has been seen to have taken up the central question of classical political philosophy—that of the best regime—and to have answered it in a way that makes the detailed provisions of a best regime less important and more simply speculative than the necessary qualities of statesmanship. His quarrel with Plato, if it be much of a quarrel, has to do with the utility of a detailed depiction of the city in speech. Much might be said to the effect that Cicero's turn to the practicable best regime and to its central figure, the statesman, is invited and in fact begun by both Plato and Aristotle. Even the necessary and moral disciplining of the philosophical eros by political duty is not unknown to Plato and Aristotle, though it may seem at times less troubling and problematic for

Cicero; thus Cicero has an easier time asserting the primacy of statesmanship among the responsibilities of this human life, and this tendency makes him all the more inclined to focus on the nature and requisites of statesmanship.

Cicero's elaboration of the best practicable regime and the role and qualities of the statesman was, as we have seen, influenced by his experience, above all then by the Roman experience. And, to be sure, his audience was expected to be primarily if not exclusively Roman. Nonetheless what he said about this best regime and the statesman was clearly meant to be of universal significance. American political theory provides strong indications that while perhaps being partly shaped by Cicero, it can even more clearly be seen as receptive in certain ways to the political wisdom of Cicero. In the closing paragraph of *The Federalist*, Publius looks to the future under an imperfect but very good constitution and cites David Hume writing nearly in paraphrase of Cicero:

> To balance a large state or society whether monarchical or republican, on general laws, is a work of so great difficulty, that no human genius, however comprehensive, is able by the mere dint of reason and reflection to effect it. The judgments of many must unite in the work. EXPERIENCE must guide their labor; TIME must bring it to perfection; And the FEELING of inconveniences must correct the mistakes which they *inevitably* fall into, in their first trials and experiments.[52]

Earlier in *The Federalist* no. 14, Publius sees the "glory" of the young American nation, in that while it has paid "a decent regard to the opinions of former times and other nations," this people has not "suffered a blind veneration for antiquity, for custom, or for names, to overrule the suggestions of their own good sense, the knowledge of their own situation, and the lessons of their own experience." Generations later, John Dewey would remind Americans that living by experience and our own good sense could not mean that a people may leave the question of the best regime implicit and unaddressed. Dewey writes of "the need of a measure" in social and political diagnosis and prescription. "In seeking this measure," he adds,

> we cannot set up, out of our heads, something we regard as an ideal society. We must base our conception upon societies which actually exist in order to have any assurance that our ideal is a practicable one. But, as we have just seen, the ideal cannot simply repeat the traits which are actually found.[53]

Americans, then, no doubt like many others, have searched anew for a way to learn from experience, to build on the past, to benefit from a favorable tradition and yet not be wholly confined by that past. Cicero and his model statesman speak quite directly to a search so framed.

Notes

1. This observation and that immediately preceding about "the guiding question" represent themes found throughout the works of Strauss. They are stated very directly in his essay "On Classical Political Philosophy" from which these and the following quotations come. See Leo Strauss, *What Is Political Philosophy?* (Westport, CT. Greenwood, 1973), 79.

2. Ibid., 80.

3. Ibid., 84–85.

4. Machiavelli's warning occurs in chapter 15 of *The Prince;* the phrasing used here is that of translator Robert Adams (New York: Norton, 1977), 44.

5. In the course of his important, ranging, and insight-filled study of the development of modern liberal political thought, R. D. Cumming gives close attention to Cicero and is the first, I believe, to employ the phrase "shift of focus" to describe Cicero's break with Plato and emphasis on "the ideal statesman." See R. D. Cumming, *Human Nature and History*, vol. I (Chicago: University of Chicago Press, 1969), 286.

6. Scipio and his circle, including Laelius, are seen by Cicero as marking not only the first opening of Roman leaders to Greek philosophy but specifically as welcoming philosophy in its Socratic form (*DR* 3:5–6). Cicero consistently and throughout his works associates himself with a Socratic tradition in philosophy; because he sees the school of the New Academy with its commitment to question-

ing and a moderate skepticism as the chief carrier of the Socratic tradition, Cicero explicitly sees the best statement of his own position in the teaching of this school.

7. One reason is that Philus, who reluctantly and against his convictions, argues in the dialogue contra the notion that justice is grounded in nature, is associated in this role with the philosophical tradition of the New Academy which Cicero again and again explicitly embraces. There is also need for caution in distinguishing Laelius and his defense of natural law from what is taken to be Scipio's and Cicero's position; see my discussion in "Cicero and the Rebirth of Political Philosophy," *Political Science Reviewer* 8 (1978): 93–94.

8. There appears to be no overall pattern regarding when Cicero uses civitas and when he uses res publica to speak of the state or polity. Thus res publica is not, as one might expect, restricted to the Roman polity or commonwealth after the fall of the monarchy and during the period conventionally known by historians as the Republican period. Given that Cicero has Scipio use the Latin etymology of res publica to define the term and link it through the idea of a people to the ideas of right and justice (*DR* 1:39). And that later (*DR* 3:43ff.) this definitional groundwork allows Scipio to observe that polities ruled by a tyrant or by a tyrannous faction or even multitude should not properly be called a res publica (*dicendum est plane nullam esse rem publicam*), there is good reason for Cicero naming this work with res publica, and describing it, as he does here, as disputatio de re publica. What he has Scipio do with the term res publica is central to the unity of the book and to its teaching. Res publica, properly understood, becomes a carrier of essential parts of Cicero's own response to the question of the best regime. At the same time that Cicero shows himself aware of a philosophically precise understanding of res publica, his dicendum est in this passage indicates a like awareness of a looser popular usage. That *DR* as a whole reflects this looser common usage should not be surprising in the light of Cicero's rhetorical training and sensitivity. A number of times in other writings, he criticized the Stoics for disabling themselves before general audiences by their insistence on using a specialized and peculiar understanding of terms. Neal Wood has reached a different and interesting conclusion in *Cicero: Social and Political Thought* (Berkeley: University of California Press, 1988), namely, that Cicero uses civitas in viewing the state "institutionally and constitutionally" and res publica when thinking of the state "in terms of common interest and right" (p. 126). Wood does not cite any of the alternate usages of civitas and res publica in *DR* in support of his conclusion but points, rather, to *De legibus* (*DL*) 2:12 and *Paradoxa stoicorum* 27, both being sources where Cicero argues, as he has done earlier here regarding res publica, that a civitas cannot be a civitas if it is not characterized by law, not any rules or orders, but just laws.

9. *DR* 1:33.

10. Ibid., 32.

11. Ibid., 35–36.

12. Ibid., 36.

13. *DR* 2:3.

14. *DR* 4:4–5.

15. Differences between Cicero and Plato on political/legal matters are suggested in a comment which Quintus, Cicero's brother, is portrayed making in Cicero's *DL* 2:17. Cicero does not speak directly to this suggestion save to affirm that he tries to imitate Plato's mode of discourse and that he does not merely translate Plato's views, for he wishes to be himself.

16. *TD* 1:39–40.

17. Cicero describes himself as "a follower of Socrates and Plato"; *De oratore* (*DO*) 1:2. He takes Plato as clearly preeminent as a philosopher; see especially *DL* 2:14. 39, 3:1, and *DR* 2:21 (Laelius speaking). At *TD* 1:22, Aristotle is held first among thinkers except for Plato, in brilliance (*ingenio*) and thoroughness (*diligentia*). In *Orator* 10, Plato is called *gravissimus auctor et magister* with respect to both thought and speech. At *DO* 3:21, Plato is presented as a teacher of the unity of knowledge and at *TD* 5:36 as a teacher of virtue as the chief good, both of these being positions very important to Cicero. References to Plato in Cicero's speeches and letters show him consistent in his high praise. In his *Pro scauro* 4, Cicero refers to Plato as the greatest (*summus*) philosopher whose written work was done *graviter et ornate*. In *Pro murena* 63, Plato is presented by Cicero as a teacher of his along with Aristotle who is free of the immoderate aspects of the philosophical life manifested in certain Stoics. See also *Pro rabirio postumo* 23, *Ep. att.* 4:16, and *Ep. Q.* 1.1.29. As to the comparative standing of Socrates

and Plato, Plato is "the philosopher" (*princeps philosophorum*) and Socrates is the source or founder of philosophy in the form it takes in Cicero's time (*princeps* or *parens philosophiae*). A fuller discussion of these descriptions and the Socrates/Plato relationship in Cicero's eyes is found in my forthcoming piece, "Cicero's Socrates: His Assessment of 'The Socratic Turn,' " in *Law and Philosophy: The Practice of Theory*, edited by W. Braithwaite, J. Murley, and R. Stone (Athens: Ohio University Press, 1991).

18. Cumming, *Human Nature*, 190.

19. *DR* 1:67–68, 2:52.

20. Strauss cites this passage (*PR* 2:52) at least five times: *Natural Right and History* (Chicago: University of Chicago Press, 1953), 122; "Plato," in *History of Political Philosophy*, edited by Leo Strauss and Joseph Cropsey (Chicago: Rand McNally, 1963), 41; *The City and Man* (Chicago: Rand McNally, 1964), 138; *The Argument and the Action of Plato's Laws* (Chicago: University of Chicago Press, 1975), 1; and *The Rebirth of Classical Political Rationalism*, edited by Thomas Pangle (Chicago: University of Chicago Press, 1989), 162.

21. *DR* 2:57.

22. Eric Voegelin, *The Ecumenic Age* (Baton Rouge: Louisiana State University Press, 1974), 128.

23. Cicero's letters and other evidence make clear that *DR* was written sometime between 55 and 51 B.C. and that *DO* was completed by 54 B.C. or shortly thereafter. These two works stand together in time and apart from the great body of Cicero's other rhetorical and philosophical writings which were done in the last years of his life, 46–43 B.C. Antonius in the dialogue seems to represent a "no nonsense" technical approach to oratory that only gradually opens to the relevance of philosophical studies.

24. *DO* 1:224–25.

25. Cicero's comment to Atticus (*Ep. att.* 2:1) that Cato, his contemporary, with his lofty and pure views would be more in place in Plato's republic than among the dregs of Romulus seems to be an indication of this popular shorthand.

26. *DO* 3:84–85.

27. *Orator* 7–10.

28. This connection cannot be explored fully within the space limitations of this essay. Suffice it here to say that Cicero's rhetorical writings involve personae who, like those of *DR*, are active public leaders and that the key rhetorical writings turn out to be defenses of the life of the statesman as the greatest service and the proper utilization of rhetorical ability and art. In his *prooemium* to the first book of *DO*, Cicero describes true eloquence as derivative from "the arts of the most prudent men" (*prudentissimorum hominum artibus*, *DO* 1:5); see also *Orator*. Crassus opens the dialogue in *DO* by describing the glory and power of speech as follows: "Nothing at all seems to be more outstanding than the power of holding an assembly of men by speech, of drawing the support of the mind of men and of directing their wills where one wishes and diverting them from what one wishes" (*DO* 1:30). In the rhetorical writing of his youth, *De inventione* 1:2, Cicero shows the public leadership function of the art from its very beginnings. See also Cumming, *Human Nature*, 265–67. J. C. Davies suggests the equivalence of Cicero's conceptions of *rector rei publicae* and *doctus orator* in "The Originality of Cicero's Philosophical Works," *Latomus* (January–March, 1971): 111.

29. *DR* 1:34.

30. *DR* 1:45.

31. This interpretation fits well with Cicero's critique, elsewhere in his writings (e.g., *De finibus* 4:65), of the Stoic conception of the perfect wise man which Cicero took to represent an unrealistic comprehensive wisdom and virtue.

32. There is then no simple congruency between reason and political order, which is to say that there is no perfect and hence stable solution to the problem of politics. At *DL* 3:23, Cicero shows that institutions favored by him and the Romans in general (as the tribunate and consulship) cannot be wholly freed from their potential for evil.

33. It is noteworthy that Polybius, who is generally thought to have influenced Cicero toward the mixed regime and who is presented in *DR* as having talked with Scipio (1:34), bans Plato's city in speech from a competition for the best constitution because Plato's city, not having been tested, is not a proven practicable model (6:47, 7–10). See Cumming, *Human Nature*, 279, n. 71. Cumming also makes the interesting suggestion (pp. 89–90) that Plato himself in the *Timaeus* is the source for Polybius banning Plato's city from competition. The suggestion is interesting partly because the *Timaeus*, having been translated by

Cicero, apparently was carefully tended to by him.

34. *Timaeus*, 2. Scipio claims he can define the best regime without a specific exemplification (*DR* 2:66); see also Polybius, 6:3, 6–10.

35. Thomas White writes that Cicero uses the "historical exemplum" for "explanatory efficacy" and for the legitimization of the concept at issue by testifying to its "workability" in "A Philosophical Examination of Cicero's Utopianism," paper for the annual meeting of the American Political Science Association (September 1981), 6.

36. Wood writes that for Cicero, "Rome is not only the best practicable state, but, with only slight modification, the ideally best state" (*Cicero's Social*, 66). My argument is that the ideally best state is the best practicable state and that Rome is the best realized exemplification of such a state. It is the best realized exemplification perhaps in part because it is the most available and the most useful exemplum under the circumstances.

37. That Cicero was not wholly or even very successful at avoiding such controversies is evident in the frequency with which his use of Rome in *DR* is taken as a comprehensive idolization of Roman customs and institutions. R. F. Hathaway probes this subsequent difficulty for Cicero's thought well, arguing that Cicero is a Socratic political philosopher first and a Roman patriot second and that he strives to use Rome and her history to point to "eternal principles," but "precisely because his rhetoric is successful, he blurs the issue of the mortality of all earthly cities; he makes us believe that history culminates in some sense in Rome," in "Cicero, *De Re Publica* II, and His Socratic View of History," *Journal of the History of Ideas* (January–March 1968): 3–4, 12. See Cumming's thoughtful struggle with the question whether Cicero's model is Rome: *Human Nature*, 239, 279 n. 72, 303, 336 n. 57.

38. *DR* 2:51.

39. At *DR* 1:69, Scipio states that significant moral failings (*vitia*) among the leaders (*principibus*) will destabilize even the mixed regime. See Cumming, *Human Nature*, 244–48, 267 for an effort to understand how Cicero's model statesman and mixed regime relate to one another.

40. *DR* 2:65ff.

41. *DR* 2:67. Note the reference to prudentissimi in *DO*; see note 28 here. Also see *DR* 6.1 and *DL* 3:5.

42. *DR* 2:45. J. Jackson Barlow has aptly described Cicero as seeing a need "for a virtually continuous process of refounding" in "The Education of Statesmen in Cicero's *De Republica*," *Policy* (Spring 1987): 367. Barlow goes on (p. 369) to recall that Cicero (*DL* 1:18–19) sets the standard of justice as "the mind and reasoning of the prudent man," that man "who combines the art of ruling with knowledge of nature." In practice, "the unchanging standard gives rise to manifestly changeable results." In a similar vein, Wood notes that the long-term goal of Cicero's statesman is the preservation of the "moderation and balance" of the mixed constitution (*Cicero's Social*, 193) and that the leading men charged with this responsibility are not a law unto themselves but servants of "a supreme law" (p. 189). The "continuous refounding" that Cicero's statesman engages in should not be seen as merely reactionary or checking evil tendencies as Cumming suggests (*Human Nature*, 274 n. 28).

43. That the model statesman was intended by Cicero as his dominant theme in *DR* or at least a co-theme with the issue of the best regime is supported by two comments of Cicero in his letters. In a letter to his brother Quintus in 54 B.C. (*Ep. Q.* 3.5.1), a time when he seems to have been working on *DR*, Cicero is found discussing his first version of the dialogue and speaks of it as being concerned with "the best regime and the best citizen" (*de optimo statu civitatis et de optimo cive*). Five years later in a letter to Atticus (*Ep. att.* 8: 11), Cicero recalls *DR* as a place where he had treated "that man," that leader and guide (*moderatorem*) of the polity, "by whom we sought to judge all things" (*quo referre velimus omnia*). Cicero also refers the reader of *DL* (3:32) to *DR* for a more exhaustive treatment of the role of the statesman and leading citizens and their influence on the moral character of a society. However, earlier, (2:23, 3:4, 13) he thrice speaks of the topic of *DR* being the best state.

44. *DR* 2:69; also *DL* 3:21–32.

45. A comment by Cicero in a letter of 60 B.C. to his brother Quintus (*Ep. Q.* 1. 1.29) reveals what Cicero seems to regard as the essential teaching (*easdem rationes*) of *The Republic* and that this teaching can be seen as directing Cicero toward an emphasis on the statesman, his qualities, and his education. The passage begins with great praise for Plato and then speaks of his teaching that states will only be happy when either the wise and learned rule

or those who rule devote themselves to learning and wisdom. In Cicero's words, what is needed in rulers is the pursuit of *doctrinam, virtutem et humanitatem*. See also *Ep. fam.* 1.9.12.

46. This injunction is one pointer toward the Dream of Scipio with which *DR* concludes (6:9–29) and in which one finds the important themes of the dialogue drawn together. The Dream makes clear that for Cicero, one can be said to know the self well only in the light of an elusive but conceivable knowledge of the whole (a point more directly stated and developed at *DL* 1:58–62), that the pull to this eternal knowledge cannot justify abandoning that highest earthly duty of statesmanship, and that virtue (*decus* or *vera gloria*) is manifest only when statesmen orient themselves finally not to public acclaim (the glory which the young rightly pursue) in their various polities but to eternal, transcendent standards. An interpretation of the Dream in the light of its dramatic detail cannot be well done within the confines of this essay concentrating as it does on the textual evidence for Cicero's shift in focus. Barlow's comments ("The Education," 361–62, 370–73) reveal much about how the Dream relates to the emphasis on statesmanship in *DR*.

47. Cumming (*Human Nature*, 263, 279 n. 72, 285) sees Cicero as identifying the ideal statesman with certain real statesmen of Roman history. Cicero's more practicable model is not, however, wholly captured by any specific historical instantiation (*Orator* 7–10), though it is best exemplified by Roman historical examples. Cicero does offer a more practicable model than the Stoic wise man (or the nearly divine man, see above, p. 240), just as with respect to the regime as a whole, Cicero offers a more practicable model than Plato's city in speech, The practicable model statesman is the key to the practicable model

(mixed) regime; the "nearly divine man" and the Stoic wise man is the key to the Platonic "city in speech." This essay has been able to provide a plausible resolution to the difficulty encountered by W. W. How when he finds Cicero at times writing of the statesman as "a purely ideal figure" and yet also finds evidence that Cicero's concept at times makes "plain references" to specific historical personages. At this same point, How makes the interesting observation that

> Cicero's *princeps* is an unofficial leader, swaying the state by his wisdom and the prestige of his past services, as did Scipio in his last years, or Cicero himself in the struggle with Antony, not a magistrate however exalted. It is, I think, significant that there is not a word of any such magistracy in the constitution laid down in the *Laws*. ("Cicero Ideal in His *De Republica*," *Journal of Roman Studies* [1930]: 41.

Cicero's statesman need not, it seems, be a magistrate—that is an actual holder of political office—but it would be going too far and in the face of other textual evidence to conclude that he cannot, by definition, be a magistrate.

48. *DR* 5:7.

49. *DR* 5:1–2, 5–6; also 1:2–3, 8.

50. *DR* 2:2.

51. Barlow, "The Education," 367.

52. *The Federalist* no. 85.

53. John Dewey, *Democracy and Education* (New York: Macmillan, 1916), 96.

Reprinted from: Walter J. Nicgorski, "Cicero's Focus: From the Best Regime to the Model Statesman." In *Political Theory*, Vol. 19 No. 2, May 1991 230–251. Copyright © 1991. Reprinted by permission of Sage Publications, Inc. ✦

Saint Augustine

In marked contrast to the claims made in American political arguments, Christianity has not always been seen as the pious glue holding society together. Indeed, immediately following the fall of Rome in 410, some authors and politicians alleged that Christianity itself was responsible for destroying the civic virtue of the Roman people and for undermining Rome's political stability. For many interpreters, Augustine's *The City of God* (composed between 413 and 425) was written largely to defend the faith from such attacks. Augustine did more than parry threats to the faith, however. He also developed an intriguing blend of classical philosophy and Christian theology that sought "to clear away the obstacles that littered the extensive common ground between educated pagans and their Christian peers, so that the pagans should cross over . . . to join the Church."[1]

Augustine's background clearly prepared him for that task. He was born in Thagaste (now Souk Ahras, Algeria) to a Christian mother and pagan father in the year 354. After moving to Carthage in 370 to finish his education in classical Latin rhetoric, Augustine began teaching in Rome in 383. The next year, he became a professor of rhetoric in Milan, then known as a center of Neoplatonism. After an impetuous young adulthood, Augustine converted to the faith of his mother in 386 and returned to North Africa to found an ascetic community. Amid the lively, if contentious, world of African Christianity, Augustine thrived and by the year 396, he had become the Bishop of Hippo (Hippo Regius, now Annaba). Augustine's simultaneously literate and popular sermons appealed to his congregation on many levels, and by the time he reached old age, he had become quite well known in the Roman Empire's intellectual circles. After contracting a fever, Augustine died in 430—just as the Vandals were conquering North Africa.

Throughout his life, even when occupied with the daily tasks of overseeing a parish, Augustine was an active thinker and a prolific writer involved in the many controversies of his day. In contrast to his philosophical exemplars (Plato, and especially Cicero), Augustine did not write a single treatise specifically devoted to political theory. Instead, throughout *The City of God*, he presents his political views in the course of discussing the issues then confronting the Christian faith. For Augustine, since having faith means assenting to something not clearly seen, it must always precede any type of authentic understanding. The prime role of reason, therefore, is to guide the individual to the right sort of faith—and hence, to the proper views on such topics as sin, free will, and grace.

Both reason and faith led Augustine to conceive of reality as composed of three natures: the divine, the corporeal, and the spiritual. Divine nature, of course, refers to God, whose chief characteristics are immutability, blessedness, and creativity. God is the ultimate ground of existence and understanding, the holder of all ideas, the bestower of all powers and the highest good. Corporeal nature refers to bodies, which are created by God and are inherently neither blessed nor wretched. Bodies are thus subject to change and to the vicissitudes of time, place, and circumstance. The focus of Augustine's thinking about human beings and society, though, is spiritual nature—the soul. Like the body, the soul is subject to change over time, but because it has free will, it may change for good or ill. Souls will thus be wretched if they identify with corporeal nature (e.g., such goods as pleasure, beauty, and strength) and will be blessed if they look toward the divine (e.g., virtue, justice, and the good). Having a properly directed will means that one would strive to do what is praiseworthy; true virtue, however, will always require the additional dimension of grace.

Augustine's primary political ideas center on his concept of the "two cities," which suggests that human beings comprise two coexistent and intermingled camps: those who live in the earthly city (the City of Man), and those who reside in the Heavenly City (the City of God). People in the earthly city live after their corporeal nature and love themselves even to the contempt of God. Most of us fall into this camp, doomed to spend our lives beset by troubles, scarcity, quarrels, and violence. Because we do not love God, an external power (the state) must regulate our unbridled passions. In such a setting, our conflicts can be managed so that we can enjoy our share of earthly goods without falling victim to an early, violent death. After the Judgment Day, however, we shall be condemned to eternal torment.

By contrast, the Heavenly City (composed of all those who love God to the contempt of self, who live after the spirit) is an order based on the love of God and characterized by the existence of true justice, peace, harmony, and wisdom. That order only materializes with the Resurrection, however. Until then, the City of God comprises the invisible body of the elect—only some of whom may be found within the visible Church, among God's representatives on earth.

The City of God

The selections from *The City of God* (Books XIV and XIX) initially present some of Augustine's mature thinking about one of his chief concerns—the problem of evil. If the people created in God's image are originally good, how could they possibly have become evil? Augustine finds that the source of that evil lies neither in an independent force nor in any inherent corruption of the flesh. Instead, people have come to live wretchedly because their souls have freely chosen to live by human, rather than divine, standards. Though all that is good comes from God, evil

(conceived as an absence, lack, or corruption of good) results from free will.

Augustine next contrasts the origins and ends, the essential natures, of the two cities. Each city has a conception of peace and justice, but the temporal versions found in the earthly city pale in comparison to their true or perfect expressions in the Heavenly City. On earth, then, even among robber bands, one can find a measure of order and justice—although it surely cannot be enough to bring forth the blessings of eternal life that ensue from God's gift of grace. Thus, the members of the Heavenly City exist as pilgrims in the world, using the earthly peace for whatever benefits may be obtained from it until the Last Judgment offers them a true and everlasting peace.

Commentaries

Rex Martin, in the article excerpted here, explores Augustine's theory of the state by examining the concept of the "two cities." Martin argues that an interpretation of Augustine's thought based on an "identification model"—a model that identifies the state with the earthly city and the church with the Heavenly City—cannot be supported by the textual evidence. In this world, though, those institutions can nevertheless function as the symbols or representatives of the two cities. What is critical for Augustine's analysis or evaluation of any institution is the nature of the community, the common values, which it embodies.

The selection from Jean Bethke Elshtain takes issue with the standard interpretation that political theorists make of Augustine's work. In her view, the complex philosophy that Augustine advances in *The City of God* and elsewhere simply cannot be reduced to a pessimistic account of human nature and politics. Recounting her own history of reading Augustine, Elshtain asserts that his thought offers subtle analyses of such important and concrete aspects of human existence as language, evil, marriage, birth, and death. Augustine's overall theme, then, is our common way of life.

Note

1. Peter Brown, *Augustine of Hippo* (Berkeley: University of California Press, 2000), 511.

Web Sources

http://ccat.sas.upenn.edu/jod/augustine.html
Augustine of Hippo. This superb site (maintained by the classical studies scholar James O'Donnell) is a comprehensive gateway to valuable materials about Augustine's life and thought.

http://www.xrefer.com/entry/551353
xrefer: Augustine (354–430). A brief summary of Augustine's life and thought from *The Oxford Companion to Philosophy.*

http://www.newadvent.org/fathers/1201.htm
St. Augustine of Hippo: City of God. An English translation of *The City of God.*

Class Activities and Discussion Items

1. Does Augustine's Christian theology provide a useful starting point for political theory? Is it a desirable starting point for understanding modern political and social life? Why or why not?

2. Research the views of some contemporary Christians (Pat Robertson, Ralph Reed, and Jim Wallis, for example) regarding the nature of social and political life. How do their views compare with those of Augustine?

3. What is meant by Augustine's concept of the "two cities?" What practical import does it have for analyzing contemporary politics? Can the concept be used to justify the creation of a theocratic state?

4. Discuss Augustine's conception of human nature. Is his view a pessimistic or optimistic one? Does his theory of human nature provide an adequate foundation for a theory of politics? Why or why not?

Further Reading

Brown, Peter. 2000. *Augustine of Hippo.* Berkeley: University of California Press. An updated version of the excellent biography that explores Augustine's personal and intellectual development.

Connolly, William. 1993. *The Augustinian Imperative.* Thousand Oaks, CA: Sage. A meditation on the contemporary relevance of Augustine's thought.

Deane, Herbert A. 1963. *The Political Ideas of St. Augustine.* New York: Columbia University Press. A classic study which argues that both realism and quietism mark Augustine's political theory.

Markus, R.A. 1970. *Saeculum: History and Society in the Thought of St. Augustine.* Cambridge: Cambridge University Press. A work that examines the connections between history, theology, and politics in Augustine's thought.

Wills, Garry. 1999. *Saint Augustine.* New York: Penguin. A readable and engaging portrait of Augustine. ✦

15
Excerpts from *The City of God*

Saint Augustine

Book XIV

Chapter 3: The Cause of Sin Arises in the Soul, Not in the Flesh; And the Corruption Resulting from Sin Is Not a Sin but Punishment

Now it may be asserted that the flesh is the cause of every kind of moral failing, on the ground that the bad behaviour of the soul is due to the influence of the flesh. But this contention shows a failure to consider man's nature carefully and in its entirety. For 'the corruptible body weighs down the soul.'[1] Hence also the Apostle, when treating of this corruptible body, first says, 'Our outer man is decaying,'[2] and later goes on thus:

> We know that if the earthly house we inhabit disintegrates, we have a building given by God, a house not made by human hands, eternal, in heaven. For in this body we do indeed sigh—as we long for our heavenly dwelling to be put on over it, hoping that when we have put it on, we shall not find ourselves naked. For we, who are in this present dwelling, feel its weight, and sigh; not that we desire to be stripped of our body; rather we desire to have the other clothing put on over it, so that what is mortal may be absorbed by life.[3]

And so we are weighed down by the corruptible body; and yet we know that the cause of our being weighed down is not the true nature and substance of our body but its corruption; and therefore we do not wish to be stripped of it, but to be clothed with the immortality of the body. For then there will still be a body, but it will not be corruptible, and therefore not a burden. Consequently, in this present life, 'the corruptible body weighs down the soul, and the earthly habitation depresses the mind as it meditates on many questions.' However, those who imagine that all the ills of the soul derive from the body are mistaken.

True, Virgil is apparently expounding Platonic teaching[4] in glorious poetry when he says,

> Of those seeds heaven is the source, and fiery
> The energy within them, did not bodies
> Hamper and thwart them, and these earthly limbs
> And dying members dull them.[5]

And he will have it that the body is to be taken as the source of all four of the most familiar emotional disturbances of the mind: desire and fear, joy and grief, which may be called the origins of all sins and moral failings.[6] Thus he adds these lines,

> Hence come desire and fear, gladness and sorrow;
> They look not up to heaven, but are confined
> In darkness, in the sightless dungeon's gloom.

However, our belief is something very different. For the corruption of the body, which weighs down the soul, is not the cause of the first sin, but its punishment. And it was not the corruptible flesh that made the soul sinful; it was the sinful soul that made the flesh corruptible.

No doubt this corruption of the flesh results in some incitements to wrongdoing and in actual vicious longings; yet we must not attribute to the flesh all the faults of a wicked life, which would mean that we absolve the Devil of all those faults, since he has no flesh. Certainly, we cannot accuse the Devil of fornication or drunkenness or any other such wickedness connected with carnal indulgence, although he is the hidden persuader and instigator of such sins. Nevertheless, he is proud and envious in the highest degree; and this moral corruption has so mastered him that he is destined because of it to eternal punishment in the prison of this murky air of ours.

Now those vices, which are predominant in the Devil, are attributed to the flesh by the Apostle, although it is certain that the Devil is without flesh. For St Paul says that enmity, quarrelsomeness, jealousy, animosity, and envy are 'works of the flesh';[7] and the fountain-head of all these evils is pride; and pride reigns in the Devil, although he is without flesh. For who is a greater enemy than he is to the saints? Who is found to quarrel with them more bitterly, to show more animosity, jealousy, and envy towards them? Yet he displays all these faults, without having flesh. So how can they be 'the works of the flesh' except in that they are the works of man, to whom, as I have said, the Apostle applies the term 'flesh'?

It is in fact not by the possession of flesh, which the Devil does not possess, that man has become like the Devil: it is by living by the rule of self, that is by the rule of man. For the Devil chose to live by the rule of self when he did not stand fast in the truth, so that the lie that he told was his own lie, not God's. The Devil is not only a liar; he is 'the father of lies'.[8] He was, as we know, the first to lie, and falsehood, like sin, had its start from him.

Chapter 4: The Meaning of Living 'By the Standard of Man' and 'By the Standard of God'

Thus, when man lives 'by the standard of man' and not 'by the standard of God', he is like the Devil; because even an angel should not have lived by the angel's standard, but by God's, so as to stand firm in the truth and speak the truth that comes from God's truth, not the lie that derives from his own falsehood. For the Apostle has this to say about man also, in another passage, 'But if the truth of God has been abundantly displayed through my falsehood'.[9] The point is that the falsehood is ours, but the truth is God's.

So when man lives by the standard of truth he lives not by his own standard, but by God's. For it is God who has said, 'I am the truth'.[10] By contrast, when he lives by his own standard, that is by man's and not by God's standard, then inevitably he lives by the standard of falsehood. Not that man himself is falsehood, since his author and creator is God, who is certainly not the au-

thor and creator of falsehood. The fact is that man was created right, on condition that he should live by the standard of his creator, not by his own, carrying out not his own will, but his creator's. Falsehood consists in not living in the way for which he was created.

Man has undoubtedly the will to be happy, even when he pursues happiness by living in a way which makes it impossible of attainment. What could be more of a falsehood than a will like that? Hence we can say with meaning that every sin is a falsehood. For sin only happens by an act of will; and our will is for our own welfare, or for the avoidance of misfortune. And hence the falsehood: we commit sin to promote our welfare, and it results instead in our misfortune; or we sin to increase our welfare, and the result is rather to increase our misfortune. What is the reason for this, except that well-being can only come to man from God, not from himself? And he forsakes God by sinning, and he sins by living by his own standard.

I have already said that two cities, different and mutually opposed, owe their existence to the fact that some men live by the standard of the flesh, others by the standard of the spirit. It can now be seen that we may also put it in this way: that some live by man's standard, others by God's. St Paul puts it very plainly when he says to the Corinthians, 'For since there is jealousy and quarrelling among you, are you not of the flesh, following human standards in your behaviour?'[11] Therefore, to behave according to human standards is the same as to be 'of the flesh', because by 'the flesh', a part of man, man himself is meant.

In fact, St Paul had previously employed the term 'animal' to the same people whom he here calls 'carnal'. This is what he said,

> For what man on earth knows the truth about a man except the spirit of the man which is in him? Similarly, no one knows the truth about God except the Spirit of God. Now we have not received the spirit of this world, but the spirit which is the gift of God, so that we may understand the gifts which God has granted us. We speak of those gifts in words which we have been taught, not by human wisdom, but by the Spirit, interpreting spiritual truths to men possessed by God's Spirit.

The 'animal' man does not grasp what belongs to the Spirit of God; it is all folly to him.[12]

It is then to such men, that is, to 'animal' men, that he says, somewhat later, 'Now I, my brothers, could not speak to you as I should to men possessed by the Spirit; I could only speak as to men of the flesh'.[13] Both these terms, 'animal' and 'carnal', are examples of the 'part for whole' figure of speech. For *anima* (the soul) and *caro* (the flesh) are parts of a man, and can stand for man in his entirety. And thus the 'animal' man is not something different from the 'carnal' man: they are identical, that is, man living by human standards. In the same way, the reference is simply to men when we read 'No flesh will be justified as a result of the works of the law',[14] and also when Scripture says, 'Seventy-five souls went down to Egypt with Jacob'.[15] In the first case 'no flesh' means 'no man', and in the second, 'seventy-five souls' means 'seventy-five men'.

Further, in the phrase, 'in words taught not by human wisdom', 'carnal wisdom' could be substituted; and in 'you follow human standards in your behaviour', 'carnal standards' would express the same meaning. This comes out more clearly in the words that follow, 'For when a man says, "I belong to Paul", and another, "I belong to Apollos", are you not merely men?'[16] Paul said earlier, 'You are "animal" ', and, 'You are carnal'. Now he makes his meaning plainer by saying, 'You are men'. That is, 'You live by man's standards, not God's. If you lived by his standards, you would be gods'.

Chapter 5: The Platonic Theory of Body and Soul; More Tolerable Than the Manichean View, but to Be Rejected Because It Makes the Nature of the Flesh Responsible for All Moral Faults

There is no need then, in the matter of our sins and faults, to do our Creator the injustice of laying the blame on the nature of the flesh which is good, in its own kind and on its own level. But it is not good to forsake the good Creator and live by the standard of a created good, whether a man chooses the standard of the flesh, or of the soul, or of the entire man, who consists of soul and flesh

and hence can be denoted by either term, soul or flesh, by itself. For anyone who exalts the soul as the Supreme Good, and censures the nature of flesh as something evil, is in fact carnal alike in his cult of the soul and in his revulsion from the flesh, since this attitude is prompted by human folly, not by divine truth.

The Platonists, to be sure, do not show quite the folly of the Manicheans.[17] They do not go so far as to execrate earthly bodies as the natural substance of evil, since all the elements which compose the structure of this visible and tangible world, and their qualities, are attributed by the Platonists to God the artificer. All the same, they hold that souls are so influenced by 'earthly limbs and dying members' that they derive from them their morbid desires and fears, joy and sadness. And those four 'disturbances' (to employ Cicero's word[18]) or 'passions' (which is a literal translation of the Greek, and is the term in common use), cover the whole range of moral failure in human behaviour.[19]

But if this is true, how is it that, in Virgil, when Aeneas is told by his father in the world below that souls will return again to bodies, he is amazed at this notion, and cries out,

Father, can we believe that souls return

To dwell beneath the sky, again to assume

The body's lethargy? Oh, what dread lust

For life under the sun holds them in misery?[20]

Must we really suppose that this 'dread lust', deriving from 'earthly limbs and dying members', still finds a place in that purity of souls which we hear so much about? Does not Virgil assert that souls have been purified from all such 'bodily infections' (as he calls them)? Yet, after that, they begin to feel the desire 'again to assume their bodies'.

Hence, even if it were true (it is in fact an utterly baseless assumption) that souls pass through a ceaseless alternation of cleansing and defilement as they depart and return, we must infer that there can have been no truth in the claim that all their culpable and perverted emotions that arise in them are derived from their earthly bodies. For we see that, on the admission of the Platonists themselves, this 'dread lust', as their renowned spokesman puts it, is so far from deriving from the body that of its own accord it urges the soul towards a bodily existence, even when the soul has been purified from all bodily infection, and has been placed in a situation outside any kind of body. Thus on their own confession, it is not only from the influence of the flesh that the soul experiences desire and fear, joy and distress; it can also be disturbed by those emotions from a source within itself. . . .

Chapter 27: The Perversity of Sinners Does Not Disturb God's Providential Design

It follows that the actions of sinners, whether angels or men, cannot obstruct the 'great works of God, carefully designed to fulfil all his decisions',[21] since in his providence and omnipotence he assigns to each his own gifts and knows how to turn to good account the good and the evil alike. Hence the evil angel had been so condemned and so hardened in evil, as the fitting retribution for his first evil will, that he could no longer have a good will; but nothing prevented God from turning him to good use and allowing him to tempt the first man, who had been created upright, that is, with a good will. For the fact is that man had been so designed that if he had trusted in God's help as a good human being he would have overcome the evil angels, whereas if in pride and self-pleasing he deserted God, his creator and helper, he would be overcome. Thus he would win a good reward with a rightly directed will that was divinely helped, but an evil retribution with a perverted will that deserted God.

Now man could not even trust in the help of God without God's help; but this did not mean that he did not have it in his power to withdraw from the benefits of divine grace by self-pleasing. For just as it is not in our power to live in this physical frame without the support of food, and yet it is in our power not to live in it at all (which is what happens to suicides), so it was not in man's power, even in paradise, to live a good life without the help of God, yet it was in his power to live an evil life; but then his happiness would not continue and a most just punishment would follow. Therefore, since God was well aware that man would fall as he did, was there any

reason why he should not have allowed him to be tempted by the malice of the jealous angel? God was perfectly certain that man would be defeated, but he foresaw with equal certainty that this same Devil was to be overcome by the man's seed,[22] helped by God's own grace, to the greater glory of the saints.

Thus it came about that God was not unaware of any event in the future, and yet he did not, by his foreknowledge, compel anyone to sin; and by the consequent experience he showed to angels and men, the rational part of creation, what a difference there was between the individual's own self-confidence and God's divine protection. Who would dare to believe or assert that it was not in God's power to ensure that neither angel nor man should fall? But God preferred not to withdraw this issue from their power, and thus to show the magnitude of their pride's power for evil and of God's grace for good.

Chapter 28: The Character of the Two Cities

We see then that the two cities were created by two kinds of love: the earthly city was created by self-love reaching the point of contempt for God, the Heavenly City by the love of God carried as far as contempt of self. In fact, the earthly city glories in itself, the Heavenly City glories in the Lord.[23] The former looks for glory from men, the latter finds its highest glory in God, the witness of a good conscience. The earthly lifts up its head in its own glory, the Heavenly City says to its God: 'My glory; you lift up my head'.[24] In the former, the lust for domination lords it over its princes as over the nations it subjugates; in the other both those put in authority and those subject to them serve one another in love, the rulers by their counsel, the subjects by obedience. The one city loves its own strength shown in its powerful leaders; the other says to its God, 'I will love you, my Lord, my strength'.[25]

Consequently, in the earthly city its wise men who live by men's standards have pursued the goods of the body or of their own mind, or of both. Or those of them who were able to know God 'did not honour him as God, nor did they give thanks to him, but they dwindled into futility in their thoughts, and their senseless heart was darkened: in asserting their wisdom'—that is, exalting themselves in their wisdom, under the domination of pride—'they became foolish, and changed the glory of the imperishable God into an image representing a perishable man, or birds or beasts or reptiles'—for in the adoration of idols of this kind they were either leaders or followers of the general public—'and they worshipped and served created things instead of the Creator, who is blessed for ever.'[26] In the Heavenly City, on the other hand, man's only wisdom is the devotion which rightly worships the true God, and looks for its reward in the fellowship of the saints, not only holy men but also holy angels, 'so that God may be all in all'. . . .[27]

Book XIX

Chapter 12: Peace Is the Instinctive Aim of All Creatures, and Is Even the Ultimate Purpose of War

Anyone who joins me in an examination, however slight, of human affairs, and the human nature we all share, recognizes that just as there is no man who does not wish for joy, so there is no man who does not wish for peace. Indeed, even when men choose war, their only wish is for victory; which shows that their desire in fighting is for peace with glory. For what is victory but the conquest of the opposing side? And when this is achieved, there will be peace. Even wars, then, are waged with peace as their object, even when they are waged by those who are concerned to exercise their warlike prowess, either in command or in the actual fighting. Hence it is an established fact that peace is the desired end of war. For every man is in quest of peace, even in waging war, whereas no one is in quest of war when making peace. In fact, even when men wish a present state of peace to be disturbed they do so not because they hate peace, but because they desire the present peace to be exchanged for one that suits their wishes. Thus their desire is not that there should not be peace but that it should be the kind of peace they wish for. Even in the extreme case when they have separated themselves from others by sedi-

tion, they cannot achieve their aim unless they maintain some sort of semblance of peace with their confederates in conspiracy. Moreover, even robbers, to ensure greater efficiency and security in their assaults on the peace of the rest of mankind, desire to preserve peace with their associates.

Indeed, one robber may be so unequalled in strength and so wary of having anyone to share his plans that he does not trust any associate, but plots his crimes and achieves his successes by himself, carrying off his booty after overcoming and dispatching such as he can; yet even so he maintains some kind of shadow of peace, at least with those whom he cannot kill, and from whom he wishes to conceal his activities. At the same time, he is anxious, of course, to be at peace in his own home, with his wife and children and any other members of his household; without doubt he is delighted to have them obedient to his beck and call. For if this does not happen, he is indignant; he scolds and punishes; and, if need be, he employs savage measures to impose on his household a peace which, he feels, cannot exist unless all the other elements in the same domestic society are subject to one head; and this head, in his own home, is himself. Thus, if he were offered the servitude of a larger number, of a city, maybe, or a whole nation, on the condition that they should all show the same subservience he had demanded from his household, then he would no longer lurk like a brigand in his hide-out; he would raise himself on high as a king for all to see—although the same greed and malignity would persist in him.

We see, then, that all men desire to be at peace with their own people, while wishing to impose their will upon those people's lives. For even when they wage war on others, their wish is to make those opponents their own people, if they can—to subject them, and to impose on them their own conditions of peace. . . .

It comes to this, then; a man who has learnt to prefer right to wrong and the rightly ordered to the perverted, sees that the peace of the unjust, compared with the peace of the just, is not worthy even of the name of peace. Yet even what is perverted must of necessity be in, or derived from, or associated with—that is, in a sense, at peace with—some part of the order of things among which it has its being or of which it consists. Otherwise it would not exist at all. For instance if anyone were to hang upside-down, this position of the body and arrangement of the limbs is undoubtedly perverted, because what should be on top, according to the dictates of nature, is underneath, and what nature intends to be underneath is on top. This perverted attitude disturbs the peace of the flesh, and causes distress for that reason. For all that, the breath is at peace with its body and is busily engaged for its preservation; that is why there is something to endure the pain. And even if the breath is finally driven from the body by its distresses, still, as long as the framework of the limbs holds together, what remains retains a kind of peace among the bodily parts; hence there is still something to hang there. And in that the earthly body pulls towards the earth, and pulls against the binding rope that holds it suspended, it tends towards the position of its own peace, and by what might be called the appeal of its weight, it demands a place where it may rest. And so even when it is by now lifeless and devoid of all sensation it does not depart from the peace of its natural position, either while possessed of it or while tending towards it. Again, if treatment with embalming fluids is applied to prevent the dissolution and disintegration of the corpse in its present shape, a kind of peace still connects the parts with one another and keeps the whole mass fixed in its earthly condition, an appropriate, and therefore a peaceable state.

On the other hand, if no preservative treatment is given, and the body is left for nature to take its course, there is for a time a kind of tumult in the corpse of exhalations disagreeable and offensive to our senses (for that is what we smell in putrefaction), which lasts until the body unites with the elements of the world as, little by little, and particle by particle, it vanishes into their peace. Nevertheless, nothing is in any way removed, in this process, from the control of the laws of the supreme Creator and Ruler who directs the peace of the whole scheme of things. For although minute animals are produced in the corpse of a larger animal, those little bodies, each and all of them, by the same law of their Creator, are subservient to their little souls in the peace that preserves their lives. And even if the flesh of dead animals is devoured by other animals, in whatever direction it is taken, with whatever substances it is united, into whatever substances it is converted and transformed, it still finds itself subject to the same laws which are diffused throughout the whole of matter for the preservation of every mortal species, establishing peace by a harmony of congruous elements.

Chapter 13: The Peace of the Universe Maintained Through All Disturbances by a Law of Nature: The Individual Attains, by God's Ordinance, to the State He Has Deserved by His Free Choice

The peace of the body, we conclude, is a tempering of the component parts in duly ordered proportion; the peace of the irrational soul is a duly ordered repose of the appetites; the peace of the rational soul is the duly ordered agreement of cognition and action. The peace of body and soul is the duly ordered life and health of a living creature; peace between mortal man and God is an ordered obedience, in faith, in subjection to an everlasting law; peace between men is an ordered agreement of mind with mind; the peace of a home is the ordered agreement among those who live together about giving and obeying orders; the peace of the Heavenly City is a perfectly ordered and perfectly harmonious fellowship in the enjoyment of God, and a mutual fellowship in God; the peace of the whole universe is the tranquillity of order—and order is the arrangement of things equal and unequal in a pattern which assigns to each its proper position.

It follows that the wretched, since, in so far as they are wretched, they are obviously not in a state of peace, lack the tranquillity of order, a state in which there is no disturbance of mind. In spite of that, because their wretchedness is deserved and just, they cannot be outside the scope of order. They are not, indeed, united with the blessed; yet it is by the law of order that they are sundered from them. And when they are free from disturbance of mind, they are adjusted to their situation, with however small a degree of harmony. Thus they have amongst them some tranquillity of order, and therefore some peace. But they are still wretched just because, although they enjoy some degree of serenity and freedom from suffering, they are not in a condition where they have the right to be serene and free from pain. They are yet more wretched, however, if they are not at peace with the law by which the natural order is governed. Now when they suffer, their peace is disturbed in the part where they suffer; and yet peace still continues in the part which feels no burning pain, and where the natural frame is not broken up. Just as there is life, then, without pain, whereas there can be no pain when there is no life, so there is peace without any war, but no war without some degree of peace. This is not a consequence of war as such, but of the fact that war is waged by or within persons who are in some sense natural beings—for they could have no kind of existence without some kind of peace as the condition of their being.

There exists, then, a nature in which there is no evil, in which, indeed, no evil can exist; but there cannot exist a nature in which there is no good. Hence not even the nature of the Devil himself is evil, in so far as it is a nature; it is perversion that makes it evil. And so the Devil did not stand firm in the truth, and yet he did not escape the judgement of the truth. He did not continue in the tranquillity of order; but that did not mean that he escaped from the power of the imposer of order. The good that God imparts, which the Devil has in his nature, does not withdraw him from God's justice by which his punishment is ordained. But God, in punishing, does not chastise the good which he created, but the evil which the Devil has committed. And God does not take away all that he gave to that nature; he takes something, and yet he leaves something, so that there may be some being left to feel pain at the deprivation.

Now this pain is in itself evidence of the good that was taken away and the good that was left. In fact, if no good had been left there could have been no grief for lost good.

For a sinner is in a worse state if he rejoices in the loss of righteousness; but a sinner who feels anguish, though he may gain no good from his anguish, is at least grieving at the loss of salvation. And since righteousness and salvation are both good, and the loss of any good calls for grief rather than for joy (assuming that there is no compensation for the loss in the shape of a higher good—for example, righteousness of character is a higher good than health of body), the unrighteous man's grief in his punishment is more appropriate than his rejoicing in sin. Hence, just as delight in the abandonment of good, when a man sins, is evidence of a bad will, so grief at the loss of good, when a man is punished, is evidence of a good nature. For when a man grieves at the loss of the peace of his nature, his grief arises from some remnants of that peace, which ensure that his nature is still on friendly terms with itself. Moreover, it is entirely right that in the last punishment the wicked and ungodly should bewail in their agonies the loss of their 'natural' goods, and realize that he who divested them of these goods with perfect justice is God, whom they despised when with supreme generosity he bestowed them.

God then, created all things in supreme wisdom and ordered them in perfect justice; and in establishing the mortal race of mankind as the greatest ornament of earthly things, he has given to mankind certain good things suitable to this life. These are: temporal peace, in proportion to the short span of a mortal life—the peace that consists in bodily health and soundness, and in fellowship with one's kind; and everything necessary to safeguard or recover this peace—those things, for example, which are appropriate and accessible to our senses: light, speech, air to breathe, water to drink, and whatever is suitable for the feeding and clothing of the body, for the care of the body and the adornment of the person. And all this is granted under the most equitable condition: that every mortal who uses aright such goods, goods designed to serve the peace of mortal men, shall receive goods greater in degree and superior in kind, namely, the peace of immortality, and the glory and honour appropriate to it in a life which is eternal for the enjoyment of God and of one's neighbour in God, whereas he who wrongly uses those mortal goods shall lose them, and shall not receive the blessings of eternal life.

Chapter 14: The Order and Law, Earthly or Heavenly, by Which Government Serves the Interests of Human Society

We see, then, that all man's use of temporal things is related to the enjoyment of earthly peace in the earthly city; whereas in the Heavenly City it is related to the enjoyment of eternal peace. Thus, if we were irrational animals, our only aim would be the adjustment of the parts of the body in due proportion, and the quieting of the appetites—only, that is, the repose of the flesh, and an adequate supply of pleasures, so that bodily peace might promote the peace of the soul. For if bodily peace is lacking, the peace of the irrational soul is also hindered, because it cannot achieve the quieting of its appetites. But the two together promote that peace which is a mutual concord between soul and body, the peace of an ordered life and of health. For living creatures show their love of bodily peace by their avoidance of pain, and by their pursuit of pleasure to satisfy the demands of their appetites they demonstrate their love of peace of soul. In just the same way, by shunning death they indicate quite clearly how great is their love of the peace in which soul and body are harmoniously united.

But because there is in man a rational soul, he subordinates to the peace of the rational soul all that part of his nature which he shares with the beasts, so that he may engage in deliberate thought and act in accordance with this thought, so that he may thus exhibit that ordered agreement of cognition and action which we called the peace of the rational soul. For with this end in view he ought to wish to be spared the distress of pain and grief, the disturbances of desire, the dissolution of death, so that he may come to some profitable knowledge and may order his life and his moral standards in accordance with this knowledge. But he needs divine direction, which he may obey with resolution, and divine assistance that he may obey it freely, to prevent him from falling, in his enthusiasm for knowledge, a victim to some fatal error, through the weakness of the human mind. And so long as he is in this mortal body, he is a pilgrim in a foreign land, away from God; therefore he walks by faith, not by sight.[28] That is why he views all peace, of body or of soul, or of both, in relation to that peace which exists between mortal man and immortal God, so that he may exhibit an ordered obedience in faith in subjection to the everlasting Law.

Now God, our master, teaches two chief precepts, love of God and love of neighbour; and in them man finds three objects for his love: God, himself, and his neighbour; and a man who loves God is not wrong in loving himself. It follows, therefore, that he will be concerned also that his neighbour should love God, since he is told to love his neighbour as himself; and the same is true of his concern for his wife, his children, for the members of his household, and for all other men, so far as is possible. And, for the same end, he will wish his neighbour to be concerned for him, if he happens to need that concern. For this reason he will be at peace, as far as lies in him, with all men, in that peace among men, that ordered harmony; and the basis of this order is the observance of two rules: first, to do no harm to anyone, and, secondly, to help everyone whenever possible. To begin with, therefore, a man has a responsibility for his own household—obviously, both in the order of nature and in the framework of human society, he has easier and more immediate contact with them; he can exercise his concern for them. That is why the Apostle says, 'Anyone who does not take care of his own people, especially those in his own household, is worse than an unbeliever—he is a renegade'.[29] This is where domestic peace starts, the ordered harmony about giving and obeying orders among those who live in the same house. For the orders are given by those who are concerned for the interests of others; thus the husband gives orders to the wife, parents to children, masters to servants. While those who are the objects of this concern obey orders; for example, wives obey husbands, the children obey their parents, the servants their masters. But in the household of the just man who 'lives on the basis of faith' and who is still on pilgrimage, far from that Heavenly City, even those who give orders are the servants of those whom they appear to command. For they do not give orders because of a lust for domination but from a dutiful concern for the interests of others, not with pride in taking precedence over others, but with compassion in taking care of others....

Chapter 17: The Origin of Peace Between the Heavenly Society and the Earthly City, and of Discord Between Them

But a household of human beings whose life is not based on faith is in pursuit of an earthly peace based on the things belonging to this temporal life, and on its advantages, whereas a household of human beings whose life is based on faith looks forward to the blessings which are promised as eternal in the future, making use of earthly and temporal things like a pilgrim in a foreign land, who does not let himself be taken in by them or distracted from his course towards God, but rather treats them as supports which help him more easily to bear the burdens of 'the corruptible body which weighs heavy on the soul';[30] they must on no account be allowed to increase the load. Thus both kinds of men and both kinds of households alike make use of the things essential for this mortal life; but each has its own very different end in making use of them. So also the earthly city, whose life is not based on faith, aims at an earthly peace, and it limits the harmonious agreement of citizens concerning the giving and obeying of orders to the establishment of a kind of compromise between human wills about the things relevant to mortal life. In contrast, the Heavenly City—or rather that part of it which is on pilgrimage in this condition of mortality, and which lives on the basis of faith—must needs make use of this peace also, until this mortal state, for which this kind of peace is essential, passes away. And therefore, it leads what we may call a life of captivity in this earthly city as in a foreign land, although it has already received the promise of redemption, and the gift of the Spirit as a kind of pledge of it; and yet it does not hesitate to obey the laws of the earthly city by which those things which are designed for the support of this mortal life are regulated; and the purpose of this obedience is that, since this mortal condition is shared by both cities, a harmony may be preserved between them in things that are relevant to this condition.

But this earthly city has had some philosophers belonging to it whose theories are rejected by the teaching inspired by God. Either led astray by their own speculation or deluded by demons, these thinkers reached the belief that there are many gods who must be won over to serve human ends, and also that they have, as it were, different departments with different responsibilities attached. Thus the body is the department of one god, the mind that of another; and within the body itself, one god is in charge of the head, another of the neck and so on with each of the separate members. Similarly, within the mind, one is responsible for natural ability, another for learning, another for anger, another for lust; and in the accessories of life there are separate gods over the departments of flocks, grain, wine, oil, forests, coinage, navigation, war and victory, marriage, birth, fertility, and so on.[31] The Heavenly City, in contrast, knows only one God as the object of worship, and decrees, with faithful devotion, that he only is to be served with that service which the Greeks call *latreia*, which is due to God alone. And the result of this difference has been that the Heavenly City could not have laws of religion common with the earthly city, and in defence of her religious laws she was bound to dissent from those who thought differently and to prove a burdensome nuisance to them. Thus she had to endure their anger and hatred, and the assaults of persecution; until at length that City shattered the morale of her adversaries by the terror inspired by her numbers, and by the help she continually received from God.

While this Heavenly City, therefore, is on pilgrimage in this world, she calls out citizens from all nations and so collects a society of aliens, speaking all languages. She takes no account of any difference in customs, laws, and institutions, by which earthly peace is achieved and preserved—not that she annuls or abolishes any of those, rather, she maintains them and follows them (for whatever divergences there are among the diverse nations, those institutions have one single aim—earthly peace), provided that no hindrance is presented thereby to the religion which teaches that the one supreme and true God is to be worshipped. Thus even the Heavenly City in her pilgrimage here on earth makes use of the earthly peace and defends and seeks the compromise between human wills in respect of the provisions relevant to the mortal nature of man, so far as may be permitted without detriment to true religion and piety. In fact, that City relates the earthly peace to the heavenly peace, which is so truly peaceful that it should be regarded as the only peace deserving the name, at least in respect of the rational creation; for this peace is the perfectly ordered and completely harmonious fellowship in the enjoyment of God, and of each other in God. When we arrive at that state of peace, there will be no longer a life that ends in death, but a life that is life in sure and sober truth; there will be no animal body to 'weigh down the soul' in its process of corruption; there will be a spiritual body with no cravings, a body subdued in every part to the will. This peace the Heavenly City possesses in faith while on its pilgrimage, and it lives a life of righteousness, based on this faith,[32] having the attainment of that peace in view in every good action it performs in relation to God, and in relation to a neighbour, since the life of a city is inevitably a social life. . . .

Chapter 24: An Alternative Definition of 'People' and 'Commonwealth'

If, on the other hand, another definition than this is found for a 'people', for example, if one should say, 'A people is the association of a multitude of rational beings united by a common agreement on the objects of their love', then it follows that to observe the character of a particular people we must examine the objects of its love. And yet, whatever those objects, if it is the association of a multitude not of animals but of rational beings, and is united by a common agreement about the objects of its love, then there is no absurdity in applying to it the title of a 'people'. And, obviously, the better the objects of this

agreement, the better the people; the worse the objects of this love, the worse the people. By this definition of ours, the Roman people is a people and its estate is indubitably a commonwealth. But as for the objects of that people's love—both in the earliest times and in subsequent periods—and the morality of that people as it proceeded to bloody strife of parties and then to the social and civil wars, and corrupted and disrupted that very unity which is, as it were, the health of a people—for all this we have the witness of history; and I have had a great deal to say about it in my preceding books. And yet I shall not make that a reason for asserting that a people is not really a people or that a state is not a commonwealth, so long as there remains an association of some kind or other between a multitude of rational beings united by a common agreement on the objects of its love. However, what I have said about the Roman people and the Roman commonwealth I must be understood to have said and felt about those of the Athenians and of any other Greeks, or of that former Babylon of the Assyrians, when they exercised imperial rule, whether on a small or a large scale, in their commonwealths—and indeed about any other nation whatsoever. For God is not the ruler of the city of the impious, because it disobeys his commandment that sacrifice should be offered to himself alone. The purpose of this law was that in that city the soul should rule over the body and reason over the vicious elements, in righteousness and faith. And because God does not rule there the general characteristic of that city is that it is devoid of true justice.

Chapter 25: True Virtues Impossible Without True Religion

The fact is that the soul may appear to rule the body and the reason to govern the vicious elements in the most praiseworthy fashion; and yet if the soul and reason do not serve God as God himself has commanded that he should be served, then they do not in any way exercise the right kind of rule over the body and the vicious propensities. For what kind of a mistress over the body and the vices can a mind be that is ignorant of the true God and is not subjected to his rule, but instead is prostituted to the corrupting influence of vicious demons? Thus the virtues which the mind imagines it possesses, by means of which it rules the body and the vicious elements, are themselves vices rather than virtues, if the mind does not bring them into relation with God in order to achieve anything whatsoever and to maintain that achievement. For although the virtues are reckoned by some people to be genuine and honourable when they are related only to themselves and are sought for no other end, even then they are puffed up and proud, and so are to be accounted vices rather than virtues. For just as it is not something derived from the physical body itself that gives life to that body, but something above it, so it is not something that comes from man, but something above man, that makes his life blessed; and this is true not only of man but of every heavenly dominion and power whatsoever.

Chapter 26: The Peace of the People Alienated from God Is Made Use of by God's People on Their Pilgrimage

Thus, as the soul is the life of the physical body, so God is the blessedness of man's life. As the holy Scriptures of the Hebrews say, 'Blessed is the people, whose God is the Lord.'[33] It follows that a people alienated from that God must be wretched. Yet even such a people loves a peace of its own, which is not to be rejected; but it will not possess it in the end, because it does not make good use of it before the end. Meanwhile, however, it is important for us also that this people should possess this peace in this life, since so long as the two cities are intermingled we also make use of the peace of Babylon—although the People of God is by faith set free from Babylon, so that in the meantime they are only pilgrims in the midst of her. That is why the Apostle instructs the Church to pray for kings of that city and those in high positions, adding these words: 'that we may lead a quiet and peaceful life with all devotion and love'.[34] And when the prophet Jeremiah predicted to the ancient People of God the coming captivity, and bade them, by God's inspiration, to go obediently to Babylon, serving God even by their patient endurance, he added his own advice that prayers should be offered for Babylon, 'because in her peace is your peace'[35]—meaning, of course, the temporal peace of the meantime, which is shared by good and bad alike.

Chapter 27: The Peace of God's Servants, a Perfect Tranquillity, Not Experienced in This Life

In contrast, the peace which is our special possession is ours even in this life, a peace with God through faith; and it will be ours for ever, a peace with God through open vision.[36] But peace here and now, whether the peace shared by all men or our own special possession, is such that it affords a solace for our wretchedness rather than the joy of blessedness. Our righteousness itself, too, though genuine, in virtue of the genuine Ultimate Good to which it is referred, is nevertheless only such as to consist in the forgiveness of sins rather than in the perfection of virtues. The evidence for this is in the prayer of the whole City of God on pilgrimage in the world, which, as we know, cries out to God through the lips of all its members: 'Forgive us our debts as we forgive our debtors'.[37] And this prayer is not effective for those whose 'faith, without works, is dead'[38] but only for those whose 'faith is put into action through love'.[39] For such a prayer is needed by righteous men because the reason, though subjected to God, does not have complete command over the vices in this mortal state and in the 'corruptible body which weighs heavy on the soul'.[40] In fact, even though command be exercised over the vices it is assuredly not by any means without a conflict. And even when a man fights well and even gains the mastery by conquering and subduing such foes, still in this situation of weakness something is all too likely to creep in to cause sin, if not in hasty action, at least in a casual remark or a fleeting thought.

For this reason there is no perfect peace so long as command is exercised over the vicious propensities, because the battle is fraught with peril while those vices that resist are being reduced to submission, while those which have been overcome are not yet triumphed over in peaceful security, but are repressed under a rule still troubled by anxieties. Thus we are in the midst of these temptations, about which we find this brief saying amongst the divine oracles: 'Is a man's life on earth anything but temptation?';[41] and who can presume that his life is of such a kind that he has no need to say to God, 'Forgive us our debts', unless he is a man of overwhelming conceit, not a truly great man, but one puffed up and swollen with pride, who is with justice resisted by him who gives grace to the humble, as it says in the Scriptures, 'God resists the proud, but he gives his favour to the humble'.[42] In this life, therefore, justice in each individual exists when God rules and man obeys, when the mind rules the body and reason governs the vices even when they rebel, either by subduing them or by resisting them, while from God himself favour is sought for good deeds and pardon for offences, and thanks are duly offered to him for benefits received. But in that ultimate peace, to which this justice should be related, and for the attainment of which this justice is to be maintained, our nature will be healed by immortality and incorruption and will have no perverted elements, and nothing at all, in ourselves or any other, will be in conflict with any one of us. And so reason will not need to rule the vices, since there will be no vices, but God will hold sway over man, and the soul over the body, and in this state our delight and facility in obeying will be matched by our felicity in living and reigning. There, for each and every one, this state will be eternal, and its eternity will be assured; and for that reason the peace of this blessedness, or the blessedness of this peace, will be the Supreme Good.

Chapter 28: The End of the Wicked

In contrast with this, however, the wretchedness of those who do not belong to this City of God will be everlasting. This is called also 'the second death', because the soul cannot be said to be alive in that state, when it is separated from the life of God, nor can the body, when it is subjected to eternal torments. And this is precisely the reason why this 'second death' will be harder to bear, because it cannot come to an end in death. But here a question arises; for just as wretchedness is the opposite of blessedness, and death of life, so war is evidently the opposite

of peace. And the question is rightly asked: What war, or what kind of war, can be understood to exist in the final state of the wicked, corresponding, by way of contrast, to that peace which is proclaimed with joyful praises in the final state of the good? Now anyone who puts this question should observe what it is that is harmful and destructive in war; and he will see that it is precisely the mutual opposition and conflict of the forces engaged. What war, then, can be imagined more serious and more bitter than a struggle in which the will is so at odds with the feelings and the feelings with the will, that their hostility cannot be ended by the victory of either—a struggle in which the violence of pain is in such conflict with the nature of the body that neither can yield to the other? For in this life, when such a conflict occurs, either pain wins, and death takes away feeling, or nature conquers, and health removes the pain. But in that other life, pain continues to torment, while nature lasts to feel the pain. Neither ceases to exist, lest the punishment also should cease.

These, then, are the final states of good and evil. The first we should seek to attain, the latter we should strive to escape. And since it is through a judgement that the good will pass to the one, and the evil to the other, it is of this judgement that I shall deal, as far as God grants, in the book which follows.

Notes

1. Wisdom 9, 15.
2. 2 Corinthians 4, 16.
3. 2 Corinthians 5, 1–4.
4. cf. Plato, *Phaedrus*, 245E–250E.
5. Virgil, *Aeneid*, 6, 730ff.
6. cf. Cicero, *Tusculanae Disputationes*, 3, 11, 24; 4, 6, 11; 12.
7. cf. Galatians 5, 19ff.
8. John 8, 44.
9. Romans 3, 7.
10. John 14, 6.
11. 1 Corinthians 3, 3.
12. 1 Corinthians 2, 11ff.
13. 1 Corinthians 3, 1.
14. Romans 3, 20.
15. Genesis 46, 27.

16. 1 Corinthians 3, 4.
17. Who ascribed the creation of flesh to an evil power, opposed to God, and co-eternal with him (Augustine of Hippo, *De Haeresibus ad Quodvultdeum*, 46); cf. Bk XI, 13n.
18. Cicero, *Tusculanae Disputationes*, 4, 6, 11.
19. cf. Bk VIII, 17.
20. Virgil, *Aeneid*, 6, 719ff.
21. Psalms 111, 2.
22. cf. Genesis 3, 15 (the 'Protevangelium').
23. 2 Corinthians 10, 17.
24. Psalms 3, 3.
25. Psalms 18, 1.
26. Romans 1, 21ff.
27. 1 Corinthians 15, 28.
28. cf. 2 Corinthians 5, 6f.
29. 1 Timothy 5, 8.
30. Wisdom 9, 15.
31. cf. Bks IV, VI, VII.
32. cf. Habakkuk 2, 4; Romans 1, 17 etc.
33. Psalms 144, 15.
34. 1 Timothy 2, 2.
35. Jeremiah 29, 7.
36. cf. 2 Corinthians 5, 7.
37. Matthew 6, 12.
38. James 2, 17.
39. Galatians 5, 6.
40. Wisdom 9, 15.
41. Job 7, 1; cf. ch. 8n.
42. James 4, 6; 1 Peter 5, 5.

Adapted from: Saint Augustine, *Concerning the City of God Against the Pagans,* translated by Henry Bettenson, pp. 550–555, 592–594, 866–867, 869–874, 877–879, 890–894. Copyright © 1972 by Henry Bettenson. Reproduced by permission of Penguin Classics. ✦

16
The Two Cities in Augustine's Political Philosophy

Rex Martin

There has been a surprisingly wide divergence of interpretations of Augustine's conception of the state, especially with respect to the political bearing of his concept of the Two Cities and to his position on the nature and role of justice in the governance of states. In this essay I wish to develop a single, coherent reading of Augustine's theory out of the themes and passages that are generally regarded as the matrix of his conception of the state and, then, to confirm and extend this reading by directing it against some of the major alternative interpretations of his theory.

What are these themes and passages which provide the agreed upon field of interpretation and reinterpretation? There is, first, the concept of the Two Cities and the political interpretation given it. Then, second, there is the well-known passage in the *City of God* (IV.4, pp. 112–13) where Augustine draws an analogy between a kingdom (*regnum*) and a robber band. Finally, we have Augustine's reflections on, and apparent reworking of, Cicero's definition of a commonwealth (*res publica*).[1] These themes and passages are all of a piece. The political interpretation placed on the idea of the Two Cities will affect the reading one gives to the "robber band" and "commonwealth" passages. The conception that one develops of the state in these passages will be a feature of the way that the idea of the Two Cities is construed. Most commentators appear to re-

gard Augustine's basic position as a consistent one. Differences have come, however, in determining exactly what this position is.

I think the simplest approach to Augustine's position is by way of the Two Cities. According to Augustine, the twofold division of the universe into the "City of God" and the "City of Earth" originated in the prideful revolt of the (now fallen) angels in heaven. As it had been in heaven so it was on earth. Men had primevally lived on earth in peace and comity (joined with one another in natural, familial affection) until the Fall, which brought sin into the world. The two cities on earth had their germ in Cain and Abel. Cain, the fratricide, built the first earthly city, "but Abel, being a sojourner, built none" (XV.1, p. 479). Thus, Augustine can say,

Accordingly, two cities have been formed by two loves: the earthly by the love of self, even to the contempt of God; the heavenly by the love of God, even to the contempt of self. . . . In the one, the princes and the nations it subdues are ruled by the love of ruling. . . . But in the other city there is no human wisdom, but only godliness, which offers due worship to the true God, and looks for its reward in the society of the saints, of holy angels as well as holy men, "that God may be all in all" (XIV.28, p. 477).

One model for interpreting Augustine's Two Cities is to *identify* the Earthly City with the state and the City of God with the institutional church. Assuming for the sake of argument that this model is fundamentally sound, we can ask what consequences for the evaluation of political life would follow from the model. As regards the state as such, when taken on its own terms, the consequence would appear to be a radical devaluation of the political side of things and a considerable measure of pessimism respecting the means and ends of man's political condition. On the other hand, the institutional church—at least in the Christian dispensation—would literally be the City of God on earth.

What political implication this would have, however, is not altogether clear. It would seem, though, that if the state could be Christianized through some special relationship with the institutional church, then a fundamentally different evaluation of such a state would be warranted. The basic point here would be to distinguish the state *per se*, on its own principles, from the state as Christianized through some organic relationship with the institutional church.[2] The function of the identification model would be to validate this distinction, to justify this way of looking at politics, and to legitimate the notion of a Christianized state.

The twofold identification which I have described, of the state with the City of Earth and of the church militant with the City of God, could lead to a "clericalist" doctrine of the state. This seems to have happened in the Middle Ages, when there was a strong current of "clericalist" rhetoric in which the identification model was asserted, or at least presupposed.[3] That we should accept this tradition of political rhetoric as an interpretation of Augustine is doubtful. For it may well be that the medieval analysis was about medieval politics rather than about Augustine and, hence, not fundamentally an interpretation of the political doctrine of the *City of God*. In modern times, however, scholarly interpretations have been advanced which lend weight to taking the clericalist doctrine, and the identification model, as a substantially correct account of Augustine's own position. As Figgis says, "Their views are stronger evidence of what Augustine meant, than is the constant use that was made of him by medieval thinkers. The medieval habit of taking tags as text-proofs, apart from the general purpose of the writer, discounts their value as evidence. Besides this there was an immediate polemical interest at stake."[4]

Although the identification model would appear to have a certain validity, or at least great historical interest, its acceptability as a substantially correct account of Augustine's position would require the support of Augustine's text, as it bears on the notion of the Two Cities and his analysis of the state. It is my own opinion that the identification model is altogether too simple to fit the salient details of Augustine's own rendering of the Two Cities, as I shall try to make clear in what follows.

Let me begin by elaborating the contention that Augustine had an essentially tripartite conception of the city of God. The first conception is that the city of God is an "eternal city"; as such it is composed of the Trinity, the unfallen or loyal angels, and the eternally predestined-to-grace portion of the human race. The eternal citizenship of the human portion, which is *potentially* eternal "in time" and *actually* eternal "at the end of time" (i.e., in the Heaven of Book XXII), is referred to by Augustine in phrases such as "the eternal life of the saints" (XII.19, p. 402) and "a future eternal priesthood" (XVII.6, p. 583).

The second conception of the city of God is that it is an association (a collective only "in concept" but taken distributively in fact) of individual persons who love God, as distinct from those who love themselves and the things of this earth. By this rubric of "two loves" Augustine divided *all* mankind into two groups, those who live after "the flesh" and those who live after "the Spirit" (XIV.1, p. 441). Members within each group have nothing in common except the peculiar characters of the "love" (or "will") which motivates them. These individuals are not corporately embodied as such in any single institution or set of institutions on earth; yet they are spoken of as forming two "cities." Accordingly, I shall refer to this as the "individualistic" conception of the city of God, for it denotes only individuals and their love.

The third conception of the city of God is that it is a visible and institutional entity. Before Christ, this entity was the Hebrew nation (not state). Christ "took away the kingdom" from Israel, because Israel had become his "enemy" (XVII.7, p. 585), and put it under his own headship in his church, the catholic church. It is especially noteworthy that Augustine used this terminology to describe what he believed to have been an *historical* occurrence, the transfer of God's institutional "kingdom" on earth from the Hebrew nation to the Christian church. . . .

As long as the institutional church is divinely directed to do God's work it *is* the city of God on earth in a most important and indispensable way. Regardless of the general character of its membership and because it always contains the greater portion of the saints on earth, the catholic church (in Augustine's opinion) goes on its pilgrimage, inheritor of the "kingdom" of God from the Hebrews, house of worship, dispenser of the sacraments, and teacher of scripture. It is the peculiar medium through which God's will is worked and is a sharer in God's grace as truly as is the "individualistic" church. Each church, admittedly in its own way and in a nonexclusive and limited sense, is an aspect of the city of God on earth. The conclusion I draw is that Augustine did not treat "City of God on earth" and "institutional church" as identical in meaning. But I have argued that there is a unique relationship here, between the City of God and the visible church, which requires some term to describe it.

Figgis has suggested the notion of a "symbol."[5] While Noah's Ark may be a symbol of the church (by way of analogy), the institutional church is not in that sense a "symbol" of the City of God. For some features of the church are not simply analogous to traits of the City of God but are, rather, actual historical functions of the City of God on earth. Perhaps the word to describe the relationship is a stronger one: the institutional church *represents* or is the *agent* of the divine City in certain of the functions the church actually performs, i.e., in worship, sacraments, scripture, and authoritative discipline. Rather than a simple identity there is an identification at certain points and for certain purposes. It is this claim which I would urge against both Figgis and Deane.[6] Although I endorse their contention that Augustine does not identify the City of God on earth with the institutional church, I claim that this fact alone does not require us to withdraw the notion of a Christianized state, since there is still the relationship of special representation.

Deane, however, wants to deny the Christianized state interpretation altogether. To accomplish this, he wants to deny not only the simple identification model but also any notion of special representation. His claim here is quite uncompromising: "No earthly state, city, or association can ever claim to be a part or a representative of the City of God. . . . Even the visible Church, which contains many of the reprobate along with the elect, is not an earthly division of the City of God, although . . . it is more closely related to that City than any earthly state or society can ever be."[7]

One might well agree with Deane, as I do, that the Christianized state is not an Augustinian notion. But I do not think that one can give as his reason that there is *no* basic relationship, either of identity or of representation, between the City of God and the institutional church in Augustine's eyes. It seems to me to run against the grain of Augustine's text to say that the institutional church is "not an earthly division of the City of God" and to suggest that it differs from (other) earthly states or societies only in degree. Rather, I contend that there is a special relationship—representation—and this might provide warrant, although an attenuated one, for retaining the notion of a Christianized state as a possible interpretation of Augustine. Indeed, Sabine has managed to squeeze the whole Christianized state doctrine through the needle's eye of the relationship of representation. He has alleged, though noting that the City of God could not be "identified precisely" with "existing human institutions," including the church, that the Kingdom of Christ was "embodied" in "the church and Christianized empire." This "conception of a Christian commonwealth" is, Sabine says, Augustine's "most characteristic idea" and is based on "a philosophy of history [i.e., the idea of the Two Cities] which presents such a commonwealth as the culmination of man's spiritual development."[8] I would agree with Sabine to this extent: the Christianized state idea must at least be left open as a possibility, given the idea of a partial identification—i.e., in the relationship of agent representation—of the city of God with the Church.

But what about the other basic member of the Two Cities, the City of Earth? Do we have any textual license to *identify* the state *qua* state and the City of Earth? In dealing with this question, I think an *a priori* move might prove helpful: I would suggest that we try to develop a parallel between the institutional church in its relation to the City of God and the state in its relation to the City of Earth. On these *a priori* grounds, we could rule out the relationship of simple identification. Moreover, Figgis's notion of a symbolic relationship would appear warranted—as the text, at a number of points, would confirm. (For example, Cain, who is the first man to be a citizen of the City of Earth, also founded the first city. He was a fratricide, as was Romulus, who founded Rome. [See XV.1, p. 479; XV.8, pp. 488–89; XV.5, pp. 482–83.].) Finally, the idea of some sort of agent representation would, on *a priori* grounds, appear appropriate.[9]

The question is, How would this representation take shape? At what point(s) would the identity hold? For an answer I think we can revert to the passage where Augustine spoke of Two Cities formed by two loves, "the earthly by love of self." There are many forms of self-love, of concern for the things of this life, that could be cited but the one Augustine specifically mentions is the "love of ruling." Obviously, this is a notion relevant to politics. But does it imply that the state as such, through the love of ruling, specifically represents the City of Earth? I do not think it was the state *per se* that Augustine had in mind, for he says, "in the one, the princes and the nations it subdues are ruled by the love of ruling" (XIV.28, p. 477).

It is not the state as such, i.e., any particular state taken at random or all of them taken together, but the *imperial state* that peculiarly represents the City of Earth. The imperial state (e.g., Assyria, Egypt, Rome) plays a role toward the City of Earth analogous to that played by the institutional church towards the City of God. This basic parallelism descends even to details. The translation of empire theme, which we have already noted in relation to the church, is found also in the succession of the great earthly empires (for example, XVIII.21, p.627).

It has been observed by Figgis (p. 53) and Deane (p. 171), in particular, that Augustine was personally an anti-imperialist. (See, for example, IV.15, p. 123.)[10] However, the connection of this attitude to the notion that the imperial state "represents" the City of Earth has not been sufficiently noted. At several points Augustine asserts the essential simi-larity of all imperial states in their motivation by love of domination and their imposition of rule by war and force, and asserts the connection of this feature of imperial states with what he called the City of Earth, a connection such that we could call these great imperial states the exemplars and institutional representatives of the City of Earth. The earthly city is the city of earthly "loves" or lusts and the master lust is the lust of domination. This lust is a form of pride; it is the pride which apes God himself. This, then, is the principle of the imperial state in its role as the agent representative of the City of Earth: "The earthly city, . . . though it be mistress of the nations, is itself ruled by its lust of rule" (I. preface, p.3; also V.19).

The notion of a basic parallelism within the Two Cities concept is, I think, substantially sound. Sabine puts the institutional aspect of the parallelism well: "Augustine did think of the Kingdom of evil as at least *represented* by the pagan empires, though not exactly identified with them. He also thought of the church as *representing* the City of God, even though the latter cannot be identified with the ecclesiastical organization" (p.190; italics added).

My analysis of Augustine's political philosophy is based on the claim that he does not *identify* either of the Two Cities with institutions on earth. The two cities have a simple corporate character and identity only beyond the Final Judgment, in Heaven and Hell. With respect to this world, the concept of the Two Cities refers primarily to two types or classifications of men. However, I have argued that there are earthly institutions that "represent" and do the work of the two cities in human history: the imperial states are special embodiments of the City of Earth and, after the advent of Christ, the institutional church is the unique and indispensable representative of the City of God.

This conception of the institutional church as the special representative of the City of God allows us neither to dismiss nor to validate the notion of a Christianized state. For it is possible that the church might appropriate some sort of political apparatus for its own purposes just as the Hebrew nation had generated a state, the Hebrew Kingdom. The issue remains open. On the other hand, it is the *imperial* state, and not the state as such, that represents the City of Earth. This fact will allow us to dispense with any identification, whole or partial, of the state *per se* with the "earthly City."[11] In short, the concept of the Two Cities on its own, although it provides the superstructure of Augustine's political doctrines, does not give us all the essential details of Augustine's political philosophy. In particular, the concept does not provide us with sufficient information to determine Augustine's notion of the nature and role of justice in the state, or to establish whether Augustine was advocating the notion of a Christianized state. It does not, in fact, provide us even with Augustine's conception of the state, since any essential link between the state as such and the City of Earth has been broken. . . .

Augustine's basic distinction is drawn between a republic and a "kingdom" of the robber band variety. Now these terms do not denote constitutional entities but, rather, principles of political and social organization. A republic is a matter of "common agreement" (which recalls Cicero's harmony of social classes) but a kingdom or regime (*regnum*) is not organized on the principle of agreement but, rather, on the principle of imposition from above. And this recalls Cicero's notion of tyranny where social harmony was replaced by the dictatorship of one man over all or of one class over the others. The only difference of any apparent importance, and it is really incidental at this point, is that Cicero's notion of popular concurrence referred to a harmony of social classes whereas that same notion in Augustine referred to a harmony of individual persons, without reference to class.

Regimes or kingdoms are structured on the principle of the lust of domination. They are in essence exactly like imperial states, and this is why the word "kingdom" (*regnum*) can be indifferently applied either to imperial states or to "domestic" regimes. The only difference is that imperial states lord it over subject peoples who were once independently organized politically while "domestic" *regna* are juntas that rule over other men in a single state. In either case a *regnum*, be it an imperial state or a regime ruling in a state, is not the property of the people but of their masters. I think Augustine's political philosophy rests on two fundamental distinctions: the one between the heavenly city of God and the "earthly republic"; the other, within the "earthly republic," between a *res publica* and a *regnum*. But the nature of this latter distinction requires further mapping.

The distinction of *regnum/res publica* is drawn by McIlwain (see p.156 where he puts *civitates* and *regna* on one side, over against *res publicae* on the other). McIlwain's point is, I think, fundamental but his way of drawing it is defective. First, he treats it as a terminological distinction which Augustine explicitly drew, whereas I suggest that Augustine's distinction was not drawn at the terminological level at all. Second, he treats the distinction as having to do with *kinds* of states, not so much constitutional kinds as religious kinds (pagan/Christian).[12] But I would assert that Augustine is not contrasting kinds of states but rather, polar political styles, principles of political organization. His distinction is drawn by preference and reflects the grounds on which the preference is based.

If anything is clear, it is that Augustine regards a state organized on the principle of "common agreement" as preferable to one organized on the principle of subjection. This is clear for the simple reason that Augustine endorses the first principle (for it is the principle of organization in Augustine's own definition), and the principle of subjection he condemned (in IV.4) as nothing better than a "grand robbery." I regard the crucial point of difference between these principles, i.e., the difference between agreement and imposition, as the ground of his basic evaluation. And it is a *political* evaluation (for there is here no contrast intended between the divine and the political but, rather, only between the political good and the political bad).[13]

It is also clear from other passages that Augustine took a negative view, morally, of the whole principle of imposition and subjection. He speaks of robbers who "invade the peace of other men" and ultimately would have a city or nation "submit itself" to their brigand's peace in a passage (XIX.12, p. 687), recalling his earlier robber band passage (in IV.4). He also speaks of "wicked men [who] wage war to maintain the peace of their own circle, and wish that, if possible, all men belonged to them, that all men and things might serve but one head, and might, either through love or fear, yield themselves to peace with [them]! It is thus that pride in its perversity apes God. It abhors equality with other men under [God]; but, instead of His rule, it seeks to impose a rule of its own upon its equals" (XIX.12, p. 689).

We have then, in Augustine's theory, two basic kinds of political values in the organization of states: the community principle, defined by basic social agreement, and the regime principle, defined by an imposed order. However, Augustine's evaluations do not end here, for he recognizes that human freedom (in its political form, i.e., common agreement as to desired political ends) can have a variety of objects. And these objects will themselves vary in moral quality, "higher interests" as opposed to "lower." What Augustine called "true justice" can never be an interest or object of the state (at least, Augustine never allowed that it could). Even strict Ciceronian justice might be unattainable, for Augustine appears to believe that human justice, with or without a proper relationship to God, would always be imperfect, even when judged by internal or human standards, like those of Cicero (XIX.23–27, pp. 705–08). But if a state were to dedicate itself to some attainable "image of justice" (but not to the impossible goal of "true justice") then presumably it would have chosen a "higher interest." Or we might infer that, if a state were to undertake certain tasks in the interest of the church, as, for example, the use of its coercive power in the maintenance of the doctrines and discipline of the church, then that would be a "higher interest." If we interpret the Christianized State notion as meaning, not that a republic can only be a Christian state or that political justice is ultimately a theological and ecclesiastical category, but simply that service to the church is a political good (a "higher interest"), then

Augustine might be said to hold this notion.[14]

Whether the highest attainable political goal is service to the church or an image of justice, I will not venture to say. But if a commonwealth can have "lower" interests and still remain a commonwealth, then it is clear that virtues like justice (i.e., an "image of justice") or service to the church are not essential to its being a commonwealth, although such virtues may be essential to its merit as a commonwealth. The "image of justice," although it is a high aspiration, is not—perhaps for that very reason—necessary to maintain the conditions for the *existence* of the commonwealth. Justice belongs then (in Reinhold Niebuhr's phrase) "not to the *esse* but to the *bene esse* of the commonwealth."

There may be, however, something other than justice that is essential to the very existence of a commonwealth as defined, and, hence, that belongs of necessity on its agenda. This is, of course, a question of fact. Put in this way, it would seem that Augustine's conclusion is not difficult to fathom. What does belong to its basic agenda, according to him, is peace.

> The earthly city, which does not live by faith, seeks an earthly peace, and the end it proposes, in the well-ordered concord of civil obedience and rule, is the combination of men's wills to attain the things which are helpful to this life. The heavenly city [on earth] makes use of this peace only because it must, until this mortal condition which necessitates it shall pass away. . . . [The heavenly city] makes no scruple to obey the laws of the earthly city, whereby the things necessary for the maintenance of this mortal life are administered; and thus, as this life is common to both cities, so there is a harmony between them in regard to what belongs to [this mortal life] (XIX.17, pp. 695–96).

Augustine's notion of peace is complex, but if we take it just in reference to the theme of commonwealth, I think it is clear that he meant it to be more than simply "law and order," the policemen's peace. It does, however, include the suppression of civil commotion and riot; but if this were all, there would be no ultimate distinction between a commonwealth and a regime. Rather what he points to is a "well-ordered concord" in which obedience follows from a rational conception of permanent and mutual interests and not from fear and repression. Augustine says, "The peace of all things is the tranquillity of order. Order is the distribution which allots things equal and unequal, each to its own place" (XIX.13, p. 690). At the basis of the Augustinian commonwealth is "order," which requires a rough, pragmatic, but effective "distribution." The Augustinian minimum political agenda is *Pax, ordo, lex, societas.*[15] Under his new definition of commonwealth, the necessary condition for one to exist is "the tranquillity of order."

How different, really, is this "tranquillity of order" from Ciceronian justice? Not very. What ultimately divides the two men, after we make the true justice/image of justice distinction, is a fine line. Augustine's "tranquillity of order" can be achieved with a rough and ready justice (i.e., imperfect even by human standards). It does not require an "absolute justice," in Cicero's phrase. If Ciceronian justice (strict fair dealing between men and between classes, giving to each his own) is an "image" of the "true justice," then Augustinian justice (the "order" requisite to tranquillity) is an image of this image. The degree to which Augustine has moved from Cicero is marked in this proposition: the true test of any state is an appropriate tranquillity.

This marks a difference, a relative devaluation of strict justice in favor of a lesser but more comprehensive good, civil peace. But it is not a rejection of justice as a political category, as Carlyle seemed to think, or of the need for some sort of rough justice; rather, it is a prudential appeal to the strictly necessary conditions for the continuing existence of the "republican" political style.[16]

Augustine's point here is simply a factual one, as was Cicero's, but they differ as to the facts. Cicero thought that a strict justice was required for the existence of a people's state (*res populi*). Augustine believed that a less than strict or perfect justice, i.e., by human standards, was required as a matter of fact. The "tranquillity of order" replaces "absolute" justice on the basic agenda for the com-

monwealth and this shift is reflected in the difference between Cicero's "definition" of a republic and Augustine's own "more feasible" one.[17]

Augustine's real break with Cicero came, not on the "definition" of the commonwealth (for they agree that it is a matter of popular concurrence in *res populi*) nor on the empirical determination of its necessary conditions (for the difference here is only one of degree and of vocabulary), but on the question of the moral status of politics. Cicero, like the great classical political philosophers Plato and Aristotle, had idealized politics. Politics had as its end the highest human good; the state was, in principle, morally adequate to men. Men could realize their true end in political association: in Aristotle's famous phrase, man is a "political animal." Cicero's emphasis on strict or absolute justice was symptomatic of this basic evaluation just as Augustine's devaluation of justice as a political necessity was symptomatic of a different evaluation.

The point is that Augustine rejected the classical idealization of the state; this is far more central than how he stood on Cicero's definition. There is a gulf of radical discontinuity between Augustine and classical politics. In this sense, Augustine can be said to have written an anti-politics. His program was to put the things of this world, even the best of states, under the things of the next, to commit oneself wholly only to what is absolute, to idealize nothing. Christian political philosophy, like the Christian himself, is a stranger here below; it can be in the world but not of it. The good state, the "republic" with meritorious common interests, can be pointed out, but the state is not a church and the church should not become a state. The church must look beyond, to the heavenly republic. This is the basic truth of the Christian religion, as it must be the constant theme of Christian political philosophy. This is, I think, the political theme of the *City of God*. It is the political meaning of the concept of the Two Cities.

Notes

1. References to and citations of the text of Augustine's *City of God* will generally occur in the body of the paper and will follow a single

style—e.g., IV.4, pp. 112–13, where the numbers denote, respectively, the book (IV), the chapter (4), and the page numbers of the passage in question. The page references are to the Modern Library edition of the *City of God*, trans. by Marcus Dods and others (New York, 1950). For Augustine's discussion of Cicero's definition see, in particular, II.21, pp. 60–63 and XIX.21, 23, 24, pp. 699–701, 706.

2. A variety of possible arrangements could be suggested as suitably satisfying the "organic relationship" in question. Among the alternatives are: (a) some sort of theocracy, (b) Caesaro-papism of the Byzantine sort, (c) a co-operative relationship between church and state within a single polity, as in Charlemagne's conception of the Holy Roman Empire, or (d) a cooperative relationship between two types of authority within a single Christian society, as in the "formula" of Pope Gelasius. It has even been said that the mere establishment of the Christian church or simply the official toleration of Christianity would be sufficient. See J. N. Figgis, *The Political Aspects of St. Augustine's "City of God"* (Gloucester, 1963; originally published in 1921), 60–61.

3. The term "clericalist" is Figgis's (64). A number of medieval thinkers can plausibly be cited as holding the clericalist doctrine on grounds of the identification model: Hildebrand (see Figgis 88–89 for discussion and citation); Engelbert of Admont (Figgis, 85, 97–98); James of Viterbo (C. H. McIlwain, *The Growth of Political Thought in the West* [New York, 1932], 159; McIlwain also cited Hildebrand, 160); the anonymous source cited in the anti-papalist tract *Rex pacificus* (H. A. Deane, *The Political and Social Ideas of St. Augustine* [New York, 1963], 232–33); and Giles of Rome (Deane, 232, 332, n. 25; Giles is also cited by McIlwain, 159n).

4. Figgis, 77. Ritschl, for example, appears to identify the state with the City of Earth (Figgis, 55, 128, n.6 for discussion and citation). Gierke holds a theocratic interpretation of the state based, again, on identifying the City of God with the church (Figgis, 77, 131, n.9). Similar views are held by Dorner and Ritschl (Figgis, 131, nn.8, 10).

5. Figgis, 51, 68. Bluhm refers to the "identification," of the city of God with the institutional church, as "only figurative": *Theories of the Political System* (Englewood Cliffs, 1965), 163.

6. Both Figgis (51–52, 121) and Deane (24, 34, 121) do, of course, deny the simple identification model. Figgis does it with the qualifica-

tion "*sans phrase*"; Deane's denial is unqualified: it is "absolutely impossible to identify the City of God . . . with the visible Christian Church in this world" (24).

7. Deane, 29 (see also 28). It is difficult to say here whether Deane is expounding Jesus's opinion or Augustine's. But he is clearly expounding Augustine later, when he says that the City of God "has no earthly representative" (120). If this remark is taken to refer exclusively to *states* I would agree, but if it is meant to include the church militant as well (as it does on 121), I cannot agree.

8. The passages cited are from G. H. Sabine, *History of Political Theory* (3d ed.; New York, 1961), 190–91. It is interesting to note that Sabine presses the Christianized State notion on Augustine, by reference to the Two Cities concept, while specifically asserting that the church "represents" the City of God "even though the latter cannot be identified with the ecclesiastical organization" (190). It is difficult to say exactly what Sabine was referring to with the phrase "Christian commonwealth." I presume that it referred, at least in part, to the "Christianized empire" of the next page. In any case, we do find Sabine endorsing the claim of James Bryce that "the theory of the Holy Roman Empire was built upon Augustine's City of God" and we do find him talking about Augustine's espousal of the notion of "a Christian state" (191–92).

9. It is interesting to note that Figgis will allow only a "symbolic" representation of the City of God by the church, and Deane not even this; but the relationship between the City of Earth and the State is treated, in each case, in a non-parallel fashion. Deane, for example, suggests that "states of this world are in some sense regarded as *parts* of the earthly city" (31, italics added; see also Deane, 30, and Figgis, 51, and 58).

10. Augustine had an ambivalent attitude toward the Romans' acquisition of empire. He does not trace it simpy to the love of ruling, but, also, includes the provocations of Rome's neighbors among the causes of empire. The empire accrued to Rome in part as the result of fighting "just wars" (IV.15, p. 123; Augustine makes this same point at III.10, p. 81). He also provides as special reason (or cause) for Rome's empire: God "helped forward the Romans, who were good according to a certain standard of an earthly state" (V.19, p. 173). At another point he says that by Rome "God was pleased to conquer the whole

world, and subdue it far and wide by bringing it into one fellowship of government and laws" (XVIII.22, p. 628; also XIX.7, p. 683). It is, in the light of this, understandable that Augustine would be reluctant to accept the "fall" of Rome (see IV.7, p. 115). The hold of the Roman myth was powerful on its loyal subjects, Christian and pagan.

11. Insofar as Augustine can be said to be concerned with the political state as such, I think we can say that he saw the state *qua* state as belonging to the things of this world, as distinct from the things of heaven. Certainly this much can be read into Augustine's oft repeated observation that Cain founded the first city (XV.1, p. 479). This, together with the fact that Augustine pointed Abel out as a shepered, not as a ruler of men, indicates that Augustine did not regard the rule of man over men as part of the economy of Eden.

12. Deane rejects McIlwain's distinction of *regnum/res publica* because he does not see that Augustine uses his terms in the way McIlwain has indicated: Deane, 297, n.28. Even more objectionable is the interpretation McIlwain puts on the distinction once he has drawn it terminologically. He says that all pagan states are *regna*, since they are, as pagan, deprived of justice but that republics would have the quality of justice; and he suggests, but does not say, that a Christianized State would be a republic. Even so, I think the distinction of *regnum/res publica*, if interpreted along the lines I am suggesting, can be used to point to a genuine principle of distinction of Augustine's political thought.

13. D'Entrèves construes Augustine as offering a value-neutral definition of the *state* (23–27). This view is, I think, mistaken. The whole notion of a "republic" was introduced and discussed in an evaluative way. In contrast to d'Entrèves I would say that Augustine was "defining" a "republic," where that term referred to a political value which could be exemplified or not in any state. The very notion of a republic, as we find it in XIX.21, for example, is itself an entirely favorably evaluated notion. (For additional discussion, see d'Entrèves's chapter, "The State—A Neologism," 28–36.)

14. Augustine came, rather reluctantly and rather late, to advocate the state coercion of

heretics and the suppression of schism by political means. See his *Correction of the Donatists*, in *Works* (trans. J. R. King; Edinburgh, 1872), III, esp. 485; also the very excellent chapter 6 on heresy by Deane, 172–220.

15. Ernest Barker, "Introduction" to J. Healey's translation of the *City of God* (London, Everyman, 1947) I, xxvii.

16. Carlyle seemed to hold the view that Augustine, in effect, simply got rid of the notion of justice as a political category: A. J. Carlyle, *A History of Medieval Political Theory in the West* (New York, originally published in 1903) I, 170, 174. Carlyle regarded this as quite momentous, out of line with literally centuries of earlier and subsequent political thought (see 169, 221). At the same time Carlyle is bemused that "Augustine seems to take the matter lightly" (166). And he was even led to conclude in another place that Augustine may not have "realized the enormous significance of what he was saying;" in F. J. C. Hearnshaw, ed., *Social and Political Ideas of Some Great Medieval Thinkers* (London, 1923), 50. But I would suggest that all this represents too simplistic a reading of Augustine's text.

17. Figgis, of course, recognizes the important role peace plays in Augustine's political thought but he does not see that what Augustine meant by peace (the "tranquillity of order") is essentially continuous with Ciceronian justice (62–64). Deane, on the other hand, tends to *equate* Augustinian peace with what Augustine called the "image" of justice (125, 136). I do not think there is adequate textual warrant for Deane's treatment; moreover, it makes the difference between Augustine's definition and that of Cicero, admittedly more apparent than real, wholly inexplicable. I would suggest that Augustine's "peace" and Cicero's "justice" do differ in name but that they point to the same kind of thing; the only difference between them is one of degree.

Reprinted from: Rex Martin, "The Two Cities in Augustine's Political Philosophy." In *Journal of the History of Ideas*, 33, pp. 195–198, 200–204, 211–216. Copyright © 1972. Reprinted with permission of the Johns Hopkins University Press. ✦

17
The Earthly City and Its Discontents

Jean Bethke Elshtain

Augustine is usually numbered among the pessimists. I'm sure many readers remember being taught Augustine in this way. Political Augustinianism belonged with Machiavellianism and Hobbesianism as a way of looking at the world that stressed evil, cruelty, violence, and a concomitant need for order, coercion, punishment, and the occasional war. Of course, one didn't actually read Augustine so much as Augustine-fragments culled from the 'political' bits in *The City of God*. Perhaps a chunk from Book I, chapter 1, on "the city of this world, a city which aims at dominion, which holds nations in enslavement, but is itself dominated by that very lust of domination."[1] Book II, chapter 21 was helpful on Augustine's alternative to Cicero's judgment (according to Scipio) of the Roman commonwealth. Book XV, chapter I, traced the lines of descent of the "two cities, speaking allegorically"; Book XIX, chapter 14, could be mined for a few precepts about the interests government should serve; chapter 15 made an argument against slavery "by nature"; and chapter 21, in which Scipio's definition of a commonwealth as advanced by Cicero makes a second appearance, also seemed pertinent. Book XIX was usually lodged as the key political text, containing what political theorists found relevant, not, of course, the debate on "Supreme Good and Evil" in chapter 1, but chapter 7 that spoke of "the misery of war even when just," as well as the most frequently excerpted chapters 14, 15, and 16, deployed in order to demonstrate

that Augustine recognized a connection between the peace and good of the household in relation to the city, or to earthly dominion more grandly defined. That, plus his rather scathing comment that what pirates do with one boat, Romans do with a navy, but the one is called brigandage while the other is named Empire, and the student would have her quick intake of Augustine Lite.

Called upon to give a lecture on Augustine for a course I took over about a month into a spring term—the year was 1972, the regular professor had taken ill suddenly, and the university in question wanted an inexpensive replacement (in other words, a graduate student)—I found that the reading list included Augustine Lite with the usual excerpts rounded up. I recall well the day I was to teach Augustine: one such session was reserved on the syllabus. It was a frigid morning during a particularly nasty winter in the Northeast. The class met at 8 A.M. Most of the students worked; indeed, some came directly to class from their night jobs.

My night job was getting up with children and, as well, I faced over an hour's drive in subzero weather in a Volkswagen mini-van with no functioning heater in order to get to class. No one was in a particularly jaunty mood. I had quickly crammed a bit of secondary reading—there had been no time to read even an abridged version of *The City of God*, and *The Confessions*, or so I had been taught, had nothing to do with politics. I decided to offer up a few bits of instant wisdom on Political Augustinianism. I called it a "way of looking at the world" and it went like this—I can be rather precise because I managed to dig out my old notes:

(1) Pessimism. Augustine does not view political order as an agency for human progress. He is extremely skeptical about the possibility that politics holds out hope for human improvement or the unfolding of the fullness of human virtue. Is not man a creature characterized by perversity of the will, plagued by fleeting desires, prone to sin, error, and perverse actions? Not too much can be expected from him.

(2) Evil is real. Man cannot be reformed.

(3) Augustine has a "tough-minded-realistic view of power." He sees power as the result of attempts to dominate. Power is not natural. It is devised by man. Power cannot be escaped; it can only be restrained.

(4) Authority must be treated with deference and respect but there is nothing inherently legitimate about it. It is a symptom of the fact that human beings do not spontaneously treat one another with love and affection.

I then asked the students: Even though political Augustinianism is not particularly attractive to us, might it not say something true about the human condition nonetheless? To be honest, I can't remember what followed. I do recall going over the nature of the two cities as formed by two loves, but as not having an "exact equivalent in this world." There are aspects of both cities in the life of this world, I claimed. The Church is not the heavenly city but prefigures it. For the Church itself is not perfect. It, too, uses powers of compulsion and control, although this is a tragic necessity, not something to celebrate or encourage. In theory, the Church can accommodate everyone and anyone: it is universalistic in principle.

The earthly city, I continued, is marked by the killing of Abel by Cain. Although violence is endemic to this city, it may promote a minimalist notion of the good, certainly better than a remorseless war of all against all. Earthly peace, though imperfect, is much to be desired. Because the political order is characterized by violence, regeneration cannot come from it: it cannot be a generative force from itself. Christians, however, can use the political order because it introduces regularity into social relations and thus helps to make possible the life of the Church.

The heavenly city, I told the by now no doubt dozing students, is important as Augustine's analysis of the earthly city makes sense only in relation to it. Condemning Roman imperialism (for the Roman *imperium* is not a genuine community, only an illusory community of coercion and force), Augustine offers an image of a city united by a shared love, one in which relations are free from earthly coercion. I ended with the question of evil. Why does God permit it to exist, to play a significant role in human life? For things are not randomly arranged. God is the creator; God brought *ordo* or order into being. Here I notice in my notes that I made a big mistake. I claimed that evil was ineradicable, for it was "brought into existence by God and can be removed only by Him." Where I derived this idea, I cannot be sure but I probably owe a public apology to those seventeen or so souls gathered on a Thursday morning in Boston over twenty years ago. Evil isn't God's doing. . . .

I concluded all those years ago by assaying what happens when one tries to make Augustine fit into the canon of Western political thought. This emerges mostly as a series of perorations on why Augustine is not a central figure for most political theorists. He does not believe living in political society transforms or completes our natures. He dissents from strong conceptions of justice. There is a rough and ready justice, to be sure, even in robber bands, but earthly justice is often little more than a principle of retribution as well as an imperfect sign of our sociality—it doesn't touch on the really important stuff.

And what is that? Here things got interesting, at least for me. I noted that Augustine criticizes Cicero's definition of a *respublica* as an association based on common agreement concerning right and on shared interests. Within the terms of this definition, Rome was never a true commonwealth. But Cicero's definition itself is wanting. A people is a gathering or multitude of rational beings united in fellowship by sharing a common love of the same things. Using such a definition, we can not only define what a society is, but we can also determine what it is that people hold dear. In proper graduate student in political theory fashion, I called Augustine's definition both "normative"—it allows us to evaluate the quality of contrasting societies—and "analytic"—it gives us a means of analyzing actual values sought and realized.[2]

Because *consensus* or *conflict* theory was much in the air then—rather like the *liberalism* and *communitarian* debate is now—I felt obliged to wade into that dispute and argued that Augustine didn't really belong in either camp. To be sure, communities are held together by what they hold dear. There is an affective aspect to it. Christians aspire to a community based on a brotherhood and sisterhood of belief. But most would consider this a- or anti-political. And there it ended—for the students but not for me.

I didn't particularly relish what I had done that day—having been forced to collect my thoughts under pressure of time and the constraints flowing from the nature and structure of a course syllabus I had not designed. I promised myself I would spend more time with Augustine. This chapter is, in part, a story of Augustine, my companion in a variety of modes of exploration, on that footpath leading out from Wittenberg and into those very peculiar villages we call universities. Over the years I took up public and private, war and peace, justice and that love of God and love of neighbor Augustine insists must be the basis of earthly life. Each encounter yielded more questions, a deepening astonishment at the apparent boundlessness of Augustine's vast curiosity, and dissatisfactions with my own take on things, for I was never sure I had quite gotten it right.

Why? Because Augustine's categories are not simple and do not comport with those most familiar to us in late-twentieth-century liberal political life. Indeed, the late George Armstrong Kelly proclaimed in 1984 that "in fair weather or foul, the Augustinian theory has little appeal for liberal society."[3] For example: Augustine's *civitas* is not a state; nor is it really a *respublica*. But if one calls it, simply, a *society*, one loses the attention and interest of political theorists, for society is what anthropologists and sociologists study unless, of course, it is *civil society* and then the reference point is either Hegel or the contemporary debate, much indebted to political thinkers and actors in Central Eastern Europe.[4] These problems are further compounded by the fact that there are so many Augustines—the pessimistic Augustine, already noted; the pluralist Augustine; the romantic Augustine; the reactionary Augustine; the sexist Augustine; the anti-sexist Augustine; even a sort of proto-socialist Au-

gustine. It is altogether too easy to slice off one chunk of Augustine and turn that piece into the *real* Augustine or the only Augustine worth salvaging. But let us perservere nonetheless.

Augustine: The Plot Thickens

In a period of soul-searching following completion of graduate school comprehensive examinations, I returned to Augustine's *Confessions* and emerged both awed and moved. But I really hadn't the faintest idea what this had to do with political theory. *The City of God*, of course, was another story, so I waded back into it as part of my consideration of the public and the private in Western political thought. Even trying to place Augustine within a private/public prism was bound to do him an injustice. I began to conjure with the ways his work intruded, impinged, pushed beyond the boundaries, and crashed through the categories political theorists work with. Peter Brown suggests that *The City of God* is such a difficult book, and such an easy text to ignore, because it is huge; it is a narrative treating literally hundreds of issues and controversies, but in ways that do not lend themselves to stipulative definitions and readily codified formulae; and, perhaps most important, it has nothing whatever to do with what Brown calls the "Rational Myth of the State," the metaphor on which classical political theory from

> the seventeenth century onwards, was based.... By myth I mean the habit of extrapolating certain features of experience, isolating them, in abstraction or by imagining an original state in which only those elements were operative, and using the pellucid myth thus created as a means of explaining what should happen today. The tendency, therefore, was to extrapolate a rational man; to imagine how reason, and a necessity assessed by reason, would lead him to found a state; and to derive from this 'mythical' rational act of choice a valid, rational reason for obeying, or reforming, the state as it now is.[5]

We moderns tend to presuppose a freestanding individual and then to posit a state that we call sovereign. What connects the individual to the state is a series of reciprocal rights and obligations. The state is the senior partner, of course, and can, if it desires, call most of the shots. The individual can proclaim rights but also has obligations. There isn't very much in-between. We *know*, of course, that there is lots of other stuff, but it goes unmentioned, untheorized, if you will.

Moving through *The City of God* with this myth of the individual and the state in my mind, but lodged there quite insecurely because I never quite got it—this story of the self and the state, for the world was so much denser, thicker, richer, and more complex than social contract metaphors and tales of rights and obligations allowed—I took up the distinction between the household and the *polis*, or the private and the public, because Aristotle had put that on the agenda explicitly and because feminists were vigorously proclaiming that the "private was the public" *tout court*, and that didn't seem quite right to me either.

It was hard not to get distracted in going through Augustine. His account of a naturalistic morality written on the hearts of sentient creatures. His critique of classical philosophy, much of it quite witty, including his unpacking of the Stoic quest for happiness and solace which culminates in suicide. The great stuff on war and peace. The discussion of languages and the ways they divide and unite us. The tongue as an instrument of domination. The emphasis on human freedom; we have free will; we can cleave to God (like the good angels, but in our own flawed human way) or turn away. But we must choose. His radical reconstruction of justice and injustice. His insistence that no one is evil by nature. Nor are we political by nature, although we are by nature social. Moreover, no man has natural dominion over his fellow men. And, of course, his powerful story of the two cities and the earthly pilgrimage of those who would be citizens in the City of God but were, at best, fitful members of the earthly city. This was tethered to the sobering material on the rising and falling of cultures, even great empires. As George Kelly observes: "St. Augustine wrote his greatest work not only to show that we are agents of some ultimate design toward which reason draws us while leaving us unsatisfied at the portals of faith but to diminish our expectations of the millennium and to cast back these disappointments on our ongoing earthly performance especially our political ones."[6]

Taken together, these insights led to the unmistakable conclusion that Augustine was subversive, shifting the center of earthly gravity away from the political order to the "solid rock" of the *civitas Dei* on pilgrimage. The Church, although not the precise referent for this City of God must, nevertheless, be an authoritative institution, one that gathers together, in its wayfaring, citizens from all races, all tongues, both sexes, and unites them into the commonality of a single but dispersed pilgrim band. Their particularity is preserved—the diversity of customs, laws, and traditions not only need not but cannot be overturned in the name of a uniform Christian society. For God loves contrasts and differences. The earthly peace preserved by these orders, though sadly wanting with reference to the ultimate, is the best that creatures in the penultimate can aspire to. Earthly peace may be illusory but it should be cherished nonetheless. The major disturbers of the peace are often those who claim to be upholding it—the great empires and great men—overtaken by a lust of sovereign dominion which disturbs and consumes the human race with frightful ills. Don't tell me so-and-so was great because he assaults and consumes the human race with his insatiable quest for earthly riches and glory, Augustine chides. This was a rich and diverse repast: how to pare it down to size in order to explicate the public and the private?

I decided to begin with Wittgenstein, having become intrigued by the fact that *The City of God* "was one of the very few books visible in Wittgenstein's sparsely decorated rooms at Cambridge and that he cited and referred to [it] often."[7] The answer to Wittgenstein's love affair with Augustine lay in the richness of Augustine's complex philosophy of language in which meaning played a central role. As well, language—its multiple possibilities of interpretation and its dispersion and difference—helps to account for the irremediable murkiness of human affairs. The relationship of words to the stuff of the world is, at best, imprecise—always riddled with ambivalence and ambiguity. Our understanding and our actions must always be imperfect, in part because, as Wittgenstein might say, when we encounter someone whose tongue is impenetrable to us we "cannot find our feet with them." In *Public Man, Private Woman*, I just scratched the surface rather than plumbing the depths of Augustine's bold forays into language and questions of what we now call hermeneutics or interpretation.

Let's take the measure, in however schematic a way, of several of his key themes. First, *contra* much of what has gone under the name Political Augustinianism, a closer look at Augustine on the nature and purpose of social forms and civic life shows us that these are not, crudely, what sin has brought into the world but what man, who is sinful, has wrought through the use of his God-given reason and his capacity for love, as well as his lust for dominance. There is a "darkness that attends the life of human society"[8] and this pertains within, and cuts across, the levels or rings or circles of human existence—the *domus*, or household; the *civitas*, or city, from clans and tribes to great and terrible empires; the *orbis terrae*, or the earth itself; finally, the *mundus*, or universe, the heaven and the earth.

Social life on all levels is full of ills and yet to be cherished. "The philosophers hold the view that the life of the wise man should be social; and in this we support them . . . heartily." The City of God itself could never have made "its first start . . . if the life of the saints were not social."[9] And yet one cannot but sigh and experience with "deep sorrow of heart" the multitude of reports on the ills attendant upon every sphere of social existence. Some are "strong enough to bear these ills with equanimity," but even such a one "cannot but feel grievous anguish, if he himself is a good man, at the wickedness of the traitors." Viciousness and shame may even, horribly, begin at home. "If, then, safety is not to be found in the home, the common refuge from the evils that befall mankind, what shall we say of the city? The larger the city, the more is its forum filled with civil

lawsuits and criminal trials, even if that city be at peace, free from alarms or—what is more frequent—the bloodshed of sedition and civil war. It is true that cities are at times exempt from those occurrences; they are never free from the danger of them."[10] What stands in the way of full use of human reason for good? Why are the anguish and the joy of human life so closely intertwined? Augustine provides a veritable hive abuzz with a swarm of explanations, among them his emphasis on the role of language.

In Book XIX, chapter 7, Augustine muses about the way in which all sentient creatures called human are divided by linguistic differences. These differences make it very hard for us to understand one another. Listen to these words:

> [T]he diversity of languages separates man from man. For if two men meet and are forced by some compelling reason not to pass on but to stay in company, then if neither knows the other's language, it is easier for dumb animals, even of different kinds, to associate together than these men, although both are human beings. For when men cannot communicate their thoughts to each other, simply because of difference of language, all the similarity of their common human nature is of no avail to unite them in fellowship. So true is this that a man would be more cheerful with his dog for company than with a foreigner. I shall be told that the Imperial City has been at pains to impose on conquered peoples not only her yoke but her language also, as a bond of peace and fellowship, so that there should be no lack of interpreters but even a profusion of them. True; but think of the cost of this achievement! Consider the scale of those wars, with all that slaughter of human beings, all the human blood that was shed![11]

This passage surely cheered the somewhat gloomy Wittgenstein! Think of what Augustine here accomplishes. He moves from the murkiness and impenetrability of language, how it divides us despite our "common human nature," to the imposition of a language on diverse peoples but at a truly terrible price. We have in this passage a drawing together of notions of human na-

ture, language, and its centrality in constituting us as living creatures; the search for
fellowship (sometimes easier to achieve with
a dog than a foreigner); and a pithy critique
of the enforced homogeneity of empire. My
specific concern in recounting this passage
in an earlier work was to think through public and private. I suggested that perhaps men
and women in past epochs spoke something
of a different language even within the
boundaries of a single linguistic community,
because men had greater access to a public
language or rhetoric than women, whose
speech was confined to the household. But
the heart of Augustine on language lies elsewhere, whatever the truth of my underdevel-
oped insight. What I am clearer on now is the
appeal of what I called "the language of
Christianity" to women in the late antique
world, because the things Christ held dear
and cherished—forgiveness, succor, devotion—helped to forge the terms of their own
lives, that and the fact that the Christian
rhetoric Augustine at first found inelegant
and even vulgar was simple and direct—told
in the language of the people, cast in the
forms of everyday speech, speech that com-
municated, speech with a liberatory moment that reached out to incorporate into a
new community—the *koinonia*—those who
were severed from the classical *polis*, women
and the poor.[12] I will have more to say on Augustine on men and women below.

I remain intrigued by the influence of Augustine on Wittgenstein, another topic less
fully written about than it might be, perhaps
because Wittgenstein has tended to be the
purview of analytic philosophers or
verstehen opponents of analytic philosophers, most of whom do not seem to have
taken up Augustine as a companion in
thought. Augustine pays meticulous attention to the performative requirements or dimensions of language and acknowledges the
importance of convention and conventional
understanding. Indeed, in most things we
must "follow the conventions in human language" because we cannot leap out of the
world and attain an Archimedean point or a
meta-language purged of earthly usage by
fallible creatures.[13] Augustine knew that no
language could be transparent, translucent,

perfectly freed from earthly habit, thicken-
ing, smudging.

Let me offer up just a few examples. Take
the following peroration on the word 'religion':

> the word 'religion' would seem, to be
> sure, to signify more particularly the
> 'cult' offered to God, rather than 'cult' in
> general; and that is why our translators
> have used it to render the Greek word
> *thrêskeia*. However, in Latin usage . . . 're-
> ligion' is something which is displayed in
> human relationships, in the family . . .
> and between friends; and so the use of the
> word does not avoid ambiguity when the
> worship of God is in question. We have no
> right to affirm with confidence that 'reli-
> gion' is confined to the worship of God,
> since it seems that this word has been de-
> tached from its normal meaning, in
> which it refers to an attitude of respect in
> relations between a man and his neigh-
> bour.[14]

Augustine performs many such 'Wittgen-
steinian' operations on central words.

The upshot of the force of linguistic convention is that we human beings have, or can
achieve, only our "creature's knowledge" and
it comes in "in faded colours, compared with
the knowledge that comes when it is known
in the Wisdom of God. . . ." Godlike wisdom
is not attainable on this earth.[15] Language is
mysterious and inexhaustible. It cannot capture the entirety of thought, try as one might,
brilliant and learned as one might be. We are
both limited *and* enabled by the "accepted
conventions of language." For example,
these conventions "allow us to 'make use' of
'fruits' and to 'enjoy' the 'use' of things; for
'fruits' are also properly the 'fruits of the
earth,' and we all 'make use' of them in this
temporal life." It is this "common meaning
of 'use' I have in mind," Augustine tells us,
when I use the word 'use.' The ways in which
words divide was not invented by philosophers but, instead, is used by them, sometimes in inventive ways. Yet no philosopher
can jump out of his or her linguistic skin.[16]

The upshot is that we "had better conform
to normal usage, as indeed we are bound to
do, and, for example, to use the phrase 'before death' "—this in a discussion of how we
distinguish life from death—"to mean before

death occurs, as in the scriptural text: 'Do not praise any man before his death.' "[17] There is much more along these lines, but perhaps these few examples will suffice to alert us to the powerful contours of Augustine's insights as a linguistic philosopher.

Let's consider next his powerful treatment of the inescapability of interpretation from *The Confessions*. Augustine begins by watching babies. . . . This is already a shocking thing for a philosopher to do and to derive epistemological value from. Augustine's is no philosophical anthropology à la Kant, wherein the philosopher devises a set of abstract propositions or presuppositions without concrete attention of any kind to any specific way of life. Augustine notices, remember, that babies throw fits and do all sorts of nasty things, in part because they are trying to make themselves understood and are failing. They get cross because others are not at their "beck and call."[18] By observing babies, he concludes that as they enter the world of speech, they come to appreciate the power of words, including their own.

Through agreed convention one learns an alphabet. But language does more: it both moves one and one is moved by it, by the representations language bears. A speech-user enamored of words and their power can easily get caught up in a spider's web of speech and become "all words," bogged down in conformity to convention in a way that is clichéd and cannot unlock the heart and the mind. A statement is "not necessarily true because it is wrapped in fine language," nor false if it is "awkwardly expressed."[19]

Suppose next that one's heart is unlocked, or is starting to open to God's truth? Can there not be some closure then, some sure and certain way to express *the* truth of things post-conversion, as it were? Alas, it is not to be. That there is truth is beyond doubt. But there is much that must be figuratively explained, including, or perhaps especially, from Scripture. Augustine tells us of his perplexity with certain passages from the Old Testament. "These passages had been death to me when I took them literally, but once I had heard them explained in their spiritual meaning I began to blame myself for my despair. . . ."[20] Literalist readings may, paradox-

ically, throw one off the trail of the truth by foreclosing a richness of possible meanings.

The blockbuster Book X of *The Confessions* provides a hermeneutical theory that is itself a dense imbrication of multiple meanings. Augustine puts the question: Why should others believe me? How do they know I am telling the truth? And he answers that there are many things one cannot prove; however, those whose ears are opened by charity will be able to listen with their hearts. We are an "inquisitive race," eager to pry, but we often do so from a harshness, a rush to destroy. There is, it seems, a condition of being that makes knowing itself possible, that can stir the heart and thus the mind. Although perfect self-knowledge is never possible, knowledge *is*. There is much we understand because we believe—not, however, from a stance of naive credulity, or because belief somehow brings inquiry to a definitive halt.[21] To the contrary: belief should spur understanding and sustain further inquiry.

The immediate matter before Augustine is memory, that great storehouse; that depth with its images to which are attached many things in its multiple folds. Epistemically, there is a mystery here, but we can gain a few rather precise intimations. When we hear certain sorts of questions—whether a thing exists, what that thing is, what sort of thing it is—the images cast by the sounds of words trigger recall and knowledge. Attention helps us to collect these scattered images, to draw them together into something recollectable, coherent, that we can offer others. But, of course, I, the curious self, want more than that. I want to understand meaning. (We have now moved to another prodigious accomplishment, Book XI of *The Confessions*.) Truth knows no language—it is "neither Hebrew nor Greek nor Latin nor any foreign speech. . . ."[22] But truth—imperfect truth given voice by human beings—is different from God's speech. God's word is not the speech of discrete words. It is spoken all at once and outside of time. We, however, are caught in time. Only outside of time is the intellect privileged to "know all at once."[23] We are on this earth. We are, therefore, immersed in a world of multiple interpretations—this from Book XII.

Augustine offers an interpretive principle with flexibility. Truth may be singular but meaning is multiple. How can it possibly bring harm "if I understand the writer's meaning in a different sense from that in which another understands it? All of us who read his words do our best to discover and understand what he had in mind, and since we believe that he wrote the truth, we are not so rash to suppose that he wrote anything which we know or think to be false."[24] The text in question is Scripture, so the principle of interpretive charity is particularly exigent. But Augustine adds flesh to the bones of this interpretive charity.

Take, for example, "In the Beginning God made heaven and earth." Augustine offers at least five plausible interpretations, all gesturing toward the truth of that claim. He proliferates examples of this sort and he doesn't stint on making each of the alternatives attractive. There is a classical hermeneutical dilemma we simply cannot get out of. Two sorts of disagreements may arise: (1) concerning the truth of the message and (2) concerning the meaning of the message. We can never plumb fully what was in an author's mind; here there can be no absolute certainty. The realm of immutable truth gives birth to many meanings; the workings of truth are varied epistemologically. "When so many meanings, all of them acceptable as true, can be extracted from the words that Moses wrote, do you not see how foolish it is to make a bold assertion that one in particular is the one he had in mind? Do you not see how foolish it is to enter into mischievous arguments which are an offence against that very charity for the sake of which he wrote every one of the words that we are trying to explain?"[25] In a world of signs, sacraments, miracles, "more things on heaven and earth" than are dreamt of in most philosophies, a truth the mind understands can be materially expressed in a variety of means; thus, "I see nothing to prevent me from interpreting the words of your Scriptures in this figurative sense."[26] I fear this, too, only scratches the surface but we must move on.

The Household and the City: The Good, the Bad, and the Ugly

In the matters of the *domus* and the *civitas*, Augustine once again complexifies our understanding. Rather than bifurcating the earthly sphere into rigidly demarcated public and private realms, Augustine finds in the household "the beginning, or rather a small component part of the city, and every beginning is directed to some end of its own kind, and every component part contributes to the completeness of the whole of which it forms a part. The implication is quite apparent, that domestic peace contributes to the peace of the city—that is, the ordered harmony of those who live together in a house . . . contributes to the ordered harmony concerning authority and obedience obtaining among the citizens."[27] (Although a contemporary feminist would emphasize "gender egalitarianism" rather than "harmony, authority and obedience" and that all-too-human dependence on others that begins in the household, Augustine's insistence on an *internal* relationship between *this* beginning and what we call civic life is not only compatible with, but a strong buttress of feminist claims that public and private are not hermetically sealed off one from the other.)

Every beginning carries within it a portion of the nature of the whole, even as the whole overlaps with, and is internally connected to, the part. The relation of *domus* to *civitas* is not a grinding of frictional parts, for these spheres of human existence do not diverge as types or in kind; rather, aspects of the whole are borne into the parts, and the integrity and meaning of the part carries forward to become an *integral* part of the whole.[28] Augustine here is engaged in a "*redefinition* of the public itself, designed to show it is life outside the Christian community which fails to be truly public, authentically political. The opposition is not between public and private, church and world, but between political virtue and political vice."[29] Augustine's unpacking of this relationship is fascinating, turning, as it does, on his recognition that the life of the household, the church, and the city is a social life, erected initially—certainly where the household and some form or semblance of society are concerned—on the ground of a naturalistic morality, a basic grammar of human actions and possibilities framed by finitude, by birth and death. Every way of life incorporates injunctions and admonitions and mounts approbrium or generates encomiums in the areas of sexuality, the taking of life, and the grounds of just or fair treatment.

If this feels or seems common-sensical, it probably should, although what is given by nature is not a sufficient basis for civic peace or domestic peace, for that matter. Augustine is convinced that were one to gather together a representative sample of humankind from the far-flung parts of the earth and ask them what they would prefer not to suffer, there would be a surprising (for him not-all-that-surprising) degree of unanimity. No one wants to be tortured or killed. Everyone wants safety and sufficient food and the like. There are rough and ready needs and givens that move people into fellowship with one another. Just as each and every human being and each and every human community is plagued by a "poverty-stricken kind of power . . . a kind of scramble for . . . lost dominions and . . . honours,"[30] so there is simultaneously present the life-forgiving and gentler aspects of loving concern, mutuality, domestic and civic peace.

Because Augustine is so often represented as a dour, late antique Hobbesian, it is worth belaboring this latter insight for a few moments. Here one must introduce two central Augustinian terms that name an earthly struggle that gestures toward ultimate things: *caritas* locked in combat with the contending force of *cupiditas*. This is old hat, so to speak, worn-smooth coin of the realm for Augustinian scholars. But let's see if we can give this a new twist, or, to sustain the metaphor, let's give the coin another toss.

There are two fundamentally different attitudes evinced within human social life and enacted by human beings. One attitude is a powerful feeling of the fullness of life. A human being will not be denuded if he or she gives, or makes a gift of the self, to others. One's dependence on others is not a diminution but an enrichment of self. The other attitude springs from cramped and cribbed pity,

from resentment, from a penury of spirit. The way one reaches out or down to others from these different attitudes is strikingly distinct. From a spirit of resentment and contempt, one condescends toward the other; one is hostile to life itself. But from that fellow feeling in our hearts for the misery of others, we come to their help by coming together with them. Authentic compassion (*com*, together; *pati*, to suffer) eradicates contempt and distance. The Christian is not afraid that he or she will lose something by offering him or herself. That is what the ethic of *caritas* is about—not moralistic self-abnegation but an abundant overflowing of the fullness of life.

There is a theology of the household and a theology of the city and they turn on the same things. Augustine deploys analogies in a free-flowing way between the two. The pirate band enjoys a semblance to empire; the robber band's ethics, to justice; even a conspiracy, a kind of peace among associates who are up to no good, exhibits a semblance to peace. For:

> Even in the extreme case when they have separated themselves from others by sedition, they cannot achieve their aim unless they maintain some sort of semblance of peace with their confederates in conspiracy. Moreover, scoundrels and robbers, to ensure greater efficiency and security in their assaults on the peace of the rest of mankind, desire to preserve peace with their associates.[31]

Augustine is second to none, including the inimitable Hobbes, in cataloging the miseries attendant upon human life, the miseries he lays on the doorstep of sin, our division (within selves and between self and others), our enthrallment to *cupiditas* and our all-too-frequent abandonment of *caritas*. We are, in other words, ignorant but it is ignorance of a particular kind, not innocent naivete (if indeed naivete is ever innocent) but prideful cognitive amputation. He writes:

> Such is the clear evidence of that terrifying abyss of ignorance, as it may be called, which is the source of all error, in whose gloomy depths all the sons of Adam are engulfed, so that man cannot be rescued from it without toil, sorrow

and fear. What else is the message of all the evils of humanity? The love of futile and harmful satisfactions, with its results: carking anxieties, agitations of mind, disappointments, fears, frenzied joys, quarrels, disputes, wars, treacheries, hatreds, enmities, deceits, flattery, fraud, theft, rapine, perfidy, pride, ambition, envy, murder, parricide, cruelty, savagery, villainy, lust, promiscuity, indecency, unchastity, fornication, adultery, incest, unnatural vice in men and women (disgusting acts too filthy to be named), sacrilege, collusion, false witness, unjust judgement, violence, robbery, and all other such evils which do not immediately come to mind, although they never cease to beset this life of man—all these evils belong to man in his wickedness, and they all spring from that root of error and perverted affection which every son of Adam brings with him at his birth. For who is not aware of the vast ignorance of the truth (which is abundantly seen in infancy) and the wealth of futile desires (which begins to be obvious in boyhood) which accompanies a man on his entrance into this world, so that if man were left to live as he chose and act as he pleased he would fall into all, or most, of those crimes and sins which I have mentioned—and others which I was not able to mention.[32]

We are no doubt grateful that Augustine stopped his listmaking when he did. This passage, taken by itself, would seem to justify the grumpiest readings of the most perfervid political Augustinian. But hold. There is more. There are countervailing influences, as we like to say. A good God's grace and mercy let's take for granted for the sake of Augustine's argument, remaining, therefore, on *terra firma* with him in order to continue to build the case. It is worth returning, at this juncture, to those containers for human social life, those forms and institutions that mark our dependence on one another, our need for trust, our capacity to mark new beginnings and to hope, our embrace—not from desperation but from yearning—of *caritas*. People yearn for earthly peace among friends. Augustine extends the definition of friend. Friends:

may mean those in the same house, such as a man's wife or children, or any other members of the household; or it can mean all those in the place where a man has his home, a city, for example, and a man's friends are thus his fellow-citizens; or it can extend to the whole world, and include the nations with whom a man is joined by membership of the human society; or even to the whole universe, "heaven and earth" as we term it, and to those whom the philsophers call gods, whom they hold to be a wise man's friends—our more familiar name for them is "angels."[33]

Mind you, friendship can never be carefree, but the "unfeigned faith and mutual affections of genuine, loyal friends" is our indispensable consolation. The "more friends we have and the more dispersed they are in different places, the further and more widely extend our fears that evil may befall them from among all the mass of evils in this present world." Should this happen, "burning sorrow . . . ravages our hearts." But this goes with the territory, so-to-speak. The "consoling delights of friendship" mean the deaths of friends must bring us sadness. "Anyone who forbids such sadness must forbid, if he can, all friendly conversation, must lay a ban on all friendly feeling or put a stop to it, must with a ruthless insensibility break the ties of all human relationships. . . ."[34]

Friendship, then, is the glue that forges our human ties, it binds husband and wife, brother and sister, friend to friend, citizen to citizen, even in the limited and flawed realm of earthly life. For the earthly city is the densely layered site of human designs. And those designs are limited by definition. A principle of interpretive charity might help us to understand and to communicate, despite the fact that each nation possesses its own language. But that household and city are alike containers for charity and cauldrons for ill-will there can be no doubt. Human society in all its aspects is twisted by life within unjust and oppressive earthly dominions and the conceptions under which those dominions order their rule. A Ciceronian definition of a people as a number of persons associated by common acknowledgement of certain rules for right and the pursuit of justice is inadequate, simply not up to the task of recognizing and deepening the work of *caritas*. Rather, as I noted above, we must look to an assemblage of persons bound together by common agreement as to the objects of love.

What are the bases for order and comity in the earthly city? Let's return to the household. Augustine assumes the ontological equality of men and women but accepts that they occupy different offices or stations. There is a basis for this both in convention and in the order of nature. But Augustine hopes to tame the occasions for the reign of *cupiditas*, for the activation of the *libido dominandi*. It follows that the father in the household should injure none and do good to all. A father who falls down on this job is worse than an "infidel." It is worth listening to what he says on this subject in his own words: "those who are genuine 'fathers of their household' are concerned for the welfare of all in their households . . . a man's house ought to be the beginning, or rather a small component part of the city. . . . The implication is quite apparent, that domestic peace contributes to the peace of the city. . . ."[35] The ground of relations of domestic peace is a well-ordered concord within the family. Both parents share responsibility for their children; women, however, should defer to their husbands, not because they are unequal to men in the order of creation, or not fully rational beings (*pace* Aristotle), but because such deference is provided for in tradition and is necessary to promote the ends of domestic peace and civic harmony. (Today, of course, we would argue that deference that flows primarily from wife to husband is not required by Augustine's commitment to ontological equality and may, in fact, exist in tension with it.)

Augustine warns that the husband's authority must never be arbitrary and cannot be absolute. He stresses the importance of households whose foundations lie in compassion and justice, tempered with mercy. A righteous domestic order is a *civitas* in miniature ruled by love, compassion, and authority in the person of Christian parents. It offers membership in the society of the faithful during their sojourn on this earth, or one

form of membership, at any rate. The Church is another body of friends. The city yet another. But the temptations of arbitrary power and excess grow greater the more power there is to be had. The life of virtue is a shared life, but so is the life of perfidy. Absolute mastery, or the urgency to acquire it, severs human beings from one another, often violently. For he who would be master—whether a brutal *paterfamilias*, a ruthless leader of a robber band, or an avaricious emperor—needs other human beings to work on and to work over, quite literally.

If *cupiditas* gains the upper hand, the result is deepening misery. Any argument that asserts that this dominion, these forms of violent or coercive imposition, is natural is wrong. For we are not, as I have already noted, political by nature. Politics results from concatenated acts of human willing, human design. Thus, Augustine can be drawn upon not only to defeat the claims of *imperium*, or to chasten these claims, but to tame the rule by fathers as well. For here things are somewhat reversed. The father's natural responsibility for, and authority within, the *domus* is *not* a political right and does not translate into one. Political authority in the *civitas* is similar to, yet different from, that of the ruler to subject. Augustine protested assimilating paternal and political authority even as he drew analogies between them.

Small wonder so few get him right. This is complicated stuff. The calling of nature may move us into fellowship with one another. But nature's reign is not sufficient unto itself. Human projects, for better or worse, must be enacted. And they must be chastened, tempered with the life-sustaining honey of *caritas*. The fullness of this honeyed life remains for the heavenly city—Augustine, in a letter, speaks of being enrolled "as a citizen of a country which is above, in holy love, for which we endure perils and toils. . . ." Earthly cities too often inflame us, they are ablaze with arms. The flowers are threaded through with thorns. To a citizen of such an earthly city, in this same letter, Augustine writes:

> Look for a moment at those very books "On the State" from which you imbibed that sentiment of a loyal subject, that "to

good men there is no limit or end of devotion to their country." [Sound familiar?] Look at them, I pray you, and notice the praise with which frugality and self-control are extolled, and fidelity to the marriage-bond, and chaste, honourable, and upright character. When a country is distinguished for these qualities, it may truly be said to be in full flower.[36]

Then and then alone. But one must remain vigilant.

There are, for example, among the pagans, more or less virtuous objects of emulation and admiration. Unfortunately, as John Milbank observes, "The Romans, like all pagans, think there can *be* virtue where there is something to be defeated, and virtue therefore consists for them, not only in the attainment and pursuit of a goal desirable in itself, but also in a 'conquest' of less desirable forces, which is always an exercise of strength *supplementary to*, although supporting, a 'right desire.' "[37]

The sin that marks the *civitas terrena* is the story of arbitrary power, or the ever-present possibility of such, untempered, as the story of this sin is, with an alternative beginning point—the privileging of peace over war; indeed the ontological priority of peace.[38] Pilgrims on this earth understand that life around them was created by human beings to achieve some good, to avoid greater evil. Augustine's work is not about flight from the world. His recurrent theme, as Peter Brown reminds us, is "our business within this common mortal life."[39] . . . [F]inally, let me turn to a controversial arena, the story of men and women in Augustine.

Male and Female, Created He Them

Augustine's principle of charitable interpretation is in place as I begin, not because I want to let Augustine off the hook but because I want to rescue him from reckless charges of misogyny, a much overused word that has become debased coin of our discursive realm. (It is worth remembering that misogyny was—for those who originated the term—a terrible disorder, the actual *hatred* of women. It was not garden variety male dominance of which the world has no doubt had quite enough. But misogyny was named

by the ancients as a derangement; thus, the misogynist was not upheld as a right-thinking sort of guy, a regular fellow.) Let's begin with Augustine's wonderfully generous definition of humanity. Men and women share a nature. The woman's mind and rational intelligence are "the equal of man's."[40] As well, the entire sentient human race belongs within one category, the human, for God created us all, male and female, diverse races, even bizarre creatures most of us would scarcely call human, though Augustine did. Celebrating God's diversity within the unity of creation, Augustine embarks on a description that delights, a discourse of "recorded monstrosities." He begins by telling us that there are many accounts—his own chief authority is Pliny's *Natural History*—of strange creatures whose existence raises some questions about human derivation and definition. There are:

the [so-called] *Sciopods* ('shadow-feet') because in hot weather they lie on their backs on the ground and take shelter in the shade of their feet. . . . What am I to say of the *Cynocephali*, whose dog's head and actual barking prove them to be animals rather than men? Now we are not bound to believe in the existence of all the types of men which are described. But no faithful Christian should doubt that anyone who is born anywhere as a man—that is, a rational and mortal being—derives from that one first-created human being. And this is true, however extraordinary such a creature may appear to our senses in bodily shape, in colour, or motion, or utterance, or in any natural endowment, or part, or quality. However, it is clear what constitutes the persistent norm of nature in the majority and what, by its very rarity, constitutes a marvel. . . . For God is the creator of all, and he himself knows where and when any creature should be created or should have been created. He has the wisdom to weave the beauty of the whole design out of the constituent parts, in their likeness and diversity. . . . If these races are included in the definition of the 'human,' that is, if they are rational and mortal animals, it must be admitted that they trace their lineage from that same one man, the first father of all mankind.[41]

To celebrate unity within the diversity of sentient humanity, and diversity within the unity, is a central feature of Augustine's work. Although Augustine doesn't focus on women as a separate consideration in his discussion of the earthly *civitas*, his enormously expanded definition of what it means to belong to the category *human*, and his insistence on a basic grammar of morality written on the human heart, touches women directly. Augustine is one of the great undoers of antique philosophies which dictated a separate and inferior female nature and consigned women to a lesser realm dictated by *necessity*. Because, for Augustine, all human life is lived on the razor's edge of necessity, and because beginnings and human regeneration are his central metaphors, women move much nearer center stage in his scheme of things. As well, the notion of moral revolt against public power opened up a range of options, duties, responsibilities, dilemmas, and reassessments not possible in pre-Christian epochs—for males and females alike.

What Augustine struggled with in the matter of men and women helps to illuminate many current debates and concerns. Adam and Eve, for example, are both responsible for the entry of sin into the world. Augustine's story of the Fall is a story of the "first human beings." His reference point is "they"—they "did not deny their sin . . . their pride seeks to pin the wrong act on another; the woman's pride blames the serpent, the man's pride blames the woman."[42] Both allowed themselves to be tempted. Both committed offenses. Both tried to pass the buck. In *De Trinitate* he insists that the woman along with the man "completes the image of the Trinity," for "human nature itself, which is complete in both sexes, has been made to the image of God, and he does not exclude the woman from being understood as the image of God."[43] He goes on to ask: "Who is it, then, that would exclude women from this fellowship, since they are co-heirs of grace," reminding his readers that through baptism male and female alike "have put on Christ." Therefore, "in their minds, a common nature is recognized, but in their bodies the division of this one mind itself is symbolized."[44]

He returns to the creation story yet another time and argues that the woman did not eat the forbidden fruit alone; therefore, it is outrageous to argue that "the woman, as it were, can be condemned without the man. Far be it from us to believe this!"[45] Performative requirements flow from this ontology of equality. "Let the husband render unto the wife due benevolence; and likewise also the wife unto the husband. The wife hath not power of her own body, but the husband; and likewise also the husband hath not power of his own body, but the wife."[46] Some might suggest, a bit cynically: "Big deal! How does this cash out?" Here it is worth quoting at some length a letter from Augustine to "Brother Eusebius." One point of the letter is to insist that no one be driven "into the Catholic communion against his will. . . ." But he has other fish to fry, an "abominable" matter concerning a "young man" who is "rebuked by his bishop for repeatedly thrashing his mother like a madman and for not withholding his unfilial hands from the body that gave him birth. . . . He threatens his mother to go over to the Donatist party and to do her to death, used as he is to thrash her with unbelievable ferocity." This "raging for his mother's blood," this gross plan of "matricide" must not be tolerated. That the young man in question is still at the altar-rails of the Catholic Church is an insult to the congregation, given his habituation to violence. Augustine tells Eusebius this cannot go on. The Church "forbids my beating my mother." Augustine then analogizes from beating "the body which bore and nurtured" this "thankless son," to the young man's beating of his other mother, that is, to abuse of *mater ecclesia*.[47] This is a fascinating discussion and only too up-to-date, but it does give us some insight into the forms of behavior the Church was attempting to halt. The story of the interdiction of infanticide by the Church is well-known, as is the fact that girl babies were more often exposed than boy babies. But the alteration in human sociality extended beyond that, as Augustine's letter indicates.

There is more. He repudiates propitiation to Fortune, represented as an unpredictable, arbitrary, erratic, and feminized cosmic force. He attacks Priapus ("that all too male god"), whose rites involved the public humiliation of virgins. He defends the violated virtues of women raped in war, insisting that women should not punish themselves, although inevitably such an event engenders a sense of shame. But violation without the will's consent cannot pollute the character. He writes: "We have given clear reason for our assertion that when physical violation has involved no change in the intention of chastity by any consent to the wrong, then the guilt attaches only to the ravishers, and not at all to the woman forcibly ravished without any consent on her part. . . . Will our opponents dare to contradict us?"[48] He goes on to tell us that in his pastoral tasks he administered consolation to women who "felt the pangs of shame," urging them "not to be ashamed at being alive, since they have no possible reason for being ashamed at having sinned."[49] Here Augustine challenges the constant attention to reputation required of noble Roman women, a demand that called upon women who had been violated to defend their honor by committing suicide. He also attacks the *Lex Vaconia*, which forbade the appointment of a woman, even an only daughter, as heir: "I cannot cite, or even imagine, a more inequitable law."[50]

Perhaps most importantly, whatever his acquiescence in the received social arrangements of his time, Augustine left as a permanent legacy a condemnation of that lust for dominion which distorts the personality, marriage, the family, and all other aspects of political and social life. "He who desires the glory of possession," Augustine notes, "would feel that his power were diminished if he were obliged to share it with any living associate," for he is one who cherishes his own manhood.[51]

Finally, there are the metaphors. God's requirement of obedience is "in a way the mother and guardian of all other virtues," not the father.[52] God's grace is given voice in Scripture through women; for example, Hannah, Samuel's mother. Augustine taxes the blindly self-righteous man who despises

himself and Christ "on account of the body which he received from a woman. . . ."[53] He says to his imagined interlocutor, "Perhaps you were put off by the unexampled birth of his body from a virgin? But this should not have presented a difficulty. The fact that a wonderful being was born in a wonderful way ought rather to induce you to accept our religion."[54] Lest anyone suspect that it is only virgin births that are wonderful to Augustine, consider his repeated use of the metaphor of laboring and giving birth to describe his own activities in trying to bring forth a transformed way of understanding his own self.[55] No man who loathed all things female could possibly characterize himself in this fleshly and feminized way. Even that city for which the *peregrinus* yearns is a mother, Jerusalem our Mother.

> By 'Jerusalem', moreover, we must understand not the Jerusalem which is enslaved along with her children, but our free mother, the Jerusalem which, according to the Apostle, is eternal in the heavens. There, after the hardships of our anxieties and worries in this mortal state we shall be comforted like little children carried on the mother's shoulders and nursed in her lap. For that unaccustomed bliss will lift us up, untrained and immature as we are, and support us with tenderest caresses.[56]

We may "rocka our souls in the bosom of Abraham," but we are held in the lap of our Mother.

Notes

1. Augustine, *The City of God*, ed. David Knowles (Baltimore: Penguin Books, 1972), p. 5. Hereafter references will be abbreviated *DCD*.

2. I was playing a bit fast and loose with "analytic" here it seems, not really thinking about the debate over positivism.

3. George Armstrong Kelly, *Politics and Religious Consciousness in America* (New Brunswick, N.J.: Transaction, 1984), p. 175.

4. See John Neville Figgis's fiddling around with the terms in *The Political Aspects of St. Augustine's City of God* (Gloucester, Mass.: Peter Smith, 1963).

5. P. L. B. Brown, "Political Society," in Robert A. Markus, ed., *Augustine: A Collection of Crit-*

ical Esays (Garden City, N.J.: Doubleday Anchor Books, 1972), p. 312.

6. Kelly, *Politics and Religious Cosciousness*, p. 261.

7. Jean Bethke Elshtain, *Public Man, Private Woman: Women in Social and Political Thought* (Princeton: Princeton University Press, 1981) p. 64.

8. Augustine, *DCD*, Book XIX, chapter 6, p. 860.

9. Ibid., chapter 5, p. 858.

10. Ibid., p. 859.

11. Ibid., chapter 7, p. 861.

12. On this see Peter Brown's wonderful book *The Cult of the Saints* (Chicago: University of Chicago Press, 1981).

13. Augustine, *DCD*, Book IX, chapter 5, p. 350.

14. Ibid., Book X, chapter 1, p. 375.

15. Ibid., Book XI, chapter 8, p. 437.

16. Ibid., Book XI, chapter 26, p. 459.

17. Ibid., Book XIII, chapter 11, p. 520.

18. *The Confessions*, Book I, pp. 25–26.

19. Ibid., Book V, p. 97.

20. Ibid., p. 108.

21. This is a rough summation of Book X, pp. 211–12.

22. Ibid., Book XI, p. 256.

23. Ibid., this is actually from Book XII, p. 289.

24. Ibid., p. 296.

25. Ibid., p. 303.

26. Ibid., Book XIII, p. 335.

27. *DCD*, Book XIX, chapter 16, p. 876.

28. Although this theme is taken up by John Milbank in *Theology and Social Theory* (London: Basil Blackwell, 1990), I here rely on my argument from *Public Man, Private Woman*. Although Milbank appears unfamiliar with my 1981 work, I offer an interpretation that prefigures his own.

29. Rowman Williams, "Politics and the Soul: A Reading of *The City of God*," *Milltown Studies* 19, no. 20 (1987): 58.

30. *DCD*, Book XI, chapter 1, p. 429.

31. Ibid., Book XIX, chapter 12, p. 866.

32. Ibid., Book XXII, chapter 22, p. 1065.

33. Ibid., Book XIX, chapter 3, p. 851.

34. Ibid., chapter 8, p. 862. Augustine's target here, of course, is Stoicism.

35. Ibid., chapter 16, p. 876.

36. Augustine, *Select Letters*, trans. J. H. Baxter (Cambridge, Mass.: Harvard University Press, 1993), no. 24 (Ep. XCI), p. 155.

37. John Milbank, *Theology and Social Theory*, pp. 390–91.

38. Both Milbank and I make this point. My discussion is in *Women and War*.

39. Brown, *Augustine of Hippo*, p. 324.

40. *The Confessions*, Book XIII, p. 344. Augustine goes on to suggest, rather vaguely, that in "sex she is physically subject to him in the same way as our natural impulses need to be subjected to the reasoning powers of the mind. . . ." But this is underargued and clearly not a central point. Here the analogy breaks down. For if woman is absolutely equal to man in nature and intelligence, the grounds for his relative authority over hers, in the interest of felicity, cannot be analogous to the mind in relation to the impulses. This is what might be called a "throw-away" line, and Augustine's account of creation itself undermines it.

41. Augustine, *DCD*, Book XVI, chapter 8, pp. 662–63.

42. Ibid., Book XIV, chapter 14, p. 574.

43. Augustine, *The Trinity* (Washington, D.C.: Catholic University of America Press, 1992), Book Twelve, chapter 7, pp. 351–52.

44. Ibid., p. 354; chapter 8, p. 355.

45. Ibid., chapter 11, p. 361.

46. *Select Letters*, no. 60, p. 503.

47. Ibid., no. 11, pp. 93–95.

48. *DCD*, Book I, chapter 19, p. 28. It is important to be clear about all this. Some have suggested that Augustine's emphasis on not having sinned in that no "willing" was there, is anemic and still leaves the woman open to "external" charges of culpability. But this radically interiorizes Augustine's discussion. Remember, he is systematically dismantling the codes of honor, among other things, that pertained among the Romans, including the self-imposed sanctions attendant upon rape in time of war—not in an ambiguous situation in a boudoir. War is a public activity. So is wartime rape. It is not a private act. By deconstructing codes that sustained a woman's destruction by her own hand given this public violation, Augustine offers an alternative *public* evaluation and code: rape in wartime is what violators do to the violated. *That* is the assumption with which one begins. There is no requirement that the woman restore her honor as her honor has not been undermined in the eyes of the new community—it is the perpetrator who has dishonored himself.

49. *DCD*, Book II, chapter 2, p. 49.

50. Ibid., Book III, chapter 21, p. 122.

51. Here I refer the reader to the extended discussion in *Women and War,* chapter 4.

52. *DCD,* Book XIV, chapter 13, p. 571.

53. *DCD,* Book X, chapter 28, p. 413.

54. Ibid., p. 415.

55. *The Confessions,* Book VIII, p. 168.

56. *DCD,* Book XX, chapter 21, p. 939.

Adapted from: Jean Bethke Elshtain, *Augustine and the Limits of Politics,* pp. 10–47. Copyright © 1995. Reprinted by permission of University of Notre Dame Press. ✦

Saint Thomas Aquinas

Thomas Aquinas was born near Naples, Italy in 1224 or 1225. The late medieval period in which he lived was one of great change. It was marked by disintegrating feudal economies, political intrigue within and among city-states and emerging nations, and the continued influence of the powerful Roman Church, despite challenges posed by pagan thought circulating through Europe in the form of newly discovered classic manuscripts.

Aquinas's parents, minor nobles, prepared Thomas early for the religious life, sending him to study with the Benedictine Monks when he was five. By about the age of 14, Thomas was sent to the University of Naples for advanced study, but soon after, he was attracted to the Dominican order of Preachers. The Dominicans were known for their intellectual pursuits and for their devotion to the poor. This was not the Order Thomas's parents had in mind for their son and they sought to dissuade him from serving with them. One tale tells of Thomas being kidnapped by his brothers and held prisoner by the family until he renounced his association with the Dominicans. The family effort was unsuccessful.

Be that as it may, Thomas was ordained and went on to study theology in Paris and Cologne. He served as a member of the faculty at the University of Paris from 1257 to 1259 and then returned to Italy where he lectured at various sites for about 10 years. During this period, he came in contact with manuscripts from the works of Aristotle which were entering the country from Moslem Spain. Aquinas began to review the pagan manuscripts and wrote extensive commentaries. Unlike many of his contemporaries, Aquinas believed it was possible to square elements of pagan philosophy with Church teaching. Much of his work can be read as an attempt to provide a synthesis of classic and theological thought. This effort placed him squarely in the middle of attacks from secular scholars who believed he misrepresented pagan sources and Church leaders who were suspicious of mixing pagan ideas with religious dogma. Together with his already rigorous schedule of lectures and studies, the burden of responding to attacks from these groups sapped his strength. He fell into ill health and died near his birthplace in 1274.

According to Aquinas there were two routes to knowledge: one through reason and the other through faith. Reason provided, even for pagans, a means for understanding one's place in the cosmos and a guide to action. Reason was the voice of natural law, the notion that God instilled in man instincts and abilities which, if correctly followed, would lead to right action. But reason alone was fallible. While it could yield knowledge of this world, it revealed little about the next. This was the job of faith, and scripture was the guide. But whether one followed the road to knowledge through reason or through faith, both roads subsisted under eternal law, the rule of God. A consequence of this teaching was to demonstrate that there was no inherent conflict between philosophy, the study of those principles that inform the experiential world, and divine revelation. This position made safe the study of philosophy and science in a world where the Church had a say in such matters.

One of the truths that natural law (as well as divine law) teaches is human sociality. The family and state, according to Aquinas (following Aristotle), are natural. Each individual is not sufficient alone to provide for his or her well-being. The state is thus the most complete form of sociality. Though achieving accord among many individuals is difficult, it is the primary responsibility of the ruler to establish unity and peace. These are necessary preconditions if people (guided by the Church) are to attend to their most important endeavor, the salvation of the soul.

The types of political regime Aquinas acknowledges are those advanced by Aristotle. For Aquinas, the question of the best regime can be answered in a twofold manner: Ideally, rule by a good monarch is to be preferred over other forms. This is the form that most closely resembles the rule of the universe by one God. However, practical problems with monarchy (including succession) demonstrate the greater resilience of mixed forms in maintaining the unity that defines the good city. Goodness inheres in the promulgation of human laws that are congruent with the dictates of natural and eternal law. Still, Aquinas's ultimate teachings about government continue to be debated among scholars, partly because his treatment of government is fragmented, with portions scattered among his *Summa Contra Gentiles*, his short treatise *On Kingship*, and his more extensive work, *Summa Theologica*.

Summa Theologica and *On Kingship*

The *Summa Theologica* (or *Summa Theologiae*), written by Aquinas between 1256 and 1272 but left unfinished, is considered his most comprehensive attempt to synthesize elements of Christian and pagan thought. The style in which it is written gives testimony to Aquinas's thoroughness and precision as a scholar. Each part of the *Summa* is divided into a set of related questions. Each question is addressed in an article. The articles begin by anticipating objections to his proposed thesis. These are followed by the statement of his own position along with authoritative support. He then develops the arguments for his philosophic position in turn and ends each article with a response to each of the objections raised earlier.

The selections below review Aquinas's teaching on the various types of law he envisioned and illustrate the way in which these laws were interconnected according to his

cosmology. Aquinas supports his views with references to classic and medieval authorities. Two of the more frequent references are to "the philosopher" and "Isidore." The former refers to Aristotle, while the latter is a reference to the 7th century Bishop of Seville who served as a source of important Church doctrines.

The selections from *On Kingship* represent a more straightforward prose style. In the selections included here, Aquinas discusses his views on various forms of government, noting the theoretical superiority of rule by one but tempering this assessment with an acknowledgement of the evils brought by tyranny, kingship gone awry.

Commentaries

Paul E. Sigmund reviews the enduring significance of Aquinas for political theory in the first commentary. As he discusses, Aquinas can be credited with developing a view of politics as a positive force in human life, accommodating traditional hierarchy with emerging notions of community and setting the parameters for discussion of difficult moral problems in the political domain by virtue of his treatment of natural law. He concludes by noting many contemporary problems, from civil disobedience to just war theory to abortion rights, for which Aquinas's views are (rightly or wrongly) often cited as providing clarity and insight.

In the second commentary, Edward A. Goerner advances the controversial position that Aquinas is not to be understood primarily as a natural law theorist, that is, one who advances the notion of universal standards for good knowable by reason but enforceable by natural punishment in accord with God's will. Rather, he argues that Aquinas is more like classic natural right theorists who emphasize virtue as the route to right action and happiness. Goerner argues that Aquinas viewed natural law as a secondary means of inducing good behavior in the special case of one who is evil and incapable of virtuous action. Viewing Aquinas in this way clears him of the often-made charge of inflexibility in his ethical and political teachings, since his natural law teaching is shown to apply only to "bad men" and not to those capable of virtue who have no need for rigid codes of conduct.

Web Sources

http://www.aquinasonline.com
Thomistic Philosophy Page. Excellent site for texts, topics, bibliography, and links to related websites. Includes frequently asked questions with understandable answers regarding St. Thomas's philosophy.

http://www.niagara.edu/aquinas
The Aquinas Translation Project. Provides translations of many of Aquinas's lesser-known works.

http://www.philosophypages.com/ph/aqui.htm
Philosophy Pages. Provides overview of Aquinas's life and teaching along with links to text material.

http://www.utm.edu/research/iep/a/aquinas.htm
The Internet Encyclopedia of Philosophy: Thomas Aquinas. Information on the life, works, and influence of Aquinas on philosophic and theological thought.

Class Activities and Discussion Questions

1. Compare Aquinas's views on obedience to unjust laws with the views of Martin Luther King, Jr. in his "Letter from Birmingham Jail." According to Aquinas's logic, was Dr. King's civil disobedience justified? Discuss the contemporary utility of Aquinas's views on obedience to unjust laws.

2. Compare Aquinas's understanding of natural law with aspects of the theory advanced by Aristotle as you understand him. In what ways are the two versions similar? In what ways are they dissimilar?

3. Compare and contrast the influence of Christianity on the political thought of Augustine and Aquinas. Could their political views hold relevance for other traditionally religious societies (e.g., Muslim nations)?

4. Compare and contrast Aquinas's views on human nature with those put for-

ward by Aristotle. In what ways does each conception succeed, and in what ways does each fail? Given your analysis, what is the relationship between a theory of human nature and a theory of politics?

5. Review the United Nation's Universal Declaration of Human Rights (http://www.unhchr.ch/udhr/index.htm) and the U.S. Declaration of Independence (http://pages.prodigy.net/krtq73aa/declare.htm). Do the views expressed in either of these documents bear any similarity to the views of Aquinas regarding the individual's duty to follow the dictates of his or her conscience regardless of the requirements of human laws? In what ways do the views of Aquinas's conflict with these declarations of rights?

Further Reading

Black, Peter. 1999. "Do Circumstances Ever Justify Capital Punishment?" *Theological Studies* 60 (2) Jun 1999: 338–345. Examines the relevance of Aquinas's views for death penalty law and Christian teaching on the death penalty.

Burns, Tony. 2000. "Aquinas's Two Doctrines of Natural Law." *Political Studies* 48 (5) Dec 2000: 929–946. Burns argues that the *Summa* contains two different and conflicting positions on natural law: one inherited from the Stoics and the other from Aristotle.

Cornish, Paul J. 1998. "Marriage, Slavery and Natural Rights in the Political Thoughts of Aquinas." *Review of Politics* 60 (3) Summer 1998: 545–561. The essay argues that Aquinas, while commenting on canon law texts, explicitly posits a subjective natural right to marry, based on the natural equality and natural liberty of all human beings. For Aquinas there are certain areas of liberty or mastery (*dominium*) that are exempt from all human authority, and wherein a person has rights to decide how to pursue natural human goods.

Finnis, John. 1998. *Aquinas: Moral, Political and Legal Theory.* New York: Oxford University Press. Excellent review of Aquinas's moral theory including discussions of freedom, reason, and human rights.

Fortin, E. 1987. "St. Thomas Aquinas." In Leo Strauss and Joseph Cropsey, eds. *History of Political Philosophy.* Chicago: University of Chicago Press. Aquinas's views from a Straussian perspective.

McInerny, Ralph M. 1997. *Ethica Thomistica: The Moral Philosophy of Thomas Aquinas,* Rev. Ed. Washington, D.C.: Catholic University of America. McInerny makes accessible Thomas's moral worldview and the philosophic premises from which it proceeds in this updated and revised edition.

O'Connor, D. J. 1967. *Aquinas and Natural Law.* London: Macmillan. Discusses Aquinas's contribution to the tradition of natural law philosophy.

Smith, Thomas W. 1995. "The Order of Presentation and the Order of Understanding in Aquinas's Account of Law." *Review of Politics* 57 (4) Fall 1995:607–640. Smith makes a distinction between the way Thomas Aquinas presents his natural law teaching to his readers in a discussion of revelation and the way he thinks human beings come to know natural law independent of special revelation.

Stump, Eleonore. 1997. "Aquinas's Account of Freedom: Intellect and Will." *Monist* 80 (4) Oct 1997: 576–597. Aquinas's views of the nature of human freedom are examined with specific regard to the inter-relatedness of intellect and will. ✦

18
Excerpts from *Summa Theologica*

Saint Thomas Aquinas

Question 91: Of the Various Kinds of Law

First Article: Whether There Is an Eternal Law?

We *proceed thus to the First Article:*

Objection 1. It would seem that there is no eternal law. Because every law is imposed on someone. But there was not someone from eternity on whom a law could be imposed, since God alone was from eternity. Therefore no law is eternal.

Obj. 2. Further, promulgation is essential to law. But promulgation could not be from eternity, because there was no one to whom it could be promulgated from eternity. Therefore no law can be eternal.

Obj. 3. Further, a law implies order to an end. But nothing ordained to an end is eternal, for the last end alone is eternal. Therefore no law is eternal.

On the contrary, Augustine says: "That Law which is the Supreme Reason cannot be understood to be otherwise than unchangeable and eternal."[1]

I answer that . . . a law is nothing else but a dictate of practical reason emanating from the ruler who governs a perfect community. Now it is evident, granted that the world is ruled by divine providence, . . . that the whole community of the universe is governed by divine reason. Wherefore the very Idea of the government of things in God the Ruler of the universe has the nature of a law. And since the divine reason's conception of things is not subject to time but is eternal, according to Proverbs viii.23, therefore it is that this kind of law must be called eternal.

Reply Obj. 1. Those things that are not in themselves exist with God, inasmuch as they are foreknown and preordained by Him, according to Romans iv.17, "Who calls those things that are not, as those that are." Accordingly the eternal concept of the divine law bears the character of an eternal law in so far as it is ordained by God to the government of things foreknown by Him.

Reply Obj. 2. Promulgation is made by word of mouth or in writing; and in both ways the eternal law is promulgated, because both the divine word and the writing of the Book of Life are eternal. But the promulgation cannot be from eternity on the part of the creature that hears or reads.

Reply Obj. 3. The law implies order to the end actively, in so far as it directs certain things to the end, but not passively—that is to say, the law itself is not ordained to the end—except accidentally, in a governor whose end is extrinsic to him, and to which end his law must needs be ordained. But the end of the divine government is God Himself, and His law is not distinct from Himself. Wherefore the eternal law is not ordained to another end.

Second Article: Whether There Is in Us a Natural Law?

We proceed thus to the Second Article:

Objection 1. It would seem that there is no natural law in us. Because man is governed sufficiently by the eternal law; for Augustine says that "the eternal law is that by which it is right that all things should be most orderly."[2] But nature does not abound in superfluities, as neither does she fail in necessaries. Therefore no law is natural to man.

Obj. 2. Further, by the law man is directed in his acts to the end. . . . But the directing of human acts to their end is not a function of nature, as is the case in irrational creatures, which act for an end solely by their natural appetite; whereas man acts for an end by his reason and will. Therefore no law is natural to man.

Obj. 3. Further, the more a man is free, the less is he under the law. But man is freer than all the animals, on account of his free will, with which he is endowed above all other animals. Since therefore other animals are not subject to a natural law, neither is man subject to a natural law.

On the contrary, A gloss on Romans ii.14: "When the Gentiles, who have not the law, do by nature those things that are of the law," comments as follows: "Although they have no written law, yet they have the natural law, whereby each one knows, and is conscious of, what is good and what is evil."

I answer that, . . . [L]aw, being a rule and measure, can be in a person in two ways: in one way, as in him that rules and measures; in another way, as in that which is ruled and measured, since a thing is ruled and measured in so far as it partakes of the rule or measure. Wherefore, since all things subject to divine providence are ruled and measured by the eternal law, as was stated above (A. 1), it is evident that all things partake somewhat of the eternal law, in so far as, namely, from its being imprinted on them, they derive their respective inclinations to their proper acts and ends. Now among all others the rational creature is subject to divine providence in the most excellent way, in so far as it partakes of a share of providence, by being provident both for itself and for others. Wherefore it has a share of the eternal reason, whereby it has a natural inclination to its proper act and end: and this participation of the eternal law in the rational creature is called the natural law. Hence the Psalmist after saying: "Offer up the sacrifice of justice," as though someone asked what the works of justice are, adds: "Many say, Who showeth us good things?" in answer to which question he says: "The light of Thy countenance, O Lord, is signed upon us";[3] thus implying that the light of natural reason, whereby we discern what is good and what is evil, which is the function of the natural law, is nothing else than an imprint on us of the divine light. It is therefore evident that the natural law is nothing else than the rational creature's participation of the eternal law.

Reply Obj. 1. This argument would hold if the natural law were something different from the eternal law, whereas it is nothing but a participation thereof, as stated above.

Reply Obj. 2. Every act of reason and will in us is based on that which is according to nature . . . for every act of reasoning is based on principles that are known naturally, and every act of appetite in respect of the means is derived from the natural appetite in respect of the last end. Accordingly the first direction of our acts to their end must needs be in virtue of the natural law.

Reply Obj. 3. Even irrational animals partake in their own way of the eternal reason, just as the rational creature does. But because the rational creature partakes thereof in an intellectual and rational manner, therefore the participation of the eternal law in the rational creature is properly called a law, since a law is something pertaining to reason. . . . Irrational creatures, however, do not partake thereof in a rational manner, wherefore there is no participation of the eternal law in them, except by way of similitude.

Third Article: Whether There Is a Human Law?

We proceed thus to the Third Article:

Objection 1. It would seem that there is not a human law. For the natural law is a participation of the eternal law, as stated above (A. 2). Now through the eternal law "all things are most orderly," as Augustine states.[4] Therefore the natural law suffices for the ordering of all human affairs. Consequently there is no need for a human law.

Obj. 2. Further, a law bears the character of a measure. . . . But human reason is not a measure of things, but vice versa, as stated in *Metaphysics* x. text. 5.[5] Therefore no law can emanate from human reason.

Obj. 3. Further, a measure should be most certain, as stated in *Metaphysics* x. text. 3. But the dictates of human reason in matters of conduct are uncertain, according to Wisdom ix. 14: "The thoughts of mortal men are fearful, and our counsels uncertain." Therefore no law can emanate from human reason.

On the contrary, Augustine distinguishes two kinds of law—the one eternal; the other temporal, which he calls human.[6]

I answer that, . . . [A] law is a dictate of the practical reason. Now it is to be observed that the same procedure takes place in the practical and in the speculative reason, for each proceeds from principles to conclusions. . . . Accordingly we conclude that just as, in the speculative reason, from naturally known indemonstrable principles we draw the conclusions of the various sciences, the knowledge of which is not imparted to us by nature, but acquired by the efforts of reason; so, too, it is from the precepts of the natural law, as from general and indemonstrable principles, that the human reason needs to proceed to the more particular determination of certain matters. These particular determinations, devised by human reason, are called human laws, provided the other essential conditions of law be observed. . . . Wherefore Cicero says in his *Rhetoric* that "justice has its source in nature; thence certain things came into custom by reason of their utility; afterward these things which emanated from nature and were approved by custom were sanctioned by fear and reverence for the law."[7]

Reply Obj. 1. The human reason cannot have a full participation of the dictate of the divine reason but according to its own mode, and imperfectly. Consequently, as on the part of the speculative reason, by a natural participation of divine wisdom, there is in us the knowledge of certain general principles, but not proper knowledge of each single truth, such as that contained in the divine wisdom; so, too, on the part of the practical reason man has a natural participation of the eternal law, according to certain general principles, but not as regards the particular determinations of individual cases, which are, however, contained in the eternal law. [Hence the necessity that human reason proceed to certain particular sanctions of law.]

Reply Obj. 2. Human reason is not of itself the rule of things, but the principles impressed on it by nature are general rules and measures of all things relating to human conduct, whereof the natural reason is the rule and measure, although it is not the measure of things that are from nature.

Reply Obj. 3. The practical reason is concerned with practical matters, which are singular and contingent, but not with necessary things, with which the speculative reason is concerned. Wherefore human laws cannot have that inerrancy that belongs to the demonstrated conclusions of sciences. Nor is it necessary for every measure to be altogether unerring and certain, but according as it is possible in its own particular genus.

Fourth Article: Whether There Was Any Need for a Divine Law?

We proceed thus to the Fourth Article:

Objection 1. It would seem that there was no need for a divine law. Because, as stated above (A. 2), the natural law is a participation in us of the eternal law. But the eternal law is a divine law, as stated above (A. 1). Therefore there is no need for a divine law in addition to the natural law and human laws derived therefrom.

Obj. 2. Further, it is written that "God left man in the hand of his own counsel."[8] Now counsel is an act of reason. . . . Therefore man was left to the direction of his reason. But a dictate of human reason is a human law, as stated above (A. 3). Therefore there is no need for man to be governed also by a divine law.

Obj. 3. Further, human nature is more self-sufficing than irrational creatures. But irrational creatures have no divine law besides the natural inclination impressed on them. Much less, therefore, should the rational creature have a divine law in addition to the natural law.

On the contrary, David prayed God to set His law before him, saying: "Set before me for a law the way of Thy justifications, O Lord."[9]

I answer that, Besides the natural and the human law it was necessary for the directing of human conduct to have a divine law. And this for four reasons. First, because it is by law that man is directed how to perform his proper acts in view of his last end. And indeed, if man were ordained to no other end than that which is proportionate to his natural faculty, there would be no need for man to have any further direction on the part of his reason besides the natural law and human law which is derived from it. But since man is ordained to an end of eternal happiness which is inproportionate to man's natural faculty . . . therefore it was necessary that, besides the natural and the human law, man should be directed to his end by a law given by God.

Secondly, because, on account of the uncertainty of human judgment, especially on contingent and particular matters, different people form different judgments on human acts; whence also different and contrary laws result. In order, therefore, that man may know without any doubt what he ought to do and what he ought to avoid, it was necessary for man to be directed in his proper acts by a law given by God, for it is certain that such a law cannot err.

Thirdly, because man can make laws in those matters of which he is competent to judge. But man is not competent to judge of interior movements that are hidden, but only of exterior acts which appear; and yet for the perfection of virtue it is necessary for man to conduct himself aright in both kinds of acts. Consequently human law could not sufficiently curb and direct interior acts, and it was necessary for this purpose that a divine law should supervene.

Fourthly, because, as Augustine says, human law cannot punish or forbid all evil deeds; since while aiming at doing away with all evils, it would do away with many good things, and would hinder the advance of the common good, which is necessary for human intercourse.[10] In order, therefore, that no evil might remain unforbidden and unpunished, it was necessary for the divine law to supervene, whereby all sins are forbidden.

And these four causes are touched upon in Psalm cxviii. 8, where it is said: "The law of the Lord is unspotted," i.e., allowing no foulness of sin; "converting souls," because it directs not only exterior but also interior acts; "the testimony of the Lord is faithful," because of the certainty of what is true and right; "giving wisdom to little ones," by directing man to an end supernatural and divine.

Reply Obj. 1. By natural law the eternal law is participated in proportionately to the capacity of human nature. But to his supernatural end man needs to be directed in a yet higher way. Hence the additional law given by God, whereby man shares more perfectly in the eternal law.

Reply Obj. 2. Counsel is a kind of inquiry; hence it must proceed from some principles. Nor is it enough for it to proceed from principles imparted by nature, which are the precepts of the natural law, for the reasons given above; but there is need for certain additional principles, namely, the precepts of the divine law.

Reply Obj. 3. Irrational creatures are not ordained to an end higher than that which is proportionate to their natural powers; consequently the comparison fails. . . .

Question 94: Of the Natural Law

First Article: Whether the Natural Law Is a Habit?

We proceed thus to the First Article:

Objection 1. It would seem that the natural law is a habit. Because, as the Philosopher says, "there are three things in the soul: power, habit, and passion."[11] But the natural law is not one of the soul's powers, nor is it one of the passions, as we may see by going through them one by one. Therefore the natural law is a habit.

Obj. 2. Further, Basil says that the conscience or "*synderesis* is the law of our mind,"[12] which can only apply to the natural law. But the *synderesis* is a habit. . . . Therefore the natural law is a habit.

Obj. 3. Further, the natural law abides in man always. . . . But man's reason, [which is involved in law], does not always think about the natural law. Therefore the natural law is not an act, but a habit.

On the contrary, Augustine says that "a habit is that whereby something is done when necessary."[13] But such is not the natural law, since it is in infants and in the damned who cannot act by it. Therefore the natural law is not a habit.

I answer that, A thing may be called a habit in two ways. First, properly and essentially: and thus the natural law is not a habit. For . . . the natural law is something appointed by reason, just as a proposition is a work of reason. Now that which a man does is not the same as that whereby he does it, for he makes a becoming speech by the habit of grammar. Since, then, a habit is that by which we act, a law cannot be a habit, properly and essentially.

Secondly, the term "habit" may be applied to that which we hold by a habit: thus faith may mean that which we hold by faith. And accordingly, since the precepts of the natural law are sometimes considered by reason actually, while sometimes they are in the reason only habitually, in this way the natural law may be called a habit. Thus, in speculative matters, the indemonstrable principles are not the habit itself whereby we hold those principles, but are the principles the habit of which we possess.

Reply Obj. 1. The Philosopher proposes there to discover the genus of virtue; and since it is evident that virtue is a principle of action, he mentions only those things which are principles of human acts, viz., powers, habits and passions. But there are other things in the soul besides these three: there are acts; thus to will is in the one that wills; again, things known are in the knower; moreover its own natural properties are in the soul such as immortality and the like.

Reply Obj. 2. Synderesis is said to be the law of our mind, because it is a habit containing the precepts of the natural law, which are the first principles of human actions.

Reply Obj. 3 This argument proves that the natural law is held habitually; and this is granted.

To the argument advanced in the contrary sense we reply that sometimes a man is unable to make use of that which is in him habitually, on account of some impediment: thus, on account of sleep, a man is unable to use the habit of science. In like manner, through the deficiency of his age, a child cannot use the habit of understanding of principles, or the natural law, which is in him habitually.

Second Article: Whether the Natural Law Contains Several Precepts, or One Only?

We proceed thus to the Second Article:
Objection 1. It would seem that the natural law contains, not several precepts, but one only. For law is a kind of precept. . . . If therefore there were many precepts of the natural law, it would follow that there are also many natural laws.

Obj. 2. Further, the natural law is consequent to human nature. But human nature, as a whole, is one, though, as to its parts, it is manifold. Therefore, either there is but one precept of the law of nature, on account of

the unity of nature as a whole, or there are many, by reason of the number of parts of human nature. The result would be that even things relating to the inclination of the concupiscible faculty belong to the natural law.

Obj. 3. Further, law is something pertaining to reason. . . . Now reason is but one in man. Therefore there is only one precept of the natural law.

On the contrary, The precepts of the natural law in man stand in relation to practical matters, as the first principles to matters of demonstration. But there are several first indemonstrable principles. Therefore there are also several precepts of the natural law.

I answer that, . . . [T]he precepts of the natural law are to the practical reason what the first principles of demonstrations are to the speculative reason, because both are self-evident principles. Now a thing is said to be self-evident in two ways: first, in itself, secondly, in relation to us. Any proposition is said to be self-evident in itself if its predicate is contained in the notion of the subject, although to one who knows not the definition of the subject it happens that such a proposition is not self-evident. For instance, this proposition, "Man is a rational being," is, in its very nature self-evident, since who says "man" says "a rational being"; and yet to one who knows not what a man is, this proposition is not self-evident. Hence it is that, as Boethius says, certain axioms or propositions are universally self-evident to all;[14] and such are those propositions whose terms are known to all, as, "Every whole is greater than its part," and, "Things equal to one and the same are equal to one another." But some propositions are self-evident only to the wise who understand the meaning of the terms of such propositions; thus to one who understands that an angel is not a body, it is self-evident that an angel is not circumspectively in a place; but this is not evident to the unlearned, for they cannot grasp it.

Now a certain order is to be found in those things that are apprehended universally. For that which, before aught else, falls under apprehension, is "being," the notion of which is included in all things whatsoever a man apprehends. Wherefore the first indemonstrable principle is that *the same thing cannot be affirmed and denied at the same time,* which is based on the notion of "being" and "not-being"; and on this principle all others are based, as it is stated in *Metaphysics* iv. text. 9. Now as "being" is the first thing that falls under the apprehension simply, so "good" is the first thing that falls under the apprehension of the practical reason, which is directed to action, since every agent acts for an end under the aspect of good. Consequently the first principle in the practical reason is one founded on the notion of good, viz., that *good is that which all things seek after.* Hence this is the first precept of law, that *good is to be done and ensued, and evil is to be avoided.* All other precepts of the natural law are based upon this, so that whatever the practical reason naturally apprehends as man's good (or evil) belongs to the precepts of the natural law as something to be done or avoided.

Since, however, good has the nature of an end, and evil the nature of a contrary, hence it is that all those things to which man has a natural inclination are naturally apprehended by reason as being good and, consequently, as objects of pursuit, and their contraries as evil and objects of avoidance. Wherefore the order of the precepts of the natural law is according to the order of natural inclinations. Because in man there is first of all an inclination to good in accordance with the nature which he has in common with all substances, inasmuch as every substance seeks the preservation of its own being, according to its nature; and by reason of this inclination, whatever is a means of preserving human life and of warding off its obstacles belongs to the natural law. Secondly, there is in man an inclination to things that pertain to him more specially, according to that nature which he has in common with other animals; and in virtue of this inclination, those things are said to belong to the natural law "which nature has taught to all animals," such as sexual intercourse, education of offspring, and so forth. Thirdly, there is in man an inclination to good, according to the nature of his reason, which nature is proper to him: thus man has a natural inclination to know the truth about God

and to live in society; and in this respect, whatever pertains to this inclination belongs to the natural law, for instance, to shun ignorance, to avoid offending those among whom one has to live, and other such things regarding the above inclination.

Reply Obj. 1. All these precepts of the law of nature have the character of one natural law, inasmuch as they flow from one first precept.

Reply Obj. 2. All the inclinations of any parts whatsoever of human nature, e.g., of the concupiscible and irascible parts, in so far as they are ruled by reason, belong to the natural law and are reduced to one first precept, as stated above, so that the precepts of the natural law are many in themselves, but are based on one common foundation.

Reply Obj. 3. Although reason is one in itself, yet it directs all things regarding man, so that whatever can be ruled by reason is contained under the law of reason. . . .

Question 95: Of Human Law

First Article: Whether It Was Useful for Laws to Be Framed by Men?

We proceed thus to the First Article:

Objection 1. It would seem that it was not useful for laws to be framed by men. Because the purpose of every law is that man be made good thereby. . . . But men are more to be induced to be good willingly, by means of admonitions, than against their will, by means of laws. Therefore there was no need to frame laws.

Obj. 2. Further, as the Philosopher says, "men have recourse to a judge as to animate justice."[15] But animate justice is better than inanimate justice, which is contained in laws. Therefore it would have been better for the execution of justice to be entrusted to the decision of judges than to frame laws in addition.

Obj. 3. Further, every law is framed for the direction of human actions, as is evident from what has been stated above. . . . But since human actions are about singulars, which are infinite in number, matters pertaining to the direction of human actions cannot be taken into sufficient consideration except by a wise man, who looks into each one of them. Therefore it would have been better for human acts to be directed by the judgment of wise men than by the framing of laws. Therefore there was no need of human laws.

On the contrary, Isidore says: "Laws were made that in fear thereof human audacity might be held in check, that innocence might be safeguarded in the midst of wickedness, and that the dread of punishment might prevent the wicked from doing harm."[16] But these things are most necessary to mankind. Therefore it was necessary that human laws should be made.

I answer that, . . . [M]an has a natural aptitude for virtue, but the perfection of virtue must be acquired by man by means of some kind of training. Thus we observe that man is helped by industry in his necessities, for instance, in food and clothing. Certain beginnings of these he has from nature, viz., his reason and his hands, but he has not the full complement, as other animals have to whom nature has given sufficiency of clothing and food. Now it is difficult to see how man could suffice for himself in the matter of this training, since the perfection of virtue consists chiefly in withdrawing man from undue pleasures, to which above all man is inclined, and especially the young, who are more capable of being trained. Consequently a man needs to receive this training from another, whereby to arrive at the perfection of virtue. And as to those young people who are inclined to acts of virtue, by their good natural disposition, or by custom, or rather by the gift of God, paternal training suffices, which is by admonitions. But since some are found to be depraved and prone to vice, and not easily amenable to words, it was necessary for such to be restrained from evil by force and fear, in order that, at least, they might desist from evil-doing and leave others in peace, and that they themselves, by being habituated in this way, might be brought to do willingly what hitherto they did from fear, and thus become virtuous. Now this kind of training which compels through fear of punishment is the discipline of laws. Therefore, in order that man might have peace and virtue, it was necessary for laws to be framed, for, as the Philosopher

says, "as man is the most noble of animals if he be perfect in virtue, so is he the lowest of all if he be severed from law and righteousness";[17] because man can use his reason to devise means of satisfying his lusts and evil passions, which other animals are unable to do.

Reply Obj. 1. Men who are well disposed are led willingly to virtue by being admonished better than by coercion, but men who are evilly disposed are not led to virtue unless they are compelled.

Reply Obj. 2. As the Philosopher says, "it is better that all things be regulated by law than left to be decided by judges";[18] and this for three reasons. First, because it is easier to find a few wise men competent to frame right laws than to find the many who would be necessary to judge aright of each single case. Secondly, because those who make laws consider long beforehand what laws to make, whereas judgment on each single case has to be pronounced as soon as it arises; and it is easier for man to see what is right by taking many instances into consideration than by considering one solitary fact. Thirdly, because lawgivers judge in the abstract and of future events, whereas those who sit in judgment judge of things present, toward which they are affected by love, hatred, or some kind of cupidity; wherefore their judgment is perverted.

Since then the animated justice of the judge is not found in every man, and since it can be deflected, therefore it was necessary, whenever possible, for the law to determine how to judge, and for very few matters to be left to the decision of men.

Reply Obj. 3. Certain individual facts which cannot be covered by the law "have necessarily to be committed to judges," as the Philosopher says in the same passage; for instance, "concerning something that has happened or not happened," and the like.

Second Article: Whether Every Human Law Is Derived from the Natural Law?

We proceed thus to the Second Article:

Objection 1. It would seem that not every human law is derived from the natural law. For the Philosopher says that "the legal just is that which originally was a matter of indifference."[19] But those things which arise from the natural law are not matters of indifference. Therefore the enactments of human laws are not all derived from the natural law.

Obj. 2. Further, positive law is contrasted with natural law, as stated by Isidore[20] and the Philosopher.[21] But those things which flow as conclusions from the general principles of the natural law belong to the natural law. . . . Therefore that which is established by human law does not belong to the natural law.

Obj. 3. Further, the law of nature is the same for all, since the Philosopher says that "the natural just is that which is equally valid everywhere."[22] If, therefore, human laws were derived from the natural law, it would follow that they too are the same for all, which is clearly false.

Obj. 4. Further, it is possible to give a reason for things which are derived from the natural law. But "it is not possible to give the reason for all the legal enactments of the lawgivers," as the Jurist says.[23] Therefore not all human laws are derived from the natural law.

On the contrary, Cicero says: "Things which emanated from nature and were approved by custom were sanctioned by fear and reverence for the laws."[24]

I answer that, As Augustine says, "that which is not just seems to be no law at all";[25] wherefore the force of a law depends on the extent of its justice. Now in human affairs a thing is said to be just from being right according to the rule of reason. But the first rule of reason is the law of nature. . . . Consequently, every human law has just so much of the nature of law as it is derived from the law of nature. But if in any point it deflects from the law of nature, it is no longer a law but a perversion of law.

But it must be noted that something may be derived from the natural law in two ways: first, as a conclusion from premises; secondly, by way of determination of certain generalities. The first way is like to that by which, in the sciences, demonstrated conclusions are drawn from the principles, while the second mode is likened to that whereby, in the arts, general forms are particularized as to details: thus the craftsman needs to determine the general form of a house to some particular shape. Some things are therefore derived from the general principles of the natural law by way of conclusions, e.g., that "one must not kill" may be derived as a conclusion from the principle that "one should do harm to no man"; while some are derived therefrom by way of determination, e.g., the law of nature has it that the evildoer should be punished; but that he be punished in this or that way is not directly by natural law but is a derived determination of it.

Accordingly, both modes of derivation are found in the human law. But those things which are derived in the first way are contained in human law, not as emanating therefrom exclusively, but having some force from the natural law also. But those things which are derived in the second way have no other force than that of human law.

Reply Obj. 1. The Philosopher is speaking of those enactments which are by way of determination or specification of the precepts of the natural law.

Reply Obj. 2. This argument avails for those things that are derived from the natural law, by way of conclusions.

Reply Obj. 3. The general principles of the natural law cannot be applied to all men in the same way, on account of the great variety of human affairs, and hence arises the diversity of positive laws among various people.

Reply Obj. 4. These words of the Jurist are to be understood as referring to decisions of rulers in determining particular points of the natural law, on which determinations the judgment of expert and prudent men is based as on its principles, in so far, to wit, as they see at once what is the best thing to decide.

Hence the Philosopher says that in such matters "we ought to pay as much attention to the undemonstrated sayings and opinions of persons who surpass us in experience, age, and prudence as to their demonstrations."[26] . . .

Question 96: Of the Power of Human Law

First Article: Whether Human Law Should Be Framed for the Community Rather Than for the Individual?

We proceed thus to the First Article:

Objection 1. It would seem that human law should be framed, not for the community, but rather for the individual. For the Philosopher says that "the legal just . . . includes all particular acts of legislation . . . and all those matters which are the subject of decrees,"[27] which are also individual matters, since decrees are framed about individual actions. Therefore law is framed not only for the community, but also for the individual.

Obj. 2. Further, law is the director of human acts. . . . But human acts are about individual matters. Therefore human laws should be framed, not for the community, but rather for the individual.

Obj. 3. Further, law is a rule and measure of human acts. . . . But a measure should be most certain, as stated in *Metaphysics* x. Since therefore in human acts no general proposition can be so certain as not to fail in some individual cases, it seems that laws should be framed not in general but for individual cases.

On the contrary, The Jurist says that "laws should be made to suit the majority of instances; and they are not framed according to what may possibly happen in an individual case."[28]

I answer that, Whatever is for an end should be proportionate to that end. Now the end of law is the common good; because, as Isidore says, "law should be framed, not for any private benefit, but for the common good of all the citizens."[29] Hence human laws should be proportionate to the common good. Now the common good comprises many things. Wherefore law should take account of many things, as to persons, as to [activities], and as to times; because the community of the state is composed of many persons and its good is procured by many actions; nor is it established to endure for only a short time, but to last for all time by the citizens succeeding one another, as Augustine says.[30]

Reply Obj. 1. The Philosopher divides the "legal just," i.e., positive law, into three parts. For some things are laid down simply in a general way: and these are the general laws. Of these he says that "the legal is that which originally was a matter of indifference, but which, when enacted, is so no longer," as the fixing of the ransom of a captive. Some things affect the community in one respect and individuals in another. These are called "privileges," i.e., "private laws," as it were, because they regard private persons, although their power extends to many matters; and in regard to these, he adds, "and further [any regulations enacted for particular cases."]—Other matters are legal, not through being laws, but through being applications of general laws to particular cases, such are decrees which have the force of law; and in regard to these, he adds "all matters subject to decrees."[31]

Reply Obj. 2. A principle of direction should be applicable to many, wherefore the Philosopher says that all things belonging to one genus are measured by one which is the [first] in that genus.[32] For if there were as many rules or measures as there are things measured or ruled, they would cease to be of use, since their use consists in being applicable to many things. Hence law would be of no use if it did not extend further than to one single act. Because the decrees of prudent men are made for the purpose of directing individual actions, whereas law is a general precept. . . .

Reply Obj. 3. "We must not seek the same degree of certainty in all things."[33] Consequently in contingent matters, such as natural and human things, it is enough for a thing to be certain, as being true in the greater number of instances, though at times and less frequently it fail.

Second Article: Whether It Belongs to Human Law to Repress All Vices?

We proceed thus to the Second Article:

Objection 1. It would seem that it belongs to human law to repress all vices. For Isidore says that "laws were made in order that, in fear thereof, man's audacity might be held in check."[34] But it would not be held in check sufficiently unless all evils were repressed by law. Therefore human law should repress all evils.

Obj. 2. Further, the intention of the lawgiver is to make the citizens virtuous. But a man cannot be virtuous unless he forbear from all kinds of vice. Therefore it belongs to human law to repress all vices.

Obj. 3. Further, human law is derived from the natural law, as stated above (Q. 95, A. 2).

But all vices are contrary to the law of nature. Therefore human law should repress all vices.

On the contrary, We read in *De libero arbitrio* i. 5: "It seems to me that the law which is written for the governing of the people rightly permits these things, and that divine providence punishes them." But divine providence punishes nothing but vices. Therefore human law rightly allows some vices, by not repressing them.

I answer that, . . . [L]aw is framed as a rule or measure of human acts. Now a measure should be homogeneous with that which it measures, as stated in *Metaphysics* x. text. 3, 4, since different things are measured by different measures. Wherefore laws imposed on men should also be in keeping with their condition, for, as Isidore says,[35] law should be "possible both according to nature, and according to the customs of the country." Now possibility or faculty of action is due to an interior habit or disposition, since the same thing is not possible to one who has not a virtuous habit as is possible to one who has. Thus the same is not possible to a child as to a full-grown man; for which reason the law for children is not the same as for adults, since many things are permitted to children which in an adult are punished by law or at any rate are open to blame. In like manner many things are permissible to men not perfect in virtue which would be intolerable in a virtuous man.

Now human law is framed for a number of human beings, the majority of whom are not perfect in virtue. Wherefore human laws do not forbid all vices from which the virtuous abstain, but only the more grievous vices from which it is possible for the majority to abstain; and chiefly those that are to the hurt of others, without the prohibition of which human society could not be maintained: thus human law prohibits murder, theft, and suchlike.

Reply Obj. 1. Audacity seems to refer to the assailing of others. Consequently it belongs to those sins chiefly whereby one's neighbor is injured; and these sins are forbidden by human law, as stated.

Reply Obj. 2. The purpose of human law is to lead men to virtue, not suddenly, but grad-ually. Wherefore it does not lay upon the multitude of imperfect men the burdens of those who are already virtuous, viz., that they should abstain from all evil. Otherwise these imperfect ones, being unable to bear such precepts, would break out into yet greater evils; thus it is written: "He that violently bloweth his nose, bringeth out blood";[36] and that if "new wine," i.e., precepts of a perfect life, is "put into old bottles," i.e., into imperfect men, "the bottles break, and the wine runneth out," i.e., the precepts are despised and those men, from contempt, break out into evils worse still.[37]

Reply Obj. 3. The natural law is a participation in us of the eternal law, while human law falls short of the eternal law. Now Augustine says: "The law which is framed for the government of states allows and leaves unpunished many things that are punished by divine providence. Nor, if this law does not attempt to do everything, is this a reason why it should be blamed for what it does."[38] Wherefore, too, human law does not prohibit everything that is forbidden by the natural law. . . .

Fourth Article: Whether Human Law Binds a Man in Conscience?

We proceed thus to the Fourth Article:

Objection 1. It would seem that human law does not bind a man in conscience. For an inferior power has no jurisdiction in a court of higher power. But the power of man which frames human law is beneath the divine power. Therefore human law cannot impose its precept in a divine court, such as is the court of conscience.

Obj. 2. Further, the judgment of conscience depends chiefly on the commandments of God. But sometimes God's commandments are made void by human laws, according to Matthew xv. 6: "You have made void the commandment of God for your tradition." Therefore human law does not bind a man in conscience.

Obj. 3. Further, human laws often bring loss of character and injury on man, according to Isaias x. 1 ff.: "Woe to them that make wicked laws, and when they write, write injustice; to oppress the poor in judgment, and do violence to the cause of the humble of My people." But it is lawful for anyone to avoid oppression and violence. Therefore human laws do not bind man in conscience.

On the contrary, It is written: "This is thanksworthy, if for conscience . . . a man endure sorrows, suffering wrongfully."[39]

I answer that, Laws framed by man are either just or unjust. If they be just, they have the power of binding in conscience, from the eternal law whence they are derived, according to Proverbs viii. 15: "By Me kings reign, and lawgivers decree just things." Now laws are said to be just—from the end, when, to wit, they are ordained to the common good—and from their author, that is to say, when the law that is made does not exceed the power of the lawgiver—and from their form, when, to wit, burdens are laid on the subjects, according to an equality of proportion and with a view to the common good. For, since one man is a part of the community, each man, in all that he is and has, belongs to the community, just as a part, in all that it is, belongs to the whole; wherefore nature inflicts a loss on the part in order to save the whole, so that on this account such laws as these which impose proportionate burdens are just and binding in conscience and are legal laws.

On the other hand, laws may be unjust in two ways: first, by being contrary to human good, through being opposed to the things mentioned above—either in respect of the end, as when an authority imposes on his subjects burdensome laws, conducive, not to the common good, but rather to his own cupidity or vainglory; or in respect of the author, as when a man makes a law that goes beyond the power committed to him; or in respect of the form, as when burdens are imposed unequally on the community, although with a view to the common good. The like are acts of violence rather than laws, because, as Augustine says, "A law that is not just, seems to be no law at all."[40] Wherefore such laws do not bind in conscience, except perhaps in order to avoid scandal or disturbance, for which cause a man should even yield his right, according to Matthew v. 40, 41: "If a man . . . take away thy coat, let go thy cloak also unto him; and whosoever will force thee one mile, go with him other two."

Secondly, laws may be unjust through being opposed to the divine good: such are the laws of tyrants inducing to idolatry or to anything else contrary to the divine law; and laws of this kind must nowise be observed because, as stated in Acts v. 29, "we ought to obey God rather than men."

Reply Obj. 1. As the Apostle says, all human power is from God . . . "therefore he that resisteth the power" in matters that are within its scope "resisteth the ordinance of God"; so that he becomes guilty according to his conscience.[41]

Reply Obj. 2. This argument is true of laws that are contrary to the commandments of God, which is beyond the scope of (human) power. Wherefore in such matters human law should not be obeyed.

Reply Obj. 3. This argument is true of a law that inflicts unjust hurt on its subjects. The power that man holds from God does not extend to this, wherefore neither in such matters is man bound to obey the law, provided he avoid giving scandal or inflicting a more grievous hurt.

Fifth Article: Whether All Are Subject to the Law?

We proceed thus to the Fifth Article:

Objection 1. It would seem that not all are subject to the law. For those alone are subject to a law for whom a law is made. But the Apostle says: "The law is not made for the just man."[42] Therefore the just are not subject to the law.

Obj. 2. Further, Pope Urban says: "He that is guided by a private law need not for any reason be bound by the public law."[43] Now all spiritual men are led by the private law of the Holy Ghost, for they are the sons of God, of whom it is said: "Whosoever are led by the Spirit of God, they are the sons of God."[44] Therefore not all men are subject to human law.

Obj. 3. Further, the Jurist says that "the sovereign is exempt from the laws."[45] But he that is exempt from the law is not bound thereby. Therefore not all are subject to the law.

On the contrary, The Apostle says: "Let every soul be subject to the higher powers."[46] But subjection to a power seems to imply subjection to the laws framed by that power. Therefore all men should be subject to human law.

I answer that, . . . [T]he notion of law contains two things: first, that it is a rule of human acts; secondly, that it has coercive power. Wherefore a man may be subject to law in two ways. First, as the regulated is subject to the regulator; and, in this way, whoever is subject to a power is subject to the law framed by that power. But it may happen in two ways that one is not subject to a power. In one way, by being altogether free from its authority; hence the subjects of one city or kingdom are not bound by the laws of the sovereign of another city or kingdom, since they are not subject to his authority. In another way, by being under a yet higher law; thus the subject of a proconsul should be ruled by his command, but not in those matters in which the subject receives his orders from the emperor, for in these matters he is not bound by the mandate of the lower authority, since he is directed by that of a higher. In this way one who is simply subject to a law may not be subject thereto in certain matters in respect of which he is ruled by a higher law.

Secondly, a man is said to be subject to a law as the coerced is subject to the coercer. In this way the virtuous and righteous are not subject to the law, but only the wicked. Because coercion and violence are contrary to the will, but the will of the good is in harmony with the law, whereas the will of the wicked is discordant from it. Wherefore in this sense the good are not subject to the law, but only the wicked.

Reply Obj. 1. This argument is true of subjection by way of coercion, for, in this way, "the law is not made for the just men: because they are a law to themselves," since they "show the work of the law written in their hearts," as the Apostle says.[47] Consequently the law does not enforce itself upon them as it does on the wicked.

Reply Obj. 2. The law of the Holy Ghost is above all law framed by man; and therefore spiritual men, in so far as they are led by the law of the Holy Ghost, are not subject to the law in those matters that are inconsistent with the guidance of the Holy Ghost. Never-

theless the very fact that spiritual men are subject to law is due to the leading of the Holy Ghost, according to I Peter ii. 13: "Be ye subject . . . to every human creature for God's sake."

Reply Obj. 3. The sovereign is said to be "exempt from the law," as to its coercive power, since, properly speaking, no man is coerced by himself, and law has no coercive power save from the authority of the sovereign. Thus then is the sovereign said to be exempt from the law, because none is competent to pass sentence on him if he acts against the law. Wherefore on Psalm L. 6: "To Thee only have I sinned," a gloss says that "there is no man who can judge the deeds of a king." But as to the directive force of law, the sovereign is subject to the law by his own will, according to the statement that "whatever law a man makes for another, he should keep himself."[48] And a wise authority says: "Obey the law that thou makest thyself."[49] Moreover the Lord reproaches those who "say and do not"; and who "bind heavy burdens and lay them on men's shoulders, but with a finger of their own they will not move them."[50] Hence, in the judgment of God, the sovereign is not exempt from the law as to its directive force, but he should fulfill it of his own free will and not of constraint. Again the sovereign is above the law in so far as, when it is expedient, he can change the law and dispense in it according to time and place. . . .

Notes

1. Augustine, *De libero arbitrio*, i. 6.
2. Augustine, *De libero arbitrio*, i.
3. The Book of Psalms.
4. Augustine, *De libero arbitrio*, i. 6.
5. St. Thomas's Commentaries on Aristotle's *Metaphysics*.
6. Augustine, *De libero arbitrio*, i. 6.
7. Cicero, *De inventione rhetorica*.
8. Ecclus, xv. 14.
9. Psalms, cxviii. 33.
10. Augustine, *De libero arbitrio*, i. 5, 6.
11. Aristotle, *Ethics*, ii. 5.
12. Damascene, *De fide orthodoxa*, iv. 22.
13. Augustine, *De bono conjugali*, xxi.
14. Boethius, *De hebdomadibus*.

15. Aristotle, *Ethics*, v. 7.

16. Isidore, *Etymologiae*, v. 20.

17. Aristotle, *Politics*, i. 2.

18. Aristotle, *Rhetoric*, i. I.

19. Aristotle, *Ethics*, v. 7.

20. Isidore, *Etymologiae*, v. 4.

21. Aristotle, *Ethics*, v. 7.

22. Ibid.

23. *Digest*, i. 3, 5.

24. Cicero, *De rhetorica ad Herennium*, ii.

25. Augustine, *De libero arbitrio*, i. 5.

26. Aristotle, *Ethics*, vi. II.

27. Aristotle, *Ethics*, v. 7.

28. *Digest*, i. 3.2.

29. Isidore, *Etymologiae*, v. 21.

30. Augustine, *De Civitate Dei*, ii. 21; xxii. 6.

31. Aristotle, *Ethics*, v. 7.

32. Aristotle, *Metaphysics*, x, text. 4.

33. Aristotle, *Ethics*, i. 3.

34. Isidore, *Etymologiae*, v. 20.

35. Ibid., 21.

36. Book of Proverbs, xxx. 33.

37. Gospel of St. Matthew, ix. 17.

38. Augustine, *De libero arbitrio*, i. 5.

39. Epistle of St. Peter, ii. 19.

40. Augustine, *De libero arbitrio*, i. 5.

41. St. Paul's Epistle to the Romans, xiii. 1, 2.

42. St. Paul's Epistle to Timothy, i. 9.

43. The Decretals of Gregory IX, CAUSA 19, 9u 2.

44. St. Paul's Epistle to the Romans, viii. 14.

45. *Digest*, i. 3, 31.

46. St. Paul's Epistle to the Romans, xiii. 1.

47. Ibid., ii. 14, 15.

48. Decretals of Gregory IX, Book I, tit. 2, c. 6.

49. Dionysius Cato, *Disticha de Moribus*, Book I, preface.

50. Gospel of St. Matthew, xxiii. 3, 4.

Adapted from: Saint Thomas Aquinas, "Summa Theologica." In *The Political Ideas of St. Thomas Aquinas,* pp. 11–18, 42–46, 55–59, 65–74. Copyright © 1953. Reprinted by permission of Benziger Publishing, a division of Macmillan/McGraw-Hill. ✦

19
Excerpts from *On Kingship*

Saint Thomas Aquinas

Chapter Two: Whether It Is More Expedient for a City or Province to Be Ruled by One Man or by Many

[16] Having set forth these preliminary points we must now inquire what is better for a province or a city: whether to be ruled by one man or by many.

[17] This question may be considered first from the viewpoint of the purpose of government. The aim of any ruler should be directed toward securing the welfare of that which he undertakes to rule. The duty of the pilot, for instance, is to preserve his ship amidst the perils of the sea and to bring it unharmed to the port of safety. Now the welfare and safety of a multitude formed into a society lies in the preservation of its unity, which is called peace. If this is removed, the benefit of social life is lost and, moreover, the multitude in its disagreement becomes a burden to itself. The chief concern of the ruler of a multitude, therefore, is to procure the unity of peace. It is not even legitimate for him to deliberate whether he shall establish peace in the multitude subject to him, just as a physician does not deliberate whether he shall heal the sick man encharged to him, for no one should deliberate about an end which he is obliged to seek, but only about the means to attain that end. Wherefore the Apostle, having commended the unity of the faithful people, says: "Be ye careful to keep the unity of the spirit in the bond of peace." Thus, the more efficacious a government is in keeping the unity of peace, the more useful it will be. For we call that more useful which leads more directly to the end. Now it is manifest that what is itself one can more efficaciously bring about unity than several—just as the most efficacious cause of heat is that which is by its nature hot. Therefore the rule of one man is more useful than the rule of many.

[18] Furthermore, it is evident that several persons could by no means preserve the stability of the community if they totally disagreed. For union is necessary among them if they are to rule at all; several men, for instance, could not pull a ship in one direction unless joined together in some fashion. Now several are said to be united according as they come closer to being one. So one man rules better than several who come near being one.

[19] Again, whatever is in accord with nature is best, for in all things nature does what is best. Now every natural governance is governance by one. In the multitude of bodily members there is one which is the principal mover, namely, the heart; and among the powers of the soul one power presides as chief, namely, the reason. Among bees there is one king bee, and in the whole universe there is One God, Maker and Ruler of all things. And there is a reason for this. Every multitude is derived from unity. Wherefore, if artificial things are an imitation of natural things and a work of art is better according as it attains a closer likeness to what is in nature, it follows that it is best for a human multitude to be ruled by one person.

[20] This is also evident from experience. For provinces or cities which are not ruled by one person are torn with dissensions and tossed about without peace, so that the complaint seems to be fulfilled which the Lord uttered through the Prophet: "Many pastors have destroyed my vineyard." On the other hand, provinces and cities which are ruled under one king enjoy peace, flourish in justice, and delight in prosperity. Hence, the Lord by His prophets promised to His people as a great reward that He will give them one head and that "one Prince will be in the midst of them."

Chapter Three: That the Dominion of a Tyrant Is the Worst

[21] Just as the government of a king is the best, so the government of a tyrant is the worst.

[22] For democracy stands in contrary opposition to polity, since both are governments carried on by many persons, as is clear from what has already been said; while oligarchy is the opposite of aristocracy, since both are governments carried on by a few persons; and kingship is the opposite of tyranny, since both are carried on by one person. Now, as has been shown above, monarchy is the best government. If, therefore, "it is the contrary of the best that is worst," it follows that tyranny is the worst kind of government.

[23] Further, a united force is more efficacious in producing its effect than a force which is scattered or divided. Many persons together can pull a load which could not be pulled by each one taking his part separately and acting individually. Therefore, just as it is more useful for a force operating for a good to be more united, in order that it may work good more effectively, so a force operating for evil is more harmful when it is one than when it is divided. Now, the power of one who rules unjustly works to the detriment of the multitude, in that he diverts the common good of the multitude to his own benefit. Therefore, for the same reason that, in a just government, the government is better in proportion as the ruling power is one—thus monarchy is better than aristocracy, and aristocracy better than polity—so the contrary will be true of an unjust government, namely, that the ruling power will be more harmful in proportion as it is more unitary. Consequently, tyranny is more harmful than oligarchy and oligarchy more harmful than democracy.

[24] Moreover, a government becomes unjust by the fact that the ruler, paying no heed to the common good, seeks his own private good. Wherefore the further he departs from the common good the more unjust will his government be. But there is a greater departure from the common good in an oligarchy, in which the advantage of a few is sought, than in a democracy, in which the advantage of many is sought; and there is a still greater departure from the common good in a tyranny, where the advantage of only one man is sought. For a large number is closer to the totality than a small number, and a small number than only one. Thus, the government of a tyrant is the most unjust.

[25] The same conclusion is made clear to those who consider the order of divine providence, which disposes everything in the best way. In all things, good ensues from one perfect cause, i.e., from the totality of the conditions favorable to the production of the effect, while evil results from any one partial defect. There is beauty in a body when all its members are fittingly disposed; ugliness, on the other hand, arises when any one member is not fittingly disposed. Thus ugliness results in different ways from many causes, beauty in one way from one perfect cause. It is thus with all good and evil things, as if God so provided that good, arising from one cause, be stronger, and evil, arising from many causes, be weaker. It is expedient therefore that a just government be that of one man only in order that it may be stronger; however, if the government should turn away from justice, it is more expedient that it be a government by many, so that it may be weaker and the many may mutually hinder one another. Among unjust governments, therefore, democracy is the most tolerable, but the worst is tyranny. . . .

Adapted from: Thomas Aquinas, *On Kingship*, translated by Gerald B. Phelan, pp. 11–15. Copyright © 1949. Reprinted by permission of the Pontifical Institute of Mediaeval Studies. ✦

20
Law and Politics

Paul E. Sigmund

Aquinas's political and legal theory is important for three reasons. First, it reasserts the value of politics by drawing on Aristotle to argue that politics and political life are morally positive activities that are in accordance with the intention of God for man. Second, it combines traditional hierarchical and feudal views of the structure of society and politics with emerging community-oriented and incipiently egalitarian views of the proper ordering of society. Third, it develops an integrated and logically coherent theory of natural law that continues to be an important source of legal, political, and moral norms. These accomplishments have become part of the intellectual patrimony of the West, and have inspired political and legal philosophers and religious and social movements down to the present day.

I. The Legitimacy of the Political Order

The challenge to which Aquinas responded was posed to medieval Christianity by the rediscovery of the full corpus of Aristotle's works, which except for some logical treatises had been unavailable to the West before the thirteenth century. Aristotle's *Politics* included descriptions and evaluations of a wide range of political experiences in fourth-century Greece that were different from the experience of the medieval feudal order. His *Metaphysics, Physics* and *Nicomachean Ethics* contained analyses of human conduct and of the external world that contrasted with the approach to legal and scriptural texts that had predominated in the medieval "schools" (which were in the process of becoming the forebears of modern universities). Operating on the basic assumption that reason and revelation are not contradictory, that "grace does not contradict nature, but perfects it," Aquinas combined tradition, Scripture, contemporary practice, and Aristotelian philosophical methods to produce a lasting and influential "Thomistic synthesis" in politics and legal theory. Central to that effort was his reliance on Aristotle's conception of teleology or final causes, which in Aquinas's thought became the working out of God's purposes in the nature of the universe and mankind that he had created.

Aquinas, however, is first a Christian, and his Aristotelianism is a Christian Aristotelianism. In contrast to Christianity, Aristotle had no conception of original sin, and, although he was not optimistic about the possibility of creating the ideal state, he was open to the possibilities of "constitutional engineering" and conscious of the wide variations in the political structures of the 158 Greek constitutions he had studied. For early Christianity and the Fathers of the Church, however, typified in the writings of St. Augustine (381–430), political life was corrupted by man's hereditary inclination to evil, and the state was a coercive institution designed to maintain a minimum of order in a sinful world. The ruler, even if he was a Christian, could only strive to moderate human power drives and impose a minimal justice on the earthly city that would make it possible for the members of the heavenly city to reach their eternal reward.[1] For the Aristotle of Book I of the *Politics*, on the other hand, man is *zoon politikon*—literally, a *polis*-oriented animal—and political life is a necessary part of his full development. "He, who is unable to live in society, or has no need because he is sufficient to himself, is either a beast or a god."[2]

In his major political work, *The Governance of Rulers* (De regimine principum, 1265–67), Aquinas correctly broadens the translation of *zoon politikon* to argue that "man is by nature a political and social animal" (Chapter 1) who uses his reason and faculty of speech to cooperate in building political communities that respond to the needs of the group and of the individuals who compose it. The political community will be a union of free men under the direction of a ruler who aims at the promotion of the common good. Government then has a positive role and moral justification. Infidel (e.g., Moslem) rulers can rule justly "since dominion and government are based on human law, while the distinction between believers and unbelievers is a matter of divine law, [and] the divine law which is based on grace does not abolish human law which is based on reason."[3]

Having said this, Aquinas then argues that the Church may for religious reasons take away the infidel's power to rule, so that the autonomy of the temporal rule is not absolute. On the question of church-state relations Aquinas is contradictory, since in some passages—notably in *The Governance of Rulers*, Chapter 15—he appears to argue for papal supremacy over all earthly rulers because "those who are responsible for intermediate ends [that is, the common good of the temporal community] should be subject to the one who is responsible for the ultimate end and be directed by his command," while in other places—STIIaIIae.60.6 and In Sent II.44.2—he states that the civil ruler is subject to the spiritual only in religious matters (although in In Sent II.44.2 he makes an exception for the pope as possessing both spiritual and secular power). In theory, it would appear that Aquinas should be a dualist or advocate of the "indirect power" of the Church, defending a moral rather than a legal or political supremacy for the Church, but, as far as the texts go, he "waffles."

M. J. Wilks has argued that by admitting the legitimacy of temporal rule in a sacral age, Aquinas was initiating the process of secularization that would ultimately destroy the intellectual and ideological power of the Catholic Church.[4] It is certainly true that Aristotle provided a rational justification for government different from that of revelation; but once the claims of reason, as exemplified by Aristotle, were admitted, there was always a possibility of conflict. For Aquinas, however, a belief that faith and reason were both valid and divinely legitimated sources of human knowledge meant that neither should be considered as dominating the other. (In fact, of course, as Aquinas implies in his discussion of divine law,[5] revelation

acts as a kind of negative check on reason although, unless the pope is the sole interpreter of the divine law, this does not in itself argue for papal supremacy over the temporal ruler.)

II. Aquinas and Constitutionalism

In addition to re-legitimizing political life, Aquinas shifted the emphasis in thinking about the best form of government. Until the thirteenth century, it was assumed that monarchy was not only the best form of government but also the only one that was in accordance with divine intention. The Neoplatonic worldview of "the great chain of being" coincided with the realities of the feudal structure to support a hierarchical structure in the universe and in society that was profoundly anti-egalitarian in its implications. The hierarchy of the angels under one God was reproduced on earth with various ranks in church, state, and society, each assigned to its position under a single monarch. As Aquinas says in *The Governance of Rulers*, Chapter 1, "In everything that is ordered to a single end, one thing is found that rules the rest," and in Chapter 2, "In nature, government is always by one." Among the bees there is a "king bee," and one God has created and rules the universe. Thus monarchy is the best form of government.

Yet from Aristotle Aquinas had also derived a view of government as rule over free men who are able to direct themselves. Moreover, he admits that a monarch can be easily corrupted and there seems to be no remedy against the tyrant but prayer.[6] The solution, Aquinas suggests, is for the community to take action to get rid of the bad ruler if this is legally possible. (In his *Commentary on the Sentences*, written when he was a young man, Aquinas went further and argued for individual action against tyrants even to the extent of tyrannicide against usurpers, although not against legitimate rulers who abuse their power.) In two other places, Aquinas advocates a mixed constitution that combines monarchy with aristocracy (in its etymological sense of the rule of the virtuous) and democracy, involving an element of popular participation—a system that he describes as both modeled on the government established by Moses and recommended by Aristotle in the *Politics*.[7]

If these passages are combined with Aquinas's belief in the supremacy of law and his recognition of the special claims of the Church as concerned with man's ultimate end, it is easy to understand why Lord Acton described Aquinas as "the First Whig" or believer in the limitation of governmental power. We should add, however, that he was also one of the first to endorse popular participation in government, despite the fact that he was writing before the emergence of national representative institutions.[8] Aquinas may also have been familiar with republican institutions in the Italian city-states, and he cites in his writings the example of the Roman republic. In addition, his *Commentary on the Politics* familiarized students and intellectuals both with Aristotle's discussions of the commonwealth (*res publica*) "in which the multitude rules for the common benefit," and with Aristotle's definition of a citizen as one who rules and is ruled in turn,[9] this tending to undermine the dominant hierarchiral and monarchical model.

The admixture of constitutional and republican elements in Aquinas's monarchism meant that centuries later, when neo-Thomists like Jacques Maritain and Yves Simon argued for a Thomistic basis for modern Christian Democratic theory, they did not have to look far to find texts to cite. This is not to say that Aquinas himself was a democrat. There is no mention of the need for explicit consent to law and government, and where he discusses participation, it is participation by corporate groups, not individuals, or by "the people" as a whole rather than through the individual voting and the majority rule of modern democracy.[10] Above all, the modern idea of religious freedom was completely alien to his thought. Heretics "have committed a sin that deserves not only excommunication by the church but their removal from the world by death [since] it is a much more serious matter to corrupt the faith that sustains the life of the soul than to counterfeit money, which sustains temporal life."[11] It is true that Aquinas admits that if there is "an error of reason or conscience arising out of ignorance and without any negligence, that error of reason or conscience excuses the will that abides by that erring reason from being evil";[12] but for him it was unthinkable that a heretic who had known the truth (as distinct from a Jew or "infidel") could be other than culpable for rejecting it.

Aquinas's view of women was also very different from that taken in modern liberal democratic theory. Contemporary feminist critics have focused on a single article in the *Summa theologiae* in which Aquinas argues that God created woman not as a helpmate to man "since he can get more effective help from another man—but to assist in procreation."[13] Even more shocking to modern sensibilities, in the same article Aquinas rejects Aristotle's description of woman as "a misbegotten man," arguing that although, as Aristotle states, women are weaker and passive "because of some material cause or some external change such as a moist south wind, woman is not something misbegotten but is intended by nature to be directed to the work of procreation."[14] He adds that woman is naturally subject to man in a mutually beneficial relationship "because man possesses more discernment of reason."

The most striking difference from modern liberalism is Aquinas's treatment of slavery. Here he is attempting to reconcile two conflicting traditions. On the one hand, Aristotle (in Book I, Chapter 5, of the *Politics*) argued that the enslavement of those who are incapable of living a moral life is justified by nature. On the other hand, the Fathers of the Church wrote that all men are equal by nature and viewed slavery as a consequence of sin. Aquinas's answer is to refer to Aristotle's argument, to describe slavery as an "addition" to the natural law "that has been found to be convenient both for the master and the slave," and to limit the master's rights over his slave in the areas of private and family life as well as the right to subsistence.[15] Yet it is not clear that he rejects Aristotle's view of natural slavery, and as late as the sixteenth century theologians at the court of Spain debated whether or not American Indians were natural slaves.[16]

In modern terms Aquinas's political thought in its original formulation (that is, before the neo-Thomist revisions) is closer to European or Latin American corporatist and integralist conservatism than to modern liberalism. In one area, however, there is less need for a drastic reformulation in order to come up with a theory that is still applicable today—and that is the Thomistic theory of natural law.

III. Natural Law

Next to the Five Ways of proving the existence of God (STIa.2), the Treatise on Law (STIaIIae.90–97) is probably the best-known part of the *Summa theologiae*. Aquinas begins with a definition of law as "an ordination of reason for the common good promulgated by the one who is in charge of the community."[17] Two comments should be made about this definition. First, by defining law as an ordination of *reason* Aquinas is saying more than simply that it is rational in character. As is clear from his explanation, he has in mind a particular type of reason—reasoning that is teleological or goal-oriented: "whenever someone desires an end, reason commands what is to be done to reach it."[18] This rational command is not a mere act of the will. When the Roman law says "the will of the prince has the force of law," it is understood that that will "must be guided by reason. . . . Otherwise the will of the prince would be iniquity rather than law."

The second point is that for Aquinas, law is based on the community, since it is ordered to the common good and "making law belongs either to the whole people or to the public personage who has the responsibility for the whole people."[19] Thus even without organized representative institutions, the ruler is obliged to keep the common good in mind when he legislates, and corrupt governments are those that are directed at the private good of the ruler rather than the common good.

Aquinas then outlines his typology of laws. At the top of the hierarchy of laws is *the eternal law,* which he defines as "the rational governance of everything on the part of God

as ruler of the universe,"[20] and identifies as divine providence.

Natural law, ranked below the eternal law, is defined by Aquinas as "the participation in the eternal law by rational creatures." That participation is through "a natural inclination to their proper action and ends."[21] What this means, as he explains in Question 94, is that reason has the capacity to perceive what is good for human beings by following the "order of our rational inclinations."[22] These Aquinas lists as self-preservation, an end that human beings share with all substances, family life and bringing up offspring, which is shared with all animals, and the goals of knowing God and living in society, which are shared with all rational creatures. These goals in turn are seen as obligatory because practical reason perceives as a basic principle that "good is to be done and evil is to be avoided," which is a self-evident principle like the principle of non-contradiction.

The brief discussion of natural law in Question 94 has been the subject of considerable critical comment and debate. Jacques Maritain used it to argue that Aquinas believed that human beings come to know the natural law intuitively through natural inclination, and that when that knowledge is articulated in rational and universal terms, it becomes something else—*the law of nations* (*ius gentium*).[23] It is clear from the text, however, that Aquinas means that knowledge of the natural law is rational knowledge that is based on our perception of natural goals or inclinations "that are naturally apprehended by reason as good." It is true that in an earlier discussion Aquinas describes *synderesis,* the capacity to understand the basic principles of morality, as beginning with "the understanding of certain things that are naturally known as immutable principles without investigation," but he then goes on to describe the way human beings make judgments on the basis of those principles "concerning what has been discovered by reasoning."[24] Applying this account to the discussion of natural law, it seems that human beings know quasi-intuitively that good is to be done and evil is to be avoided, but that they use their reason to make judgments that identify the basic human goods that are the object of our natural inclinations.

Others besides Maritain have attempted to de-emphasize the rational and propositional character of Aquinas's theory. Michael Novak, for example, describes Aquinas's natural law theory as "the traditional pragmatism . . . not a set of generalizations but a set of individual intelligent actions,"[25] and E.A. Goerner argues that natural law is only an imperfect, second-best standard of morality, while "natural right" (*ius naturale*) is the "equitable but unformulatable virtue of the prudent and the just."[26] Morton White also misrepresents Aquinas's theory of natural law when he describes it as deductive in character, on the model of a system of logic.[27]

Aquinas states explicitly that adultery, homosexuality, usury, drunkenness, gluttony, suicide, murder, lying, and the breaking of promises are opposed to nature and therefore forbidden by natural law.[28] His argument is not intuitive, pragmatic, or deductive, but teleological in terms of the nature and purposes of human beings in relation to a given type of action. Those purposes can come into conflict, as Aquinas recognizes, but he believes that such conflicts are not irreconcilable, and that apparent contradictions can be resolved by the use of reason, since the world has been created and continues to be guided by a rational and purposive God.

Aquinas built his theory of natural law by taking a number of Aristotelian concepts and combining them in a way that is different from the way they were used by Aristotle. Whether or not he was faithful to the spirit of Aristotle can be argued,[29] but a comparison of Aquinas's discussion of natural law with the relevant passages in Aristotle's writings reveals that Aquinas has combined quite disparate elements in Aristotle—the *phronesis* of the *Nicomachean Ethics*, the description of final causality in the *Physics*, the discussion of the natural basis of government, slavery, property, etc., in Book I of the *Politics*, the ambiguous treatment of natural justice (not natural law) in Book V of the *Ethics*, and the description of law as reason in Book III of the *Politics*—into a new synthesis that makes the determination of natural ends (based on natural inclinations) a central consideration in the development of a workable theory of natural law.

The originality of Aquinas's theory is evident when it is compared, for example, with discussions of natural law in Gratian's *Decretum* or *Concordance of Discordant Canons*, the major source book for canon law in the thirteenth century. Gratian describes natural law as "what is contained in the Old and New Testaments," following this with quotations from Isidore of Seville's *Etymologies* stating that "Divine laws come from nature" and, in a formulation borrowed from the introductory passages of the *Digest* of Roman Law, "Natural law is the law that is common to all nations."[30]

For Aquinas *the law of nations* is related to natural law as "conclusions from principles," conclusions that enable people to relate to one another in all societies.[31] Aquinas therefore classifies the law of nations as a type of *human law*, that is, the particular applications of natural law derived by reason, while he calls the more specific and variable applications of human law "civil law" (from *civitas* = "city"). Both varieties of human law are derived from natural law, and if human law disagrees with natural law, "it is no longer a law, but a corruption of law."[32]

When Aquinas discusses the application of natural law through human law, he allows for a good deal more flexibility than one might expect, given the absolute character of the prohibitions of natural law. Thus evils like prostitution, usury, and the widespread exercise of the religious rites of heretics or infidels may be tolerated "so as not to prevent other goods from occurring, or to avoid some worse evil."[33] The "secondary" precepts of natural law, which "follow as immediate conclusions from first principles," can be changed "in a few cases because some special reasons make its precepts impossible to observe,"[34] although, except for the mention of polygamy in the Old Testament, there is no further discussion of the difference between the two types of principles.

It is also possible for there to be additions to the natural law of "provisions that are useful to human life." In addition to slavery, already mentioned, property is cited as an addition to resolve the contradiction between the statement of Isidore of Seville, reflecting a common view of the Fathers of the Church, that "possession of all things and universal freedom are part of the natural law" and Aristotle's arguments in favor of the natural character of private property and slavery. For Aquinas, "neither separate possessions nor slavery resulted from nature, but they were produced by human reason for the benefit of human life."[35] Despite what appears to be a parallel treatment of the two cases of property and slavery, however, it is clear from other passages, cited earlier, that Aquinas is much more favorable to Aristotle's view of the natural law basis of private property (within limits such as a starving man's need for the means of subsistence)[36] than he is to his argument for natural slavery.

Two other concepts derived from Aristotle serve to provide flexibility in Aquinas's application of the natural law. The first is prudence, which he describes as a virtue by which human beings choose the right means for the attainment of ends that are identified by practical reason.[37] Some modern interpreters of Aquinas's political thought put great emphasis on prudence, particularly in the area of the conduct of international relations, where, it is claimed, the norms of natural law can be applied only in a modified way. Others are more insistent that even in the case of modern war, natural law prohibitions against the killing of the innocent, for example, even indirectly, are still binding.[38]

Equity is a second source of flexibility that Aquinas derived from Aristotle's *Nicomachean Ethics* (V 10). Aquinas's word for equity is not its Latin cognate, *aequitas*, but Aristotle's original Greek term, *epieikeia*. This is the power of the ruler to depart from the letter of the law when its literal application would violate its spirit.[39] An example that Aquinas gives is the opening of the gates of a besieged city after the legal hours of closure in order to admit defenders of the city being pursued by the enemy. The exceptions, however, may not violate the divine law or the "general precepts" of natural law.[40]

In the area of sexual morality, which is part of the divine law, there is no departure from the Christian doctrine that sexual ex-pression is permitted only within the bonds of monogamous marriage, although Aquinas admits that polygamy was tolerated in the Old Testament. Fornication and adultery are seriously wrong because they operate against the natural goals of family life, especially the upbringing of children. Because this is "the natural ordering of the sex act that is appropriate to mankind," masturbation, sodomy, and bestiality are also unnatural vices, in increasing order of seriousness.[41]

Did Aquinas believe that these sins should be made the subject of legislation? On the one hand, like Aristotle he believed that the object of government was to promote virtue. On the other hand, as noted above, he was also willing to allow for considerable legislative flexibility "to avoid greater evils," and human law can prohibit only "the more serious vices, especially those that harm others and which must be prohibited for human society to survive."[42]

On the other hand, Aquinas's discussion of sexual pleasure as divinely intended (and as more intense before the Fall) implies a more positive view of sexuality than earlier Christian writers had held.

The teleological approach to natural law also affected Aquinas's discussion of usury, which in the Middle Ages was defined broadly as the charging of interest for lending money. Citing Aristotle's discussion in Book I of the *Politics*, Aquinas asserts that because money is not in itself productive, but only a means of exchange, it is wrong to receive payment for a loan of money. But he admits that "human law allows usury not because it considers it just, but to avoid interference with the useful activities of many people."[43]

There are two other issues where Aquinas's natural law theory has been relevant for public policy down to the present day, abortion and the just war. Deliberate abortion of the fetus is for Aquinas equivalent to murder, but only after "quickening" or "ensoulment," which Aquinas, following Aristotle, believed occurred forty days after conception in the case of males, and eighty days thereafter for females.[44] However, contrary to what some contemporary polemicists have argued,

Aquinas believed that abortion even before ensoulment was a sin, although not the sin of murder. He did not discuss the case where the mother's life is directly threatened, but given his biblically based opposition to doing evil so that good may come of it (Romans 3:8), it is unlikely that he would have approved.

Aquinas was not the originator of the just war theory. Cicero had defended the wars of Rome as just, and Augustine had discussed the problem of the legitimate use of defensive violence by Christian rulers. What Aquinas did was to systematize its conditions, setting out three: declaration by the ruler whose duty it is to defend the commonwealth, a just cause (in particular, self-defense), and a right intention.[45] Possibly equally important was his description of what came to known in ethics as the principle of "double effect."[46] In discussing whether killing an unjust aggressor in order to defend one's life would be using evil means to achieve a good end, Aquinas argues that one intends only the defense of one's own life but not the killing that may inevitably result, and that only the minimally necessary force may be used. This passage has been cited in connection with the debate on the morality of nuclear warfare, with the defenders of nuclear deterrence arguing that it is not immoral to target military objectives that may incidentally have the unintended (but inevitable) effect of killing innocent people.[47]

IV. Aquinas's Legacy

As we have seen, Aquinas's thought on the topics of this chapter continues to be influential to the present day. Initially, he was only one of many writers of *Summae*, and he was even regarded with some suspicion because of the Church's condemnation of the doctrines of the Latin Averroists.[48] Despite the fact that Aquinas expressly opposed the Averroists in detail, some propositions drawn from his works were condemned by the bishop of Paris in 1277 in a general condemnation of Averroism. In 1323, however, Aquinas was declared a saint; his writings were widely taught, especially by the Domin-

ican order to which he belonged; and when the Council of Trent assembled in the middle of the sixteenth century, his *Summa theologiae* was placed on the altar along with the Bible as a source from which to draw answers to the arguments of the Protestant reformers. In 1879, his teachings were declared to be the official philosophy of the Roman Catholic Church by Pope Leo XIII, and, at least until the Second Vatican Council (1962–1965), they were the principal basis of theological and philosophical instruction at Catholic seminaries and in most Catholic universities.

His political ideas were developed by sixteenth-century Jesuit theorists such as Suarez and Bellarmine and through them influenced Grotius and other early writers on international law. His theory of natural law was adapted late in sixteenth-century England by Richard Hooker in his *Laws of Ecclesiastical Polity*, and through Hooker influenced John Locke. Aquinas's views on property, the family, and sexual morality have been widely cited in papal encyclicals; and a modernized version of his politics, which endorses democracy, religious pluralism, and human rights, has become the ideological basis of significant Christian Democratic parties in Germany, the Low Countries, Italy, Chile, Venezuela, and Central America. His statement on the invalidity of unjust laws was cited by Martin Luther King in his *Letter from Birmingham Jail*, and he has inspired many contemporary Catholic social theorists to argue for the establishment of a "communitarian" society that avoids the excessive individualism of capitalism and the collectivism of socialism.

Protestant Christians are critical of the excessive rationalism and optimism of Thomistic ethics, and of his refusal to recognize that there are contradictions between a rationalistic teleological natural law theory and certain aspects of the message of Christ, such as sacrificial love, martyrdom, rejection of wealth and worldly possessions, and "turning the other cheek." Radicals are suspicious of Aquinas's emphasis on the "natural" character of social systems that they insist are subject to human control and conditioned by economic structures. At least until the twentieth-century Neo-Thomist changes in favor of democracy, freedom, human rights, and religious pluralism, liberals were suspicious of Thomism's clericalism, implicit authoritarianism, sexism, and hierarchical outlook that seemed to prefer order to freedom.

Recognizing that many of Aquinas's views on society and politics that are unacceptable today (such as his monarchism, his qualified acceptance of slavery, his attitudes toward Jews, his defense of the burning of heretics, his belief in the natural inferiority of women) were historically conditioned or the result of an uncritical acceptance of Aristotle, the modern reader, like a number of contemporary moral and social philosophers (such as John Finnis, Alasdair MacIntyre, and Alan Donagan),[49] can still find relevant Aquinas's belief in the human capacity to identify goals, values, and purposes in the structure and functioning of the human person that can be used to evaluate and reform social, political, and legal structures, and to make a sustained argument based on evidence and clear statements of one's assumptions and the conclusions derived from them. This belief, which is really a faith that the meaning of human life is, at least in part, accessible to human reason, is an important element in the continuing attraction of what some of his followers like to call the perennial philosophy (*philosophia perennis*).

Notes

1. Augustine, *The City of God*, Bk. XIV, ch. 28; Bk. XIX, chs. 6, 13.

2. Aristotle, *Politics*, I.2.

3. Aquinas, *Summa Theologiae* (ST), IIaIIae.10. 10.

4. Wilks, Michael. 1963. *The problem of Sovereignty in the Later Middle Ages; The Papal Monarchy with Augustinus Triumphus and the Publicists*. Cambridge [Eng.]: University Press.

5. ST IaIIae 91.4.

6. Aquinas, *De regimine principum* (DRP), 6.

7. *In Sent Scriptum super libros Sententiarum* (In Sent.), II.44.2.exp.; ST IaIIae.95.4; 105.I.

8. The English Parliament dates its foundation in its present form to 1265, the year Aquinas began to write *De regimine principum*.

9. Aquinas, St. Thomas. 1963. "Commentary on the *Politics*." In R. Lerner and Muhsin Mahdi, eds. *Medieval Political Philosophy*. Ithaca, New York: Cornell University Press, pp. 314 and 332.

10. ST IaIIae.105.I.

11. ST IIaIIae.II.3.

12. ST IaIIae.19.6.

13. ST IaIIae.92.I.

14. Aristotle, *On the Generation of Animals*, IV 2.

15. *Summa Contra Gentiles* (SCG), III, 81; ST IIaIIae.57.3; ST IIaIIae.94.5, ad 3; IIaIIae. 104.5.

16. Hanke, L. 1959. *Aristotle and the American Indians*. Chicago: Regenery.

17. ST IaIIae.90.4.

18. ST IaIIae.90.I.

19. ST IaIIae.90.2.

20. ST IaIIae.91.I.

21. ST IaIIae.91.2.

22. ST IaIIae.94.2.

23. Maritain, J. 1951. *Man and State*. Chicago: University of Chicago Press, ch. 4.

24. ST Ia.79.12.

25. Novak, M. 1967. *A Time to Build*. New York: Macmilan, p. 342.

26. Goerner, E. A. 1983. "Thomistic Natural Right." *Political Theory* 2.

27. White, M. 1959. *Religion, Politics and Higher Learning*. Cambridge: Harvard University Press, pp. 124 ff.

28. ST IaIIae.94.3; IIaIIae.47.2; 64.5; 78; 88.3; 110.3; 154.2.

29. See, for example, Jaffa, H. V. 1952. *Thomism and Aristotelianism*. Chicago: University of Chicago Press.

30. D.1.c.1 and 7, translated in Sigmund, P. E. 1981. *Natural Law in Political Thought*. Washington: University Press of America.

31. ST IaIIae.95.4.

32. ST IaIIae.94.I. Cf. Kretzmann, N. 1988. "Warring Against the Law of My Mind: Aquinas on Romans 7." In T. Morris, ed. *Philosophy and the Christian Faith*. Notre Dame: University of Notre Dame Press.

33. ST IIaIIae.10.11; 78.1.

34. ST IaIIae.95.5.

35. Ibid., obj. 3.

36. ST IIaIIae.66.7.

37. ST IaIIae.57.5. See also QVDC 13.

38. For the two views see Novak , M. 1983. *Moral Clarity in the Nuclear Age.* Nashville: Thomas Nelson; and Finnis, J. with Boyle, J. and Grisez, G 1984. *Nuclear Deterrence, Morality, and Realism.* New York: Oxford University Press.

39. ST IIaIIae.120.

40. ST IaIIae.96.6; 97.4.

41. ST IaIIae.154.II.

42. ST IaIIae.96.I.

43. ST IIaIIae.78.I.

44. In Sent IV.31.2.

45. ST IIaIIae, 40.I.

46. ST IIaIIae.40.7.

47. See Ramsey, P. 1961. *War and the Christian Conscience.* Durham: Duke University Press, pp. 39ff.

48. See Aertsen, J. A. 1988. *Nature and Creation: Thomas Aquinas's Way of Thought.* Leiden: E.J. Brill. Chapter 1.

49. Finnis, J. 1980. *Natural Law and Natural Rights.* New York: Oxford University Press; McIntyre, A. 1988. *Whose Justice? Which Rationality?* Notre Dame: University of Notre Dame Press; Donagan, A. 1977. *The Theory of Morality.* Chicago: University of Chicago Press.

21
On Thomistic Natural Law

The Bad Man's View of Thomistic Natural Right

Edward A. Goerner

The most important thing that can be done for Thomistic studies in ethics and politics is to make clear that neither the notion of law in general nor of natural law in particular is the foundation of his ethical and political teaching. On the contrary, his teaching about virtue is the foundation of his doctrine. Within the teaching about virtue the natural law doctrine plays quite a subordinate role whose character is, furthermore, quite different from what it is commonly presented to be.

This essay presents only the case for the first part of that broad claim. It argues that the treatment of natural law in the *Summa Theologiae*, if carefully read in context, clearly indicates two crucial things that have commonly been overlooked. First, the natural law is only a second-best, imperfect, and supplementary standard for right action according to nature. Second, the primary and perfect standard of naturally right action is to be found in those parts of the *Summa* that deal with virtue. It would take another, and probably longer, essay to explicate Thomas's treatment of that perfect standard.[1] So this essay only takes the first step. It summarizes the main evidence *within the teaching on law* for rejecting the categorization of St. Thomas Aquinas as primarily a natural law thinker. That evidence also suggests the possibility that a careful treatment of Thomas's teaching on virtue would reveal him as a classical natural right, as opposed to natural law, thinker.

With the late Leo Strauss, I take a natural law theorist to be one who holds that the stan-

dard of natural morality is a law or laws in the sense of universally valid propositions about what it is right or wrong, by nature, to do or not do. Thus to know whether an act is right or wrong it suffices to know whether it conforms to the law or not. That is how Strauss presents Thomas and it is how modern writers about Thomas have generally presented him, whether they are political philosophers or historians of political thought.[2]

In contrast, the natural right theorist is one who, while agreeing that acts may be right or wrong by nature, does not agree that the standard for such rightness is a law or laws in the sense of universally valid propositions. He holds, with Aristotle for example, that objective rules of right are, at best, generalizations that are not universally valid but are changeable according to circumstances (*Ethics* v. 7. 1134b 17–35). Thus the standard of natural right is the judgment of the virtuous man in particular cases rather than any universally valid law. As Leo Strauss puts it: "There is a universally valid hierarchy of ends, but there are no universally valid rules of action."[3]

What is at stake here is of the greatest importance. Thomistic natural law, as commonly interpreted, "is free from the hesitations and ambiguities characteristic of the teachings" of classical natural right. It surpasses in "definiteness and noble simplicity" the classical natural right teaching. But, in so doing, it considerably restricts the "latitude" of statesmanship. In sum, Thomas's natural law teaching can be said to have failed to avoid "the Scylla of 'absolutism.'" The absolutistic and legalistic cast of teachings about natural law tends to provoke the modern revolt, especially in the form of natural rights doctrines, against classical teachings about natural right.[4]

But if Thomas's doctrine about natural law is not such as it has been commonly interpreted, and if he actually places it in a wholly subordinate position to a doctrine of classical natural right, then Aquinas's relationship to modern natural rights theorizing needs to be drastically rethought. The purpose of this essay is merely to take the first step by summarizing the evidence in the Thomistic teaching about law itself, which suggests that the effort required for so deep a revision of our common conceptions about Thomistic political ethics will be fruitful.

I would like to focus the argument exclusively on the so-called[5] "Treatise on Law" in the *Summa Theologiae*. That is not only the most famous and influential passage in St. Thomas's writings where natural law is mentioned but it is also his most comprehensive and systematic treatment of the subject. . . .

The "Treatise on Law" contains a number of strange arguments that draw the careful reader's attention to issues that do not appear on a superficial reading. Moreover, Thomas himself introduces the whole *Summa Theologiae* with a prologue in which he says that the work is written for beginners. He quotes St. Paul (I. Cor. 3: 1–2) saying: "I gave you milk to drink, not meat." Some of the strange arguments that Thomas makes seem designed precisely to call the attention of the mature reader to the fact that the surface argument is indeed milk rather than meat, good for beginners but not good enough for everyone. Indeed, some of those passages seem designed to tell those who are weaned or ready to be weaned how to find the meat. Thomas also says in the Prologue that the order of the parts of his work has been especially fitted to beginners. That is according to the order of teaching and learning (*ordo disciplinae*) rather than "according to what the order of explication of texts requires or according as the occasion for disputing offers itself." So the mature and careful reader ought to be especially concerned with the order within which Thomas places his discussion of law and ought to ask how that context is especially suitable to the teaching of beginners. Naturally, one may wonder why the meat could not be presented directly to beginners. But that question must wait until the natures of the milk, and of the meat, and of the beginners are clear. So let us begin.

Rule by Law and Rule by the Virtuous

In the "Treatise on Law" St. Thomas does not ask directly whether the full standard of natural morality (as distinguished from su-pernatural morality) is the natural law or something else. Nevertheless, the question is raised obliquely in question 95, article 1: "Whether it be useful that some laws be laid down by men?"[6] There he specifically raises an objection (obj. 2) to human lawmaking by citing Aristotle (*Eth.* v. 4. 1132a 27) to the effect that "animate justice is better than inanimate which is contained in laws" and that, therefore, justice ought to be done according to the will of the judge rather than according to a law and the will of a judge. This is the middle objection of three. Thomas deals with the other two in a single sentence each, but the reply to this second objection requires two paragraphs and is almost as long as the body of the article itself. The reply has three distinct arguments none of which alone nor all of which together constitute a full reply to the objection.

Since the objection starts with a citation from Aristotle, the reply to it does also. The objection, as noted above, was drawn from the *Nicomachean Ethics*. The context there is that of a general account of the virtue of justice. The reply to the objection, on the other hand, is drawn from the *Rhetoric* (i. 1. 1354a 31–1354b 22) where the issue is the use of rhetoric to sway the passions of judges and how this perversion of the judicial process can be prevented.

So the reply to the objection bases itself on a text from the *Rhetoric* where the relative merits of the animate justice of the judge and the inanimate justice of the law are directly weighed by Aristotle only in a narrow context—a less theoretical context (conceding specific imperfections) than the broad and theoretical context of the passage in the objection itself. One who is looking for meat must ask whether the reply would have gone the same way if the broad, theoretical context of the objection had been accepted. Let us look at the argument of the reply in somewhat greater detail.

St. Thomas simply paraphrases Aristotle's argument in the *Rhetoric*. The first point is that it is easier to find enough wise men to make good laws than to find enough wise men to judge all cases. But notice that this argument does not deny, in principle, the original objection that animate justice is better than inanimate justice. It simply poses a practical difficulty in the way of obtaining the very best justice in most situations and offers a solution for that statistically normal, but morally abnormal, majority of situations.

Second, lawmakers are said to consider, long beforehand, what is best and to consider many cases, whereas judgment on particular cases is under the press of time. But that argument applies only to judges who lack the leisure and inclination to think on such matters before the case. If they lack leisure, it would be hard to see how they had become wise. If they lack the inclination to think on such matters, even though they know that they are to be judges, then they are surely not wise. So the wise judge will be one who has considered many cases over a long time to discover what is usually most just and who adds to that his prudential judgment of the individual case before him, which may have peculiar features requiring a decision unlike the usual one that would be formulated as a law.

Third, he notes that lawgivers judge about universals, and not about particulars and about matters in the future rather than the present. In judging present particulars men are more easily swayed from the course of justice by some personal passion or interest. Again, the argument has great practical force for the general run of situations but does not deal with the objection in principle since it *assumes* judges whose virtue is imperfect.

In a society not addicted to lawsuits one might find enough wise men to act as judges, wise men with the leisure and inclination to meditate on matters of justice, wise men sufficiently mature in virtue not to be deflected by personal passion or interest. In such a society the dictum of the *Rhetoric* that it is better for all to be regulated by law rather than the will of judges is untrue.

But St. Thomas did not set out to answer whether it is *always* useful to have the laws decide as much as possible and the judges as little as possible any more than Aristotle did in the *Rhetoric*. The argument in the *Rhetoric* makes clear that Aristotle is talking about the problems caused by the practice of foren-

sic rhetoric before *popular* law courts and democratic assemblies of the Athenian type, i.e., before a mass of men who do not have the leisure for the study of matters of justice, and who, are not preeminent (by definition) in wisdom and virtue. Now medieval judicial practice was not the same as the Athenian but, no more than Aristotle in Athens, could St. Thomas assume that medieval judges and juries were ordinarily wise men in the philosophic sense. The milk-drinkers, the beginning students in theology, are given sound practical advice likely to help the cause of justice in most cases, but those capable of eating meat can see that the matter is not theoretically quite what it seems on the surface.

Our concern here is not with the organization of human judicial systems, but with the divine government of the world by natural law. The primary governor by natural law is not man, according to St. Thomas, but God, in whose eternal law men only participate by what is called natural law (q. 93, a. 6, resp). So the question at issue here is whether the divine government of the world insofar as it affects human action is *first and foremost* to be spoken of as a government by law or, on the other hand, is first and foremost to be spoken of in analogy with the government of comprehensive kingship or all-kingship, the *omnimodum regnum . . .* of Book III of Aristotle's *Politics* (1276a 8–9). Indeed the last reference to Aristotle in question 95, with which we have been dealing, is to Book III, ch. 7 of the *Politics* where Aristotle sets up his typology of constitutions, including kingship, a subject that Aristotle concludes by the discussion of all-kingship at the end of Book III.

The "Treatise" on law shows God as governing the world by law, i.e., governing as a law-giver and judge rather [than] as an all-king. But the careful reader will notice that none of the reasons why men find it useful to have their wise men be lawgivers rather than kings applies to God. All the arguments that St. Thomas borrows from the *Rhetoric* to establish the superiority of rule by law to rule by men are arguments based on some human defect: (1) there are too few wise men; (2) men find it hard to judge particular cases under pressure of time; (3) men are deflected from doing justice by their passions. But, surely, none of those defects are thought by St. Thomas to be found in God too. So the question arises as to whether God *does* rule men as a law-giver rather than as an all-king and, if so, why?

The first thing to notice is that the treatment of God as governing the world by law is not the first treatment of the divine government of the world in the *Summa*. Earlier, in the First Part, St. Thomas speaks of the divine government as a government by providence. There he makes clear that divine providence is perfect government, and that perfect government is government of individuals as such rather than a government that controls only species or classes as would a law (I, q. 92, art. 1, resp.; I, q. 103, art. 6, resp.). The issue here is a major one, and Thomas calls our attention to the fact that his teaching differs from most of the philosophic tradition. He says his claim, that God governs the universe by a providence that governs each individual being, is at odds not only with Democritus and the Epicureans, who denied all providence, but also with "others," whom he doesn't name, who taught that corruptible substances were not subject to divine government of their individual being but only in their species. The "others" seem to be mainly Aristotle and Averroes (cf. *In I Sent.*, d. xxxix, q.2, a.2).

In short, St. Thomas seems to say two grossly incompatible things about the divine government of the world in the *Summa*. In the First Part he says God governs individuals by providence, i.e., like an all-king rather than a lawgiver. In the "Treatise on Law" he says that God governs the world by the eternal law (of which natural law is the human participation) and that laws treat things in general classes rather than as individuals. How are we to reconcile those arguments? To raise such a question fruitfully requires some attention at first to the overall order or structure of the work, an order to which Thomas explicitly calls attention in the Prologue.

Fear of the Law and the Freedom of Virtue

The *Summa Theologiae* is divided into three main parts of which the first two are of interest to us here. The First Part deals with God and His creative work. The Second Part deals with the principles of human action. One might even speak of the First Part as Thomas's theology, and of the Second Part as his ethics. It is in this theology, i.e., in the First Part, that Thomas goes to great pains to insist upon God's governing the universe by a providence that deals with individuals. It is only in his ethics, i.e., in the Second Part, that he speaks of God governing the world by law.

The ethics, or Second Part, is itself divided into two parts, since ethics can be treated in two ways. The principles of human action can be treated in general terms; that is the burden of the First Part of the Second Part, (cf., I–II, prologue). The principles of action can also be treated in particular, i.e., in terms of particular virtues and vices; that is the burden of the Second Part of the Second Part (cf., II–II, prologue). The "Treatise" on Law falls in the First Part of the Second Part. That is to say God is presented as governing the world by the eternal law (in which man participates by natural law) only in that part of the *Summa* that deals with ethics in general. A consideration of the specific order of this First Part of the Second Part and of the place of the "Treatise" on Law within it will help in understanding how the eternal and natural laws are to be understood.

The treatment of ethics in general (i.e. I–II) opens with a discussion of the ultimate end of man as the first principle of human action. It comes to the conclusion that the end of human action is a specific human act, by nature contemplation and by grace the direct vision of the divine essence (qq. 1–5). The question then arises as to how one might be enabled to perform such an act. So there follows a discussion of human action and passion (qq. 6–48). Human acts are said to be led to their proper end by two sorts of principles: intrinsic or interior and extrinsic or exterior.

The intrinsic principles are the human powers as developed in the virtues (qq. 49–70). Insofar as man acts by virtue, intellectual and practical, he realizes in himself the latent image of God; he is, albeit only in a secondary way, an intellectual causal source of order in the created world. However, man is defective in this regard: he sometimes does things badly out of ignorance and sometimes out of sin and vice (qq. 71–89). Now if men always knew everything they were capable of knowing, both as individuals and societies, and never acted maliciously, the order of the world intended by God's government would be realized. But men obviously do not always act virtuously. Thomas thus looks for the means whereby God, who cannot fail of His purposes, achieves His intended universal order in spite of human weakness, i.e., in spite of the fact that men do not of their own inner desire do the works of virtue. That is to say, Thomas looks for external or exterior principles of human acts, causes other than the habitually virtuous human powers.

Here is where the "Treatise on Law" comes in the *Summa Theologiae* (qq. 90–108). Law is the first of two ways by which God, as the extrinsic principle of good human acts, leads men to do good deeds in spite of themselves and their weakness. But law is not a sufficient external corrective for vice. The second way that God achieves the correction of men is grace. The externality of grace is less than that of law, since grace conforms the desire of the soul in such a way that it can even be said to be a quality of the soul (q. 110). Consequently, law, as most external, is discussed first, and then grace. Both discussions constitute a long digression from the discussion of virtue which had to be left off after a general treatment in order to confront the problem of vice and its relation to the ability of God to govern the world. Only after the treatment of God's external correctives (law and grace) for human defect does St. Thomas return to the subject of the virtues, the detailed treatment of which forms the whole of the Second Part of the Second Part.

This, then, is the context within which the "Treatise" on Law must be read. Men are not born perfect in virtue. They are born only with a capacity for virtue from the fulfillment of which they are powerfully distracted by ignorance and malice. The role of law is merely that of a corrective for a defect. Law is "a kind of training (*disciplina*) that compels by fear of punishments" (q. 95, art. 1 resp.). Law, whether human or divine, habituates men to avoiding evil and doing good *for fear of punishment. Sometimes* they grow to take pleasure in so acting. Then they no longer do the acts of the virtuous out of fear, but only out of virtue itself, i.e., of their own will. Of course, some men never come to virtue. For them the law must always be ready with its punishments so that the rest of the community can be left in peace (q. 92, art. 2 and q. 95, art. 1, resp.). At its worst, law is a kind of barrier to complete social disorder. At its best, it is merely a propaedeutic to virtue. Consequently, law, including natural laws, must be understood in relation to that for which it is a propaedeutic, namely virtue. Any full understanding of Thomas's ethics and politics, both natural and supernatural, must focus primarily on his treatment of virtue rather than law.

This point is confirmed by a review of the particular theological problems that Thomas is faced with in writing a book on theology for beginners. On the level of theological ethics, rather than natural ethics, Thomas has to deal with the relationship of the law of Moses, the Old Law, as he calls it, to the grace of Christ. There is a special danger that a careful Christian writer on these matters needs to face. There is a considerable danger of antinomianism in the Christian tradition, reflected in both the New Testament and the Church fathers. Thus, St. Paul says, "Where the spirit of the Lord is, there is liberty" (2 Cor. 3:15) and St. James speaks of the Gospel as "the law of perfect liberty" (Jas. 1:25) and St. Augustine says, ironically, "there is little difference between the Law and the Gospel, fear [*timor*] and love [*amor*]" (*Contra Adimant.*, xvii) all of which St. Thomas cites. But there is not only a permanent *danger* of Christian antinomianism. There was a very serious range of powerful antinomian currents in medieval society. It was not unheard of for milk drinkers to throw off all restraints, claiming the liberty of the Gospel. A whole range of more or less interrelated politico-ecclesiastical movements claimed one sort or another of Spirit-filled perfection that put them above all secular and ecclesiastical authority and the laws of those authorities, natural or divine. This is not the place for a discussion of those movements, but it is important to note that St. Thomas himself draws attention to the problem by devoting article 4 of question 106 precisely to the claim that the New Law of grace (and thus all ecclesiastical law and authority based on it) is to be superceded by an age of the Holy Spirit in which "spiritual men" in "a more perfect state" will rule (*principabuntur*). It is precisely this kind of milleniaristic enthusiasm (represented by the speculations of such men as Abbott Joachim of Fiore) for existence under supposedly Spirit-filled *perfecti* beyond all law, lay and ecclesiastical, that is common enough in the middle ages and that St. Thomas refutes for his theological beginners. The denial of a Third Age of the Spirit is part of St. Thomas's very nuanced treatment of the Gospel as the New Law with which the treatment of law concludes and toward which it is aimed. Having treated the Old Law—the letter, he turns to the Gospel—the Spirit. But he argues for a certain continuity between the law of Moses and the Gospel: even the Gospel is experienced as law, is presented in writing and in dogmas and in required external acts such as sacraments. Consequently, even the Gospel can be called a law, the New Law. That is the case even though the "New Law is principally the grace itself of the Holy Spirit" (q. 106, art. I resp.). Only in a secondary way does the Gospel contain such things as rules and external acts that dispose one to the reception of grace. And grace itself is distinct from law (q. 90, prologue). Therefore it is dealt with in the so-called "Treatise" on grace that, following the "Treatise" on law, concludes the First Part of the Second Part.

In short, the careful reader notes that St. Thomas, a theologian who must write to beginning theologians about such heady stuff as the liberty of the Gospel and the supremacy of Spirit over letter, of love over fear and command, is very careful to validate the letter, and constraint, and fear, and command as having a due function in the education and public order of men. And he is very careful to do that before speaking of the heady stuff of grace. And he is careful not to separate them (though he distinguishes them) so that grace itself is accompanied by an appropriate legal propaedeutic. Nevertheless, it is grace, it is love, it is the prompting of the Holy Spirit that is the center and standard of his *Christian* moral teaching.

One other point needs to be made about Thomas's treatment of law and virtue in his theological or supernatural ethics before returning to his natural ethics. First, there is a dynamic of human development, both individually and socially, from innocence to sin, to law, to grace, to virtue. Socially the development in question is the history of innocence and fall into sin, followed by the law given by Moses, then the Gospel announced by Christ followed by the full life of the theological virtues: faith, hope and charity (see e.g., q. 98, arts. 1 and 6).

The case of natural morality is similar. Natural law and natural virtue are the analogues, respectively, of the supernatural Old Law and supernatural virtue. There is even a considerable overlap since the supernatural Old Law is said to contain, among other things, the natural law (q. 98, art. 5, resp.), which had become obscured even for good men by the "exuberance of sin" (q. 98, art. 6, resp.). Note that the implication is that the natural law is known, at least partly, in a social manner—a point that we shall return to.

In any case, the natural law, like all law (cf., q. 92, art. 2, ad 3), is an external constraint effective through fear of punishment whereas natural virtue is an internal principle effective by love of the good. Thus natural law is, at best, propaedeutic to virtue as the Old Law is propaedeutic to supernatural virtue. Consequently, the teachings about virtue must be theoretically prior (even though some of them are temporally subsequent) to the teachings about law, since the perfect is always theoretically prior to the imperfect and the end is theoretically prior to the means. That is to say, a full understanding of Thomas's natural ethics must rest on his teaching about natural virtue rather than about natural law.

But the foregoing argument may be granted and still the objection be raised: all that has been said so far seems to apply only to the motive for which good is done and evil avoided (i.e., fear of punishment vs. pleasure in good deeds) but not to the content of morality. As to content, Thomas may envisage good and evil seen from the perspective of the virtuous man to be identical to the content of the natural law. Then the charge against Thomas's ethics still stands: it is inflexible, unpolitically (even antipolitically) inflexible and, thus, unreasonable.

I have already suggested the broad grounds on which one ought to suspect that such an objection is mistaken, namely Thomas's argument in the First Part that government that touches particulars is superior to government that only reaches classes of things (I, q. 22, art. 2, resp.; I, q. 103, art. 6, resp.). But let us see how he treats the matter in the "Treatise" on Law.

St. Thomas calls attention to the problem in a strange passage in the "Treatise" (q. 91, art. 1, resp.; and cf. art. 2, resp.). He writes:

> Now it is evident, supposing that the world is ruled by divine providence, as is stated in the First Part, that the whole community of the universe is governed by the divine reason. And, therefore, the very idea of the government of things, existing in God as in the principle of the universe, has the nature of law.

St. Thomas calls that law (of Providence) the eternal law (*lex aeterna*). The natural law (*lex naturalis*) is said, in the next article, to be a human participation in the eternal law, a participation in divine providence. One's surprise at this seeming identification of law and providence is sustained when one notes that Thomas does indeed think that laws do not deal with particulars (q. 91, art. 1). This surprising identification of two things that had previously been most clearly distinguished seems designed to encourage the mature and reflective reader to proceed most cautiously.[7]

There is a common element in rule by law and rule by providence: both involve the rule of a community by reason (q. 91, art. 1). The general subject under discussion here is the ruling of the universe by the divine reason. The specific subject under discussion in the ethical part of the *Summa Theologiae* is God's government of the universe through man as a secondary cause who, by virtue of his reason, is endowed with free choice (I, q. 22, art. 2, ad 2). The specific part of that subject under discussion in the "Treatise" on Law is God's manner of governing human affairs so as to achieve His intended universal order in spite of the fact that human beings are not always virtuous. The problem is this: how can God constrain human action to conform to His natural order without destroying the essence of man which is to be a reasonable creature with free choice? Thomas's answer is the natural law.

All of Thomas's discussions of divine government necessarily proceed from its analogy with human experiences of government because one cannot talk directly about God's essence or activity inasmuch as we do not know them (I, q. 12). Consequently, talk about God governing man through the medium of natural law rests on the primary experience of human government by law. Thomas, as we have already seen, lays out the reasons for government by law in response to the question: "whether it was useful for laws to be laid down by men?" (q. 95, art. 1). He there argues that there is in man only a natural *aptitude* for virtue, but that aptitude has to be developed to reality by some kind of training. It is important here to note how broad Thomas's notion of human virtue is. It includes the ability to master the means to food and clothing. But all that man has *naturally* for such purposes is "reason and hands." All the rest, in the way of tools and technique, he has to acquire by some training (*disciplina*). The problem is that discipline or training is not itself pleasant. So the perfecting of virtue "chiefly consists in withdrawing man from undue pleasures, to which men are especially inclined, and most of all the young with respect to whom discipline is more efficacious." So he needs a trainer. Now some young men are inclined to virtue by a naturally good disposition, or by custom, or rather by a divine gift, and they can be trained by paternal discipline which works by admonitions. But there are others, inclined to vice, who cannot easily be moved by words. They "have to be restrained from evil by force and fear" so that they leave others in peace. Sometimes these unruly chaps, from being habituated to act well, come rather to like and to do voluntarily what before they did for fear of punishment "and so they become virtuous men."

Such training could be given by individual virtuous trainers or by human laws. We have already seen Thomas's argument that such discipline is normally the work of human legislation rather than the work of virtuous individuals governing particular cases. I argued there that the lack of virtuous rulers had no direct and obvious analogy in the divine government of the world. But it can now be seen that such a lack does, in fact, have an analogy in the indirect mode of governing the world that Thomas attributes to God in his notion of natural law. Insofar as men have a share in governing the world (a share that Thomas sees as expanding with the development of technique and tools), God governs the world by secondary causes that have reason and free choice. If God retains a control over the actions of those human agents by a natural law it will have to be understood by analogy to the operation of human law. That is to say nature itself had to be structured in such a way that violators of the natural law are punished by nature itself. Furthermore, the natural relationship between the act and its punishment will have to be seen by human reason or the punishment could not have the deterrent and training effects that Thomas attributes to law in general.

Now, how ought such a natural law be envisaged as operating? On the surface, the beginner, the "drinker of milk," will notice Thomas saying that the natural law is unchangeable in its first principles (q. 94, art. 5); and he will notice that the natural law's first and common precepts are known to all whereas only its secondary precepts (which are like proximate conclusions drawn from these principles) are not known to all (q. 94, art. 6, resp.). That seems to sustain, at least in part, the charge that Thomas's natural law teaching is unpolitically and, so, unreasonably inflexible. But one wonders: how general are those first precepts or principles of natural law? Are they as legalistically inflexible as charged? How are they promulgated naturally? How are they made efficacious through fear of punishment?

None of those questions is directly answered in what is surely a marvelously brief treatment by Thomas of so celebrated a subject, a treatment whose surface certainly seems to encourage a certain legalism. Nevertheless, Thomas gives a few striking clues as to how to answer such questions. I should like to follow up one of them in detail.

The Case of the German Robbers

Although the first precepts of natural law are known to all men, according to Thomas, they are evidently of the most general nature, as one gathers from occasional examples. Drawing from Caesar's *De bello gallico* (vi. 23), he remarks that "among the Germans robbery or raiding (*latrocinium*) was not thought to be unjust although it is expressly against the law of nature" (q. 94, art. 4, resp. and cf. art. 6, resp.). The only other case he mentions of a precept of the natural law being unknown among some men is that of "vices against nature" where the reference to Romans 1:24 makes clear that it is a question of sexual perversion. So natural law precepts forbidding robbery and sexual perversion must be only secondary precepts because the primary precepts are known to all. A little reflection on the case of robbery among the Germans can help to clarify both how natural law works, what sort of contents it has, and how it relates to virtue.

Let us assume with Thomas (q. 94, art. 6, resp.) that robbery or raiding or piracy or freebooting is prohibited by one of those secondary precepts of the natural law that are nevertheless very close to the first principles which are known by all. How is it that they could not have known that robbery was against a precept of the natural law? Moreover, since the Germans knew that precept in Thomas's time and were, one must presume, punished by nature when they broke it, were they not punished by nature in Caesar's time? Or is it that they were punished in

Caesar's time but did not know it was a punishment? We cannot assume that they knew they were punished but chose to break the law anyway, because Thomas says they didn't even know robbery was unjust and so could not see any natural consequences as a punishment.

To begin with, Caesar's famous raiding or robbing Germans did not think all robbery was just. They only thought it good if practiced against people outside the community of the raiders, as is clear from the passage in Caesar to which Thomas referred. A society that thought all robbery was good would be a society with no stable property, and, therefore, scarcely any technical mastery of nature.

Insofar as some fairly extensive human artifice is prerequisite to, and contributes to, satisfying the general human inclination to individual self-preservation, to biological and cultural procreation, to the leisure for sociability and learning—all of which men naturally desire (q. 94, a. 2. resp.)—men cannot, without suffering the consequences, either argue or act as if robbery is simply good.

In the context of the very crude economy of the Germanic tribes, based on a mixture of hunting, gathering, agriculture and herding, a substantial amount of raiding other groups and being raided by them existed without utterly undermining the economic structure upon which group life rested. Raiding can be viewed as a kind of hunting-gathering activity. It is, furthermore, a more attractive mode of acquiring wealth than farming to a people that have not yet harnessed themselves to the hard discipline of agriculture. Finally, contact with the Roman Empire allowed for a vast expansion of the raiding ethic without immediately disastrous consequences.

For a long time, the Empire maintained a high level of material prosperity rooted in stable property over vast areas west and south of the Rhine. That structure was rich enough to withstand great amounts of raiding over a long period of time during which the Germans did not find it necessary to take any responsibility for maintaining the productivity of the Roman economy, nor did they find that their raids permanently diminished the booty anymore than picking raspberries this year prevents next year's crop. Only when the raiding began to take on the proportions of whole peoples moving through and sacking the Empire did the Roman economy collapse and the seemingly inexhaustible source of booty dry up. Then the invading hordes, conquerors of an indigenous agricultural population, began the long, hard political process of reconstituting an order that suppressed the endemic robbery of the Dark Ages. In order to enjoy what was left of what they had taken from the Romans and in order to raise the defense forces necessary to protect it from the next wave of robbers, the Franks, for example, worked to set up a stable order of property that allowed the slow economic redevelopment of Gaul and parts of Germany. They had learned from nature itself the precept forbidding raiding.

Now laws, according to Thomas, discipline the unvirtuous, training them through fear of punishment. A natural law must punish through consequences that in some way flow naturally from the crime. The kind of training through punishment that the natural law imposes would seem to be just the sort of slow social learning process whereby Germanic, northern Europeans, who liked nothing better than a good raid, had been painfully and imperfectly learning for a millennium that robbery, *as a way of life*, doesn't pay for technically developed societies living together.

The natural law prohibition of robbery, so understood, fits Thomas's definition of law (q. 90, a. 4, resp.). It is a rule of reason, first of all of the reason or intelligible principle in the order of nature itself and secondly of human reason that comes to know it. It is directed at the common good of society rather than the good of some individual. Finally, it is promulgated in the way peculiar to natural law. The rational creature, he says (q. 91, art. 2, resp.), has a share of Providence, by "being provident for itself and others." That "being provident" by men is natural in that man has a natural inclination to his "proper act and end." But the natural law does not promulgate the forms and modalities of property relationships, which necessarily vary according to the economic activities with which they are associated. They have to be worked out by reason in relation to the particular economy of a society. So human law, in the article immediately following that on natural law (i.e., q. 91 art. 3), works out the particulars of such things as property.

But then it necessarily follows that robbery (*lactrocinium*) is only understood in a very general sort of way by natural law since property[8] is itself only defined in its particulars by human law. And the prohibition of robbery by natural law only comes to be effectively promulgated through the slow process by which peoples come to know the relationships between stable property and the relatively high levels of economic development upon which depend high development of the leisured pursuits of sociability and learning, in other words, of civilization. Men are naturally but imperfectly drawn to these last as to their appropriate act and end.

If natural law as a whole is understood analogously to the foregoing treatment of robbery, then it is a kind of crude, rough and external rule of right that comes to be known by discovering the relationship between behavior outside the rule and the natural consequences of that behavior. Then the consequences are seen as punishments for violating the order of nature. And only then do human lawmakers devise new laws with a view to the social reform required by the discovery of this precept of the natural law.

But what kind of wisdom is necessary to legislate against robbery? Is it not possible for a leader, even mad with avarice but disciplined by cunning and calculation, to legislate against robbery for a people who have relished it? Will he not find it useful to urge his less-than-perfectly virtuous people to accept his new laws because, under new circumstances, their (and his) acquisitive desires can be more fully indulged in a system of widespread security of property and its attendant economic expansion? That kind of sagacity seems to be produced by the encounter of reason and the laws of nature, i.e., a law naturally efficacious through fear of the natural consequences of violating it.

In short, natural law is the bad man's view of natural right.[9] It was precisely in terms of

controlling even the bad men that Thomas introduced the whole discussion of such external principles controlling human acts as natural law. But such base wisdom is unlikely to be the full standard of naturally right-doing for men. Will the full standard of ethics not have to be that seen by the wise and virtuous, whether individuals or communities?

One could grant all of this and still argue: perhaps the ethical standard of the wise and virtuous might add other things to the standard of the natural law, but still be identical to the latter in matters that it touches, such as robbery. In that case the charge that natural law is unpolitically and, therefore, unreasonably inflexible would still stand. Perhaps a closer look at the case of robbery will provide an answer.

Let us assume that a people of raiders, like the Franks, have come to discover the natural precept against raiding and that raiding has been additionally prohibited by human legislation and rather successfully repressed in fact.... Let us further assume that a community of such people is suffering from a most severe famine due to unseasonable floods, while a neighboring community is blessed with such abundance that considerable food rots for lack of demand. Assume that the former have no money to buy the latter's surplus and that the latter refuse to give it away. Will the natural law precept against raiding or robbery prohibit the starving from taking by force from the rich the means to subsistence? If it can reasonably be argued that it would prohibit such a raid, then the charge against natural law teaching that it is unreasonably inflexible will be a fair charge.

But recall that the natural law is promulgated to men by way of their reasoned discovery of the good or bad consequences of doing one thing or another, and that it is efficacious by fear of the punishment in the form of bad consequences that naturally flow from doing the prohibited acts. Will the starving men of the first community think that some raiding and its attendant economic disorder is worse, more unjust, or more morally unfitting, than allowing the community to starve to death while food rots among the rich? They will only think such nonsense insofar as they have somehow become captivated by the unnatural and rigid legalism that both the opponents and many of the proponents of natural law ethics have saddled it with.

But, if they undertake raids to get the wherewithal to satisfy their hunger, there are a whole range of important questions left: how much raiding is justified? how many will be killed? how long should the raiding go on? who should do it? if it goes on for a long time, how many young men will be lured by that experience into a love of the vicious, murderous, but exciting life of the freebooter? how can peaceful relations ever be reestablished with the neighbors? how can the wounds be bound up, healed and cleansed? Those are questions that the crude, rough and ready, external constraint of the natural law does not easily go far to answering.

As Thomas points out, the natural law's precepts, except for its most general platitudes (e.g., do good and avoid evil), may fail to be *right* in some cases even when known (q. 94, art. 4, resp.). That is the case because the natural rightness or wrongness of human acts is ultimately to be understood according to Thomas in terms of the natural end of mankind. That is the reason that he begins the ethical part of the *Summa* with a discussion of the end of human life (I–II, qq. 1–5), which he believes Aristotle has demonstrated to be the happiness of contemplative wisdom (I–II, q. 3 and cf. SCG, Bk. III, chs. 37–47).

From the point of view of the roots of universal order, perceived by the contemplative, it is possible to judge intelligently how far a particular moral rule does or does not aid in developing, in realizing, the final end of man. That is the role of the wise man who, knowing and willing the end, by rational necessity wills the means thereto (q. 90, art. 1, ad. 3). But law, as has been shown is precisely for those who do not perfectly know and will the final end. The unwise only will their human happiness imperfectly, perhaps only this or that subordinate part of it or perhaps the whole of it but ill understood (it was in that sense I called them "bad"). So the nat-

ural law precepts only tend to converge *toward* the wisdom of the virtuous sage or philosopher.

Consequently, the standard of right in such a difficult case as I asked the reader to assume cannot be the general propositions of the natural law, rules of which even "bad" men can see the wisdom. The full standard of right can only be the judgement of the temperate wisdom of a virtuous man who can choose well because he knows and loves the good rather than the judgment of the intemperate, the unwise, or the vicious who nevertheless refrains from some evils for fear of the consequences. To gain an adequate understanding of Thomas's ethics, one must go primarily to his teaching about virtue which precedes and follows the excursus on law (i.e., to I–II, qq. 1–89 and II–II).

The Rhetorical Problem

If I am right in the foregoing argument that Thomas's natural ethics is fundamentally a natural right teaching rather than one of natural law, the question nevertheless arises: how is it that his natural ethics has been so widely mistaken for an ethics of natural law? There seem to be a number of reasons, at least one of them due to Thomas's editors rather than to Thomas himself.

He himself did not divide the *Summa Theologiae* into "treatises." That seems to be the work of later editors. But, once the work is separated into distinct treatises, the reader interested in political theory is easily led to take the "Treatise" on Law and read it as if it were meant to be taken as a separate work rather than, as I have argued, an integral and theoretically quite subordinate part of a larger and theoretically seamless whole.

Still, it must be said that the format that Thomas adopts for the work surely allows, if it does not actually encourage, just such a misunderstanding and misediting as culminates in the separate publication of sections of the whole work as if they were separate treatises. Thomas writes in the formal question and answer format of the medieval schools. A highly systematic writer, he groups the questions so that the work can be mistaken for a kind of reference encyclopedia to which one has recourse to look up questions that occur at random. Such a practice became easy once editors added schematic tables of contents with the questions grouped under "Treatise" headings.

In any case, Thomas wrote for beginners in theology in an academic system in which a degree did not require some special evidence of saintly sagacity. So just as he found it prudent to emphasize the continuity from supernatural law to grace to virtue, he seems to have found it wise to do analogously with the continuity from natural law to philosophy to virtue for men who, though they had studied philosophy, were not necessarily philosophers in the sense of virtuous sages. In both cases showing the substantial overlap between law and philosophy or grace tends to restrain the newly learned from a certain sophomoric conceit that they are simply beyond any need to consult the law.

Finally, the brevity of Thomas's remarks on natural law (given its minor role in the work as a whole) is such that there is no place for much elaboration of the content of those crucial terms: "primary precepts" (unchangeable) and "secondary precepts" (changeable). But the Western Church has a powerfully legalistic thrust to its morality. Resting on the Roman legal tradition, the Church had developed an elaborate body of canon law and an elaborate system of ecclesiastical courts for dealing with morals. In such an environment it was practically inevitable that there grow up a tradition in which Thomas's teaching on law should be given a role and an interpretation he had not intended. My suspicion is that the unfortunate emphasis on Thomas's natural law teaching is something that develops especially with the split in the western church at the Reformation and Counter-Reformation which tend to reinforce the naturalistic and legalistic strands in Catholicism. Whether that suspicion is true is a matter for careful and extensive historical research. But, however such research may turn out, the time has come for political theorists to return to Thomas's text, as it was written, and to focus on his teaching about virtue rather than on law.

Notes

1. For the main lines of such an investigation see Leon John Ross, *Natural Right and Natural Law in Thomas Aquinas*, Ph.D. dissertation, University of Chicago, 1971.

2. Leo Strauss, *Natural Right and History* (Chicago: Univ. of Chicago Press,1953), pp.162–164 and cf., Harry V. Jaffa, *Thomism and Aristotelianism* (Chicago: Univ. of Chicago Press, 1952), pp. 167–188.

   Although the historians of political thought do not commonly make Strauss' distinction between natural law and natural right in so direct a fashion, they are one with Strauss in emphasizing the centrality of the concept of natural law in St. Thomas's ethical and political theory. . . .

3. *Natural Right and History,* p. 162.

4. Ibid., pp. 163–164.

5. Thomas's text itself is not separated into parts under "treatise" titles. The practice of assigning titles to groups of questions in the *Summa Theologiae* and calling those sections "treatises" is the work of editors of Thomas rather than of Thomas himself. This fact is of some importance to later parts of my argument.

6. All references to the *Summa Theologiae,* unless otherwise noted, are to the First Part of the Second Part. All translations, unless otherwise noted, are my own.

7. I am here following the Straussian procedure of assuming that, when one encounters a great thinker making what seems to be such a blunder as would shame an intelligent schoolboy one ought seriously to entertain the possibility that the thinker himself was aware of it—all the more so when he is a writer as systematic as Thomas Aquinas.

8. Perhaps I should remark that the property in question is not necessarily or exclusively private property. It may just as well be communal property.

9. It is not, of course, a question of absolute badness. To begin with, nothing is absolutely bad for Thomas since existence itself is good. Furthermore, laws, including natural law, are effective precisely insofar as those subject to them are not utterly bereft of rational judgment in moral matters. They are effective only insofar as bad men are still not so corrupted that they are unable to see precisely that the punishment is worse than the crime. (If they are so mad as to think the punishment good, the law is useless.) That is the minimum kind of human goodness of judgment

and will that even bad men have to some degree. Without it human life in a common world would be an utterly unbearable chaos.

Reprinted from: Edward A. Goerner, "On Thomistic Natural Law: The Bad Man's View of Thomistic Natural Right." In *Political Theory*, Volume 7, Issue 1, pp. 101–122. Copyright © 1979. Reprinted by permission of Sage Publications, Inc. ✦

Christine de Pizan

Born in Venice circa 1364, de Pizan was the daughter of a physician and astrologer who was called to the court of King Charles V of France in 1368. By 1380, de Pizan had entered a happy marriage to Etienne de Castel, a royal secretary. Ten years later, however, both her father and her husband died in quick succession. She thus became a widow, embroiled in legal difficulties, and faced with the task of supporting not only her three children, but also her mother and a niece. Beset by various misfortunes, de Pizan both consoled and educated herself by reading books in history, the sciences, and poetry. During these studies, she found instruction and inspiration in a book by Eustache Deschamps on the craft of writing poetry. De Pizan thus turned to writing commissioned poems and ballads as a means of earning a living.

Christine de Pizan soon became fairly well known as a literary figure in many of the courts of Europe. Even today, many scholars regard her as the first female professional writer. But just as she was a *professional* writer, she was also a self-consciously *female* writer. Her concerns and experiences took center stage in her work, with de Pizan often appearing as a character and independent voice. In many respects, she "was the first writer to address the tradition of misogyny prevalent in both the society and literature of her time from a female perspective. She made herself a champion for women by illustrating their achievements in culture and history and by emphasizing their intellectual equality."[1] Though some scholars regard her as a protofeminist, others have reminded us that de Pizan by no means advocated any fundamental transformation of established social roles.

One can see both her feminism and her caution in the moral and political works that de Pizan began to write in the early 15th century. Composed during a time when French court politics was riven by conflict and intrigue, her prose works underscored such important Christian ideals as virtuous conduct, compassion for others, and stoic acceptance of misfortune. Just prior to her death in 1430, amid the political disarray confronting France at the time, she devoted her last major work to telling the story of Joan of Arc. During the next century, Christine de Pizan achieved the literary immortality she had long desired.

The Book of the City of Ladies

The Book of the City of Ladies (1405) has sometimes been described as an early feminist utopia. De Pizan begins the book by noting that the philosophers and poets of the past had all come to the same conclusion: "that the behavior of women is inclined to and full of every vice."[2] Since her conversations with women as well as her own experience showed that women were quite otherwise, de Pizan wonders why men have been so eager to believe the worst about women. In the book, her lamentations result in a vision of three crowned ladies—the virtues of Reason, Rectitude, and Justice—who guide de Pizan's creation of a symbolic city of ladies. In that city, built by and for women, "the most worthy among them would be invited to dwell, free from the demands and the preoccupations of the world."[3]

In the book, each virtue comes to de Pizan to assist her in building a distinct portion of the city. Each also provides *exempla*, stories of worthy women, to show that what men have been saying about women throughout history is demonstrably false. Reason, for example, details the stories of women who have made important discoveries, founded civilizations, and fought bravely. Rectitude tells stories that show the good and noble character of most women—such as daughters who love and care for their parents, or wives who show great patience and constancy of heart. The book's final part presents the words of Justice, with her tales of the saints and her introduction of the Virgin Mary, Queen of Heaven, who is to rule over the city. De Pizan closes with the admonition for women to be well-informed so they may defend their honor and to show their virtue so that men's lies will be seen for what they are.

The Book of the Body Politic

Christine de Pizan wrote *The Book of the Body Politic* (1406) for Louis of Guyenne, the teenage heir to the throne of France. Like other books in the "mirror for princes" genre, it was designed to both educate and entertain a current or future monarch. In this work, a simplified version of John of Salisbury's detailed metaphor of the body politic provides the structure for the argument. John's work, *Policraticus*, is not mentioned directly as the source of the image, but in de Pizan's hands, the metaphor works as follows: the prince is the head, the nobles and knights are the hands and arms, while the common people function as the belly, legs, and feet. Her goal appears to be that of teaching each estate or class in the community the proper moral duties for its station in life.

Indeed, the lesson of the book is that, since virtue alone brings happiness, it ought to regulate the whole of life for each estate. Part One of the book identifies three virtues necessary for the prince, who must love God, love the good, and love justice, if the body politic is to become and remain healthy. Part Two suggests that, although the cardinal virtues remain the same for all classes, the knights and nobles must possess additional sources of merit—skill at arms, honor, loyalty, as well as a practical wisdom suited to warfare. Employing metaphors reminiscent of Plato's *Republic*, de Pizan asserts that, just as the prince must be a good shepherd, these knights and nobles should serve the role of effective guard dogs. In the final part of the book, de Pizan urges the common people to do their work humbly and obediently. They are also told to remain loyal to the prince, though she urges the prince to act with such compassion and respect that the people have no great desire to rebel. For de Pizan, the long-term guarantee of health for the body politic lies in whatever concord and unity the estates may achieve.

Commentaries

Edward Wheat's essay recaps the argument of *The Book of the City of Ladies* and places it in the context of Western political theory. He highlights several themes in the book, such as the essential equality of men and women, in order to support his view that de Pizan's work marks the origin of feminist discourse. Wheat also employs a Straussian strategy of interpretation to show that the second part of the book, where de Pizan challenges a number of mistaken views about women, is the most central to understanding her political thought. Finding some foreshadowing of Machiavelli in de Pizan's work, this essay argues that she was in many ways a modern thinker.

Kate Forhan, who translated *The Book of the Body Politic*, presents a detailed examination of the ways in which both John of Salisbury and Christine de Pizan used that key metaphor. In both sets of hands, the metaphor underscores the importance of interdependence to the health and survival of the community. There are important differences between John and Christine, however, differences that can be traced to their respective times and audiences. Written in a time of peace, John's book was primarily directed toward courtiers (medieval bureaucrats, essentially) and stressed the importance of following administrative procedure. Writing for a prince during a time of political upheaval, however, de Pizan chose to focus her narrative more on the concepts of virtue and harmony.

Notes

1. Renate Blumenfeld-Kosinski, "Introduction," in *The Selected Writings of Christine de Pizan*,

ed. Renate Blumenfeld-Kosinski (New York: W.W. Norton, 1997), xv.

2. Christine De Pizan, *The Book of the City of Ladies* (New York: Persea Books, 1998), 4.

3. Charity Cannon Willard, *Christine de Pizan: Her Life and Works* (New York: Persea Books, 1984), 136.

Web Sources

http://www.pinn.net/~sunshine/whm2000/pizan5.html

http://www.pinn.net/~sunshine/march99/pizan3.html
Sunshine for Women. These profiles of de Pizan include a biographical sketch, a list of her major works, and a summary of *The Book of the City of Ladies.*

http://faculty.msmc.edu/lindeman/piz1.html
Christine de Pizan. Contains a helpful timeline, biography, and bibliography.

http://www.aug.edu/langlitcom/humanitiesHBK/handbook_htm/pizan_intro.htm
The Humanities Handbook. Offers a profile of Christine and excerpts from *The Book of the City of Ladies.*

http://dhushara.tripod.com/book/renewal/voices2/pizan.htm
Christine de Pizan. Extracts from *The Book of the City of Ladies*, billed as "essential reading for transforming the world."

Class Activities and Discussion Items

1. Compare and contrast the influence of Christianity on the political thought of Augustine, Aquinas, and de Pizan.

2. Read aloud some of the exemplary stories of women's achievements found in *The Book of the City of Ladies.* Have the class find similar stories that Christine might use if she were writing today.

3. Discuss whether or not Christine de Pizan is a feminist.

4. Discuss the metaphor of the body politic as used by John of Salisbury and Christine de Pizan. How useful is that metaphor for understanding contemporary political life?

5. What qualities does de Pizan think should characterize the prince, the nobility, and the people? Why are these qualities important?

Further Reading

Blumenfeld-Kosinski, Renate, ed. 1997. *The Selected Writings of Christine de Pizan.* New York: W.W. Norton. Introduction to her chief works of poetry and prose, accompanied by critical essays on de Pizan's relationship to contemporary feminism.

Brabant, Margaret, ed. 1992. *Politics, Gender and Genre: The Political Thought of Christine de Pizan.* Boulder, CO: Westview Press. Important collection of essays that examine de Pizan's thought from several perspectives.

Desmond, Marilynn, ed. 1997. *Christine de Pizan and the Categories of Difference.* Minneapolis: University of Minnesota Press. Essays exploring the medieval context of, and various themes within, the literary corpus produced by de Pizan.

Willard, Charity Cannon. 1984. *Christine de Pizan: Her Life and Works.* New York: Persea Books. A valuable and comprehensive biography. ✦

22
Excerpts from *The Book of the City of Ladies*

Christine de Pizan

1. Here Begins the Book of the City of Ladies, Whose First Chapter Tells Why and for What Purpose This Book Was Written.

I.1.1 Following the practice that has become the habit of my life, namely the devoted study of literature, one day as I was sitting in my study, surrounded by books on many different subjects, my mind grew weary from dwelling at length on the weighty opinions of authors whom I had studied for so long. I looked up from my book, deciding then to leave subtle questions in peace and to read some lyric poetry for pleasure. With this intention, I searched for some small book, and by chance a strange volume came into my hands, not one of my own but one which had been given to me for safekeeping along with some others. When I held it open and saw from its title page that it was by Mathéolus, I smiled, for though I had never seen it before, I had often heard that like other books it discussed respect for women. I thought I would browse through it to amuse myself. I had not been reading for very long when my good mother called me to refresh myself with some supper, for it was evening. Intending to look at it the next day, I put it down. The next morning, again seated in my study as was my habit, I remembered wanting to examine this book by Mathéolus. I started to read it and went on for a little while. Because the subject seemed to me not very pleasant for people who do not enjoy lies, and of no use in developing virtue or manners, given its lack of integrity in diction and theme, and after browsing here and there and reading the end, I put it down in order to turn my attention to more elevated and useful study. But just the sight of this book, even though it was of no authority, made me wonder how it happened that so many different men—and learned men among them—have been and are so inclined to express both in speaking and in their treatises and writings so many devilish and wicked thoughts about women and their behavior. Not only one or two and not even just this Mathéolus (for this book had a bad name anyway and was intended as a satire) but, more generally, judging from the treatises of all philosophers and poets and from all the orators—it would take too long to mention their names—it seems that they all speak from one and the same mouth. They all concur in one conclusion: that the behavior of women is inclined to and full of every vice. Thinking deeply about these matters, I began to examine my character and my conduct as a natural woman, and, similarly, I discussed this with other women whose company I frequently kept, princesses, great ladies, women of the middle and lower classes in great numbers, who graciously told me of their private experiences and intimate thoughts, in order to know in fact judging in good conscience and without favor—whether the testimony of so many famous men could be true. To the best of my knowledge, no matter how long I confronted or dissected the problem, I could not see or realize how their claims could be true when compared to the natural behavior and character of women. Yet I still argued vehemently against women, saying that it would be impossible that so many famous men—such solemn scholars, possessed of such deep and great understanding, so clear-sighted in all things, as it seemed—could have spoken falsely on so many occasions that I could hardly find a book on morals where, even before I had read it in its entirety, I did not find several chapters or certain sections attacking women, no matter who the author was. This reason alone, in short, made me conclude that, although my intellect did not perceive my own great faults and, likewise, those of other women because of its simpleness and ignorance, it was however truly fitting that such was the case. And so I relied more on the judgment of others than on what I myself felt and knew. I was so transfixed in this line of thinking for such a long time that it seemed as if I were in a stupor. Like a gushing fountain, a series of authorities, whom I recalled one after another, came to mind, along with their opinions on this topic. And I finally decided that God formed a vile creature when He made woman, and I wondered how such a worthy artisan could have deigned to make such an abominable work which, from what they say, is the vessel as well as the refuge and abode of every evil and vice. As I was thinking this, a great unhappiness and sadness welled up in my heart, for I detested myself and the entire feminine sex, as though we were monstrosities in nature. And in my lament I spoke these words:

I.1.2 "Oh, God, how can this be? For unless I stray from my faith, I must never doubt that Your infinite wisdom and most perfect goodness ever created anything which was not good. Did You yourself not create woman in a very special way and since that time did You not give her all those inclinations which it pleased You for her to have? And how could it be that You could go wrong in anything? Yet look at all these accusations which have been judged, decided, and concluded against women. I do not know how to understand this repugnance. If it is so, fair Lord God, that in fact so many abominations abound in the female sex, for You Yourself say that the testimony of two or three witnesses lends credence, why shall I not doubt that this is true? Alas, God, why did You not let me be born in the world as a male, so that all my inclinations would be to serve You better, and so that I would not stray in anything and would be as perfect as a male is said to be? But since Your kindness has not been extended to me, then forgive my negligence in Your service, most fair Lord God, and may it not displease You, for the servant who receives fewer gifts from his lord is less obliged in his service." I spoke these words to God in my lament and a great deal more for a very long time in sad reflection, and in my folly I considered myself most unfortunate because God had made me inhabit a female body in this world.

2. Here Christine Describes How Three Ladies Appeared to Her and How the One Who Was in Front Spoke First and Comforted Her in Her Pain.

So occupied with these painful thoughts,I.2 my head bowed in shame, my eyes filled with tears, leaning my cheek on my hand, elbow propped on the pommel of my chair's armrest, I suddenly saw a ray of light fall on my lap, as though it were the sun. I shuddered then, as if wakened from sleep, for I was sitting in a shadow where the sun could not have shone at that hour. And as I lifted my head to see where this light was coming from, I saw three crowned ladies standing before me, and the splendor of their bright faces shone on me and throughout the entire room. Now no one would ask whether I was surprised, for my doors were shut and they had still entered. Fearing that some phantom had come to tempt me and filled with great fright, I made the Sign of the Cross on my forehead.

Then she who was the first of the threeI.2 smiled and began to speak, "Dear daughter, do not be afraid, for we have not come here to harm or trouble you but to console you, for we have taken pity on your distress, and we have come to bring you out of the ignorance which so blinds your own intellect that you shun what you know for a certainty and believe what you do not know or see or recognize except by virtue of many strange opinions. You resemble the fool in the prank who was dressed in women's clothes while he slept; because those who were making fun of him repeatedly told him he was a woman, he believed their false testimony more readily than the certainty of his own identity. Fair daughter, have you lost all sense? Have you forgotten that when fine gold is tested in the furnace, it does not change or vary in strength but becomes purer the more it is hammered and handled in different ways? Do you not know that the best things are the most debated and the most discussed? If you wish to consider the question of the highest form of reality, which consists in ideas or celestial substances, consider whether the greatest philosophers who have lived and whom you support against your own sex have ever resolved whether ideas are false and contrary to the truth. Notice how these same philosophers contradict and criticize one another, just as you have seen in the *Metaphysics* where Aristotle takes their opinions to task and speaks similarly of Plato and other philosophers. And note, moreover, how even Saint Augustine and the Doctors of the Church have criticized Aristotle in certain passages, although he is known as the prince of philosophers in whom both natural and moral philosophy attained their highest level. It also seems that you think that all the words of the philosophers are articles of faith, that they could never be wrong. As far as the poets of whom you speak are concerned, do you not know that they spoke on many subjects in a fictional way and that often they mean the contrary of what their words openly say? One can interpret them according to the figure of grammar called *antiphrasis*, which means, as you know, that if you call something bad, in fact, it is good, and also vice versa. Thus I advise you to profit from their works and to interpret them in the manner in which they are intended in those passages where they attack women. Perhaps this man, who called himself Mathéolus in his own book, intended it in such a way, for there are many things which, if taken literally, would be pure heresy. As for the attack against the estate of marriage—which is a holy estate, worthy and ordained by God—made not only by Mathéolus but also by others and even by the *Romance of the Rose* where greater credibility is averred because of the authority of its author, it is evident and proven by experience that the contrary of the evil which they posit and claim to be found in this estate through the obligation and fault of women is true. For where has the husband ever been found who would allow his wife to have authority to abuse and insult him as a matter of course, as these authorities maintain? I believe that, regardless of what you might have read, you will never

see such a husband with your own eyes, so badly colored are these lies. Thus, in conclusion, I tell you, dear friend, that simplemindedness has prompted you to hold such an opinion. Come back to yourself, recover your senses, and do not trouble yourself anymore over such absurdities. For you know that any evil spoken of women so generally only hurts those who say it, not women themselves."

3. Here Christine Tells How the Lady Who Had Said This Showed Her Who She Was and What Her Character and Function Were and Told Her How She Would Construct a City with the Help of These Same Three Ladies.

The famous lady spoke these words to me,I.3.1 in whose presence I do not know which one of my senses was more overwhelmed: my hearing from having listened to such worthy words or my sight from having seen her radiant beauty, her attire, her reverent comportment, and her most honored countenance. The same was true of the others, so that I did not know which one to look at, for the three ladies resembled each other so much that they could be told apart only with difficulty, except for the last one, for although she was of no less authority than the others, she had so fierce a visage that whoever, no matter how daring, looked in her eyes would be afraid to commit a crime, for it seemed that she threatened criminals unceasingly. Having stood up out of respect, I looked at them without saying a word, like someone too overwhelmed to utter a syllable. Reflecting on who these beings could be, I felt much admiration in my heart and, if I could have dared, I would have immediately asked their names and identities and what was the meaning of the different scepters which each one carried in her right hand, which were of fabulous richness, and why they had come here. But since I considered myself unworthy to address these questions to such high ladies as they appeared to me, I did not dare to, but continued to keep my gaze fixed on them, half-afraid and half-reassured by the words which I had heard, which had made me reject my first impression. But the most wise lady who had spoken to me and who knew in her mind what I was thinking, as one who has insight into everything, addressed my reflections, saying:

I.3.2 "Dear daughter, know that God's providence, which leaves nothing void or empty, has ordained that we, though celestial beings, remain and circulate among the people of the world here below, in order to bring order and maintain in balance those institutions we created according to the will of God in the fulfillment of various offices, that God whose daughters we three all are and from whom we were born. Thus it is my duty to straighten out men and women when they go astray and to put them back on the right path. And when they stray, if they have enough understanding to see me, I come to them quietly in spirit and preach to them, showing them their error and how they have failed, I assign them the causes, and then I teach them what to do and what to avoid. Since I serve to demonstrate clearly and to show both in thought and deed to each man and woman his or her own special qualities and faults, you see me holding this shiny mirror which I carry in my right hand in place of a scepter. I would thus have you know truly that no one can look into this mirror, no matter what kind of creature, without achieving clear self-knowledge. My mirror has such great dignity that not without reason is it surrounded by rich and precious gems, so that you see, thanks to this mirror, the essences, qualities, proportions, and measures of all things are known, nor can anything be done well without it. And because, similarly, you wish to know what are the offices of my other sisters whom you see here, each will reply in her own person about her name and character, and this way our testimony will be all the more certain to you. But now I myself will declare the reason for our coming. I must assure you, as we do nothing without good cause, that our appearance here is not at all in vain. For, although we are not common to many places and our knowledge does not come to all people, nevertheless you, for your great love of investigating the truth through long and continual study, for which you come here, solitary and separated from the world, you have deserved and deserve, our devoted friend, to be visited and consoled by us in your agitation and sadness, so that you might also see clearly, in the midst of the darkness of your thoughts, those things which taint and trouble your heart.

"There is another greater and even more I.3 special reason for our coming which you will learn from our speeches: in fact we have come to vanquish from the world the same error into which you had fallen, so that from now on, ladies and all valiant women may have a refuge and defense against the various assailants, those ladies who have been abandoned for so long, exposed like a field without a surrounding hedge, without finding a champion to afford them an adequate defense, notwithstanding those noble men who are required by order of law to protect them, who by negligence and apathy have allowed them to be mistreated. It is no wonder then that their jealous enemies, those outrageous villains who have assailed them with various weapons, have been victorious in a war in which women have had no defense. Where is there a city so strong which could not be taken immediately if no resistance were forthcoming, or the law case, no matter how unjust, which was not won through the obstinance of someone pleading without opposition? And the simple, noble ladies, following the example of suffering which God commands, have cheerfully suffered the great attacks which, both in the spoken and the written word, have been wrongfully and sinfully perpetrated against women by men who all the while appealed to God for the right to do so. Now it is time for their just cause to be taken from Pharaoh's hands, and for this reason, we three ladies whom you see here, moved by pity, have come to you to announce a particular edifice built like a city wall, strongly constructed and well founded, which has been predestined and established by our aid and counsel for you to build, where no one will reside except all ladies of fame and women worthy of praise, for the walls of the city will be closed to those women who lack virtue."

4. Here the Lady Explains to Christine the City Which She Has Been Commissioned to Build and How She Was Charged to Help Christine Build the Wall and Enclosure, and Then Gives Her Name.

I.4.1 "Thus, fair daughter, the prerogative among women has been bestowed on you to establish and build the City of Ladies. For the foundation and completion of this City you will draw fresh waters from us as from clear fountains, and we will bring you sufficient building stone, stronger and more durable than any marble with cement could be. Thus your City will be extremely beautiful, without equal, and of perpetual duration in the world.

I.4.2 "Have you not read that King Tros founded the great city of Troy with the aid of Apollo, Minerva, and Neptune, whom the people of that time considered gods, and also how Cadmus founded the city of Thebes with the admonition of the gods? And yet over time these cities fell and have fallen into ruin. But I prophesy to you, as a true sybil, that this City, which you will found with our help, will never be destroyed, nor will it ever fall, but will remain prosperous forever, regardless of all its jealous enemies. Although it will be stormed by numerous assaults, it will never be taken or conquered.

I.4.3 "Long ago the Amazon kingdom was begun through the arrangement and enterprise of several ladies of great courage who despised servitude, just as history books have testified. For a long time afterward they maintained it under the rule of several queens, very noble ladies whom they elected themselves, who governed them well and maintained their dominion with great strength. Yet, although they were strong and powerful and had conquered a large part of the entire Orient in the course of their rule and terrified all the neighboring lands (even the Greeks, who were then the flower of all countries in the world, feared them), nevertheless, after a time, the power of this kingdom declined, so that as with all earthly kingdoms, nothing but its name has survived to the present. But the edifice erected by you in this City which you must construct will be far stronger, and for its founding I was commissioned, in the course of our common deliberation, to supply you with durable and pure mortar to lay the sturdy foundations and to raise the large walls, all around, high, wide, and with mighty, entrenched towers, blockhouses, moats, and palisades, just as is fitting for a city with a strong and lasting defense. Following our plan, you will set the foundations deep to last all the longer, and then you will raise the walls so high that they will not fear anyone. Daughter, now that I have told you the reason for our coming and so that you will more certainly believe my words, I want you to learn my name, by whose sound alone you will be able to learn and know that, if you wish to follow my commands, you have in me an administrator so that you may do your work flawlessly. I am called Lady Reason; you see that you are in good hands. For the time being then, I will say no more."

5. Here Christine Tells How the Second Lady Told Her Name and What She Served as and How She Would Aid Her in the Building of the City of Ladies.

When the lady above finished her speech, I.5.1 before I could resume, the second lady began as follows: "I am called Rectitude and reside more in Heaven than on Earth, but as the radiance and splendor of God and messenger of His goodness, I often visit the just and exhort them to do what is right, to give to each person what is his according to his capacity, to say and uphold the truth, to defend the rights of the poor and the innocent, not to hurt anyone through usurpation, to uphold the reputation of those unjustly accused. I am the shield and defense of the servants of God. I resist the power and might of evildoers. I give rest to workers and reward those who act well. Through me, God reveals to His friends His secrets; I am their advocate in Heaven. This shining ruler which you see me carry in my right hand instead of a scepter is the straight ruler which separates right from wrong and shows the difference between good and evil: who follows it does not go astray. It is the rod of peace which reconciles the good and where they find support and which beats and strikes down evil. What should I tell you about this? All things are measured by this ruler, for its powers are infinite. It will serve you to measure the edifice of the City which you have been commissioned to build, and you will need it for constructing the façade, for erecting the high temples, for measuring the palaces, houses, and all public buildings, the streets and squares, and all things proper to help populate the City. I have come as your assistant, and this will be my duty. Do not be uneasy about the breadth and long circuit of the walls, for with God's help and our assistance you will build fair and sturdy mansions and inns without leaving anything vague, and you will people the City with no trouble."

6. Here Christine Tells How the Third Lady Told Her Who She Was and Her Function and How She Would Help Build the High Roofs of the Towers and Palaces and Would Bring to Her the Queen, Accompanied by Noble Ladies.

I.6.1   Afterward, the third lady spoke and said, "My friend Christine, I am Justice, the most singular daughter of God, and my nature proceeds purely from His person. My residence is found in Heaven, on Earth, or in Hell: in Heaven, for the glory of the saints and blessed souls; on Earth, for the apportionment to each man of the good or evil which he has deserved; in Hell, for the punishment of the evil. I do not bend anywhere, for I have not friend nor enemy nor changeable will; pity cannot persuade me nor cruelty move me. My duty is only to judge, to decide, and to dispense according to each man's just deserts. I sustain all things in their condition, nothing could be stable without me. I am in God and God is in me, and we are as one and the same. Who follows me cannot fail, and my way is sure. I teach men and

women of sound mind who want to believe in me to chastise, know, and correct themselves, and to do to others what they wish to have done to themselves, to distribute wealth without favor, to speak the truth, to flee and hate lies, to reject all viciousness. This vessel of fine gold which you see me hold in my right hand, made like a generous measure, God, my Father, gave me, and it serves to measure out to each his rightful portion. It carries the sign of the fleur-de-lis of the Trinity, and in all portions it measures true, nor can any man complain about my measure. Yet the men of the Earth have other measures which they claim depend upon and derive from mine, but they are mistaken. Often they measure in my shadow, and their measure is not always true but sometimes too much for some and too little for others. I could give a rather long account of the duties of my office, but, put briefly, I have a special place among the Virtues, for they are all based on me. And of the three noble ladies whom you see here, we are as one and the same, we could not exist without one another; and what the first disposes, the second orders and initiates, and then I, the third, finish and terminate it. Thus I have been appointed by the will of us three ladies to perfect and complete your City, and my job will be to construct the high roofs of the towers and of the lofty mansions and inns which will all be made of fine shining gold. Then I will populate the City for you with worthy ladies and the mighty Queen whom I will bring to you. Hers will be the honor and prerogative among all other women, as well as among the most excellent women. And in this condition I will turn the City over to you, completed with your help, fortified and closed off with strong gates which I will search for in Heaven, and then I will place the keys in your hands." . . .

8. Here Christine Tells How, Under Reason's Command and Assistance, She Began to Excavate the Earth and Lay the Foundation.

I.8.1   Then Lady Reason responded and said, "Get up, daughter! Without waiting any longer, let us go to the Field of Letters. There the

City of Ladies will be founded on a flat and fertile plain, where all fruits and freshwater rivers are found and where the earth abounds in all good things. Take the pick of your understanding and dig and clear out a great ditch wherever you see the marks of my ruler, and I will help you carry away the earth on my own shoulders."

I.8.2   I immediately stood up to obey her commands and, thanks to these three ladies, I felt stronger and lighter than before. She went ahead, and I followed behind, and after we had arrived at this field I began to excavate and dig, following her marks with the pick of cross-examination. And this was my first work:

I.8.3   "Lady, I remember well what you told me before, dealing with the subject of how so many men have attacked and continue to attack the behavior of women, that gold becomes more refined the longer it stays in the furnace, which means the more women have been wrongfully attacked, the greater waxes the merit of their glory. But please tell me why and for what reason different authors have spoken against women in their books, since I already know from you that this is wrong; tell me if Nature makes man so inclined or whether they do it out of hatred and where does this behavior come from?"

Then she replied, "Daughter, to give you a way of entering into the question more deeply, I will carry away this first basketful of dirt. This behavior most certainly does not come from Nature, but rather is contrary to Nature, for no connection in the world is as great or as strong as the great love which, through the will of God, Nature places between a man and a woman. The causes which have moved and which still move men to attack women, even those authors in those books, are diverse and varied, just as you have discovered. For some have attacked women with good intentions, that is, in order to draw men who have gone astray away from the company of vicious and dissolute women, with whom they might be infatuated, or in order to keep these men from going mad on account of such women, and also so that every man might avoid an obscene and lustful life. They have attacked all

women in general because they believe that women are made up of every abomination."

"My lady," I said then, "excuse me for interrupting you here, but have such authors acted well, since they were prompted by a laudable intention? For intention, the saying goes, judges the man."

"That is a misleading position, my good daughter," she said, "for such sweeping ignorance never provides an excuse. If someone killed you with good intention but out of foolishness, would this then be justified? Rather, those who did this, whoever they might be, would have invoked the wrong law; causing any damage or harm to one party in order to help another party is not justice, and likewise attacking all feminine conduct is contrary to the truth, just as I will show you with a hypothetical case. Let us suppose they did this intending to draw fools away from foolishness. It would be as if I attacked fire—a very good and necessary element nevertheless—because some people burnt themselves, or water because someone drowned. The same can be said of all good things which can be used well or used badly. But one must not attack them if fools abuse them, and you have yourself touched on this point quite well elsewhere in your writings. But those who have spoken like this so abundantly—whatever their intentions might be—have formulated their arguments rather loosely only to make their point. Just like someone who has a long and wide robe cut from a very large piece of cloth when the material costs him nothing and when no one opposes him, they exploit the rights of others. But just as you have said elsewhere, if these writers had only looked for the ways in which men can be led away from foolishness and could have been kept from tiring themselves in attacking the life and behavior of immoral and dissolute women—for to tell the straight truth, there is nothing which should be avoided more than an evil, dissolute, and perverted woman, who is like a monster in nature, a counterfeit estranged from her natural condition, which must be simple, tranquil, and upright—then I would grant you that they would have built a supremely excellent work. But I can assure you that these attacks on all women—when in fact there are so many excellent women—have never originated with me, Reason, and that all who subscribe to them have failed totally and will continue to fail. So now throw aside these black, dirty, and uneven stones from your work, for they will never be fitted into the fair edifice of your City.

I.8.4 "Other men have attacked women for other reasons: such reproach has occurred to some men because of their own vices and others have been moved by the defects of their own bodies, others through pure jealousy, still others by the pleasure they derive in their own personalities from slander. Others, in order to show they have read many authors, base their own writings on what they have found in books and repeat what other writers have said and cite different authors.

I.8.5 "Those who attack women because of their own vices are men who spent their youths in dissolution and enjoyed the love of many different women, used deception in many of their encounters, and have grown old in their sins without repenting, and now regret their past follies and the dissolute life they led. But Nature, which allows the will of the heart to put into effect what the powerful appetite desires, has grown cold in them. Therefore they are pained when they see that their 'good times' have now passed them by, and it seems to them that the young, who are now what they once were, are on top of the world. They do not know how to overcome their sadness except by attacking women, hoping to make women less attractive to other men. Everywhere one sees such old men speak obscenely and dishonestly, just as you can fully see with Mathéolus, who himself confesses that he was an impotent old man filled with desire. You can thereby convincingly prove, with this one example, how what I tell you is true, and you can assuredly believe that it is the same with many others.

I.8.6 "But these corrupt old men, like an incurable leprosy, are not the upstanding men of old whom I made perfect in virtue and wisdom—for not all men share in such corrupt desire, and it would be a real shame if it were so. The mouths of these good men, following their hearts, are all filled with exemplary, honest, and discreet words. These same men detest misdeeds and slander, and neither attack nor defame men and women, and they counsel the avoidance of evil and the pursuit of virtue and the straight path.

"Those men who are moved by the defect I.8.7 of their own bodies have impotent and deformed limbs but sharp and malicious minds. They have found no other way to avenge the pain of their impotence except by attacking women who bring joy to many. Thus they have thought to divert others away from the pleasure which they cannot personally enjoy.

"Those men who have attacked women I.8.8 out of jealousy are those wicked ones who have seen and realized that many women have greater understanding and are more noble in conduct than they themselves, and thus they are pained and disdainful. Because of this, their overweening jealousy has prompted them to attack all women, intending to demean and diminish the glory and praise of such women, just like the man—I cannot remember which one—who tries to prove in his work, *De philosophia*, that it is not fitting that some men have revered women and says that those men who have made so much of women pervert the title of his book: they transform 'philosophy,' the love of wisdom, into 'philofolly,' the love of folly. But I promise and swear to you that he himself, all throughout the lie-filled deductions of his argument, transformed the content of his book into a true philofolly.

"As for those men who are naturally given I.8.9 to slander, it is not surprising that they slander women since they attack everyone anyway. Nevertheless, I assure you that any man who freely slanders does so out of a great wickedness of heart, for he is acting contrary to reason and contrary to Nature: contrary to reason insofar as he is most ungrateful and fails to recognize the good deeds which women have done for him, so great that he could never make up for them, no matter how much he try, and which he continuously needs women to perform for him; and contrary to Nature in that there is no naked beast anywhere, nor bird, which does not naturally love its female counterpart. It is thus quite unnatural when a reasonable man does the contrary.

I.8.10 "And just as there has never been any work so worthy, so skilled is the craftsman who made it, that there were not people who wanted, and want, to counterfeit it, there are many who wish to get involved in writing poetry. They believe they cannot go wrong, since others have written in books what they take the situation to be, or rather, *mis*-take the situation—as I well know! Some of them undertake to express themselves by writing poems of water without salt, such as these, or ballads without feeling, discussing the behavior of women or of princes or of other people, while they themselves do not know how to recognize or to correct their own servile conduct and inclinations. But simple people, as ignorant as they are, declare that such writing is the best in the world." . . .

19. The End of the Book: Christine Addresses the Ladies.

I.19.1 My most honored ladies, may God be praised, for now our City is entirely finished and completed, where all of you who love glory, virtue, and praise may be lodged in great honor, ladies from the past as well as from the present and future, for it has been built and established for every honorable lady. And my most dear ladies, it is natural for the human heart to rejoice when it finds itself victorious in any enterprise and its enemies confounded. Therefore you are right, my ladies, to rejoice greatly in God and in honest mores upon seeing this new City completed, which can be not only the refuge for you all, that is, for virtuous women, but also the defense and guard against your enemies and assailants, if you guard it well. For you can see that the substance with which it is made is entirely of virtue, so resplendent that you may see yourselves mirrored in it, especially in the roofs built in the last part as well as in the other parts which concern you. And my dear ladies, do not misuse this new inheritance like the arrogant who turn proud when their prosperity grows and their wealth multiplies, but rather follow the example of your Queen, the sovereign Virgin, who, after the extraordinary honor of being chosen Mother of the Son of God was announced to her, humbled herself all the more by calling herself the handmaiden of God. Thus, my ladies, just as it is true that a creature's humility and kindness wax with the increase of its virtues, may this City be an occasion for you to conduct yourselves honestly and with integrity and to be all the more virtuous and humble.III.19.2

And you ladies who are married, doIII.19.2 not scorn being subject to your husbands for sometimes it is not the best thing for a creature to be independent. This is attested to by what the angel said to Ezra: Those, he said, who take advantage of their free will can fall into sin and despise our Lord and deceive the just, and for this they perish. Those women with peaceful, good, and discrete husbands who are devoted to them, praise God for this boon, which is not inconsiderable, for a greater boon in the world could not be given them. And may they be diligent in serving, loving, and cherishing their husbands in the loyalty of their heart, as they should, keeping their peace and praying to God to uphold and save them. And those women who have husbands neither completely good nor completely bad should still praise God for not having the worst and should strive to moderate their vices and pacify them, according to their conditions. And those women who have husbands who are cruel, mean, and savage should strive to endure them while trying to overcome their vices and lead them back, if they can, to a reasonable and seemly life. And if they are so obstinate that their wives are unable to do anything, at least they will acquire great merit for their souls through the virtue of patience. And everyone will bless them and support them.

So, my ladies, be humble and patient,III.19.3 and God's grace will grow in you, and praise will be given to you as well as the Kingdom of Heaven. For Saint Gregory has said that patience is the entrance to Paradise and the way of Jesus Christ. And may none of you be forced into holding frivolous opinions nor be hardened in them, lacking all basis in reason, nor be jealous or disturbed in mind, nor haughty in speech, nor outrageous in your acts, for these things disturb the mind and lead to madness. Such behavior is unbecoming and unfitting for women.

III.19.4 And you, virgin maidens, be pure, simple, and serene, without vagueness, for the snares of evil men are set for you. Keep your eyes lowered, with few words in your mouths, and act respectfully. Be armed with the strength of virtue against the tricks of the deceptive and avoid their company.

III.19.5 And widows, may there be integrity in your dress, conduct, and speech; piety in your deeds and way of life; prudence in your bearing; patience (so necessary!), strength, and resistance in tribulations and difficult affairs; humility in your heart, countenance, and speech; and charity in your works.

III.19.6 In brief, all women—whether noble, bourgeois, or lower-class—be well-informed in all things and cautious in defending your honor and chastity against your enemies! My ladies, see how these men accuse you of so many vices in everything. Make liars of them all by showing forth your virtue, and prove their attacks false by acting well, so that you can say with the Psalmist, "the vices of the evil will fall on their heads." Repel the deceptive flatterers who, using different charms, seek with various tricks to steal that which you must consummately guard, that is, your honor and the beauty of your praise. Oh my ladies, flee, flee the foolish love they urge on you! Flee it, for God's sake, flee! For no good can come to you from it. Rather, rest assured that however deceptive their lures, their end is always to your detriment. And do not believe the contrary; for it cannot be otherwise. Remember, dear ladies, how these men call you frail, unserious, and easily influenced but yet try hard, using all kinds of strange and deceptive tricks, to catch you, just as one lays traps for wild animals. Flee, flee, my ladies, and avoid their company—under these smiles are hidden deadly and painful poisons. And so may it please you, my most respected ladies, to cultivate virtue, to flee vice, to increase and multiply our City, and to rejoice and act well. And may I, your servant, commend myself to you, praying to God who by His grace has granted me to live in this world and to persevere in His holy service. May He in the end have mercy on my great sins and grant to me the joy which lasts forever, which I may, by His grace, afford to you. Amen.

Here Ends the Third and Last Part of the Book of the City of Ladies.

Adapted from: Christine de Pizan, *The Book of the City of Ladies*, translated by Earl Jeffrey Richards, pp. 3–20, 254–257. Copyright © 1982, 1998 by Persea Books, Inc. Reprinted by permissions of Persea Books Inc. (New York). ✦

23
Excerpts from *The Book of the Body Politic*

Christine de Pizan

Part One: On Princes

Here begins the Book of the Body Politic which speaks of virtue and manners and is divided into three parts. The first part is addressed to princes, the second to knights and nobles, and the third to the universal people.

Chapter 1: The First Chapter Gives the Description of the Body Politic

If it is possible for vice to give birth to virtue, it pleases me in this part to be as passionate as a woman, since many men assume that the female sex does not know how to silence the abundance of their spirits. Come boldly, then and be shown the many inexhaustible springs and fountains of my courage, which cannot be stanched when it expresses the desire for virtue.

Oh, Virtue, noble and godly, how can I dare to flaunt myself by speaking of you, when I know that my understanding neither comprehends nor expresses you well?

But what comforts me and makes me bold is that I sense that you are so kind that it will not displease you if I speak of you, not about what is most subtle, but only in those areas which I can conceive or comprehend. So, I will speak about you as far as it concerns the teaching of good morals, by speaking first of the industry and rule of life for our superiors; that is, princes, whose majesties I humbly supplicate not to take wrongly nor disdain such a small intelligence as mine, that such a humble creature dares undertake to speak about the way of life for higher ranks.

And may it please them to remember the teaching of the Philosopher, who said, "Do not disdain the wise words of the insignificant despite your own high position." Next, by the grace of God, I hope to speak on the manner of life of knights and nobles. And then, thirdly, on the whole universal people.

These three types of estate ought to be one polity like a living body according to the words of Plutarch who in a letter which he sent to the Emperor Trajan compared the polity to a body having life. There the prince and princes hold the place of the head in as much as they are or should be sovereign and from them ought to come particular institutions just as from the mind of a person springs forth the external deeds that the limbs achieve. The knights and nobles take the place of the hands and arms. Just as a person's arms have to be strong in order to endure labor, so they have the burden of defending the law of the prince and the polity. They are also the hands because, just as the hands push aside harmful things, so they ought push all harmful and useless things aside. The other kinds of people are like the belly, the feet, and the legs. Just as the belly receives all that the head and the limbs prepare for it, so, too, the activity of the prince and nobles ought to return to the public good, as will be better explained later. Just as the legs and feet sustain the human body, so, too, the laborers sustain all the other estates.

Chapter 2: Which Describes How Virtuous Felicity Is Symbolized

First we have to discuss virtue, to the benefit of the rule of life for the three different estates. Virtue must regulate human life in all its works. Without it, no one can have honor. Whatever the degree of honor, Valerius says, honor is the plentiful food of virtue. And on this subject, Aristotle said, "Reverence is due to honor as a testimony of virtue," which means that honor must not be attributed but to a virtuous person, because he is not speaking about the powerful nor about the rich, but the virtuous. According to him, only the good are honored. Nothing is more desired by noble hearts than honor. As he says himself in the fourth book of the *Ethics*, neither power nor riches is without honor. Now it is true that kings and powerful princes are especially invested with honor, and as a consequence, virtue, so it is appropriate to distinguish the aspects of virtue. In chapter 20 of his book, *The City of God*, St. Augustine says that the philosophers say that virtue is the objective of all human good and evil. That is, human happiness comes from being virtuous.

Now it is fitting that there is great delight in happiness, otherwise it would not be happiness, and this joy and happiness ancient philosophers described and symbolized in this manner: Felicity is a very beautiful and refined queen seated on a royal throne, and the virtues are seated around her and look at her, waiting to hear her commands, to serve her, and to obey. She commands Prudence to inquire how she can stay healthy and in good condition so that she can reign a long time. And she commands Justice to do everything that she should and keep the laws so that there will be peace. And she commands Courage that if any pain should come to her body, to moderate it by resisting it with virtuous thought. She commands Temperance to take wine, food and other delectable things in moderation so that anything she takes is for a reason and not to her detriment. This description allows one to understand that to be virtuous is nothing more than to have in one everything that attracts good and which pushes away evil and vice. Thus, in order to govern the body of the public polity well, it is necessary for the head to be healthy, that is, virtuous. Because if it is ill, the whole body will feel it. Therefore we begin by speaking of medicine for the head, that is, for the king or princes, and, since this is a work beginning with the head, we will take first the "head" of age, that is the childhood of the prince who is brought up on the responsibility of his parents. . . .

Chapter 6: Here It Tells What the Young Prince Should Do When He Begins to Govern

When the time comes that the son of the prince has grown, and come of age to rule, and comes into his heritage by succession, whether it is a kingdom or another lordship, just as the fruit appears after the tree blossoms, so in him ought to appear the perfection of virtue, following the example of the wise king of France, Charles V. Because from the moment of his coronation, even though it was in the flower of his youth, no one could find anything dishonest in him and he occupied his time in suitable and virtuous things. I have plainly spoken elsewhere of him in my book on his deeds and good manners.

The virtues of a prince are seen in three things, without which he will not achieve this crown of reputation, good name, and consequently, honor. The first and most important, is to love, fear, and serve God without dishonesty, but with good deeds rather than spending time withdrawn in long prayers.

Another is this: he ought solely to love the good and benefit of his country and his people. All his ability, power, and the study of his free time ought to be for this, rather than his own benefit. The third is that he must love justice above all, guarding it and keeping it without restraint, and must do equity to all people. By keeping these three points well, the prince will be crowned with glory in heaven and on earth.

Now we will continue our work as before: Just as part one speaks of the head, that is the prince or princes, so we continue to discuss the first of our three points. From the first which is to love God, we will follow the many branches of virtue which stem from it, and likewise, the other two points. . . .

Chapter 8: Of the Observance Towards God and Toward the Law Which the Prince Ought to Practice

The good prince who loves God will know his commandments by memory, and how the worthy name of God must not be taken in vain. To this purpose he will proclaim an edict throughout his land, which will forbid on pain of severe punishment anyone swearing on or denying his Creator. Alas, there is great need in France at present for such an edict, because it is horrible that the whole of Christendom has the custom of such disrespect toward the Savior. One can scarcely hear any other language, whether it be in jest or another manner of speech, but everyone swears horribly at every word about the torments of the passion of our redeemer, and they forsake and deny him. I believe that the pagans of old would not have treated their gods and idols so!

All these things the good prince ought to forbid, because they are opposed to and disapproved by the Christian religion and could be the cause of the wrath of God and the subversion of kingdoms and countries where they take place, as some prophesies tell. And so, the good prince who loves God will carefully observe and keep the divine law and holy institutions in everything that is worthy and devout (which I will not discuss for reasons of brevity, and also because most people would prefer to hear of less boring things). But the good prince that keeps and observes these things ought to believe firmly that God will guard, defend, and increase him in virtue of soul and body. And why should he not have faith in God, the living, all powerful, and just, whenever the pagans trusted that their needs would be met generously, because of the worship that they gave to their gods and their idols? It appears, by what Valerius says, that the city of Rome desired to serve the gods conscientiously, and he said, "Our city has always set aside everything for the service of the gods," even those things that concerned the honor of the sovereign majesty, that is, the emperors, because they had, he says, firm belief that in doing thus they acquired the rule and the governance of the world, and also because of this "the emperors of our city have generally not abandoned the constant service of holy things."

This suffices for the first point of the first part, on the virtue of the prince, which should to be founded on and should demonstrate the fact that he loves and serves God.

Chapter 9: How a Good Prince Ought to Resemble a Good Shepherd

Now we have discussed the first point on which the goodness of the prince ought principally to be founded, so next we shall speak of the second point, that is, that the good prince ought especially to love the public good and its augmentation more than his own good, according to the teaching of Aristotle's *Politics*, which says that tyranny is when the prince prefers his own good over the public good. This is against royal lordship as well, for he ought to care more for the benefit of his people than his own. Now he shall be advised on how to demonstrate this love.

The good prince who loves his country will guard it carefully, following the example of the good shepherd. As he guards his sheep from wolves and evil beasts, and keeps them clean and healthy so that they can increase and be fruitful and yield their fleece whole, sound, and well nourished by the land on which they are fed and kept, so that the shepherd will be well paid by their fleece, shorn in time and in season. But the rich good shepherd who gives them to others to keep because he cannot take care of all his flocks himself, provides himself with good and capable help. So he takes good, careful servants, wise and hard working in their craft, whom he understands and knows are loyal and prefer his interest. So he orders that those servants be equipped with good strong dogs with iron collars, well trained by being brought to the field to chase off wolves. So they let them loose at night in the fold so that thieves coming for the sheep are attacked by them. By day, they keep them tied to their belts while the sheep graze peacefully in the fields. But if these servants feel any fear of wolves or evil animals coming out of the woods or mountains, they then unleash the dogs, and let them run after them and nip at their heels. And to give the dogs greater boldness against the wolf or evil animal the servants run after them with good ironclad staffs. And if any sheep goes out of the flock, the good hounds go after it and, without doing it harm, they bring it back to the flock. In this manner, the wise servants defend and take care of them so well that they yield a good account to the head shepherd.

Just so, the good prince is mindful of the defense and care of his country and people, even though it is impossible in person. In every place he has responsibility, he will always provide himself with very good assistance, in deeds of knighthood and for other things; that is, the brave leaders whom he knows are good and loyal and who love him, such as constables, marshals, admirals and others, to whom he gives responsibility for furnishing other good soldiers, well-taught and experienced in war, whom he binds to him by an oath, not to leave without permission and are so ready to do his business that if needed they will go attack his enemies, so that the country is not despoiled, pillaged, nor the people killed. This does not mean that the soldiers themselves should pillage and despoil the country like they do in France nowadays when in other countries they dare not do so. It is a great mischief and perversion of law when those who are intended for the defense of the people, pillage, rob, and so cruelly, that truly short of killing them or setting their houses on fire, their enemies could do no worse. This is not the right manner of warfare, which ought to be just and without extortion, and if not, the soldiers and the princes that send them to war are in great peril of the wrath of God falling on them and punishing them severely. Before God, there is no doubt that the justifiable curses of the people, when they have been oppressed too much, can cause evil fortune to fall, as, for example, one finds in many places in Holy Scripture; for everyone ought to know that God is just, and all this is the fault of an evil order. For if soldiers were well paid, one could restrict them on pain of punishment to take nothing without paying for it, and by this means they could find provisions and everything that they needed economically and plentifully. It is too greatly astonishing how people can live under such a law without any compassion from the soldiers for the pity of their life. But the Holy Spirit, father of the poor, will visit them! Now, if a shepherd had a dog that ran after his sheep, he would hit him with his staff. It is not a thing a good prince who loves God and his people should bear, and just as one unleashes the dogs at night in the fold to keep them from thieves, so must the head keep watchmen and spies along the borders so that the country and the people are not surprised by thieves or by some trickery, and so that they can know the plans of their enemies.

The soldiers ought to have yet another duty. Just as the good dog brings back the strayed sheep, so they ought to bring back the common people or others who from fear or dread or evil want to rebel and take the wrong side. They ought to bring them back to the right path either by threats or by taking good care of them. Although it displeases some and surprises others, I compare the noble office of arms to the nature of the dog because, truly, the dog naturally has many characteristics which the good man-at-arms ought to have. The dog loves his master marvelously and is very loyal to him. And the man-at-arms should be also. He is tough and exposes himself to death for his master and when he is committed to guarding any place he is very alert and has excellent hearing in order to run after evil doers or thieves. He will not bite the friends of his master but naturally sniffs at them, nor does he bite the neighbors nor those of the household where he is fed, but he guards them instead. He is very tough and fights with great skill. He has a good understanding, knowledge, and is very amiable to those who do him kindness. And all these characteristics are those of the good soldier.

Chapter 10: On the Same Subject

Let us return to our first topic: the good shepherd who takes care that his sheep are well kept and healthy. The good prince will not put all his responsibilities onto his ministers, but will make himself available to his subjects so as to hear as many pleas as he can. He will not fear nor despise the pitiful supplications of the people, but kindly condescends to their requests for mercy and justice. So he takes care that they are not pressured more than is reasonable, nor "devoured" by bad ministers and officers.

To speak clearly on this would take great leisure and space and perhaps the truth will displease some; but without doubt, it is a great pity when the truth is quieted and muted either from fear or from favoritism. On this subject, Seneca speaks in the sixth book in the twenty-first chapter of *On Benfices*. "I will show you," he says, "What those who are raised to high rank need most, although one thinks they have everything; that is, that someone would tell them the truth." This sentence is true because the servitors around princes do not seek their good but their individual benefit, and many of these tend to flatter and say what will please their lord and thus by their blandishments blind them. As it is written in chapter 15, book 3 of the *Politics*, the flatterer is the enemy of all virtues and he is a nail in the eye of his acquaintances. And on the subject of these officers, both the good and bad ones, without writing too much about them or about their deeds, I wish to God that princes studied who the people were they have around them, and who the people are that they have around them in the administration of their affairs, and knew their deeds well. For I believe that there is nothing more vile or corrupt than the conscience of some of them in their perversities.

But there are some of great evil and malice who conspire to hide their vices in darkness by coloring their virtues brightly. But they cannot hide the experiences others have of their deeds and words; as beautiful as they seem, there is no truth in them. They manifest their iniquities to those who suffer at their hands. But this is not apparent to the lords before whom they dissimulate, and no one dares tell the truth for fear of the lord's displeasure with those who tell the truth, for the lord does not want to hear evil spoken of his men. And there is a common saying around the court: My lord has very good manners since he refuses to hear those who speak evil of his people. Alas, "good manners" ought to include the desire to hear the truth! But if anyone is accused falsely through envy, as can happen, when the lord has inquired into the truth, he ought to punish and dismiss the accuser as an envious liar; in this way his people will fear to do evil and will cease the evils they have done. But these things the good prince should not allow.

He ought to desire that his subjects perform their best in whatever office God has placed them. The nobles ought to do what they ought to do, the clerics attend to their studies, and to the divine service, the merchants to their merchandise, the artisans to their craft, the laborers to the cultivation of the earth, and thus each one whatever his rank, ought to live by good policy, without extortion nor over-charging, so that each

may live properly under him, and that they love him as a good prince ought to be loved by his people, and that he have from them the legal revenue that is reasonable to collect and take from his country, without gnawing to the bone his poor commoners. When asked why he did not collect larger taxes from his people, the Emperor Tiberias responded, Valerius tells us, "the good shepherd shears his sheep only once a year; he does not fleece them all the time, nor skin them so that he draws blood." ...

Chapter 21: How a Good Prince, Despite Being Good Natured and Kind, Ought to Be Feared

The nature of justice and what it serves and to what extent is well known and understood; it is appropriate for the good prince to punish (or have punished) evildoers. And so I will pass by this for a time and proceed to that which also befits the good prince: The virtue of justice, which renders to each that which is his due, according to his power. If he keeps this rule, which is just, he will not fail to do equity in everything, and thus, he will render to himself his due. For it is rational that he has the same right he gives to everyone, which means that he would be obeyed and feared by right and by reason, as is appropriate to the majesty of a prince.

For in whatever land or place where a prince is not feared, there is no true justice. How it is appropriate for the prince to be feared is shown by the worthy man Clearcus who was Duke of Lacedemonia (which is a large part of Greece where there once was a marvelously valiant people). This duke was so chivalrous and great a warrior that his people were more afraid to flee than to die. He told them that soldiers should be more afraid of their prince than death and their enemies. Because of his words and also the punishment that he gave malefactors and cowards, they gave themselves without sparing, by which they achieved marvelous things. There is no doubt that the good prince ought to be feared despite being gentle and benign. His kindness ought to be considered a thing of grace which one ought to particularly heed rather than scorn. It is for this reason the ancients painted the goddess of lordship as a seated lady of very high rank on a royal throne, holding in one hand an olive branch and in the other a naked sword, showing that rule must include kindness and mercy as well as justice and power.

The good prince, as was said before, is governed by old sages and gives to everyone his due, as is in his power. And he prefers that these good and meritorious persons, are honored for their virtues, according to the wise saying: "Rise in the presence of the bald man." In times past, the old and wise were honored most, especially by the Lacedemonians who were honorable Greeks. This began with the introduction of the laws of Lycurgus, the noble and brave king who governed them. Then they had beautiful customs and maintained them a long time. Once upon a time, a very old man went to the theater in Athens to see the games. The theater was a place for the young men to wrestle each other, if armed, in jousts or battles, or in other ways, but none of the citizens of Athens would give up a place for this old man to sit down, so he went around to the place where the legates, which we call ambassadors, of Lacedemonia sat, who had come with a message to Athens. According to their custom those who were young honored the old, and they all stood up and set him in a honorable place among them. And when the people [of Athens] saw this they greatly approved of the noble custom of this foreign city, and said among themselves, "we know well what is right, but we should pay attention to the foreigners." . . .

Chapter 32: How It Is Proper for the Good Prince to Take His Recreation in Any Honest Diversion After His Great Labor

So that my intention be clearly understood, and so that I not be proved to be mistaken in my present work, when I said that the prince ought to be busy all the time; these words should not be taken absolutely, because one would not want the prince to be extremely over burdened. This is not my intent and so I say that the prince and likewise all who are burdened with high and important occupations must sometimes cease work and rest in leisure. And on this Valerius, whose words are more authoritative than mine, said on this subject: there are two kinds of idleness of which one ought to be avoided. This one causes virtue to disappear and makes life foolish and impotent in all good works, and renders one inclined to lust and accompanies the inclination to sensuality. Ovid spoke of this kind of idleness in his book the *Remedy of Love:* "If you put aside your idleness, the arts of the God of love are lost."

The other idleness I understand to be without vice. It is virtuous, and sometimes through it virtue may be acquired. It is sometimes appropriate for nobles and excellent men for the restoration of their natural vigor, so that the moderate cessation of labor, makes them more lively for work. For this moderate idleness recreates the natural virtues and strengthens them for better work. And so Ovid said, "he who has no rest cannot endure long by nature."

Valerius gives the example of Scipio and Lelius who were hard-working and worthy knights, who were such good companions and friends, that just as they were companions in the hardest labor, so they were in rest, in idleness, and in recreation, amusing themselves in honest sports, when it was time for them to play.

Chapter 33: How the Good Prince Who Knows That He Does His Duty in All Virtue Ought Reasonably to Desire Praise and Glory

Now it is time to bring to an end the first part of my book, on the introduction of princes to a virtuous life. For an abyss could be filled with all the sayings and stories of good habits which a prince should cultivate. But it seems to me better to exclude length by speaking generally of all the virtues. If he followed those discussed here, then there would be songs of glory and praise about him like once greeted the great and worthy prince of Athens Themistocles! Once it happened that singers of songs and ancient epics came before him. One of the knights asked him in jest what song would be most pleasing to hear. He answered "The one that says truly that I am virtuous and that I have done good and noteworthy deeds." Thus a well-conducted prince is worthy of praise, but the one who does not act virtuously does not have willing praise from the common estimation, but only in what he merits. It should not surprise us if the one who is worthy, virtuous and who does good deeds is praised for them! For it is known, according to the ancients, that high princes and noblemen of times past were greedy for glory and that they had the desire to acquire such glory by virtue, as one can see by their worthy deeds. It appears quite natural that everyone desires his own perfection, and so the person who is sovereign over all worldly creatures desires the testimony and proof of his perfection. And as the Philosopher says, glory and honor bring reverence, which shows that one has in him the dignity that is shown, and the desire to be honored is rooted and joined to human nature. But not everyone desires the pain of acquiring it. And the means by which honor and praise should be acquired is virtuous works, says the Philosopher. No other means is worthy of glory, as Tully says in the first book of *On Duties*. Despite what anyone says, everyone ought to be honored because of virtue and living well. No honor, praise or worldly glory is sufficient reward for virtuous deeds and excellence. According to Aristotle, one can lawfully desire a reward for good deeds to attract others to similar virtues. And Tully says that one scarcely finds anyone who after great and virtuous labors does not desire glory and honor as part of his reward. And because of such honor and glory, Aristotle says (in the third book of *Ethics*) the strength and great courage of virtuous men is identified and proven, who by their deeds have been honored. The unworthy and vicious ones are despised and blamed. But Socrates said that those who chose the way of glory just had to show by their deeds that they were as everyone would be believed, which means good. Socrates warns of those who have the appearance of right and virtue without the deeds, as hypocrites do. So the good prince who desires to reach paradise, as well as glory and praise in the world from all people, will love God and fear God above everything. And he will love the public good of his kingdom or country more than his own as well. He ought to do justice without hindrance and to justly render to each his own according to the power which is his. As justice commands he will be humane, generous, and merciful to his dependents as was described before. And in doing so, he will acquire praise through his good merits, not only during his life, but eternally, as Valerius said about the excellent prince Julius Caesar, who by his merits and good deeds after his death was reputed to be a god. For the ancients of old, who did not yet have the faith, when they saw a person, a man or woman who surpassed others in any superiority of grace, believed that such virtue could not be without divine virtue. And Julius Caesar had many great virtues. Above all others, he was just and merciful. They said that such virtue in a man could not perish in leaving life, and his soul ascended to heaven, deified.

Here ends the first part of this book.

Part Two: On Knights and Nobles

Here begins the second part of this book, which addresses chivalrous nobles.

Chapter 1: The First Chapter Describes How These Nobles Are the Arms and Hands of the Body Politic

Having concluded speaking to princes whom we described according to Plutarch as the head of the living image of the body politic and exhorting them to a virtuous life, it is appropriate in this second part of the present book to keep our promise and speak of the arms and hands of this image which, according to Plutarch, are the nobles, knights, and all those of their estate. In order to follow the style already begun, we ought to discuss their introduction to virtue and good manners, and particularly to deeds of chivalry, for they are responsible for guarding the public, according to the writings of the authors. While the same virtue is just as appropriate and necessary for the ordinary person, the simple knight, or the noble, as for princes, nevertheless, the estates differ in their way of life, in their conversation, and kinds of activity; thus it is suitable for my treatment of the subject to differ as well. The thing that is appropriate for the prince to do is not appropriate for the simple knight or the noble, and likewise the opposite. But there is no doubt that one can speak the same to nobles as to princes when it concerns the aforementioned virtues. This means that it is also their part to love God and fear Him above all else, to care for the public good for which they were established, to preserve and love justice according to their competences; just as it is for princes and other human beings. To be humane, liberal, and merciful, to love the wise and good and to govern by their advice, and likewise they should have all the other virtues, which I do not think I will describe for them, as it suffices to have described them once. What I have said before concerning the virtues serves each estate in the polity, and each individual person, therefore I will not proceed much longer in this form. For it is sufficient to speak of the manner in which everyone ought to do his own part in the order that God has established, that is, nobles do as nobles should, the populace does as it is appropriate for them, and everyone should come together as one body of the same polity, to live justly and in peace as they ought. That is what I had in mind when I was speaking of teaching them good morals. So I will begin my subject, as I did in the beginning of the first part where I spoke of the way to educate the children of princes. Now I will begin by speaking on how the ancient nobles educated their children, as it is written in their histories. . . .

Chapter 5: How There Are Six Good Conditions That Are Necessary for Nobles and Knights, and the First of the Six

It seems to me that according to the writings of the authors on the manners of noblemen, six conditions are especially necessary if they desire honor due for their merits. Otherwise their nobility is nothing but a mockery. The first is that they ought to love arms and the art of them perfectly, and they ought to practice that work. The second condition is that they ought to be very bold, and have such firmness and constancy in their courage that they never flee nor run from battles out of fear of death, nor spare their blood nor life, for the good of their prince and the safe keeping of their country and the republic.

Otherwise they will endure capital punishment through sentence of the law, and be dishonored forever.

Thirdly, they ought to give heart and steadiness to each other, counselling their companions to do well, and to be firm and steadfast.

The fourth is to be truthful and to uphold their fealty and oath. Fifthly, they ought to love and desire honor above all worldly things. Sixthly, they ought to be wise and crafty against their enemies and in all deeds of arms. To those who observe them and keep these conditions well there will be honor. But it is no doubt more difficult to do these things than it is to speak of them! Therefore, Aristotle said that the greatest honor is found where the greatest difficulty is.

On the first condition that the noble ought to have, which is to love and practice arms, and keep them right, we can give the examples of many noble knights. But since we have begun with the history of the Romans, let us continue with them, for it seems to me that they particularly loved warfare, and as a consequence were very noble (that is, the good ones who are mentioned in the writings of the ancient authors where their deeds are told). And although they loved arms well, they also observed knightly discipline, that is they kept right in suitable things by rules, so that they failed in nothing. Those who broke the established rules were punished. Valerius said that the discipline of chivalry, that is, keeping the rules and order appropriate to it, was the highest honor and firm foundation of the empire of Rome. Moreover, he said that they won their great victories, they secured the state, and the certain position of happy peace and tranquility because they kept this discipline well. Valerius gives us many examples of how they kept their discipline. Among others, he tells of a great rebellion in Sicily against the Romans. A consul, that is, one of their princes or high captains, was sent before a great army. He was called Calpurnius Piso. He sent one of his captains to lead a company of soldiers to guard a port against his enemies. But he was surprised by a great multitude of these people so that he and his army were forced to give up their arms. When Calpurnius the consul heard of this it seemed to him that they had not had sufficient watch guards, so when he [the captain] returned he shamed him publicly: he had him dressed in the clothing that the nobles wore, which was called a "toga," and as a sign that he had dishonored his nobility by giving himself up so easily, he had the fringe taken off, and forbade him to ride as long as the army did. And he was not allowed to stay with the other knights, that is, soldiers mounted on horseback, of whom he was captain. And he and his men were placed among the slingers, who were mere boys and foot soldiers, of no price, who used slings. . . .

Part Three: On the Common People

Here begins the third part of this book, which is addressed to the universal people.

Chapter 1: The First Chapter Discusses How the Estates Must Unite and Come Together

In the first part of this book concerning the instruction of princes, we depicted the aforementioned prince or princes as the head of the body politic, as planned before. Thereafter followed the second part, on the education of nobles and knights, which are the arms and the hands. In this part, with God's help, let us continue with what we can pluck from the authorities on this subject of the life of the body of the aforementioned polity, which means the whole of the people in common, described as the belly, legs, and feet, so that the whole be formed and joined in one whole living body, perfect and healthy. For just as the human body is not whole, but defective and deformed when it lacks any of its members, so the body politic cannot be perfect, whole, nor healthy if all the estates of which we speak are not well joined and united together. Thus, they can help and aid each other, each exercising the office which it has to, which diverse offices ought to serve only for the conservation of the whole community, just as the members of a human body aid to guide and nourish the whole body. And in so far as one of them fails, the whole feels it and is deprived by it.

Thus it is appropriate to discuss the way the final parts of the body should be maintained in health and in well-being, for it seems to me that they are the support and have the burden of all the rest of the body, thus they need the strength and the power to carry the weight of the other parts. This is why, just as we said earlier, the good prince must love his subjects and his people, and we spoke of the office of nobles which is established to guard and defend the people.

It is suitable to speak of the love, reverence, and obedience that his people should have for the prince. So let us say to all universally: all the estates owe the prince the same love, reverence, and obedience. But after I have said something about the increase of virtue in their life and manner of living, perhaps I will discuss the three ways the different classes ought to express the generalized principle. And because sometimes there are complaints among the three different estates—princes, knights, and people—because it seems to each of them that the other two do not do their duty in their offices, which can cause discord among them, a most prejudicial situation, here is a moral tale told as a fable:

Once upon a time there was great disagreement between the belly of a human body and its limbs. The belly complained loudly about the limbs and said that they thought badly of it and that they did not take care of it and feed as well as they should. On the other hand, the limbs complained loudly about the belly and said they were all exhausted from work, and yet despite all their labor, coming and going and working, the belly wanted to have everything and was never satisfied. The limbs then decided that they would no longer suffer such pain and labor, since nothing they did satisfied the belly. So they would stop their work and let the belly get along as best it might. The limbs stopped their work and the belly was no longer nourished. So it began to get thinner, and the limbs began to fail and weaken, and so, to spite one another, the whole body died.

Likewise, when a prince requires more than a people can bear, then the people complain against their prince and rebel by disobedience. In such discord, they all perish together. And thus I conclude that agreement preserves the whole body politic. And so attests Sallust, "in concord, little things increase, and by discord, great things decrease." . . .

Adapted from: Christine de Pizan, *The Book of the Body Politic,* pp. 3–5, 11, 14–19, 38, 55–59, 63–64, 90–91. Edited and translated by Kate Langdon. Copyright © 1994. Reprinted by permission of Cambridge University Press. ✦

24

'Now a New Kingdom of Femininity Is Begun . . .'

The Political Theory of Christine de Pizan's *The Book of the City of Ladies*

Edward M. Wheat

Introduction

Christine de Pizan's *The Book of the City of Ladies* (1405) is the first substantial work of political theory by a woman, preceding Mary Wollstonecraft's *A Vindication of the Rights of Woman* (1792) by almost 400 years. This bold fifteenth century book presents a detailed examination of the treatment of women by previous authors—literary and philosophical, secular and sacred—and their treatment by men in daily life. In doing so Christine discusses many themes that exercise feminists today. But it is not just the feminist themes that make the book interesting and significant. The work is also a studied attempt at political theory in a more general sense, one very much in the tradition of Western political philosophy. In *The Book of the City of Ladies*, Christine offers her readers a political utopia, a "city in words," to illuminate the problems of the political realm and serve as a guide to political thought and practice.

Though the book is clearly an important political theoretical work, assessing the precise relationship of Christine de Pizan and *The Book of the City of Ladies* to the tradition

of Western political theory is somewhat problematic. Christine was well known in her time as an important writer, a spokesperson on the status of women, and an astute commentator on politics and society. She was born c. 1364 in Venice. Thomas, her Italian father, was a physician and was appointed a councillor and scientific adviser at the court of Charles V of France. Her father supported her early education, and through additional rigorous self-study she eventually attained an education at least as good as the education typically available to males of her social status. She was married at fifteen to Etienne Castel of Picardy, one of the Royal Secretaries (notaries) at the court of Charles VI. Through her father and husband Christine thus had an insider's view of court politics. (There is some evidence that she herself worked as a court scribe.) She bore three children, was widowed at 25, and did not remarry. Following her husband's untimely death, Christine supported herself, her children, her mother, her two brothers, and her niece with her writing (Anderson and Zinsser 1988, 79–80; Willard 1984, 35–39, 44–47; Wisman 1984, xiv). She was quite probably the only woman of her time to make her living as a writer.

Over her forty-year writing career, Christine wrote lyric and epic poetry, essays, biography, autobiography, literary criticism, a textbook on military strategy, and a variety of historical and political works (Yenal 1982). Most of her works were originally written on commission, and they were very well received and widely appreciated. Several of her major works were translated into English. The fact that she wrote before the invention of printing in Europe limited the potential circulation of her works. When she was 54, she retired to a convent at Poissy and completed one final work, appropriately enough a long poem celebrating Joan of Arc. She died c. 1431.

Several of Christine's works were printed in French and English translations after her death, including a printed English edition of *The Book of the City of Ladies* in 1521, but by the late sixteenth century her works were out of print and rapidly became inaccessible and unknown except to medievalists, specialists in French literature, and collectors of rare manuscripts. In 1982 *The Book of the City of Ladies* was finally rendered into modern English, and Christine began to receive some recognition as a political thinker (see the articles in Brabant 1992), though her relationship to the history of Western political theory is still unclear. Is she a feminist? Is she a medieval thinker? A modern thinker? Is she merely a polemicist?

Chronologically, Christine stands between Marsilius of Padua and Machiavelli. Though *The Book of the City of Ladies* was published over a century and a quarter before Machiavelli's *The Prince* and is often classified as a late medieval work (Cohen & Fermon 1996), the following analysis, which includes comparison with some of the characteristics and ideas of *The Prince*, will suggest that Christine's book is better understood as an important work of modern political thought. Her emphasis on reason, her self-conscious individualism, her critique of religious and philosophical authorities, her egalitarian feminist argument, and her treatment of the centrality of power in political life clearly mark her as a modern.

The Book of the City of Ladies

In Part One of *The Book of the City of Ladies* (hereinafter *BCL*), Christine introduces herself and tells why and for what purpose she wrote the book. In the initial scene, three "crowned ladies" appear to her in her study and announce that they have come to bring her out of ignorance and to help her "establish and build the City of Ladies" (Pizan 1982, 11). Authorial dialogue with allegorical figures was a popular medieval literary device, and in *BCL* Christine converses with the traditional allegorical figures Reason and Justice, and significantly, with her own literary creation, Droiture, or Rectitude (right thinking, right doing) (Warner 1982, xv). The remainder of Part One is a dialogue between Christine and Lady Reason on several questions concerning women's status in philosophy, literature, society, and politics. In Part Two, the longest of the parts, Lady Rectitude continues the dialogue with Christine, and their interchange shifts to ques-

tions of everyday man-woman relationships, the marriage bond, the education of women, women's virtue, and great services rendered to various past societies and peoples by women. Lady Justice takes over the dialogue in the much shorter Part Three, and lectures Christine on the lives and contributions of several Christian saints and martyrs.

'Come Back to Yourself . . .'

Part One of *BCL* begins: "One day as I was sitting alone in my study surrounded by books on all kinds of subjects, devoting myself to literary studies, my usual habit, my mind dwelt at length on the weighty opinions of various authors whom I had studied for a long time." Several points can be made about this initial sentence. Assuming the reader is aware that the author is a woman, the startling information is conveyed that she has a mind, and not only that, she has a room of her own, in fact a study filled with books, in which she devotes herself, and has devoted herself for a long time, to the solitary study of "weighty opinions." Thus at the very beginning of the book appear two of its main themes, the natural intellectual abilities of women and the central importance of life-long study and education, especially women's education. These are points that Christine insists on, and they are argued throughout the book.

Christine then relates how the book came to be written. She says that she was in her study perusing a book by Matheolus and she began wondering "how it happened that so many different men—and learned men among them—have been and are so inclined to express both in speaking and in their treatises and writings so many wicked insults about women and their behavior" (Pizan 1982, 3–4). Vexed by this question she "thinks deeply" about it and begins "to examine [her] character and conduct as a natural woman" (Pizan 1982, 4). Based on her understanding of her own character and on many previous conversations that she had with "princesses, great ladies, women of the middle and lower classes," she realizes that the slanders of these learned men could not possibly be true. She notes that she had always dismissed her doubts as the product of the "simpleness and ignorance" of her intellect:

> And so I relied more on the judgement of others than on what I myself felt and knew. I was so transfixed in this line of thinking for such a long time that it seemed as if I were in a stupor. Like a gushing fountain, a series of authorities, whom I recalled one after another, came to mind, along with their opinions on this topic. . . . As I was thinking this, a great unhappiness and sadness welled up in my heart for I detested myself and the entire feminine sex, as though we were monstrosities in nature. (Pizan 1982, 4–5)

Gerda Lerner comments: "Here, for the first time in the written record, we have a woman defining the tension every thinking woman has experienced—between male authority denying her equality as a person and her own experience" (1993, 258–259).

Like Socrates—as portrayed by Plato in the *Apology*—Christine is confused about fundamental questions and has sought answers from the traditional authorities. She intuits that these answers are wrong, but she lacks the wisdom, she thinks, to confute them. She is kept in a "stupor," or to borrow a term from Mary Daly, she is "spooked," by their reputations for wisdom (1978, 321–337). Sitting in her study "occupied with these painful thoughts" she is startled by a ray of light that falls on her lap "as though it were the sun" (Pizan 1982, 6). It startles her because she was "sitting in a shadow where the sun could not have shone at that hour" (1982, 6). Looking up, she espies the three crowned ladies—Reason, Rectitude, and Justice—and the dialogue begins. Reason tells Christine,

> we have come to bring you out of the ignorance which so blinds your own intellect that you shun what you know for a certainty and believe what you do not know or see or recognize except by virtue of many strange opinions. . . . It also seems that you think that all the words of the philosophers are articles of faith, that they could never be wrong. . . . Come back to yourself, recover your senses, and do not trouble yourself anymore over such absurdities. (Pizan 1982, 6, 7, 8)

In this same passage Reason gives four examples of the philosophers whose words about "the question of the highest form of reality" should not necessarily be taken as articles of faith, but should be subject to critical examination: Plato, Aristotle, Saint Augustine, and the Doctors of the Church (Pizan 1982, 6–7). In the place of their exalted opinions, Reason suggests, Christine should seek "clear self-knowledge" (Pizan 1982, 9).

As these passages demonstrate, *BCL* is Socratic in form. It is a dramatic dialogue; it engages and questions all sources of traditional authority; the ideas of all classes are given credence, including those of "the middle and lower classes"; as the dialogue proceeds there is progressive clarification and enlightenment; there is continual use of Platonic imagery; Christine receives wisdom from an oracle, in her case three oracles, and the oracular answer is the same as that of the Oracle at Delphi—Know (and trust) Thyself. And, most importantly, like the *Republic*, the purpose of *BCL* is the building of an ideal polis, a "city in words." Lady Reason commands Christine, "Get up daughter! Without waiting any longer, let us go to the Field of Letters. There the City of Ladies will be founded . . ." (Pizan 1982, 16). It will be a city "extremely beautiful, without equal, and of perpetual duration in the world" (Pizan 1982, 11). In a passage reminiscent of Socrates likening himself to a midwife of ideas in the *Apology*, Christine declares that despite her ignorance she is a "handmaiden," ready to help the three Ladies "build and construct in the world from now on a new city" (Pizan 1982, 15).

Reason tells Christine at one point that she and the other Ladies do not often appear to humans, but that they have come to her because of her "great love of investigating the truth through long and continual study . . . solitary and separated from the world." They will reward her for her diligence by helping her to construct a City on the Field of Letters for "all valiant women" who have until now lacked the weapons necessary to win "a war in which women have had no defense" (Pizan 1982, 10). What women need, in other words, is what Christine already has, discipline, learning, and a study of one's own. *BCL* will reveal this to all women, and the book itself, when completed, will be a weapon for their use.

As the dialogue of Part One proceeds, Christine questions Reason about women's intellectual abilities. Reason responds that "although there are ignorant women, there are many women who have better minds and a more active sense of prudence and judgement than most men" (Pizan 1982, 35). "They have minds skilled in conceptualizing and learning, just like men . . ." and "they have minds that are freer and sharper [than those of men] whenever they apply themselves" (Pizan 1982, 63). Christine insists throughout her book on the necessity of education for all women and their ability to take advantage of it. The final paragraph of *BCL* begins with a command by Christine, "In brief, all women—whether noble, bourgeois, or lower-class—be well-informed in all things. . . ." (Pizan 1982, 256).

Another of the central teachings of *BCL* is that virginity, chastity, celibacy (both in and out of marriage), and principled widowhood are often necessary to secure women's autonomy, freedom, and power. If you have a choice, don't marry; if you marry, be as celibate as possible; if you are widowed, don't remarry. Throughout the stories of the great legendary and historical women in her book, Christine has recourse to certain phrases that she repeats again and again. "She had such a great and lofty heart that not for a day in her life did she deign to couple with a man, but remained a virgin her entire lifetime." "This lady was so high-minded that she never condescended to couple with a man, remaining a virgin her whole life." "With her considerable force of mind, this lady remained a virgin her entire life." "She was so high-minded that she did not deign to take a husband or to couple with a man." "This lady was quite chaste during her marriage as well as during her widowhood . . ."(Pizan 1982, 33, 42, 48, 61, 74, 157). And so on. Christine sets a demanding ascetic standard for her ladies. A rigorously disciplined mind is the key to feminine power and autonomy, and chastity, or control of one's sexuality, is conducive to maintaining one's high-mindedness. Women must not "set themselves adrift in the dangerous and damnable sea of foolish love" (Pizan 1982, 202).

Christine, Lady Reason, and Lady Rectitude discuss the exemplary lives of some historical ladies who performed well in public roles that are normally thought to be the preserve of males—politics, statesmanship, war, science, and philosophy—as well as the lives of women from myth and Homeric legend. In presenting these *exempla*, Christine translates and adapts freely from other authors, a common literary practice of the time (Forhan 1994, xviii; Lewis 1964, 5, 11–12). In this case, she relies heavily on Boccaccio's *de claris mulieribus*. Barbara Hooper argues that in presenting these exemplary female lives Christine "reconstructs the idea of woman, countering male discourse with what may be the first feminist theory, the first feminist 'plan'. . . . " (1992, 46–47; see also Kelly 1984).

As already discussed, a principal teaching of Part One of *BCL* is the appropriateness of intellectual work and the scholarly life for women. In terms of politics, statesmanship, and war, Reason cautions Christine against those who say "that women do not have a natural sense for politics and government," and promises to give her "examples of several great women rulers who have lived in past times" (Pizan 1982, 32). In this regard she instructs Christine at some length on the history of the Amazons, whose kingdom "founded and powerfully upheld, lasted more than eight hundred years" (Pizan 1982, 51). "In large battalions constituted solely of ladies and maidens, they advanced on their enemies and laid waste to their lands with fire and the sword, and no one could resist them. . . . They so delighted in the vocation of arms that through force they greatly increased their country and their dominion, and their high fame spread everywhere" (Pizan 1982, 41). Lady Reason tells Christine the stories of several Amazon queens and princesses, but notes that there were so many of these valiant stateswomen, Amazons and otherwise, who met and outperformed men at their own game that "to name all of them one by one could bore readers" (Pizan 1982, 42).

In response to Christine's query "whether there was ever a woman who discovered hitherto unknown knowledge," Reason tells Christine that after Carmentis had to leave Arcadia, her home, because of a regime change, she sailed to the river Tiber, disembarked, and built a fortress on the Palentine that became the foundation of Rome. "After discovering that the men of that country were all savages, she wrote certain laws, enjoining them to live in accord with right and reason, following justice. She was the first to institute laws in that country which subsequently became so renowned and from which all the statutes of law derive" (Pizan 1982, 71). Later she invented and "established the Latin alphabet and syntax, spelling, the difference between vowels and consonants, as well as a complete introduction to the science of grammar." Of Carmentis' accomplishment Reason remarks that "one can say that nothing more worthy in the world was ever invented" (Pizan 1982, 72), since "thanks to her, men have been brought out of ignorance and led to knowledge" (Pizan 1982, 78).

Reason also tells Christine the stories of many women, such as Sappho, who excelled in learning, poetry, and philosophy. Of the Roman woman Proba, Reason remarks that she "had such a noble mind and so loved and devoted herself to study that she mastered all seven liberal arts and was an excellent poet and delved so deeply into the books of the poets, particularly Virgil's poems, that she knew them all by heart" (Pizan 1982, 65). After years of study Proba went on to create her own great works, combining stories from the Scriptures with matter from the great poetry of the classical tradition, of which no less an authority than Boccaccio remarked that it was not just admirable that "such a noble idea would come into a woman's brain, but it is even more marvelous that she could actually execute it" (Pizan 1982, 65–66).

In other stories Reason attributes to women the invention of cultivation, the art of making armor from iron and steel, the fashioning of flutes, fifes, and other wind instruments, the construction of gardens and planting, the science of dying wool, the sci-ence of the extraction of silk from silkworms, and "the building of cities and towns of permanent construction" (Pizan 1982, 76). Of this last feat, attributed to Queen Ceres, Reason remarks that "she transformed the minds of vagabond and lazy men by . . . leading them from the caverns of ignorance to the heights of contemplation and proper behavior" (Pizan 1982, 78), thus attributing the creation of civilization itself to a woman. Christine expresses her deep gratitude to Reason for enlightening her on these matters, because "the typical opinions and comments of men claim that women have been and are useful in the world only for bearing children and sewing" (Pizan 1982, 77). The burden of Part One has been to challenge such "typical opinions."

'Now a New Kingdom of Femininity Is Begun . . .'

In Part Two of *BCL* the discussion turns more to the everyday personal interaction of men and women in courtship, marriage, childbearing, and so on. And here the dialogue takes on a harder edge; from this point on in Part Two the dialogue shifts away from praise of exemplary women to direct attack on men for their attitudes to women and their baiting of women. Husbands, sons, the Emperors of Rome, Popes and Churchmen, the behavior of all men, regardless of station, is subjected to scrutiny and condemnation. After a preliminary discussion in the first six sections of some other great women in history, Christine asks Lady Rectitude in the seventh section to help her understand a "practice with widespread currency among men—and even among some women—"

> that when women are pregnant and then give birth to daughters, their husbands are upset and grumble because their wives did not give birth to sons. . . . Why does it happen, my lady, that they grieve so? Are daughters a greater liability to their parents than sons, or less loving and more indifferent toward their parents than sons are? (Pizan 1982, 110)

Rectitude answers that simplemindedness and ignorance account for much of this misperception, but that it is also a result of the belief of fathers that daughters are a financial liability and are likely to be deceived when they are young and naive, which would bring discredit on the family. Rectitude tells the stories of many women who exhibited much more filial piety than sons, and she also disposes of the economic argument, pointing out that if one looks closely, over a lifetime sons often cost their parents much more than daughters. "And if you consider the anger and worry which many sons cause their parents—for they often get involved in harsh and bitter riots and brawls or pursue a dissolute life, all to the grief and expense of their parents—I think that this anguish can easily exceed the worries which they have because of their daughters" (Pizan 1982, 111). She adds to this the suggestion that "if you are very attentive, you will find more sons than daughters who are . . . corrupt" (Pizan 1982, 112).

Shortly after this discussion, Rectitude announces in section twelve, very close to the center of *BCL*, that they have completed the foundation, houses, palaces and defensive turrets of the city and that

> It is therefore right that we start to people this noble City now, so that it does not remain vacant or empty, but instead is wholly populated with ladies of great excellence, for we do not want any others here. How happy will be the citizens of our edifice, for they will not need to fear or worry about being evicted by foreign armies, for this work has the special property that its owners cannot be expelled. Now a New Kingdom of Femininity is begun, and it is far better than the earlier kingdom of the Amazons, for the ladies residing here will not need to leave their land in order to conceive or give birth to new heirs to maintain their possessions throughout the different ages, from one generation to another, for those whom we now place here will suffice quite adequately forever more. (Pizan 1982, 116–117)

Like Queen Ceres, Christine is building a city, but The City of Ladies is a kallipolis, a city in words like Plato's *Republic*, and though it may never be actualized on earth it will be perennially available to those who wish to guide their individual lives by its precepts and laws. Though a city in words, it is "in the world" as a book, and this is very important; as Reason has stated earlier: "natural sense can only last as long as the lifetime of the person who has it, and when he dies, his sense dies with him. Acquired learning on the other hand, lasts forever . . . and it is useful for many people insofar as it can be taught to others and recorded in books for the sake of future generations" (Pizan 1982, 88). The book is a weapon, a source of intellectual countervailing power, for those who wish to counterattack in the "war in which women have had no defense" (Pizan 1982, 10).

In a series of interchanges, Christine and Rectitude discuss the common views of female psychology and behavior held by men and expressed in their behavior and in the writings of theological and cultural authorities. Christine complains that the authorities argue that marriage is unhappy for men "because of women's faults and impetuosity, and because of their rancorous ill-humor" (Pizan 1982, 118). The authorities say women are untruthful, gossipers, expensive to maintain, betrayers of their husband's confidences and interests, frivolous, immoral, and, as Christine sums up at one point, "Men, especially writing in books, vociferously and unanimously claim that women in particular are fickle and inconstant, changeable and flighty, weak-hearted, compliant like children, and lacking all stamina" (Pizan 1982, 164).

The authorities Christine and Rectitude have in mind share "a common attitude which took its tone from the Church," as expressed by the great 13th century encyclopaedist Vincent de Beauvais in his *Speculum historiale*: woman is "the confusion of man, an insatiable beast, a continuous anxiety, an incessant warfare, a daily ruin, a house of tempest . . . a hindrance to devotion" (Tuchman 1978, 222). Though she appears to be unaware of Christine de Pizan's work and decries "the paucity of political thinking during the middle ages," Diana Coole has argued that Western feminists from the medieval period to the present have faced two culturally sanctioned philosophical arguments denigrating women and relegating them to the private, non-political sphere: the scriptural arguments stemming from the two accounts of the creation of woman in Genesis coupled with the Pauline commentaries, and a secular argument stemming from classical political theory, especially the naturalistic teleology of Aristotle. The latter, of course, was carried to Christine's time in the writings of St. Thomas Aquinas and the Fathers of the Church (1993, 35, 40–52). In her dialogue with Lady Rectitude, Christine directly confronts these arguments.

Rectitude's responses to Christine's various queries and statements are premised in an idea already advanced by Lady Reason in Part One, the divine equality of men and women. "God created the soul and placed wholly similar souls, equally good and noble in the feminine and in the masculine bodies" (Pizan 1982, 23). Lady Rectitude restates the point: "There is not the slightest doubt that women belong to the people of God and the human race as much as men, and are not another species or dissimilar race" (Pizan 1982, 187). Christine's discussion of male/female equality rests on St. Augustine's belief that God created the soul, not the body, "which allowed her to stress the equality of the sexes regardless of their bodily differences" (Lerner 1993, 144).

Continuing the strategy of BCL up to this point, Rectitude relates the stories of many great ladies of the past whose behavior refutes the various slanders brought by men against women. In section 47 of Part Two, however, the strategy abruptly shifts to direct attacks upon representative males. Rectitude tells Christine of the inconstancy and weakness and corruption of several Roman emperors, including Claudius, Nero, Galba, and Otho. Not only emperors, but religious authorities as well are subjected to Rectitude's censure:

Let me also tell you about the popes and churchmen, who must be more perfect and more elect than other people. But whereas in the early Church they were holy, ever since Constantine endowed the Church with large revenues and riches, the remaining holiness . . . well, you only have to read through their histories and chronicles . . . you need only consider

whether the words and deeds of temporal and spiritual princes show much firmness and constancy. The point is clear—I will not say more. (Pizan 1982, 169)

Rectitude condemns men for their hypocrisy in blaming women for their own obvious faults, pointing to "all the evil kings in various countries, disloyal emperors, heretical popes, and other unbelieving prelates filled with greed." In fact, "you will never find such perversion in women as you encounter in a great number of men," and "women should bless and praise God who placed their precious souls in feminine vessels" (Pizan 1982, 169, 170).

Just before the passages on the faults of the emperors and religious authorities, Christine poses a question. "I am . . . troubled and grieved when men argue that many women want to be raped and that it does not bother them at all even when they verbally protest. It would be hard to believe that such great villainy is actually pleasant for them" (Pizan 1982, 161). Rectitude ridicules this notion and instructs Christine with the story of Lucretia, who was raped by Tarquin, committed suicide, and in whose memory a "fitting, just, and holy" law was passed that mandated execution for the crime of rape (Pizan 1982, 162), and with the story of "the noble queen of the Galatians," who was violently raped by an officer of the Roman army while she was a prisoner of war. The Queen bided her time, contrived through a ruse to be alone with the officer when the ransom came and then, "the lady, who had a knife, stabbed him in the neck and killed him. She took his head and without difficulty brought it to her husband and told him the entire story and how she had taken vengeance" (Pizan 1982, 163). Christine replies that Lady Rectitude had given her "a remarkable account of the marvelous constancy, strength, endurance, and virtue of women" (Pizan 1982, 164).

Later in Part Two Christine comes back to the question of sexuality, a subject "that goes somewhat beyond the temperament of reason," and remarks to Rectitude that "a natural behavior of men toward women and of women toward men prevails in the world which is not brought about by human institutions but by the inclination of the flesh, and in which men and women love one another with a very strong love strengthened in turn by foolish pleasure" (Pizan 1982, 186). Christine complains that though both sexes possess natural sexuality, males complain that it is women that are deceitful in matters of the heart. Ovid justifies his attack on women in his "Ars amatoria," Christine notes, by saying that it is for the common good that the deceptions of women be made public.

The Goddess defers to Christine on the subject of natural sexuality and women's deceit, saying "Dear friend, as for the charge that women are deceitful, I really do not know what more I can say to you, for you yourself have adequately handled the subject, answering Ovid and the others in your 'Epistre au Dieu d'Amour' and your 'Epistres sur le Roman de la Rose'" (Pizan 1982, 187). In further response, Rectitude relates stories of several women who were not deceitful and were constant to their men unto death, but before this Rectitude undertakes to respond to Ovid's claim that to reveal the ruses of women is in the interest of the common good, saying that this itself is deceitful, since

> the common good of a city or land or any community of people is nothing other than the profit or general good in which all members, women as well as men, participate and take part. But whatever is done with the intention of benefiting some and not others is a matter of private and not public welfare. (Pizan 1982, 187)

Since men and women (according to Christine) equally possess natural sexuality, Rectitude argues that the deceit of men and the traps they lay for women should also be publicized for the common good. "Therefore I conclude that if these men had acted in the public good that is for both parties—they should also have addressed themselves to women and warned them to beware of men's tricks just as they warned men to be careful about women" (Pizan 1982, 188).

This interchange points to an interesting egalitarian, even "democratic" political argument that runs throughout *BCL*. In these passages, the natural equality and sexuality of men and women that Justice proclaimed

in Part One and Rectitude reiterated in Part Two serves as the basis of a discussion of the common good as it applies to "a city or land or any community of people." The City of Ladies itself is said at several different points to be populated by "women from all classes" (Pizan 1982, 214). According to one scholar, "no writer before Christine showed as much interest in the situation of the poor; no one spoke of them with such feeling or kindness" (Brian Woledge, quoted in Reno 1992, 176). Exemplary stories are told of all classes of women from prostitutes to queens. The unrelenting attacks on the traditional hierarchies of sacred and secular governmental and literary authorities that occur throughout the book are part of this democratic argument, as is the strong insistence on the education of women and the recurrence throughout the book of the Socratic idea of the value of self-knowledge. And women are said to have "a natural sense for politics and government" (Pizan 1982, 32). During her telling of the story of Veturia, a noble lady of Rome, Rectitude remarks offhandedly but pointedly that "it is extremely dangerous for a people to be governed at the will of a single individual" (Pizan 1982, 150).

Another theme that is strongly related to Christine's democratic/egalitarian argument runs throughout Parts One and Two of *BCL*—a cogent critique of socially constructed gender roles. Christine's concern with this dates from 1399 when she became involved in a public debate about an extremely popular literary work, Jean de Meung's *Roman de la rose*, a maliciously satiric poem with misogynist elements. Christine wrote a long poem critical of de Meung's portrayal of women and exchanged a number of letters with male literary authorities that were publicly circulated. This exchange was an early moment in the *querelle des femmes*, a debate on the status of women that lasted for more than three centuries in Europe and "represented the first serious discussion of gender as a social construct in European history" (Lerner 1993, 146; see also Kelly 1984, 66–72; Willard 1994, 138–141). Putting her ideas in modern terminology (Elshtain 1992, 4; cf. Pateman [1983] 1991; Pateman 1988, 224–227), she accepts that there are biological differences of sex and that this entails somewhat different social roles, but she disputes the way socially constructed private and public gender roles have traditionally been defined and the terrible abuse that these imposed definitions have often justified.

Earlier, Christine had asked Lady Reason why, if women "have minds skilled in conceptualizing and learning, just like men," women are not learned in the sciences. Lady Reason answers, "Because my daughter, the public does not require them to get involved in the affairs which men are commissioned to execute. . . ." "If it were customary to send daughters to school like sons, and if they were then taught the natural sciences, they would learn as thoroughly and understand the subtleties of all the arts and sciences as well as sons" (Pizan 1982, 63). Interestingly, Lady Rectitude later remarks of Christine's own case that whereas Christine's father was unusual in that he encouraged her in her studies, her mother "who wished to keep you busy with spinning and silly girlishness, following the common custom of women, was the major obstacle to your being more involved in the sciences" (Pizan 1982, 154–155). Here, as in other places in her writings, Christine offers intimate autobiographical evidence for her historical and theoretical arguments. The individualism this reveals is striking; for Christine the personal is, indeed, political. And by the end of Parts One and Two of *BCL* her stern prescription for individual female autonomy and personal empowerment has been clearly outlined: self-knowledge, self-trust, life-long study, an ascetic life-style, principled celibacy, and recourse for intellectual countervailing power to *The Book of the City of Ladies*.

'Be Well Informed in All Things . . .'

In the final and shortest part of *BCL*, Christine steps back and allows Lady Justice to dominate the dialogue. Justice nominates the Virgin Mary to rein as Queen over the City of Ladies and proceeds to populate the city with numerous female Christian saints and martyrs whose stories she tells to Christine. Christine remains completely silent during Justice's eighteen-section monologue. Only in the nineteenth and final section of Part Three—"The End of the Book: Christine Addresses the Ladies"—does Christine regain her authorial voice, and when she does it is to utter some somewhat surprising statements.

In her final address, Christine rejoices at the completion of her task and exhorts the ladies to be well informed in all things and to use the City as a refuge and as a weapon of defense against "enemies and assailants." All this is to be expected; but given the critical and egalitarian argument of Parts One and Two, it is somewhat disquieting to come to the end of Part Three of *BCL* and find Christine writing the following: "And you ladies who are married, do not scorn being subject to your husbands, for sometimes it is not the best thing for a creature to be independent," and supporting this idea with quotations from scripture (Pizan 1982, 255). Christine says that she hopes that women will be lucky and have "peaceful, good, and discrete" husbands, but that even those wives who have "cruel, mean, and savage" husbands should be patient and "strive to endure them" while endeavoring to bring them back to a seemly life. So at the close of *BCL*, it appears, we have an acceptance of the traditional hierarchies and double standards that have received such a battering during the argument of Parts One and Two.

One way to explain this is to say that Christine's critique takes place within a framework of unquestioned Christian belief and dogma. But the place of Christianity in Christine's political theory is a vexed subject. In Parts One and Two of *BCL* she attacks the writings of religious thinkers and the behavior of clergy. In an important study of Christine's use of the metaphor of the "body politic" in one of her later polemical works, Kate Langdon Forhan concluded that "despite Christine's apparent piety, [her] matter-of-fact attitude toward the clergy may indicate that her religious belief is more conventional than inspired" (1992, 45; see also Forhan 1994, xxii). At points Christine seems to give sacred writings the same status as secular writings, or even a somewhat lower status, though she refers to the classical histories themselves as "fictions" (Pizan 1982, 103). She has Lady Justice refer to the story of Jesus and the Apostles as a "holy legend" (Pizan 1982, 252). She remarks to her own creation, Rectitude, "Indeed, my lady, what you say is as true as the Lord's Prayer" (Pizan 1982, 155). Yet the few extant accounts of her life and works assume she was a believing Christian. Marina Warner calls her "a devout Christian woman" (Warner 1982, xvi).

Earl Jeffrey Richards argues cogently that Christine simply wanted men to live up to their professed Christian standards, and this argument has some merit. In this account, her use of Christianity is to overcome oppression. In this view, she is similar to Martin Luther King and other modern reformers in her commitment to radicalizing Christian values. She presents herself as a Christian, and her book can be seen as a complement to Saint Augustine's *City of God*: "By juxtaposing the two cities Christine did not intend that her City of Ladies rival the City of God, but that her political vision be understood as participating in a Christian tradition of political philosophy" (Richards 1982, xxix). This sort of argument justifies Christine's seeming turnabout at the close of her book, but perhaps there is another way of looking at it.

A Manual for Princesses?

Christine began her writing career as a poet, and her biographer Charity Cannon Willard notes that she was attracted very early by the idea of hidden meaning in poetry (1984, 68). In the closing stanzas of one of her poems, "This Mask No Grief Reveals," Christine acknowledged this aspect of her poetics:

So no plaint nor appeal
My aching heart can show
And mirth, not tears, bestow;
Those my gay rhymes conceal.
May this mask no grief reveal
So it is I conceal
The true source of my ditty,
Instead I must be witty
To hide the wound that does not heal.
Let this mask no grief reveal.
—(Willard 1994, 55)

Covert techniques of literary exposition were common in Christine's time, and they have a long history in political philosophy. Might it be that in her prose works Christine indulged in a form of the "secret" or "esoteric" writing that Leo Strauss argued is often a necessary strategy of political philosophy due to its subversive nature (Strauss 1969, 29–53)?

In Christine's time most written texts were produced under a patronage or commission system, and indeed most of Christine's works were so produced. Her first major prose work, *The Book of the Deeds and Good Customs of the Wise King Charles V* (1404), was commissioned by Philip, the Duke of Burgundy, the King's brother. The title indicates the somewhat hagiographic nature of the book, yet scholars have argued that even in the works she produced on commission from the Duke of Burgundy and various other royal authorities Christine often criticized her patrons and many of the institutions and practices of her time and found "ways to say more than she could sometimes write explicitly" (Reno 1992, 179; see also Forhan 1994, xvi–xvii).

The fact that *BCL* was not a commissioned work is important. Since Christine wrote and published the book on her own, it is much more explicitly critical than her other works, and she defers much less to traditional and status-quo ideas. Given the nature of her times, however, she could not be completely explicit, and read carefully *BCL* can be seen to embody a variety of covert techniques. Christine deploys her own literary creation, Lady Rectitude, in Part Two of *BCL*, which is appreciably longer than the other two Parts. She sandwiches many of her most interesting and radical ideas between somewhat more moderate discussions in Part One and a very conventional, and much shorter, discussion of Christian saints and martyrs in Part Three. In Part Two, where she announces the beginning of the "New Kingdom of Femininity," she directly attacks males, in the form of the ultimate patriarchs—the emperors of Rome, popes and churchmen, and husbands. She also comes more to the fore herself—the sayings of Rectitude, her literary creation, are said to be as true as the Lord's Prayer; she talks of her own experience, using it as evidence; she also directly discusses natural sexuality, and women's sexual freedom, and Christine is lauded by Rectitude as an expert in the subject.

A comparison of the section titles of Parts One, Two, and Three, provides textual evidence for the idea that Christine means the Parts of *BCL* to have different "weights." At the beginning of Part One, when Christine describes the initial scene in her study and the appearance of the Ladies, the titles have initial stock phrases like "Here Christine describes . . . ," "Here Christine tells. . . ." Once she begins conversing with Lady Reason, the titles with Christine's name in them all begin "Christine asks . . . " and in those titles with Lady Reason's name, Reason most often "speaks," as in "Here Reason speaks of a queen of France. . . ." In Part Two, Christine's name first appears in the title of section seven, "Christine speaks to Rectitude," and thereafter in Part Two, with only one exception, when Christine again "asks," she "speaks" to and with Lady Rectitude. Christine also begins frequently using the construction "Then I, Christine said . . . " or "I Christine spoke . . . " within the text of the sections of Part Two. By contrast, in Part Three Lady Justice does all the "speaking," and Christine's name does not appear in any but the title of section nineteen, the final section of the book, "The end of the book: Christine addresses the ladies." The "I, Christine" construction is not used at all in Part Three. Perhaps these are hints to the attentive reader of *BCL* that Christine's real teaching is to be sought primarily in Part Two of the book.

It seems possible that she, as Leo Strauss argues of Machiavelli and other political philosophers, trusts that many readers will leaf through the first few pages of the book, begin scanning the titles of the numbered sections, lose patience, and skip over the more troublesome matter of Part Two to the end to read her more familiar and comforting scripturally based account of religious saints and martyrs. She even inserts a bit of filler at the beginning of Part Two in case a reader skips from the first few pages of Part One to the beginning of Part Two. She cunningly suggests this approach to the casual reader on the first page of *BCL* when she describes her encounter with Matheolus' book. On the second day of reading his book she says that she found it to be unpleasant and full of lies and that she completed it by "browsing here and there and reading the end" (Pizan 1982, 3). This puts Christine's acceptance of the traditional hierarchy within Christian marriage put forth on the last few pages of the book in a very different light. The closing discussion serves to distract the casual reader from the central fact that there are no men in the City of Ladies and softens the impact of the openly secular and separatist argument of the book as a whole. Only the serious reader will engage the central arguments of Parts One and Two.

In Christine's time there was, of course, an accepted tradition of religious female separatism dating from the 3rd century of the Christian era (Lerner 1993, 24–25). But Christine's separatist city is quite different than a cloistral retreat (within a patriarchal institution) for religious purposes; the *raison d'être* of *BCL* is general female empowerment. Christine's "city in words" serves as a safe haven, an intellectual fortress, from which all women can begin to reclaim their rightful place in the secular social and political world.

Is there anything beyond her secular egalitarian arguments, her overt attacks on male authorities, her open discussion of natural sexuality, and her separatist political principles that can account for her elaborate concealments? Is it possible that Christine wrote *BCL* as a "manual for princesses" over a hundred years before Machiavelli wrote his manual for princes?

There are many similarities between the two books. The concealment of central principles is one similarity. Another is their use of history. Both Christine and Machiavelli use history in a particular way; they appeal to history as an experiential and authoritative base for their teachings, but as many scholars have noted, Machiavelli modifies history to suit his purposes and teach his lessons. Marina Warner has noted the same of Christine's use of history and mythology: "To achieve her vindications of women, Christine alters her source material in the most surprising ways, sometimes refreshing, sometimes bizarre." Socrates' wife, Xanthippe, who is traditionally portrayed as shrewish, "emerges from Christine's pages as loyal and devoted and wise" (1982, xv, xvi; see also Lerner 1993, 259–260; Willard 1984, 92, 136).

There are some stylistic similarities as well. Christine's book is based on an architectural metaphor that recurs throughout. She refers to ink as the mortar of the city, her pen as a means of fortification, great ladies' lives as the foundation stones of the wall, and so on. Machiavelli adopts many architectural metaphors throughout *The Prince*, likening the establishment of a secure political base to the building of a house or the construction of a wall. Both use hunting metaphors as well (Machiavelli 1992, 5, 19, 34, 41; Pizan 1982, 12, 38, 256).

Yet another similarity to Machiavelli's ideas is the ascetic standard that Christine prescribes for the ladies of her city. In *The Prince*, Machiavelli argues that a successful prince must exert rigid control over his passions and appetites; the prince must be disciplined, studious, and must engage constantly in military training. Most important, the prince must be frugal and chaste: he must "keep his hands off the property of his subjects or citizens, and off their women" (Machiavelli 1992, 46). Christine decrees a regimen of constant rigorous intellectual study and self-improvement. And she argues that celibacy is necessary for woman's autonomy.

An idea that is often cited as one of Machiavelli's central political teachings is found in an inchoate form in Christine's book. Machiavelli taught that no matter how strenuously a virtuous Prince might prepare for eventualities, no matter how much wisdom and prudence he brings to bear, it is impossible to secure a principality forever. There will always be the chance events that bring down a kingdom. Fortuna, or fortune, will fell even the wisest and most prudent Prince (Machiavelli 1992, 68). Similarly, in the story of Queen Dido, the founder of Carthage, told in Part One of *BCL*, Lady Reason praises the Queen for her "prudence and attentiveness," but notes that even this great female lawgiver "lived for a long time in glory and would have lived so the rest of her life if Fortune had not been unfavorable to her, but Fortune, often envious of the prosperous, mixed too harsh a brew for her in the end" (Pizan 1982, 95).

Read in a certain way, Christine gives the same notorious twist to the concept of "virtu," or virtue, in *BCL* as does Machiavelli in *The Prince* (on Machiavelli's redefinition of the word virtu, see Berlin 1992; de Alvarez 1989, xix–xxii). Though Christine constantly exhorts her ladies to "cultivate virtue," Brabant and Brint point out that in *BCL* she does not give a catalogue of deadly sins or "identify immutable moral principles" (1992, 209) as do many other writers of her time. Recall the story related earlier of "the noble queen of the Galatians," violently raped by an officer of the Roman army while she was a prisoner of war. The wronged lady managed to stab her defiler to death through a ruse, cut off his head, and deliver same to her husband as proof of her vengeance. At the beginning of the section the Queen is described as "quite beautiful, simple, chaste, and virtuous" (Pizan 1982, 162). Then there is the story told in the scriptures of the widow, Judith, who was upright, beautiful, and "above all chaste and virtuous" (Pizan 1982, 144). Judith saved the people of Israel by agreeing to come to Holophernes' bed and then sneaking in and cutting off his head with his own sword. The people of Israel were saved by this "honest woman" (Pizan 1982, 145). One final example will suffice. Artemisia, Queen of Caria, "possessed strong virtue, moral wisdom, and political prudence." The neighboring Rhodians did not like the idea of a female ruler and planned to attack Caria. Hearing of this, Artemisia left the city, tricked them into thinking that the city had capitulated, and then slipped back into the city and "captured and killed all the princes" (Pizan 1982, 55–57).

It does not take strenuous analysis to read in these passages the identical notorious distinction between private and public virtue that is found in the writings of Niccolo Machiavelli and other modern political thinkers. Many of the great ladies profiled in *BCL* combine virtue in their private dealings with the intellect, guile, and willingness to get their hands dirty and use force that constitutes Machiavellian *virtu* in public life. They are, like Judith, also willing to use their sexuality to advance public ends, and this is justified; it does not compromise their virtue. The great ladies are often both Lions (force) and Foxes (guile). *BCL* is a manual for princesses with a very modern message. Though she went to some lengths to conceal her "unladylike polemics" (Laennec 1993) in her work, Christine appears to develop the Argument of the Dirty Hands sixty-four years before Machiavelli was born.

Conclusions: Christine and Political Philosophy

Christine de Pizan is a critical theorist, if we follow John Dryzek's characterization of critical theory as a "theory addressed to a specific audience and designed to liberate them from their sufferings"; a theory that "strives to interpret the condition of a group of sufferers, make plain to them the cause of their suffering, and by sketching a course of relief, demonstrate that their situation is not immutable" (1990, 19, 185). In *BCL*, Christine directly attacks the misogynistic arguments and actions of the secular and sacred authorities of history and her own time, and she offers a course of relief: education, especially as regards the collective experience and history of women; control of one's sexuality; and the safespace provided by her book. The specific audience her theory addresses is, of course, women. Though Sheila Delany (1992) and other scholars argue that the use of the modern term "feminist" to refer to Christine and her works is somewhat misleading and anachronistic, her work is profoundly and radically feminist in Carolyn Heilbrun's sense of the term: "A feminist . . . questions the gender arrangements in society and culture . . . and works to change them; the desired transformation gives more power to women while simultaneously challenging both the forms and the legitimacy of power as it is now established" (1990, 3).

Though the thrust of her work is feminist, Christine's dialogue explicitly participates in a broader tradition of political philosophy stemming from the classical Greeks. Like the Socratic dialogues of Plato, a central purpose of *BCL* is human liberation through study and dialectical thought. The arguments of *BCL* embody a critique of various forms of domination, including the domination of institutionalized religion, but the critique is based partially in a radicalized and purified Christianity that looks forward 125 years to the European Reformation. Situated chronologically on the cusp of the Modern between Marsilius of Padua and Machiavelli, Christine advances arguments reminiscent of the universalism and hierarchicalism of the classics but more congenial to the relativism and individualism of the moderns. If political science, following in the choppy wake of other disciplines, ever gets around to revising and expanding its canon of central thinkers, Christine will surely be a candidate for inclusion.

There is one certainty: Christine de Pizan is a founder of feminist political theoretical discourse, and she should be more widely recognized as such. She forcefully argues for female autonomy and equality against the arguments of history and the practices of her own culture, and she correctly identifies women's lack of education as a central cause of their condition. Feminism is traditionally seen as dating back some 200 years to Mary Wollstonecraft's manifesto "The Vindication of the Rights of Woman" (1790). But feminism, at least theoretical feminism, is nearly 600 years old. What Christine de Pizan wrote in her book in 1405 can be said of her book, "Now a new Kingdom of Femininity is begun."

References

Anderson, Bonnie S. and Judith P. Zinsser. 1988. *A History of Their Own: Women in Europe from Prehistory to the Present, Vol II.* New York: Harper and Row.

Berlin, Isaiah. 1992. "The Question of Machiavelli." In *The Prince: A Norton Critical Edition*, 2nd ed., Robert M. Adams, ed. New York: Norton.

Brabant, Margaret and Michael Brint. 1992. "Identity and Difference in Christine de Pizan's *Cité des Dames.*" In *Politics, Gender, and Genre: The Political Thought of Christine de Pizan*, Margaret Brabant, ed. Boulder, Colorado: Westview Press.

Cohen, Mitchell and Nicole Fermon, eds. 1996. *Princeton Readings in Political Thought: Essential Texts Since Plato.* Princeton, New Jersey: Princeton University Press.

Coole, Diana. 1993. *Women in Political Theory: From Ancient Misogyny to Contemporary Feminism*, 2nd ed. Boulder, Colorado: Lynne Rienner Publishers.

Daly, Mary. 1978. *Gyn/Ecology: The Metaethics of Radical Feminism.* Boston: Beacon Press.

de Alvarez, Leo Paul S. 1989. "Introduction." *The Prince.* Prospect Heights, Illinois: Waveland Press.

Delany, Sheila. 1992. "History, Politics, and Christine Studies: A Polemical Reply." In *Politics, Gender, and Genre: The Political Thought of Christine de Pizan*, Margaret Brabant, ed. Boulder, Colorado: Westview Press.

Dryzek, John. 1990. *Discursive Democracy: Politics, Policy, and Political Science.* New York: Cambridge University Press.

Elshtain, Jean Bethke. 1992. "Introduction." In *Politics, Gender, and Genre: The Political Thought of Christine de Pizan*, Margaret Brabant, ed. Boulder, Colorado: Westview Press.

Forhan, Kate Langdon. 1992. "Polycracy, Obligation, and Revolt: The Body Politic in John of Salisbury and Christine de Pizan." In *Politics, Gender, and Genre: The Political Thought of Christine de Pizan*, ed. Margaret Brabant. Boulder, Colorado: Westview Press.

——. 1994. "Introduction." In Christine de Pizan, *The Book of the Body Politic*, Kate Langdon Forhan, ed. Cambridge, England: Cambridge University Press.

Heilbrun, Carolyn G. 1990. *Hamlet's Mother and Other Women.* New York: Columbia University Press.

Hooper, Barbara. 1992. " 'Split at the Roots': A Critique of the Philosophical and Political Sources of Modern Planning Doctrine." *Frontiers* 13(1): 45–80.

Kelly, Joan. 1984. "Early Feminist Theory and the *Querelle des Femmes.*" In *Women, History, and Theory: the Essays of Joan Kelly.* Chicago: University of Chicago Press.

Laennec, Christine Moneera. 1993. "Unladylike Polemics: Christine de Pizan's Strategies of Attack and Defense." *Tulsa Studies in Women's Literature* 12(1): 47–59.

Lerner, Gerda. 1993. *The Creation of Feminist Consciousness: From the Middle Ages to 1870.* New York: Oxford University Press.

Lewis, C. S. 1964. *The Discarded Image: Art Introduction to Medieval and Renaissance Literature.* Cambridge, England: Cambridge University Press.

Machiavelli, Niccolo. 1992. *The Prince.* Robert M. Adams, ed. New York: W .W. Norton.

Pateman, Carole. 1988. *The Sexual Contract.* Stanford: Stanford University Press.

——. [1983] 1991. "Feminist Critiques of the Public-Private Dichotomy." In *Contemporary Political Theory*, Paul Edwads, ed. New York: Macmillan.

Pizan, Christine de. 1982. *The Book of the City of Ladies.* New York: Persea Books.

Reno, Christine M. 1992. "Christine de Pizan: 'At Best a Contradictory Figure'?" In *Politics, Gender, and Genre: The Political Thought of Christine de Pizan*, Margaret Brabant, ed. Boulder, Colorado: Westview Press.

Richards, Earl Jeffrey. 1982. "[Translator's] Introduction." In Christine de Pizan, *The Book of the City of Ladies.* New York: Persea Books.

Strauss, Leo. 1969. *Thoughts on Machiavelli.* Seattle: University of Washington Press.

Tuchman, Barbara W. 1978. *A Distant Mirror: The Calamitous 14th Century.* New York: Alfred A. Knopf.

Warner, Marina. 1982. "Foreword." In Christine de Pizan, *The Book of the City of Ladies.* New York: Persea Books.

Willard, Charity Cannon. 1984. *Christine de Pizan: Her Life and Works.* New York: Persea Books.

——, ed. 1994. *The Writings of Christine de Pizan.* New York: Persea Books.

Wisman, Josette A. 1984. "Introduction." In Christine de Pizan, *The Epistle of the Prison of Human Life with an Epistle to the Queen of France and Lament on the Evils of the Civil War.* New York: Garland Publishing, Inc.

Yenal, Edith, ed. 1982. *Christine de Pisan [sic]: A Bibliography of Writings by Her and About Her.* Metuchen, N.J., & London: The Scarecrow Press, Inc.

25
Polycracy, Obligation, and Revolt

The Body Politic in John of Salisbury and Christine de Pizan

Kate Langdon Forhan

The conventional account of Christine de Pizan's *Livre du corps de policie* is that it was influenced by John of Salisbury's *Policraticus.*[1] This characterization is based on Christine's use of the corporate metaphor, with specific attribution to Plutarch, for which the *Policraticus* is the only source—for the very good reason that the text of pseudo-Plutarch was John's own invention.[2] However, while no systematic exploration of any further similarities or differences has been made, the question of influence is significant for a variety of reasons. First, both works were ostensibly written for the instruction of princes, a genre that can be highly revealing of political philosophy. Second, other well-known aspects of John's thought, for example, his theory of tyrannicide, are significant milestones in the history of political ideas and, thus form a part of Christine's intellectual context. Finally, and most important, the use of the body politic metaphor has shaped Western political thought in ways that we only dimly appreciate today when we use phrases like "right hand man" or "head of state." The metaphor has been used by such varied figures as Hobbes and Rousseau, but its transmission through the Middle Ages to the modern is an important, but little developed, area of study.

In this chapter, I will examine the use of the metaphor by both John and Christine in order to answer the following questions: First, in what ways does their use of the metaphor differ, and how do those differences reflect a changing view of the body politic? Second, in what ways do their different uses of the speculum genre reflect larger differences in their own political thought?

The *Policraticus*

In 1153, after twenty years of civil war, a king of tremendous promise and energy sat upon the throne of England. The neglect and isolation that had characterized the reign of Stephen was in great contrast to Henry II's passion for reorganization, efficiency, and administration. A whole generation of highly trained, able, and articulate administrators, from Chancellor Thomas Becket to Exchequer clerk Richard Fitznigel, would transform the kingdom. It is this world that John of Salisbury addressed in his *Policraticus*, presented to Chancellor Thomas Becket in 1159.

The *Policraticus* is the first medieval and Christianized attempt to reconcile the demands of practical politics with an equally exigent moral philosophy, on the model of the great Republics of Cicero and Plato. Like his contemporaries, John addresses issues central to his age, such as the relationship between secular and temporal power and the primacy of the contemplative life. But, by combining these problems with reflections on how to be a good prince or courtier, John reformulates the entire issue: How can the courtier be active in political life and remain a moral being? Both thinker and actor in some of the most dramatic events of his age, John contrives to think himself out of his historical circumstances in order to elaborate a new political theory. Most important is the reorientation of political life that John envisions.

In the twelfth century, the dominant metaphors for describing the polity emphasized hierarchy and subordination to authority. By changing the metaphor used to describe politics, John intends to show that its true nature is "polycratic" and to emphasize the interdependence of political actors, whether groups or individual persons. The corporate metaphor has a long and venerable history, but in the *Policraticus*, a far more elaborate version of the metaphor appears than had been seen before. In John's work, the head, that is, the prince, and the soul, which represents the clergy, are shown to be indispensable to the well-being of the whole body (as are, it should be noted, all other parts of the body, including the feet, or peasantry). John's use of the metaphor stresses neither duality nor subordination but interdependence. Although the soul is superior to the body, the body politic cannot survive without all its members. This striking new use of a powerful political metaphor enables John to address problems of political violence, the nature of justice, and the concept of liberty, all within a larger context of the whole society and its relationship to the philosophic good.

John's Audience

The twelfth-century courtier was what we would call a "bureaucrat:" a government official, often an administrator or magistrate. He was an educated man and a cleric, with some training in philosophy, logic, and rhetoric as well as theology and law. Moreover, his placement was as likely to be in secular government as in ecclesiastical circles. By playing these two different roles in his society, the clerical administrator or secretary was at the very least cognizant of a gap between the life for which he had been prepared and the life in which he found himself. In a more extreme situation, the individual could easily be subject to the sometimes conflicting interests of king and church. On the one hand, by virtue of his education, the individual had been taught to value the life of the mind and the pursuit of the good, as well as the salvation of his soul. The great masters of the schools in Paris had taught him that the pursuit of the good, the goal of philosophic life, was accessible only to those who lived apart from the world in the monastery. He had learned that clerics, due to their sacramentally endowed status, ought to enjoy a privileged position. He had been schooled in

the importance of order, codification, and the uniform application of law.

On the other hand, secular rulers were not likely to tolerate secretaries or ambassadors whose opinions or actions countered their own interests or expressed some other loyalties. Codification and institutionalization of various customs could and did limit a ruler's field of action. The cleric's fidelity to his bishop, to canon law, and to the papacy could bring him into conflict with his king, with custom, and with national interests. Furthermore, the cleric engaged in public life would appear to be excluded from the pursuit of philosophy and the highest good.

The *Policraticus* addresses the problem of reconciling the apparently discordant values of the clerical "bureaucrat;" to allow him to lead the philosophical life in the world of action. The life of the philosopher, that is, of the lover of wisdom, had to be shown to be identical with the Christian life. Furthermore, this life had to be shown to be accessible to those who live far from the silence of the monastery. Otherwise, how could the man in the world, the prince, the magistrate or the courtier, pursue wisdom and the good life? How in the midst of temptation and conflicting loyalties could he attain salvation?

The originality of the work is expressed in four areas. An extensive education in the classics had left John deeply impressed by the political ideals of Greek and Roman authors, especially Cicero. The Ciceronian statesman—articulate, well educated, and virtuous—was to be the model for the twelfth-century public man. The Roman model was not, however, perfectly suited to the twelfth century because of at least one glaring difference: unlike Cicero's Rome, John's England was Christian.

Second, another classical theme, the idea of virtue as moderation rather than asceticism, is invigorated and Christianized by John. He desired to see the virtues practiced in a revalidated public life.

Third, the structure of the *Policraticus* is distinctive: It spirals, preparing the reader for each successive step. Books 1–3 deal with the preparation of the individual for the pursuit of virtue. The courtier is an ordinary sinful human being, caught up in the temptations of court life. The king is an "ordinary" king, pursuing his own pleasures and own interests. His follies are explained, his life is reordered, his mistakes are finally left behind. In Books 4–6, purged of folly, the individual is shown the "polycratic" nature of the just society. If all its members are virtuous, then the just society will appear. Finally, in Books 7–8, the individual can turn his attention to the acquisition of the good and thereby to a true understanding of ideas—only hinted at before—such as justice, virtue, knowledge, and liberty. Because of this structure, themes introduced early in the work can be reintroduced later when their real significance can be better understood. The most notable example of a concept treated in this fashion is tyranny, but the ideas of virtue, liberty, and knowledge are discussed similarly.

Fourth, the work is intended for a nonmonastic audience. The *Policraticus* is about human nature and purpose and the highest good that a person can achieve. The highest good, unlike the good in John's Roman models, has to be shown to be compatible with the Christian good, that is, God. Moreover, it must be possible to achieve that good in the world of politics. The *Policraticus*, unlike, for example, the *Rule* of Benedict, is not intended for men and women living in a cloister. It is intended for those who, like Thomas Becket, to whom the work is dedicated, and John himself, lived in the center of the turmoil, excitement, power, and temptation of a medieval court.

John has a fundamentally classical view of politics. Through the exploration of the relationship between individuals and their society, he indicates that the moral choices an individual makes affect others. They have, therefore, political consequences. This is a very classical view of what Aristotle calls "universal" justice, but it is modified by John's own view that persons have rights and responsibilities that are related to, and dependent on, moral judgments, which become, in fact, political judgments. Paradoxically, John's descriptions of court life are curiously remote from the day-to-day experience a clerical courtier like John would

have had, but for good reason. It is far more important to John that his audience develop the public virtues appropriate to court life than that he spell out the details of administration. Only when the courtiers and princes are truly "civilized" in the classical sense of the word, and the individual virtues proper to their positions developed, can there be universal justice.

John's Body Politic: Twelfth-Century Political Physiology

The description of the corporate metaphor begins with a letter to the young Emperor Trajan, purportedly written by his tutor, Plutarch, that John says was followed by a political treatise called the Instruction of Trajan. It was in this political work that he claims to have found the corporate metaphor. This use of Plutarch as an authority would have resonated with John's medieval audience because Trajan was the virtuous pagan, the philosopher-king, later to be immortalized by Dante as the pagan who abides in the heaven of the Just (*Paradisio* 20. 43–45). By using Trajan (of whose legend John is an important transmitter), John establishes a relationship of the same significance as that between Aristotle and Alexander the Great, a relationship that gives the letter tremendous authority for John's readers. In brief, the head is the prince; the soul is the Church; the heart is the senate; eyes, ears, and tongue are the magistrates and governors; the hands are officials and soldiers; the sides are the prince's attendants; the stomach and intestines are the financial officers; and the feet are the agricultural laborers.

Differences in the twelfth century understanding of physiological function give the metaphor a distinctive twist. The king as head, for example, connotes a different kind of leadership than it does for us. Wisdom and intelligence were considered by medical science to be located in the heart; thus it is not the king's decision-making power that gives him the right to rule but literally his position, his greater height, his ability to lead because he can see over those around him. It is the senate or council that is the heart of the body politic and thus the seat of wisdom and the will. Interestingly, in contrast to Christine de Pizan's physiology, John does not even mention the "middle classes." Merchants and artisans are omitted completely from his discussion. The peasantry, however, John describes as essential without giving much explicit detail, mentioning that without the feet, the body must creep slowly and shamefully across the ground, although to have included them at all in his description of society was very unusual. Especially important in contrast to Christine de Pizan is the role of the clergy as the soul of the body, because without a soul, John reminds us in a later chapter, the body is dead.

John's development and use of the corporate metaphor emphasizes inclusion, mutuality, and interdependence rather than hierarchy and subordination. John envisioned a society where responsibility is interdependent, as are the members of a human body, and where institutional arrangements could exist that would protect administrators and other groups from the follies or foibles of a king. This is a foundation on which later political thinkers would build theories of consent, of limited government, and of checks and balances.[3]

The implications of a politics of inclusion can even mean legitimate tyrannicide, a position, as we shall see, not directly addressed by Christine de Pizan.[4] The *Policraticus* is unique in its recognition that tyranny is something that happens when a society is not ruled polycratically, and when rulers and ruled forget their purpose—the quest for wisdom and virtue. John discusses several forms of despotic behavior—domestic, political, and ecclesiastical—and suggests different remedies for each. Tyrannicide may be considered only in the case of despotic secular rulers.

This discussion of tyranny takes place toward the end of Book 7, where the context is the desire for the Good. At this point in the work, the reader has been purged of his follies, placed on the path to virtue, and the true nature of the body politic has been explained to him. It is a society of laws and institutions designed to foster the health of the entire body. It is also a "polycratic" society, with

each member or organ of the body working in harmony with the others. The body is healthy when those members are actively engaged in the pursuit of the highest Good.

John is aware that the nature of the Good has preoccupied philosophers in the past. What is it? Power, glory, fame, wealth, and sensual pleasure are all possibilities that have been presented by pagan philosophers, and John has discussed each of these, following the model of his mentors, primarily Cicero, Augustine, and Boethius. On secular tyrants, John believes that it was as a consequence of disobedience and error that kings were established. The people, in their stupidity, undiscipline, and wickedness, "forced God, whom they had despised, to give them a king," so that the king might take their sons, "and make them his charioteers, and take their daughters to bake his bread and cook his food, and take their fields and lands to distribute at his pleasure among his servants, and in short, oppress the whole people under the yoke of slavery." (*Policraticus*, 2. 358; Dickinson, 350).[5]

The idea that kingship is inherently oppressive is further supported in the *Policraticus* by events from Roman history illustrating the fact that "more often than not, power was in the hands of bad men" (*Policraticus*, 2. 360; Dickinson, 352). Tyranny is clearly an "abuse of power entrusted by God to man" (*Policraticus*, 2. 359; Dickinson, 351). Tyrannicide may be a consequence of abuse. Since all power has its origins in God, it is fundamentally good, but when exercised abusively, power can become evil. God can turn evil into good and use it for his own good purposes. Tyrannical churchmen, however, should not be killed or executed, but they should not consider themselves above canon law or divine retribution just because, according to the doctrine of the two swords, they are outside the purview of the king's law. The metaphor of the body necessitates the view that it is wrong for a person to attack the priesthood. Although a body can receive wounds and still survive, the end of the soul signals the death of the entire body. The choice of the priesthood as the soul in the body politics constrains as well as enriches the significance of the metaphor.

All tyrants will suffer. This is the counsel in the *Policraticus* to all members of the body politic; virtue is essential from head to toe. The *Policraticus* is a treatise designed to help princes and courtiers learn how to live. If they reorder their priorities and practice virtue, liberty and happiness will be theirs. If they persist in the vices, certain consequences are equally inevitable: slavery, tyranny, and, ultimately, death. Although the ambiguity of John's argument for or against tyrannicide has been much debated, it is quite clear that he has strong views on tyranny and the use of institutions that can serve to inhibit its development, as well as a sense that kingship may be an inherently oppressive institution that must be restrained.

Le Livre du Corps de Policie

While often described as "inspired" by the *Policraticus*, Christine de Pizan's *Livre du corps de policie* has not been closely examined with respect to John of Salisbury's work. In *Corps de policie*, Christine uses the corporate metaphor and attributes it to Plutarch without further attribution to John of Salisbury or the *Policraticus*.[6] To what degree did the *Policraticus* inspire or influence *Corps de policie*? Why, given John's considerable reputation, was he not explicitly cited as the source of the metaphor? I shall address these fascinating questions.

Christine's Audience

When *Corps de policie* was written between, late 1404 and 1407, France hovered on the brink of civil war. The growing disability of Charles VI trapped France between the two powerful personalities of his brother, Louis, Duke of Orleans, and his uncle Philip Duke of Burgundy. The crisis was partly resolved with the assassination of Louis of Orleans in November 1407 and the eventual exoneration of his assassins on the grounds of tyrannicide.

Although *Corps de policie* was dedicated to Charles VI and the princes of the royal family, in *Livre de la paix*, Christine mentions the former was written for the benefit of the dauphin, Louis of Guyenne.[7] Presumably anyone concerned about the moral and political education of princes would have found it useful. Although the work is ostensibly addressed to the different classes of society, its first recipients were royal. Christine's audience and therefore her purpose were quite different from John of Salisbury's. He was writing primarily to those who advised princes, to courtiers, prelates, and administrators. He could, indeed, was obligated to warn them about the roots of tyranny and despotism in princes and in each other. He stresses tyranny as a human failing. In contrast, Christine's audience was princely. Any discussion for remedies to tyranny would have to be oblique at most. In a time of what was virtually a civil war, her position was delicate and her advice discreet, but there is, nonetheless, a warning to tyrants.

Christine's Body Politic and Fourteenth-Century Physiology

Both the *Policraticus* and *Corps de policie* have a tripartite structure, a convention they share with many other medieval works. The organization of Christine de Pizan's *Corps de policie* is very different from that of the *Policraticus*, however. Her organizational principle is hierarchical rather than developmental or symphonic. The three sections of the work are addressed to princes, to aristocrats and nobles, and to the "universal people," and thus roughly parallel the structure of her other work, *The Treasury of the City of Ladies*. As Diane Bornstein notes,[8] the three parts of the *Corps de policie* correspond to three common genres of the period: the prince's speculum, the knight's manual of chivalry, and, addressed to the common people, a treatise on the three estates. Each part of the work is ostensibly directed to its particular audience, which is quite different from John's work, all of which is aimed at administrators and courtiers.

In the first chapter, Christine introduces the metaphor of the body: "[Plutarch], in a letter which he sent to the Emperor Trajan, compares the polity to a body having life; in which the prince or princes hold the place of the head since they are or ought to be sovereign. And from them should come the particular institutions just as from the understanding of humans the outside works that the members accomplish springs forth" (Lucas, 2).[9]

As in the *Policraticus*, the prince is also the head, but neither why he should rule nor the nature of kingship is discussed. But implicit in this brief passage is a different view of kingship, one that stems perhaps from a new understanding of human physiology. Christine's prince leads at least in part by virtue of his "entendement," his judgment and understanding, now located physiologically in the head and no longer in the heart as they were in the twelfth century. The King's Council or "heart" is not mentioned and the administrators have disappeared. The physiology of the body politic is completely different.

Considerable attention is given to the nurturing and education of the prince, a subject that John completely ignores.[10] In his early childhood, the prince is to be fed simple food and given an orderly schedule for play and work. He should hear Mass and say his prayers daily. He is to be taught his letters, reading and grammar in Latin, logic, and if he shows any intellectual gifts, philosophy as well. His teacher should be a man of good character who uses positive reinforcement in his teaching, and who can act as a role model for the prince and his other charges. As the prince matures, he should be placed in the home of a guardian, a wise but authoritative knight, who will be as much concerned about the prince's manners as his physical health. He should teach the prince not only to be a knight (the arts of war, leadership, and weaponry) but also self-discipline and self-control (to rise early, to hear Mass and morning prayer, to speak well to people, and to control his words and expression). The prince needs to be brought into council sometimes to learn to govern well and to deal with all types of people. Once he is old enough to rule, Christine emphasizes, he must be aware of seigneurial responsibility. The prince should remember that his high estate is due to the grace of God and that much will be expected of him.

In her descriptions of good rule and her choice of illustrations, Christine's use of authority is quite different from John's. His source of maxims on kingly behavior is Deuteronomy, each dictum followed by several exempla from Roman sources, often recounted at length and with loving detail. Christine gives no "auctor" but instead three principles of good rule. The first is love of God, shown in deeds rather than prayers. Second is love of the good of his people and kingdom rather than self-interest. This in particular is shown in the development of the charming virtues of generosity, humanity, and meekness, which make a prince lovable. The third principle is to love justice and act with equity toward all his people. Despite her emphasis on the prince's good manners and congenial air, Christine writes that he should also be feared, so that his commands are taken seriously. In general, Christine's most revered source for practical advice and for exempla is "celui noble auteur Valere" (Lucas, 41).[11] She also quotes Seneca, Cicero, Aristotle, and Boethius, among others, but not primarily for stories; rather, they provide the maxims, or punch lines, for Valerius's tales.

Part 2 is addressed to nobles, the hands and arms of the body politic, whose function is to defend the rights of the prince and the common people. Just as hands put aside what is bad, so should the knights and nobles push aside what is evil and unprofitable. Still within a hierarchical understanding of the body politic, Christine reminds us that some things that are appropriate to princes are not appropriate for knights and nobles—but virtue belongs to both.

This section of the work includes another description of child-rearing practices, comparing what she believed to be the austere conventions of Rome with the less strict customs of her own day. Her emphasis, attributed to Anselm, is on personal virtue, physical asceticism, and silence. Six attributes are especially important for knights and nobles: knowledge of arms, hardiness, encouragement of others, keeping one's word, the desire for glory, and wisdom and cunning in battle. These are illustrated with stories from Roman experience, with considerable emphasis placed on the importance of truth and honoring one's word, a somewhat pointed lesson in time of civil war.

In Part 3, emphasis is very strong on the use of the physiological metaphor to stress mutual dependence. All of the parts of the body are to work together for the welfare of the entire community. Not only are they to help each other, but each is to exercise its own office for the conservation of the whole body.Thus the prince is to love and care for the whole people, the knights and nobles are to guard and defend them, and, in turn, the people are to love, revere, and obey the prince.

The people are the belly, the legs, and the feet of the body politic. As the legs and feet bear the weight of the body, so do the laboring people sustain all the other estates through their work. By the early fifteenth century the medieval social order had grown more complex than the simple "three orders" of the twelfth century. The development of a "middle" class of merchants, artisans, and burghers over the intervening two centuries affected not only economic life but political ideas as well. In contrast to the *Policraticus*, *Corps de policie* develops the roles of these "lesser members" in arresting detail. Whereas John uses his discussion of the feet or peasantry to validate the peasants' role in society for a perhaps indifferent audience and thereby underlines the importance of "polycracy," Christine addresses the people themselves. Her "mirror" includes their behavior, with particular emphasis on burghers, merchants, and artisans practicing their trades honestly. Unlike John of Salisbury, Christine reveals a more subtle and detailed knowledge of classes other than the traditional three orders of warriors, priests, and peasants. She presents these upper ranks of the common people as having a political duty toward the orders below them, their own bourgeois responsibility to represent the people to the prince and his council and to advise the people themselves. This view—that although the people have no right to revolt, higher ranks of citizens have a duty to petition the king on their behalf and to act as intermediaries for them—is one that develops later into a French political theory of representation; it is quite unlike the behavior expected of the English merchant class of the same period:

> These people should involve themselves in the governing of the cities in all which concerns the merchant class and the common people, so that they are well governed. For the common poeple rarely have great prudence in words about those things which concern politics and so they should not meddle in the ordinances established by princes. The burghers and wealthy must take care that the common people are not hurt so that they have no reason to evilly conspire against the prince or the council. (Lucas, 184)[12]

Roman examples of good behavior and proper class relations play a less important role in Part 3, but the increase in tales and maxims from Scripture reflect learning considered appropriate for its supposed audience and its anticipated place in society. Many of these scriptural references stress subordination and obligations to rulers (Titus 3, 1 Peter 2, Matthew 22, Exodus 22), as, in this part of the work, do the stories from Valerius. Not all of these stories are as obsequious as this might suggest, since they sometimes close with an interesting twist. For example, the tale of Straton ends with the hero's being confirmed as king on his sovereign's deathbed, and his children heirs after him, "for the good he had done his lord" (Lucas, 176).

Striking to the reader of John of Salisbury is the disappearance of the soul in the body politic and with that disapperance, a new role assigned to the clergy. The clerical class is now part of the people and as such has a greatly diminished and less-privileged position. In John's use of the metaphor, the church was the soul of the body politic, and without it, the body is dead. By contrast, in Christine's body, although there is emphasis on the clerical student and the importance of study, the clergy is not a group set apart. Although they are worthy of honor, they are neither princes nor knights, and their function is to provide prayers and rituals, as a baker provides bread. They are members of the body politic and therefore important, but they are not its soul, not essential to its being, or being itself. Despite Christine's apparent piety, this rather matter-of-fact attitude toward the clergy may indicate that her religious belief is more conventional than inspired. John of Salisbury's understanding of the purpose of life and of society is fundamentally a religious one: Philosophy is love of wisdom, which is the love of God. Christine's view reflects a far greater secularization and an increased regard for national interests, concepts alien to John's thought.

A third very different aspect of Christine's body politic is the substantive political advice that is given. In John's work, the individual is to exercise moderation in his pursuits, particularly the activities of his leisure. Although individual virtue is very important, John's emphasis is on the development of institutional procedures for the administration of the king's justice. The *Policraticus* insists that the king's officers should receive regular compensation to remove the temptation of bribery, they should swear an oath of office to distinguish their personal from public responsibilities, and they should follow administrative rules and procedures. By contrast, Christine's work is directed to the development of virtue and manners appropriate to each class and its responsibilities. Hers is not a theoretical work but a practical one. She does not examine the nature of rule, the role of institutions, or the concepts of justice.

One story that Christine and John share illustrates their characteristic differences in a truly remarkable way. The fable of the revolt of the members against the stomach is first told by John of Salisbury in the *Policraticus*. He attributes the fable to Nicholas Breakspear, the English pope, Adrian IV, whom John knew well, but although he may have heard the story in the papal court, it is found in Livy's *History of Rome* (Book 2. 32).[13] There, although the fable is metaphorically neutral, that is, no body part is attributed to a particular group in society, the fable is used to show the resentment of the common people toward the patrician class.

In John's version, the body parts in the fable are assigned the same roles that they have in his metaphor in the rest of the Policraticus; the revolt is raised by the jealous "members"—soldiers, administrators, and common people—against what they see as the greedy and lazy "stomach," tax collectors and the financial officers of the kingdom. In revenge, the members decide to starve the stomach, and of course, eventually they grow weak themselves from lack of nourishment. In John's work, the fable is used to stress interdependence and is closely followed by the analogy of the bees, a classical image for an orderly kingdom.

In *Corps de policie*, the fable is told differently. Although in Christine's physiology, the stomach is the part of the universal people, in her use of the fable the belly is the prince; thus it is against him that the people revolt. For Christine, the moral of the story is as follows: "When the prince asks more of the people than they can provide, . . . the people complain about the prince and rebel in disobedience. In such discord, the whole [body] perishes" (Lucas, 168).[14]

In Christine's hand, the fable becomes a warning for princes, the more startling given her generally cautious approach to political questions.

An examination of the manuscripts offers support for this thesis. Christine de Pizan is well known for having carefully supervised the production of her manuscripts, particularly in the choice of illuminations for presentation copies.[15] The illustrations for *Policie* provide an appropriate introduction to each part of the work. Since, as Robert G. Calkins reminds us,[16] illuminations have a signaling effect, marking important parts of the book and even interpretations of its text, her choice of subjects to be painted forms a kind of "subtext" synthesizing important elements of her argument.[17] The first miniature (47r), introducing Part One, shows the enthroned figure of "felicite vertueuse" surrounded by the cardinal virtues: courage, temperance, justice, and prudence. Part 2, addressed to the nobility, is introduced by a courtier teaching a young man (137r).

By contrast, Part 3, while ostensibly addressed to the "universal people," shows two nobles being attacked and murdered by five commoners; ruffians armed with daggers and swords. The illumination provides a significant and pointed pictorial "sub-text," indicating the effects of misrule. This part of the work was clearly intended to be read by princes, since the text is a warning to the nobility to apply the lessons of the book or pay the consequences of death by violence. Here, Christine's habitual political caution, combined with her desire to be taken seriously by princes oblivious to the needs of their people, keeps her from acknowledging John of Salisbury, well-known theorist of tyrannicide, as her source, not only of this fable, but of the corporate metaphor itself.

Conclusion: Polycracy and the Politics of Seigneurial Responsibility

It seems clear that Christine de Pizan's quite distinctive use of the corporate metaphor does not represent a self-conscious adaptation of the polycratic metaphor of John of Salisbury, but rather the use of an elegant figure of speech that provided a way to enter into the problem of writing advice to princes. John's model of the body politic was in a sense a convenience, a vehicle for presenting her own quite different political ethic that had been shaped by the very different needs of her own time, a political ethic of seigneurial responsibility. Yet given the similarity of themes, the question might well be, why does she not cite John of Salisbury much more? Why Valerius as her source of exempla and not John?

There is ample evidence that the text of the *Policraticus* was both well known and widely cited in the Paris of the late fourteenth century. The library of Charles V had both a Latin manuscript and a French translation by Denys Foulechat (which disappears from library inventories after having been borrowed by Louis, Duke of Anjou, in 1380).[18] Excerpts from the *Policraticus* were also plentiful. Not only were there extracts of pseudo-Plutarch, but John's varied Roman and scriptural exempla had been particularly popular with Franciscan preachers, and his legal maxims with the masters of schools of law. Specific anecdotes, for example, the story of Trajan and the virtuous widow, and the comments of Adrian IV on the papacy, had found their way into a wide variety of works, sometimes misattributed. Christine clearly had access to a wide variety

of sources for the ideas of John of Salisbury, but the evidence is inconclusive as to which she may have used.

John's usefulness to Christine as a literary source in a strict sense was more limited. The *Policraticus* did of course serve in the transmission of classical knowledge to the later Middle Ages, but by the early fifteenth century, Christine had direct access to complete works that had been available to John in only fragmentary form, most notably the political and ethical works of Aristotle, but including scores of other works as well— even medical texts, which might have been useful in developing a physiological metaphor.

There is one curious exception in the discussion of John of Salisbury's influence on Christine de Pizan. From the preceding paragraphs it would be easy to conclude that Christine was totally unaware of John's political thought and that her use of material from the *Policraticus* was merely borrowing, and very possibly unselfconscious borrowing at that except for two curious facts. She never refers to him by name in *Corps de policie*[19] and yet there are references to him in the contemporaneous *Livre des trois vertus*. Second, on the themes of tyranny and tyrannicide, John was an important political authority in the late fourteenth and early fifteenth centuries. Christine was writing during the unstable reign of Charles VI, and questions of political legitimacy, tyranny, and the rights of subjects to oppose policies were very topical and widely discussed in sermons, public speeches, and the like. Jean Gerson refers to arguments in the *Policraticus* in sermons dating from 1392 to 1409; and in a public speech at court in November 1405, he links the *Policraticus* with Aristotle's teaching on tyranny. This use of John's political theory would culminate after the completion of *Corps de policie* in 1407, when Master John Petit, a distinguished university scholar and theologian, justified the assassination of Louis, Duke of Orleans, on John's theory of tyrannicide and consequently maintained that the brutal murder was both honorable and lawful.[20] Whether or not this is an accurate understanding of John's theory of tyrannicide, the climate of opinion in the early fifteenth century would certainly describe John of Salisbury's political thought as controversial. Perhaps Christine's avoidance of explicit reference to John of Salisbury was an exercise in discretion, since her manuscript carries its own very subtle warnings for princes.

The essential differences between the two works are best understood by examining the differences in the audiences they address and their authorial intention. John's society was newly at peace, and the roles of political actors were being freshly defined. He writes within the context of a society undergoing institutionalization, where horizons seem unlimited and the future bright. Yet there is the risk that Henry II, in his desire to control his hard-won kingdom, would trample the liberties of others and behave tyrannically.

Christine's work, by contrast, is written during the reign of an incapacitated king, on the edge of civil war, where institutions are apparently in disarray and society is in danger of dissolution because of unbridled private interests. Changing the political institutions cannot stop the bloodshed, greed, and aggression. Her focus as a political writer must stress not only interdependence but also obligation, both individual and collective. The crisis of her time is not a tyrannical ruler, but a weak one; thus her politics must be more than a politics of inclusion: It must be a politics of responsibility, representation, and political obligation.

Notes

An earlier version of this paper was originally presented at the twenty-fifth annual International Congress on Medieval Studies, Kalamazoo, Michigan, 1990. My thanks to Charity Cannon Willard, whose comments on the paper were as graceful as they were useful. I am also grateful to the staff of the manuscript room at the Bibliothèque Nationale in Paris for their cheerful assistance.

1. Christine de Pizan, *Le Livre du corps de policie*, trans. Robert Lucas (Geneva, 1967), xxi. (Referred to hereafter as "Lucas.") See also Gianni Mombello, "Quelques aspects de la pensée politique de Christine de Pisan d'après ses oeuvres publiée," in *Culture et politique en France à l'époque de l'humanisme*

et de la Renaissance, ed. Franco Simone (Turin, 1974), 43–153, 56.

2. The case against the independent existence of the *Institutio* is to my mind very convincing. In part it is circumstantial; John never quotes from it directly, for example, whereas the *Policraticus* cites other sources profusely; moreover no other reference or copy of the *Institutio*, unassociated with John of Salisbury, has ever been found. Janet Martin has shown that the stratagems attributed by John of Salisbury to Plutarch actually come from the same manuscripts of Frontinus and Heiric that are used in the *Policraticus*. Martin concludes, "There is no possibility, then, that John was deceived by an existing pseudo-Plutarch that included these exempla in this form." See her "John of Salisbury as Classical Scholar," in *The World of John of Salisbury*, ed. Michael Wilks, (Oxford: Basil Blackwell, 1984), 195. Finally the *Institutio* is not listed in the *Catalogue of Lampias*, which listed over two hundred of Plutarch's works. (In Book 5 of the *Policraticus*, John makes reference to a letter he claims was written by Plutarch to the emperor Trajan—Ed.) Nonetheless in 1976, Max Kerner revived the argument that it was a work of late antiquity, now lost. He based his argument, first, on the belief that other scholars in Canterbury would have been aware of such an attempt at forgery and, second, on detection of earlier patterns of thought and expression in the *Institutio* as presented by John ("Institutio" 1976). Kerner's reexamination of the question serves as a reminder that proof of a negative is very difficult to establish. Definitive evidence to resolve the debate may never appear. See Max Kerner, "Zur entstenhungsgeschichte dur institutio traiani," *Deutches archiv* 32 (1976), 558–71. For further discussion on this debate, see my dissertation, "The Twelfth Century 'Bureaucrat' and the Life of the Mind: John of Salisbury's *Policraticus*," Johns Hopkins University, 1987.

3. For a fuller explanation, see Cary Nederman, "The Physiological Significance of the Organic Metaphor in John of Salisbury's *Policraticus*," *History of Political Thought* 8 (Summer 1987), 211–223, and my dissertation, "The Twelfth Century 'Bureaucrat.'"

4. The debate on John's position on tyrannicide is as old as the *Policraticus* itself. For a review of the modern debate and a telling argument, see Cary Nederman, "A Duty to Kill: John of Salisbury's Theory of Tyrannicide," *Review of*

Politics 50 (Summer 1988), 365–389. See my article, "Salisburian Stakes: The Uses of 'Tyranny' in John of Salisbury's *Policraticus*" in *History of Political Thought* 11, (Autumn, 1990), 397–407.

5. Ioannis Saresberiensis, *Policraticus*, ed. C.C.I. Webb, (Oxford: Oxford University Press, 1909), 1:232. All English translations are from John of Salisbury, *Stateman's Book*, trans. John Dickinson (New York: Russell and Russell, 1963), referred to as "Dickinson." The translator worked from Webb's critical edition but did not translate the entire work, only Books 4–6 and parts of 7. Despite its shortcomings, it remains the standard English translation. Fortunately, new translations are forthcoming.

6. In the Lucas edition there is only one reference to the *Policraticus* and that is to a story about Titus the Emperor. The Middle English translation refers to the *Policraticus* in a discussion on flattery, and although I have not yet examined the other extant French manuscripts, I understand that they do too. This omission may be limited to Lucas edition. In neither the Lucas edition nor the Middle English translation is the *Policraticus* cited as the source of Plutarch's letter.

7. *Le Livre de la paix*, ed. Charity Cannon Willard (The Hague, 1958), 174.

8. Diane Bornstein, *The Middle English Translation of Christine de Pizan's Livre du Corps de Policie* (Heidelberg, 1977), 8.

9. "[Plutarch] qui en une epistre qu'il envoya a Trajan l'empereur compare la chose publique a une corps aiant vie, auquel le prince ou les princes tiennent le lieu du chef en tant qu'ilz sont ou doivent estre souverains et d'eulx doivent venir les singuliers establissemens tout ainsi comme de l'entendement de l'omme sourdent et viennent les foraines euvres que les membres achievent." There is at present no published English translation of this work. I am presently working on my own translation for Cambridge University Press. (Translations of this work in this text are mine.)

10. Not that John was unconcerned with education. His *Metalogicon* discusses the purpose and methods of a liberal arts education, and the *Policraticus* examines the role of education in the acquisition of wisdom, but neither work surveys the care and nurturing of the young.

11. In Lucas's text this is rendered "acteur." In his introduction he cites the same line as "auteur" (cf. p. xxxix). Bornstein's *Middle English* text quite rightly renders this "auctor" (p. 70). Why Christine and some other writers of the late Middle Ages should have found Valerius so captivating remains to be addressed.

12. "Ces gens cy se doivent entremettre des faitz et besoingnes des cites dont ilz sont que toutes choses qui apertiennent a la marchandise et au fait du commun soit bien gouvernees. Et pour que le menu peuple n'a mie communement grande prudence en parole, mesmes en fait qui touche policie, dont ne se doivent mesler des ordonnances d'icelle establies par les princes, doivent prendre garde les bourgoys et les gros que pour chose qui en soit faicte le commun ne s'en empeche ne n'en face aucune conspiracion mauvaise contre le prince ou le conseil."

13. Another possible source is the very attenuated fable in Aesop, which is not given any political content or significance in the original source. Although this may have been Livy's inspiration, it is unlikely to have been either John's or Christine's source of the tale because it is devoid of political meaning. I believe the *Policraticus* to be the more likely source for Christine simply because of its greater availability.

14. "Quant le prince demande plus au peuple qu'il ne peut fournir et que peuple murmure contre prince et se rebelle par desobeissance; tel discort perit tout ensemble."

15. See the enlightening study by Sandra Hindman, *Christine de Pizan's Epistre Othéa: Painting and Politics at the Court of Charles VI* (Toronto: Pontifical Institute of Mediaeval Studies, 1986).

16. Robert G. Calkins, *Programs of Medieval Illumination* (Lawrence: University of Kansas Press, 1984).

17. I develop this argument further in my paper, "Narrative and Synthesis in Walter de Milemete's *The Noble, Wise, and Prudent King*" presented at the twenty-sixth annual International Congress on Medieval Studies, Kalamazoo, Michigan, 1991.

18. Leopold Delisle, *Recherches sur la librairie de Charles V* (Paris, 1907).

19. She refers once to *Policraticus* in Lucas's edition in reference to the Emperor Titus. All references to the body politic are attributed to Plutarch in Lucas's edition. The Middle English translation, which derives from a different manuscript line, refers to the *Policraticus*.

20. See Amnon Linder, "The Knowledge of John of Salisbury in the Late Middle Ages," *Studi Medievali,* ser. 3, 18 (1977), 348–349.

Part III

Enter Modernity

If the medieval outlook was shaped by Christian and classical ideas, the Renaissance (usually dated from the middle of the 14th century) both accepted and challenged them. For humanist scholars such as Petrarch (1304–1374) and Desiderius Erasmus (1469–1536), the classical world supplied the basic learning that one should acquire, but in many respects, that world was clearly relegated to the past. As such, the humanist approach favored by scholars in the provincial capitals of Italy and elsewhere came to be marked by a philosophical flexibility that allowed it to reevaluate the contributions of ancient thought and culture.

Without a doubt, the Renaissance was a time of scientific advance and artistic experimentation. It was also a time of political contrasts and philosophical change. Politically, in large states such as France and England, the sort of monarchy limited by feudal obligations and the claims of natural law gave way to a more or less absolute one. In Italy, by contrast, there were so many competing states that no overarching authority developed. Even the Church began to lose whatever special claim to authority it once had as a series of popes behaved in ways that were no different from secular rulers. Indeed, the image we have of political life in the Renaissance ranges from the highly refined court described in *The Courtier* (1528) by Baldassare Castiglione (1478–1529) to the pervasive corruption and greed criticized by Thomas More (1478–1535) in his *Utopia* (1516).

Philosophically, especially among writers on politics, the prevailing approach was to redirect thinking. An individualistic stress on making one's way in the world soon came to replace medieval Christianity's emphasis on community and interdependence. Renaissance thinkers had little use for the *vita contemplativa*, the monastic ideal of isolation and spiritual contemplation. For them, the life of action was where one should devote one's energies. Parallel to this advocacy of action was "the proliferation of independent areas of inquiry, each intent on staking out its autonomy, each concerned to develop a language of explanation suited to a particular set of phenomena, and each proceeding without benefit of clergy."[1]

As we noted in the Introduction, the political theory of Niccolò Machiavelli can be seen as marking the transition from the ancient world to the modern. An enthusiast for ancient republics, Machiavelli nonetheless realized that he confronted a quite different political situation than Cicero had. Where Plato had imagined an ideal community, Machiavelli turned his attention to actually existing ones. Where Aristotle theorized about ensuring the good life and Augustine contemplated the nature of sin, Machiavelli asserted that the mundane realities of statecraft were the proper subject of political theory. And where thinkers such as Aquinas and de Pizan encouraged rulers to abide by Christian principles and duties, Machiavelli pointedly observed that all too many people act in accordance with other, more secular values. In the spirit of novelty and experimentation characteristic of the Renaissance, then, Machiavelli employed traditional genres, whether the mirror for princes or the history, for non-traditional—that is, modern—aims.

Note

1. Sheldon Wolin, *Politics and Vision: Continuity and Innovation in Western Political Thought* (Boston: Little, Brown, 1960), 199.

References

Best, Judith A. 1980. *The Mainstream of Western Political Thought*. New York: Human Sciences Press.

Germino, Dante. 1972. *Modern Western Political Thought: Machiavelli to Marx*. Chicago: Rand McNally.

Wolin, Sheldon. 1960. *Politics and Vision: Continuity and Innovation in Western Political Thought*. Boston: Little, Brown. ✦

Niccolò Machiavelli

No name is more synonymous with politics, especially as politics is popularly conceived, than that of Niccolò Machiavelli. Machiavelli's reputation is based largely on the amoral, if not immoral, advice he gave in *The Prince*, written in 1513. Indeed, the book became so readily despised that at one time the name "Old Nick" was a synonym for the Devil. Although his works have been somewhat more charitably interpreted in recent years, the view persists that Machiavelli was little more than a "teacher of evil" who urged political rulers to disregard conventional norms and values. Beyond the appeal of tasting forbidden fruit, however, scholars have found other significant contributions in Machiavelli's work. Offering a rational, empirical analysis of the modern state and politics, his writings (although appearing in the form of practical maxims) are considered a key forerunner of contemporary political science. Moreover, he also advocated a politics of civic republicanism and freedom that continues to shape a number of currents in democratic thought.

The diverse, contradictory character of Machiavelli's writings is, to some extent, mirrored in his life. Born in 1469, Machiavelli spent his early career as a diplomat and administrator for his native city of Florence. Though he never attained the rank of ambassador, he conducted several diplomatic missions and became something of an expert in military affairs. When the Florentine republic fell and was replaced by the rule of the Medici family in 1512, Machiavelli was forced out of office and began a lifetime of study in the fields of history and politics. After years of seeking favors from the Medici, Machiavelli returned to public service in 1525, only to be removed with the Medici themselves a year later. Machiavelli

died soon afterward, unable to win the trust of Florence's new republican leaders.

Machiavelli believed regimes fall into two types, principalities and republics. In *The Prince*, he offers advice on how to acquire and maintain a principality. To do so, a wise ruler would follow the path set forth by necessity, glory, and the good of the state. Only by combining machismo, martial spirit, and political sagacity can a ruler fulfill one's duty to the state and achieve historical immortality. By contrast, Machiavelli turns his attention in the *Discourses* (a commentary on a history of Rome written by Titus Livius, also known as Livy) to the creation, maintenance, and renovation of a republican government. His chief concern is to show how republican governments can promote stability and freedom while avoiding the debilitating effects of corruption. For Machiavelli, glory (whether princely or republican) is the definitive political ambition—one pursued within limits set by reason, prudence, fortune, and necessity.

The Prince

Machiavelli's *The Prince* is an intriguing little book of advice to any ruler interested in conquering or reforming a state. Though of humble origin, Machiavelli feels he can give such advice not only because of his lengthy study of public affairs, but also because "one needs to be a ruler to understand properly the character of the people, and to be a man of the people to understand properly the character of rulers."[1] From this realistic standpoint, not one based in utopian conceptions of politics, Machiavelli examines the traits for which rulers are praised or blamed. In the selections reprinted below, he argues that the wise ruler should possess the following: (1) an ability to be both good and bad, both loved and feared; (2) such character traits as boldness, ruthlessness, independence, discipline, and self-control; and (3) a reputation for generosity, mercy, trustworthiness, and piety. He advises the prince to do whatever is necessary, no matter how apparently vicious, since people are ultimately concerned only with outcomes—that is, with the good of the state. Of course, even a vicious prince must nevertheless contend with the fickle nature of changing circumstances, the capriciousness of fortune.

The *Discourses*

In the *Discourses* (1519), Machiavelli suggests that, while the founder or reformer of a state should act alone or even ruthlessly, maintaining a state over the long haul requires a virtuous, democratic rule by the many. Here it should be noted that maintenance does not mean simple persistence; it also connotes the promotion of freedom and political stability, the avoidance of corruption and decadence. The selections from Book One thus illustrate both Machiavelli's classical scholarship and his disillusionment with princely rule. Machiavelli begins by outlining a typology of forms of government and the cycle through which governments pass from virtuous to corrupt forms. This leads quite naturally to a general discussion of corrupt peoples and institutions, and the means to renovate and reconstitute political life. Once that reconstitution occurs, Machiavelli (upon comparing the respective virtues and vices of masses and princes) recommends popular rule as the path to political stability, security, and glory.

Commentaries

In the introduction to his translation of *The Prince*, Harvey C. Mansfield, Jr. summarizes the essential argument of the book. His primary focus is on the qualities that the "new prince" should exhibit in order to secure his rule. In order to be an effective ruler, then, the prince should owe nothing to anyone, rely upon his own arms, ally himself with the people rather than the nobles, and most importantly, learn how not to be good. Mansfield leaves no doubt that, in this most famous of works on politics, Machiavelli

himself was definitively Machiavellian. In other words, because he separated the conduct of politics from all connection to justice and morality, Machiavelli deserves the bad reputation that he has long since acquired.

One long-standing dispute among Machiavelli scholars has concerned the extent to which *The Prince* can be reconciled with the *Discourses*. In this context, John Leonard examines the vocabulary that Machiavelli employs in his defense of the extraordinary actions necessary to remedy political and social decadence. Leonard makes the case that the concepts of *virtù* and *bontà* have little to do with Christian virtue or goodness; instead, they respectively refer to such pursuits as glory and patriotism. Whether he is advising princes or peoples, Machiavelli's chief concern is to preserve the public sphere from the corrupting influences of private interests.

Note

1. Niccolò Machiavelli, *The Prince*, ed. Quentin Skinner and Russell Price (Cambridge: Cambridge University Press, 1988), 4.

Web Sources

http://www.utm.edu/research/iep/m/machiave. htm
The Internet Encyclopedia of Philosophy. A biographical profile and a summary of *The Prince*.

http://www.historyguide.org/intellect/machiavelli.html
Niccolò Machiavelli, 1469–1527. A brief profile with links to texts by Machiavelli.

Class Activities and Discussion Items

1. Have the class read and report on some of the works that have been modeled (more or less) after *The Prince*—for example, Gary Hart's *The Patriot*, Dick Morris's *The New Prince*, L.F. Gunlick's *The Machiavellian Manager's Handbook for Success*, or even Claudia Hart's *A Child's Machiavelli*. Discuss to what extent these works reflect either the letter or the spirit of Machiavelli's views.

2. What qualities does Machiavelli think a prince should have? Compare his views with those of de Pizan.

3. Is Machiavelli merely an advocate of violence, wickedness, and power-seeking? Why or why not?

4. What does Machiavelli mean by *virtù*? What import does the concept have for both princely and republican rule?

5. What is the relationship between Machiavelli's views expressed in *The Prince* and those expressed in the *Discourses?* Are they consistent or inconsistent? Why?

Further Reading

De Grazia, Sebastian. 1989. *Machiavelli in Hell.* Princeton, NJ: Princeton University Press. An engaging and rewarding intellectual biography that won a Pulitzer Prize.

Dietz, Mary. 1986. "Trapping the Prince: Machiavelli and the Politics of Deception." *American Political Science Review* 80 (September): 777–799. Captivating article which suggests that the scheming Machiavelli, even while advising princes, was an advocate of civic republicanism.

Hulliung, Mark. 1983. *Citizen Machiavelli.* Princeton, NJ: Princeton University Press. Regards Machiavelli's emphasis on the pursuit of glory as subversive of the humanist or republican tradition.

Pitkin, Hannah. 1984. *Fortune is a Woman: Gender and Politics in the Thought of Niccolò Machiavelli.* Berkeley: University of California Press. Identifies Machiavelli's ambivalence toward manhood and autonomy as the source of his fear of and contempt for feminine power.

Pocock, J.G.A. 1975. *The Machiavellian Moment: Florentine Political Thought and the Atlantic Republican Tradition.* Princeton, NJ: Princeton University Press. Noteworthy study of the nature and impact Machiavelli's republican ideas.

Skinner, Quentin. 1981. *Machiavelli.* New York: Hill and Wang. Brief but excellent introduction to Machiavelli's life and thought.

Strauss, Leo. 1958. *Thoughts on Machiavelli.* Glencoe, IL: Free Press. The classic case for regarding Machiavelli as a teacher of evil. ✦

26
Excerpts from *The Prince*

Niccolò Machiavelli

Chapter XV: The Things for Which Men, and Especially Rulers, Are Praised or Blamed

It remains now to consider in what ways a ruler should act with regard to his subjects and allies.[1] And since I am well aware that many people have written about this subject I fear that I may be thought presumptuous, for what I have to say differs from the precepts offered by others, especially on this matter. But because I want to write what will be useful to anyone who understands, it seems to me better to concentrate on what really happens rather than on theories or speculations. For many have imagined republics and principalities that have never been seen or known to exist.[2] However, how men live is so different from how they should live that a ruler who does not do what is generally done, but persists in doing what ought to be done, will undermine his power rather than maintain it. If a ruler who wants always to act honourably is surrounded by many unscrupulous men his downfall is inevitable. Therefore, a ruler who wishes to maintain his power must be prepared to act immorally when this becomes necessary.

I shall set aside fantasies about rulers, then, and consider what happens in fact. I say that whenever men are discussed, and especially rulers (because they occupy more exalted positions), they are praised or blamed for possessing some of the following qualities. Thus, one man is considered generous, another miserly (I use this Tuscan term because *avaro* in our tongue also signifies someone who is rapacious, whereas we call *misero* someone who is very reluctant to use his own possessions); one is considered a free giver, another rapacious; one cruel, another merciful; one treacherous, another loyal; one effeminate and weak, another indomitable and spirited; one affable, another haughty; one lascivious, another moderate; one upright, another cunning; one inflexible, another easy-going; one serious, another frivolous; one devout, another unbelieving, and so on.

I know that everyone will acknowledge that it would be most praiseworthy for a ruler to have all the above-mentioned qualities that are held to be good. But because it is not possible to have all of them, and because circumstances do not permit living a completely virtuous life, one must be sufficiently prudent to know how to avoid becoming notorious for those vices that would destroy one's power and seek to avoid those vices that are not politically dangerous; but if one cannot bring oneself to do this, they can be indulged in with fewer misgivings. Yet one should not be troubled about becoming notorious for those vices without which it is difficult to preserve one's power, because if one considers everything carefully, doing some things that seem virtuous may result in one's ruin, whereas doing other things that seem vicious may strengthen one's position and cause one to flourish.

Chapter XVI: Generosity and Meanness

To begin, then, with the first of the above-mentioned qualities, I maintain that it would be desirable to be considered generous; nevertheless, if generosity is practised in such a way that you will be considered generous, it will harm you. If it is practised virtuously, and as it should be, it will not be known about, and you will not avoid acquiring a bad reputation for the opposite vice. Therefore, if one wants to keep up a reputation for being generous, one must spend lavishly and ostentatiously. The inevitable outcome of acting in such ways is that the ruler will consume all his resources in sumptuous display; and if he wants to continue to be thought generous, he will eventually be compelled to become rapacious, to tax the people very heavily, and raise money by all possible means. Thus, he will begin to be hated by his subjects and, because he is impoverished, he will be held in little regard. Since this generosity of his has harmed many people and benefited few, he will feel the effects of any discontent, and the first real threat to his power will involve him in grave difficulties. When he realises this, and changes his ways, he will very soon acquire a bad reputation for being miserly.

Therefore, since a ruler cannot both practise this virtue of generosity and be known to do so without harming himself, he would do well not to worry about being called miserly. For eventually he will come to be considered more generous, when it is realised that, because of his parsimony, his revenues are sufficient to defend himself against any enemies that attack him, and to undertake campaigns without imposing special taxes on the people. Thus he will be acting generously towards the vast majority, whose property he does not touch, and will be acting meanly towards the few to whom he gives nothing.

Those rulers who have achieved great things in our own times have all been considered mean; all the others have failed. Although Pope Julius cultivated a reputation for generosity in order to become pope,[3] he did not seek to maintain it afterwards, because he wanted to be able to wage war. The present King of France[4] has fought many wars without imposing any special taxes on his subjects, because his parsimonious habits have always enabled him to meet the extra expenses. If the present King of Spain[5] had a reputation for generosity, he would not have successfully undertaken so many campaigns.

Therefore, a ruler should worry little about being thought miserly; he will not have to rob his subjects; he will be able to defend himself; he will avoid being poor and despised and will not be forced to become rapacious. For meanness is one of those vices that enable him to rule. It may be objected that Caesar obtained power through his open-handedness, and that many others have risen to very high office because they were open-handed and were considered to be so. I would reply that either you are already an established ruler or you are trying to become a ruler. In the first case, open-handedness is harmful; in the second, it is certainly necessary to be thought open-handed. Caesar was one of those who sought power in Rome; but if after gaining power he had survived, and had not moderated his expenditure, he would have undermined his power. And if it should be objected that many rulers who have been considered very generous have had remarkable military successes, I would reply: a ruler spends either what belongs to him or his subjects, or what belongs to others. In the former case, he should be parsimonious; in the latter, he should be as open-handed as possible. A ruler who accompanies his army, supporting it by looting, sacking and extortions, disposes of what belongs to others; he must be open-handed, for if he is not, his soldiers will desert. You can be much more generous with what does not belong to you or to your subjects, as Cyrus, Caesar and Alexander were. This is because giving away what belongs to others in no way damages your reputation; rather, it enhances it. It is only giving away what belongs to yourself that harms you.

There is nothing that is so self-consuming as generosity: the more you practise it, the less you will be able to continue to practise it. You will either become poor and despised or your efforts to avoid poverty will make you rapacious and hated. A ruler must above all guard against being despised and hated; and being generous will lead to both. Therefore, it is shrewder to cultivate a reputation for meanness, which will lead to notoriety but not to hatred. This is better than being forced, through wanting to be considered generous, to incur a reputation for rapacity, which will lead to notoriety and to hatred as well.

Chapter XVII: Cruelty and Mercifulness; And Whether It Is Better to Be Loved or Feared

Turning to the other previously mentioned qualities, I maintain that every ruler should want to be thought merciful, not cruel; nevertheless, one should take care not to be merciful in an inappropriate way. Cesare Borgia was considered cruel, yet his harsh measures restored order to the Romagna, unifying it and rendering it peaceful and loyal. If his conduct is properly considered, he will be judged to have been much more merciful than the Florentine people, who let Pistoia be torn apart, in order to avoid acquiring a reputation for cruelty. Therefore, if a ruler can keep his subjects united and loyal, he should not worry about incurring a reputation for cruelty; for by punishing a very few he will really be more merciful than those who over-indulgently permit disorders to develop, with resultant killings and plunderings. For the latter usually harm a whole community, whereas the executions ordered by a ruler harm only specific individuals. And a new ruler, in particular, cannot avoid being considered harsh, since new states are full of dangers. Virgil makes Dido say:

Res dura, et regni novitas me talia cogunt moliri, et late fines custode tueri.[6]

Nevertheless, he should be slow to believe accusations and to act against individuals, and should not be afraid of his own shadow. He should act with due prudence and humanity so that being over-confident will not make him incautious, and being too suspicious will not render him insupportable.

A controversy has arisen about this: whether it is better to be loved than feared, or vice versa. My view is that it is desirable to be both loved and feared; but it is difficult to achieve both and, if one of them has to be lacking, it is much safer to be feared than loved.

For this may be said of men generally: they are ungrateful, fickle, feigners and dissemblers, avoiders of danger, eager for gain. While you benefit them they are all devoted to you: they would shed their blood for you; they offer their possessions, their lives, and their sons, as I said before, when the need to do so is far off. But when you are hard pressed, they turn away. A ruler who has relied completely on their promises, and has neglected to prepare other defences, will be ruined, because friendships that are ac-

quired with money, and not through greatness and nobility of character, are paid for but not secured, and prove unreliable just when they are needed.

Men are less hesitant about offending or harming a ruler who makes himself loved than one who inspires fear. For love is sustained by a bond of gratitude which, because men are excessively self-interested, is broken whenever they see a chance to benefit themselves. But fear is sustained by a dread of punishment that is always effective. Nevertheless, a ruler must make himself feared in such a way that, even if he does not become loved, he does not become hated. For it is perfectly possible to be feared without incurring hatred. And this can always be achieved if he refrains from laying hands on the property of his citizens and subjects, and on their womenfolk. If it is necessary to execute anyone, this should be done only if there is a proper justification and obvious reason. But, above all, he must not touch the property of others, because men forget sooner the killing of a father than the loss of their patrimony. Moreover, there will always be pretexts for seizing property; and someone who begins to live rapaciously will always find pretexts for taking the property of others. On the other hand, reasons or pretexts for taking life are rarer and more fleeting.

However, when a ruler is with his army, and commands a large force, he must not worry about being considered harsh, because armies are never kept united and prepared for military action unless their leader is thought to be harsh. Among the remarkable things recounted about Hannibal is that, although he had a very large army, composed of men from many countries, and fighting in foreign lands, there never arose any dissension, either among themselves or against their leader, whether things were going well or badly. This could be accounted for only by his inhuman cruelty which, together with his many good qualities, made him always respected and greatly feared by his troops. And if he had not been so cruel, his other qualities would not have been sufficient to achieve that effect. Thoughtless writers admire this achievement of his, yet condemn the main reason for it.

That his other qualities would not have sufficed is proved by what happened to Scipio, considered a most remarkable man not only in his own times but in all others, whose armies rebelled against him in Spain. The only reason for this was that he was over-indulgent, and permitted his soldiers more freedom than was consistent with maintaining proper military discipline. Fabius Maximus rebuked him for this in the senate, and called him a corrupter of the Roman army. And when Locri was ravaged by one of Scipio's legates, the inhabitants were not avenged by him, and the legate was not punished for his arrogance, all because Scipio was too easy-going. Indeed, a speaker in the senate who wished to excuse him said that there were many men who were better at not committing misdeeds themselves than punishing the misdeeds of others. This character of his would eventually have tarnished his fame and glory, if he had continued his military command unchecked; but since he was controlled by the senate, this harmful quality was not only concealed but contributed to his glory.

Returning to the matter of being feared and loved, then, I conclude that whether men bear affection depends on themselves, but whether they are afraid will depend on what the ruler does. A wise ruler should rely on what is under his own control, not on what is under the control of others; he should contrive only to avoid incurring hatred, as I have said.

Chapter XVIII: How Rulers Should Keep Their Promises

Everyone knows how praiseworthy it is for a ruler to keep his promises, and live uprightly and not by trickery. Nevertheless, experience shows that in our times the rulers who have done great things are those who have set little store by keeping their word, being skilful rather in cunningly confusing men; they have got the better of those who have relied on being trustworthy.

You should know, then, that there are two ways of contending: one by using laws, the other, force. The first is appropriate for men, the second for animals; but because the former is often ineffective, one must have recourse to the latter. Therefore, a ruler must know well how to imitate beasts as well as employing properly human means. This policy was taught to rulers allegorically by ancient writers: they tell how Achilles and many other ancient rulers were entrusted to Chiron the centaur, to be raised carefully by him. Having a mentor who was half-beast and half-man signifies that a ruler needs to use both natures, and that one without the other is not effective.

Since a ruler, then, must know how to act like a beast, he should imitate both the fox and the lion, for the lion is liable to be trapped, whereas the fox cannot ward off wolves. One needs, then, to be a fox to recognise traps, and a lion to frighten away wolves. Those who rely merely upon a lion's strength do not understand matters.

Therefore, a prudent ruler cannot keep his word, nor should he, when such fidelity would damage him, and when the reasons that made him promise are no longer relevant. This advice would not be sound if all men were upright; but because they are treacherous and would not keep their promises to you, you should not consider yourself bound to keep your promises to them.

Moreover, plausible reasons can always be found for such failure to keep promises. One could give countless modern examples of this, and show how many peace treaties and promises have been rendered null and void by the faithlessness of rulers; and those best able to imitate the fox have succeeded best. But foxiness should be well concealed: one must be a great feigner and dissembler. And men are so naive, and so much dominated by immediate needs, that a skilful deceiver always finds plenty of people who will let themselves be deceived.

I must mention one recent case: Alexander VI was concerned only with deceiving men, and he always found them gullible. No man ever affirmed anything more forcefully or with stronger oaths but kept his word less. Nevertheless, his deceptions were always effective, because he well understood the naivety of men.

A ruler, then, need not actually possess all the above-mentioned qualities, but he must certainly seem to. Indeed, I shall be so bold as to say that having and always cultivating them is harmful, whereas seeming to have them is useful; for instance, to seem merciful, trustworthy, humane, upright and devout, and also to be so. But if it becomes necessary to refrain, you must be prepared to act in the opposite way, and be capable of doing it. And it must be understood that a ruler, and especially a new ruler, cannot always act in ways that are considered good because, in order to maintain his power, he is often forced to act treacherously, ruthlessly or inhumanely, and disregard the precepts of religion. Hence, he must be prepared to vary his conduct as the winds of fortune and changing circumstances constrain him and, as I said before, not deviate from right conduct if possible, but be capable of entering upon the path of wrongdoing when this becomes necessary.

A ruler, then, should be very careful that everything he says is replete with the five above-named qualities: to those who see and hear him, he should seem to be exceptionally merciful, trustworthy, upright, humane and devout. And it is most necessary of all to seem devout. In these matters, most men judge more by their eyes than by their hands. For everyone is capable of seeing you, but few can touch you. Everyone can see what you appear to be, whereas few have direct experience of what you really are, and those few will not dare to challenge the popular view, sustained as it is by the majesty of the ruler's position. With regard to all human actions, and especially those of rulers, who cannot be called to account, men pay attention to the outcome. If a ruler, then, contrives to conquer, and to preserve the state, the means will always be judged to be honourable and be praised by everyone. For the common people are impressed by appearances and results. Everywhere the common people are the vast majority, and the few are isolated when the majority and the government are at one. One present-day ruler, whom it is well to leave unnamed, is always preaching peace and trust, although he is really very hostile to both; and if he had practised them he would have lost either reputation or power several times over. . . .

Chapter XXV: How Much Power Fortune Has over Human Affairs, and How It Should Be Resisted

I am not unaware that many have thought, and many still think, that the affairs of the world are so ruled by fortune and by God that the ability of men cannot control them. Rather, they think that we have no remedy at all; and therefore it could be concluded that it is useless to sweat much over things, but let them be governed by fate. This opinion has been more popular in our own times because of the great changes that have taken place and are still to be seen even now, which could hardly have been predicted. When I think about this, I am sometimes inclined, to some extent, to share this opinion. Nevertheless, so as not to eliminate human freedom, I am disposed to hold that fortune is the arbiter of half our actions, but that it lets us control roughly the other half.

I compare fortune to one of those dangerous rivers that, when they become enraged, flood the plains, destroy trees and buildings, move earth from one place and deposit it in another. Everyone flees before it, everyone gives way to its thrust, without being able to halt it in any way. But this does not mean that, when the river is not in flood, men are unable to take precautions, by means of dykes and dams, so that when it rises next time, it will either not overflow its banks or, if it does, its force will not be so uncontrolled or damaging.

The same happens with fortune, which shows its powers where no force has been organised to resist it, and therefore strikes in the places where it knows that no dykes or dams have been built to restrain it. And if you consider Italy, which has been the seat of these changes, and which has given rise to them, you will see a countryside devoid of any embankments or defences. If it had been protected by proper defences, like Germany, Spain and France, the flood would not have caused such great changes or it would not have occurred at all. But I have said enough in general terms about resisting fortune.

Considering the matter in more detail, I would observe that one sees a ruler flourishing today and ruined tomorrow, without his having changed at all in character or qualities. I believe this is attributable, first, to the cause previously discussed at length, namely, that a ruler who trusts entirely to luck comes to grief when his luck runs out. Moreover, I believe that we are successful when our ways are suited to the times and circumstances, and unsuccessful when they are not. For one sees that, in the things that lead to the end which everyone aims at, that is, glory and riches, men proceed in different ways: one man cautiously, another impetuously; one man forcefully, another cunningly; one man patiently, another impatiently, and each of these different ways of acting can be effective. On the other hand, of two cautious men, one may achieve his aims and the other fail. Again, two men may both succeed, although they have different characters, one acting cautiously and the other impetuously. The reason for these different outcomes is whether their ways of acting conform with the conditions in which they operate. Consequently, as I have said, two men, acting differently, may achieve the same results; and if two men act in the same way, one may succeed and the other fail. From this, again, arise changes in prosperity; because if a man acts cautiously and patiently, and the times and circumstances change in ways for which his methods are appropriate, he will be successful. But if the times and circumstances change again, he will come to grief, because he does not change his methods. And one does not find men who are so prudent that they are capable of being sufficiently flexible: either because our natural inclinations are too strong to permit us to change, or because, having always fared well by acting in a certain way, we do not think it a good idea to change our methods. Therefore, if it is necessary for a cautious man to act expeditiously, he does not know how to do it; this leads to his failure. But if it were possible to change one's character to suit the times and circumstances, one would always be successful.

Pope Julius II always acted impetuously, and found the times and circumstances so suited to his ways that he was always successful. Consider the first expedition he made to Bologna, while messer Giovanni Bentivoglio was still alive. The Venetians were opposed to it, and so was the King of Spain; there were also discussions with the King of France about such an enterprise. Nevertheless, acting with his usual indomitable spirit and impetuosity, he led the expedition personally. This initiative caught the King of Spain and the Venetians off guard and constrained them to be passive spectators, the latter through fear and the former because of his desire to recover the whole of the Kingdom of Naples. On the other hand, Julius involved the King of France: for that King saw the Pope moving and, because he wanted to cultivate the Pope's friendship with a view to reducing the power of Venice, he decided that he could not refuse him troops without offending him very openly. With this swift initiative, then, Julius achieved what no other pope, acting with consummate prudence, could have attained. If he had not left Rome until everything had been agreed and settled, as any other pope would have done, he would never have succeeded. For the King of France would have contrived to find countless excuses, and the others would have produced countless reasons why the Pope should hesitate. I shall not discuss his other actions, which were similar in character, and all turned out well for him. The shortness of his pontificate did not permit him to taste of failure. But if circumstances had changed so that it was imperative to act cautiously, he would have been undone; for he would never have deviated from the methods that were natural to him.

I conclude, then, that since circumstances vary and men when acting lack flexibility, they are successful if their methods match the circumstances and unsuccessful if they do not. I certainly think that it is better to be impetuous than cautious, because fortune is a woman and if you want to control her, it is necessary to treat her roughly. And it is clear that she is more inclined to yield to men who are impetuous than to those who are calculating. Since fortune is a woman, she is always well disposed towards young men, because they are less cautious and more aggressive, and treat her more boldly. . . .

Notes

1. A ruler's conduct towards subjects is treated in Chs. XV–XVII, towards allies (*amici*) in Ch. XVIII.

2. M. apparently refers both to some ancient writers (e.g., Plato, in his *Republic*) and to more recent ones who emphasised ideals and the duties of rulers.

3. I.e., by bribes.

4. Louis XII.

5. Ferdinand the Catholic.

6. Virgil, *Aeneid*, 563–4: 'Harsh necessity and the newness of my kingdom force me to do such things, and to guard all the frontiers.'

Adapted from: Niccolò Machiavelli, *The Prince*, translated by Quentin Skinner and Russell Price, pp. 54–63, 84–87. Copyright © 1988. Reprinted by permission of Cambridge University Press. ✦

27
Excerpts from the *Discourses*

Niccolò Machiavelli

2. How Many Kinds of State There Are and of What Kind Was That of Rome

I propose to dispense with a discussion of cities which from the outset have been subject to another power, and shall speak only of those which have from the outset been far removed from any kind of external servitude, but, instead, have from the start been governed in accordance with their wishes, whether as republics or principalities. As such cities have had diverse origins, so too they have had diverse laws and institutions. For either at the outset, or before very long, to some of them laws have been given by some one person at some one time, as laws were given to the Spartans by Lycurgus; whereas others have acquired them by chance and at different times as occasion arose. This was the case in Rome.

Happy indeed should we call that state which produces a man so prudent that men can live securely under the laws which he prescribes without having to emend them. Sparta, for instance, observed its laws for more than eight hundred years without corrupting them and without any dangerous disturbance. Unhappy, on the other hand, in some degree is that city to be deemed which, not having chanced to meet with a prudent organizer, has to reorganize itself. And, of such, that is the more unhappy which is the more remote from order; and that is the more remote from order whose institutions have missed altogether the straight road which leads it to its perfect and true destiny. For it is almost impossible that states of this type should by any eventuality be set on the right road again; whereas those which, if their order is not perfect, have made a good beginning and are capable of improvement, may become perfect should something happen which provides the opportunity. It should, however, be noted that they will never introduce order without incurring danger, because few men ever welcome new laws setting up a new order in the state unless necessity makes it clear to them that there is need for such laws; and since such a necessity cannot arise without danger, the state may easily be ruined before the new order has been brought to completion. The republic of Florence bears this out, for owing to what happened at Arezzo in '02 it was reconstituted, and owing to what happened at Prato in '12 its constitution was destroyed.

It being now my intention to discuss what were the institutions of the city of Rome and what events conduced to its perfection, I would remark that those who have written about states say that there are to be found in them one of three forms of government, called by them *Principality*, *Aristocracy* and *Democracy*, and that those who set up a government in any particular state must adopt one of them, as best suits their purpose.[1]

Others—and with better judgement many think—say that there are six types of government of which three are very bad, and three are good in themselves but easily become corrupt, so that they too must be classed as pernicious. Those that are good are the three above mentioned. Those that are bad are the other three, which depend on them, and each of them is so like the one associated with it that it easily passes from one form to the other. For *Principality* easily becomes *Tyranny*. From *Aristocracy* the transition to *Oligarchy* is an easy one. *Democracy* is without difficulty converted into *Anarchy*. So that if anyone who is organizing a commonwealth sets up one of the three first forms of government, he sets up what will last but for a while, since there are no means whereby to prevent it passing into its contrary, on account of the likeness which in such a case virtue has to vice.

These variations of government among men are due to chance. For in the beginning

341

of the world, when its inhabitants were few, they lived for a time scattered like the beasts. Then, with the multiplication of their offspring, they drew together and, in order the better to be able to defend themselves, began to look about for a man stronger and more courageous than the rest, made him their head, and obeyed him.

It was thus that men learned how to distinguish what is honest and good from what is pernicious and wicked, for the sight of someone injuring his benefactor evoked in them hatred and sympathy and they blamed the ungrateful and respected those who showed gratitude, well aware that the same injuries might have been done to themselves. Hence to prevent evil of this kind they took to making laws and to assigning punishments to those who contravened them. The notion of justice thus came into being.

In this way it came about that, when later on they had to choose a prince, they did not have recourse to the boldest as formerly, but to one who excelled in prudence and justice.

But when at a yet later stage they began to make the prince hereditary instead of electing him, his heirs soon began to degenerate as compared with their ancestors, and, forsaking virtuous deeds, considered that princes have nought else to do but to surpass other men in extravagance, lasciviousness, and every other form of licentiousness. With the result that the prince came to be hated, and, since he was hated, came to be afraid, and from fear soon passed to offensive action, which quickly brought about a tyranny.

From which, before long, was begotten the source of their downfall; for tyranny gave rise to conspiracies and plots against princes, organized not by timid and weak men, but by men conspicuous for their liberality, magnanimity, wealth and ability, for such men could not stand the dishonourable life the prince was leading. The masses, therefore, at the instigation of these powerful leaders, took up arms against the prince, and, when he had been liquidated, submitted to the authority of those whom they looked upon as their liberators. Hence the latter, to whom the very term 'sole head' had become odious, formed themselves into a government. Moreover, in the beginning,

mindful of what they had suffered under a tyranny, they ruled in accordance with the laws which they had made, subordinated their own convenience to the common advantage, and, both in private matters and public affairs, governed and preserved order with the utmost diligence.

But when the administration passed to their descendants who had no experience of the changeability of fortune, had not been through bad times, and instead of remaining content with the civic equality then prevailing, reverted to avarice, ambition and to seizing other men's womenfolk, they caused government by an aristocracy to become government by an oligarchy in which civic rights were entirely disregarded; so that in a short time there came to pass in their case the same thing as happened to the tyrant, for the masses, sick of their government, were ready to help anyone who had any sort of plan for attacking their rulers; and so there soon arose someone who with the aid of the masses liquidated them.

Then, since the memory of the prince and of the injuries inflicted by him was still fresh, and since, having got rid of government by the few, they had no desire to return to that of a prince, they turned to a democratic form of government, which they organized in such a way that no sort of authority was vested either in a few powerful men or in a prince.

And, since all forms of government are to some extent respected at the outset, this democratic form of government maintained itself for a while but not for long, especially when the generation that had organized it had passed away. For anarchy quickly supervened, in which no respect was shown either for the individual or for the official, and which was such that, as everyone did what he liked, all sorts of outrages were constantly committed. The outcome was inevitable. Either at the suggestion of some good man or because this anarchy had to be got rid of somehow, principality was once again restored. And from this there was, stage by stage, a return to anarchy, by way of the transitions and for the reasons assigned.

This, then, is the cycle through which all commonwealths pass, whether they govern themselves or are governed. But rarely do they return to the same form of government, for there can scarce be a state of such vitality that it can undergo often such changes and yet remain in being. What usually happens is that, while in a state of commotion in which it lacks both counsel and strength, a state becomes subject to a neighbouring and better organized state. Were it not so, a commonwealth might go on for ever passing through these governmental transitions.

I maintain then, that all the forms of government mentioned above are far from satisfactory, the three good ones because their life is so short, the three bad ones because of their inherent malignity. Hence prudent legislators, aware of their defects, refrained from adopting as such any one of these forms, and chose instead one that shared in them all, since they thought such a government would be stronger and more stable, for if in one and the same state there was principality, aristocracy and democracy each would keep watch over the other. . . .

18. How in Corrupt Cities a Free Government Can Be Maintained Where It Exists, or Be Established Where It Does Not Exist

It will not, I think, be foreign to my purpose nor contrary to the plan of my previous discourse to consider whether in a corrupt city it is possible to maintain a free government where it exists, and whether, when there has been none, it can be set up. In regard to this question I maintain that in either case it will be a very difficult thing to do. It is, moreover, almost impossible to lay down rules, for the method to be adopted will of necessity depend upon the degree of corruption. None the less, since it is well to take account of all cases, I do not propose to shelve the question. I suppose then an exceedingly corrupt state, whereby the difficulty will clearly be intensified, since in it there will be found neither laws nor institutions which will suffice to check widespread corruption. Because, just as for the maintenance of good customs laws are required, so if laws are to be observed, there is need of good customs. Furthermore, institutions and laws made in

the early days of a republic when men were good, no longer serve their purpose when men have become bad. And, if by any chance the laws of the state are changed, there will never, or but rarely, be a change in its institutions. The result is that new laws are ineffectual, because the institutions, which remain constant, corrupt them.

In order to make this point more clear I would point out that in Rome there was a constitution regulating its government, or rather its form of government, and then laws enabling the magistrates to keep the citizens in order. To the constitution determining its form of government pertained the authority vested in the people, the senate, the tribunes, and in the consuls, the method of applying for and of appointing to magisterial posts, and its legislative procedure. These institutions underwent little or no change in the course of events, whereas there were changes in the laws which kept the citizens in order. There was, for instance, the law concerning adultery, the sumptuary law, a law concerning ambition, and many others. These laws were introduced step by step as the citizens became corrupt. But since the institutions determining its form of government remained unchanged and, when corruption had set in, were no longer good, these modifications of the laws did not suffice to keep men good, though they might have helped had the introduction of new laws been accompanied by a modification of the institutions.

That it is true to say that such institutions would not be good in a corrupted state is clearly seen in two important cases, in the appointing of magistrates and in the making of laws. The Roman people had never given the consulate or any other important office in the city except to such as had applied for the post. This institution was at the outset good, because only such citizens applied for posts as judged themselves worthy to fill them, and to be rejected was looked upon as ignominious; so that everybody behaved well in order to be judged worthy. This procedure, when the city became corrupt, was extremely harmful; because not those who had more virtue, but those who had more power, applied for magistracies, and the powerless, though virtuous, refrained from applying through fear. This inconvenience did not come about all at once, but by stages, as is the case with all inconveniences. For when the Romans had conquered Africa and Asia, and had reduced the greater part of Greece to subjection, they had become secure as to their liberty nor had they any more enemies whom there was ground to fear. This sense of security and this weakness on the part of their enemies caused the Roman people in appointing to the consulate to consider not a man's virtue, but his popularity. This drew to that office men who knew better how to get round men, not those who knew better how to conquer enemies. They then turned from those who had more popularity and gave it to those who had more power. Thus owing to the defectiveness of this institution it came about that good men were wholly excluded from consular rank.

Again, a tribune or any other citizen could propose to the people a law, in regard to which every citizen was entitled to speak either in favour of it or against, prior to a decision being reached. This institution was good so long as the citizens were good, because it is always a good thing that anyone anxious to serve the public should be able to propose his plan. It is also a good thing that everyone should be at liberty to express his opinion on it, so that when the people have heard what each has to say they may choose the best plan. But when the citizens had become perverse, this institution became a nuisance; because only the powerful proposed laws, and this for the sake, not of their common liberties, but to augment their own power. And against such projects no one durst speak for fear of such folk; with the result that the people were induced, either by deceit or by force, to adopt measures which spelt their own ruin.

In order to maintain Rome's liberty, therefore, when corruption had set in, it was necessary in the course of its development to introduce new institutions just as there had been made new laws; for different institutions and a different procedure should be prescribed for the governed according as they are good or bad, since similar forms cannot subsist in matter which is disposed in

a contrary manner. Now defective institutions must either be renovated all at once as soon as the decline from goodness is noticed, or little by little before they become known to everybody. Neither of which courses is possible, I maintain. For if the renovation is to take place little by little, there is need of someone who shall see the inconvenience coming while yet it is far off and in its infancy. But it may quite easily happen in a state that no such person will ever arise, or, should he arise in point of fact, that he will never be able to persuade others to see things as he does himself; for men accustomed to a certain mode of life are reluctant to change it, especially when they have not themselves noticed the evil in question, but have had their attention called to it by conjectures. While with regard to modifying institutions all at once when everybody realizes that they are no good, I would point out that, though it is easy to recognize their futility, it is not easy to correct it; for, to do this, normal methods will not suffice now that normal methods are bad. Hence it is necessary to resort to extraordinary methods, such as the use of force and an appeal to arms, and, before doing anything, to become a prince in the state, so that one can dispose it as one thinks fit.

But, to reconstitute political life in a state presupposes a good man, whereas to have recourse to violence in order to make oneself prince in a republic supposes a bad man. Hence very rarely will there be found a good man ready to use bad methods in order to make himself prince, though with a good end in view, nor yet a bad man who, having become a prince, is ready to do the right thing and to whose mind it will occur to use well that authority which he has acquired by bad means.

It is on account of all this that it is difficult, or rather impossible, either to maintain a republican form of government in states which have become corrupt or to create such a form afresh. Should a republic simply have to be created or to be maintained, it would be necessary to introduce into it a form of government akin rather to a monarchy than to a democracy, so that those men whose arrogance is such that they cannot be corrected by legal processes, may yet be restrained to some extent by a quasi-regal power.[2] To try to make them become good in any other way would be either a most brutal or an impossible undertaking—the kind of thing that Cleomenes did, as I said above; for that he might rule alone, he killed the ephors, and for the same reasons Romulus killed his brother and Titus Tatius killed the Sabine, and afterwards both of them made good use of their authority. It should, however, be noted that neither the one nor the other had subjects steeped in corruption, which in this chapter we have taken as the basis of our argument; so that both were able to resolve on such steps, and, having done so, to camouflage their plan. . . .

58. The Masses Are More Knowing and More Constant Than Is a Prince

Nothing is more futile and more inconstant than are the masses. So says our author, Titus Livy, and so say all other historians. For in the records of the actions men have performed one often finds the masses condemning someone to death, and then lamenting him and ardently wishing he were alive. The Roman people did this in Manlius Capitolinus's case: first they condemned him to death, then urgently wished him back. Of this our author says that 'soon after he had ceased to be a danger, the desire for him took hold of the people'. And again, when describing the events which happened in Syracuse after the death of Hieronymus, the nephew of Hiero, he says: 'It is of the nature of the masses either servilely to obey or arrogantly to domineer.'

I know not whether the view I am about to adopt will prove so hard to uphold and so full of difficulties that I shall have either shamefully to abandon it or laboriously to maintain it; for I propose to defend a position which all writers attack, as I have said. But, however that may be, I think, and always shall think there can be no harm in defending an opinion by arguments so long as one has no intention of appealing either to authority or force.

I claim, then, that for the failing for which writers blame the masses, any body of men one cares to select may be blamed, and especially princes; for anyone who does not regulate his conduct by laws will make the same mistakes as the masses are guilty of. This is easily seen, for there are and have been any number of princes, but of good and wise ones there have been but few. I am speaking of princes who have succeeded in breaking the bonds which might have held them in check; among which I do not include those kings who were born in Egypt when that most ancient of ancient realms was governed in accordance with the law, nor those born in Sparta, nor those born in France in our own times, for the kingdom of France is better regulated by laws than is any other of which at present we have knowledge. Kings who are born under such conditions are not to be classed among those whose nature we have to consider in each individual case to see whether it resembles that of the masses; for, should there be masses regulated by laws in the same way as they are, there will be found in them the same goodness as we find in kings, and it will be seen that they neither 'arrogantly dominate nor servilely obey'. Such was the Roman populace which, so long as the republic remained uncorrupt, was never servilely obsequious, nor yet did it ever dominate with arrogance: on the contrary, it had its own institutions and magistrates and honourably kept its own place. But when it was necessary to take action against some powerful person, it did so, as is seen in the case of Manlius, of the Ten, and in the case of others who sought to oppress it. Also, when it had to obey dictators or consuls in the public interest, it did so. Nor is it any wonder that the Roman populace wanted Manlius Capitolinus back when he was dead, for what they wanted was his virtues, which had been such that his memory evoked everyone's sympathy, and would have had power to produce the same effect in a prince, for all writers are of opinion that virtue is praised and admired even in one's enemies. Again, had Manlius, in response to this desire, been raised from the dead, the Roman populace would have passed on him the same sentence as it did, have had him arrested and, shortly after, have condemned him to death: though, for that matter, one also finds that reputedly wise princes have put people to death and then wished them alive again; Alexander, for instance, in the case of Cleitus and other of his friends, and Herod in the case of Mariamne. But the truth is that what our historian says of the nature of the masses is not said of the masses when disciplined by laws, as were the Romans, but of undisciplined masses, like those of Syracuse, which made the same kind of mistakes as do men when infuriated and undisciplined, just as did Alexander the Great and Herod in the cases cited.[3]

The nature of the masses, then, is no more reprehensible than is the nature of princes, for all do wrong and to the same extent when there is nothing to prevent them doing wrong. Of this there are plenty of examples besides those given, both among the Roman emperors and among other tyrants and princes; and in them we find a degree of inconstancy and changeability in behaviour such as is never found in the masses.

I arrive, then, at a conclusion contrary to the common opinion which asserts that populaces, when in power, are variable, fickle and ungrateful; and affirm that in them these faults are in no wise different from those to be found in certain princes. Were the accusation made against both the masses and princes, it would be true; but, if princes be excepted, it is false. For when the populace is in power and is well-ordered, it will be stable, prudent and grateful, in much the same way, or in a better way, than is a prince, however wise he be thought. And, on the other hand, a prince who contemns the laws, will be more ungrateful, fickle and imprudent than is the populace. Nor is inconstancy of behaviour due to a difference in nature, for they are pretty much the same, or, if one be better than the other, it is the populace: it is due to the greater or less respect which they have for the laws under which both alike are living.

If we consider the Roman populace it will be found that for four hundred years they were enemies to the very name of king and lovers of glory and of the common good of their country. Of both characteristics the Roman populace affords numerous and striking examples. And, should anyone bring up against me the ingratitude the populace displayed towards Scipio, my answer is that I have already discussed this question at length and have there shown the ingratitude of the populace to be less than that of princes. While in the matter of prudence and stability I claim that the populace is more prudent, more stable, and of sounder judgement than the prince. Not without good reason is the voice of the populace likened to that of God; for public opinion is remarkably accurate in its prognostications, so much so that it seems as if the populace by some hidden power discerned the evil and the good that was to befall it. With regard to its judgement, when two speakers of equal skill are heard advocating different alternatives, very rarely does one find the populace failing to adopt the better view or incapable of appreciating the truth of what it hears. While, if in bold actions and such as appear advantageous it errs, as I have said above, so does a prince often err where his passions are involved, and these are much stronger than those of the populace.

It is found, too, that in the election of magistrates the populace makes a far better choice than does the prince; nor can the populace ever be persuaded that it is good to appoint to such an office a man of infamous life or corrupt habits, whereas a prince may easily and in a vast variety of ways be persuaded to do this. Again, one finds that when the populace begins to have a horror of something it remains of the same mind for many centuries; a thing that is never observed in the case of a prince. For both these characteristics I shall content myself with the evidence afforded by the Roman populace, which in the course of so many hundreds of years and so many elections of consuls and tribunes did not make four elections of which it had to repent. So much, too, as I have said, was the title of king hated that no service rendered by one of its citizens who ambitioned it, could render him immune from the penalties prescribed. Besides this, one finds that cities in which the populace is the prince, in a very short time extend vastly their dominions much more than do those which have always been under a prince; as Rome did after the expulsion of the kings, and Athens after it was free of Pisistratus.

This can only be due to one thing: government by the populace is better than government by princes. Nor do I care whether to this opinion of mine all that our historian has said in the aforesaid passage or what others have said, be objected; because if account be taken of all the disorders due to populaces and of all those due to princes, and of all the glories won by populaces and all those won by princes, it will be found that alike in goodness and in glory the populace is far superior. And if princes are superior to populaces in drawing up laws, codes of civic life, statutes and new institutions, the populace is so superior in sustaining what has been instituted, that it indubitably adds to the glory of those who have instituted them.

In short, to bring this topic to a conclusion, I say that, just as princely forms of government have endured for a very long time, so, too, have republican forms of government; and that in both cases it has been essential for them to be regulated by laws. For a prince who does what he likes is a lunatic, and a populace which does what it likes is unwise. If, therefore, it be a question of a prince subservient to the laws and of a populace chained up by laws, more virtue will be found in the populace than in the prince; and if it be a question of either of them loosed from control by the law, there will be found fewer errors in the populace than in the prince, and these of less moment and much easier to put right. For a licentious and turbulent populace, when a good man can obtain a hearing, can easily be brought to behave itself; but there is no one to talk to a bad prince, nor is there any remedy except the sword. From which an inference may be drawn in regard to the importance of their respective maladies; for, if to cure the malady of the populace a word suffices and the sword is needed to cure that of a prince, no one will fail to see that the greater the cure, the greater the fault.

When the populace has thrown off all restraint, it is not the mad things it does that are terrifying, nor is it of present evils that one is afraid, but of what may come of them, for amidst such confusion there may come to be a tyrant. In the case of bad princes it is just the opposite: it is present evils that are terrifying, but for the future there is hope, since men are convinced that the evil ways of a bad prince may make for freedom in the end. Thus one sees the difference between the two cases amounts to the same thing as the difference between what is and what must come to be. The brutalities of the masses are directed against those whom they suspect of conspiring against the common good; the brutalities of a prince against those whom he suspects of conspiring against his own good.[4] The reason why people are prejudiced against the populace is because of the populace anyone may speak ill without fear and openly, even when the populace is ruling. But of princes people speak with the utmost trepidation and the utmost reserve.

Nor does it seem to me foreign to my purpose, since I find the topic attractive, to discuss in the next chapter on which more reliance can be placed, on confederations made by a republic or on confederations formed by a prince. . . .

Notes

1. Here Machiavelli follows Polybius very closely, and in so doing virtually repeats Aristotle's classification of Book III of the *Politics* (see Walker, Vol. II, pp. 7–8).

2. *Discourses* I.16, 17 and 18 all show how Machiavelli would handle the transition from servitude to freedom and republican institutions according to the basic principle, set out most clearly in *Discourses* III.9, of conformity with 'the times' or circumstances. The difficulties are great, as he says in *Discourses* I.17 and 18 and in I.49, so great that 'quasi-regal' power may be needed to contain dissident elements during the transition (see also *Discourses* I.55). But this is fully consistent both with what he says about the need for dictatorship in times of emergency and his general view that a '*potestà regia*' is one of the '*qualità*' in the mixture of elements that go to make up even (or particularly) a flourishing republic.

3. His optimistic view of '*il popolo*' . . . is not contradicted even in *The Prince*, although there their fickleness and unpredictability—from the point of view of a prince—is naturally stressed. (See *Prince* 6, 9 and 17.)

4. Machiavelli does not in fact explain why the masses should ruthlessly defend the common good while a prince is more likely to fight back for his own good. But, of course, there never is any philosophical discussion of the meaning of 'common good'; it never seems to occur to Machiavelli that the phrase could have any meaning apart from, in some sense, the aggregation of the interests of the actual inhabitants. His philosophical simplicity saved him from a lot of irrelevant nonsense.

In this discourse, however, both his thesis about the most appropriate circumstance for which type of government gets stated at its most general, and we see him introducing the dimension of *time* as the solvent of apparent contradictions: 'If princes are superior to populaces in drawing up laws, codes of civic life, statutes and new institutions, the populace is . . . superior in sustaining what has been instituted.' Amid all the 'political development' literature of today, I will suspect that there are general grounds for thinking this proposition (albeit at a high level of abstraction) is true.

28
Introduction to
The Prince

Harvey C. Mansfield, Jr.

Anyone who picks up Machiavelli's *The Prince* holds in his hands the most famous book on politics ever written. Its closest rival might be Plato's *Republic*, but that book discusses politics in the context of things above politics, and politics turns out to have a limited and subordinate place. In *The Prince* Machiavelli also discusses politics in relation to things outside politics, as we shall see, but his conclusion is very different. Politics according to him is not limited by things above it, and things normally taken to be outside politics—the "givens" in any political situation—turn out to be much more under the control of politics than politicians, peoples, and philosophers have hitherto assumed. Machiavelli's *The Prince*, then, is the most famous book on politics when politics is thought to be carried on for its own sake, unlimited by anything above it. The renown of *The Prince* is precisely to have been the first and the best book to argue that politics has and should have its own rules and should not accept rules of any kind or from any source where the object is not to win or prevail over others. *The Prince* is briefer and pithier than Machiavelli's other major work, *Discourses on Livy*, for *The Prince* is addressed to Lorenzo de' Medici, a prince like the busy executive of our day who has little time for reading. So *The Prince* with its political advice to an active politician that politics should not be limited by anything not political, is by far more famous than the *Discourses on Livy*.

We cannot, however, agree that *The Prince* is the most famous book on politics without immediately correcting this to say that it is the most infamous. It is famous for its infamy, for recommending the kind of politics that ever since has been called Machiavellian. The essence of this politics is that "you can get away with murder": that no divine sanction, or degradation of soul, or twinge of conscience will come to punish you. If you succeed, you will not even have to face the infamy of murder, because when "men acquire who can acquire, they will be praised or not blamed" (Chapter 3). Those criminals who are infamous have merely been on the losing side. Machiavelli and Machiavellian politics are famous or infamous for their willingness to brave infamy.

Yet it must be reported that the prevailing view among scholars of Machiavelli is that he was not an evil man who taught evil doctrines, and that he does not deserve his infamy. With a view to his preference for republics over principalities (more evident in the *Discourses on Livy* than in *The Prince*, but not absent in the latter), they cannot believe he was an apologist for tyranny; or, impressed by the sudden burst of Italian patriotism in the last chapter of *The Prince*, they forgive him for the sardonic observations which are not fully consistent with this generous feeling but are thought to give it a certain piquancy (this is the opinion of an earlier generation of scholars); or, on the basis of Machiavelli's saying in Chapter 15 that we should take our bearings from "what is done" rather than from "what should be done," they conclude that he was a forerunner of modern political science, which is not an evil thing because it merely tells us what happens without passing judgment. In sum, the prevailing view of the scholars offers excuses for Machiavelli: he was a republican, a patriot, or a scientist, and therefore, in explicit contradiction to the reaction of most people to Machiavelli as soon as they hear of his doctrines, Machiavelli was not "Machiavellian."

The reader can form his own judgment of these excuses for Machiavelli. I do not recommend them, chiefly because they make Machiavelli less interesting. They transform him into a herald of the future who had the luck to sound the tunes we hear so often today—democracy, nationalism or self-determination, and science. Instead of challenging our favorite beliefs and forcing us to think, Machiavelli is enlisted into a chorus of self-congratulation. There is, of course, evidence for the excuses supplied on behalf of Machiavelli, and that evidence consists of the excuses offered by Machiavelli himself. If someone were to accuse him of being an apologist for tyranny, he can indeed point to a passage in the *Discourses on Livy* (II 2) where he says (rather carefully) that the common good is not observed unless in republics; but if someone else were to accuse him of supporting republicanism, he could point to the same chapter, where he says that the hardest slavery of all is to be conquered by a republic. And, while he shows his Italian patriotism in Chapter 26 of *The Prince* by exhorting someone to seize Italy in order to free it from the barbarians, he also shows his fairmindedness by advising a French king in Chapter 3 how he might better invade Italy the next time. Lastly, it is true that he sometimes merely reports the evil that he sees, while (unnecessarily) deploring it; but at other times he urges us to share in that evil and he virtuously condemns half-hearted immoralists. Although he was an exceedingly bold writer who seems to have deliberately courted an evil reputation, he was nonetheless not so bold as to fail to provide excuses, or prudent reservations, for his boldest statements. Since I have spoken at length on this point in another place, and will not hesitate to mention the work of Leo Strauss, it is not necessary to explain it further here.

What is at issue in the question of whether Machiavelli was "Machiavellian"? To see that a matter of the highest importance is involved we must not rest satisfied with either scholarly excuses or moral frowns. For the matter at issue is the character of the rules by which we reward human beings with fame or condemn them with infamy, the very status of morality. Machiavelli does not make it clear at first that this grave question is his subject. In the Dedicatory Letter he approaches Lorenzo de' Medici with hat in one hand and *The Prince* in the other. Since, he says, one must be a prince to know the nature of peoples and a man of the people to know the nature of princes, he seems to offer Lorenzo the knowledge of princes he does not have but needs. In accordance with this half-serious promise, Machiavelli speaks about the kinds of principalities in the first part of *The Prince* (Chapters 1–11) and, as we learn of the necessity of conquest, about the kinds of armies in the second part (Chapters 12–14). But at the same time (to make a long story short), we learn that the prince must or may lay his foundations on the people (Chapter 9) and that while his only object should be the art of war, he must in time of peace pay attention to moral qualities in such manner as to be able to use them in time of war (Chapter 14, end).

Thus are we prepared for Machiavelli's clarion call in Chapter 15, where he proclaims that he "departs from the orders of others" and says why. For moral qualities are qualities "held good" by the people; so, if the prince must conquer, and wants, like the Medici, to lay his foundation on the people, who are the keepers of morality, then a new morality consistent with the necessity of conquest must be found, and the prince has to be taught anew about the nature of peoples by Machiavelli. In departing from the orders of others, it appears more fitting to Machiavelli "to go directly to the effectual truth of the thing than to the imagination of it." Many have imagined republics and principalities, but one cannot "let go of what is done for what should be done," because a man who "makes a profession of good in all regards" comes to ruin among so many who are not good. The prince must learn to be able not to be good, and use this ability or not according to necessity.

This concise statement is most efficacious. It contains a fundamental assault on all morality and political science, both Christian and classical, as understood in Machiavelli's time. Morality had meant not only doing the right action, but also doing it for the right reason or for the love of God. Thus, to be good was thought to require "a profession of good" in which the motive for doing good was explained; otherwise, morality would go no deeper than outward conformity to law, or even to superior force, and could not be distinguished from it. But professions of good could not accompany moral actions in isolation from each other; they would have to be elaborated so that moral actions would be consistent with each other and the life of a moral person would form a whole. Such elaboration requires an effort of imagination, since the consistency we see tells us only of the presence of outward conformity, and the elaboration extends over a society, because it is difficult to live a moral life by oneself; hence morality requires the construction of an imagined republic or principality, such as Plato's *Republic* or St. Augustine's *City of God*.

When Machiavelli denies that imagined republics and principalities "exist in truth," and declares that the truth in these or all matters is the effectual truth, he says that no moral rules exist, not made by men, which men must abide by. The rules or laws that exist are those made by governments or other powers acting under necessity, and they must be obeyed out of the same necessity. Whatever is necessary may be called just and reasonable, but justice is no more reasonable than what a person's prudence tells him he must acquire for himself, or must submit to, because men cannot afford justice in any sense that transcends their own preservation. Machiavelli did not attempt (as did Hobbes) to formulate a new definition of justice based on self-preservation. Instead, he showed what he meant by not including justice among the eleven pairs of moral qualities that he lists in Chapter 15. He does mention justice in Chapter 21 as a calculation of what a weaker party might expect from a prince whom it has supported in war, but even this little is contradicted by what Machiavelli says about keeping faith in Chapter 18 and about betraying one's old supporters in Chapter 20. He also brings up justice as something identical with necessity in Chapter 26. But, what is most striking, he never mentions—not in *The Prince*, or in any of his works—natural justice or natural law, the two conceptions of justice in the classical and medieval tradition that had been handed down to his time and that could be found in the writings on this subject of all his contemporaries. The grave issue raised by the dispute whether Machiavelli was truly "Machiavellian" is this: does justice exist by nature or by God, or is it the convenience of the prince (government)? "So let a prince win and maintain a state: the means will always be judged honorable, and will be praised by everyone" (Chapter 18). Reputation, then, is outward conformity to successful human force and has no reference to moral rules that the government might find inconvenient.

If there is no natural justice, perhaps Machiavelli can teach the prince how to rule in its absence—but with a view to the fact that men "profess" it. It does not follow of necessity that because no natural justice exists, princes can rule successfully without it. Governments might be as unsuccessful in making and keeping conquests as in living up to natural justice; indeed, the traditional proponents of natural justice, when less confident of their own cause, had pointed to the uncertainty of gain, to the happy inconstancy of fortune, as an argument against determined wickedness. But Machiavelli thinks it possible to "learn" to be able not to be good. For each of the difficulties of gaining and keeping, even and especially for the fickleness of fortune, he has a "remedy," to use his frequent expression. Since nature or God does not support human justice, men are in need of a remedy; and the remedy is the prince, especially the new prince. Why must the new prince be preferred?

In the heading to the first chapter of *The Prince* we see that the kinds of principalities are to be discussed together with the ways in which they are acquired, and then in the chapter itself we find more than this, that principalities are classified into kinds by the ways in which they are acquired. "Acquisition," an economic term, is Machiavelli's word for "conquest"; and acquisition determines the classifications of governments, not their ends or structures, as Plato and Aristotle had thought. How is acquisition related to the problem of justice?

Justice requires a modest complement of external goods, the equipment of virtue in Aristotle's phrase, to keep the wolf from the door and to provide for moral persons a certain decent distance from necessities in the face of which morality might falter or even fail. For how can one distribute justly without something to distribute? But, then, where is one to get this modest complement? The easy way is by inheritance. In Chapter 2, Machiavelli considers hereditary principalities, in which a person falls heir to everything he needs, especially the political power to protect what he has. The hereditary prince, the man who has everything, is called the "natural prince," as if to suggest that our grandest and most comprehensive inheritance is what we get from nature. But when the hereditary prince looks upon his inheritance—and when we, generalizing from his case, add up everything we inherit—is it adequate?

The difficulty with hereditary principalities is indicated at the end of Chapter 2, where Machiavelli admits that hereditary princes will have to change but claims that change will not be disruptive because it can be gradual and continuous. He compares each prince's own construction to building a house that is added on to a row of houses: you may not inherit all you need, but you inherit a firm support and an easy start in what you must acquire. But clearly a row of houses so built over generations presupposes that the first house was built without existing support and without an easy start. Inheritance presupposes an original acquisition made without a previous inheritance. And in the original acquisition, full attention to the niceties of justice may unfortunately not be possible. One may congratulate an American citizen for all the advantages to which he is born; but what of the nasty necessities that prepared this inheritance—the British expelled, Indians defrauded, blacks enslaved?

Machiavelli informs us in the third chapter, accordingly, that "truly it is a very natural and ordinary thing to desire to acquire." In the space of a few pages, "natural" has shifted in meaning from hereditary to acquisitive. Or can we be consoled by reference to Machiavelli's republicanism, not so prominent in *The Prince*, with the thought that acquisitiveness may be natural to princes but is not natural to republics? But in Chapter 3 Machiavelli praises the successful acquisitiveness of the "Romans," that is, the Roman republic, by comparison to the imprudence

of the king of France. At the time Machiavelli is referring to, the Romans were not weak and vulnerable as they were at their inception; they had grown powerful and were still expanding. Even when they had enough empire to provide an inheritance for their citizens, they went on acquiring. Was this reasonable? It was, because the haves of this world cannot quietly inherit what is coming to them; lest they be treated now as they once treated others, they must keep an eye on the have-nots. To keep a step ahead of the have-nots the haves must think and behave like have-nots. They certainly cannot afford justice to the have-nots, nor can they waste time or money on sympathy.

In the Dedicatory Letter Machiavelli presents himself to Lorenzo as a have-not, "from a low and mean state"; and one thing he lacks besides honorable employment, we learn, is a unified fatherland. Italy is weak and divided. Then should we say that acquisitiveness is justified for Italians of Machiavelli's time, including him? As we have noted, Machiavelli does not seem to accept this justification because, still in Chapter 3, he advises a French king how to correct the errors he had made in his invasion of Italy. Besides, was Machiavelli's fatherland Italy or was it Florence? In Chapter 15 he refers to "our language," meaning Tuscan, and in Chapter 20 to "our ancients," meaning Florentines. But does it matter whether Machiavelli was essentially an Italian or a Florentine patriot? Anyone's fatherland is defined by an original acquisition, a conquest, and hence is always subject to redefinition of the same kind. To be devoted to one's native country at the expense of foreigners is no more justified than to be devoted to one's city at the expense of fellow countrymen, or to one's family at the expense of fellow city-dwellers, or, to adapt a Machiavellian remark in Chapter 17, to one's patrimony at the expense of one's father. So to "unify" one's fatherland means to treat it as a conquered territory—conquered by a king or republic from within; and Machiavelli's advice to the French king on how to hold his conquests in Italy was also advice to Lorenzo on how to unify Italy. It appears that, in acquiring, the new prince acquires for himself.

What are the qualities of the new prince? What must he do? First, as we have seen, he should rise from private or unprivileged status; he should not have an inheritance, or if he has, he should not rely on it. He should owe nothing to anyone or anything, for having debts of gratitude would make him dependent on others, in the widest sense dependent on fortune. It might seem that the new prince depends at least on the character of the country he conquers, and Machiavelli says at the end of Chapter 4 that Alexander had no trouble in holding Asia because it had been accustomed to the government of one lord. But then in Chapter 5 he shows how this limitation can be overcome. A prince who conquers a city used to living in freedom need not respect its inherited liberties; he can and should destroy such cities or else rule them personally. Fortune supplies the prince with nothing more than opportunity, as when Moses found the people of Israel enslaved by the Egyptians, Romulus found himself exposed at birth, Cyrus found the Persians discontented with the empire of the Medes, and Theseus found the Athenians dispersed (Chapter 6). These famous founders had the virtue to recognize the opportunity that fortune offered to them—opportunity for them, harsh necessity to their peoples. Instead of dispersing the inhabitants of a free city (Chapter 5), the prince is lucky enough to find them dispersed (Chapter 6). This suggests that the prince could go so far as to make his own opportunity by creating a situation of necessity in which no one's inherited goods remain to him and everything is owed to you, the new prince. When a new prince comes to power, should he be grateful to those who helped him get power and rely on them? Indeed not. A new prince has "lukewarm defenders" in his friends and allies, because they expect benefits from him; as we have seen, it is much better to conciliate his former enemies who feared losing everything (compare Chapters 6 and 20).

Thus, the new prince has virtue that enables him to overcome his dependence on inheritance in the widest sense, including custom, nature, and fortune, and that shows him how to arrange it that others depend on

him and his virtue (Chapters 9, 24). But if virtue is to do all this, it must have a new meaning. Instead of cooperating with nature or God, as in the various classical and Christian conceptions, virtue must be taught to be acquisitive on its own. Machiavelli teaches the new meaning of virtue by showing us both the new and the old meanings. In a famous passage on the successful criminal Agathocles in Chapter 8, he says "one cannot call it virtue to kill one's fellow citizens, betray one's friends, to be without faith, without mercy, without religion." Yet in the very next sentence Machiavelli proceeds to speak of "the virtue of Agathocles."

The prince, we have seen in Chapter 15, must "learn to be able not to be good, and to use this and not use it according to necessity." Machiavelli supplies this knowledge in Chapters 16 to 18. First, with superb calm, he delivers home-truths concerning the moral virtue of liberality. It is no use being liberal (or generous) unless it is noticed, so that you are "held liberal" or get a name for liberality. But a prince cannot be held liberal by being liberal, because he would have to be liberal to a few by burdening the many with taxes; the many would be offended, the prince would have to retrench, and he would soon get a name for stinginess. The right way to get a reputation for liberality is to begin by not caring about having a reputation for stinginess. When the people see that the prince gets the job done without burdening them, they will in time consider him liberal to them and stingy only to the few to whom he gives nothing. In the event, "liberality" comes to mean taking little rather than giving much.

As regards cruelty and mercy, in Chapter 8 Machiavelli made a distinction between cruelties well used and badly used; well-used cruelties are done once, for self-defense, and not continued but turned to the benefit of one's subjects, and badly used ones continue and increase. In Chapter 17, however, he does not mention this distinction but rather speaks only of using mercy badly. Mercy is badly used when, like the Florentine people in a certain instance, one seeks to avoid a reputation for cruelty and thus allows disorders to continue which might be stopped with a very few examples of cruelty. Disorders harm everybody; executions harm only the few or the one who is executed. As the prince may gain a name for liberality by taking little, so he may be held merciful by not being cruel too often.

Machiavelli's new prince arranges the obligation of his subjects to himself in a manner rather like that of the Christian God, in the eye of whom all are guilty by original sin; hence God's mercy appears less as the granting of benefits than as the remission of punishment. With this thought in mind, the reader will not be surprised that Machiavelli goes on to discuss whether it is better for the prince to be loved or feared. It would be best to be both loved and feared, but, when necessity forces a choice, it is better to be feared, because men love at their convenience but they fear at the convenience of the prince. Friends may fail you, but the dread of punishment will never forsake you. If the prince avoids making himself hated, which he can do by abstaining from the property of others, "because men forget the death of a father more quickly than the loss of a patrimony," he will again have subjects obligated to him for what he does not do to them rather than for benefits he provides.

It is laudable for a prince to keep faith, Machiavelli says in Chapter 18, but princes who have done great things have done them by deceit and betrayal. The prince must learn how to use the beast in man, or rather the beasts; for man is an animal who can be many animals, and he must know how to be a fox as well as a lion. Men will not keep faith with you; how can you keep it with them? Politics, Machiavelli seems to say, as much as consists in breaking promises, for circumstances change and new necessities arise that make it impossible to hold to one's word. The only question is, can one get away with breaking one's promises? Machiavelli's answer is a confident yes. He broadens the discussion, speaking of five moral qualities, especially religion; he says that men judge by appearances and that when one judges by appearances, "one looks to the end." The end is the outcome or the effect, and if a prince wins and maintains a state, the means will always be judged honorable. Since

Machiavelli has just emphasized the prince's need to appear religious, we may compare the people's attitude toward a successful prince with their belief in divine providence. As people assume that the outcome of events in the world is determined by God's providence, so they conclude that the means chosen by God cannot have been unworthy. Machiavelli's thought here is both a subtle attack on the notion of divine providence and a subtle appreciation of it, insofar as the prince can appropriate it to his own use.

It is not easy to state exactly what virtue is, according to Machiavelli. Clearly he does not leave virtue as it was in the classical or Christian tradition, nor does he imitate any other writer of his time. Virtue in his new meaning seems to be a prudent or well-taught combination of vice and virtue in the old meaning. Virtue for him is not a mean between two extremes of vice, as is moral virtue for Aristotle. As we have seen, in Chapter 15 eleven virtues (the same number as Aristotle's, though not all of them the same virtues) are paired with eleven vices. From this we might conclude that virtue does not shine of itself, as when it is done for its own sake. Rather, virtue is as it takes effect, its truth is its effectual truth; and it is effectual only when it is seen in contrast to its opposite. Liberality, mercy, and love are impressive only when one expects stinginess (or rapacity), cruelty, and fear. This contrast makes virtue apparent and enables the prince to gain a reputation for virtue. If this is so, then the new meaning Machiavelli gives to virtue, a meaning which makes use of vice, must not entirely replace but somehow continue to coexist with the old meaning, according to which virtue is shocked by vice.

A third quality of the new prince is that he must make his own foundations. Although to be acquisitive means to be acquisitive for oneself, the prince cannot do everything with his own hands: he needs help from others. But in seeking help he must take account of the "two diverse humors" to be found in every city—the people, who desire not to be commanded or oppressed by the great, and the great, who desire to command and oppress the people (Chapter 9). Of these two humors, the prince should choose the people. The people are easier to satisfy, too inert to move against him, and too numerous to kill, whereas the great regard themselves as his equals, are ready and able to conspire against him, and are replaceable.

The prince, then, should ally with the people against the aristocracy; but how should he get their support? Machiavelli gives an example in the conduct of Cesare Borgia, whom he praises for the foundations he laid (Chapter 7). When Cesare had conquered the province of Romagna, he installed "Remirro de Orco" (actually a Spaniard, Don Remiro de Lorqua) to carry out a purge of the unruly lords there. Then, because Cesare thought Remirro's authority might be excessive, and his exercise of it might become hateful—in short, because Remirro had served his purpose—he purged the purger and one day had Remirro displayed in the piazza at Cesena in two pieces. This spectacle left the people "at the same time satisfied and stupefied"; and Cesare set up a more constitutional government in Romagna. The lesson: constitutional government is possible but only after an unconstitutional beginning.

In Chapter 9 Machiavelli discusses the "civil principality," which is gained through the favor of the people, and gives as example Nabis, "prince" of the Spartans, whom he calls a tyrant in the *Discourses on Livy* because of the crimes Nabis committed against his rivals. In Chapter 8 Machiavelli considers the principality that is attained through crimes, and cites Agathocles and Oliverotto, both of whom were very popular despite their crimes. As one ponders these two chapters, it becomes more and more difficult to find a difference between gaining a principality through crimes and through the favor of the people. Surely Cesare Borgia, Agathocles, and Nabis seemed to have followed the same policy of pleasing the people by cutting up the great. Finally, in Chapter 19, Machiavelli reveals that the prince need not have the support of the people after all. Even if he is hated by the people (since in fact he cannot fail to be hated by someone), he can, like the Roman emperor Severus, make his foundation with his soldiers (see also Chapter 20). Severus had such virtue, Machiavelli says, with an unobtrusive com-

parison to Cesare Borgia in Chapter 7, that he "stupefied" the people and "satisfied" the soldiers.

Fourth, the new prince has his own arms, and does not rely on mercenary or auxiliary armies. Machiavelli omits a discussion of the laws a prince should establish, in contrast to the tradition of political science, because, he says, "there cannot be good laws where there are not good arms, and where there are good arms there must be good laws" (Chapter 12). He speaks of the prince's arms in Chapters 12 to 14, and in Chapter 14 he proclaims that the prince should have no other object or thought but the art of war. He must be armed, since it is quite unreasonable for one who is armed to obey one who is disarmed. With this short remark Machiavelli seems to dismiss the fundamental principle of classical political science, the rule of the wise, not to mention the Christian promise that the meek shall inherit the earth.

Machiavelli does not mean that those with the most bodily force always win, for he broadens the art of war to include the acquisition as well as the use of arms. A prince who has no army but has the art of war will prevail over one with an army but without the art. Thus, to be armed means to know the art of war, to exercise it in time of peace, and to have read histories about great captains of the past. In this regard Machiavelli mentions Xenophon's "Life of Cyrus," as he calls it (actually "The Education of Cyrus"), the first and best work in the literature of "mirrors of princes" to which *The Prince* belongs. But he calls it a history, not a mirror of princes, and says that it inspired the Roman general Scipio, whom he criticizes in Chapter 17 for excessive mercy. Not books of imaginary republics and principalities, or treatises on law, but histories of war, are recommended reading for the prince.

Last, the new prince with his own arms is his own master. The deeper meaning of Machiavelli's slogan, "one's own arms," is religious, or rather, antireligious. If man is obligated to God as his creature, then man's own necessities are subordinate or even irrelevant to his most pressing duties. It would not matter if he could not afford justice: God commands it! Thus Machiavelli must look at the new prince who is also a prophet, above all at Moses. Moses was a "mere executor of things that had been ordered by God" (Chapter 6); hence he should be admired for the grace that made him worthy of speaking with God. Or should it be said, as Machiavelli says in Chapter 26, that Moses had "virtue," the virtue that makes a prince dependent on no one but himself? In Chapter 13 Machiavelli retells the biblical story of David and Goliath to illustrate the necessity of one's own arms. When Saul offered his arms to David, David refused them, saying, according to Machiavelli, that with them he could not give a good account of himself, and according to the Bible, that the Lord "will deliver me out of the hand of this Philistine." Machiavelli also gives David a knife to go with his sling, the knife which according to the Bible he took from the fallen Goliath and used to cut off his head.

Must the new prince—the truly new prince—then be his own prophet and make a new religion so as to be his own master? The great power of religion can be seen in what Moses and David founded, and in what Savonarola nearly accomplished in Machiavelli's own time and city. The unarmed prince whom he disparages in Chapter 6 actually disposes of formidable weapons necessary to the art of war. The unarmed prophet becomes armed if he uses religion for his own purposes rather than God's; and because the prince cannot acquire glory for himself without bringing order to his principality, using religion for himself is using it to answer human necessities generally.

The last three chapters of *The Prince* take up the question of how far man can make his own world. What are the limits set on Machiavelli's political science (or the "art of war") by fortune? At the end of Chapter 24 he blames "these princes of ours" who accuse fortune for their troubles and not their own indolence. In quiet times they do not take account of the storm to come, but they should—they can. They believe that the people will be disgusted by the arrogance of the foreign conquerors and will call them back. But "one should never fall in the belief you can find someone to pick you up." Whether successful or not, such a defense is base, be-cause it does not depend on you and your virtue.

With this high promise of human capability, Machiavelli introduces his famous Chapter 25 on fortune. He begins it by asking how much of the world is governed by fortune and God, and how much by man. He then supposes that half is governed by fortune (forgetting God) and half by man, and he compares fortune to a violent river that can be contained with dikes and dams. Turning to particular men, he shows that the difficulty in containing fortune lies in the inability of one who is impetuous to succeed in quiet times or of one who is cautious to succeed in stormy times. Men, with their fixed natures and habits, do not vary as the times vary, and so they fall under the control of the times, of fortune. Men's fixed natures are the special problem, Machiavelli indicates; so the problem of overcoming the influence of fortune reduces to the problem of overcoming the fixity of different human natures. Having a fixed nature is what makes one liable to changes of fortune. Pope Julius II succeeded because the times were in accord with his impetuous nature; if he had lived longer, he would have come to grief. Machiavelli blames him for his inflexibility, and so implies that neither he nor the rest of us need respect the natures or natural inclinations we have been given.

What is the new meaning of virtue that Machiavelli has developed but flexibility according to the times or situation? Yet, though one should learn to be both impetuous and cautious (these stand for all the other contrary qualities), on the whole one should be impetuous. Fortune is a woman who "lets herself be won more by the impetuous than by those who proceed coldly"; hence she is a friend of the young. He makes the politics of the new prince appear in the image of rape; impetuous himself, Machiavelli forces us to see the question he has raised about the status of morality. Whether he says what he appears to say about the status of women may be doubted, however. The young men who master Lady Fortune come with audacity and leave exhausted, but she remains ageless, waiting for the next ones. One might go so far as to wonder who is raping whom, cautiously as it were, and whether Machiavelli, who has personified fortune, can impersonate her in the world of modern politics he attempted to create.

Reprinted from: Harvey C. Mansfield, Jr., "Introduction" to *The Prince*, by Niccolò Machiavelli, pp. vii–xxiv. Copyright © 1985. Reprinted by permission of The University of Chicago Press. ✦

29
Public Versus Private Claims

Machiavellianism from Another Perspective

John Leonard

Machiavellianism is frequently conceived of as a derivative of the term Machiavellian. The Oxford English Dictionary, beginning with its definition of Machiavellian, reads:

> Of, pertaining to, or characteristic of Machiavelli, or his alleged principles; following the methods recommended by Machiavelli in preferring expediency to morality; practicing duplicity in statecraft or in general conduct; an instance of this.

This derivation of Machiavellianism from Machiavellian has the effect of shifting attention from the foundations of Machiavelli's theory, which are reduced to the principle that expediency should always be placed ahead of morality, and focusing it on various methods and practices consistent with this principle.

The aim of this article is to present a broader interpretation of Machiavelli's theoretical concerns, one which seeks neither to support nor refute the common understanding of Machiavellianism but to go beyond it. To this end the problem of Machiavelli's attitude toward virtue is examined in the context of crucial terms in his conceptual vocabulary, and this examination is used in turn to shed light on other aspects of Machiavelli's thought.

1. Why *Virtù* Is Never Virtue

The first task in assessing the place of virtue in Machiavelli's political thought is to see if we can locate something that resembles virtue in his writings. The first word to consider, both because Machiavelli uses it frequently and because in appearance it resembles virtue, is *virtù*. *Virtù* is, in fact, a standard equivalent of the English word virtue in contemporary Italian, and because it can be translated as virtue without apparent damage in some of the places Machiavelli uses it, *virtù* is often rendered as virtue in English translations of Machiavelli. This way of finding virtue in Machiavelli's writings is a false trail, but at the same time a promising one.

Virtue involves adherence to some set of moral principles. *Virtù* as Machiavelli uses the term is closer to the Latin *virtus* in its connotation of manly valor and signifies an excellence that manifests itself most clearly in military and political affairs, perhaps because it is associated most prominently with the capacity to act boldly at critical moments. Evidently *virtù* is not the same thing as virtue. A translator sensitive to the diverse contexts in which Machiavelli uses *virtù*, Allan Gilbert, recognizes that there is a problem with translating *virtù* as virtue when he translates *virtù* as ability in contexts in which virtue, with its moral connotations, is obviously out of place, such as Machiavelli's reference in Chapter 17 of *The Prince* to Hannibal's "inhuman cruelty . . . together with his infinite *virtù*." But this method of sometimes translating *virtù* as virtue and sometimes as something else according to context is more misleading than the clumsiness involved in consistently translating *virtù* as virtue, for such clumsiness at least reveals the incompatibility of the terms despite contexts in which they seem compatible at first sight.[1]

Chapter 8 of *The Prince* provides an interesting example of a context in which *virtù* at first sight appears equivalent to virtue. Machiavelli writes,

> Neither can one call it *virtù* to kill one's citizens, to betray one's friends, to be faithless, without pity, without religion; by these means rule may be acquired, but not glory.

Virtue seems a perfectly acceptable substitute for *virtù* in this passage because one certainly cannot call it virtue to kill one's citizens, betray one's friends, etc. But a moment's reflection leads to the realization that this is too obvious to require statement. Either Machiavelli is making an obvious point about what is inconsistent with morality, a proceeding which in the context of *The Prince* as a whole would be distinctly anomalous, or he is making a less obvious but important point about what is inconsistent with *virtù*. It will be necessary to return to this point later. Here it is enough to note that *virtù* turns out not to be equivalent to virtue even in contexts that at first glance suggest such equivalence.

The Prince contains no word equivalent to virtue but it does include a list of moral qualities and a phrase that indicates Machiavelli's view of what it would mean to live in accordance with these qualities. The list appears in Chapter 18 of *The Prince*, in which Machiavelli says a prince should seem to be compassionate, faithful, humane, sincere, and religious. The phrase, which occurs in Chapter 15, is "to make a profession of goodness in all things."[2] To make such a profession would presumably mean to live a life dedicated to the exemplification of the moral qualities listed in Chapter 18. Thus *The Prince* reveals Machiavelli's awareness of what would constitute a high standard of virtue. But Machiavelli does not want the prince to comply with this standard, only to seem to do so. His reasoning on this point helps clarify the incompatibility of virtue and *virtù*.

It is in Chapter 15 of *The Prince* that Machiavelli states his intention of writing for "he who understands" and contrasts this method with that of those who imagine states that have "never been seen nor known to exist in reality." He then proceeds to justify his choice on the grounds that there is such a difference between how men live and how they ought to live that he who departs from what is done for the sake of what should be done will learn his ruin rather than his preservation. The phrase "to make a profession of goodness in all things" occurs in this connection; he who wants to make a profession of goodness in all things, says Machiavelli, must bring about his ruin among the many who are not good.

Machiavelli deduces from this the proposition that a prince must learn how not to be good. He repeats this principle in Chapter 18, in which he advises that the prince should not part from the good without need, but should be able to enter into the bad when to do so is necessary for the maintenance of his position. The words good and bad here take on a moral emphasis deriving from the preceding list of moral qualities, and Machiavelli makes clear what he means by entering into the bad when, referring to these qualities, he says the prince must be able to act, "contrary to faith, contrary to charity, contrary to humanity, contrary to religion." This ability, evidently contrary to virtue, is consistent with *virtù*, as Machiavelli indicates in his treatment of Hannibal's "inhuman cruelty." This cruelty, says Machiavelli, was necessary to maintain order among Hannibal's mixed force of mercenary troops and thus was an essential aspect of Hannibal's excellence as a general, and for this reason Machiavelli includes it among Hannibal's "infinite *virtù*."

That such a quality could be included within *virtù* reveals its difference from virtue. It also raises the question whether *virtù* is defined solely in terms of success in the pursuit of military or political power.

Machiavelli's discussion of what is not *virtù* assumes special significance in this connection. It has been noted that in Chapter 8 of *The Prince* Machiavelli either makes an implausible argument for what is not virtue or some sort of argument for what is not *virtù*. Machiavelli says that it cannot be called *virtù* to kill one's citizens, betray one's friends, and be without honor, piety, and religion because although such methods can lead to rule they cannot lead to the acquisition of glory. If virtue is substituted for *virtù* Machiavelli is doing something very curious, for instead of making the obvious point that such acts and qualities cannot be called virtue because they are directly opposed to it, he is saying that they cannot be called virtue because they cannot lead to glory. Using glory to define virtue in this context makes little sense. But if we read *virtù* as *virtù* the attempt to set a boundary on it through the use of glory makes considerable sense. By limiting the ascription of *virtù* to actions that are consistent with the acquisition of glory Machiavelli can deny *virtù* to actions that involve "entering into the bad" out of choice rather than necessity. At the same time, and unlike virtue, glory is compatible with entering into the bad out of necessity. Thus glory is useful to Machiavelli because it is compatible with the necessities of public life while providing a standard for rejecting its worst excesses.

By employing glory as a critical standard Machiavelli reveals his awareness of the problem posed for political action by the incompatibility of virtue and *virtù*. At its core Machiavellian *virtù* represents pure efficacy unconstrained by any imperative except that of attaining one's end. For *virtù* to play a constructive role in politics such efficacy must be constrained to serve the needs of the public sphere. This is the basis of Machiavelli's appeal to glory. The effectiveness of this appeal will be considered later. At this point it is time to enter the world of the *Discourses* and consider another incompatibility, that of virtue and *bontà*.

2. Why *Bontà* Is Never Virtue

Machiavelli's *Discourses* differs from *The Prince* alike in its subject matter and its method. *The Prince* is concerned with the exigencies of princely government in the harsh political climate of Machiavelli's Italy. Thus, for example, Machiavelli's reference to states that have never been known to exist is designed to throw into relief the necessities imposed by the political realities of his day. This contrast serves Machiavelli's purposes in *The Prince*, but it also reflects *The Prince* as a whole in leaving no room between the harshness of the reality it describes and the fatuity of utopian thinking for consideration of what a well-ordered state that could exist in reality would look like.

In the *Discourses* Machiavelli opens the way to such consideration by taking as his model a state that actually did exist in an earlier period. This state is the Roman republic

as Livy depicts it, and Machiavelli's method is to present the *Discourses* as a commentary on the first ten books of Livy's *History of Rome*. Because Machiavelli represents the Roman republic as a model state in the *Discourses* the role of virtue in public life should reveal itself in this work if it has a place anywhere in Machiavelli's thought.

A careful examination of Machiavelli's comments in the *Discourses* concerning the role of the popular element in Roman society reveals an emphasis on the concept of *bontà*. *Bontà* is worthy of consideration on several grounds. First, it represents Machiavelli's nearest approach to a workable concept of virtue. Second, this little discussed concept is of great importance to Machiavelli, being as important to his well-ordered state as *virtù*.

Chapter 55, Book 1 of the *Discourses* opens with an example of the Roman people's *bontà*. A similar example occurs in Chapter 13 of Book 1, though the word itself does not appear in Chapter 13.[3] Both examples concern oaths that are interpreted by the nobility in a way that threatens the people with the loss of something they desire. In both cases the people have a plausible excuse for evading the obligation created by the oath, and it is their decision not to break the oath outright that makes it possible to come to a workable compromise with the nobility.

In Chapter 13 Machiavelli recounts Livy's story of a feud between the nobles and the people that was interrupted by a slave revolt that succeeded in occupying the Capitol. The nobles called on the people to help put down the revolt whereas the Tribunes argued that no aid should be rendered until the nobles agreed to a proposed law for a committee to devise ways of limiting the power of the Consuls. The people decided to aid in the recapture of the Capitol and swore an oath to obey the Consul's orders. The attack was a success but the Consul was killed. His replacement, seeking to keep the people from renewing their consideration of the disputed law, ordered them out of the city to do battle against a neighboring state. The Tribunes protested that because the oath was made to the previous Consul it was no longer binding, but because the oath did not specify this the people were afraid of breaking it. Thus the Tribunes were forced to compromise with the nobility by promising to drop consideration of the law for a year in exchange for the Consul's promise not to order the people to war during that period.

In Chapter 55 Machiavelli relates how trouble flared up between the people and the nobles when the commander of a victorious Roman army decided to offer a tenth of the spoils of combat to Apollo. The Senate accordingly directed each member of the army to turn over a tenth of his spoils. The common soldiers protested, understandably enough, because they had not participated in the vow and the spoils were their only remuneration for the hardships and dangers of military service. But instead of evading the order individually by cheating, as they could easily have done, and thus invalidating the vow, they chose to protest openly and in a body. This open protest led to a compromise in which the people were released from their obligation and the vow was fulfilled by other means.

The *bontà* of the people in these examples is linked with their fear of breaking oaths. *Bontà* is normally translated as goodness, and inasmuch as the goodness in these examples seems to derive from a form of piety *bontà* appears to have something in common with Christian virtue. But the role of Roman religion with respect to *bontà* is very different from, though just as important as, the role of Christianity with respect to Christian virtue. For although Christianity reinforces admonitions to virtue with warnings of the punishments in store for sinners, it also establishes the principle that true virtue consists in obeying moral precepts out of an inner conviction of their rightness rather than out of fear. Roman religion reinforces *bontà* through fear of the gods, but its purpose in so doing is not to remind men of the wages of sin. The goal of Roman religion is rather to invest the concept of obedience to public authority with a sense of religious awe. It is this use of religious awe or piety to which Machiavelli refers in both his examples of *bontà*. *Bontà* does not lead to the creation of a moral sense in the individual, but it does provide a peaceful means of controlling an armed populace.

That Machiavelli is concerned with *bontà* as an aid in maintaining the public sphere is confirmed by his description of the cause and effect of the loss of religious belief among a people. In Chapter 12, Book 1 of the *Discourses* he says that when religion begins to speak with the voice of the rich and powerful, and this is discovered by the people, "men become unbelievers and disposed to upset every good order." In other words, the loss of religious belief on the part of the people, caused by its shortsighted manipulation by the wealthy and powerful (a manipulation that proves they do not share this belief) leads to the loss of the *bontà* that helps control threats to public order.

Bontà is the closest Machiavelli comes to a workable concept of virtue, but it is a substitute for virtue rather than virtue by another name. In *The Prince* Machiavelli's rejection of virtue had to do with the practical requirements of survival in a disordered political environment. The reason virtue is also absent in Machiavelli's model state and the consequences of its absence remain to be considered.

Extraordinary Action and Its Enemy

Machiavelli's analysis of government begins with the institutional structure of political power. A well-ordered state, be it republic or princedom, is in the first instance one in which the structure of political power is well designed to meet the needs of that particular state. But he also shows great sensitivity to the fact that the usefulness of political institutions depends on their authority in the eyes of the citizenry and that a diminution of this authority can lessen the capacity of those institutions to meet the needs of the state.

Machiavelli's discussion of the Roman republic as a model state reveals two of his fundamental political premises. One is that a state that provides an institutional channel for popular participation in public affairs is potentially stronger than a state that makes no such provision. The other is that widespread participation in public affairs requires the highest possible esteem for public authority among all classes of citizens. Any lessening of this esteem signifies the onset of corruption, which manifests itself in inattention to, or self-serving uses of, the laws and religion. The prevention of such corruption requires sanctions against the misuse of the qualities associated with *virtù* as well as the reinforcement of the *bontà*, the almost religious awe with which public authority and its representatives were regarded at the time of the state's founding.

The importance of preventing corruption and various methods of combating it make up the subject matter of Chapter 1, Book 3 of the *Discourses*. The eradication of corruption is linked with a symbolic refounding of a state or religion through the revitalization of its orders. Machiavelli describes three ways by which such a refounding can occur. One is the appearance of danger in the form of a foreign threat so great that it seems capable of destroying the state. Such a threat may serve as a sort of shock therapy that brings the leaders and citizens back to the observance of the principles on which the state was founded. This method is clearly a dangerous one. A state content to rely on extrinsic accident to combat corruption would not be likely to have a long history.

Machiavelli next turns to a pair of methods that he lists under the category of intrinsic prudence. The first of these methods is legislative. The second is that of personal actions that set a good example for the citizens. Either the *virtù* of a new order created by legislation or the *virtù* exhibited by a citizen at a critical juncture can bring a state back to health. But of these two forms of *virtù* the one embodied in legislation suffers from the defect that it does not inspire men to obedience in itself. Thus Machiavelli concludes his discussion of rejuvenation by means of new orders with the comment: "Those orders need to be brought to life by the *virtù* of a citizen, who boldly agrees to execute them against the power of those who transgress them."

Machiavelli expands on this statement by providing a list of the kind of actions he has in mind. These actions are all taken from Roman history, and most of them are executions. The list begins with the execution of Brutus's sons and continues with the execution of the Ten Citizens, Spurius Melius, Manlius Capitolinus and the son of Manlius Torquatus. It concludes with several prosecutions that did not result in executions. For Machiavelli the importance of all these actions resides in the fact that, "because they were extreme and noteworthy, whenever one of them occurred it made men retire to their place."

The connection between the extreme and noteworthy quality of these actions and their exemplary effect is revealed in Chapter 3, Book 1 of the *Discourses*. In this chapter Machiavelli notes that Brutus not only voted to condemn his sons to death for treason but actually attended their execution. He refers to this conduct as an example rare in all the records of historical events and claims that the severity exhibited by Brutus on this occasion was not merely useful but necessary to the maintenance of Roman liberty. What makes Brutus's action so extraordinary is the emphatic manner in which he resolved the conflict between the private affection of a father for his sons and the public duty of protecting the orders of the state. By not only condemning his sons to death but witnessing their execution Brutus made a public statement of the citizen's primary duty to maintain the state, a statement that renewed both the respect of the citizens for the state's laws and orders and their fear of transgressing those laws and orders.

A second look at the extraordinary actions listed in Chapter 3, Book 1 of the *Discourses* reveals that the offenses involved are ones that in every case pose threats to the authority of the public sphere. In every case this threat is also enhanced by the existence of a private bond between the transgressors and some or all of their judges that might conduce to leniency. It is in these circumstances that harsh punishments take on the character of extreme and noteworthy actions. This is so because in such circumstances these actions function, to borrow a phrase, by using punishment to make a memory.[4] Extraordinary actions are thus of particular importance in cases in which some obvious threat to public authority conceals the less evident threat of a conflict between personal feelings of affection or obligation and the good of the state.[5] That it is this latter threat to which Machiavelli is particularly sensitive is underscored by his treatment of two actions in which harsh punishment is thwarted by private pleadings.

One of Machiavelli's examples in Chapter 1, Book 3 of the *Discourses* is the prosecution of Papirius Cursor's master of cavalry. This prosecution was extreme and noteworthy because Papirius asked that his master of cavalry be condemned to death for having given battle contrary to orders even though the latter had been victorious. At the end of Chapter 31, Book 1 of the *Discourses* Machiavelli notes that the father of Papirius's master of cavalry argued against this punishment on the grounds that the Romans did not treat even their defeated commanders in such a fashion. But although earlier in the chapter Machiavelli approves the Roman practice of not punishing their generals for mistakes made in the course of military operations it would be a mistake to construe this as indicating support for the father's plea. For in Chapter 36, Book 3 of the *Discourses* he quotes with approval Livy's account of Papirius's speech in favor of the death penalty. The point of this speech is that an army cannot maintain good order unless discipline is strictly enforced. From this perspective the intervention of his father in the prosecution of the master of cavalry was clearly contrary to the interests of the state.

Another instance of a father interceding for his son is recounted in Chapter 22, Book 1 of the *Discourses*. Horatius, the sole survivor of a combat between three brothers from Rome and three brothers from the neighboring state of Alba, returned home in triumph, but shortly afterward killed his sister when he heard her lament the death of one of the Alban brothers, to whom she had been married. Horatius was put on trial for his life and was acquitted. According to Machiavelli this acquittal owed more to his father's prayers for the life of his last son than Horatius' recent services to the state. Two chapters later Machiavelli returns to this topic and states that although, superficially considered, it might have seemed an act of ingratitude had

the Roman people condemned Horatius to death after he had saved Rome, they were actually to blame for having acquitted him. Machiavelli's reasoning is that meritorious actions should never be allowed to mitigate punishment for crimes because examples of such mitigation might encourage men to whom the state owed a debt of gratitude to think they could plot against it with impunity.

Machiavelli's fears that private ties will be used to undermine the state center on leaders and potential leaders, for it is when men of prominence and ability seek the satisfaction of private ends at the expense of the state's laws and orders that the public sphere is most gravely threatened. It is with respect to such threats that the absence of virtue from Machiavelli's theory of politics is revealed as a major problem for what he seeks to accomplish.

Bontà, based as it is on religious credulity, is of considerable importance in controlling the populace but has much less bearing on the control of leaders. Yet the maintenance of *bontà* depends on a state's leaders, for when they become corrupt, religious disillusionment is sure to follow. Thus Machiavelli's fundamental problem is how to keep the most prominent and able members of the state on the path of *virtù* as he defines it: that is, as consistent with glory and, consequently, complementing the needs of the state. This problem is compounded by the ineffectiveness of the image of glory to keep men to the desired standard of conduct. In Chapter 10, Book 1 of the *Discourses* Machiavelli extols both the public and private advantages of actions that strengthen states and religions, including the advantage of a glorious reputation, and emphasizes the disadvantages of actions that harm public institutions. But though he says that given a choice between praiseworthy and blameworthy actions no one would mistake one for the other, he goes on to say that despite this, in practice most men, "deceived by a false good and a false glory," end up in the ranks of those who deserve more blame than praise.

The ineffectiveness of representations of glory to prevail over the urgings of private desire in any but a few cases explains

Machiavelli's necessary reliance on extraordinary action. Extraordinary action must fill the gap left by the absence of virtue because the majority of men are incapable of internalizing not only virtue but any code of conduct that requires them to define their own good in terms of a wider good. Thus Machiavelli feels he must rely on a purely external, public form of action that can cow the temptation to break laws and overthrow orders, but which has no roots in the private sphere and no connection with private values. Rather, extraordinary action is a response to a vision of private ties as posing a potential threat to public life. It is important to inquire why this vision should dominate Machiavelli's thinking even in the consideration of his model state. . . .

Conclusion

Machiavellianism is normally understood as the doctrine that no principle or moral scruple should be regarded as binding if it stands in the way of the acquisition or maintenance of political power. On examination, this interpretation stands revealed as a mixture of truth and inaccuracy.

The focus of Machiavelli's political thought is the good of the public sphere. He considers the pursuit of virtue to be incompatible with this good, yet his concern for public life and its fragility makes him highly critical of the means by which power is acquired and maintained. Thus in both *The Prince* and the *Discourses* Machiavelli judges the means by which power is acquired in terms of its effect on the maintenance of the public sphere over time. It is for the purpose of making this connection that Machiavelli attempts to link *virtù* and glory,[6] and the importance he attaches to maintaining *bontà* is likewise related to the needs of the public sphere.

What is troubling in Machiavelli's thought is not an uncritical admiration of power but his view that any conflict between the public and private spheres of life should be resolved in favor of the former. For Machiavelli there seems to be no possibility of mediation between these spheres. The threat posed to the public sphere by private claims and impulses is viewed as insidious, omnipresent, and, insofar as it has its roots in the family, ineradicable.[7]

The consequences of this viewpoint are twofold. First, not only the founding of the public sphere but its continuation must be made dependent on religious credulity and exemplary punishments in the form of extraordinary acts. Second, because the public sphere is represented as the only valid locus of self-assertion, the legitimate expression of private feelings of aggression and ambition is confined to this sphere. This channeling process, although it creates a tremendous dynamism in the public sphere, must also create an agonistic political life that poses a constant threat to the laws and orders established to contain it and give it expression, extraordinary acts notwithstanding.

The absence of virtue in Machiavelli's political thought is not the result of shallow and unprincipled cynicism but of a deeply rooted pessimism concerning the ability of most men to internalize a code of conduct that clashes with immediate self-interest combined with an exaltation of the public sphere as an arena of conflict in which the practice of Christian virtue would amount to self-martyrdom. A theory of politics based on such views is not without problems, but as portrayed by Machiavelli it offers insights and opportunities for thought that are lost to view when Machiavellianism is confused with a version of his thought that is little more than a stalking-horse for moral censure.

Notes

1. For a translation of *The Prince* in which *virtù* is rendered as virtue even in the unlikely context of Machiavelli's reference to Hannibal's cruelty, see the Luigi Ricci/E.R.P. Vincent translation of *The Prince* in the Modern Library College Editions' *The Prince and the Discourses* (Random House, 1950). Gilbert's translation is included in Volume 1 of *Machiavelli: The Chief Works and Others*, trs. Allan Gilbert (Duke University Press, 1965).

2. To "make a profession" of a quality can either mean to avow it in one's actions or to feign it. Here the term must be understood in the former sense and without any implication of

pretence. Otherwise Machiavelli's whole critique of this conduct and his argument in favor of making a false profession of goodness in Chapter 18 are unintelligible. Worth noting is the resemblance of making a profession of goodness in this context to making a profession of religious faith at the risk of martyrdom.

3. As explained below, the importance of religion and honesty in both chapters is the usefulness of these qualities in maintaining respect for public authority and the laws that uphold the public sphere and it is this respect that Machiavelli characterizes as *bontà* in Chapter 55. It is for this reason that he clinches the argument in Chapter 13 concerning the importance of religion with a quotation from Livy in which the latter connects the decline of religion with the interpretation of laws and oaths on the basis of self-interest.

4. The formulation is Nietzsche's and occurs in Section 13 of the second essay of *On the Genealogy of Morals*. The whole of this section and the last paragraph of Section 15 provide insights that can be fruitfully applied to Machiavelli's discussion of the function of extraordinary acts in Chapter 1, Book 3 of the *Discourses*.

5. This same potential conflict and the importance of dealing with it decisively also appear in Machiavelli's accounts of extraordinary acts in his own times. See, for example, his account of Cesare Borgia's execution of a trusted subordinate in Chapter 7 of *The Prince* (an action Machiavelli says is "worthy of notice and imitation by others") and that of Caterina Sforza's renunciation of her children in Chapter 6, Book 3 of the *Discourses*.

6. In Chapters 6 through 9 of *The Prince* Machiavelli discusses different ways of acquiring power in terms of their relation to its maintenance. A ruler who cannot maintain himself once he takes power is of no use to his state. At the same time, a ruler who destroys the public sphere to gain power when he could have achieved power without doing so is subject to censure, as Machiavelli implies in Chapter 8 of *The Prince* and states openly in Chapter 10, Book 1 of the *Discourses*, in which he defines glory and infamy in terms of what is beneficial and harmful to the establishment and maintenance of states and religions. Machiavelli's interest in power has to do not with the maintenance of the ruler per se but with the protection of the public sphere, though admittedly his conflation of ruler and public sphere in the concept of the state (*lo stato*) as he employs it in *The Prince* confuses the issue in that work.

7. Francesco Guicciardini, in his fragmentary but interesting commentary on Machiavelli's *Discourses*, reacts with displeasure to two aspects of the work. One is Machiavelli's foreshortening of the historical distance between the early Rome of Livy's description and the Italians of the early 16th century. The other is what Guicciardini perceives to be Machiavelli's excessive pleasure in the concept of extraordinary action. The first source of displeasure reveals Guicciardini's early sensitivity to the problem of anachronism. The second may spring from an equal sensitivity to the fact that Machiavelli's advocacy of extraordinary action to maintain a sharp division between the public and private spheres is fundamentally antagonistic to Guicciardini's aristocratic conception of politics.

Reprinted from: John Leonard, "Public versus Private Claims: Machiavellianism from Another Perspective." In *Political Theory*, Volume 12, Issue 4, pp. 491–501, 504–506. Copyright © 1984 by Sage Publications, Inc. Reprinted by permission of Sage Publications, Inc. ✦

About the Editors

Joseph Losco is professor and current chairman of the political science department at Ball State University in Muncie, Indiana. He has published in the fields of political theory, bioethics, and public policy. Among his publications are *Human Nature and Politics* (with Albert Somit, 1995) and *Higher Education in Transition: The Challenges of the New Millennium* (with Brian Fife, 2000). He is a member of the Executive Council of the Association for Politics and the Life Sciences and on the Biopolitics Research Committee of the International Political Science Association.

Leonard Williams is professor of political science at Manchester College in North Manchester, Indiana. He has published in the fields of political theory, political communication, and electoral politics. Among his publications are *American Liberalism and Ideological Change* (1997), essays in *Women and Elective Office* (1998) and *The Year of the Woman* (1994), as well as articles in *New Political Science* and *The Social Science Journal*. He has served as president of the Indiana Academy of the Social Sciences and the Indiana Political Science Association. ✦

About the Contributors

Allan Bloom was professor in the Committee on Social Thought and the College and the co-director of the John M. Olin Center for Inquiry into the Theory and Practice of Democracy at the University of Chicago until his death.

Jean Bethke Elshtain is the Laura Spelman Rockefeller professor of social and political thought at the Divinity School of the University of Chicago.

Kate Langdon Forhan is professor of political science at Siena College in Loudonville, New York.

Edward. A. Goerner is professor of government and international studies at Notre Dame University in South Bend, Indiana.

Dale Hall is professor of political theory and government at University College at the University of Wales, Swansea.

Laurie Johnson (Bagby) is professor of political science at Kansas State University in Manhattan, Kansas.

John Leonard received his Ph.D. in political theory from the University of California at Berkeley.

Harvey C. Mansfield, Jr. is the William R. Kenan, Jr. professor of government at Harvard University.

Rex Martin holds joint appointments as professor of philosophy at the University of Kansas in Lawrence and professor of political theory and government at the University of Wales, Swansea.

Cary J. Nederman is professor of political science at the University of Arizona, Tucson.

Walter J. Nicgorski is professor of government and international studies at the University of Notre Dame.

Mary P. Nichols is professor of political science at Fordham University in New York.

C. D. C. Reeve is professor of philosophy at Reed College in Portland, Oregon.

Paul E. Sigmund is professor and director of the Latin American studies program at Princeton University in Princeton, New Jersey.

Edward M. Wheat is emeritus professor of political science at the University of Southern Mississippi in Hattiesburg, Mississippi.

Neal Wood is professor of political science at York University in Ontario, Canada. ✦

CPSIA information can be obtained
at www.ICGtesting.com
Printed in the USA
FFOW01n0945160915
16885FF